Inside Citrix® MetaFrame XP™

A System Administrator's Guide to Citrix MetaFrame XP/1.8™ and Windows® Terminal Services

Inside Citrix® MetaFrame XP™
A System Administrator's Guide to Citrix MetaFrame XP/1.8™ and Windows® Terminal Services

Ted Harwood

✦✦ Addison-Wesley

Boston • San Francisco • New York • Toronto • Montreal
London • Munich • Paris • Madrid
Capetown • Sydney • Tokyo • Singapore • Mexico City

Inside Citrix® MetaFrame XP™
A System Administrator's Guide to
Citrix MetaFrame XP/1.8™ and Windows®
Terminal Services

The publisher offers discounts on this book when ordered in quantity for special sales.

For more information, please contact:

Pearson Education Corporate Sales Division

201 W. 103rd Street

Indianapolis, IN 46290

(800) 428-5331

corpsales@pearsoned.com

Visit AW on the Web: www.awprofessional.com

ISBN 0-73571-192-5

5 6 7 8 9 10 OPM 07 06 05

Fifth printing, February 2005

Publisher
John Wait

Publishing Manager
Sondra Scott

Production Manager
Gina Kanouse

Managing Editor
Kristy Knoop

Acquisitions Editor
Elise Walter

Development Editor
Laura Loveall

Product Marketing Manager
Kathy Malmloff

Publicity Manager
Susan Nixon

Project Editor
Suzanne Pettypiece

Copy Editor
Keith Cline

Indexers
Cheryl Lenser
Lisa Stumpf

Manufacturing Coordinator
Jim Conway

Book Designer
Louisa Klucznik

Cover Designer
Aren Howell

Proofreader
Sarah Cisco

Composition
Jeff Bredensteiner

❖

To Karen, my love. To Justin and Joshua, my joy.

❖

Table of Contents

About the Author

Ted Harwood is currently Windows Systems Manager for Southern Wine & Spirits in Miramar, Florida. He is the author of one of the first books on Windows Terminal Server and Citrix MetaFrame, *Windows NT Terminal Server and Citrix MetaFrame* (ISBN: 1562059440), published by New Riders Publishing in 1998, and has been working extensively with server-based computing solutions for the past eight years. Harwood is a Microsoft Certified Systems Engineer, Novell Master Certified NetWare Engineer, Cisco Certified Network Administrator, and a Certified Citrix Enterprise Administrator. He also holds a bachelor of science degree in Computer Information Systems from the University of the State of New York and is currently working toward his master's degree in Business Administration.

When not working or studying, Harwood enjoys spending time with his wife and children. You can reach him directly at tharwood@southernwine.com.

About the Technical Reviewers

These reviewers contributed their considerable hands-on expertise to the entire development process for *Inside Citrix MetaFrame XP*. As the book was being written, these dedicated professionals reviewed all the material for technical content, organization, and flow. Their feedback was critical to ensuring that *Inside Citrix MetaFrame XP* fits our readers' need for the highest quality technical information.

Brian Craig Cumberland is currently completing his Ph.D in Management Information Systems and Strategy at Washington State University. He also is the lead author of *Microsoft Windows NT Server 4.0 Terminal Server: Technical Reference Guide* (ISBN: 0735606455), published by Microsoft Press in 1998 and a Technical Editor for Harwood's previous book, *Windows NT Terminal Server and Citrix MetaFrame*, published by New Riders. Prior to joining Washington State University, Cumberland spent five years at Microsoft Corporation, most recently as a technical evangelist in Microsoft research.

Cumberland, in addition to the upcoming completion of his Ph.D, holds a master's in Business Administration from Indiana University and bachelor's degree from Texas A&M University. He has spent the last 12 years in the Information Technology industry and currently consults with a wide range of corporations and organizations on the strategic utilization of information technology assets. You can reach him directly at `craigcu@wsu.edu`.

Rob Harper is the Manager for System Engineering for Latin America and Caribbean Group. Prior to joining Citrix, as an MCT, he became familiar with Citrix technologies after training a group of Citrix engineers on NT domain structures. Intrigued, Harper jumped on board at Citrix as a system engineer working the southeast territory out of Atlanta, Georgia, in 1997. In 1999, he moved to Florida as a Senior System Engineer with Citrix covering the Florida territory. Currently, he is helping individuals drink the Citrix "KoolAid" in the LACG region and spreading the Citrix word globally. He holds a bachelor's of science degree from the University of Florida and is currently pursuing a master's in Business Administration from the University of Miami specializing in international business. He is 30, married to his lovely wife, Kristin, and planning a comeback to the intramural basketball leagues to follow in the footsteps of Jordan. He can often be found eating at McDonald's, which may hurt his comeback.

Acknowledgments

Although the work you hold may seem to be the result of a few, it truly requires the support of many. I am deeply grateful for all those who both directly and indirectly contributed to the completion of this book.

My heartfelt thanks goes first, and always, to my wife. Without her unrequiting support, this book would not have been completed. With her help I was able to find much-needed calm in the middle of the inevitable ruckus of having children. I owe deep gratitude to both her family and mine for all of their help along the way.

I also would like to thank the many people at New Riders Publishing who helped with this book. It is always a pleasure to work with you all. Hopefully, some day I will have a chance to shake some of the many unseen hands that have contributed to getting this work into print.

Many thanks go to the outstanding technical editors on this project, Craig Cumberland and Rob Harper. Craig's constructive commentary and technical input on Microsoft Terminal Server were essential in ensuring the accuracy of the writing. Rob's extensive real-world Citrix experience was invaluable and helped provide important insight and balance to the book.

Last but far from least, I would like to thank all those I work with at Southern Wine & Spirits who helped along the way. Although my first book was an overly intense effort done solely after-hours, on this book I was graciously granted the time off I needed. Thanks goes to Bobby Burg, Jose Curtis, and Richard Talboy for their trust in me and their untiring support. In addition, many thanks go to the people on the Network and Windows Systems groups at Southern who did an outstanding job of covering for me in my absence.

Introduction

Microsoft Terminal Servers remain the most powerful and widely used implementation of server-based computing technology today. In Windows 2000 Terminal Server, Microsoft has added many new and important features. These added features make Windows 2000 Terminal Server alone a good solution for many companies' application deployment needs.

Like its predecessor, Windows 2000 Terminal Server's main purpose is to distribute Windows 2000 desktops to remote Terminal Server clients using server-based technology. By using server-based technology to distribute these desktops, Terminal Server extends the reach of your Windows applications.

Citrix MetaFrame XP is an add-on product available for either Windows NT 4.0 or 2000 Terminal Server. It adds on to and complements the existing features available in these products. Using Citrix MetaFrame XP, you can publish your applications instead of having users run them from a Terminal Server desktop. In addition, MetaFrame XP offers better printer management capabilities, a centralized management console, and support from non-Windows client connections such as UNIX, DOS, and Macintosh workstations.

For Citrix MetaFrame 1.8 administrators who are considering upgrading to Citrix MetaFrame XP, you will find MetaFrame XP's core design to be very different, but also much more scalable than that of MetaFrame 1.8.

In this book, you will learn the inner workings of both of these products and how to integrate them effectively into the diverse environments of today's enterprise networks.

Although this book focuses mainly on Citrix MetaFrame XP and 1.8 running on Windows 2000 Terminal Server, those who support Terminal Server–only solutions or Citrix MetaFrame on Windows NT 4.0 Terminal Server should not feel left out. You will find plenty of material that is applicable to you. The majority of the tips, techniques, and concepts covered here apply equally well for all platform combinations.

Although Microsoft's next release of their Windows server platform, Windows .NET Terminal Server has not been released as of this writing, you will find coverage of some of the many new features that you can expect in this product when it is released.

Who This Book Is For

This book is primarily for system administrators and consultants who are responsible for implementing a Terminal Server and Citrix MetaFrame solution. However, there also is significant coverage for those who find that Terminal Services alone provides all the features they need.

This is a technical book written by an engineer for engineers. You will find real-world solutions, top-ten tips, command and technical article references, lists of technical resources and web sites available, and lots of technical coverage that will hopefully help you when you need it the most. It assumes a basic familiarity with Windows server and workstation administration.

Web Site for the Book

In conjunction with the material in this book, you will find a simple companion web site that provides useful links and reference material related to Citrix MetaFrame, Windows Terminal Services, and server-based computing at www.thinwizard.com, which also is available from www.awl.com/cseng/titles/0-735-71192-5. For more information about the companion web site, see the inside back cover of this book.

How This Book Is Organized

Inside Citrix MetaFrame XP is organized into five main parts. Each part covers a related set of Terminal Server and Citrix MetaFrame topics. Each of those parts is divided into chapters. They are organized as follows.

Part I: Planning a Windows Terminal Server and Citrix MetaFrame Solution

The first part of the book provides a technical overview of Terminal Server and MetaFrame. The chapters in this part will provide the necessary introduction for those who are new to server-based computing technology or who want a better understanding of how this technology has been implemented in Terminal Server and MetaFrame. In addition, you will learn about how to best plan your Terminal Server or Citrix MetaFrame solution.

Chapter 1, "Introduction to Server-Based Computing," introduces the server-based computing model by introducing the concept of the application pyramid. You will find out how Terminal Server works and distributes desktops using server-based computing technology. You also will learn about the different types of thin client hardware available.

Chapter 2, "Introduction to Windows Terminal Server," is where you are introduced to the many applications that Terminal Server is best suited for and the applications for which you would want to use other solutions. You will learn all about the features in both Windows NT 4.0 and 2000 Terminal Server. In addition, you will learn about some of the features to be expected in Windows .NET Terminal Server.

Chapter 3, "Introduction to Citrix MetaFrame 1.8 and MetaFrame XP," introduces you to all the features in both of these products. You will see the features of these products compared side-by-side. In addition, you will learn what the most important reasons are for adding Citrix MetaFrame to your Terminal Server solution.

Chapter 4, "Understanding the Costs and Benefits of a Terminal Server Solution," covers the many benefits and also the costs of a Terminal Server solution. You can use this information to help prepare the cost/benefit analysis you might need to get your Terminal Server project approved.

Chapter 5, "Licensing Terminal Server and Citrix MetaFrame," is dedicated to the complete coverage of this complex and often poorly understood topic. You will learn how licensing works with both Terminal Server and Citrix MetaFrame and how to license your servers correctly.

Chapter 6, "Planning a Terminal Server and Citrix MetaFrame XP Solution," covers the many important steps you need to take to plan your Terminal Server solution properly, including how to set up and place your Terminal Server licensing servers. You also will learn all about the many new concepts involved in a Citrix MetaFrame XP solution such as zones, data collectors, and the data store. In addition, recommended migration techniques for both Terminal Server and Citrix MetaFrame version migrations are discussed.

Chapter 7, "Planning for the Installation of Terminal Server and Citrix MetaFrame," covers the many important aspects of pre-installation planning such as sizing servers and configuring the hardware.

Part II: Implementing a Windows Terminal Server and Citrix MetaFrame Solution

Part II is the core of the book. Here is where you will learn what you need to know to get Terminal Server and MetaFrame working on your network.

Chapter 8, "Installing Windows 2000 Terminal Server and Citrix MetaFrame XP," guides you through installing Windows 2000 Terminal Server and Citrix MetaFrame XP. You will learn the specific steps you need to follow during the installation and how the installation differs from that of standard Windows 2000 Servers. Citrix MetaFrame XP administrators also will learn how to set up the data store for MetaFrame XP, how to install MetaFrame XP on your Terminal Servers, and how to activate the licenses for the product.

Chapter 9, "Setting Up Terminal Server Users," discusses the special Terminal Server user properties that you can set for both Windows NT 4.0 and 2000 domain users. You will then learn how to properly set up your Terminal Server users and groups. You also will learn about how to set up logon scripts for your users in this chapter.

Chapter 10, "Setting Up Terminal Server Connections," shows how to create and manage the connections used by both Terminal Server and Citrix MetaFrame clients to connect to the server.

Chapter 11, "Installing RDP Clients for Windows," guides you through installing the Windows Terminal Services Client (RDP) software on Windows-based operating systems. In addition, you will learn some of the many techniques available for helping automate the installation of the clients.

Chapter 12, "Installing and Deploying ICA Clients," is dedicated to explaining how to best install and deploy the client software for Citrix MetaFrame servers.

Chapter 13, "Installing Applications," gives you guidance on the technically challenging topic of how to integrate your applications into Terminal Server's multiuser environment. You will learn the technical details of how applications use the Registry and how to troubleshoot common application problems.

Chapter 14, "Policies and Desktop Management," looks at the important aspects of administering Terminal Server desktops, such as how to lock them down properly using profiles and policies. You will learn about the difference between policies in Windows NT 4.0 and Group Policy objects in Windows 2000, and recommend policies to implement for Windows 2000.

Chapter 15, "Application Publishing and Load Management with Citrix MetaFrame," covers how to publish your applications using Citrix MetaFrame XP. For administrators who are using MetaFrame XPa and XPe, you also will learn how to load balance your published applications using Citrix's load-management capabilities.

Chapter 16, "Dial-In and VPN Access," covers how to provide remote access to your Terminal Server or Citrix MetaFrame solution using dial-in and VPN access.

Part III: Deploying Applications on the Internet

In Part III you will learn about how to create your own web sites for access to applications on either Terminal Server alone or Terminal Server with Citrix MetaFrame. In addition, you will learn what it takes to provide access to those web sites through firewalls and proxy servers.

Chapter 17, "Firewalls and SSL Relay," covers how to set up your firewall and proxy servers correctly for access to both Terminal Servers and Terminal Servers with Citrix MetaFrame. You will learn the ports that you need to open on your firewall and the many different design options you have.

Chapter 18, "Running Applications on the Web Using the Terminal Services Advanced Client," will show you how you can set up Microsoft's freely available Terminal Services Advanced Client to provide web access to your Terminal Server.

Chapter 19, "Deploying Applications over the Web Using NFuse and Wireless Technologies," covers how to use Citrix's freely available NFuse product to set up an application web portal. Your users will be able to log on to this portal from their web browser and run their applications through Citrix.

Part IV: Advanced Terminal Server and MetaFrame Topics

The final chapters in this book make up a solutions guide for Terminal Server and MetaFrame. Each of these chapters covers a specific advanced topic of Terminal Server or MetaFrame solution in detail.

Chapter 20, "Advanced Printing Techniques," covers what you need to know to effectively set up and troubleshoot printer auto-creation. Citrix MetaFrame XP administrators also will learn all about the new printer management capabilities built into that product.

Chapter 21, "Performance Tuning and Resource Management," is a very important chapter that will help you ensure that your Terminal Server hardware is adequate for its intended purpose. It also will help you establish a performance baseline to measure against for future needs.

Chapter 22, "Securing Your Server," is another important chapter that covers what you need to do to lock down your server properly.

Chapter 23, "Advanced Application Installation and Installation Management," covers advanced techniques for automating the installation of your server applications. Citrix MetaFrame XPe administrators will learn the specifics of how to deploy applications across the server farm using Installation Manager.

Chapter 24, "Advanced Network Management and Monitoring," discusses how you can setup a network monitoring system for your Terminal Server solution. In addition, Citrix MetaFrame XPe administrators will learn about how to set up SNMP monitoring of their Citrix server farm using XPe Network Manager software.

Chapter 25, "Terminal Server and NetWare," is for the many administrators who need to integrate their Terminal Server solution with Novell NetWare. You will learn about Netware-related topics, such as using the IPX/SPX protocol with Citrix, installing the NetWare client, and integrating your solution with ZENworks.

Chapter 26, "Disaster Recovery Techniques and Enhancing Reliability," is a very important chapter that will help you design your Terminal Server solution to be as reliable as possible. You will learn how you can set up your solution for quick recovery in case of disaster.

Chapter 27, "Network Load Balancing for NFuse and Terminal Servers," shows you how to use other third-party software and features built into Microsoft Windows 2000 to make the most of your Terminal Server solution, without having to purchase Citrix MetaFrame. You will learn about such things as how to setup load sharing using Microsoft's Network Load Balancing.

Part V: Appendixes

The appendixes cover some additional topics of interest beyond the scope of the main material.

Appendix A, "Thin Client Hardware Solutions," lists some of the many manufacturers of thin client hardware solutions, including manufacturers of thin client terminals, handheld devices, and low-end desktops.

Appendix B, "Third-Party Software and Utilities for Terminal Server and MetaFrame," describes some of the many incredibly useful third-party software packages and utilities that you can use with your Terminal Server and Citrix MetaFrame solution.

Appendix C, "Web Sites, Newsgroups, and Other Resources," lists the many web sites and newsgroups that contain valuable information on Terminal Server and MetaFrame. In addition, you will learn about some of the other technical support resources that are available for these two products.

Appendix D, "History of Terminal Server and Citrix MetaFrame," provides an interesting historical perspective on these two products.

Appendix E, "Terminal Server and MetaFrame Command Reference," is a thumb-tabbed reference of the many commands included with Terminal Server and MetaFrame. Important Terminal Server–related commands that you can use by purchasing the Windows 2000 Resource Kit or by downloading freely available utilities are covered as well.

Appendix F, "Citrix and Microsoft Technical Article Reference," is an easy-to-use index of the most important Terminal Server and Citrix MetaFrame–related technical articles on both Microsoft's and Citrix's web site. This is a good reference to go to check first to find articles on resolutions to common problems and also technical articles that provide detailed information on particular Citrix and Terminal Server issues.

Conventions Used

Throughout this book, certain conventions are used to convey the material in a standard and understandable fashion.

Terminology Used

It is important that this book covers a wide range of different versions of both Windows Terminal Server and Citrix MetaFrame so that the information provided is as useful and relevant as possible for your environment. However, covering this wide range of topics means that it is also important that consistent terminology is used throughout the book. Using consistent terminology helps ensure that it is clear what version is being referred to in a particular sentence. The following is the list of terminology used in this book:

- **Windows NT 4.0 Terminal Server**   Refers specifically to Windows NT 4.0 Terminal Server Edition.
- **Windows 2000 Terminal Server**   Refers specifically to a Windows 2000 Server with Terminal Services installed.
- **Windows 2000 Terminal Services**   Refers to the Terminal Services themselves.
- **Terminal Server**   Shorthand reference that refers in general to either Windows 2000 Terminal Server or Windows NT 4.0 Terminal Server. Normally is shorthand for Windows 2000 Terminal Server because that is the focus of the book.
- **Windows .NET Terminal Server**   Refers to the next release of Windows 2000 Server. You will learn about some of the many new features projected to be released in this version. The Windows .NET

Terminal Server line should be available within a few months after the release of this book.

- **Citrix MetaFrame**   General reference to Citrix MetaFrame 1.8 or XP
- **MetaFrame XP or 1.8**   Specific reference to that version of Citrix MetaFrame.
- **MetaFrame XPs, XPa or XPe**   Used when discussing a feature specific to a particular subversion of MetaFrame XP. For example, "You need to install Terminal Services on a Windows 2000 Server for it to be a Windows 2000 Terminal Server."

This terminology usage also makes is simpler when referring to multiple products in the same sentence. For instance, "You will find this feature in both Windows NT 4.0 and 2000 Terminal Server" or "Citrix MetaFrame enables you to publish applications to your users."

Author's Notes and Sidebars

There are two types of "notes" in this book: Author's Notes and Sidebars. The examples that follow show what they look like and what they contain:

Author's Note

Author's notes are short notes that cover information related to the topic at hand or exceptions to the information being presented.

[Sidebar Topic Name]

Throughout the book you will find numerous sidebars. These sidebars provide you with important information that applies to the topic at hand and is taken from real-world experiences.

Typographical Conventions

This book follows a few typographical conventions:

- A new term is set in *italics* the first time it is introduced.
- Program text, functions, variables, and other "computer language" are set in a fixed-pitch font—for example, `setwallpaper ("")`.

- Many times a particular value will need to be supplied by you for a command or file path. This is indicated by enclosing a short description of the value in brackets (for example, [Value Description]). You should replace the brackets and value description with the appropriate value needed for the command or path. If this value is an optional value, it will be indicated as such in the text.

- Often in the book, there is reference to a particular file or folders on your server or on a product CD. Because the drive letters used for servers and the CD drive vary by machine, the following terms are used instead to indicate particular locations. The variables enclosed in percent signs (%) are actual environment variables on the system. You can view a list of these variables by going to the command prompt on the machine and entering **SET**.

  - **%systemdrive%**   The system drive of the server or workstation. Normally, the C: drive or M: drive if your server drives have been remapped.

  - **%systemroot%**   The root of the Windows NT or 2000 operating system on the machine. Normally this location is c:\winnt or c:\windows.

  - **%programfiles%**   The default location for the installation of programs on a Windows NT or 2000 machine. Normally this location is c:\program files.

  - **%userprofile%**   The location for a particular user's profile folder (on Windows 2000).

  - **[cd]:**   The CD drive on the machine. There is no environment variable for this particular value, so it is indicated in brackets instead. Normally this value is actually either d:\ or e:\.

  - **%homedrive%**   The drive letter for a user's home directory. You can arbitrarily assign this drive letter during user creation.

  - **%homepath%**   The path for the home directory for the user. The combination of %homedrive% and %homepath% make up the full pathname for the user's home directory.

I

Planning a Windows Terminal Server and Citrix MetaFrame Solution

1

Introduction to Server-Based Computing

Y OU ARE NOW ENTERING INTO AN EXPLORATION of a very important area of Windows server technology called *server-based computing*. This technology will give wings to your business applications, enabling your users to access them from wherever they are with little regard to the speed of their connection or the capabilities of their computers. It is a technology you can use to roll out new applications or upgrade existing ones for hundreds of people in a matter of minutes rather than months or days. With all of this technology's amazing potential, however, it also can be one of the most challenging both to comprehend and to implement.

This chapter provides a high-level overview of today's server-based computing landscape. Much like looking at a map before starting a long journey, this overview will help you find the safest and most expeditious path to reach your destination. This chapter is intended for those who are at the start of their server-based computing journey and need a better general understanding of the different server-based technologies available today. It is important that you obtain a good perspective and that you know your options before you begin your travels. Without this perspective, you are likely to get lost in the details without reaching your intended destination or run into unnecessary trouble along the way.

Although Windows Terminal Server and Citrix MetaFrame are the main server-based technologies covered in this book, in this chapter, you will also gain a wider perspective of the many software solutions available today that utilize server-based technology. Using portal technology, which is covered later in this chapter, these solutions can often be integrated with a Terminal Server/MetaFrame solution to provide a comprehensive and powerful synergy. In addition you will learn about the many hardware devices that you can use as part of server-based solutions.

Benefits of Server-Based Technology

A server-based software solution is a solution in which lightweight pieces of software, referred to as *thin clients*, are used to control heavier and more processor-intensive applications. These heavier applications are most often run at a central data-processing location. Much like using leverage to move a large weight, a small but powerful thin client can remotely run much larger and more robust applications. As you will see in Chapter 2, "Introduction to Windows Terminal Server," this broad definition of server-based software technology includes not just Terminal Server and Citrix MetaFrame, but also Java, ActiveX, DHTML, and other software solutions capable of this behavior.

The reason "thin clients" are called thin is twofold. First, the client software is generally small in size compared to most business applications. Second, because of this small size, the corresponding hardware requirements tend to be very minimal. This has given rise to many thin client hardware solutions, such as thin client terminals, that are specifically designed to support thin client software solutions.

Although thin client terminals are designed to run thin client software, that does not mean that only thin client terminals can run thin client software. Microsoft's main thin client software solution, the Remote Desktop Protocol client, can be run on most every version of the Windows operating system. In addition, Citrix's thin client software, the Independent Computing Architecture client, will run on even a larger variety of platforms, including most versions of UNIX, Macintoshes, EPOC, and even DOS.

Although the thin client software is normally less than a few megabytes, it is capable of remotely controlling applications that are hundreds of megabytes in size. This capability is due to the fact that most thin clients act as graphical interface interpreters, leveraging the processing capabilities of powerful remote servers by viewing, controlling, and interacting with applications running on those remote servers.

In a server-based software solution, because application processing is handled almost entirely by the server and not by the client, the solution is easier to scale. One of the main differences between workstation and server class hardware is the emphasis on scalability in server hardware design. Most servers are designed to make it easy to add extra drives, processors, peripheral cards, and other hardware as needed. Also administrators can scale a smaller number of servers centrally instead of having to upgrade a large number of client workstations.

This relatively simple idea of using a small piece of software to control a powerful central server farm has many benefits, some of which might not be obvious on the surface.

Thin Clients Use Few Network Resources

One of the many business reasons for using server-based technology is the need for running business applications across slow connections. Because thin clients are interpreters, they mainly handle the display of information from an application and the user response rather than more network intensive functions, such as data querying and file transfer. This means that instead of an application sending enormous amounts of data down to a client, as is typical with many client/server applications, only that information necessary for display is sent. Using server-based technology for applications is necessary to run them across slower and expensive wide area network connections. By being able to effectively run applications across wide area network connections, businesses are more easily able to centralize their applications and resources for better efficiency.

Thin Clients Make Application Upgrades Easy

Server-based technology makes application upgrades and patches a breeze. In a traditional environment in which full applications are installed on local workstations, every machine has to be visited to upgrade the application. Some corporations automate this process using application packaging and deployment technologies. However, limitations—such as limited workstation resources for the application or limited network resources for handling the transfer of the application install package—still need to be faced. No facts are available to prove this one way or the other. Speculation on our part is not warranted.

In a centralized environment using server-based computing technology, normally only the central application needs to be updated. If a workstation's thin client software itself needs an update, the update process can often be automated centrally and takes very little time because of the small size of the client.

Server-Based Computing Helps Centralize Management

Many businesses are driving toward a centralized information systems management model. In other words, as companies grow larger, great efficiencies can often be gained by bringing together your computer systems under one roof or at least the management of those systems at one location. The server-based computing model is ideal for this environment because thin clients enable you to easily centralize your applications.

Centralization is also important in terms of resource usage. By moving systems centrally, businesses can afford to hire better-trained and more highly skilled support staff at the central location. This helps improve the reliability of these systems and the ability to support these systems effectively.

Server-Based Computing Allows Businesses to Adapt Quickly

One very important benefit of server-based computing technology is that it allows for quick adaptation. In today's often hyper-competitive business environment, server-based technology can give your company a leg up on the competition by allowing it to respond to changing business needs more quickly. Not only are application upgrades much quicker and easier to implement, but the rollout of new applications is also much easier using server-based computing technology.

Server-Based Computing Helps Reduce Total Cost of Ownership

The final benefit of server-based technology that has been much discussed is how it can help reduce a business's *total cost of ownership* (TCO). Over the years, this has mainly referred to the cost of ownership of personal computers and the resultant support costs. Server-based technology effectively reduces an organization's desktop support and PC replacement costs, especially on new software rollouts. Because thin clients can be managed centrally, you generally need fewer people to support them. Also because they have very minimal hardware requirements, there is seldom reason to upgrade a workstation to run a new version of software that is deployed using server-based computing technology.

The Evolution of Server-Based Computing

Server-based technology is all about extending the reach of your applications, or, in other words, application ubiquity. No matter where you are or how you are connected, you should have easy and secure access to your applications. Much like the well-known remote-control product pcAnywhere, whose goal is to provide access to your PC's desktop from any-where, server-based computing technology's main goal is to provide access to your applications from anywhere. Although there are many ways to make this possible today, it has taken many years of application evolution and the advent of server-based technology to bring us to this point. Before going into the specifics of how different approaches to server-based computing technology work, the general concepts of server-based technology need to be covered so that you gain a better understanding of the applications that they are intended to deploy.

The PC Application Pyramid

Most PC applications today can be classified as either Tier 1, Tier 2, or Tier 3 applications in an application pyramid. Separating each tier in the pyramid is some type of connecting medium, such as a network, modem, serial line, or application interface, which provides for multiple users on the lower tier to connect to the tier above. See Figure 1.1.

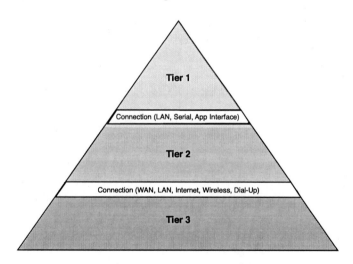

Figure 1.1   The application pyramid.

Single-Tier Applications

During the formative years of PC applications back in the 1980s, most appli-cations were single-tier applications (see Figure 1.2). A strictly single-tier application is self-contained and does not require any external connection to function. Because networks were not readily available, most businesses that used PCs had no choice but to run single-tier applications. Older word pro-cessing and spreadsheet applications are typical single-tier applications.

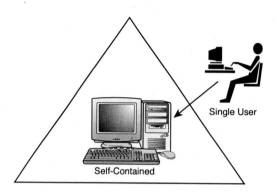

Figure 1.2   Single-tier application.

Dual-Tier Applications

The biggest problem with single-tier applications was their isolation. As businesses grew, so did the need to share information and for employees to use applications that would allow them to work together with common sets of data. Hence, businesses quickly began to focus on building networks to allow for easier communication between people, between applications, and between applications and a central data source.

The advent of networks was a driving force for the production of dual-tier applications. Dual-tier applications have both a component that runs on the client at Tier 2 and a component that runs on the server at Tier 1 (see Figure 1.3). That server also typically contains the data source for the application and handles all or part of the data processing. These types of applications are traditionally referred to as *client/server applications*. Although many Tier 2 applications can be run on a single workstation, they are ultimately designed for multiple people running Tier 2 client software to be able to access a Tier 1 server that contains the information that needs to be shared.

Most accounting applications are dual-tier applications, such as Microsoft (formerly Great Plains) Dynamics. Dynamics has both a client component and a server component. The Tier 1 server component contains the accounting data and is designed to be accessed by multiple users running Tier 2 Dynamics client software.

Author's Note

As the number of tiers an application runs in increases, so does the reliance on the reliability, performance, and security of the connections between tiers. This concept will be reinforced several times in this book and is critical to fully understand. If you deploy an application using server-based computing technology without closely considering the reliability, performance, and security of the connections it relies on, the project will likely fail.

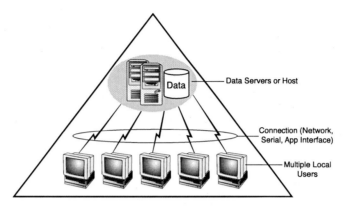

Figure 1.3 Dual-tier applications.

Heavy Applications at Tier 2

Tier 2 applications can be divided into two categories: heavy or light. *Heavy applications*, such as many accounting and reporting applications, generally take up a large amount of resources on the computers on which they are installed. They tend to take up a lot of drive space when installed, often a large amount of memory and processing time when running, and most importantly make heavy use of their connection to the Tier 1 data source. The heaviness of these applications can make them difficult to widely deploy. If the application makes heavy use of the connection, you must have a fast local connection or pay for an expensive wide area network connection for the application to perform adequately. A slower dial-up or Internet connection will likely not be a practical option for this type of application because application response time will be unacceptable. If the application makes heavy use of your computer's resources, you must purchase more robust and more expensive computer hardware to support it.

Even with these disadvantages, heavy applications tend to have the most features and most options for the user. Developers are not as limited by deployment considerations when designing heavier applications and instead concentrate on features. The features that these applications offer are important to businesses and the shear number of features means that a business can purchase a single application that is very flexible and fulfills many business needs. Some examples of heavy Tier 2 applications are accounting applications and database applications. Office suites, such as Microsoft Office, can be considered Tier 2 applications as well when they are used to access a document across a network on a Tier 1 file server.

Light Applications at Tier 2

Light applications, on the other hand, tend to use very little drive space, are easy to deploy and install, take up very little local memory or processing time, and use relatively little network resources. Because of the light hardware requirements, light (or in other words, thin) applications can often be run on a wide array of devices—from dedicated thin client terminals to handheld computers. Some examples of these types of applications are lighter editions of terminal emulation applications, and email software. A properly optimized server-based application can easily be run across slow connections, such as dial-up lines.

Compared to heavy applications, light ones at Tier 2 tend to have fewer features. Although they might perform one or two tasks very well, such as sending and receiving email, there will likely be less associated options for the user, such as contact management or scheduling.

As an administrator, deploying a handful of Tier 2 light applications might meet specific needs very well, but if light applications are used to meet all business needs, you can end up with a disjointed collection of applications that are difficult to support. Most businesses choose a smaller number of heavier applications, such as Microsoft Office, rather than a large number of simpler, lighter applications that provide similar functionality. Not only do users get more options, but also businesses can take advantages of the synergies that an integrated product suite can offer, such as the ability to easily pass information between office applications.

Three-Tier Applications

Well, of course, businesses want it all; they want all the features of heavy applications but the ease of deployment and limited use of resources that light applications offer. In addition, because of the large resource requirements of Tier 2 applications, many businesses continued to run into scalability issues with their most heavily used applications, forcing them to have to do mass workstation upgrades to support new application suites. In the early 1990s, companies such as Citrix began to capitalize on this need by building Tier 3 software solutions to these problems using server-based technology.

Although many possible variations of Tier 3 application structures exist, in this book a Tier 3 client application, such as Citrix's ICA client, remote controls a more processor-intensive, server-based application on Tier 2. The heavy Tier 2 server application then accesses the data on Tier 1. This type of application solution is referred to as a *three-tier application* (see Figure 1.4).

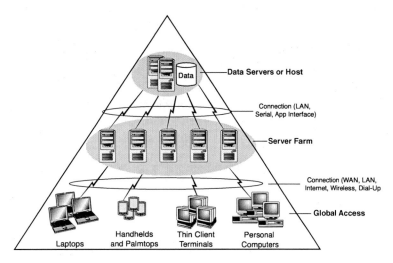

Figure 1.4   Three-tier application.

Tier 2 is conceptually where your Terminal Servers and Citrix MetaFrame servers would reside. Because most of the processing happens at Tier 2, very little data needs to pass between the Tier 3 thin client and the Tier 2 server.

The majority of the data is passed between the Tier 2 server and the Tier 1 data source. For this solution to work efficiently, the connection between the server and the data source needs to be connected together by a high-speed network, preferably a local area network.

Whether you are talking about a single application solution that has components on each tier, or a combination of applications, such as Microsoft Dynamics running on Citrix MetaFrame, the concept is the same. At Tier 3, you run a lightweight application or application component, which interfaces with a heavy, more processor- and resource-intensive application on Tier 2. This application in turn uses a data source at Tier 1.

Applications designed using a three-tier model or that are three-tier-enabled using technology such as Citrix MetaFrame offer the best of both worlds. They are easy to deploy because the Tier 3 client tends to be very small in size and requires few resources. They also can offer the powerful features and capabilities handled by their Tier 2 components.

Some Tier 3 applications are designed to run as plug-ins or applets that work with common browsers. Because browsers are commonly available and have built-in capability to easily download plug-ins from a central source, deployment of Tier 3 applications can be as simple as pointing your users to a web page.

The Three-Tier Model in Practice

To drive home the three-tier concept, a practical example is in order.
This will help enforce why an understanding of the three-tier concept is
important when deciding where Terminal Server and Citrix MetaFrame
technology fits best in a business.

Many web-based reporting applications, such as Crystal Enterprise, are
designed to be a complete three-tier application solution. Crystal Enterprise
is one example of this type of application. Crystal Enterprise has a Tier 3
browser-based client that works with most standard browsers and enables
the user to run, schedule, and view reports across the Internet.

Within Tier 2 are the Crystal Enterprise reporting servers that handle web
page display, report generation, and other core tasks that are very resource-
intensive. Within Tier 1 are the data sources from which the reports are
created.

Because Crystal Enterprise is already a three-tier application, you most
likely do not need three-tier enabling technology, such as Citrix MetaFrame,
to make this application easy to deploy.

If you look carefully at this product, however, you'll still see an area
that needs the assistance of server-based computing technology. Although
Crystal Enterprise provides a Tier 3 browser plug-in for viewing and running reports, the one thing Crystal Enterprise does not have is a set of
full-featured report design tools that run at Tier 3. For report designers to
create new reports for Crystal Enterprise, they run Crystal's Windows-based
Tier 2 reporting application, which is called *Crystal Reports*. As you will see
in this book, server-based technologies are an ideal choice for deploying
heavy Tier 2 applications, such as Crystal Reports. By using a server-based
computing solution to three-tier enable Crystal Reports, you can easily
extend the reach of this application across your enterprise, enabling report
designers at branch offices to make reports off of a central data source.

Introducing Terminal Server and Citrix MetaFrame

Now that you have a better understanding of the type of applications that
server-based computing technology can help, this section introduces the
premier server-based computing solution today, Microsoft Terminal Server
and Citrix MetaFrame. Microsoft Terminal Server was first introduced in
1997 as a specially enhanced version of Windows NT Server 4.0. This product was referred to as *Windows NT Server 4.0, Terminal Server Edition* (or, as
referred to throughout this book, *Windows NT 4.0 Terminal Server*). Building
on technology licensed from Citrix, Microsoft, with cooperation from

Citrix, rewrote its operating system to support multiple interactive remote users. Much like remote-control clients, such as pcAnywhere, allow access to an individual computer user's desktop from a remote computer, by using Microsoft's *Remote Desktop Protocol* (RDP) client, users can access their own "Windows" desktop through the Terminal Server. From this desktop, users can run applications at the server just like they would on their local workstation. Unlike most remote-control products that allow only one user access to one remote desktop at a time, however, Terminal Server allows for multiple people to remotely access their own desktop environment simultaneously from a single Windows Terminal Server.

When Microsoft released the next version of its operating system, Windows 2000 Server, it included Terminal Services as an installable option that is part of the core operating system installation instead of rewriting and releasing a separate version of the operating system. This move of Terminal Services to the core operating system indicates Microsoft's strong commitment to thin client technology and helps ensure your investment in this technology. In this book, a Windows 2000 server with Terminal Services installed is referred to as a *Windows 2000 Terminal Server.*

In the soon to be released Windows .NET Terminal Server, Terminal Services again are available as part of the core operating system components. Although, as of this writing, it has not been decided whether Terminal Services will be available for all versions of Windows .NET Terminal Server, it will definitely be available.

Author's Note

Although this book's focus is mainly on Windows 2000 Terminal Server, as much information as possible is presented on the upcoming Windows .NET Terminal Server from Microsoft. This information is based on features and functionality currently in beta, so it is very possible that some of the features and functionality discussed with regard to Windows .NET Terminal Server will not make the final release.

Although Microsoft's Terminal Server product might contain all the features you need for your project, many businesses choose to install the add-on product from Citrix, which is called *MetaFrame.*

Citrix MetaFrame, the Citrix flagship product, builds on the basic capabilities of Microsoft Terminal Server by adding important features and enhancements, such as application publishing, load balancing, and thin client software that is written for a much wider range of operating systems.

Author's Note

The history of the development of Citrix MetaFrame and how it led to Microsoft's development of Terminal Server is covered in Appendix D, "History of Terminal Server and Citrix MetaFrame." This appendix makes for some rather interesting reading and provides an important historical perspective that will help you gain a deeper understanding of the often-complicated decisions behind the development and licensing of these products.

Understanding Terminal Services and Citrix MetaFrame

To better understand how both Terminal Server and Citrix MetaFrame work, the three components that make up this server-based technology solution—the server, the protocols, and the thin clients—are discussed in this section. As these components are discussed, remember that one of the main benefits of Terminal Server and Citrix MetaFrame is that they are three-tier enabling products. In other words, they enable you to take an existing Tier 2 application and extend the reach of that application by running it from a thin client on Tier 3.

The Server

Microsoft has made the process of making a Windows 2000 server a Terminal Server very simple by making Terminal Services an optional Windows component. The creation of a Windows 2000 Terminal Server can be done by just clicking the Terminal Services check box in the Add/Remove Windows Components dialog box, either during the installation of Windows 2000 Server or after. For previous Windows Terminal Server 4.0 administrators who had to purchase and install a completely separate version of Windows NT Server 4.0 to create a new Terminal Server, this new modularity is a very welcome enhancement!

Installation of the separately purchased Citrix MetaFrame product is also just as easy. After you create a Windows 2000 Terminal Server by adding Terminal Services, just purchase and install Citrix MetaFrame. Citrix MetaFrame installs on top of Terminal Server just as any other application would. However, MetaFrame is designed to build on Terminal Services' core capabilities to add additional features and capabilities. Chapters 4 through 7 cover the planning necessary and the installation process itself in detail.

Terminal Services as a Desktop Server

Adding Terminal Services to your Windows 2000 server can be thought of as turning your Windows 2000 server into a desktop server. When you log on to the console of a Windows 2000 server with a particular logon name, you receive your own desktop. If you log on to the console with a different name, you will receive a different desktop. So by keeping separate profiles for each user who logs on, the core operating system already is capable of providing separate desktops. Because there is only one console, however, two users cannot access their own desktops at the same time on the server. When you add Terminal Services to Windows 2000 Server, it provides the functionality for multiple users to receive their personal desktops remotely running Microsoft's Terminal Services client.

Running Tier 2 Applications on the Server

Because your desktop runs on the server itself, when you run applications on that server, you are taking advantage of the more robust processing power, added memory, and reliability that a server class computer can offer. In other words, the Terminal Server becomes your own remote, high-power workstation! Heavy Tier 2 applications, such as reporting applications, can often run faster and more efficiently on a Terminal Server because they can take advantage of the hardware scalability for which servers are designed.

It is important to realize that in most cases, your applications run on Windows 2000 Terminal Server just as they would on any 32-bit Microsoft Windows operating system. Other than the fact that you are remote controlling your application on a Terminal Server instead of running it locally, your application will function exactly the same. As will be reinforced throughout this book, it helps to start thinking of your Windows 2000 Terminal Server desktop as a high-powered Windows 2000 workstation, especially when troubleshooting application problems.

It is also important to realize that applications running on Terminal Server share server resources with other applications running on the server. If you do not plan for the capacity of your servers correctly when deploying applications through Terminal Server, your high-powered Terminal Server "workstation" will quickly become bogged down by all the applications running simultaneously. As you will see in Chapter 21, "Performance Tuning and Resource Management," you can use many techniques to size and tune your Terminal Servers.

The Protocols

Both Microsoft and Citrix have each developed their own network protocol for handling the communication between the Terminal Server and the thin client. As mentioned earlier, Microsoft's thin client protocol is referred to as the RDP and is used when the server is communicating with Microsoft's

Terminal Services—in other words, RDP client software. Citrix's protocol is called the *Independent Computing Architecture* (ICA) protocol and is the protocol used by the server to communicate with Citrix's client software—or in other words, the ICA clients.

Both ICA and RDP are highly efficient thin client protocols designed to work well over low-bandwidth connections. Their main job is providing a defined structure for carrying the desktop display information to the client, while returning keyboard and mouse movements from the client to the server. As is shown in Figure 1.2, the Terminal Server's job is to keep the client updated with any changes to the desktop running on the server by encapsulating and sending those changes down to the client using either RDP or ICA. Because the Terminal Server has to keep all of its clients up-to-date with the latest changes to their associated desktops running on the server, when people are actively using applications on the desktop, the server can become very busy!

Microsoft's Remote Desktop Protocol

Microsoft's RDP is based on the T.120 series network conferencing protocols, initially defined by the *International Telecommunications Union* (ITU) in 1996. Even before the development of Windows Terminal Server 4.0 in 1996, Microsoft had been using the T.120 protocol series for more than a year in its NetMeeting videoconferencing product. Building on the desktop sharing capabilities of NetMeeting, Microsoft extended this protocol series to meet the needs of a multiuser Terminal Server environment.

Microsoft's first edition of the RDP protocol was version 4.0, chosen to match the version of the Windows NT Server operating system with which it was designed to run. The current version of the RDP protocol used with Windows 2000 Terminal Server is version 5.0 and contains significant improvements over 4.0, as you will see in detail in Chapter 2. Microsoft is currently working on version 5.1 of this protocol for Windows .NET Terminal Server, which as of this writing is in the beta stages of development.

Citrix's Independent Computing Architecture Protocol

The Citrix ICA protocol is made available when you purchase and install Citrix MetaFrame on your Terminal Server. ICA has been around for many years and has become a de facto thin client protocol standard in the industry. Citrix has gone to great lengths to support external development using its ICA protocol and has encouraged its implementation for a wide variety of thin client hardware and software solutions.

Although ICA and RDP have the same main goal, they differ significantly in terms of the features they inherently support and in their implementation. Because both ICA and RDP are considered upper-layer protocols, they need to rely on transport protocols underneath, such as TCP/IP, to carry them across the network. RDP works only on top of TCP/IP. This means you first must have TCP/IP installed and communicating between the client and the server for RDP to be able to communicate. On the other hand, ICA is designed to be more open and will work on top of TCP/IP, IPX, SPX, NetBIOS (NetBEUI), and direct serial. More importantly, ICA and RDP and their associated thin clients support different sets of features, as you will learn in Chapter 2 and 3, "Introduction to Citrix MetaFrame 1.8 and MetaFrame XP."

The Thin Client

The final piece in a Terminal Server and MetaFrame solution is the thin client. Microsoft's and Citrix's thin clients are responsible for re-creating the Windows 2000 desktop for the user from the information they receive from the server via the thin client protocol. They also take the mouse movements and keyboard input from the user, translate those movements into thin client protocol packets, and send them back to the server. Depending on the version and functionality of your thin client, they also might handle COM and LPT port communication between the thin client and the server, sound, file transfers, printing, and more. The goal of a thin client is to make it seem both to the user and to the remote application that the application is running locally.

Microsoft Terminal Services Client

Two types of thin clients work with Terminal Server. The first is the Terminal Services client or RDP client. This client, written by Microsoft, comes with Windows 2000 Terminal Server. It can be installed and run from most Windows operating systems, including Windows for Workgroups, Windows 95/98/ME, Windows NT/2000, and Windows CE.

As you will see in Chapter 18, "Running Applications on the Web Using the Terminal Services Advanced Client," Microsoft also makes an ActiveX version of this client called the *Terminal Services Advanced Client* (TSAC), which enables you to remotely control desktops and applications running on a Terminal Server within your Microsoft's Internet Explorer web browser.

Citrix ICA Client

The second client is referred to as the *Citrix ICA client.* This client can either be installed from the server after you have installed Citrix MetaFrame by sharing the client directory, or it can be downloaded directly from the Citrix web site.

Unlike the Terminal Services client, which can be installed only on Windows or Internet Explorer, the Citrix ICA client will run on most every type of popular operating system and browser available today. Citrix has ported its client to all versions of Windows as well as most versions of UNIX, including Linux, the Macintosh, EPOC, Java, IBM OS/2, and even good old DOS.

Like the Microsoft RDP client, Citrix also makes an ActiveX version of its client that will work with a Microsoft Internet Explorer web browser. In addition, Citrix also has made available a version that will run on Netscape and Java-enabled devices.

At the start of this chapter, server-based technology was referred to as a technology "that gives wings to your Windows applications." This is truly the case with Citrix MetaFrame and Terminal Server because by using the Citrix version of server-based computing technology, not only can you run your applications from anywhere in the world, but you also can run them from nearly any device or operating system!

Other Server-Based Computing Technology Software Solutions

Although Citrix MetaFrame and Microsoft Terminal Services are the most prevalent server-based computing technologies today, it is important to understand other available server-based solutions. Some day you, as an administrator, might have to defend your choice of MetaFrame and Terminal Server versus other available solutions. You also will likely face the challenge of integrating server-based technology solutions together using portal and web development technologies.

Although many of the short topics that follow, such as Java and ActiveX, are not thin client solutions in themselves, they are the prevalent tools used today for building the Tier 3 client piece of three-tier, server-based solutions. Notice also that the majority of server-based solutions covered here, including Terminal Server and MetaFrame, are designed to run well across the Internet. The enormous growth and reach of the Internet has made it an ideal communications medium for server-based computing technologies. Server-based solutions that work across the Internet and can be integrated with widely available web browsers can be accessed from around the world.

Java-Based Thin Client Solutions

Java is a development language that was created by Sun Microsystems back in the mid-1990s. Java was created from the beginning to enable developers to write their applications once and run them anywhere. Although not every Java application is a Tier 3 thin client, it is an excellent choice for the development of these types of clients and is a key part of many of today's three-tier thin client solutions.

Java differs from other programming languages in that it is designed to be interpreted and compiled on-the-fly rather than distributed in a precompiled form.

Java applications are interpreted and compiled locally by a small application called a *Java Virtual Machine*. Much like Citrix has worked on making its ICA client available on multiple platforms, Sun has endeavored to port its Java Virtual Machine to as many platforms as possible and continually encourage its inclusion in all types of thin client devices.

Java Tier 3 applications are commonly deployed as downloadable Java applets, which can be run from Java Virtual Machines embedded in most common browsers. When used to control and communicate with a Tier 2 server application and a Tier 1 database, Java is a key component in three-tier thin client applications.

Java is not only a language used to develop Tier 3 client-side applications, but also can be used to develop integrated server-side applications running at Tier 2 using technology such as Java Server Pages and Java servlets.

Web Browser–Based Thin Client Solutions

Although web browsers were originally intended for the display of information across the Internet, they have become much more interactive in recent years. Using languages such as Perl, CGI, DHTML, ActiveX, and Java, both simple and complex three-tier solutions can be easily developed. Using these solutions, multiple remote users can interact with Tier 2 web servers and Tier 1 data sources.

Although these types of applications are very powerful, most full three-tier web solutions remain very expensive to purchase and even more expensive to custom develop. This expense is often a key factor in the decision as to whether to three-tier enable an existing application, purchase an end-to-end three-tier solution, or custom develop a three-tier solution using web development technologies. Even with this expense, however, some businesses find that full three-tier solutions have an excellent return on the investment because they can easily be widely deployed and can scale very well.

Citrix MetaFrame for UNIX

Much like MetaFrame 1.8/XP for Windows is designed to extend the reach of your Windows applications to most any platform, MetaFrame for UNIX can do the same for your UNIX applications and Java applications that run on UNIX. Currently in version 1.1, this product will enable you to run UNIX applications, such as Sun Microsystems Star Office suite, on most varieties of UNIX, Macintosh, OS/2, DOS, and of course all versions of Windows. Like MetaFrame for Windows, MetaFrame for UNIX is a three-tier-enabling application for UNIX-based applications. Currently, the product can be installed on Sun Microsystems Solaris, HP UX, and IBM's AIX UNIX operating systems.

Microsoft's .NET Movement and Server-Based Computing

For more than a year now, Microsoft has been loudly pronouncing the virtues of .NET. For many supporters of server-based computing, the purpose and eventual impact of this movement is unclear. .NET has definite potential for the creation of powerful three-tier applications on the Internet. However, like the Java Virtual Machine, which must be installed on a client for Java applications to run, or the Visual Basic Runtime Components, which are necessary for Visual Basic applications to work, applications written for the .NET framework rely on a relatively large client-side set of application components called the *Common Language Runtime* (CLR). Microsoft's intention over the next several years is to port the CLR to a wide range of operating systems, starting with Windows.

For Microsoft, the most important goal of the .NET movement is using it as part of its continued efforts to move away from a conventional business software-licensing model and toward subscription-based licensing. Therefore, the .NET framework is optimized for the widespread deployment of applications as services across the Internet. If the .NET movement proves successful, it is Microsoft's hope that it will push developers to produce a large variety of powerful Internet applications that will be available by subscription, starting with .NET versions of many of its own products.

Specific "Thin Client" Hardware Solutions

Although three-tier software solutions have mainly been discussed so far, part of any three-tier solution is choosing what hardware to run the Tier 3 client on. Over the years, hundreds of different hardware solutions have been created that can support server-based computing. In this section, you learn about the most prevalent ones available today.

Thin Client Terminals

Thin client terminals represent the next step in the evolution of the old green-screen terminal. Although several varieties of thin client terminals are available today, most can run Windows applications remotely on a Terminal Server using a preloaded Microsoft Terminal Services client and/or Citrix ICA client.

Author's Note

Whereas in the past most thin client terminals were based on either Windows CE or Windows NT OEM operating systems, you can now find terminals in the market that are based on various versions of Linux. For this reason, these devices are referred to as *thin client terminals* in this book, rather than Windows-based terminals.

In situations in which you currently use terminals or terminal emulation, using thin client terminals with Terminal Server is an excellent choice. Thin client terminals are well suited for task-oriented workers. The following are some of the many advantages of using this hardware solution rather than personal computers for your thin client project:

- Like text-based terminals, thin client terminals are very easy to install and inexpensive to maintain.
- Using thin client terminals with Terminal Server, users can run most Windows applications that they can run on a PC.
- Thin client terminals are generally less expensive and require less electricity than PCs.
- Most thin client terminal vendors include standard terminal emulation software on their terminals, such as 3270, 5250, and Wyse terminal emulation software.
- Web browsers are available for many thin client terminals.
- Thin client terminals are more secure than PCs because they have no local storage.

For a listing of some of the many thin client terminals available, refer to Appendix A, "Thin Client Hardware Solutions."

Handhelds and Wireless Technology

Although thin client terminals are excellent choices for the corporate environment, they are not designed to be portable. To address the need for portability, many manufacturers produce handheld devices. A wide variety of these types of devices are on the market; manufacturers are constantly in search of the best combination of portability and functionality.

Handhelds based on the Windows CE operating system or some newer palmtops based on the Windows operating system—such as the Sony VAIO, HP Joranda, and Compaq iPAQ—can easily run either Microsoft Terminal Services client or the Citrix ICA client. Although the capabilities of these small devices are generally limited, they can be made to remotely run full-featured applications from a Terminal Server by using server-based technology.

One very promising technology that has not yet reached its full potential is wireless. By integrating wireless capabilities with handheld devices, users can access information and run corporate applications from wherever they travel. Although wireless vendors are quickly building larger and faster wireless networks, however, users today still face many problems with limited coverage and unpredictable performance. This area of thin client technology is growing at a very fast rate and will increasingly become a major driving force for three-tier thin client solutions as the networks are more fully built out. Citrix is pursuing this market aggressively by making ICA clients available for wireless devices such as cell phones.

Personal Computers

Thinking of personal computers as thin client devices is almost sacrilegious to some. However, personal computers not only make very effective thin client devices, but also low-end PCs can be as inexpensive as thin client terminals. For administrators who want the greatest level of flexibility to respond to future business needs, personal computers remain a top choice. Although you can use a PC as a simple thin client terminal and run all of your applications off of a Terminal Server, you also have the choice of running some of those applications, such as a web browser, on the local workstation. Thin client technology also can be used to extend your existing investment in PC technology by enabling you to run newer, more processor-intensive Tier 2 applications at the server instead of being forced to purchase new computers to run them effectively.

Application Service Providers

Application service providers (ASPs) are businesses dedicated to providing applications and services to other businesses using server-based technology. Because of the relative newness of this business model, there are an almost unending variety of ASPs, applications, and services that they provide. Although many ASPs have tried and failed to be everything to everyone, a number of ASPs have focused on providing vertical applications using server-based technology to particular markets and have fared very well.

To provide applications to customers, many ASPs choose to use MetaFrame and Terminal Server technology. MetaFrame in particular is a good option for many ASPs because it offers the ability to easily publish applications to the widest variety of client devices.

Portal Technology

The idea of being able to get all of your applications and business information using server-based technology solutions wherever you are and no matter how you are connected is a compelling concept. As you can see by this chapter, however, a huge variety of different server-based solutions are available. Companies who have implemented, or are considering implementing, multiple server-based solutions are beginning to see the power of being able to bring all the different services these solutions provide together into a single service and information web portal.

The recent purchase of Sequoia's enterprise portal software by Citrix and the wide acceptance of their NFuse application portal are strong indications of how important this technology will soon be to businesses around the world. Using portal technology, you can bring together your entire web-based initiatives into a single comprehensive and secure web interface (see Figure 1.5).

Note how the web browser display is sectioned into different windows, each of which has a customization control so that you can close it or edit the contents. Note also in this example the inclusion of Citrix applications in the portal using NFuse technology. Most enterprise portal offerings, such as those by PlumTree, Viador, and Yahoo!, offer the ability to make your applications available in your personal portal using their built-in capability to tightly integrate with NFuse.

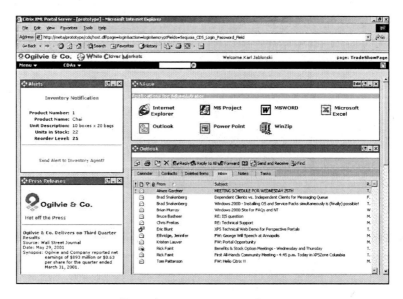

Figure 1.5   Corporate portal page.

With most portal products, your users log on through a web browser and receive back their view of the business and the information and services they need. Some of the many examples of information sources and services that can be integrated into portal software today include the following:

- Windows applications using NFuse technology
- General and industry-specific business news
- Reports and graphs
- Stock prices and graphs
- Document sharing and storage
- Email, scheduling, and contact management services
- Employee directories

Keep your eye out for future innovations by companies such as Citrix in the area of portal technology. Undoubtedly, many amazing and important business products will be produced as thin client technology continues to evolve!

2

Introduction to Windows Terminal Server

IT IS TIME TO BEGIN YOUR EXPLORATION of the core architecture and features of the Windows 2000 Terminal Server operating system. Because Terminal Server is implemented as an installable service on Windows 2000, you will find that much of the core capability to handle Terminal Services is now an integral part of the operating system. In this chapter, you will first learn how key components of Windows 2000 operating system have been written to support a multiuser environment.

Next, the features of Terminal Services in Windows 2000 versus those in Windows Terminal Server 4.0 are covered. There also is extensive coverage of the many feature enhancements you can expect in the release of Windows .NET Terminal Server.

For those who want more, this discussion is followed by coverage of core features now available in Windows 2000, such as the Installer Service and Active Directory, which can play a big role in your Terminal Server deployment.

Terminal Server Architecture

Before getting into the details of Windows 2000 Terminal Server architecture and how it differs from the preceding version, you need to understand the main differences between a standard Windows 2000 server and one that is running Terminal Services.

The fundamental difference is that Terminal Server architecture supports multiple sessions or desktops running at the same time, whereas Windows 2000 Server alone supports only one—the console. Each session running on a Terminal Server must be isolated from the actions of all other sessions.

Terminal Server mainly handles this need by assigning each new session a unique session ID. The session ID is used to keep track of and keep separate each session's resources by creating a separate namespace for those resources.

Sessions

To view the session IDs currently in use on your server, several utilities are available. The Terminal Services Manager is probably the simplest and easiest to use. To view the current session IDs on your server, follow these steps:

1. Install Terminal Services on your Windows 2000 server as shown in Chapter 8, "Installing Windows 2000 Terminal Server and Citrix MetaFrame."

2. Go to Administrative Tools in the Programs section of your Start menu and run Terminal Services Manager.

3. In the window that appears, highlight your Terminal Server by clicking it.

4. On the right side of the screen, click the Sessions tab.

A window similar to the one shown in Figure 2.1 will appear. This figure shows several sessions: the console, two idle sessions, two listening sessions for ICA and RDP, and one active terminal session.

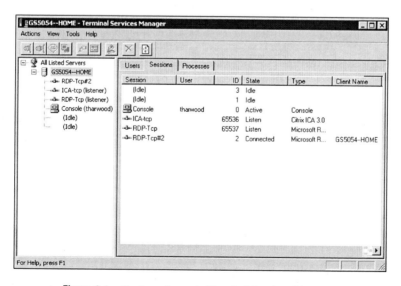

Figure 2.1   Sessions shown in Terminal Services Manager.

The Console Session

The console session, which is the session used by whoever is logged on to the console of the server, is always assigned session number 0. The console session can be accessed only from the console of the server and cannot be accessed from a Terminal Services client.

Idle Sessions

The two idle sessions are special sessions created by Terminal Services in an idle state. If the Terminal Server were to go through the entire session creation process every time someone attempted to connect using the Terminal Services Client, users would run into slow connection times and would be unable to connect when too many people tried to log on at once. To reduce the amount of time it takes to set up a new user with a session, Terminal Server by default creates two idle sessions. The next person who logs on is assigned one of these two sessions while Terminal Server goes through the more time-intensive process of creating a new one in the background.

To see this concept in action, note the session number assigned to one of the idle sessions before logging on and then log on to the Terminal Server using the Terminal Services client. One of the idle sessions will become your active session. A new idle session will quickly be created to replace the one you just used and will be assigned the next sequential session ID number.

Idle sessions are an important concept in the Terminal Server world. The default of two sessions can be adjusted and should be, as you will see in Chapter 21, "Performance Tuning and Resource Management."

Listening Sessions

Special sessions are also created for the resources necessary for each listening connection protocol. In the example shown in Figure 2.1, a listening session is created for RDP/TCP and ICA/TCP. Listening sessions are assigned a session number starting with 65537. Each additional listening session is assigned the next lower session number. These special-purpose sessions are closely related to idle sessions. Their purpose is to listen for session requests on their assigned protocol. They handle the initial session setup and assign the incoming session request to the next available idle session.

Connected and Disconnected Terminal Sessions

When the session establishment process is complete, the user's session enters a connected state. There is one terminal session for every Terminal Services client connected to the box.

Although sessions are initially assigned a connected state, if a user discon-nects from his session, the session enters a disconnected state. This is a very cool concept, because in a disconnected state the user's applications are still running at the server! This means that even if a momentary glitch occurs on the network causing you to lose your connection to Terminal Server, your session will remain running on Terminal Server. The next time you connect you will be brought back to where you left off. Because you can fine-tune this behavior in a lot of ways, this feature is covered in greater detail in later chapters.

Although many components of Windows 2000 Server run differently when Terminal Services is installed, the three most significant components are the Object Manager, Win32 subsystem, and the Virtual Memory Manager.

Components of the Terminal Server Architecture

One of the goals of this chapter is to provide a thorough understanding of the underlying structure of Terminal Server. You will find that a thorough understanding of the operating system's operation at this level will help you to better troubleshoot Terminal Server and optimize its performance.

This section starts with the Terminal Server architecture diagram shown in Figure 2.2, and as you proceed through this section, the function of each part of the diagram is explained. As each part is described, refer back to the archi-tecture diagram to see how a specific part fits in with the whole architecture.

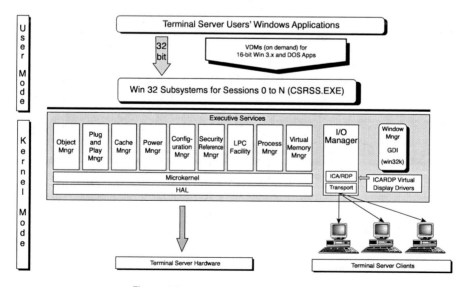

Figure 2.2   Terminal Server architecture.

Components of the Terminal Server operating system run in one of two modes: user or kernel.

Kernel Mode

In kernel mode, an application has direct access to the hardware. Examples of kernel mode applications are the *hardware abstraction layer* (HAL), microkernel, Virtual Memory Manager, and device drivers. Because the applications are running in kernel mode, the system is not protected from them, and as a result, they must be written and tested very carefully. One poorly written application can lock up or crash the entire system.

When a kernel-mode application crashes, most often you will receive the infamous "blue screen of death" and be forced to reboot your Terminal Server to recover.

User Mode

In user mode, an application can access hardware and operating system resources only through the Win32 subsystem. This layer of isolation provides a great amount of protection and portability for applications. Examples of applications running in the user mode are DOS applications, Windows 3.x (16 bit), Windows 32, POSIX, and OS/2. If a user-mode application crashes, the crash affects only the process in which the application is running. By using Task Manager, you can just delete the frozen process. All other applications continue to run without interruption.

User Mode Crashes and Dr. Watson

One important tool for troubleshooting user-mode applications crashes is Dr. Watson. When a user-mode application crashes, it normally will create a log entry in the Dr. Watson log with detailed developer-level information on the state of the system before the crash. Although you will likely find these logs nearly undecipherable, to a developer, they provide important clues as to why the application crashed. As an administrator, these logs will help you when working with application developers to isolate application problems, so that they can develop the necessary patches. On the other hand, in a Terminal Server environment, leaving Dr. Watson enabled can cause session lockups when applications fail. If you are not actively pursuing an application problem, it is best to disable Dr. Watson on your server. This is done through a Registry change that you will find covered in Chapter 21.

The underlying difference between kernel and user mode has to do with the processor privilege level. Kernel mode is often referred to as *privileged mode*. On most modern processors, you can run an application at different privilege levels. Intel processors have four privilege levels or rings in which applications can run: 0–3. In reality, kernel mode refers to programs that run at privilege level 0. These programs have unrestricted access to all hardware and memory in the system. Programs running at privilege level 0 can set the privilege level for programs that they call. In contrast, user mode refers to applications and subsystems set by the kernel to run in privilege level 3.

In this mode, applications are "boxed-in." The processor allows them to work only within their own memory areas. The processor also restricts them from directly accessing I/O, such as disk drives, communications ports, and video and network cards. To access these devices, applications must make a special gated call to a kernel-mode program that handles the hardware.

Author's Note

One very important difference between Windows NT 4.0 Terminal Server and Terminal Services in Windows 2000 is that parts of the printing subsystem have been moved from the kernel mode to the user mode. For those who have experienced the dreaded "blue screen of death" because of a printer driver problem in WTS 4.0, this is a welcome change. Now if a printer has a problem the operating system can stop the process without blue screening the server.

Kernel-Mode Components

A description of the components that make up Terminal Server must start at the heart of the operating system and work outward. The following sections first describe the microkernel and HAL in detail and their relation to each other. These are the core components of the operating system. Next, the Executive Services, which run in kernel mode, are covered.

Microkernel

Notice in Figure 2.2 that many of the modular components of the Terminal Server operating system are built around a microkernel. The microkernel is a small and very efficient program that handles the core functions of the operating system.

The microkernel's primary responsibility is to manage the operating system's workload. As a manager, the microkernel takes the tasks assigned to it by the applications and divides the work between the server's microprocessors. In a multiprocessor system, the efficiency of the microkernel is critical. Without an efficient microkernel, some processors become overburdened while others remain idle.

The microkernel actually resides in either NTOSKRNL.EXE or NTKRNLMP.EXE in the SYSTEM32 directory. The NTKRNLMP.EXE file is the multiprocessing version of NTOSKRNL.EXE. It is specially written to handle multiprocessor synchronization.

Processes and Threads

Terminal Server applications and the operating system itself divide their work between processes and threads. The Process and Thread Manager handles the creation and terminations of these threads. A *process* is a program under control of the Windows 2000 operating system that in essence is given its own room in memory and resources to work with by the operating system. When a process is started, an address space is set up for it. A process has its own variables and can request from the operating system its own access to the hardware below it. The operating system keeps track of what each process is doing by assigning it a unique process ID. Furthermore, Terminal Server keeps track of the processes that each session is running by assigning them session IDs.

For processes to get any work done, they divide their work into threads and have the operating system execute them. A *thread* is a piece of executable code that can be run on a single processor. The microkernel works by dispatching these threads to the processors based on their priorities.

Hardware Abstraction Layer

The hardware abstraction layer is what the microkernel communicates through when it needs to send threads to the processors or I/O devices. The HAL shields the microkernel from the differences in the hardware below it.

In Windows NT 4.0, the HAL contained not only code for communicating with the processors, but also with the system bus. In Windows 2000, bus drivers can be written separately by manufacturers.

The HAL also is used by many device drivers to access the hardware. The HAL shields these drivers from the differences in the structure of the hardware below them by providing a uniform interface.

Changing the HAL in Windows 2000

With Windows 2000, Microsoft has set up Windows for you to be able to easily change the HAL as needed using Device Manager. This is a nice benefit for Terminal Server administrators who often might start with a single-processor server with the intention of upgrading it with additional processors as needs grow. With WTS 4.0 you would either have to use a special utility from the manufacturer to upgrade from a single- to multiprocessor HAL or reinstall the box from scratch.

To view which HAL you are currently running and be able to change the HAL, run the Device Manager by following these steps:

1. Right-click the My Computer icon on the console and select Properties.

2. From the System Properties window that appears, click the Hardware tab.

3. Click the Device Manager button to run Device Manager.

4. Click the Computer icon to expand.

Underneath the Computer icon, as shown in Figure 2.3, you will see which type of HAL is currently installed on your system. You can change the HAL by following these steps:

1. Right-click the name of the HAL and select Properties.

2. Select the Driver tab in the window that appears.

3. Click Update Driver and follow the wizard.

From the wizard you will be able to have it either redetect the correct HAL, let you choose from one of the built-in HALs, or let you install one from a disk provided by the manufacturer.

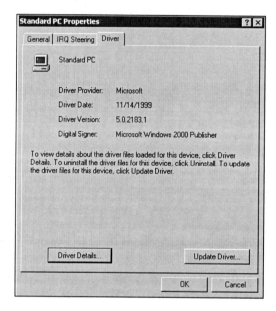

Figure 2.3   Changing the HAL in Windows 2000.

Executive Services

There are 11 primary Executive Services. These are the basic kernel-mode components that the applications running in user mode utilize through the Win32 API:

- Object Manager
- Plug and Play Manager
- Cache Manager
- Power Manager
- Configuration Manager
- Security Reference Monitor
- Process Manager
- Virtual Memory Manager
- Local Procedure Call Facility

- I/O Manager
- Windows Manager and Graphical Device Interface

Refer to Figure 2.2 for a general idea of how these components relate. The Executive Services are all kernel-mode components that provide the operating system services used by the applications running on Terminal Server. The following sections describe each of the kernel-mode components.

Object Manager

One of the most important components in the Executive Services suite is the Object Manager. Because Windows 2000 is an object-oriented operating system, most of its resources are treated as objects. The Object Manager is in charge of creating, tracking, protecting, and deleting system objects. The Object Manager is responsible for objects used in both kernel mode and user mode. The Object Manager keeps track of both global objects used by all sessions and session-specific objects that applications running in a particular session create.

The following are examples of some of the objects under Windows 2000:

- Port objects
- Memory objects
- Process objects
- Thread objects
- File and directory objects

In the multiuser environment of Terminal Server, each session must keep its objects separate from those of the other sessions. To keep them separate, Terminal Server adds the session ID to the object name for each object created within the session.

Plug and Play

One of the great new benefits with Windows 2000 is true Plug and Play capability. This new Executive Service is responsible for monitoring for new devices and loading the correct drivers when devices are added. In addition, the Plug and Play Manager is responsible for assigning system resources to hardware such as IRQ and I/O port numbers.

Cache Manager

The Cache Manager's job is to constantly monitor file access by system processes. It then determines which files are being loaded most often and loads them into memory. Having commonly accessed files in memory rather than on disk greatly speeds up system file-serving performance.

Power Manager

The Power Manager handles system power management and can be configured for such things as putting the CPU or hard drive to sleep if the system has been in an idle state for too long. The Power Manager's behavior is controlled by the Power Options in Control Panel.

Configuration Manager

The Configuration Manager's responsibility is to manage the system Registry. Because the Registry is critical to operating system functionality, the Configuration Manager has been designed to take steps to ensure the reliability of the Registry and to control how changes occur to it.

Security Reference Monitor

For an operating system to be secure, not every application or user can have access to all resources on the system. This is especially important with Terminal Server, in which several users can access the same resources remotely. If the operating system is not protected, for example, a single Terminal Server user could accidentally delete a critical system file that everyone needs. The Security Reference Monitor provides both authentication and auditing services to protect your server from instances such as these.

Process Manager

In the earlier discussion about the microkernel, processes are described as being part of applications and having threads. The Process Manager keeps track of all processes running on the system and their associated threads. The Process Manager also handles the opening and closing of processes and threads.

Every process is assigned a security access token when it first starts. The Process Manager works closely with the Security Reference Monitor to ensure that the process goes through the appropriate security checks before accessing protected objects.

Virtual Memory Manager

The applications that run on your Terminal Server need memory to hold their data and code. The Virtual Memory Manager is responsible for keeping track of this memory and assigning it to your programs.

In older operating systems such as MS-DOS, a set amount of memory was available and only one program was loaded into it at a time. Under Terminal Server, several users can simultaneously run multiple applications on the same server. For these applications to work together properly, each is given its own block of virtual memory. Applications are allowed to access only their own memory and are blocked from accessing others' memory. In this way, each application runs in its own protected space in the Terminal Server's memory.

The Virtual Memory Manager maps virtual addresses used by processes into actual physical locations in the computer's memory. Each process running on Windows 2000 Terminal Server is given up to a 2GB virtual address space within which to work. In addition, the operating system itself reserves a virtual 2GB address space for its use.

The magic of the Virtual Memory Manager is that although you might not actually have this amount of memory, it appears to your applications as if this amount is available. If you have a program that runs out of room, the Virtual Memory Manager swaps other portions of memory to the hard disk to make room for the running application. To your application, the memory still appears as one contiguous space.

The Virtual Memory Manager also provides very important performance information to your system. On Terminal Server, having the right amount of memory to handle all users and applications is critical. If not enough memory is available, the response time slows down tremendously for all users because the Virtual Memory Manager must swap out memory to disk to make room. In Chapter 21, you learn how to use Performance Monitor to effectively monitor how much memory you are using and how much you need.

The 2GB Limit

If you are using standard Windows 2000 Server, the maximum memory that it will support is 4GB. Because 2GB of that is automatically used by the operating system, your Terminal Server applications are left with 2GB of working room. Although this might seem like a lot, as processor speeds increase, Terminal Servers that support large numbers of light users can run into memory bottlenecks.

You might think that by Windows 2000 Microsoft would have found a way to get around this 2GB limit. Well they have, sort of. Using the new *Address Windowing Extensions* (AWE) programming, interface developers can now create applications that can make use of up to 64GB of system memory. If you are running Windows 2000 Advanced Server, which supports up to 8GB of memory, or DataCenter Server, which supports up to 64GB, your users can take advantage of this extra room only if applications running on the server have been written to the AWE interface. With the exception of a handful of heavy-duty server-based applications, such as SQL Server 2000, very few applications today are written to make use of this extra space.

The reason behind why Microsoft has struggled with this limitation is that Windows 2000 is a 32-bit operating system. Because of this, applications are capable of addressing up to only 4GB of memory at a time. To totally eliminate this limitation, Microsoft is diligently working on a 64-bit version of its server operating system that will run on Intel's upcoming 64-bit Itanium processors.

Local Procedure Call Facility

The *Local Procedure Call Facility* (LPC) handles the client/server communication between applications and subsystems and between processes. It handles only those calls that occur locally. The actual request is sent to the Win32 subsystem, which in turn sends the request to the appropriate Executive subsystem for display. This level of complexity is hidden from the application, which must only call the procedure and receive a response.

Terminal Server makes extensive use of LPCs. The Terminal Server service (TERMSRV.EXE), which handles most of the background administration necessary on Terminal Server, uses LPCs to communicate with other processes. When new connections need to be made, for example, the Terminal Server service calls the *Session Manager* (SMSS) to create idle connections that wait for new users who need to log on.

I/O Manager

The I/O Manager handles all input and output to your system's devices, and as such, it is probably one of the busiest subsystems. The I/O Manager includes a Cache Manager that handles caching all disk and network input/output. Whether you are connecting your clients to the Terminal Server via the network, serial ports, or modems, the I/O Manager is the main Terminal Server subsystem through which they will interact. Because of this, it is important that you keep up with new releases of I/O drivers, so that you always have the most up-to-date and efficient versions.

Windows Manager and Graphical Device Interface

The Windows Manager and *Graphical Device Interface* (GDI) are responsible for handling all Win32 API video requests by applications. They are the kernel-mode components of the Win32 subsystem. How the Windows Manager and GDI relate to the Win32 subsystem is diagrammed in Figure 2.2. The code that makes up the kernel-mode Windows Manager and GDI are part of the WIN32K.SYS system file. Every new session on Terminal Server starts up a separate instance of this file.

User-Mode Components

So far, the discussion has focused on kernel-mode components. The applications the users are running are in user mode. For Terminal Server to support as many types of applications as it does, it has subsystems that emulate the native environments in which these applications would run. There are environment subsystems for DOS, Windows 16-bit, POSIX, and text-based OS/2 applications. All these subsystems are designed to basically convert the foreign application's calls into calls that Terminal Server's native environmental subsystem, the Win32 API, can understand.

Win32 Subsystem

The Win32 subsystem handles most Win32 API calls. All user-mode applications communicate with the Terminal Server operating system through this API. Because Terminal Server is a strictly controlled operating system, all interaction between applications and hardware must occur through the Win32 API. Applications that try to improperly bypass the operating system and access hardware directly are shut down or stopped by Terminal Server. This level of application security brings a great amount of stability to the operating system. Even poorly written applications do not have the capability to lock up the entire operating system with an improper direct hardware call, such as a direct disk write. This is very important for Terminal Server because it typically is running several applications simultaneously for several users.

The Win32 API, supported by the Win32 subsystem, is an object-oriented set of functions and procedures that allows the application to control all aspects of the operating system. One of the main advantages of an API is the layer of isolation it provides to the operating system. As long as the Win32 API stays the same, the entire kernel can be rewritten, and Win32 applications would still run.

The Win32 subsystem can be divided into two subsystems: the Executive and the Console. The Executive subsystem resides in the kernel mode; it is made up of the Windows Manager and GDI. The Executive handles the majority of the graphics-related Win32 API calls. The Console runs in the user mode and provides text window support, hard-error handling, and shutdown.

The system file that makes up the user-mode portion of the Win32 subsystem is the *Client Server Runtime Subsystem* executable (CSRSS.EXE). Every instance of CSRSS also starts an instance of the WINLOGON process (WINLOGON.EXE), which is responsible for the initial handling of the client logon, and pass-thru authentication after the client has already logged on.

On Windows 2000 Server, only a single instance of this subsystem is created by the *Session Manager* (SMSS.EXE). This instance handles the graphical display of the server console. Because Terminal Server must keep track of multiple desktops simultaneously, each new session created on it must be assigned its own Win32 subsystem.

Viewing the Win32 Subsystem in Action

You can view the multiple instances of CSRSS.EXE and WINLOGON.EXE by going into Windows Task Manager. To access Task Manager, follow these steps.

1. Press Ctrl+Alt+Del while logged on at the server console or open Windows Security under the Settings section of the Start menu.

2. In the Windows Security window that appears, click the Task Manager button.

3. When the Task Manager window appears, click the Processes tab.

4. Check the box next to Show processes from all users.

5. Under the View menu, select Select Columns.

6. From the Select Columns window that appears, make sure Session ID and Username are checked, and then click OK.

A window similar to the one shown in Figure 2.4 will display. Notice that six sessions are shown and for each session there is an instance of CSRSS and WINLOGON. If you were to scroll down, you would also see the instance of CSRSS and WINLOGON for the console, session 0.

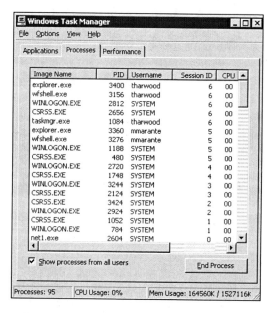

Figure 2.4   Win32 subsystem shown running in Task Manager.

DOS and Windows 16-Bit Applications

To run DOS applications, you need a converter to take the application's device calls and convert them to Win32 API calls that Terminal Server can understand. The module that does this is the *Virtual DOS Machine* (VDM). The VDM simulates a DOS environment for DOS applications. It provides simulation for the following:

- Standard DOS 21 Interrupt services
- ROM BIOS calls
- Device calls, such as to the keyboard or video

When a DOS application runs on Terminal Server, it is assigned three threads. The first thread is the one in which the application runs. The second thread provides a heartbeat to simulate timer interrupts for the MS-DOS applications. Many DOS applications rely on the timer interrupt to time various procedures and to control the execution of programs. The third thread is for console I/O.

Windows 2000 Terminal Server Features

Now that you have a good understanding of the architecture that makes Terminal Server possible, it is time to explore its many features. Microsoft is very dedicated to the continual improvement of server-based technology in its products and has implemented many significant improvements in Windows 2000 Terminal Services over those available in WTS 4.0. These improvements have mainly been enabled by the new version of the *Remote Desktop Protocol* (RDP). As discussed in the preceding chapter, RDP is Terminal Server's thin client protocol. In addition to improvements in RDP, several additional features have been added to the operating system that are important to consider when implementing server-based solutions, such as Windows Load Balancing, Disk Quotas, and Intellimirror to mention just a few.

Author's Note

Although the main focus of this book is on Windows 2000 Terminal Services, wherever possible, glimpses into the upcoming Terminal Services features in Windows .NET Terminal Server are included. It is important to note that the name Windows .NET Terminal Server has not been finalized by Microsoft as of this writing. In this book, however, Windows .NET Terminal Server refers to the next edition of Windows 2000 Server from Microsoft, currently codenamed Whistler. Also be aware that as of the writing of this version of the book, Windows .NET Terminal Server is still in development, so there is the possibility that the features covered might differ slightly or that new features will be added by the time the final product is released.

Features in the Remote Desktop Protocol

The RDP 5.0 protocol, included with Windows 2000 Terminal Services, has significant improvements over both the features and capabilities of the preceding RDP 4.0 client as shown in Table 2.1. In comparison to the Citrix ICA client, which is covered in more detail in the next chapter, RDP 4.0 did not have nearly the number of features and was not nearly as efficient over low-speed connections. However, RDP 5.0 represents the first truly robust thin client protocol from Microsoft. Although installing Citrix MetaFrame still retains several important advantages to Microsoft Terminal Server, Microsoft has begun closing the gap with this release of Terminal Server. Table 2.1 shows some of the many feature improvements in RDP 5.0.

Author's Note

To take advantage of the new features in version 5.0 of the RDP protocol, it is important to note that they are available only if you use the version of the Terminal Services client that comes with Windows 2000 Server and only if it is used with a Windows 2000 Terminal Server. Although the new Terminal Services client is backward compatible with WTS 4.0, not all the features will be enabled when connecting to that platform. Remember that Windows NT 4.0 Terminal Server supports only the features in RDP 4.0 and not 5.0.

Table 2.1   **RDP Feature Comparison**

Feature	WTS 4.0 RDP 4.0	Windows 2000 RDP 5.0	Windows .NET Terminal Server RDP 5.1
Capability to reconnect to disconnected sessions	X	X	X
Encryption – 40-bit and 128-bit RC4	X	X	X
Compression available	X	X	X
Printer auto-creation		X	X
Bitmap and glyph caching in RAM	X	X	X
Capability to display 256 colors	X	X	X
Session remote control (shadowing)		X	X
Persistent bitmap and glyph caching to disk		X	X
Automatic detection and installation of client printers		X	X

Feature	WTS 4.0 RDP 4.0	Windows 2000 RDP 5.0	Windows .NET Terminal Server RDP 5.1
Encryption		X	X
Compression highly optimized and on by default		X	X
Clipboard redirection		X	X
LPT and COM port redirection		X	X
Rudimentary load-balancing capability using NLB		X	X
Audio redirection			X
Drive mapping			X
Capability to display up to 16 million colors			X
Supports logon with Smart Cards			X
Rudimentary load-balancing using NLB with session reconnect capability			X

Enhanced Performance

Several steps have been taken to enhance the performance of the RDP protocol in version 5.0, especially over low-speed connections, as follows:

- Compression has been enabled by default in the Terminal Services client 5.0. In version 4.0, compression was off by default. Through extensive testing, Microsoft found that enabling compression had less effect on processor performance than originally thought and offered significant reduction in the amount of data that needed to be transferred.

- In addition to the RAM caching of commonly used screen bitmaps, Microsoft has added the capability to do persistent caching to disk. This means that Terminal Server will now remember the common screen components that your applications use between sessions. In other words, the more you use your applications, the more efficient their use across the Terminal Services client becomes.

- Significant tuning has improved the performance of both their compression algorithm and reduced the number of screen updates necessary over high-latency connections, such as dial-up connections.

Persistent Caching to Disk

For those who are not familiar with how this feature works, imagine your users run one or two applications from their Terminal Server desktop every day. When they log on to Terminal Server without bitmap caching, the server would have to send down a full snapshot of whatever was currently running on their desktop. With bitmap caching, the client caches commonly used bitmaps in local memory. Instead of sending down the entire display to the client, the server sends only those components not already in the client's local cache. In addition to caching these bitmaps in memory, RDP 5.0 allows for them to be automatically cached to disk, which greatly improves the performance between sessions.

56-Bit Encryption

Although RDP 4.0 had 40-bit, one-way (low), 40-bit, two-way (medium), and 128-bit, two-way (high) encryption available, in RDP 5.0 Microsoft added 56-bit encryption. In version 5.0, the RDP client will use 56-bit encryption rather than 40-bit encryption if the client is running on a Windows 2000 workstation. Encryption in version 5.0 still uses the same RC4 encryption algorithm that was used before.

Printer Auto-Creation

New to RDP 5.0, client printers can be automatically detected and installed during logon. This is an incredibly valuable feature for enterprise deployments; because as you will see in later chapters, supporting users printers can be very challenging. With WTS 4.0 without MetaFrame, you would be forced to manually map your users' printers. For large deployments, printer management would become a significant burden for administrators.

LPT, COM, and Clipboard Redirection

Another important feature new to RDP 5.0 is the automatic redirection of LPT ports, COM ports, and the Clipboard. When clients log on to Windows 2000 Server, their local LPT and COM ports are automatically detected by the server and made available to applications. In this way, users can now print to printers and communicate with other locally attached devices using applications running on Terminal Server.

In the same way, Clipboard redirection enables you to copy contents from an application running on Terminal Server to your local Clipboard and vice versa.

Session Remote Control

A very valuable administrative support tool, previously only available with Citrix MetaFrame, was the ability to remotely control another user's session. This feature is now included with RDP 5.0.

Features Available in Windows .NET Terminal Server

As you can see from Table 2.1, Microsoft is continuing to add significant improvements to its thin client software. Perhaps the most important and sought-after feature is the ability to automatically map user drives. Currently, if you need the ability for your users to save information to their local drives from applications running on Terminal Server, you have to manually set up connections to network shares or purchase Citrix MetaFrame. With the addition of this new feature, when you log on to Terminal Server in Windows .NET Terminal Server, your local drives will appear automatically as drives available to your applications.

In addition, other significant features are slated to be included, such as audio redirection, the ability to display up to 16 million colors, and Smart Card logons. A new Session Directory Service is planned to be included, which keeps track of which server is running which Terminal Server connection. In this way, Terminal Services clients can automatically reconnect to their session running on Terminal Server farms that have some type of load-sharing enabled.

Finally, although not an RDP feature, Microsoft is currently intending to release 64-bit versions of Windows .NET Terminal Server for the Intel Itanium processor. As a Terminal Server administrator, this will enable you to eventually get past the 2GB memory barrier of today. However, although you will likely be able to run your 32-bit applications in a Windows on Windows emulation mode, you will not be completely free of the 2GB barrier until your applications have been recompiled as 64-bit applications.

Terminal Server and Remote Desktops

Although Citrix's main focus is to provide easy remote access to your applications, Microsoft is increasingly using Terminal Server technology as a means for easy desktop remote control. In Windows 2000 Server, you have the choice of whether you want to use the technology for simple remote control of your server's desktop or for more robust desktop and application serving for multiple users. If you use it for only remote control, no additional licensing cost applies. This feature is valuable to administrators who need secure remote access to their servers and in the past have had to purchase and install third-party remote-control software to achieve this.

With Windows XP and Windows .NET Terminal Server, Microsoft has renamed the Terminal Server client to be the *Remote Desktop client*. In Windows XP, this client is installed by default. In addition, Windows XP can easily be set up for remote access without needing to purchase third-party remote-control software. This allows for easy remote support of these systems by administrators and support centers.

Useful Windows 2000 Features for Terminal Servers

Windows 2000 Server includes several very important and useful features that can be taken advantage of for Terminal Servers. This section covers the most important of those features.

Disk Quotas

New to Windows 2000 Server is the built in capability to enforce disk quotas. This feature can be very useful for Terminal Server administrators who need to limit the amount of space that their users can take on a particular file server. This is especially useful for limiting the size of user home directories and common areas. Disk Quotas are set per user and per logical drive, which means that for them to be effective, you need to dedicate logical drives for a single user purpose. As users save information to this drive, the amount of space they use is tallied up. If they attempt to exceed their quota, they receive a Drive Out of Space error.

Active Directory

Perhaps the most important boon to Terminal Services is Active Directory. For administrators who are constantly nesting security accounts from multiple domains into their Terminal Server, Active Directory enables them to consolidate these domains into a single Active Directory or a manageable handful.

Another big benefit of Active Directory is *group policy objects* (GPOs). One of the big problems with WTS 4.0 policies is that they "tattoo" your machine. Tattooing refers to the manner in which Windows NT 4.0 policies are applied. When a machine logs on to a network and a Windows NT 4.0 policy is applied to that machine, that policy setting remains on that machine. To remove a Windows NT 4.0 policy setting, you have to set the policy to be deleted and then the user has to log on again to get rid of it. Suppose, for example, that you set a policy for a particular logon banner to appear on your clients. When they log on to the network, this Windows NT 4.0 policy is applied and the users see the logon banner. If one of the users is a consultant with a laptop, however, when he leaves and goes back to his company, the policy will still be in effect on his workstation. The network administrator at the consultant's company would then have to remove the policy manually.

With Windows 2000, the GPOs applied at logon are automatically removed when the user logs off. This completely avoids the problem of tattooing. In addition, policies are refreshed periodically while users are logged on. This means that as an administrator, you can make a Windows 2000 group policy take effect without having to have users log off and then log back on to the domain.

In addition, many new policies have been added, including security policies, application-specific policies, desktop control policies, and the ability to install applications using policies. This last feature is very important for Terminal Server administrators, because in a pure Windows 2000 environment, it can be used to publish Terminal Server applications. An example of how to implement this feature is shown in Chapter 27, "Network Load Balancing for NFuse and Terminal Servers."

Network Load Balancing

Network Load Balancing (NLB) is a feature available in the Advanced and DataCenter versions of Windows 2000 Server. NLB allows for load sharing among up to 32 servers on the same network segment. This new service was initially designed with web servers in mind, but will work well in a Terminal Server environment. Unlike the Citrix MetaFrame version of load balancing, the Microsoft version does not have the capability to divert incoming sessions based on a real-time evaluation of which server can best handle them. It is therefore more of a load-sharing technique similar to DNS Round-Robin rather than a load-balancing one.

For Terminal Server–only shops, NLB is a viable option for not only load sharing, but also for ensuring high availability of their Terminal Server solutions. In Chapter 27, you will find specific guidance on how to best set up NLB for your Terminal Servers.

Author's Note

Be aware that NLB is not inherently designed to handle disconnecting and reconnecting to the same session by clients. By enabling an NLB feature called *Client Affinity* after a client has made the first connection to an NLB server, however, it will continue to make a connection to the same server on future attempts. In this way, if the client leaves a session in a disconnected state, the client can reconnect to it.

In Windows .NET Terminal Server the new Session Directory Service is designed to get around this problem.

Windows Scripting

Windows 2000 includes built-in support for significantly more advanced scripting capabilities than WTS 4.0. Using VBScript, administrators can develop advanced scripts for their Terminal Servers instead of relying on third-party scripting tools such as Kixtart.

3

Introduction to Citrix MetaFrame 1.8 and MetaFrame XP

ONE MAJOR QUESTION ON THE MINDS of many administrators is whether they need MetaFrame, the add-on product for Terminal Server from Citrix. Out of the box, Windows 2000 Terminal Server is a very powerful product with many significant enhancements since the last version. It is possible that the features that are available in Terminal Server alone might be all that you need. On the other hand, many administrators have chosen to purchase Citrix MetaFrame based on the unique needs of their environment. This chapter explores MetaFrame features in detail, comparing both the features in MetaFrame 1.8 to MetaFrame XP and the difference in features between Terminal Server alone and Terminal Server with MetaFrame.

Understanding MetaFrame

MetaFrame is an add-on product from Citrix that you install on your existing Terminal Server. Citrix makes two versions of MetaFrame for the Windows Server platforms: MetaFrame 1.8 and MetaFrame XP. As discussed in Chapter 8, "Installing Windows 2000 Terminal Server and Citrix MetaFrame," the installation process is very simple. You install it from the server console using the MetaFrame CD, which normally takes less than 20 minutes.

The MetaFrame installation adds many features to the Terminal Server operating system. It integrates very smoothly into existing Terminal Server deployments, and your existing Terminal Server clients will still be able to connect just as they did before MetaFrame was added. With the addition of

MetaFrame, however, you can take advantage of its many features only by installing and using Citrix MetaFrame *Independent Computing Architecture* (ICA) client software on the client workstations. This client software is included on the MetaFrame CD and can be easily deployed in several ways, including through the web by using the freely available web-based Citrix ICA client install components. In Chapter 11, "Installing RDP Clients for Windows," you will learn all about the many ways to deploy both types of clients.

In a Citrix MetaFrame world, your Citrix servers are referred to as being part of a *server farm*. As discussed in this chapter and many times throughout this book, one of Citrix MetaFrame's most important advantages over Terminal Server alone is the many ways in which it brings together the capabilities of your individual Citrix servers into a single, more powerful server farm. This focus on synergy enables you to more easily centralize your server-based computing solution than you can currently do with Windows 2000 Terminal Services alone.

Citrix MetaFrame 1.8 and XP

Although this book's main focus is on Citrix MetaFrame XP, if you are a Citrix MetaFrame 1.8 administrator, you should definitely not feel left out. You will find plenty of excellent real-world tips, Registry changes, and ideas that are just as applicable to you as they are to Citrix MetaFrame XP administrators. If you are considering upgrading to MetaFrame XP at some point in the near future, this chapter will provide you with the details you need to help make your decision.

One reason this book covers both is because of the indefinite commitment by Citrix to continue both the support and sales of MetaFrame 1.8. This gives you plenty of time to plan and budget for your migration to MetaFrame XP and enables you to get the most value out of your existing investment in 1.8. However, future development efforts by Citrix currently focus mainly on MetaFrame XP. Therefore, although Citrix intends to continue to add features to its MetaFrame XP product line and to test and support it on new operating systems such as Windows .NET, Citrix has not committed to doing the same with 1.8.

MetaFrame 1.8 and MetaFrame XP Core Features

Citrix MetaFrame 1.8 and MetaFrame XP both share many core features that complement what you find in Terminal Server alone. Whether these features are important enough to purchase MetaFrame depends on the specific needs of your business and what you are trying to accomplish using this technology.

The sections that follow will give you a better understanding of the main differences between MetaFrame and Terminal Server to help you better decide for yourself. These sections provide a list of those features that are shared by both Citrix MetaFrame 1.8 and MetaFrame XP.

Author's Note

Remember that, unless noted, these features are available only after you have installed MetaFrame on the server and have changed the clients to the MetaFrame ICA client.

Citrix ICA

Like Microsoft's Remote Desktop Protocol (RDP) client, Citrix makes its own version of server-based computing client software. This client uses the Citrix ICA protocol and is referred to as the *ICA client*. The ICA protocol that the client relies on is an integral and important piece of Citrix's server-based computing architecture. Many of the features that MetaFrame adds to Terminal Server are actually the result of features within the ICA protocol.

ICA handles the diversity of information required to be communicated in a server-based computing environment by using virtual channel technology. Each virtual channel within the ICA protocol can be used for different functionality on the client side. For example, graphics display and printing both have their own separate virtual channels within ICA.

Unlike RDP, which only works with TCP/IP, the ICA protocol can run on top of several different lower-layer transport protocols, such as TCP/IP, IPX/SPX, and NetBEUI. Support also exists for the ICA protocol over direct serial and dial-up connections.

Program Neighborhood

The Program Neighborhood interface (see Figure 3.1) provides users with a single location to go to for access to all of their Citrix applications. Unlike the Terminal Server Connection Manager, which only enables you to make connections for a single server or application, the Citrix Program Neighborhood enables you to connect to a collection of Citrix servers referred to as a *Citrix farm* and a collection of Citrix applications, not just one. The applications that have been published for you on this farm automatically appear in your Citrix Program Neighborhood when you connect. As you will see in the next section, this is an especially important feature for many administrators.

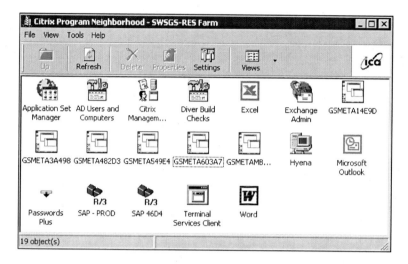

Figure 3.1   Citrix Program Neighborhood

Pass-Thru ICA Client

Citrix also makes a special version of the Program Neighborhood referred to as the Pass-Thru ICA client. The Pass-Thru ICA client is a special version of Program Neighborhood that is installed on the MetaFrame server by default. Because not all implementations of the ICA client include the Program Neighborhood, by using the Pass-Thru ICA client you can provide a single interface from which these users can run their applications.

Often this client is used when deploying thin client terminals. Instead of setting up thin client terminals to run their applications from a full Terminal Server desktop, many administrators choose to have them run applications from the more easily controlled Program Neighborhood. This is done by setting up a connection on the terminal to the Pass-Thru ICA client.

Publishing and Embedding Applications

Application publishing remains as one of the most significant feature differences between Terminal Server and MetaFrame. With application publishing in MetaFrame, you can push out icons for new applications running on the MetaFrame server just by adding users to a group. The icons then automatically appear in a user's Program Neighborhood or are published to their local Start menu or desktop the next time the user attaches to the server farm. For administrators who want to be able to roll out new applications quickly or upgrade existing ones, this feature is an incredible time saver.

With application publishing, you also can restrict which users or groups are allowed access to individual applications. This gives you much more control over what applications your user can use. Finally, besides using the freely available NFuse application, which is covered later in this chapter. Citrix automates the process of creating the HTML code necessary to run your applications on a web server and embed them within a web page. Remote users can then run your applications by using standard web browsers.

Application-Centric Versus Desktop-Centric

An important conceptual difference that you should understand between Terminal Server and MetaFrame is that in its current release Terminal Server continues to take a desktop-centric approach and not an application-centric one as does MetaFrame. With Terminal Server, you can manually set up connections to particular applications. Unless you have a pure Windows 2000 server, a 2000 or XP workstation environment, and use Intellimirror technology, however, there is no easy way to automatically publish applications running on Terminal Server.

The desktop-centric approach means your users in essence have two desktops. Because users have direct access to a desktop provided at the server, you need to take great care to lock down the desktop properly. If a user accidentally deletes or overwrites a critical file, it can bring down the entire server and affect all the users. As an administrator you need to be especially careful if you choose to use a desktop-centric approach that you lock down desktops tightly. Chapter 14, "Policies and Desktop Management," provides specific instructions on how to do this.

If you take a more application-centric approach, as you are able to with MetaFrame, and publish applications to your users rather than desktops, users do not see or have access to their Terminal Server desktop. To the user, this is a more seamless experience because applications running on MetaFrame appear to run just as any other application running on their local desktop.

On the other hand, if you intend to deploy thin client terminals, you might want users to have their own desktop from Terminal Server because there is no local desktop on most thin client terminals. In this case, application publishing might not be an important feature. Instead, it is more important whether the thin client terminals you choose include an RDP client if you want to run them on Terminal Server alone.

Client Platform Independence

Citrix is working constantly to provide support for the widest range of client operating systems. Compared to Terminal Server, MetaFrame currently supports a much wider variety of clients. Microsoft currently develops client software only for the following versions of its own operating systems and web browser application:

- Windows NT 3.51, NT 4.0, 2000, and XP
- Windows 95/98/Me
- Windows for Workgroups 3.11
- Windows CE (built into many thin client terminals)
- Internet Explorer using the ActiveX-based Terminal Services Advanced Client

If you have non-Windows clients on which you want to run Windows applications, you must purchase the MetaFrame add-on. With MetaFrame, you can run Windows terminal sessions on all versions of the Windows operating systems listed previously plus the following:

- Macintosh Client 68030/040 and Power PC-based systems
- Most flavors of UNIX, including HP-UX, Sun Solaris/x86 and Solaris/Sparc, SunOS, Compaq Tru64, HP/UX, SGI, SCO, IBM AIX, and Linux
- DOS 4.0 and above
- OS/2 v2.1/3.0/4.0
- EPOC/Symbian OS
- Java applet version, which will run on any platform that supports the Java SDK 1.1 and above
- Netscape Navigator and Communicator using a downloadable plug-in

Keep in mind that the list of clients supported by MetaFrame is growing constantly. For the latest list of clients supported by the product, check out the Citrix web site at www.citrix.com.

Hardware Independence

Citrix does not just want clients to run on a much greater variety of operating systems than is possible with Terminal Server, but also on a greater variety of hardware. In most all cases with Microsoft clients, they are designed to run on Microsoft operating systems that run on Intel-based hardware platforms. The Citrix client will run on several versions of UNIX and other operating systems that work on non-Intel-based hardware platforms, such as Solaris/Sparc and Macintosh workstations. In addition, the Citrix client is supported on a wider range of thin client terminals, such as those not based on the Windows CE platform.

Citrix support of a wider range of hardware setups truly helps extend the value of your existing hardware investment. With Citrix, no matter what hardware or operating system you have, you will always be able to run the latest Windows-based applications with the processing power of a high-performance server. One anecdote that helps give perspective is how Citrix, when first selling its thin client solution in the early to mid 1990s, used to go to trade shows and demo Windows-based applications running on an IBM AT running DOS. This is a poignant demonstration of Citrix platform independence. If you still have an old IBM AT in the closet with a VGA card, you could actually make use of it to run modern Windows applications, even today, at speeds that would rival that of a modern high-end workstation!

Web Application Publishing Using NFuse

Web application publishing is one of the most important capabilities that Citrix offers. This alone is often a reason for administrators to purchase Citrix over just Terminal Server. Web application publishing is easily accomplished in Citrix using the freely available NFuse software. For MetaFrame 1.8 administrators, this software can be downloaded from the web site for free. For MetaFrame XP customers, the option to install NFuse is now made part of the installation process. This integration of NFuse into the install process is an indicator of how important and widely accepted this technology has become.

Citrix NFuse is a set of customizable web-based application components that provide an infrastructure for publishing applications to the web. Out of the box, you can use NFuse to quickly create a virtual web-based Program Neighborhood for your users. When users log on to the NFuse web site you created, a logon window displays. After entering their credentials, they are shown the icons for all the applications that have been published to them from the Citrix server farm.

In case the user does not have the client software installed, Citrix includes freely available web-based client install components, which can be used to deploy preconfigured clients to your users with the click of a button.

Although NFuse can provide a complete solution out of the box, it was originally intended to provide a programming interface that developers could use to more closely integrate NFuse features with their web-based applications. For this reason, NFuse is very modular and its programming interfaces are well documented.

Columbia and NFuse

NFuse began as a simple proof of concept type-project code named Charlotte. Citrix wanted to prove that by using server-based computing technology, you could extend easily the reach of all of your corporate applications to the web. The result of this proof of concept in reality was a set of tools and application components that you could use to develop your own web-based Citrix MetaFrame solution. The intended audience for these tools was the web developer community and not corporate Citrix MetaFrame administrators.

Although NFuse 1.0 and 1.51 came with some sample web sites showing what you could do, they lacked the important features needed for large deployments. Administrators were faced with either having to make do with the lack of features or investing in costly web development resources to create the functionality needed.

In response to the growing demand for a more feature-rich, turnkey solution, Citrix started an internal web development project code named Columbia. Columbia version 5.x is a set of web pages written using Microsoft's ASP technology, which is designed to work with the application components contained in NFuse 1.51. The results of the Columbia 5.x project are incorporated into the version of NFuse that comes with MetaFrame XP.

As of the writing of this book, Columbia 6.x has been released. This version includes significantly more features than were available in Columbia 5.x. Columbia 6.x also is written using Microsoft ASP technology, but it is designed to work with the application components provided with NFuse 1.6.

Figure 3.2 shows a sample screenshot of a web site that uses NFuse 1.6 technology. Users can click on any of the icons for the applications shown, and the applications will launch from their browser. The only component needed is a small web ICA client that can be automatically downloaded from the site.

Although NFuse started as an experiment, it is quickly becoming a truly valuable business tool. Some level of web development knowledge, however, still is very useful when working with NFuse. By implementing the set of web pages that are available for free as part of the Columbia project, you can quickly create an almost turnkey corporate application port. You will learn all about how to setup a web site like this in Chapter 19, "Deploying Applications over the Web Using NFuse and Wireless Technologies."

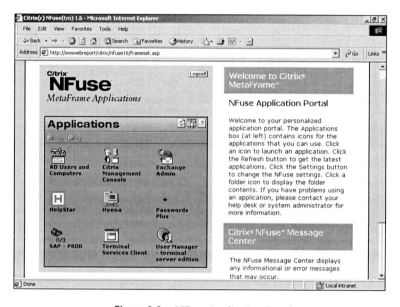

Figure 3.2   NFuse Application Portal.

Server Protocol Independence

Both RDP and ICA rely on an underlying transport protocol to carry them across the network. The Microsoft RDP protocol supports two types of protocol transports: TCP/IP, and TCP/IP across RAS for remote access.

In contrast, the MetaFrame ICA protocol works on top of IPX/SPX, NetBIOS (NetBEUI), and TCP/IP. ICA supports RAS for remote access, but RAS is not necessary because it also supports dial-in asynchronous connections directly into MetaFrame. If you have an environment in which you do not want to be limited to just TCP/IP, or you need support for direct dial-in connections to the Terminal Server, MetaFrame might be for you.

Seamless Windows

Seamless Windows works with published applications to make them appear as if they are a local application running on the workstation. When you run a published application using Seamless Windows, the title bar is removed and the application window can be resized just as if the application were running locally.

In addition to providing a uniform appearance for your applications, Seamless Windows takes up only one connection on MetaFrame, no matter how many application sessions have been opened. This allows for the seamless integration of multiple published applications onto your users' desktops without taking up multiple licenses on the farm.

SpeedScreen 3

Both Microsoft and Citrix have taken many steps with their respective thin client protocols to improve user experience with applications running on Terminal Server by reducing the amount of time it takes to update the screen. Those who have used other remote-control products have probably experienced painfully slow screen updates on slow connections. If this were the case with Terminal Server, users would not want to run their applications on the server because the response time would be too slow.

Both MetaFrame and now Terminal Server support persistent caching across sessions of commonly used screen graphics, such as icons and bitmaps. In addition, both support caching of screen components in memory on the client. However, only with MetaFrame do you get the more advanced screen update performance enhancements available in SpeedScreen 3.

Normally, when users type information into dialog boxes in their application, a significant delay can occur before they can see what they type. This is because the keystrokes must be sent to the server, the application on the server must display the characters typed in the dialog box, and then the server must send back the character display to the client before the client can see what he typed.

Using the Latency Reduction Manager tool provided with SpeedScreen 3, administrators can enable virtual local mouse and keyboard response for particular applications on the server. In other words, users will be able to see what they type and the results of their mouse actions even before the application does. This is a huge benefit for users trying to run applications on Citrix across high-latency connections such as wireless and satellite. This technology is included in MetaFrame XP, but only available by purchasing the separate Feature Release 1 for MetaFrame 1.8.

TAPI Support for Direct Asynchronous Connections

MetaFrame includes support for direct-asynchronous connections to the server. This means you can easily set up a modem bank for dial-in access to your Citrix server. Although this is possible using RAS with Terminal Server, MetaFrame support for this feature is built into the client. This allows for a single-click connection approach from the client instead of having to connect with RAS first and then make a second connection to the Terminal Server. MetaFrame works with existing modems already defined on the user's desktop for the client or on the server, by using TAPI support.

Automatic Client Update

MetaFrame is set up to automatically update your client software with the latest version as your client's logon. The administrator can distribute new versions of a client to all users of the server by just installing the new client at the server.

Multimonitor Support and True Color

With both MetaFrame XP and MetaFrame 1.8 and with Feature Release 1, clients can run their applications on multiple monitors. Therefore, you can bring together several monitors to form a single virtual display that users can use. This feature proves very handy for presentations and trade shows where you need to demonstrate an application running on Citrix for a large audience. It also is often used by large financial institutions when a large display is necessary.

In addition, MetaFrame supports up to 16-bit color or 24-bit color using the ICA thin client. Terminal Server currently supports only 256. This can be a vital feature for businesses that need to deploy applications that display photos or are graphical in nature (such as Internet Explorer).

Author's Note

Microsoft is currently expected to support 16 million colors with its RDP v5.1 client that will come with Windows .NET.

Local Device Redirection

For many people, the automated local device redirection capabilities of MetaFrame are a very important feature. Although Windows 2000 Terminal Server has caught up significantly in this area, MetaFrame supports redirection for local drives and audio that Windows 2000 Terminal Server does not.

So what is device redirection? *Device redirection* makes it appear to your applications that they are running locally on your machine. With device redirection, your applications can save files to your local drives, print to your local printers, communicate with your local COM ports, and more, even though they are actually running on the Terminal Server. The following list identifies the devices that can be redirected automatically in both Terminal Server alone and with Citrix MetaFrame:

- **Printers**   You can print to any of your local printers from any Windows program running on Terminal Server. Your local printers automatically appear as [Computer Name]#[Printer Name] on Windows NT 4.0 Terminal Server and \\Client\[Computer Name]#[Printer Name] on Windows 2000 Terminal Server after you log on. This nomenclature differentiates them from the printers that were already set up on the server before you logged on.

Author's Note

Although Terminal Server and MetaFrame both implement printer redirection, significant differences apply to their implementation. For more detailed coverage of these differences, refer to the "Printer Auto-Creation and Drive Mapping" sidebar later in this chapter or see Chapter 20, "Advanced Printing Techniques."

- **COM and LPT ports**   COM and LPT port redirection enables you to use your local COM and LPT ports with a program running on MetaFrame. This often proves very important if you are running DOS applications on MetaFrame. Because DOS applications cannot print to Windows printers, the only way for them to print is through the LPT or COM ports. People who use locally attached printers find this to be an important feature because it enables applications running on Terminal Server to print to those printers. Finally, you can even communicate with other local devices, such as a handheld attached by a serial port, so that you can synchronize your data with an application running on Terminal Server.

- **Clipboard redirection**   Clipboard redirection enables you to cut and paste from applications running on MetaFrame to applications running locally. This feature truly makes your applications appear as if they are running locally and not remotely to the users.

Two other device redirections, available only with MetaFrame, are very important to a lot of companies: local drives and audio redirection. The following is a description of both:

- **Local drives**   Many users need to be able to save from their applications to their local drives. By default, when you log on to a MetaFrame server, your local drives become available to the applications on your MetaFrame desktop. This means you can both easily access data on your local drive from any program running on MetaFrame and also save data to your local drive.

Author's Note

Because the server's C: drive and your local C: drive are the same letter, MetaFrame offers you the option during install to move the server's drives higher in the alphabet, such as starting with *M*. This way, your local drives retain their original drive letters when you log on. You also can map drives to your local resources just by mapping them to \\CLIENT\[*drive or port name*].

Even though your local drives do not automatically become part of your desktop with Terminal Server alone, you can still map to them using net shares. To do this, you would share your local drive on the network and then map to it manually or through a script when you log on. In large enterprise deployments, however, this technique can be very tedious to implement and can open up numerous security holes if the shares are not carefully locked down. Also traffic to and from the share is not compressed or encrypted, as it would be if you were using MetaFrame and an ICA client.

- **Audio redirection**   Multimedia applications running on MetaFrame can play sounds and music on your local speakers. MetaFrame gives you control of the audio quality and thus the amount of bandwidth it takes for sending the audio across the network to the clients. This feature is intended primarily for LAN environments in which network bandwidth is not much of an issue. Client computers can play 8- or 16-bit mono or stereo. WAV files at 8, 11.025, and 44.1KHz.

Author's Note

As noted in Chapter 2, "Introduction to Windows Terminal Server," these last two features are currently slated to be included in Windows .NET Terminal Services.

Shadowing

One justly heralded feature that used to be available only with MetaFrame is shadowing. With shadowing, MetaFrame enables an administrator to basically remotely control any user's Terminal Server session. With the release of Terminal Server 2000, Microsoft has enabled you to do the same from the Terminal Services Manager. Both implementations are cross-compatible, meaning you can remotely control RDP sessions from ICA and vice versa.

This feature proves very handy for remote technical support because you can see the user's desktop and troubleshoot a problem by just shadowing her session. As discussed in the "Shadowing Enhancements" section later in this chapter, Citrix has added features to its basic shadowing capabilities with the release of MetaFrame XP that are not available in Terminal Server.

Author's Note

Citrix MetaFrame includes several enhancements to this remote control feature that are not available with Terminal Services alone, including a Shadowing Taskbar, many-to-one shadowing, logging of shadowing, and per-server shadowing control.

MetaFrame 1.8 and the MetaFrame 1.8 Add-On Services

MetaFrame 1.8 has been around for several years and comes in two separate editions: one for Windows NT 4.0 Terminal Server and the other for Windows 2000 with Terminal Services. MetaFrame 1.8 is currently at service pack level 3 and is a robust and highly reliable server-based solution.

Much like Terminal Server, MetaFrame 1.8 allows for the serving of desktops and applications to multiple users using a thin client protocol, which in the case of MetaFrame is the ICA protocol. Unlike Terminal Server, however, MetaFrame includes advanced application publishing capabilities, the capacity to support non-Window-based clients, and several other important features that many businesses find critical for their thin client deployments.

Citrix also sells several add-on products or services for Citrix MetaFrame 1.8 that add important features, such as Load Balancing Services, Resource Management Services for integrated system and application monitoring, Installation Management Services for application imaging, automated installation, and Feature Release 1—a general feature enhancement to 1.8 sold separately. These products are licensed per server and, with the exception of Load Balancing Services, do not come on the MetaFrame 1.8 CD. Finally, there is Citrix NFuse, a freely available product that works with both Citrix MetaFrame 1.8 and MetaFrame XP to allow for easy publishing of your applications to the web.

The following sections cover only those features and services that are available for Citrix MetaFrame 1.8. If you are only interested in MetaFrame XP, then skip ahead to the "What's New in MetaFrame XP" section.

Load Balancing Services

One reason that many administrators find compelling for the purchase of Citrix MetaFrame and the additional Citrix product for load balancing is its advanced load-balancing capabilities. Load balancing makes the most efficient use of your servers by evenly distributing the users across them, based on easily modified load-measurement criteria. Citrix Load Balancing Services also can be used for balancing the user load based on the hardware capabilities of the server. If you want to load balance your applications across two servers (one being a larger four-processor server and the other being a slower single-processor server with less available memory), you (as an administrator) can easily balance the user load between the two, so that more users are sent to the higher performance server than the lower performance one. Load balancing is a good solution for high availability as well, and for ease of maintenance. If a server goes down, or is taken down, users can log back on to the next available server.

The tools and capabilities for load balancing are installed already when you install Citrix MetaFrame 1.8. However, they are not available until you purchase and install a per-server Load Balancing License from Citrix.

With load balancing, you publish your application across a group of MetaFrame servers, which is referred to as that application's *load-balancing server group*. This server group can be any collection of two or more servers in the server farm. At the point new users attempt to connect to a particular load-balanced application, a master server in the server farm evaluates, based on the criteria you established, which server in the application's load-balancing server group to place the user on. If you find that any of the servers in the load-balancing server group are found to be constantly over- or underutilized, you can use the Load Balancing Administration tool to adjust the criteria for that server.

Each server periodically reports its load or any changes to that load to the current master server in the server farm. In MetaFrame 1.8, this master server is called the *master browser*. As discussed later in this chapter, the master browser performs many critical functions in a server farm and is the glue that brings all the servers together into one synergetic whole.

If any of the servers in the load-balanced pool fail or are shut down, the master browser detects this, so that it will not send further users to that server. Any users who were on the failed server will need to reconnect to the application, they then will be directed to the next most available server that is part of that application's load-balanced server group.

The reported server load can be adjusted using the following criteria. By increasing one of these criteria, you give it more weight in the load-balancing decision-making process:

- Number of current users versus licensed users
- Number of current users versus a set maximum number of users
- Paging file usage
- Swap file activity
- Processor utilization
- Number of sessions and memory load

Load Sharing Versus Load Balancing

When making the choice of whether to purchase load balancing, it is important to understand the difference between what Citrix load balancing offers versus the methods of setting up load sharing with Terminal Server.

In a load-balancing solution, such as that offered by Citrix Load Balancing Services, a heuristic process is used to intelligently balance the load between servers. With Citrix MetaFrame 1.8, this process is handled by the master browser, which also keeps track of session information. If the user disconnects from the server leaving his session running, when he next attempts to connect he will be returned to his disconnected session.

A load-sharing solution is one in which incoming session requests are evenly distributed across a set of load-shared servers without considering the load on the servers. Two load-sharing solutions are available with Terminal Server: DNS round-robin and Network Load Balancing.

DNS round-robin is a load-sharing solution often used in the world of web and FTP servers. With DNS round-robin, you create several name records (A records) on your DNS server for the same host name, each with the IP address of one of your Terminal Servers. When a client requests the host name, the DNS server returns the next IP address in the list in round-robin fashion. In this way, users are evenly distributed across the servers in the DNS round-robin list. DNS round-robin is supported by most versions of BIND and by Microsoft DNS services in both Windows NT 4.0 and Windows 2000. The main disadvantage of DNS round-robin for load sharing is that if one of the servers fails, the DNS server has no mechanism to detect this. Connection requests will continue to be sent to the failed server until the administrator manually removes the server's DNS entry.

Network Load Balancing (NLB) is a more intelligent load-sharing solution from Microsoft and is available as part of Windows 2000 Advanced and DataCenter Servers. With network load balancing you can load share up to 32 Terminal Servers. Each server participating in load sharing has its own individual IP address, but also shares a common virtual IP address with the rest of the servers. By default, new connection requests directed to the common address are equally distributed across the load-shared servers. However, you also can manually load balance the servers by specifying what percentage of the load you want directed to a particular server. Unlike DNS round-robin, network load balancing is designed to dynamically detect and recover from a failed server in the load share.

As of this writing, no third-party load-balancing solutions are available for Terminal Server other than Citrix. Although NCD had made a load-balancing solution in the past (called *NCD ThinPath*) for Terminal Server, this product has now been discontinued.

Resource Management Services

Resource Management Services (RMS) is an application and system resource management tool designed specifically for Citrix MetaFrame. Unlike Load Balancing Services, which is installed but not enabled when you install MetaFrame, RMS must be installed separately from CD. After it is installed and configured to communicate with any ODBC-compliant database, MetaFrame will periodically send current application and system-related information to the database. You can query this information at anytime using the provided Resource Management tool. The following system and application information is gathered and reported on by RMS:

- **Application usage** Application usage statistics such as how often and for how long particular applications are run. Other statistics gathered include how many times an application was used, how much of that time a user spent actively working on the application, and how much memory the application used. Processor utilization and memory usage of an application on a per-user basis is analyzed as well. This can be very important to look at to see exactly what an application is taking up on the server instead of having to rely on third-party white papers. You also can use this tool to see how a new application added to the server might affect the other applications in terms of processor or memory.

- **Usage billing** RMS enables you to easily create billing reports based on application or system resource usage. This proves valuable for administrators whose corporations charge back internally for system usage.

- **System monitoring** Within the RMS management tool, you can view a collection of stoplight icons representing your server's current health. In addition, the health of any other Citrix server running RMS can be included in the display, giving you an overall systemwide view. A red light indicates health problems, and detailed instructions on how to correct the problem are available.

Installation Management Services

Installation Management Services (IMS) enables you to easily package and publish applications across your entire server farm with the click of a button. This service is especially valuable for larger Citrix server deployments where application installs and updates can take up significant administrative time.

Another advantage of using IMS versus manually installing applications is that it ensures your applications are installed identically across servers. This can be a great time saver if you have applications that require Registry or other setting changes to run efficiently on Terminal Server. These changes will be replicated with every new installation using IMS.

Finally, with IMS, uninstalling an application is made just as easy as installing it. You just have to unpublish the application from a server, and it will be removed remotely for you.

Feature Release 1

Feature Release 1 is a collection of several new features and feature enhancements that add to the base capabilities of the MetaFrame 1.8 product. Included with Feature Release 1 are improvements such as the support of greater color depth and video resolution, improved application response time using SpeedScreen 3 technology, multimonitor support, and advanced encryption capabilities (which used to be offered as a separate SecureICA product).

Feature Release 1 also includes the new XML service. This is an important feature addition. It allows for the enumeration of applications and other Citrix-related queries to happen in a more secure fashion than before. In addition, the XML service is the one used by NFuse web sites for application enumeration.

What's New in MetaFrame XP

So with all these great features in MetaFrame 1.8, why go ahead with the upgrade or new purchase of MetaFrame XP? Well, with MetaFrame XP, not only have there been many significant feature improvements and additions, the core architecture of how a server farm works has been greatly improved as well. Looking forward, MetaFrame XP is the best choice for the future because of the Citrix commitment to continue the improvement of this product. Although the bell has not tolled yet for Citrix 1.8, Citrix does not intend to release future feature enhancements for MetaFrame 1.8.

For those who have existing MetaFrame 1.8 server farms, Citrix has taken many steps to make the transition to MetaFrame XP as easy as possible. Using the provided "interoperability mode" or mixed mode in MetaFrame XP, you can migrate your MetaFrame 1.8 servers one server at a time to MetaFrame XP, while still keeping them all part of the same server farm. Although a new version of the Citrix ICA client software does come with XP, your older versions of the software will still work; and by using the Citrix ICA Client Update Service, you can centrally update your users' client software as they log on. In addition to using the mixed-mode approach, several other approaches might make more sense when upgrading your 1.8 server farm to XP. Chapter 6, "Planning a Terminal Server and Citrix MetaFrame XP Solution," covers these approaches in detail.

MetaFrame XPs, XPa, and XPe Compared

Citrix makes three different editions of its MetaFrame XP product: MetaFrame XPs, XPa, and XPe. These products can be differentiated as follows:

- **MetaFrame XPs**   This starter edition of MetaFrame includes only the base MetaFrame XP feature set and is intended for small to medium-size business deployments. For MetaFrame 1.8 administrators, purchasing MetaFrame XP would be much like purchasing MetaFrame 1.8 without any add-ons.

- **MetaFrame XPa**   The advanced edition of MetaFrame includes the base product plus the Load Manager. This is the MetaFrame 1.8 equivalent of purchasing MetaFrame 1.8 and Load Balancing Services. However, as you will soon be shown, there have been many improvements in MetaFrame load balancing with Load Manager in XP.

- **MetaFrame XPe**   The enterprise version is the top-of-the-line edition that includes Load Manager, Resource Manager, Installation Manager, and SNMP monitoring capabilities in the new Network Manager. It is the MetaFrame 1.8 equivalent of purchasing MetaFrame with Load Balancing Services, Resource Management Services, and Installation Management Services. In addition, although all these add-on products have been improved in XPe, XPe also includes the Network Manager component, which offers the ability for tight integration into SNMP monitoring packages.

Although this discussion goes through the new features and functionality of MetaFrame XP in more detail, the following sections refer to Table 3.1, a feature comparison table.

Table 3.1   **MetaFrame 1.8 and MetaFrame XP Simplified Feature Comparison Table**

Feature	MF 1.8	MF XPa	MF XPs	MF XPe
Application publishing and other basic MetaFrame capabilities	X	X+	X+	X+
Load balancing	MF+LB		X+	X+
Resource management	MF+RMS			X+

Installation services for packaging and publishing	MF+IMS	X+
SNMP Monitoring and Management		X

X = Has the capability
X+ = Has the capability, but has several improvements over the similar capability in MetaFrame 1.8

Citrix Management Console

With MetaFrame XP, Citrix has combined several of its administration tools into a single Java-based management console called the *Citrix Management Console* (CMC). This single management interface can be used to manage and monitor all the Citrix servers in your enterprise. You can use the CMC to perform the following functions:

- Application publishing
- License management
- Server monitoring
- Shadowing remote sessions
- Printer driver management
- Load balancing (XPs/XPe only)
- Application distribution using Installation Management (XPe only)
- Resource monitoring and management (XPe only)

Much like Microsoft's Management Console or Novell's Network Administrator, the CMC is designed to be modular. As new products are installed, such as Resource Management, they "plug-in" to the CMC instead of installing their own set of management tools. This is a welcome change for MetaFrame 1.8 administrators who often had to learn and use a multitude of different management tools to manage their server farms.

The CMC also helps make management of Citrix more secure. Before with MetaFrame 1.8, if you had to have full access to Citrix management tools, you needed administrative access to the server or domain the server was a part of. With the CMC you can instead choose which users from which domains have access and grant them either full access or just read-only. Before you get into the CMC, it will prompt you for your username, password, and domain before granting you access to the console.

Centralized Printer Driver Management

Now with MetaFrame XP, you can centrally and more easily manage the albatross of all Citrix administrators, printers, and their drivers! From the CMC you can now do the following with printers:

- **Auto-replicate drivers**   You can now automatically replicate printer drivers across your server farm using a particular server as the driver source. Prior to MetaFrame XP, you had to manually install the printer drivers to all servers in the farm so that your users could print no matter what server they logged on to.

- **Enforce driver compatibility**   Now you can enforce the use of only drivers that you deem safe on your server farm or allow everything but a set of drivers that you deem unsafe to be used. For Citrix administrators who have been to "printer driver hell" before, this added level of control provides a welcome relief.

- **Centrally control driver mapping**   Using the CMC GUI interface, you can now control printer driver mappings across the farm. Prior to MetaFrame XP, if you needed to map a particular driver to a user's printer, you had to manually edit the printer driver mapping text file on the server. If you wanted this change to take place across the farm, you had to manually copy the file across to each server.

- **Auto-create network printers**   You also can now ensure that particular users automatically receive a particular network printer, regardless of whether they have it installed locally.

- **Enforce client printer mappings**   If a thin client terminal has a printer attached locally, you can set it up using CMC, so that no matter what server the terminal connects to, the printer will be available from the desktop.

Printer Auto-Creation and Drive Mapping

For readers who are new to Citrix, the idea behind and importance of printer mappings might not be readily apparent. The following aside gives you a brief background as to why they are necessary. Printing is a very important topic in the Citrix/Terminal Server world and is covered in full in Chapter 20. Be sure to also read about the new Universal Printer Driver feature available in Feature Release 1 for MetaFrame XP in the "MetaFrame XP Feature Release 1" section later in this chapter.

Users very often need to be able to print from the applications they run off of Terminal Server. By default, both Terminal Server 2000 and Citrix MetaFrame attempt to auto-create a user's local desktop printers on his Terminal Server desktop. As the user logs on to the server, the server attempts to match up the driver for each printer configured on the user's local desktop to the equivalent printer driver that is available for Windows 2000 Terminal Server. Ideally, when the auto-creation process is complete, users should be able to print to the same printers from their Terminal Server desktop and applications as they can from their local desktop.

Unfortunately, this process is more difficult than it sounds. The main problem is that users can connect from everything from Windows CE to Windows XP, and from even more operating systems in the case of Citrix. Because printer driver names tend to differ from OS to OS, the server does not always know which driver it should load when it attempts to auto-create the users' printers on their Terminal Server desktop. Citrix and Microsoft have both handled this problem by creating driver-mapping tables that translate a user's printer driver name to the correct Terminal Server printer driver name.

Suppose, for example, that you need to print from an application running off of your Terminal Server desktop to an HP 1600C printer that you normally print to from your local desktop. The driver name on your local desktop might be HP DeskJet 1600C ColorSmart. However, the correct driver to use on Terminal Server 2000 is the built-in HP DeskJet 1600C driver. Because the driver names are not the same, Terminal Server would normally not recognize the driver and not auto-create the printer when you log on. This would mean the user would have to manually create the printer to be able to print to it from Terminal Server. This could be difficult at best for the user and more than likely end up in a support call to the help desk. As an administrator, you are much better off if you add an entry to the printer-mapping table on Terminal Server specifying that every time it sees a client log on with an HP DeskJet 1600C ColorSmart, it should load the HP DeskJet 1600C Driver. In this way, both this user's printer and any others who use an HP DeskJet 1600C will have the printer correctly auto-created each time they log on.

Centralized License Configuration ("Per-Farm" Licensing)

Even though licenses are pooled in Citrix MetaFrame 1.8, the licenses are still installed at a server level. In addition, with Citrix MetaFrame 1.8, you must first purchase a base server license, which includes 15 user licenses, and then add user license "bump" packs as needed. This costly base license scheme made it difficult for many organizations to add servers to their server farm as needed even if they already had enough connection licenses for their users.

Now with MetaFrame XP, you install your connection licenses as part of the farm using the CMC instead of to a particular server. When you first purchase MetaFrame XP, you purchase a single MetaFrame XP "starter system," which includes 20 connection licenses. This gives you a special license code that you use when you set up the first server in your Citrix MetaFrame XP farm. These 20 connection licenses are added to your farm's XPe, XPa, or XPs initial license pool depending on which starter product you purchased.

You can now add as many servers as you want to the server farm without having to purchase a new base license for each new server. Therefore, you can now have a server with 2 licenses, for example, a server with 10 licenses, and another server with 8 licenses (all as part of the 20-connection starter system). All the licenses will pool, regardless of which subnet they are on. Basically, you choose where you want your licenses to lie and how many servers you want to bring into the farm.

Instead of entering a new base license code, you use a much shorter product code that is provided with your "starter system." This product code identifies the type of licenses users of this server will retrieve from the common license pool when they connect, either XPe, XPa, or XPs. Normally, you use the same product code across all of your servers in the farm, so that they all pull licenses from the same pool.

When you need to add additional licenses to the farm, just purchase a 5-, 10-, 20-, or 50-user license "bump" pack for the appropriate edition of XP and add it to the central license pool using the CMC.

Shadowing Enhancements

Several security improvements have been made to the shadowing features, including the following:

- **Server-level shadowing control** This new capability enables you to disable shadowing or enforce user notification on shadowing at a server level.

- **Shadow logging** Shadowing events can now be logged to the event log on servers.

- **Shadow indicator box** Shadowed users now have a box appear when they are shadowed, indicating that shadowing is in progress.

Application Load Balancing (XPa and XPe Only)

With the new Load Balancing Services available in Citrix MetaFrame XPa and XPe, you have more granular and more centralized control over the load balancing of your servers and now applications. The new Load Balancing Manager integrates with the CMC and provides the following enhancements to Load Balancing Services in 1.8:

- **Application load balancing** You can now balance your applications based on the user load of the application itself.

- **Application scheduling** Access to applications can now be scheduled using the Load Balancing Manager.

- **IP range restrictions** You can restrict what IP ranges have access to which applications.

- **Load monitoring** The current load of your servers can now be monitored in a graphical format from the CMC.

Installation Management (XPe Only)

Several improvements in XPe have been made to the Installation Management Services available as an add-on to MetaFrame 1.8. The following are the most significant:

- **Ability to package service packs and unattended installs**
  Installation Services now supports the ability to package service packs and other applications that can be installed unattended using command-line parameters.
- **File packaging**   Files and folders can now be easily published across the farm.
- **Scheduling and server reboots**   Installation of applications can now be scheduled for off-hours and the server automatically rebooted for applications that require reboots.
- **CMC integration**   Installation management is now tightly integrated into the CMC.

SNMP Monitoring (XPe Only)

The final main new feature, available only in the XPe edition of MetaFrame XP, is SNMP monitoring and better integration with SNMP network management. Now you can monitor and manage certain aspects of your server farms from commonly available SNMP management packages. This enterprise-class feature is an excellent enhancement for Citrix MetaFrame administrators who lacked enterprise-class management capabilities in previous versions. In addition, for users of HP OpenView and Tivoli, special integration has been included with MetaFrame XPe, so that these packages can run the CMC from their management interfaces.

MetaFrame XP Feature Release 1

As with MetaFrame 1.8, the first feature release for MetaFrame XP is now available. This feature release is not one to be missed. There are several very important features available in this release including the following:

- **Universal Printer Driver**   Perhaps the most important and widely requested feature is the Universal Printer Driver. As covered in the previous "Printer Auto-Creation and Drive Mapping" sidebar, problems with printer auto-creation are one of the leading causes of problems with Citrix MetaFrame. Although techniques exist to significantly minimize these problems, you still have to manually install drivers for users' printers that are not in the driver list. Now with the Universal Printer Driver and the latest ICA client, if the correct driver is not found for a printer, the universal driver is used. This universal driver can be used for most grayscale printing needs and handles graphic resolution up to 300 dpi.

- **Program Neighborhood Agent**   One really great feature available with Feature Release 1 is the Program Neighborhood Agent. This agent is smaller in size than the full Program Neighborhood but still retains all of its important features. It also enables you to centrally control settings for all of your users and push down icons from application icons to users' Start menus, desktops, and/or system trays. One other big advantage of the Program Neighborhood Agent over Program Neighborhood alone is the Auto-Refresh feature. Because the Program Neighborhood Agent is designed to run in the background and refresh user applications automatically, any changes you make to published applications on the Citrix server farm are periodically pulled down by the agent running on the clients. This circumvents the problem with Program Neighborhood that users needed to go into the application set and manually refresh their icons to receive the latest changes. The Program Neighborhood Agent works in conjunction with NFuse and requires the setup of an NFuse 1.6 web site to function.

- **Content Publishing**   If users locally have applications that they can use to view or modify documents, they do not necessarily need to run the viewer application on Citrix. With Feature Release 1, you now can publish content in addition to applications. Publishing content simply publishes a link to a file, document, or other type of content that is available for the users on the network to users' Program Neighborhood. When they click on the link, the content will be downloaded and brought up with the local viewer. You can use Content Publishing to publish important documents, forms, sound files, video files, and even links to web pages all with the same ease with which you can publish an application.

- **NetWare Directory Services (NDS) Support**   Many improvements for the support of NDS have been included in Feature Release 1. For Novell shops, Feature Release 1 is a must.

- **Application CPU Prioritization**   With Feature Release 1, you can set different priorities for different applications running on your Citrix servers.

- **Parameter Passing**   Command-line parameters now can be passed from clients to applications running on Citrix. This enables tighter integration of Citrix applications with users' local desktop environments.

- **Connection Control**   This new feature enables you to control the maximum number of concurrent instances of a particular application on a server or the maximum number of connections across the farm.
- **Citrix Web Console**   With Feature Release 1, you can setup a web-based console that provides basic administrative access to your Citrix MetaFrame server farm, including the ability to reset, disconnect, and shadow sessions on the farm.
- **Other features**   Many other minor improvements have been made in several areas with Feature Release 1, including enhancements to the CMC, SSL encryption, auto-reconnect for broken connections, and more.

Feature Release 1 is sold as a separate add-on product for MetaFrame XP. Although you can download Feature Release 1 with Service Pack 1 free from the Citrix web site, you will not be able to take advantage of all of its features unless you purchase, enter, and activate the Feature Release 1 license. Feature Release 1 should also be available to those with Subscription Advantage. If you have purchased Subscription Advantage for your Citrix MetaFrame XP servers, you will have access to the Feature Release 1 license code through the secure myCITRIX web site (www.citrix.com/mycitrix).

MetaFrame XP Architecture

One of the most significant changes that comes with MetaFrame XP is an entirely new core architecture. This architecture is designed to be highly scalable and more easily centralized than the architecture that supported MetaFrame 1.8. This new architecture is referred to as the *Independent Management Architecture* (IMA). Before looking at the details of IMA, it's important that you understand what this architecture refers to and how it worked before MetaFrame XP.

The Way It Worked in MetaFrame 1.8

In MetaFrame 1.8, when you first connect to a server farm, you are directed to the farm's ICA master browser. The master browser's main job is to assign a connection license to you and to connect you to the server that hosts the application you are trying to run. If the application is load balanced, the master browser will determine which of the servers in the application's load-balancing server group to send you to based on their reported load. If you disconnect your session and try to reconnect, it is the master browser that keeps track of the location of your disconnected session, so that you can reconnect seamlessly.

The master browser can perform these important tasks by keeping track of the following information:

- **License pooling** The master browser keeps track of the connection licenses installed on each server and pools them together into a single license count. This pool of licenses is made available to all people who use the farm.

- **Application publishing information** A list of all the applications published on each server in the farm is collected by the master browser, along with specific application information (such as which server the application runs on).

- **Load-balancing information** The list of applications that are load balanced in the farm is kept track of by the master browser.

- **User and session information** Information about which users are logged on and what applications they are running is kept by the master browser. In addition, the master browser keeps track of disconnected sessions.

- **Server information** The list of servers in the farm, along with their current status, is kept by the master browser. With MetaFrame 1.8, servers need to periodically refresh the master browser with their information, so that the master browser knows they are still active.

By default, in MetaFrame 1.8 the servers in a particular MetaFrame server farm initiate an election process when they are first started to choose an ICA master browser for the farm. In addition, because of the criticality of the ICA master browser service, a backup browser is chosen in case the master browser fails. If the farm makes use of more than one protocol, such as TCP/IP and IPX, a separate master browser and set of backup browsers (by default two) are elected for each protocol.

Limits of MetaFrame 1.8 Architecture

The idea of the master browser is core to the functionality of Citrix MetaFrame 1.8. However, the method of implementing this functionality in 1.8 has certain limits, which are especially apparent in large Citrix deployments:

- **Information is decentralized.** In MetaFrame 1.8, application and licensing information is first kept track of by the individual servers and then pooled together by the master browser. To pool together this information, the servers must constantly keep the master browser up-to-date with any changes. In large environments, this can produce significant amounts of network traffic and inhibit scalability.

- **Difficult to extend across the WAN.**   Using a MetaFrame 1.8 feature called *ICA gateways*, you could extend your server farm across a WAN. However, ICA gateways were not originally designed for widespread use within an enterprise. The use of multiple ICA gateways can quickly degrade both server farm and WAN performance.
- **License pooling across a WAN is not supported.**   In MetaFrame 1.8, there is no way to pool licenses across multiple subnets because all the servers rely on broadcasts for license advertisement. You are basically limited to one farm per subnet.

The Independent Management Architecture

For many years, with all of its issues, the architecture of MetaFrame 1.8 was adequate for most deployments. As deployments grew larger and more expansive, however, administrators began to feel the pain of an architecture that did not scale well in the enterprise. Hence, in Citrix MetaFrame XP, the architecture has been completely revamped. As mentioned previously, the new architecture is now called the *Independent Management Architecture* (IMA).

With MetaFrame XP, the master browser concept has been replaced by a *data collector* (DC). The DC's job is to keep track of licensing-, application-, and other important farm-related information, much like the master browser did in MetaFrame 1.8. In MetaFrame XP, servers can now be grouped together by assigning them to particular zones when they are first installed. Servers that are a member of a common zone elect a single DC to handle the farm information for that zone.

So far DCs sound like they do pretty much the same thing as master browsers did in 1.8, so what is the advantage of the new architecture? The advantage is the data store. The *data store* is the central repository for all the same farm-related information that the master browser in MetaFrame 1.8 used to keep. However, the centralized nature of the data store circumvents many of the problems caused by the decentralized nature of the master browser. It also has made it possible for the centralization of the server farm management using the new CMC management tool.

The data store can be configured as either a local Microsoft Access database on one of the servers in the farm or on a central SQL Server or Oracle database server. The Access database is recommended for small farms comprised of fewer than 20 servers. For larger farms, take advantage of the more robust capabilities of either SQL Server or Oracle for your data store server.

The combination of DCs and a data store represent a more centralized and much more scalable architecture with which you can build your server farm.

Choosing the Data Store Platform

Although you do have a choice of platforms for the data store, in reality, you will find that a Microsoft SQL database is used for most large professional installations. This platform provides a robust and reliable database solution that is heavily tested by Citrix when they make improvements to MetaFrame XP.

Finding the Right Fit

Even with all of this information, it can still be difficult to make the right choice as to what you should purchase to meet the needs of your server-based computing solution. The following general tips, however, might help you best decide:

- **Use Terminal Server without MetaFrame or Terminal Server with MetaFrame 1.8 for small deployments.**   MetaFrame XP is currently geared for medium, large, and very large scale deployments. Even though you can use the Access Data Store for small deployments, you will likely realize a greater level of reliability with a Microsoft SQL or Oracle Data Store. This, in effect, can make Citrix MetaFrame cost-prohibitive for small installations, especially those that are for less than 25 users. If money is not an issue for a small deployment, then Citrix MetaFrame XP is definitely the way to go.

- **Use Terminal Services for basic server remote access.**   If you want to setup a lights-out computer room, Terminal Services is a great solution.

- **Use MetaFrame XPs or XPa for medium to large size deployments.**   MetaFrame XPs and XPa are good choices for medium to large size deployments. Use XPa if you need load management capabilities.

- **Use MetaFrame XPe for large to very large scale deployments.** MetaFrame XPe's advanced management capabilities are especially geared for large scale deployments. If you need the ability to centrally and easily deploy applications across the farm, manage farm resources, and integrate farm management with enterprise-class network management tools, then you need MetaFrame XPe.

- **NFuse is a big selling point for Citrix MetaFrame.**   NFuse technology alone adds incredible value to your Citrix MetaFrame solution. Using NFuse, you can make all of your applications on Citrix MetaFrame available to anyone with a web browser. This can make the deployment of your Citrix solution incredibly easy and quick. In addition, NFuse can be used to provide a "virtual workplace" for people in case of disaster. During a disaster, your key employees still need access to critical corporate applications. By setting up a NFuse web site at a disaster recovery location, you can provide easy and centrally configurable access to any application in case of disaster.

4

Understanding the Costs and Benefits of a Terminal Server Solution

NOW THAT YOU HAVE A BETTER UNDERSTANDING of the features of MetaFrame and Terminal Server, it is time to discuss planning the implementation. Proper planning is essential to ensure that the solution will meet your company's business needs.

If you are at the start of your thin client project, you will probably be expected by your management to justify the costs of the project versus the expected benefits. This chapter begins with a discussion of the costs and benefits of using server-based technology versus other available solutions. You will learn how to calculate the return on investment for your Terminal Server solution, what the costs and benefits involved are, and about the concept of Total Cost of Ownership. This chapter concludes with a top-ten list of Terminal Server solutions, along with a list of situations in which other solutions might work better.

Understanding Return on Investment

Deploying a Terminal Server solution can provide huge cost benefits for many companies. However, it is important to understand where that value lies in this type of solution, so that you can mine the value most effectively.

Unless you are an application service provider that charges for use of applications running on Terminal Server, no direct revenue is generated by its deployment. However, Terminal Server is capable of running applications that have a direct effect on revenue. This in itself makes the benefits of the solution more challenging to measure and more difficult to explain.

Many senior executives demand a thorough *return on investment* (ROI) study before approving the funding for any new technology department. An ROI study's goal is to calculate the expected business benefit versus the business cost of a project over its intended life span.

ROI studies make simple business sense. Businesses do not want to spend time and money on projects that do not contribute to the bottom line. Even if your company does not require this level of rigor, learning how to prepare an ROI study will help justify your support of the investment in this technology.

It is important to realize that not all Terminal Server solutions by themselves have a positive ROI. As covered in Chapter 1, "Introduction to Server-Based Computing," Terminal Server is a three-tier-enabling technology. One of its main benefits is that it can be used to extend the reach of your important business applications, and by itself it is likely not a direct source of business revenue. In other words, to calculate true ROI, you also must look at the business benefit gained by the applications that will run on Terminal Server.

On the other hand, in many cases senior management might have already decided on the business value of the deployment of a particular application. They might be coming to you to deploy this application and want to know the costs involved in the deployment. In cases like this, you could forego a more rigorous ROI study and instead do a simpler cost comparison between using Terminal Server to deploy the application and using another solution.

Either way, whether doing a detailed ROI study or a simpler cost comparison, it is important to ensure management understands not only the short-term but also the long-term benefits of a Terminal Server solution. Once you make the investment in a Terminal Server infrastructure, you can reap many future dividends from this investment as your company grows.

Suppose, for example, that you build a Terminal Server infrastructure today to deploy a particular application. When management wants to deploy another application or upgrade the existing one, you already have the infrastructure in place to do this easily and quickly. Even if you have to upgrade your server farm to handle the additional user load, the initial time and money spent gaining the support knowledge and building the infrastructure is not wasted.

Calculating Return on Investment

To calculate the ROI, you need to first focus on both the costs and benefits of the Terminal Server solution. In your ROI study, you can highlight the costs and benefits of each solution and make your recommendation.

To determine the ROI on a solution, you need to determine the following as accurately as possible. The variable name for each value is given in parentheses after the title. After you have all the values, you can plug them into the ROI formula toward the end of this section to get your ROI.

- **Quantifiable benefits per month (QuantBen)**   These benefits are direct, easily measurable monetary returns or benefits from the use of Terminal Server technology. An example of these types of benefits is billing fees for the use of Terminal Server such as those often charged by application service providers or those that are billed back internally at many corporations. You also could include cost savings versus the solution that is in place currently or versus another proposed solution.

- **Intangible benefits per month (IntBen)**   These benefits are harder to quantify but are significant benefits to the users of Terminal Server technology. Examples are increased user productivity and increased customer retention or satisfaction. Many of these benefits might be related to the features of the applications that Terminal Server is going to be used to deploy and not Terminal Server itself.

- **Implementation or fixed costs (ImpCst)**   One-time costs are the initial costs of building the infrastructure for Terminal Server. These costs are very easy to estimate and include the costs of licensing the product, hardware costs, consulting fees, and training.

- **Recurring costs per month (RecCst)**   These costs are the charges necessary for the ongoing maintenance and support of Terminal Server. They include administrator salaries, software support fees, support contracts, and software subscription costs. You need to break down these costs per month.

- **Solution life span in months (LifeSpan)**   The solution life span is the expected amount of time in months that this solution is intended to last before needing to be replaced or have significant upgrades. This is a very important measure on an ROI project.

Two numbers need to be produced from the ROI study: the break-even point and the return percentage. The first number is the number of months to break even. The break-even point is calculated as follows. Make sure that all of your costs and benefits, except for the implementation cost, are calculated per month.

Break Even in Months = ImpCst / (QuantBen + IntBen − RecCst)

The second number is the return percentage. Return is represented as a percentage of your initial investment or implementation cost. Here is how to calculate the return:

ROI = 100 ⋆ ((QuantBen + IntBen − RecCst) ⋆ LifeSpan)/ ImpCst) − 100

Going Through an Example

You can think of the ROI much like the return on a stock investment. ROI is a measure of the percentage return. If ROI is 10 percent, over the life span of your solution, you expect to realize a 10-percent return on your investment.

ROI is best used with Terminal Server when comparing one technical solution versus a Terminal Server solution. You could compare an existing solution's ROI over a period of time to replacing that solution with a Terminal Server solution. If you do not have a solution in place for the need, you might calculate the ROI for a Terminal Server solution versus a similar solution using some other product. Whether you are comparing your solution to an existing solution or another solution, make sure you are comparing what the ROI will be over the same period of time.

Suppose, for example, that you implement a Terminal Server solution to deploy a sales-reporting application to your sales force. This solution is designed to replace the current "green-screen" and bar-paper solution that is in place. There is a one-time equipment and software cost for the entire solution of $48,000 (ImpCst). This includes the costs for the consulting services to set up the hardware, deploy the solution, and train the sales staff.

You figure that this solution should last 4 years without having to replace the equipment (or 48 months, LifeSpan).

You do not believe you will have to add any additional support staff to support this solution after it is up and running, because there are only two servers in the solution and there is already a help desk in place that can handle calls for this server. You decide not to add support staff costs into the ROI calculation in this scenario because they will be the same whether you stay with the old solution or you replace it with a Terminal Server solution. In many other scenarios, however, support costs can lead to significant savings compared to other solutions, because you can centralize your support and might be able to eliminate the need for support staff at remote locations. In addition, many will argue that Terminal Servers require less support staff in general than deploying an application to individual workstations and having to support all of those workstations.

You do intend to sign a yearly support contract with a local integrator and are planning for software upgrade costs for both the sales-reporting application and for Terminal Server and Citrix MetaFrame. You divide your estimate of these costs over 4 years by 48 months to come up with a recurring cost of $1200 per month (RecCst).

After talking to the sales department, they estimate the information provided by the sales reporting solution can make the company more competitive than with the current system and can lead to an additional $400 in sales profit per month on average over the next 4 years. The current sales reporting solution provides a net profit of about $600 per month, so the total return of this solution will be $1200 per month (QuantBen). Using the net profit of a solution is the simplest approach. However, some executives might want to see how you got to that net profit. In that case, you might need to put things such as sales staff salary, operating costs, and revenues into the final ROI report. Either way, make sure you take exactly the same approach to your calculations when compare two solutions.

In addition, with the Terminal Server solution, sales staff will retrieve their own reports. In the past, a position was dedicated to generating green-bar sales reports for sales once a week. With the Terminal Server solution, this position is no longer needed. In this situation, you would include the salary cost for this position in the ROI for the existing solution and not put it into the ROI for the Terminal Server solution. Remember that you are comparing two possible solutions in this scenario.

The sales team also believes that customer retention will be greatly improved because they will be able to understand customers' needs and buying habits better by using the information in the sales reports. They estimate that this will lead to about $1200 in profit per month (IntBen) due to increased customer retention.

With this information, you can calculate the ROI for the Terminal Server solution as follows:

ROI = 100 $\star$ (((1200 + 1200 − 1200) $\star$ 48) / 48000 − 1))

ROI = 100 $\star$ ((57600/48000) − 1) = 100 $\star$ .2 = 20%

This ROI means that over a period of 4 years you can expect a return of about 5 percent per year from a Terminal Server solution. At this point, you would normally go through the same ROI calculation for the existing "green-screen" solution, put the results of both of these ROIs into a report, and then present this report to the decision makers at your company. Because the green-screen solution requires a dedicated position to handle the reports and because those reports do not provide as good of information as the reports in the sales-reporting tool, you will likely find the Terminal Server solution has a better return in comparison.

Although the exact technique of how your company does ROI studies will likely vary, always remember to use the same approach when evaluating two solutions to get a fair comparison. If you add in support costs for one solution, for instance, make sure you also add in support costs for the solution to which you are comparing it. Exactly what you include in your ROI comparison is up to you; however, the following sections will give you a better idea of where the costs and benefits are in a Terminal Server solution.

Costs and Benefits of Terminal Server Versus Alternative Solutions

Terminal Server is never the only solution to consider in today's complex business world. Depending on your situation, you might have to justify the purchase of Terminal Server versus another competing solution. The following sections cover some of the different general solutions that you might find being considered versus a Terminal Server solution. For each solution, the comparative advantages and disadvantages of a Terminal Server solution are compared.

Terminal Server Versus a Two-Tier Application

If your business has a two-tier application, there are often many methods of extending the reach of the application without having to use a Terminal Server to three-tier enable it. Business managers might push for just installing the two-tier application at remote locations instead of risk running the application on Terminal Server, a platform that they do not understand. However, this is the type of situation in which Terminal Server's many benefits often make the better solution for both reasons that might be obvious and for many reasons that are not.

To address these concerns, you need to look closely at the two-tier solution they are proposing versus three-tier enabling the application with Terminal Server. The following are the likely problems, both obvious and not so obvious, that you need to highlight in your ROI study when you compare the two solutions.

Decreased Hardware Costs

Most Tier 2 applications require significant PC hardware to run properly. Make sure you closely analyze the application's hardware requirements and evaluate whether the level of hardware required is already deployed. In many cases, you will find that to roll out a Tier 2 application, you also have to upgrade hardware. Be sure to include not only the hardware costs to do this, but also the cost of any resources necessary, such as contracted technicians. These types of costs go under Implementation Costs for the ROI that you generate for the alternative solution.

On the other hand, to ensure your study is fair, make sure to include all the server hardware costs for the Terminal Server solution under Implementation Costs in your Terminal Server solution ROI. Although you might not have to upgrade your workstations, you will have to buy significant hardware at a server level.

Decreased Network Costs

Decreased network cost is a critical cost that is often left out of most ROI studies. Often when two-tier applications are deployed across the wide area network, the extra traffic generated by the two-tier application degrades network performance. Users then begin complaining about performance of not only the two-tier application, but also other applications that before had plenty of bandwidth to use. The easiest response is to upgrade the network bandwidth. However, this is an expensive and ongoing cost that is rarely accounted for in the ROI study. This type of cost goes under Ongoing Cost on the alternative solution.

Wide Area Network Performance and Terminal Server

A Terminal Server connection generally uses between 15 and 25Kbps of network bandwidth per concurrent connection. Although this is significantly less than most two-tier applications use, it is an important factor to be considered when evaluating how well your Terminal Server solution will perform across the WAN. Suppose, for example, that you have a remote site with a 56Kbps connection that has 10 users who need access to the application running on Terminal Server. If all 10 users attempt to connect at once, the 56Kbps line will quickly become overutilized. This will equate into slow response times for the users.

To ensure that your network has sufficient capacity, you need to first estimate the maximum number of concurrent users you expect will actively be using the application on Terminal Server during the busiest times of the day (MaxConc). Next, make an estimate of the amount of growth in users that you want to be able to handle before you need to upgrade the line speed (ExpGrw). Suppose, for example, that you do not want to have to upgrade the line speed for at least a year, and that within the year another 5 users will be added. In this case, ExpGrw will be 5.

You can then use the following formula to obtain a rough guess for each wide area network connection as to whether there is enough capacity:

Terminal Server Line Usage = 85 * Line Speed in Kbps / ((MaxConc + ExpGrw) * 20)

The 85 in the formula is a conservative estimate. Generally, you do not want to go past 85-percent line usage for an extended period of time. At around 85 percent, you will quickly start running into performance and response time problems both with your Terminal Server users and users of other network applications at the site.

The one significant factor that this formula does not take into account is your current usage of these network connections. If you are having performance and response-time problems on your wide area network today, your Terminal Server solution will compound the problems. Before deploying any Terminal Server solution, you also need to make sure that there is sufficient capacity on your wide area network and that response times are good. Also check to make sure that no large file transfers occur during the day, when users are using Terminal Server. Large file transfers can easily monopolize the line during the time of transfer, causing very slow performance for your Terminal Server sessions. You can circumvent this problem on many routers by giving a higher priority to your Terminal Server traffic than to file-transfer traffic. Ideally, file transfers should be scheduled for after-hours if possible.

Most network monitoring packages can give you a good picture of what your average response time is on your network and how heavily your connections are being used. Response time is a measure of how long it takes for a packet to travel from a Terminal Server client to the Terminal Server and back. As a general rule of thumb, you want to ensure that your average response time is less than 250ms or $1/4$ second to every site where Terminal Server users will be. This will ensure that response time will be adequate for extended Terminal Server use. Make sure to measure this during the times of the day when they will be using it the most. If users begin complaining about slow response time, check to ensure that response time to the site is less than 250ms. Chapter 24, "Advanced Network Management and Monitoring," discusses response time in more detail.

Although 250ms is a good rule of thumb for WAN connections, with remote access over dial-up lines or wireless, you might not be able to consistently get less than 250ms in response time. You can expect response times to be slower in most cases over these types of solutions. Although these type of connections are generally slower, however, users will still be able to access Terminal Server remotely even up to response times of around 500ms.

In addition, if you can find your average line usage, check what the average line usage is during the times of day that you expect your Terminal Server users will be busiest. You can add this percentage to the expected Terminal Server Line Usage calculated previously to get a better estimate of what your true line usage will be. If this figure is greater than 85 percent, you should consider either increasing the line speed before deploying Terminal Server or finding ways to reduce the network traffic at this time of day.

Increased Productivity

Applications that require significant amounts of processing, such as reporting and accounting applications, tend to have very poor response time on low-end workstations and especially across wide area network connections. By running these applications on a high-end server, your users can gain significant efficiencies and better response times. A calculation or query that might have taken 15 minutes on a low-end workstation will take a fraction of the time when run on a high-end server. For this reason, it is important to understand when creating the ROI study what often-used functions within the application require significant processing power. Test these functions on a typical workstation and on the application running on a high-end server. You can use a measure of time saved in terms of salary as a Tangible Benefit in the ROI equation for the Terminal Server solution.

Network and Server Stability

Productivity can easily be ruined by an unstable network or an unstable server with a Terminal Server solution. A Terminal Server solution puts a greater reliance on the stability of your network and server farm than do most two-tier applications. When designing your Terminal Server solution, you need to ensure that you build sufficient redundancy into your solution to be able to easily recover from common server hardware failures. In addition, you should evaluate whether sufficient redundancy is built in to the network to support the level of reliability you need for your solution. The best place to address these concerns is in the ROI study. In this way, you can ensure that these concerns and how they intend to be handled are documented for management to read.

Faster Rollout and Upgrades

The rollout of a two-tier application to remote locations normally requires the tedious process of burning CDs, creating install instructions, and then working with each site on the install. With Terminal Server the clients are small enough that they can easily be downloaded and installed from the web. You do not need to make individual install instructions for each two-tier application you want installed; instead, just make the appropriate RDP or ICA clients available on the web and let the users download and install them. The clients can both be set up for single-click installs that require little or no user intervention. The client software is also small enough to be emailed as an attachment out to remote locations. Compare this to heavy two-tier applications, which can be easily hundreds of megabytes in size, and you can see why the small size of thin clients is a definite advantage. With MetaFrame, an easy-to-install, web-based package for deploying ICA clients is already freely available on its web site.

Upgrades are also incredibly simple using a Terminal Server solution. This is an often forgotten cost with two-tier deployments. Most two-tier application publishers update their applications at least once per year. With a two-tier application deployment, this means you have to go through the tedious manual process of rolling out the new application again. With a Terminal Server solution, you just upgrade the application at the server, and all the users will get the new application when they log on next. For in-house applications that are upgraded more often, the ease with which you can roll out new upgrades is a strong reason by itself for the deployment of the application through Terminal Server.

Another often overlooked aspect with two-tier deployments is future hardware costs. Heavy two-tier applications generally do not get any smaller with each upgrade; instead they tend to get significantly bigger as developers add more features. Even though you might not have to upgrade your hardware today to support the two-tier application, it is likely that the application will grow to the size in the future that hardware upgrades will be necessary.

When you roll out the next version, you will have to deal with users who do not have enough drive space, memory, or processing power to run the application. This can slow down deployments considerably and add additional hardware costs as computers need to be upgraded. To estimate for this, take the current hardware requirements for the application and estimate the percentage growth of the application over a year. You can roughly base this estimate on the difference between the preceding version of the application and the current. You can use this number and your knowledge of existing PC hardware capabilities to determine at what point the PCs will need to be upgraded to support the new application. Sometimes with a Terminal Server solution, you might need to upgrade the RDP or ICA client itself to take advantage of new features and functionality. This again is very easy to do by either setting up a client download web site or emailing out the client. In the case of MetaFrame, you just upgrade the client at the server, and the server will automatically push it out and install it for users who do not have it already when they log on.

Both the extra time necessary for the rollout of a two-tier application and any additional resources necessary for this rollout should be included in the ROI for the two-tier solution. The additional cost for rolling out future upgrades and any likely additional hardware costs should also be included with the two-tier ROI, but under Ongoing Costs. You will need to estimate how many months apart on average updates come out for the application, estimate the costs involved for rolling out the new application manually, including likely additional hardware costs, and then divide these by the number of months to get a monthly cost estimate.

Three-Tier Enablement Versus Three-Tier Applications

Building a case for using a Terminal Server solution to three-tier enable an existing two-tier application versus using a three-tier application can be tough. Because of the efficiencies gained with three-tier applications, many software development companies have spent considerable time porting their two-tier solution to a three-tier, web-enabled one.

These three-tier solutions do not suffer the same limitations as covered in the preceding section on deploying a two-tier application. Hardware and network costs are normally not an issue because the web-based applications tend to be very lightweight. Productivity is not normally an issue because three-tier applications rely just as heavily on the processing power of a central server farm as does a Terminal Server solution. Rollouts and upgrades are simplified because plug-ins can automatically be downloaded from a web site. However, many possible reasons for going with a Terminal Server solution still need to be fully investigated and put into the ROI study.

Limited Features

Many limitations with today's web-based development tools make it difficult for application developers to fully port their two-tier applications to the web or to create new three-tier solutions. When comparing the two solutions, whether they are from the same software company or not, you need to carefully compare the features available in the two-tier version versus the three-tier version. Often you will find a more limited set of features available in the three-tier solution.

Pay especially close attention to the printing, display, and file management capabilities of the three-tier application versus the two-tier version. A document printed or displayed on a three-tier application might not be formatted in the same manner as with a two-tier application. You also might likely find limitations in the manner in which files are saved and opened.

Although feature limitations are difficult to directly relate to costs in the ROI, they need to be analyzed and mentioned in the ROI for a fair comparison between the two solutions.

Making Full-Featured Three-Tier Applications

The reason developers continue to struggle with making full-featured, three-tier applications is the thin client dilemma. If they try to build too many features into the three-tier application, it no longer will be a lightweight, easy-to-deploy application. Developers struggle to pack in as many features as they can into as light a weight three-tier application as possible.

Both Sun Microsystems Java and Microsoft .NET are designed to help address these limitations. Both solutions rely on having a common set of application components already included in most web browsers. In the case of Java, this common set of components is called a *Java Virtual Machine* (JVM). With .NET it is called the *Common Language Runtime* (CLR). By already having core application components available on the browser, application developers do not have to include this code in their three-tier applications. This makes it easier for them to build lightweight, feature-filled, three-tier applications.

Two-tier Applications Still Necessary

Beware of two-tier components that might be necessary in the three-tier solution. Take for example a reporting application, such as those made by Brio, Hyperion, or Crystal Decisions. These companies have successfully been able to port the ability to view your data and work with it via the web using easily downloadable three-tier components. However, supporting applications such as their heavy-duty, feature-filled report layout and design tools are still heavy two-tier applications. If these applications are needed at remote locations, you will likely need Terminal Server to deploy them. Make sure to evaluate whether this is the case and to include this in your ROI study.

Building a Corporate ASP Using Portal Technology

If you can't beat them with a Terminal Server solution, join them instead! Using portal technology, such as the Citrix NFuse product, you can bring together the best of both worlds, your three-tier enabled applications on Terminal Server and your three-tier web-based applications, all into a single secure web interface. If you are considering deploying both three-tier applications and three-tier-enabled applications using Terminal Server, make sure to consider including portal technology in your plans. Portal can help bring together your solutions, making them easier to deploy and to support.

You will learn more about building your own application portal in Chapter 19, "Deploying Applications over the Web Using NFuse and Wireless Technologies." Although including portal technology might increase Implementation Costs in the ROI, it will likely provide long-term benefits by providing a powerful infrastructure for the deployment of future applications.

Desktop Replacement and Extending PC Hardware Life

For thin client technology purists, desktops are a thing of the past. Instead of running applications on desktops, all applications should be run on a central server farm for true server-based computing. Although this ideal has often been sought after, few corporations have been able to truly obtain it. There have been several reasons for this lack of corporate-wide acceptance of thin client terminals.

- **Desktops are relatively inexpensive** Desktops are relatively inexpensive compared to most true thin client devices—especially newer "thinner" desktops designed for the task-oriented worker, such as the Compaq iPAQ. These "thinner," less-expensive desktops, if set up properly, can be very easy to support.

- **Flexibility** Some corporations that have chosen to replace all of their desktops with thin client devices find that they can lose some level of flexibility. Thin client devices tend to be difficult to upgrade and can become outdated just like desktops can. In addition, many departments eventually find themselves needing to run at least a handful of applications, such as telephony applications, locally that are not designed to run in a pure server-based computing environment. Many of these applications can be easily run on desktops; however, they cannot be run on thin client terminals.

- **Political reasons**   There are often significant political barriers to any desktop replacement project. Users do not often like losing the control that they get when they have direct access to their own desktop. For task-oriented workers, this might be a moot point; however, knowledge workers might have legitimate business concerns with losing control of their desktop.

- **Working while traveling**   Traveling users often need to work on documents while in their hotel or on the road. Because thin clients have no local storage, it is impossible to work on documents while traveling unless always connected. Currently, this is not very practical with the state of wireless technology. When wireless technology matures by becoming faster, less expensive, and more widely available, this reason will be less important.

Using "Thinner" Desktops or Thin Client Terminals

Although desktops are not dead, neither is thin client technology by any means. Even though replacing all desktops might not make sense, you will likely find many departments at your corporation that could benefit from "thinner" desktops and thin client technology. By replacing select desktops with thin client terminals or purchasing "thinner" desktops for groups of users whose job requirements fit well with thin client technology, you can realize true long-term savings.

Often the best fit for wide-ranging thin client deployments is for task-oriented workers. A task-oriented worker is typically one who has limited computer training, whose main job involves repetitive task-based work, and who generally only needs to work with a handful of applications. Examples of this type of worker are abound in most corporations. Workers such as data-entry clerks, accounting staff, call center staff, and order-entry personnel are just a few of the many examples of task-oriented workers.

If your project involves implementing a Terminal Server solution for a brand new group, you likely have a lot of leeway in choosing what hardware to use for the workstations. In this case, be sure to carefully consider all the options. You will find a list of common thin client hardware offerings, including examples of the newer class of "thinner" desktops, in Appendix A, "Thin Client Hardware Solutions." You might want to highlight the many advantages of thin client hardware in your ROI study, especially if you need to compare your solution to another solution where full desktops are necessary.

If you intend to install the thin client software on existing desktops, you might want to consider a couple of things in your ROI. First, consider the possibility of replacing the existing desktops with either thin client terminals or a "thinner" class of desktops. These desktops could then be reused elsewhere where their local processing capability is more important. For fast-growing companies, where the desktops will be quickly reused, this can be an excellent cost-saving option and will greatly extend your existing PC hardware investment.

The second thing you need to consider in the ROI is the hardware savings realized by extending the life of your PC hardware investment. If you are comparing the Terminal Server solution to another solution that is not based on thin client technology in your ROI, be sure to calculate and include the additional future hardware upgrade and replacement costs that might be necessary. As mentioned in the earlier section on decreased hardware costs, the toll on your PC hardware by heavy two-tier applications and their likely future upgrades quickly adds up. This hardware toll leads to additional PC upgrade and replacement costs that would not be necessary with a thin client solution.

Terminal Replacement

Many corporations still have tens or hundreds of legacy green-screen terminals. Although these hardware terminals have paid for themselves many times over through their long lifetime, they are inflexible single-purpose devices that can only run text-based applications from the host. If your Terminal Server project involves replacing green-screen terminals with thin client hardware, there are several costs and benefits to consider on the ROI.

Your choice of thin client hardware is still very important. Thin client terminals are a great choice for this situation. Most thin client terminals take minutes to set up rather than the hours often necessary for even the "thinnest" of desktops. When a thin client terminal is connected to the network and powered on, it will use DHCP to automatically configure its IP settings. The only steps you normally will have to take are to add the connection entries at the main menu for the host and Terminal Server connections that the users need. Keep in mind when evaluating thin client terminal solutions that many solutions also come with central management software. This software can be a great time saver because you can in effect publish new connection entries to all of your thin client terminals from your workstation without having to visit any of them. See Appendix A for a list of the features that these devices normally have.

When putting the ROI together for this type of solution, be sure to include the costs for the new network drops and equipment that might be necessary for terminal replacement in the Implementation Costs. If you intend to replace existing green-screen applications with Windows-based applications, one benefit that is not often considered is the reduced training costs for GUI applications. The cost savings could be significant, especially if there is high turnover for the employees who use the green-screen terminals.

Understanding the Total Cost of Ownership

This section takes you on a comparative walk through the typical life of a personal computer, showing the many hidden costs of a PC-based solution versus a server-based solution using Terminal Server. These costs are what add up to the TCO for a personal computer. You will find in general the thinner your hardware solution, the less the TCO will be. Thinner hardware is simply less expensive to support in the long run.

When you put together your ROI study or discuss a server-based solution with management, these points are very important to bring up. Although PCs might initially seem like a good investment for your users to management, there are many other options, such as thin client terminals and the newer class of "thinner" desktops, that can save your company an enormous amount of money in the long run.

In the scenario that follows, you are a network administrator for a large company. The scenario shows how administration is made easier with Terminal Server versus the purchase of a power PC and how deploying Terminal Server can save you money.

The Initial Purchase

PC Based   Your company buys a personal computer ($1200–$2200) for a new user or for upgrading the computer of an existing user.

Terminal Server Based   Your company buys a thin client terminal or "thin" desktop ($500–$1200) for the same user. If you had older, unused PCs, you could also save money by installing them as Terminal Server clients. The hardware requirements are fewer for a Terminal Server client than for most modern operating systems.

Installing or Upgrading the Computer

PC Based   The technical department spends an hour or two unboxing the PC, installing the corporate software, setting up the user on the network, and installing the PC on her desk. If this is an upgrade, the tech support individual spends a few more hours transferring data and application settings and making sure the user has the applications and capabilities she had before.

Terminal Server   The technicians spends 15 minutes unboxing the terminal, setting up the user on the network, and installing the terminal, and the RDP or ICA client will already be installed. Upgrades are rarely necessary, unless the user needs a bigger monitor. Upgrading takes fewer than 5 minutes because data and applications are stored centrally.

Virus Removal

PC Based   Because the PC reports that it has a virus, you go to the user's desk, do a virus scan, and find that the user has infected his PC. You clean the PC and all of the floppy disks.

Terminal Server Based   Virus protection is done at the server. Because thin client terminals and most "thin" desktops do not use floppy disks, the most likely source of infection is email. The boot sector and all system files are locked using NTFS, so viruses will have a difficult time causing significant damage. By running virus protection software, the administrator is notified immediately upon infection and the server is scanned periodically.

Software Upgrades and Rollouts

PC Based   When a rollout of a new client occurs, you and a group of technicians go from PC to PC and install the client from a network share. If users experience problems, such as missing files as a result of the rollout, you must go to their desks to resolve the problems. Software could also be rolled out using automated application deployment solutions, such as Microsoft SMS or Veritas WinInstall, to save time for large deployments.

Terminal Server Based   Application installation for all of your users can be done from your desk. You install or upgrade the applications at the server and not the desktop. In the case of Citrix, you publish the new application by adding users to a group and the next time they log on they will have the new icon available in their Program Neighborhood. With Terminal Server, you could either use central thin client terminal management software to push out a new icon to your thin client terminals or use a logon script to push out the connection file to your "thin" desktops.

Hardware Problems

PC Based   Suppose a user can't remove a floppy disk from the drive. After a half hour of fiddling with it, the user finds that the label is stuck badly in the drive. You need to take the entire machine to get the floppy disk drive replaced or cleaned out. Perhaps, then, someone else calls in with a hard drive that won't boot. You find that the hard drive is dead and replace it with a new one. Because the new drive does not have anything on it, you spend an hour or two formatting the drive, installing the operating system, gathering the correct drivers, and installing user applications.

Terminal Server Based   The main points of failure on a thin client terminal are the monitor, keyboard, and mouse. If any of these fail, they can be replaced very quickly and easily. If the server fails, however, everyone is affected. Because of this, it's important to invest in high-reliability hardware options, such as RAID 5 or disk-mirroring RAID 1. If a RAID 5 drive fails, in many systems it can be replaced while the system is running without losing any data or causing downtime. If you are instead using a "thin" desktop, most come with a CD that enables you to quickly reinstall the operating system. Because the applications are mostly run centrally, there is little else to install other than the RDP or ICA client.

Software Problems

PC Based   A user's application keeps giving her general protection faults. All your other users are running the same application with no problems. You reinstall the application and the problem disappears.

Terminal Server Based   The protected environment of Terminal Server keeps applications and users separate. Still, it is important to maintain tight control of the applications they can run. By using the Shadow feature, you can remotely control any user's session to assist him with a software problem, without leaving your desk.

Data and Hardware Security

PC Based   Take, for example, the following common data and hardware security problems with PCs:

- The user has been storing documents on his hard drive, and they were accidentally deleted. He will have to re-create the documents because there is no central backup.

- Unbeknownst to you, a user is secretly copying product design documents and other mission-critical information to a Zip drive. The next week the person quits to work for a competitor, taking the Zip disks with him.

- Your PC storage room has been broken into. Some equipment and memory are missing.

Terminal Server Based   Applications and data are all backed up centrally. Because data is not stored locally, there is little chance of user data loss.

Thin client terminals have no local storage, so pilfering large amounts of company data is not an easy task. The auditing feature on Windows NT also enables you to track data use down to a file level.

Thin client terminals are not as susceptible to theft as desktop are because thin client terminals require a network server to operate. The cases on thin client terminals are also often sealed.

Remote Access

PC Based   To give a user remote access from home, you must request that a phone line be installed and also order and install remote-access software and a modem on her machine at work. When other users see that user's ability to remotely access the network, they begin to request remote access also. If instead you choose to set up a shared remote-access solution, such as RAS or VPN, the slow connection speeds still limit users on the types of applications they can run remotely.

Terminal Server Based   You can set up remote access for hundreds of users by installing and configuring a modem bank for the server. Because users share a bank of modems and phone lines, you do not have to dedicate a phone line per user, saving your company money on phone costs. Terminal Server is also an excellent solution for remote-access needs because it has very tight, centralized security.

WAN Access

PC Based   When a user relocates, you must move his PC to a remote branch. Some of the user's financial applications require access across the WAN to corporate data. The user finds that these applications run very slowly across the wide area network. For the user to work at an acceptable speed, you must install an expensive, fast WAN link.

Terminal Server Based   Terminal Server works very well across a WAN. Because you are remotely controlling a session running at corporate, only screen updates must go across the line. The user will be able to run the application remotely at nearly the same speed as he runs it at corporate. The bandwidth required is minimal compared to that taken by running an application at corporate without using Terminal Server.

User-Created Problems

PC Based   The user finds a screen saver at the local computer store or some free software online that is too tempting to resist. He installs the screen saver and other applications, which eats up so much memory that his business applications crash regularly on that machine. The user complains to you about the crashing, but doesn't inform you about the screen saver. After a half hour of searching for the problem, including a virus scan and ScanDisk, you discover the screen saver and remove it.

Terminal Server Based   With Terminal Server, users can easily be prevented from installing their own applications. By using policies, you can lock down the desktop tightly.

Hardware Obsolescence

PC Based   You spend a lot of time doing the "computer shuffle." The president complains that the PCs at the local computer store are twice as fast as what is on his desktop. After you upgrade his PC, he requests you give his old computer to his secretary. You spend several hours installing all the correct applications for the president, cleaning up his old PC, installing applications for the secretary, moving data, and moving the PCs. The secretary's old computer is too old for anyone else to use and ends up in storage.

Terminal Server Based   Because the processing occurs at the server, with Terminal Server, users' thin client terminals are far less likely to become obsolete. The president might want a bigger monitor. If so, replacing his and giving the old one to his secretary will take just a few minutes.

Wrapping Up

As you can see, the cost in terms of your time in a PC-only environment can quickly add up. By establishing a network using Terminal Server, you can use this time more productively by implementing solutions that would make your company more competitive and your job more interesting. It is important to keep in mind, however, that Terminal Server is meant to fill particular needs, not to replace every PC in your organization. You will find many situations in your environment where Terminal Server is an ideal fit, but you will also find many situations where another solution might work better. The most successful Terminal Server administrators are the ones who understand the business needs of their company and are able to find the best fit for Terminal Server technology in meeting those needs.

Top-Ten Terminal Server Solutions

Terminal Server will not cure all of your computer woes. There are situations in which Terminal Server is the ideal solution, just as there are situations in which Terminal Server is not well suited. The following is a short list of the top-ten recommended uses for this product:

1. **Replacing text-based terminals**   Terminal Server is a great solution for upgrading your existing terminals. Many companies such as banks need to give employees access to mainframes and minicomputers, but also want them to be able to take advantage of the capabilities of modern Windows applications such as email. Terminal Server puts your investment in Windows-based applications and legacy host computers together on one desktop.

2. **Extending the use of legacy equipment**   The closet full of old PCs you might currently be thinking of getting rid of could make excellent thin client terminals. Terminal Server will squeeze new life out of your old computers by giving them the capability to run applications as fast as new ones.

3. **Making your heterogeneous environment more homogenous**
   Terminal Server greatly extends the reach of your Windows applications. You have probably experienced the need to run a Windows application on a non-Windows platform, or have waited months for a software company to release clients for all your operating systems. With Terminal Server, you can immediately extend any Windows application across all of your different types of clients.

4. **Remote access**   With Terminal Server, your mobile work force can dial in and access a Windows desktop or Windows applications running on Terminal Server. They will be able to run them remotely at nearly the same speed as they can run the applications at the office.

5. **Centralizing administration and computer resources**   Many companies find that centralizing computer resources offers great efficiencies of scale. Terminal Server is a great fit for companies that are in the process of doing this. With Terminal Server you can easily centralize the applications that are run at branch offices, by running them on a central collection of Terminal Servers.

6. **Centralizing accounting, reporting, and data entry**   One of the most common uses of Terminal Server is to help centralize accounting, reporting, and data-entry applications. As data is being centralized, it is important to consider how access to that data will still be provided to

remote locations. Often companies just try to run their branch office applications across the WAN. This usually leads to performance problems and the need to purchase additional expensive bandwidth. Before this decision is made, demonstrate the same application running remotely on Terminal Server to your management. In almost all cases, the application will run much faster and use less WAN bandwidth when running on Terminal Server.

7. **Public access terminals**   Because terminals can be locked down and because of their ease of management, they are great solutions for kiosks, information terminals, research machines, student labs, and other means of providing information and access to applications to the public. Even inside a corporation, they have great possibilities. Many legal firms have libraries where legal assistants and lawyers can do research. A few thin client terminals could be put in the library to run a checkout application, legal research program, library database, and Internet browser.

8. **Customer service and point of sale**   Terminal Server clients make very flexible point-of-sale terminals. Terminal Servers are a great solution for point of sale, where sales representatives need access to special information. For example, a realty office could use Windows-based terminals to display its database of homes to buyers. A central database could be updated regularly with pictures of the homes available, their interiors, and their features. Queries could be quickly done against this database to generate a list of prospective homes. Other pertinent real-estate applications could also be distributed to employees' desktops, such as a mortgage calculator or contract form maker.

9. **Harsh environments**   Thin client terminals are a good solution for harsh environments because they are relatively inexpensive and secure and they are easy to replace. They also are resistant to pilfering. Examples of this application would be terminals on a factory floor, in a machine shop, or on the workbench.

10. **Building the corporate portal**   Last but not least, Terminal Server is the best solution out there for building a corporate application portal. By developing a custom solution using the Terminal Server Advanced Client or using the free portal capabilities that Citrix NFuse provides, you can quickly build a powerful corporate portal for your users. This one point of access, through the web, can result in incredible benefits for your users. You not only can deploy your applications quickly and easily to users, but also other important information such as company news, reports, and other web-based applications.

When Not to Use Terminal Server

Just like you need to be able to recognize situations in which Terminal Server is an ideal fit, you also need to be able to quickly recognize where other solutions might work better. Following is a list of five common situations in which the use of Terminal Server is not recommended:

1. **Applications requiring heavy calculation** Users who often run processor-intensive applications, such as developers, spreadsheet power-users, and report designers, will significantly tax the resources of the server. Be careful when having them run their applications on Terminal Server; they will take up a large piece of the processing time, leaving less for other Terminal Server users. Although Terminal Server is likely the best solution for running these types of applications across the WAN, if your users have local access to the data, it might be less expensive to run the applications on their local workstation.

2. **Applications using animation** Because the only thing that goes across the wire are screen updates, if your screen is changing constantly, you will bog down the network with these updates.

3. **Publishing/drawing programs** Publishing applications, such as desktop publishers, CAD applications, image editing, and drawing programs, are most often better run locally than off a Terminal Server. These applications place a significant burden on both the processing time and network bandwidth available. If you do decide to run them on Terminal Server, remember that you will need to use Citrix MetaFrame to display more than 256 colors.

4. **Unstable network** Without a network, your users are dead in the water. If you frequently have network outages, are low on network bandwidth, have users who can't take any downtime, or do not have redundancy built into your network, you should either consider other options or take steps to increase the reliability of the network before implementing Terminal Server.

5. **Users requiring the ability to work locally** Some users might need to work while traveling where the network might be inaccessible. Until wireless technologies have matured to the point that users can have fast, reliable access to the network wherever they are, running these applications locally is probably the best bet.

5

Licensing Terminal Server and Citrix MetaFrame

THIS CHAPTER COVERS TERMINAL SERVER and Citrix licensing in detail. Understanding the many complexities of both Terminal Server and Citrix licensing is a big part of any planning process for these products. You will need this understanding to accurately put together and be able to explain the licensing costs for a Terminal Server solution.

Before you will be able to plan for a Terminal Server deployment and accurately estimate the costs, you need to understand how the licensing works. Unfortunately, truly understanding Microsoft Terminal Server and Citrix licensing can be a daunting task. Both Microsoft and Citrix take very different approaches to licensing.

Author's Note

Both MetaFrame and Terminal Server have gone through many licensing changes over the past few years. Although the basic concepts covered here have remained the same, some of the details have changed. Although this information is accurate as of today, even by the time this book is published there might be additional changes to licensing. You can find the latest licensing information by contacting your local reseller or searching for the information at the following web site addresses:

Microsoft: www.microsoft.com/business/licensing

Citrix: www.citrix.com

Citrix Licensing

Citrix licensing for MetaFrame and all of its predecessors has always been based on a concurrent user-licensing scheme. This means that when you are estimating the costs of a Terminal Server solution that includes Citrix MetaFrame, you need to determine what the maximum number of concurrent users will be. The "Server Sizing" section in Chapter 8, "Installing Windows 2000 Terminal Server and Citrix MetaFrame," discusses some simple ways to come up with a rough number of concurrent users for your situation.

Licensing MetaFrame 1.8

With MetaFrame 1.8 for Windows NT 4.0 and 1.8 for 2000, you first have to buy a base license for every MetaFrame server you install. This base license includes 15 concurrent user licenses. For some administrators, this licensing scheme is tedious. Even if you just want to set up a test server or a server that would never have 15 users on it at a time, you still need to buy an expensive base license.

On the other hand, if you need more than 15 concurrent licenses, you just buy 5, 10, 20, or 50-user Citrix user license packs or "bump-packs." You then install them on whichever Citrix server needs them.

License Pooling

By default, all the licenses you install for all the servers in a particular farm are pooled together into a single license count. By default, when users connect to Citrix MetaFrame, they take a license from the central license pool and not the server to which they connect. In Citrix MetaFrame 1.8, the server farm's master browser is the one that pools together the licenses and keeps track of their usage. This is an important feature with Citrix MetaFrame because it helps make sure your licenses are being used efficiently.

One relatively new feature with MetaFrame 1.8 is that even if you run multiple applications across multiple servers at the same time, you take up only one connection license from the license pool. Remember, however, that licenses are pooled together within a single server farm. If you run applications on multiple Citrix server farms, you will take up one license for each farm to which you are concurrently connected.

Licensing MetaFrame XP

With MetaFrame XP, Citrix has changed its licensing approach. Instead of needing to buy a base license for every server in your server farm, you need to buy only a single MetaFrame XP Starter System and then add user-connection license packs as needed. This Starter System includes 20 concurrent user licenses.

The Starter System comes in three different editions: XPs, XPa, and XPe. Each edition has a different set of features. The XPs edition is the starter edition and includes all the basic MetaFrame features, such as application publishing and the ICA protocol. XPa is considered the advanced edition and enables application and server load-balancing management capabilities. XPe is the enterprise edition and includes all the features of XPa, plus advanced management capabilities through SNMP network management, installation management, and resource management. A detailed list of the differences in features between these three editions is provided in Chapter 3, "Introduction to Citrix MetaFrame 1.8 and MetaFrame XP."

Unlike MetaFrame 1.8, which has a separate version for Windows NT 4.0 and 2000 Terminal Server, MetaFrame XP includes install software for both. With this Starter System, you get *one* set of install CDs you can use to install MetaFrame XP on *all* of your servers in a single farm, including both Windows NT 4.0 Terminal Servers and Windows 2000 Servers with Terminal Services installed.

Remember that the Starter System is licensed only for a single farm. If you intend to set up MetaFrame XP on multiple farms, you need to purchase a Starter System for each farm. In addition, you need to purchase the connection licenses that are needed for users on that farm because connection licenses between farms are not pooled.

Although having multiple farms can become expensive, one of the big advantages of MetaFrame XP is its capability to more easily merge multiple farms into one. Using MetaFrame XP, you can easily have a single farm spread across multiple subnets without the need for ICA gateways. Unlike MetaFrame 1.8, licenses can now be pooled easily across subnets using MetaFrame XP.

Author's Note

Citrix intends to make an edition of MetaFrame XP for Windows .NET Terminal Server. This edition will be sent to existing MetaFrame XP customers with Subscription Advantage, so that they can extend their XP solution to the Windows .NET platform. With Citrix MetaFrame XP, all you pay for is the connection licenses you need. How many platforms you want to install the product on is up to you to decide.

MetaFrame Product Code

In MetaFrame XP, your licenses are pooled together within a Citrix server farm. However, there are now three separate license pools, one for XPe, XPs, and XPa. The license used by your server when you log on depends on that server's MetaFrame Product Code (MPC). This product code is an eight-digit alphanumeric code separated by a dash in the middle (A123-B456, for example).

The product code is initially entered during the server install. However, it can be easily modified later from within the Citrix Management Console (CMC) by right-clicking the server name and selecting Set MetaFrame Product Code as shown in the test farm in Figure 5.1. You also can view the current product code for your server by looking under the Information tab in the server's Properties window. You can get to this window by right-clicking the server in the CMC and selecting Properties.

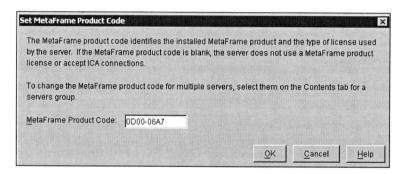

Figure 5.1   Changing the product code.

Mixed XPe, XPa, and XPs Farms

Setting up your servers with different product codes can be useful in larger deployments to save money. If you purchase MetaFrame XPe, for example, it also includes the product codes for MetaFrame XPa and XPs. This means you can make a select group of servers into MetaFrame XPa or XPs servers by entering the XPa or XPs product code for those servers. When users log on to those servers, they take a less-expensive MetaFrame XPa or XPs license out of the connection license pool rather than a MetaFrame XPe license. Although you do not get to enjoy the features offered by XPe on those particular servers, they are still part of the main farm.

Product Licenses

When you first set up a MetaFrame XP server farm, the first license you need to enter and activate is the product license. The product license refers to the license for MetaFrame XPe, XPa, or XPs. It is normally provided for you with your MetaFrame XP CD kit or electronically through the Citrix Subscription Advantage web site at www.citrix.com/services/ subscription/default.htm.

Normally, you will receive both the product licenses and the product codes for the product you purchased and any products below it. If you purchase MetaFrame XPe, for example, you should receive the product licenses and product codes for XPs and XPa as well. This way you can install all three product licenses on your server farm if desired.

Each product license, whether it is for XPe, XPa, or XPs, can be installed only once on your farm. After that, the only licenses you can install are additional connection licenses.

Each server you add to the farm will take a copy of one of the product licenses that are available on the farm. The product that server is licensed for depends on what product code you enter when you install it. If a server's product code is blank or the associated product license has not been installed in the farm, the server will not be properly licensed. When users log on, they will receive an error message indicating the licensing problem until the server is licensed properly.

This is a very important point to understand. Suppose, for instance, that you have a MetaFrame XPa server farm and have entered and activated the MetaFrame XPa product license for the farm. Then, on any server in the farm, you should be able to enter the product code for XPa, and it will automatically grab a copy of the master XPa license. If you enter the product code for XPe, however, because there is no product code for XPe in the farm, the server will not be licensed.

To check which product licenses are available in your farm for use by the servers, just go into the Citrix Management Console, select Licenses, and click the Product tab (see Figure 5.2). Notice in Figure 5.2 that four product licenses have been entered into the farm, one for MetaFrame 1.8, XPs, XPa, and XPe.

These product licenses are available in this farm. To use one of these licenses for one of your servers, just change the product code to the appropriate product (XPe, XPa or XPs). If the server can successfully obtain a copy of the product license for that code from the farm, you will be able to see it in the CMC. To view which product license a server is running, select the server under the Servers folder in the CMC, and then click the Licenses tab on the right.

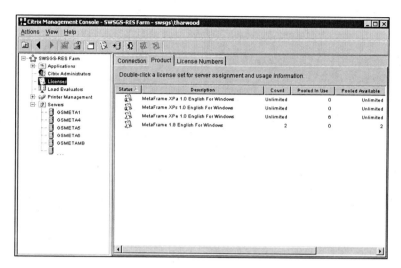

Figure 5.2   Farm product licenses.

Using QFARM to Verify Servers Are Licensed Properly

You can use a simple command-line utility called QFARM to verify that your product licenses and product codes are set up correctly. From any server in the farm, enter the command `qfarm /laod`. You will see the load statistics for all of your servers. If any of the servers report an erroneous load statistic of `22000`, that particular server has a license problem. To fix it, change the product code on the server to the product code for one of the product licenses you have in the farm. If you have a MetaFrame XPe product license in the farm, for example, change the product code on the server to the MetaFrame XPe product code.

Connection Licenses

After you have the product itself licensed correctly, it is time to decide on how many connection licenses you will need for your users. The MetaFrame XPe, XPa, and XPs starter kits come with 20 initial user-connection licenses for your farm. If you need more than 20 concurrent users to be able to connect to the farm, you need to purchase additional Citrix user-connection license packs. These are normally available in increments of 5, 10, 20, and 50 users. You need to purchase enough connection licenses to handle the maximum projected number of concurrent users you will have across your farm.

If you will have a 5-server farm and you expect the maximum concurrent number of users per server will be 25, you need to purchase a minimum total of 125 connection licenses for the farm.

MetaFrame 1.8 Licenses and Upgrade Connection Licenses

Those of you who are upgrading from MetaFrame 1.8 pay close attention to this part. If you have been provided upgrade connection licenses from Citrix through Subscription Advantage or have purchased them, you need *to enter your MetaFrame 1.8 product license* into the farm to validate the upgrade connection licenses. Normally, this is done for you automatically by the install process if you upgrade an existing MetaFrame 1.8 server in place. If you do a clean install of MetaFrame XP, however, you need to enter the product license for MetaFrame 1.8 to activate the MetaFrame XP upgrade licenses.

Subscription Advantage

When you are deciding on what licenses you need to get, you also need to decide whether to purchase them with Subscription Advantage. Subscription Advantage gives you upgrade protection for one year from the time you activate the license. After that year is up, you need to pay an annual maintenance fee to have access to the latest upgrades available from Citrix. Citrix will mail you new product upgrades as they are released, once you are a member of the Subscription Advantage program.

From both an administrative and business standpoint, Subscription Advantage is highly recommended. Many of the new features that come out with newer versions of the product make administrators' lives much easier and greatly improve the performance and functionality of the product.

Citrix has recently standardized two different types of updates that you are qualified for under Subscription Advantage: feature releases and product upgrades. Feature releases are important feature enhancements and additions that are released more frequently than product upgrades. They are based on customer feedback on the product releases and allow for Citrix to provide some feature enhancements without the release of an entirely new product.

Product upgrades are major version upgrades to a product such as the upgrade from MetaFrame 1.8 to MetaFrame XP. If you had MetaFrame 1.8 with Subscription Advantage when MetaFrame XP was released, you would have received the install CDs and been able to apply for the product and license codes you needed to upgrade to XP.

Feature Release 1 for MetaFrame XP

As of this writing, Citrix has already released its first feature release for MetaFrame XP, called simply *Feature Release 1*. Feature Release 1 is actually bundled with the first service pack for MetaFrame XP. This feature release/service pack combo is available for free download from the Citrix web site.

Although you can download and install the feature release at any time, to enable the features in the feature release, you need to enter the product license and activate it. Once activated, the features available in the feature release can be used.

You can get the product license for the feature release in two ways. If you are purchasing MetaFrame XP from scratch, you need to order the feature release separately. If you have MetaFrame XP with Subscription Advantage, however, you should receive a registration code for the feature release for free.

Microsoft Terminal Server Licensing

The Microsoft approach to licensing differs significantly from the Citrix approach. Instead of charging for concurrent user licenses like Citrix, Microsoft charges per seat. If you are licensing just Terminal Server alone, you just need to add up the number of seats that you will be installing the Terminal Services client on and the number of Windows 2000 Server licenses you will need, and then use these numbers to get a quote. If you are licensing both Terminal Server and MetaFrame, however, you need to purchase the correct licenses for *both* products. Your connection to Citrix MetaFrame relies on your connection to Terminal Server.

Three basic licenses are involved in most Terminal Server 2000 deployments:

- **Windows 2000 Server License**   Provides the license you need to install and use your Windows 2000 server. Terminal Services is included with all editions of Windows 2000 Server, so there is no additional server-related charge for its installation.

- **Windows 2000 Terminal Server Client Access License (CAL)** Each license grants the right for a single workstation or client device to connect to your Windows 2000 Terminal Server via the Terminal Services or ICA client. This is a per-seat license. One license must be purchased for every device on the network that will connect to the Terminal Server using Terminal Services unless you are using Windows 2000 as the client.

- **Windows 2000 Server Client Access License**   Each license grants the right for a single workstation or client to connect to and use the resources of Windows 2000 servers on the network. Unlike other server products, Terminal Server cannot be legally licensed using per-server Windows 2000 CALs, only per-seat licenses. You must purchase a Windows 2000 CAL for every device on your network that will connect to the server.

Windows 2000 Server License

Windows 2000 Server comes in three different editions: Windows 2000 Server, Windows 2000 Advanced Server, and Windows 2000 DataCenter Server. The first choice you need to make when putting together your Terminal Server project is which type of Terminal Server you are going to purchase.

To make this choice, you need to better understand the differences between these three products. The main difference, as you can see in Table 5.1, is that Advanced Server and DataCenter Server support significantly more memory and processors than plain Windows 2000 Server. Although ideally they would make good choices for a Terminal Server, in practice most applications today are not written to take advantage of the extra memory and processing power available. Check with the software companies for the applications you intend to use on Terminal Server to be sure before you make your decision. In addition, Terminal Services are not supported with the server clustering capabilities available with DataCenter Server.

Table 5.1 **Comparison of Windows 2000 Edition**

Operating System Edition	CPUs	Max Memory	Comments
Windows 2000 Server	4	4GB	
Windows 2000 Advanced Server	8	8GB	Supports NLB and 2 node clusters
Windows 2000 DataCenter Server	32	~64GB	Supports NLB and 4 node clusters

For these reasons, plain Windows 2000 Server is the most common choice by Terminal Server and Citrix administrators. The one exception to this practice is that if you want to be able to load share your Terminal Servers using Microsoft Network Load Balancing, all the servers need to be Windows 2000 Advanced Servers. If instead you intend to use the more advanced load-balancing capabilities available in Citrix MetaFrame XPa, XPe, or 1.8 with Load Balancing Services, just Windows 2000 Server should be adequate.

Limitations of 32-Bit Computing

The truth is we still have a long ways to go before running hundreds or even thousands of concurrent users on a single Terminal Server will be practical. It is very rare today to see more than 150 concurrent users on a single Terminal Server, even on ones that are maxed out in both memory and processors. One barrier that you are likely to run into is the memory limitations caused by using 32-bit technology.

By default, Terminal Server provides only 2GB of working room for applications and 2GB for system processes. Even if you put more than 4GB of memory in your system, the most a single application will be able to access is 2GB. Although there are ways in Advanced Server and DataCenter Server for applications to access additional memory, most applications today, with the exception of a few heavy-duty server applications, such as SQL Server, are not written to take advantage of the extra memory.

Even though 4GB seems like a lot of memory, when you are running 150 users on a box you can run into limitations quickly. If you have 150 users on the box at the same time, for example, each user will have somewhere around 13 to 25MB of memory space available assuming the server has the full 4GB of memory installed and depending on how much space the system needs. This is not a whole lot of working room for many of today's more advanced applications, such as reporting applications.

Microsoft's upcoming 64-bit version of Windows .NET Terminal Server is designed to work with the Intel 64-bit Itanium chip. The 64-bit bus of the Itanium processor will definitely help get around this limitation. However, your applications will have to be recompiled as 64-bit before they will be able to take advantage of the extra hardware capacity that will be available in a 64-bit operating system. For now, you are best off spreading the load across multiple servers using either Microsoft load-sharing or Citrix load-balancing technologies.

Terminal Server Client Access Licenses

For every seat where you will be installing the Terminal Services client, you need a Windows 2000 TS Client Access License (TS CAL). A Windows 2000 Terminal Services CAL is not a separate product or a installable piece of software, but just a license that gives you the legal right for a workstation to connect to a Terminal Server and use Terminal Services. The Windows 2000 TS CAL is a separately purchased license from Microsoft. It is not part of other CALs available from Microsoft, such as the BackOffice or Core CAL.

The Windows 2000 TS CAL is included with both Windows 2000 and Windows XP Professional Workstation. For every workstation that is not either Windows 2000 or XP, however, you will need to purchase a Windows 2000 TS CAL for that workstation to connect to a Windows 2000 Terminal Server. This even includes non-Windows workstations, such as UNIX or Macintosh workstations, which connect to a Terminal Server with MetaFrame.

The following are some examples of connection options that require you to purchase a TS CAL:

- Windows 95/98/Me workstation using the RDP or ICA client to connect to Terminal Server
- Windows NT 4.0 via RDP or ICA (Remember that Windows NT 4.0 only "includes" a Windows NT 4.0 TS CAL and not the Windows 2000 TS CAL needed to connect to a Windows 2000 Terminal Server.)
- Handheld Win CE device using the RDP or ICA client
- Thin client terminal using either RDP or ICA client
- Any UNIX workstation connecting to Citrix MetaFrame through the ICA client
- A Macintosh connecting to Citrix MetaFrame through the ICA client

With Windows 2000, Microsoft has begun enforcing the TS CAL licensing requirement by requiring that you set up a Terminal Services Licensing server. The Terminal Services Licensing server keeps track of Terminal Server CAL usage on the network by assigning a Windows 2000 TS CAL to every workstation that connects to Terminal Servers on that network. This TS CAL is normally assigned by embedding it in the local Registry of the machine. If the Terminal Services Licensing server has no more TS CALs available, unlicensed workstations are not allowed to connect.

This enforced licensing practice is a *big change* from what you might be used to with Windows NT 4.0 Terminal Server edition. Even though NT 4.0 TS CALs were legally required for each workstation, this requirement was not enforced by the system. Instead, it was up to you to ensure that the correct number of NT 4.0 TS CALs were purchased.

Although licensing is now enforced, you do have a 90-day grace period from the point you install Terminal Server before it starts enforcing the licensing requirements.

Terminal Server Licensing Scenarios

Suppose, for example, that you are deploying a Terminal Server solution for your main office and two branch offices. At your main office, you have 50 Windows 2000 workstations where users will be accessing Windows Terminal Server. At each branch office, you have 5 Windows 98 workstations from which users will be accessing the server. In this case, you need to purchase only 10 TS CALs to cover the Windows 98 workstations at the branch offices. The Windows 2000 workstations at the main office are already covered because each Windows 2000 workstation includes a TS CAL.

Suppose further that you are setting up a computer lab at a school with 20 Windows NT 4.0 workstations that will be used to run applications off of a Terminal Server. This lab is heavily used by the school's students throughout the week. The school has at most 550 students over the course of a year who use the computers in the lab. In this case, you need only 20 Windows 2000 TS CALs, one for each Windows NT 4.0 workstation. How many students use the workstations is irrelevant because Terminal Server is licensed per seat.

Upgrading from Windows NT 4.0 Terminal Server

If you are upgrading from Windows NT 4.0 Terminal Server, you likely already have several Windows NT 4.0 TS CALs. However, these cannot legally be used to connect to a Windows 2000 Terminal Server. You need to either purchase new Windows 2000 TS CALs or upgrade your existing ones to meet the licensing requirements of Windows 2000 Terminal Server.

Unfortunately, as of October 1, 2001, Microsoft no longer permits users to purchase a version upgrade license for upgrading from a Windows NT 4.0 CAL to a Windows 2000 TS CAL. These types of licenses no longer are available in the channel. As of this writing, however, you do have the option of purchasing an Upgrade Advantage license for your Windows NT 4.0 CALs as long as you are already in a volume licensing agreement with Microsoft. An Upgrade Advantage license allows you to upgrade your Windows NT 4.0 CAL to the latest version for the term of the volume licensing agreement that you have. This option is available currently until July 2002. For more information, contact your local Microsoft representative or talk to your reseller.

Terminal Services Licensing Server

With the release of Windows 2000 Terminal Services, Microsoft has created a special service that you need to install on one of your Windows 2000 servers to keep track of your TS CALs on the network. The service is called *Terminal Services Licensing* and can be installed on your server through the Add/Remove Windows Program Wizard in Control Panel. Once installed and activated, this server becomes your Terminal Services Licensing server for your network. This server does not necessarily have to be a Terminal Server. If you need this server to support licensing for Terminal Servers in multiple domains or across the WAN, however, you need to install it on a Windows 2000 domain controller. This is the recommended configuration.

After you roll out your Terminal Server solution, you have a 90-day grace period before you need to activate a licensing server on your network and add your TS CAL licenses to it. After the 90-day grace period, your Terminal Server will begin checking whether clients are properly licensed before allowing them to connect to the server.

When a client attempts to connect to a Windows 2000 Terminal Server after the server's 90-day grace period has expired, the server will check whether the client already has a TS CAL in its Registry. It will then verify that this TS CAL is valid with the Terminal Services Licensing server. If the client does not already have a Windows 2000 TS CAL, the Terminal Server requests a TS CAL on behalf of the client from the Terminal Services Licensing server. This license is taken from the license pool and then assigned to the client. The client will now be able to connect to the Terminal Server.

When planning your licensing strategy, you have to be much more careful in Windows 2000 than you had to be with Windows NT 4.0 Terminal Server. Although the Terminal Services Licensing service was a part of every Windows NT 4.0 Terminal Server, it is only with Windows 2000 server that license usage is enforced. If you try to connect to your Terminal Server after the 90-day grace period and your workstation needs a TS CAL, you will not be able to connect unless there is a licensing server available and it has licenses left.

Licensing Complexities

Because of the many licensing complexities, licensing problems on both Terminal Server and Citrix MetaFrame are very common. Support forums and other online Terminal Server and Citrix MetaFrame communities are filled with licensing problems and answers. However, the majority of these questions can be more easily answered by following a few simple rules. For a good summary coverage, see the "Top-Ten Licensing Questions and Answers," at the end of this chapter.

Client Access Licenses

Just when you thought you had enough of licensing requirements, along comes the requirement to purchase Windows 2000 CALs. The Windows 2000 Client Access License or just plain CAL differs from the TS CAL in that it gives you license to make use of the resources of the server itself and not Terminal Services specifically. Although Windows 2000 CALs can be configured for either per-server or per-seat licensing, the only supported licensing with Terminal Server is per-seat. What this means is that you will need to buy a Windows 2000 CAL *in addition* to a TS CAL for each workstation or device that will attach to your Terminal Server.

Many corporations have already purchased Windows CALs so that their workstations are licensed to connect to their Windows servers. However, you need to make sure with Windows 2000 Terminal Server that you buy Windows 2000 CALs and not NT 4.0 CALs. If you intend to use your NT 4.0 CALs for this solution, check with your local vendor to determine your options to upgrade these CALs to Windows 2000 CALs.

Also, if you intend to use Citrix MetaFrame to deploy applications to non-Windows machines, this licensing requirement also applies to those machines.

Suppose, for example, that you have 30 Sparc workstations on which you want to run Windows applications using Citrix MetaFrame. You need to purchase 30 TS CALs and 30 Windows 2000 CALs so that the machines are properly licensed for using Windows 2000 Terminal Services.

Suppose further that you have a main office with 50 Windows 2000 workstations and a branch office with 20 Windows Me workstations that all need access to a Terminal Server. In this case, you would need 70 Windows 2000 CALs, one for each workstation. In addition you would need 20 TS CALs for the branch offices Windows Me workstations. The Windows 2000 workstations at the main office already have TS CALs.

Author's Note

For those who prefer to purchase BackOffice (now called Core) CALs rather than the plain Windows 2000 CAL, it is important to note that the TS CAL is not included because Terminal Server is not part of the BackOffice suite.

Putting It All Together

Now that you understand the licensing for both products, it's time to start putting it together so that you can get an accurate cost estimate for your project. First you need to come up with a number for the following items:

- **Total number of seats (NumSeats)**   Includes the total number of all the devices and workstations, including non-Windows workstations and thin client terminals, that you will be installing the Terminal Services client onto for access to your Terminal Server(s).

- **Total number of servers (NumServ)**   The number of servers that you estimate you will need for your project.

- **Number of Windows 2000 or XP workstations (NumTSCAL)** This is the total number of Windows 2000 or XP workstations that you have that will be used for connecting to the Terminal Server.

- **Number of Windows 2000 CALs (NumCAL)**   This is the total number of Windows 2000 CALs that you currently have for the workstations that will be connecting to the Terminal Server.

You can use the following formula to figure out the cost of your Terminal Server project:

Total Cost = (NumServ) $\star$ (Cost of Windows 2000 Server, Advanced or DataCenter as chosen) + (NumSeats − NumTSCAL) $\star$ (Cost of TS CAL) + (NumSeats − NumCAL) $\star$ (Cost of Windows 2000 CAL)

If you will be using MetaFrame 1.8 or XP for your solution, you also need to add in their concurrent licensing costs. Remember that with MetaFrame you need to figure out what the maximum number of concurrent users will be across the server farm. The number of seats for MetaFrame is irrelevant because it is licensed per connection and not per seat.

With MetaFrame 1.8, your costs will be the base license for each server, which includes 15 concurrent user licenses and enough additional concurrent user bump-packs to bring you up to the maximum number of concurrent users you expect. In addition, if you need load balancing, RMS, or IMS, you will need to add in the per-server costs for those products.

The licensing for MetaFrame XPa, XPs, and XPe is a little bit simpler. You will need to purchase the 20-user Starter System for whichever product you choose and enough license bump-packs to bring you up to the total number of concurrent users you expect.

Author's Note

Actual licensing requirements are subject to change at any time, so be sure to get the advice of your local Microsoft and Citrix resellers before making purchases.

Although there might be some variance by the time you read this book, this section helps give you some important background and hopefully a better understanding of Terminal Server and Citrix licensing.

Alternative Licensing Arrangements

The unusual nature of Terminal Server and Citrix licensing has been the source of much debate. The biggest problem has been with application service providers or others who want to deploy applications using Terminal Server over the web. Because Terminal Server relies on a per-seat licensing scheme, this makes deployment impractical on a large scale. To better meet the needs of this type of solution, both Microsoft and Citrix have several alternative licensing arrangements and programs available.

Terminal Server Internet Connector License

If you intend to deploy applications across the Internet, you might want to consider purchasing the Terminal Server Internet Connector License rather than the traditional TS CAL and Windows 2000 CALs. The Terminal Server Internet Connector License is a per-server license that allows you to serve up to 200 concurrent connections on that licensed server. Although this sounds great for corporations that want to deploy applications on the Internet, there are two big catches:

- **Only anonymous users allowed**   You can deploy applications only to anonymous and not named users. In other words, your site cannot use some types of logon mechanisms, such as NFuse, to authenticate users.
- **Only non-employees allowed**   Only people who are not employed by your company are legally allowed access to connect to your Terminal Server.

Unfortunately, these caveats are pretty big and limit the use of this license mainly for demonstration purposes. You also could use this license for setting up some type of public kiosk.

Corporate Licensing Programs

Both Citrix and Microsoft offer several different corporate licensing programs for large-volume purchases of their thin client technology. You can receive huge savings if you qualify for one of these programs. Before you pay the full package price on these products, make sure you investigate whether you qualify for one of them. The details of these programs are not covered here; your local Citrix or Microsoft reseller can quickly fill you in on the latest details and help you determine whether you qualify.

Top-Ten Licensing Questions and Answers

To help reinforce this important topic, the following list presents frequently asked questions and their answers with regard to both Terminal Server and Citrix MetaFrame licensing.

1. I am planning a Terminal Server project for our office. We intend to put together a 2-server Windows 2000 Terminal Server solution that will be accessed by all 50 of our users. Everyone currently has Windows 98. What licenses do I need?

   You will need to purchase the following software:

   50 Windows 2000 TS CALs

   50 Windows 2000 CALs

   2 Windows 2000 Server licenses

2. I also have 10 Macintoshes that need access to the applications on the servers. How much would it cost to set these users up with Citrix MetaFrame? I don't expect more than 20 users will be connected at a time to the servers.

In this case you would need to purchase these additional items:

1 MetaFrame XPa or XPs Starter Pack (includes 20 concurrent user-connection licenses)

10 Windows 2000 CALs for the Macs

10 Windows 2000 TS CALs for the Macs

3. We intend to roll out Microsoft Office to all of these users. Because only 20 users will be connecting at a time, can I just purchase 20 licenses?

If your product is licensed per seat like Microsoft Office, you need to purchase a copy for every seat (or in other words, 60 copies). If you are deploying software that is licensed per concurrent user, however, you need to purchase only 20 licenses. Refer to the individual application's licensing policy.

4. I already have 2 Windows NT 4.0 Terminal Servers and 50 Windows NT 4.0 TS CALs. We also have 2 base licenses of Citrix MetaFrame 1.8. Can I just upgrade these to get to Windows 2000 with MetaFrame XP?

In the case of Citrix MetaFrame 1.8, the answer is currently yes. Citrix has both base-license and connection-license upgrades available. In the case of Windows NT 4.0 Terminal Server, however, you would have had to purchase Upgrade Advantage on the licenses to be able to upgrade to the latest product. As of this writing, Microsoft no longer has version upgrade licenses available. However, Upgrade Advantage licenses will still be available until July 2002 if you already have a volume licensing agreement with Microsoft (that is, Open or Select).

5. Well, I bought all the software I needed for a Terminal Server and Citrix MetaFrame XPa solution. However, when I installed Terminal Services on my servers, it did not ask for any license codes. It appears that multiple people can connect to my Terminal Servers with no problems. When do I need to enter a license code?

Terminal Server gives you a 90-day grace period, from the time Terminal Services is first installed, before it starts checking licensing. Make sure to set up and activate a Terminal Services Licensing server on your network before this 90-day period expires; otherwise after 90 days, your clients will no longer be able to connect! Activating the Terminal Services Licensing server involves contacting the Microsoft Licensing Clearinghouse, either through the Internet or by phone. They will provide the licensing codes you need to add licenses to and activate the Terminal Services Licensing server. You can find explicit instructions on how to do this in Chapter 8.

6. Now I have finished setting up and activating one of the servers as a Terminal Services Licensing server and am beginning the installation of MetaFrame XPa. It is asking for a licensing code. What code is this?

During the installation of your first MetaFrame XPa server, you will have to enter the product license code for XPa. The product license code is normally located on a sticker affixed to the MetaFrame install CD pack. This license is not assigned to this particular server, but is made available to all the servers that you will be installing in this farm.

7. Now it is asking for a product code. What is this and why do I need to enter it?

The product code indicates the product type for the server you are installing. For the product code to work correctly, you must have already installed the associated product license in the farm. Product codes are per-server and are entered every time you set up a new server. Product licenses are only entered once per farm.

In this situation, you enter the product code for MetaFrame XPa. You will find the product code, next to the product license for XPa on the sticker on the CD.

8. Now I am setting up the second server, and it is asking for a license code again. I thought you only had to install the product license once per farm.

You do have to install the product license only once. You should be able to skip past the license prompt this time without having to enter one. If you have connection licenses you want to add, you can add them at this prompt.

9. It is asking for the product code for the second server. Should I enter the same product code that I did for the first?

Yes. Normally you want to enter the same product code for all of your servers in a server farm. In this case, you would enter the MetaFrame XPa product code on all your servers, which means they would all be XPa servers and share the same product features. You could enter a different product code, such as an XPs product code, only if the XPs product license were already entered into the farm. This type of mixed product environment, although possible, is not recommended.

10. I entered all the licenses I think I should have; however, every time I log on to the server I get a Citrix error message stating that no licenses are available. What's up?

If you are upgrading from MetaFrame 1.8, make sure that the MetaFrame 1.8 license exists in the farm. Go into the CMC, click Licenses, click the Product tab, and look for a MetaFrame 1.8 license. If you are using upgrade licenses, you need to have a MetaFrame 1.8 license entered into the farm, otherwise they will not work. Normally, this license will automatically be brought in when you upgrade a MetaFrame 1.8 server. If you do a clean install, however, you must manually enter the license.

Planning a Terminal Server and Citrix MetaFrame XP Solution

6

THIS CHAPTER PROVIDES AN IN-DEPTH discussion of both Terminal Server and Citrix MetaFrame XP design, so that you understand how best to implement these products in your environment. You will learn about such planning issues as how to properly place your licensing servers for Terminal Server, and how to set up your MetaFrame XP farm correctly. This chapter lays very important groundwork, especially for those who intend to deploy an enterprise-wide Terminal Server or MetaFrame XP solution.

Planning for Terminal Server

Terminal Server does not have as many different aspects that you need to plan for like MetaFrame. Just because the planning requirements are less, however, does not mean that they are not important. In this chapter, you will learn several of the important factors you need to plan for with a Terminal Server solution. You also will learn about items such as planning your Terminal Server licensing setup, which applies for both Terminal Servers with MetaFrame and without.

Migrating from Windows NT 4.0 Terminal Server

If you will be migrating from Windows NT 4.0 Terminal Server, it is a good time for a fresh rebuild. Upgrades from Windows NT 4.0 Terminal Server to Windows 2000 are not a supported option.

It is also a very good time to start implementing imaging technology. Install a fresh Windows 2000 server in the lab, do your performance tuning and common application installations, and then image it. Chapter 8, "Installing Windows 2000 Terminal Server and Citrix MetaFrame," contains explicit instructions on how to create an image of your server.

Be sure to document the server installation and application installation thoroughly. Now is a good time to create a good base set of documents to ease future support.

How Terminal Services Licensing Works

As part of the planning process for both Terminal Server and Terminal Server with MetaFrame, you need to decide how you will handle Terminal Services licensing and on what Windows 2000 server you will install the Terminal Services Licensing service. Before making these decisions, however, you first need to understand exactly how the process works.

Windows 2000 Terminal Services Licensing service can be installed only on a Windows 2000 server. Even though there is a licensing service on Windows NT 4.0 Terminal Server, this licensing service monitors licensing only for clients that log on to the local Windows NT 4.0 Terminal Server. In Windows 2000, Terminal Server licenses are not only monitored by the Windows 2000 Licensing server, but also are enforced.

You can set up any Windows 2000 server as your licensing server just by adding the Terminal Services Licensing component in the Windows Components section of the Add/Remove Programs utility in Control Panel.

During the installation you need to choose whether you are setting up a *Domain/Workgroup Licensing Server* (DLS) or an *Enterprise Licensing Server* (ELS) as shown in Figure 6.1.

A DLS server is designed for use in an environment where your Windows 2000 Terminal Servers are either a member of their own workgroup or they are a member of a Windows NT 4.0 domain. If a Terminal Server is a member of a workgroup or NT 4.0 domain, it will send out a broadcast request when it needs to find a licensing server. Because of this, the DLS server needs to be on the same broadcast domain or network as the Terminal Servers for licensing to work.

An ELS server is designed for use in an Active Directory environment and must be set up on a Windows 2000 domain controller. Only when installing the licensing service on a domain controller will you have the option to select for the server to be an ELS. Notice in Figure 6.1 that this option is grayed out. This is because the server in the example is not a domain controller.

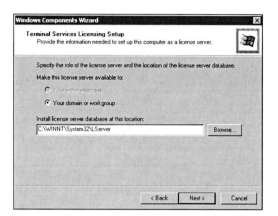

Figure 6.1   Setting Up a Terminal Services Licensing server.

If your Terminal Servers are a member of a Windows 2000 Active Directory domain, you need to set up one or more of your domain controllers as either a DLS or an ELS. The difference is that all ELSs in a tree are recorded in the Active Directory, and are available for licensing for all domains in that tree. A Terminal Server that is a member of an Active Directory domain will request a license as follows:

1. Generates a list of all the domain controllers in its own domain.

2. Queries all the domain controllers to determine which ones are running the Terminal Services Licensing service and selects one at random from which to retrieve the license.

3. If none of the domain controllers are running and the license service or a license is not available, the Terminal Server will query the Active Directory for the ELS by looking for the list of servers under the following container:

   ```
   LDAP://CN=TS-Enterprise-License-Server,CN=[Site
   Name],CN=Sites,Configuration-container
   ```

4. It then randomly picks from one of these servers to obtain the license.

Setting Up a Preferred Licensing Server

If any of your Terminal Servers are a member of a workgroup or NT 4.0 domain and you need them to retrieve their licenses from a remote Terminal Server Licensing server that is not in its broadcast domain, you need to manually specify in the Registry that that server is the preferred licensing server. The following instructions cover how to do this:

1. First make sure that you can ping the licensing server by name from the Terminal Server that needs access to it.

2. Run REGEDIT on the Terminal Server and browse to the following Registry key:

   `HKEY_LOCAL_MACHINE\SYSTEM\CurrentControlSet\Services\TermService`

3. Add a new string (REG_SZ) value named `DefaultLicenseServer`, with a value set to the server name of the preferred licensing server.

Terminal Services Licensing Server Placement

Now that you understand how the Terminal Services Licensing server system works, you can better decide how to set it up. The following are some general tips:

- If any of your Terminal Servers are a member of an Active Directory domain, you must install the licensing service on one of the Active Directory domain controllers.

- Be very careful when upgrading a Windows NT 4.0 domain to 2000, that you also ensure you install a licensing service on one of the new domain controllers. If you do not, licensing will fail on your network.

- Always make sure you set up at least two licensing servers for redundancy in large Terminal Server deployments.

- Setting up a domain controller as an ELS is preferred, instead of setting it up as a domain/workgroup server in most environments.

- If you want to localize licensing requests in an Active Directory environment, install the licensing service on the local domain controllers.

- If any of your Terminal Servers are a member of a Windows NT 4.0 domain or workgroup, you will need to have either a DLS or ELS on the same broadcast domain as the server.

- If you need a Terminal Server that is a member of a workgroup or NT 4.0 domain to retrieve licenses from a server outside of its network, set its preferred licensing server in the Registry as shown previously.

Making Sure Terminal Services Licensing Is Working

You can verify that licensing is working properly in Terminal Server by checking the following in the System event log:

1. Look for a periodic 1010 error in the event log that indicates that the Terminal Server is not able to reach a licensing server.

2. Make sure when clients connect you do not get errors in the event log indicating a failure to assign a license.

Activating Your Licensing Servers

Remember that you only have 90 days to activate your licensing server. Until the server is activated and licenses are added, it will not be able to serve out licenses to Terminal Server users.

Activating your licensing server can be done by phone, fax, or across the Internet through the Microsoft Licensing Clearinghouse. Chapter 8 contains explicit instructions on how to do this.

Client Licensing Issue Hotfix

The licensing scheme has a couple of problems. First is that the license is permanently assigned to a workstation by default. This license code is recorded in the Registry of the workstation. If this workstation is reformatted, the workstation will lose the license and will take another license once it is rebuilt and connects to Terminal Server. Also if you give the workstation to another user who does not need Terminal Server, this license is "lost" because there is no way to return it to the central license pool for use by someone else. In both of these situations, you would have to contact the Microsoft Licensing Clearinghouse to add the "lost" licenses back to the Terminal Server. For ASPs, whose customer base might change daily, this licensing practice can be a real pain in the neck because customers basically take the licenses with them if they decide to no longer use the ASP.

For this reason, Microsoft has made a post-Service Pack 2 hotfix available. This hotfix modifies the default behavior of the licensing assignment. Instead of permanently assigning a license, a Terminal Server will lease a license for a random number of days between 52 and 89. If a client does not reconnect within that timeframe, the license is returned to the central pool. This way, if a workstation is put to another use and does not reconnect to Terminal Server, its license will be re-added to the license pool after a maximum of 90 days.

It is important to realize that only new licenses assigned after the hotfix is applied will have this behavior. Any licenses that have already been assigned will remain permanently assigned. If you need to reuse these permanently assigned licenses, you must call the Microsoft Licensing Clearinghouse to reissue them.

This hotfix also affects another behavior of Terminal Services licensing. Normally a license is permanently assigned to a workstation once the connection to a Terminal Server is made, before the user logs on. After you apply the hotfix, a temporary license is assigned when you first connect. After you log on, this license is activated.

For more information on this fix, along with download instructions, refer to Microsoft Article Q287687.

Removing a TS CAL from the Registry

In some situations you might want to remove a TS CAL that has already been assigned to a computer—for example, if you have some clients deployed already before the hotfix was installed and you want them to pull a new leased license from the pool rather than use their existing permanent license. In this case, you need to do the following:

1. Run REGEDIT.

2. Browse to HKEY_LOCAL_MACHINE\Software\Microsoft\MSLicensing\Store.

3. Remove any keys that start with LICENSExxx.

Planning for MetaFrame XP

If you are a MetaFrame 1.8 administrator who is planning on migrating to MetaFrame XP or if you are planning to install a new MetaFrame XP server farm, this section is for you. MetaFrame XP has a very different enterprise-class structure than you might be used to with MetaFrame 1.8. However, Citrix has endeavored hard to ensure that your migration from 1.8 to XP goes as smoothly as possible. Before delving into different migration or installation scenarios, you first need to understand some basic MetaFrame XP concepts.

Basic MetaFrame XP Concepts

Chapter 3, "Introduction to Citrix MetaFrame 1.8 and MetaFrame XP," briefly discussed the new architectural concepts in MetaFrame XP, covering the differences between the architecture in MetaFrame 1.8 and that in MetaFrame XP. Now it is time to go into MetaFrame XP architecture in more detail and provide some examples, so that you can better understand how it works in the enterprise.

Remember from the discussion in Chapter 3 the new items in MetaFrame XP terminology, which are covered in the sections that follow.

Independent Management Architecture (IMA)

Citrix's *Independent Management Architecture* (IMA) is the term used to describe the brand new architectural model used in Citrix MetaFrame XP. Each server in a Citrix MetaFrame XP server farm runs the IMA service. This service communicates with other servers in the enterprise using the new IMA protocol. It is this service and the communication between Citrix MetaFrame XP servers that allows them to work together as an integrated whole for serving applications out to your users.

Server Farm

In the Citrix world, Citrix servers are grouped together into what are called *server farms*. Each server farm is assigned a unique name by the administrator at the point of installing MetaFrame XP on the first server in the farm. This server farm and all the applications that are published within it are managed as a single unit using the *Citrix Management Console* (CMC).

Data Store (DS)

Each *server farm* has only one central *data store* (DS). The DS holds the following farm-specific information:

- **Licensing**   All of your Citrix MetaFrame XP licenses.
- **Published applications**   Information regarding any application that has been published for any server in the server farm.
- **Printers**   Printer and printer mapping information.
- **Server information**   Basic information on servers that are part of the farm is kept track of in the DS, such as server name, product code, and zone.
- **Citrix administrators**   Users who are allowed to log on to the CMC and what rights they have to administer the farm.
- **Trust relationships**   Because users from different domains might access servers in your farm, it is important to track the domain membership and trust relationships of the servers.

The DS can either be installed as a local Access database on the first server in the farm, or you can install it centrally on either a Microsoft SQL or Oracle database server. If you choose to install it as a local Access database on the first server in the farm, your other servers will access it indirectly by making an indirect connection to the database through this server. If you are running it centrally on a SQL or Oracle database, however, your servers can access the DS directly across the network without going through another server. Citrix does provide the option of accessing the central Oracle or SQL database indirectly through another server; however, it is recommended to set up your servers to directly connect to the database instead.

By default, every server in the farm makes contact with the DS upon initial startup of the IMA service and at 10-minute intervals thereafter.

Local Host Cache (LHC)

The DS is so critical for server farm functionality that Citrix decided to have servers cache a subset of the DS locally, in case the central DS or access to it fails. This local cache of the DS is referred to as the *local host cache* (LHC). It is kept in a small Microsoft Access database (IMALHC.MDB) in the install directory for MetaFrame XP on that server.

If the main DS for the farm goes down, all the servers in the farm will continue to function for 48 hours off of the information in their LHC. In addition, the LHC plays an important role in server performance. For certain types of requests, such as application enumeration or server enumeration, the server can retrieve this information from its LHC instead of sending a query across the network.

Zones

In MetaFrame XP, servers within a server farm can now be logically grouped into zones. This is a significant departure from the architecture of a MetaFrame 1.8 server farm and is very important to understand, especially in large enterprise or ASP environments where there are hundreds of Citrix servers. As a large server farm administrator, you can divide your server farm into zones to help with network traffic utilization and server processor utilization caused by large numbers of server information updates.

By default, when you install the first server in the farm, it creates an initial zone for the farm named after the subnet that the server is on. If the first server you install MetaFrame XP on is on subnet 192.168.10.0, for example, it will create a new zone named 192.168.10.0, and it will be the first member of that zone.

As you install MetaFrame XP on additional servers and add them to the farm, you are given the option to join the default zone or to join a new or existing zone. If you decide to join the default zone in this scenario, your server's zone name will become 192.168.10.0.

Zone Data Collectors (ZDC)

Servers that are members of the same zone share information through their *zone's data collector* (ZDC). The ZDC then shares information with the rest of the ZDCs in the farm. The role of the ZDC is very similar to the role of the master browser in Citrix MetaFrame 1.8. An election takes place when new servers are brought online in the zones or the old ZDC is brought offline. Through this election process, one of the servers in the zone will be designated as the ZDC.

The ZDC's job is to keep track of the following changes that are reported to it by servers in its zone:

- **Server load**   The server load is calculated by each server and reported to that server's ZDC upon any change in the load.

- **Client connections**   Any logon, logoff, disconnect, or reconnect of a client to a server is reported by that server to its ZDC.

- **Published applications**   Information on the usage of published applications is reported to the ZDC by each server.

- **Server changes**   Changes to the IP address of the server or server shutdowns and startups are reported to the ZDC.

- **License usage**   Real-time license usage is reported to the ZDC.

The ZDC pools together all of this information for the servers in its zone. The ZDC also immediately reports any changes to the rest of the ZDCs in the server farm. In that way, all ZDCs know about the server load, client connections, active published applications, and license usage for all servers in the farm.

The ZDC also is responsible for ensuring that all the servers in its zone are still active. By default, if the ZDC does not hear from a particular server for more than one minute, it will send a special ping to each server in the zone to ensure that the server responds.

Qfarm Versus Qserver

To display which server in your MetaFrame XP server farm zone is currently acting as the ZDC, run the command qfarm.exe from the command prompt. The server with the *D* next to it is the ZDC for that zone.

Qfarm is the replacement for the qserver command used in MetaFrame 1.8. If you are running in mixed mode, you can still list the master browser from a MetaFrame XP server. In mixed mode, your MetaFrame XP servers still run the ICA Browser service and participate in the MetaFrame 1.8 master browser process. Because the browser version of your XP servers is greater than that of the MetaFrame 1.8 servers, they will normally take over as the master browser for your MetaFrame 1.8 server farm in mixed mode.

MetaFrame XP Design Decisions

You need to make three very important decisions before you deploy your MetaFrame XP solution. First, you need to decide on what platform your DS will reside. Your DS is a critical part of Citrix MetaFrame XP functionality. Although moving the DS at a later time is possible, you will be better off in the long run deciding on where it should go before you begin your deployment.

The second decision you need to make is how to set up the zones for your server farm. If you have fewer than 100 servers in your farm, and they are all at the same location, your decision is easy: Use only one zone—the default zone. If your server farm will contain more servers or you have a significant number of servers across the WAN, however, you need to consider dividing your server farm up into zones. This section discusses how to decide how many zones you will need.

The third and final decision you need to make is how many server farms you need. Although scalability in MetaFrame XP makes it easier to support a single farm in even the largest deployments, there are some advantages to be considered with using multiple farms.

Data Store Placement

The current release of MetaFrame XP supports having the DS on either a local Access database on one of the servers in the farm or a central SQL or Oracle database server. MetaFrame XP is supported only on the following versions of these databases:

- Access 4.x
- SQL Server 7.0 with Service Pack 2 or SQL 2000
- Oracle 7.34, 8.06, 8.15, 8.16

The decision about where to put the DS is mainly about performance. A local Access database solution is an excellent solution for server farms of fewer than 50 servers that are on the same network. However, the server you choose to run the DS on needs to be very reliable, have enough system power, and have enough capacity to handle the demands of your server farm.

A DS for 100 servers will take up roughly 20MB, which is not a whole lot. For performance reasons, however, do not put the DS on the system drive, instead put it on the application drive. Because the DS is installed in your Citrix MetaFrame XP install directory, this means that when you install Citrix on your DS server, you should install it on your application drive and not your system drive. Although putting it on the system drive is a valid option, putting it on a separate drive can improve performance because it will not have to compete with the often heavy use of the system drive. In addition, as you will be shown in Chapter 8, the system drive space can quickly get used up on Terminal Server, causing system-wide problems. To help avoid this, it is recommended to install all applications on the application drive.

The Data Store and MDAC

It is not a good idea to load applications on your Access DS server that install local database components. These database components can overwrite the DLLs that the DS relies on and cause farm-wide problems. As you will see in the section "Using Dedicated Zone Data Collectors," dedicating a server for use as a DS server is a good idea. Microsoft packages together their database access components into a *Microsoft Data Access Component* (MDAC) package. There are several different versions of the MDAC and many applications will install components from it when they are installed. These components are mainly updates to the ODBC drivers on the system that reside in the system directory of the servers as ODBC[*type*].DLL drivers.

Several different MDACs are available for download at the Microsoft web site (www.microsoft.com/data). However, Citrix supports only MDAC 2.5. MDAC 2.6, which is also available and comes with many applications, is not supported and might cause problems on your DS server. Do not install MDAC 2.6 on your DS server or applications that rely on its components. Because MDAC components become an integral part of operating system functionality, it is very difficult to downgrade to an older version without reloading the operating system. Although technically this might be possible, there is no supported way to do this. Your best bet is to just avoid MDAC 2.6 altogether.

You can load your Access DS on either Windows NT 4.0 Terminal Server or Windows 2000. Realize, however, that Windows NT 4.0 TSE does not come by default with MDAC 2.5. Before you set up any Windows NT 4.0 TSE server with MetaFrame XP, it is recommended to download and install MDAC 2.5 on the server.

If you have more than 100 servers or have a large distributed Citrix server farm environment, it pays to put your database on an enterprise-class database system. Both SQL Server and Oracle are excellent enterprise-class database systems, and will perform equally as well as a DS server. In addition, both products support database replication. If you have a small number of very large data centers—each with more than 50 Citrix servers, you should investigate the possibility of replicating your database between these two locations. SQL Server and Oracle support real-time database replication and this configuration is supported by Citrix. Replication is also a good choice if you have a disaster recovery data center with a backup server farm at the disaster recovery center.

Author's Note

In Chapter 8, you will be shown how to best set up your DS on either Access, SQL, or Oracle. Later, in Chapter 26, "Disaster Recovery Techniques and Enhancing Reliability," several DS disaster recovery techniques are discussed in more detail, including replication.

Setting Up Zones

Each ZDC receives updates every time someone logs on to, logs off of, disconnects, or reconnects from any server in the zone. In addition, server changes and load changes are immediately reported to the ZDC. This means the ZDC can become very busy, very quickly in large server farms. For this reason, if your farm has more than 50 servers at the same location, it is recommended to divide your servers up into zones.

In addition, zones are useful to set up for every remote location where there are five or more Citrix servers. Especially remote locations that are across slower or heavily used WAN connections.

Using Dedicated Zone Data Collectors

If your server farm has more than 50 servers, it is a good idea to dedicate one of the servers for use as a ZDC. You should plan for this in advance by selecting a server with adequate processing power to handle the need. A small, but fast single-processor- or dual-processor-capable server will work well as a ZDC for zones up to 50 servers. Also expect to use up to 32MB for handling zone update information. Because the operating system alone can take up to 150MB, you want to make sure that a dedicated ZDC has a minimum of 256MB of memory.

The ZDC and Domain Trusts

One important thing that is often overlooked in choosing ZDCs is trust relationships. If you have a multidomain environment where you publish applications to users from different domains, you need to be very careful with the trust relationships and domain memberships of your servers. Citrix MetaFrame does not always handle trust relationships correctly when servers in the same farm, under the same ZDC, are members of different domains. To avoid problems in this situation, make sure that the server you choose for a ZDC is a member of a domain that has trust relationships to all the domains that applications are published to in the zone.

If you are using an Access database as your DS, the DS server also will be the default ZDC. If you are using a SQL or Oracle DS, however, or if your farm has multiple zones, you will need to manually set the preferred ZDC to be the one you want to dedicate.

Dedicated Access Data Store Servers

Even in farms with fewer than 20 servers that use an Access DS, you should consider dedicating a server for use as both the DS and ZDC. One advantage of MetaFrame XP is that you do not need to purchase a base license for your servers to install MetaFrame XP, as you did in MetaFrame 1.8. This means you can afford to install MetaFrame XP on any server you choose. In smaller farms, an older single-processor server will work just fine as a dedicated DS and ZDC. By dedicating a server to be used as the DS, you not only ensure the best farm performance, but also a higher level of reliability.

Choosing a Single Farm Versus Multiple Farms

It used to be very difficult to work across multiple farms with Citrix. With the advent of the new multifarm capabilities of NFuse and other efforts by Citrix to make their ICA client work better across multiple farms, choosing whether to deploy a single- or multiple-farm solution is not as easy of a decision.

Many of the most significant architectural improvements of MetaFrame XP are geared toward meeting the needs of large enterprise server farms, by providing a structure that has the capacity to consolidate multiple farms into a single larger server farm. If you are careful when designing a single-farm solution, by taking steps such as having dedicated ZDCs and a central or replicated DS, you can efficiently scale your solution to hundreds of servers. For large corporate ASPs, having a single farm and a single point of management can make administration much easier.

On the other hand, MetaFrame XP does not yet have the capability to divide out farm administration effectively for huge farm deployments. Although you now have to log on to the CMC to manage the farm, you are either granted read access or full access to the entire farm. For commercial ASPs, setting up multiple farms can provide the isolation they need to ensure the reliability and security of the thin client solutions they provide for customers. For corporations where IS administration is heavily delegated and different divisions own clusters of their own Citrix servers, centralizing the server farm would be a difficult and nonbeneficial task. By building a multi-farm Citrix NFuse portal, you could provide central access to applications on all the farms, yet maintain the administrative separation.

Naming Standards

As discussed in Chapter 15, "Application Publishing and Load Management with Citrix MetaFrame," naming standards are very important to set up early in a farm's design, especially for large farm deployments or farms that are expected to grow rapidly. You should set up naming standards for your servers, published applications, and security groups. One nice feature in the MetaFrame XP CMC is that you can now organize your published applications into folders. This makes administration simpler and faster when you have hundreds of applications in your farm.

Migrating to MetaFrame XP

Setting up a brand new MetaFrame XP server takes proper care and planning, but does not present as many challenges as migrating from an older Citrix server farm to XP. When you are migrating from an existing system, your goal is to add functionality and improve the system without affecting existing users. This is kind of like the magician's trick of pulling out the tablecloth from under the glasses without letting the water in them spill. If you have an existing MetaFrame or even WinFrame deployment, this section is where you will learn the "magic" you need to know to make the migration successful.

Setting Up a Test MetaFrame XP Lab

The first step you should take in any migration is to set up a test MetaFrame XP lab. This is important for several reasons. It will give you a chance to start getting used to MetaFrame XP administration. MetaFrame XP administration has many differences from what you might be used to in prior versions. First, there is now a central management tool called the Citrix Management Console. Many of the features of this tool are different and they need to be learned well to administer a MetaFrame XP server farm successfully. In addition, you will be able to test your applications and application publishing on MetaFrame XP thoroughly. Your applications that currently work with older versions of Citrix should work without a problem on MetaFrame XP. However, the operative word is *should* and not *will*; this means test your applications well before switching to MetaFrame XP.

When setting up your test lab, you should use a minimum of two servers to be able to simulate the different scenarios you will need to test and understand. For larger migrations, set up a test lab with at least three servers. Unless you intend to do extensive performance testing, you can use workstations with Windows NT 4.0 TSE or Windows 2000 Server installed on them.

It is very important to thoroughly understand the following items before you begin your migration. (You can use the material in this book to learn the concepts and then reinforce those concepts in the lab.)

- How existing published applications are migrated to XP.
- How licensing is handled in mixed mode and in native mode. Licensing works very differently in MetaFrame XP, and you need to understand it thoroughly.
- How published applications are managed in mixed mode.
- Switching from mixed mode to native mode.
- The role of the ZDC and DS.
- Setting up the DS.
- How to effectively use the CMC.
- How to add printer drivers and replicate printer drivers across the farm.
- How Load Management works with the CMC.
- Resource Management (RM) and Installation Management (IM).

When you initially set up the test farm, install the version of Citrix you will be migrating from in the farm on both servers. Make sure to install the same service pack level on the servers as you run in the farm. Next, install your most critical applications on the servers and publish them. Now that you have a small-scale environment of what you might have at work, test out the different migration scenarios to see which one works best for you.

If you are using any of the special services available with MetaFrame 1.8, such as Load Balancing, Remote Management Services, or Installation Management Services, be sure to test these thoroughly in the test environment. Load Balancing is now managed via the CMC in MetaFrame XP and has several new options. In addition, you need to follow special procedures if you intend to load balance applications in mixed mode. Remote Management Services also are managed via the CMC and are significantly different from before. Finally, Installation Management Services requires special procedures to migrate properly to Citrix MetaFrame XP.

To get a better feel for administering users on the test farm, enlist the help of a few key users in the Citrix user community who can help you test the farm in action. Publish their applications on the test farm and have them use it on a day-to-day basis. As discussed in Chapter 12, "Installing and Deploying ICA Clients," you can easily set up the ICA client, so that a user has access to applications in both farms. This is an especially important step if you intend to used mixed mode for the migration of your server farms.

Published Applications and the Migration to XP

At the very end of the MetaFrame XP installation process, MetaFrame XP will ask whether you want to upgrade your MetaFrame 1.8 applications, so that they will be available in MetaFrame XP. This is a convenient feature of the install that will make upgrades to XP very easy. However, published applications can be a very fickle item. It pays to be very careful with published applications and ensure that they are upgraded successfully during a migration.

First, you should record your published application settings, so that you can re-create them quickly in case of problems migrating published applications. You need to record the exact name of the published application as it appears in the *Published Application Manager* (PAM). An easy way to do this is to just take a screen shot of the PAM screen. Also record the groups assigned to the application, the servers it is run on or is load balanced across, and the command-line parameters used to run the application.

Second, you should set up at least one test user per domain that receives applications from the Citrix server farm. If you publish applications only to users in a single domain, setting up this test user should be easy.

1. Create a test user called **ctx[*domain name*]**.

2. Add this user to all groups in the domain that applications are published to. Make sure that the user is not an administrative-level user.

3. Connect to your server farm using the ICA client and make sure the user gets all the icons for the applications and that each application works. If an application requires any special install procedures, go through that for the application.

4. After each server is migrated or after migrating all the servers at once, make sure that the test user still receives all the published applications and that the user can run them all with no problems.

5. If you have multiple domains, set up one test user on each of the domains and follow the previous steps for each user.

This technique will save you a lot of headaches because you will be able to ensure that all of your published applications migrated correctly. In addition, you will have a good set of test users to troubleshoot with in case there are any future problems with published applications.

The Importance of the Published Application Name

Be very careful to record the published application names exactly before you upgrade to MetaFrame XP. Depending on how you deploy your applications, changing the published name of the application will most often "break" the published icon for the users. If you choose to publish an icon on the user's Start menu or desktop when publishing applications and then change the application name, for example, the icons will no longer work. They will get changed or taken away only once a successful connection is made to the Citrix server farm. If your users are used to working out of Program Neighborhood and know how to manually refresh their applications, however, there should be no problems so long as you warn your users ahead of time of the need to refresh their applications.

Migration Technique 1: The All-or-Nothing Approach

The "all-or-nothing approach" means picking an open window, such as a Saturday or weeknight to migrate all of your servers to MetaFrame XP simultaneously. When you get used to how MetaFrame XP migrations work in a test environment, you will see how easy and quick it is to migrate from MetaFrame 1.8 to MetaFrame XP. The all-or-nothing approach is recommended for environments of up to 20 servers that are all at the same location, and where there are good maintenance windows for upgrades.

This is definitely a migration technique for the brave hearted, but is not necessarily a foolhardy technique. The key to a successful all-or-nothing migration is plenty of testing and practice. You should plan for at least two weeks to two months of migration testing before you and your team will be ready to undertake the all-or-nothing migration, depending on the size of your environment. Make sure you thoroughly understand all the topics listed in the preceding section on setting up a test MetaFrame XP lab. You want to make sure that if something does go wrong you know how to fix it quickly!

Make sure that you record your published applications and set up test users as covered in the preceding section. You need to make sure they all work after the migration.

Although an upgrade of MetaFrame 1.8 to MetaFrame XP should work fine and will save time, a clean install is preferred, especially for the DS server if you will be using a local Access database. To perform a clean install, you need to uninstall MetaFrame 1.8, reboot, and then install MetaFrame XP. If you do a clean install, you will have to republish any applications that were on that server back into MetaFrame XP. You also will have to reestablish load balancing for these applications. Make sure that in the maintenance window you choose that you have enough time to do a clean install of MetaFrame XP on your servers and republish applications in case you need to.

If you do not feel comfortable with doing the migration on your own, this is an excellent technique that a local Citrix reseller (or Citrix Consulting Services) can help you with.

The main risks of the all-or-nothing migration technique are as follows:

- A significant amount of time needs to be taken for testing the migration.
- A large open maintenance window is needed for the migration, during which users will likely not be able to connect to the farm.
- You and your support staff need a high level of practice with MetaFrame XP. There will be very little time to respond to issues if they do come up.
- This solution is not well suited for farms larger than 20 servers or that are spread across multiple sites.

The main benefits of all-or-nothing migration technique are as follows:

- You do not have to run your farm in mixed mode, with its inherent risks and lack of functionality, during production.
- Very fast technique for rapid upgrades.
- Excellent technique if you can afford outside consulting to assist with the migration. Because it is quick, it will be inexpensive.

Migration Technique 2: Parallel Farms

The parallel-farms technique involves building a new MetaFrame XP server farm and migrating your servers and applications to the new farm. Using the NFuse multifarm capability, you can seamlessly move users between the farms without them knowing that the change is taking place. Alternatively, you could set up two different farms in the Citrix Program Neighborhood on the clients and train users to be able to pull up their applications from the new farm. The parallel-farms technique can be used for upgrading any size existing server farm to MetaFrame XP. It is especially suited to environments where a clean install is required for upgrades or for environments that are using NFuse extensively already.

Just as with the all-or-nothing technique, you need to document your published applications thoroughly and test them before and after the migration of any server.

With the parallel-farm technique, you have the option of either doing a clean uninstall of MetaFrame 1.8 and then reinstalling MetaFrame XP, or formatting the server and doing a clean install of the entire server from scratch. Although the first option is easier, you need to consider several advantages to the second option:

- You might want to develop and deploy a better and more reliable server building standard. Now is a good time to put it into place.

- You might want to develop and deploy server imaging technology, to ensure all your servers can be quickly rebuilt. Citrix now supports server imaging. In Chapter 8, you will learn how to image a MetaFrame XP server correctly.

- You are moving to a MetaFrame XPe server farm and want to use Installation Management Services for all of your application installs in the future.

If you do take this as an opportunity to rebuild your servers from scratch, make sure you document both the server rebuild steps and the application install steps thoroughly. You should already have notes on how your applications were originally installed on your servers. If not, before you start migrating your servers over, do some test installs of the application in the test lab.

If you are using NFuse technology or plan to deploy it to help with the migration, you will find all the information you need in Chapter 19, "Deploying Applications over the Web Using NFuse and Wireless Technologies." If you intend to set up the clients to log on to both farms, however, you will find information on how to do that in Chapter 12. In Chapter 12, you also will learn how to set up a web site where your users can download new clients that are automatically installed with no user intervention and are preconfigured with the farm settings that you need. You can use this to deploy clients that are configured to be able to log on to both farms, before you start your migration. This makes the migration easier because you can focus on moving your servers, instead of having to deal with client upgrades and server migrations at the same time.

One disadvantage of this technique is that if you are load balancing across two or more servers, you will have to migrate those servers over at the same time to be able to maintain the load-balanced configuration.

If you are migrating from a large enterprise server farm with a dedicated master browser, the master browser should be the last server migrated over and not the first. It is recommended to start your migration by installing MetaFrame XP on a new server that will be the ZDC and the DS server, if using Access, for the new farm. This is a much different approach from either the all-or-nothing or the mixed-mode migration approaches, because with these approaches, the first server you should migrate is the master browser. Keep this in mind when planning the migration because you will need to keep the master browser up in the old farm until all the servers have been moved over.

The main drawbacks of the parallel-farms migration technique are as follows:

- More time-consuming than the all-or-nothing technique
- More complicated because you have to work with two farms
- Cannot be made completely seamless for your users unless they all currently use NFuse
- Difficult to do if you are doing load balancing across more than two servers

The main benefits of the parallel-farms migration technique are as follows:

- No need for running in mixed mode
- Good for migrating the smallest to the largest farms
- Good for migrating distributed farms or multiple farms into a single enterprise-wide farm
- Can be seamless for your users if you use NFuse for the migration
- Enables you to change the server farm name to a new name
- Allows for a more gradual and less-risky migration than the all-or-nothing approach
- Works well for migrating multifarm environments to a single farm or distributed farm environments
- Fewer problems likely because you will be using clean installs
- Good opportunity for setting up server and application imaging

Migration Technique 3: Mixed-Mode Migration

The last major migration technique is the "mixed-mode migration." With this technique, you gradually migrate your MetaFrame 1.8 servers to MetaFrame XP in the same farm. The MetaFrame XP servers remain in mixed mode during the migration, which means that they will emulate MetaFrame 1.8 functionality, so that the farm appears as one. The clients will notice no difference because the server farm name stays the same and all applications are migrated over.

Although this might seem like an excellent and easy way to move your servers over, it is not a recommended migration technique, especially on larger farms. Even though it is covered here for the sake of completeness, it is important that you understand the risks of using mixed mode as part of your migration plan.

First, mixed mode is not as well tested as native mode. Citrix has spent the majority of its development and testing efforts making sure that MetaFrame XP in native mode is as reliable as possible; this is not to say mixed mode will not work, but there is a higher likelihood of running into unusual problems.

Second, mixed mode is not recommended to be used for an extended period of time by Citrix. If you run into problems while you are in mixed mode, the likely recommendation will be to move to native mode as quickly as possible. If all of your planning relies on mixed mode being stable enough to give you time to move your servers over gradually, and you run into problems, you will be forced to either quickly roll back to MetaFrame 1.8 or convert the rest of your servers over to MetaFrame XP and switch to native mode.

Third, mixed mode requires double work and can cause performance problems and intermittent glitches in farm behavior. When a MetaFrame XP server is running in mixed mode, all the farm-related information that it normally communicates to other XP servers, by the IMA service using TCP/IP, also has to be communicated to other MetaFrame 1.8 servers using the ICA Browser service. In larger farms, this added communication burden can cause intermittent problems such as dropped connections.

If you decide to migrate using the mixed-mode technique, despite the warnings, make sure to test your published applications before and after the migration. This is especially important to do after you set up your first MetaFrame XP server—because the first MetaFrame XP server in mixed mode will become the master browser, which means that MetaFrame XP will now be responsible for keeping track of your published applications. You need to make sure this transition happened smoothly by ensuring that your test users are all receiving and are able to run all the applications they could run before the move.

In a mixed-mode MetaFrame XP farm, the applications published in MetaFrame XP using the CMC are pooled with the applications published with the PAM in MetaFrame 1.8 to give the appearance to the clients of a single farm with a single set of applications.

As you move servers over to MetaFrame XP, you will start managing their published applications using the CMC. When you upgrade a server that already has published applications on it, you will be asked whether you want to migrate them to MetaFrame XP. If you do, those applications will be migrated and their configuration information will be recorded in the MetaFrame XP DS. When you log on to the CMC, you will now see the migrated application under the Application folder. If you now go into the PAM on MetaFrame 1.8, you will no longer see the applications! This is because as you move servers over to MetaFrame XP, their applications should no longer be managed and are no longer accessible from the legacy PAM tool. The PAM tool is to be used only for managing published applications on the MetaFrame 1.8 servers that have not been migrated over yet.

The first server you should migrate over if you use this technique is your dedicated master browser, if you have one. If not, choose one of your lesser-used servers or a server that you can dedicate in the future as the ZDC in XP.

The reason for this is that the first server you migrate will automatically become both the master browser for the 1.8 server farm and the ZDC for the MetaFrame XP farm, even if you have another server in the 1.8 farm set to always become the master browser. Because MetaFrame XP has a higher browser version number than MetaFrame 1.8, it takes over as master browser. See the next section, "Master Browser and ZDC Considerations," for more information regarding the Master Browser service.

In mixed mode, all MetaFrame XP servers in the farm run both the Program Neighborhood and ICA Browser services. They participate in MetaFrame 1.8 browser elections and emulate MetaFrame 1.8 browser and Program Neighborhood communications. To MetaFrame 1.8 servers and to users, the farm appears no different from what the MetaFrame XP servers were in 1.8.

To run in mixed mode, you need to install the first MetaFrame XP server into a new farm with exactly the same farm name as the existing MetaFrame 1.8 server farm. You will then be prompted whether you want the XP farm to operate in mixed mode with the existing MetaFrame 1.8 server farm.

After you have migrated the first server over, you can verify that it is participating as a master browser in the MetaFrame 1.8 farm by running MetaFrame 1.8 QSERVER.EXE from the command prompt on one of the MetaFrame 1.8 servers. You will see the letter *M* next to the current master browser, which should be the MetaFrame XP server. If you do not see the server in the list, make sure the farm name is exactly the same on the MetaFrame XP server and then try rebooting the XP server or just stopping and starting the ICA Browser service.

If you need to migrate over applications that are load-balanced, it is highly recommended to migrate over all the load-balanced servers at the same time. If there are too many to make this practical, you can use a technique to load balance applications between MetaFrame 1.8 and MetaFrame XP running in mixed mode. To do this, you need to first unpublish the application from both the MetaFrame 1.8 servers using the PAM and from the MetaFrame XP servers using CMC, if it has been published on XP. Now republish the application on the MetaFrame XP servers using the CMC and then republish the application using exactly the same name across the MetaFrame 1.8 servers using PAM, in that order. Because the name is the same, the application will automatically be load balanced across the servers it is published to on both the XP and 1.8 side of the mixed-mode farm.

After the last server has been migrated over to MetaFrame XP, you need to switch the MetaFrame XP farm back into native mode. This operation is best scheduled for after-hours because it makes significant changes to the farm. To switch the farm to native mode, follow these steps:

1. Log on to the CMC.

2. Right-click the MetaFrame XP server farm name and select Properties.

3. From the Properties window that appears, click the Interoperability tab.

4. Uncheck the check box next to Work with 1.8 Servers in the Farm.

After you uncheck this check box, a message will be sent to all XP servers in the farm to run in native mode. The XP servers will then all shut off their ICA Browser and Program Neighborhood services and begin communicating solely through the IMA service. Be sure to use your test user IDs to ensure that all the published applications are still being published correctly. If you run into problems because of the switch to native mode, you can quickly switch the farm back to mixed mode by rechecking the box.

Master Browser and ZDC Considerations

In both the all-or-nothing and mixed-mode migration techniques, you want to ensure that the first server migrated over remains as the master browser during the migration. Instability in the master browser can cause a lot of problems with the remaining MetaFrame 1.8 servers. This server should also normally be dedicated as the ZDC for the new MetaFrame XP server farm. Both the master browser for a MetaFrame 1.8 server farm and the ZDC for a zone in XP are determined by a very similar election process. In MetaFrame 1.8, the election process was based on the following criteria in order of importance starting with the most important:

- Version number of the ICA browser (most recent version wins)
- Configured to always attempt to become master browser using the Citrix Server Administration tool
- Server is a Windows 2000 domain controller
- Length of time the ICA Browser service has been active
- Server name

Because the highest version number always wins, when you install your first MetaFrame XP server running in mixed mode with an existing MetaFrame 1.8 farm, the XP server automatically becomes the master browser. In addition, the next MetaFrame XP server installed will become the backup browser for the farm. You can actually still manage the preferences of which MetaFrame XP server will be the master browser using the Citrix Server Administer tool by highlighting the MetaFrame XP server running in mixed mode, clicking the ICA Browser tab on the right, and changing the During Master ICA Browser Election setting. Make sure this setting is set to Always Attempt To on the XP server you want to be the master browser and No Preference on new MetaFrame XP servers that you bring into the farm. After all the servers have been migrated and you are in native mode, this setting has no effect.

The election process in MetaFrame XP for the ZDC is a completely separate and different process from the ICA master browser election. In MetaFrame XP, the IMA service holds a new election when changes occur in the zone, such as a new server coming online or an existing data collector going offline. By default, the first server in the farm is given the master ranking of one, meaning that it is the most preferred to win data collector elections. As new servers are added to the farm, they are given the default master ranking of three. The following are the criteria, in order of importance, for the election of a data collector in a zone:

- Master version number of the IMA service.
- Master ranking number of the server. The master ranking number is on a scaled of 1 to 4, with 1 being the highest priority.

- Highest host ID. The host ID is a randomly assigned number between 0 and 65535 that is generated when MetaFrame XP is first installed.

This criteria means that in the default zone, the first server installed on the farm, will always win the election because its master ranking number is 1, unless you install a newer version of MetaFrame or a patch that changes the master version number.

Setting the Data Collector Preference

Because of the way the election process works in MetaFrame XP, it is best to make sure that the first server you set up is the one you intend to be the dedicated data collector for the default zone. If this server goes down, however, the election for the next data collector will be essentially random because the remaining servers will all be set to a master ranking of 3. Also, if you will be deploying a large farm with multiple zones, you need control over which servers will be the data collectors. The following instructions show you how to change the master ranking and thus which server is the preferred data collector in a zone:

1. Open REGEDT32.EXE.

2. Scroll down to HKLM\Software\Citrix\IMA\Runtime.

3. Change the UseRegistry value to 1.

4. Change the MasterRanking to whatever rank, between 1 and 4, that you want to assign this server (with 1 being the highest).

5. Stop and then start the IMA service.

Remember the default master ranking is 3 for every server except the first one installed on a farm, which is 1. If you want to ensure that a server will never become a ZDC, change the value to 4. If you want it to be the preferred backup browser in case the ZDC fails, set it to 2. If you want it to be the ZDC for a particular zone, set it to 1.

Remember that it is not recommended to run the ZDC for the default zone on a different server from the server that contains the DS, if you are using a local Access DS.

ICA License Gateways and Mixed Mode

If you currently have ICA gateways in your environment, it is very important that you read and understand this section before you upgrade to MetaFrame XP. In the MetaFrame 1.8 world, you generally set up ICA gateways on both sides of a WAN to enable the master browsers on each side of the WAN to talk to one another. This had several beneficial effects, when the ICA gateways worked properly, such as the ability to pool your licenses together, spread your farm across the WAN, allow remote clients to browse for servers at the data center, and even load balance applications across the WAN for the sake of disaster recovery.

There are two types of ICA gateways: a standard ICA gateway and a ICA license gateway. The standard ICA gateway supports ICA browsing functionality across the WAN, such as being able to list servers, load balance applications, and consolidate a server farm across the WAN. An ICA license gateway supports the same functionality; however, in addition license pooling has been enabled on the ICA gateway servers on both sides of the WAN.

The problem with MetaFrame XP and ICA gateways happens when you migrate to XP using the mixed-mode technique or any time your MetaFrame XP farm is in mixed mode and shares the same farm name as a MetaFrame 1.8 farm on the network. Remember that in mixed mode, the first MetaFrame XP server you upgrade will always take over as the master browser. In addition, in mixed mode on XP, license pooling ICA gateway functionality is not supported. Instead, when you run XP in mixed mode and your farm has XP servers that are across subnets, any connection licenses you install on XP are shared equally between those subnets.

Suppose, for example, that you have a MetaFrame 1.8 server farm spread across two data centers, an East Coast and a West Coast data center. The East Coast data center has 20 servers, each server has the base 15 licenses and the server that is the master browser has a 50-user bump pack, for a total of 350 connection licenses (20 * 15 base + 50 bump). The West Coast data center has a server farm with 10 servers, each server has the base 15 user licenses plus the master browser has a 50-user bump pack for a total of 200 connection licenses (10 * 15 base + 50 bump). You set up a license pooling ICA gateway between the two sites, so that the licenses are pooled together. This means that there are a total of 550 connection licenses available on the farm.

Now you begin your upgrade at the West Coast data center and upgrade one of the smaller servers, which is not currently the master browser, to MetaFrame XP running in mixed mode. Because MetaFrame XP will always win browser elections, the MetaFrame XP server you installed will immediately become the master browser for the West Coast. Because MetaFrame XP does not support license pooling across ICA gateways, the license pooling with the East Coast will stop working. This normally will take 48 hours to occur because the backup browsers will still cache the pooled licenses. After 48 hours, however, the West Coast will have only its local set of 200 connection licenses available minus the 15 licenses that were on the server you changed over to XP, for a total of 185 connection licenses. The East Coast will still have its local set of 350 connection licenses.

MetaFrame XP does support license pooling in mixed mode with MetaFrame 1.8. This means that even though license pooling will stop working across the WAN through the ICA gateway, it should still work on the local subnet between the licenses you have on the XP server and the licenses on the 1.8 servers. In this example, suppose that you installed 200 licenses on the MetaFrame XP server. In this case, these 200 licenses would be pooled with the remaining 185 connection licenses for a total on the West Coast of 385 licenses.

Next you upgrade the master browser server on the East Coast to MetaFrame XP running in mixed mode. Remember that when you upgrade a server, its licenses are not automatically brought into XP; you need to manually add licenses to XP and activate them. Because the master browser had the 50-user bump pack and the 15-user base license, your East Coast license count drops down by 65 to 285 after 48 hours.

Now that you have XP servers on both coasts they will equally share their pooled licenses across the WAN. You currently have only 20 licenses. This means 100 licenses will be given to the West Coast XP master browser and 100 licenses will be given to the East Coast XP master browser by default.

Using the CMC, you can adjust this license sharing across subnets. Instead of giving 100 licenses to the East Coast and 100 to the West Coast, for example, you could give 50 to the East Coast and 150 to the West Coast. This is done under the Interoperability tab found by right-clicking the farm name in the CMC and selecting Properties. From here you can adjust the license count given to every subnet on which you have an XP server, in mixed mode only.

After you have migrated all of your servers and switched to native mode, your licenses are pooled together across the farm into a single count. Although you are in mixed mode, however, it is important to remember that licenses are divided across subnets and that license pooling ICA gateways will no longer work.

Licensing Considerations in Mixed Mode

Because of the many changes in how licensing works with MetaFrame XP, it is very important to ensure that license migration planning and license testing are an integral part of your migration planning for the project. The following is recommended:

- **Use mixed mode for as short a time as possible.**   The licensing complexities caused by mixed mode make it difficult to implement. In addition, the limited testing of MetaFrame XP in mixed mode means there is a strong likelihood that you will run into unusual licensing problems.

- **Remember the 48-hour rule.** Because backup browsers cache licensing information for 48 hours, you will not see the effects of the changing you make in licensing until that time. Be sure you understand what changes will take place after that 48 hours expire.

- **Add all of your MetaFrame XP licenses and activate them when in production.** When you roll out your first production MetaFrame XP server, add all of your licenses and activate them on the server. In this way there should be plenty of licenses available as you migrate the remaining servers.

- **Do not activate licenses while testing.** To avoid activation headaches, do not active your licenses while you are still testing MetaFrame XP.

- **Use QSERVER.EXE to check licenses before and after every upgrade.** When migrating using the mixed-mode or all-or-nothing techniques, make sure to double-check your license count before and after every server upgrade, especially before and after the first server upgrade.

- **Watch license distribution carefully while in mixed mode.** Keep a close eye on how licenses are being distributed while in mixed mode from the Interoperability tab of the farm's Properties dialog box in the CMC. If the farm is spread across a WAN, make sure to adjust the license counts as needed under this tab.

- **Be careful of multihomed servers.** One gotcha often overlooked is multihomed master browsers. By default, in mixed mode, MetaFrame XP will divide the licenses available across each subnet. If you have a multihomed master browser, your license count available to the servers on each subnet will be half of the total count. Use the Interoperability tab to adjust as needed. Remember that even if you have a dual-NIC server and do not intend to make it multihomed, MetaFrame will still think it is multihomed because it has two cards.

- **Manually assign licenses to individual servers.** If you run into unusual or unexpected licensing problems while in mixed mode, try manually assigning licenses to individual servers as needed. This will help stabilize the licensing and give you direct control over what licenses are available.

- **Do not confuse Terminal Server licensing issues with MetaFrame.** Make sure you thoroughly understand how Terminal Server licensing works before undertaking your migration. It is very easy to confuse licensing errors between the two. The event log will normally give you more information on what the nature of the license problem is that your are having.

- **Do not change Terminal Server licensing during MetaFrame migration.**   You are best off making sure your Terminal Server licensing is stable and set up correctly before undertaking a MetaFrame XP migration. If you make changes to both licensing systems simultaneously, it will be easy to confuse licensing problems that might arise.

- **Use a separate server for Terminal Server licensing.**   The Terminal Server Licensing service can reside on any Windows 2000 Terminal Server on your subnet or on a domain controller if you are using Active Directory. It is better to have this on a separate server than your MetaFrame XP servers, so that it is not affected by the migration. Make sure to plan how you will handle Terminal Services licensing before you migrate to XP.

- **Know your master browsers.**   Using QSERVER.EXE, keep track of which server is the master browser before and after any server migrations. You should plan in advance where you want your master browser to be during the migration and follow up to ensure it is where you expect. Remember that unless disabled, MetaFrame XP will always become the master browser in mixed mode.

Using QSERVER.EXE to Check Licensing

Before you begin your migration, go to the command prompt on one of your MetaFrame 1.8 servers and run QSERVER.EXE. You will see a list of all the servers in your farm, how many licenses are available, and how many are being used by each server. The output will look similar to the following from a test-three server farm:

```
Server                Transport Conns Free  Total  Network Address
------------------    --------- ----------------   ------------------
META1                 TCP/IP    0     43    45     192.168.10.208 B
META2                 TCP/IP    0     43    45     192.168.10.227 B
META3*                TCP/IP    2     43    45     192.168.10.228 M
```

In this case, META3 is the master browser as noted by the *M* next to the network address for META3. The META3 server is set up to elect two backup browsers, which are META1 and META2.

Because META3 is the master browser, it is responsible for license pooling in the farm. Each server has a base license of 15 licenses, so META3 pools them together, making a total license count of 45.

After you upgrade each server to XP, use QSERVER.EXE to keep track of license count changes for the farm. Although QSERVER.EXE is a MetaFrame 1.8 tool, it is available on MetaFrame XP and provides a good way to view how license pooling is behaving on the server farm while in mixed mode.

Planning for Service Packs

You should make installing at least Service Pack 1 an important piece of your MetaFrame XP deployment plan. Service Pack 1 contains many critical hotfixes that will save you from a lot of headaches. Whether you choose to install Service Pack 1 or a newer service pack from Citrix, if available, always review the currently available hotfixes available on the Citrix web site. Choose to install any that you think are important for your environment.

When installing the service packs and hotfixes on your servers, remember that it is critical to install exactly the same service packs and hotfixes on all servers in a farm. Citrix MetaFrame is not very forgiving at all when it comes to mixing service packs or hotfixes in the same server farm. In many cases, a particular service pack or hotfix makes important changes to data structures. If you deploy these fixes unevenly, you could risk corrupting your IMA DS or creating even uglier situations.

Installation Management Services and Upgrading to MetaFrame XP

If you have created packages in Installation Management Services 1.0 on MetaFrame 1.8, it is important to upgrade them to MetaFrame XP before beginning the MetaFrame XP upgrade on each server. The Application Packaging and Delivery CD that accompanies MetaFrame XPe includes an application called IM_APP_UPGRD.EXE. It is located under the \support\debug\i386 directory. Run this application directly before installing MetaFrame XP, and your 1.0 application packages will be converted, so that they will be brought into MetaFrame XPe successfully. After the upgrade, you can install these applications only using the Installation Management Services on MetaFrame XP, so it is a good idea to make a backup of these packages before upgrading.

7

Planning for the Installation of Terminal Server and Citrix MetaFrame

THE KEY TO SUCCESSFUL TERMINAL SERVER installation is proper planning. Although you learned many of the more general steps involved in planning a solution in Chapter 6, "Planning a Terminal Server and Citrix MetaFrame XP Solution," it is now time to get down to the specifics. In this chapter, you will learn how to size your server properly, how to best set up the hardware on your server, and what choices during the install process are important to decide on in advance.

Next there will be a discussion on documentation. Good documentation is critical for a successful Terminal Server implementation and the best time to start documenting your servers is now, before the installation begins.

Preparing for Terminal Server

You will find that the actual installation process for Terminal Services is deceptively easy in Windows 2000. When you are finished, the server will still appear the same as before.

Even though it might look and act like a standard Windows 2000 server, however, it is an entirely different animal from your other servers. Not only are hardware requirements calculated differently, but also the administration of the server requires a higher level of knowledge of Windows server technology and a more systematic approach.

You will find that a deeper understanding of basic Windows features such as the Registry, profiles, policies, and file security is vital for the effective administration of Terminal Server and for the ability to efficiently troubleshoot problems that might come up.

You also need to take a very systematic and disciplined approach to the implementation and administration of your Terminal Servers. This approach starts with the creation of detailed server documentation, as you will be shown in the "Documentation During the Planning and Testing Stage" section later in this chapter, in which you record the configuration of both your servers and their applications as you install. You can then use these documents as a template for the creation of additional servers as your server farm grows, ensuring that your servers and applications are installed consistently and correctly.

A Terminal Server solution is a server-based computing solution. In a server-based solution, your servers are a critical part of the system. The clients rely on them heavily because application processing happens at the server. This increased emphasis on the server equates to the need for a different approach, especially in file security, reliability, and performance, which are covered in the following sections.

File Security

Security is always important on your servers. However, with Terminal Server security requirements reach a new level. With standard Windows 2000 Server, you normally gave access to your server's data by using shares and then assigning rights for users to the share or the folders beneath it. Because users access the server across the network, they can see only what you decided to share with them.

With Terminal Server, users get a desktop on the server itself. This is the security equivalent of letting all of your Terminal Server users into the computer room so that they can walk up to the server console and log on locally! Users not only have access to network shares from their Terminal Server desktop, but they also can run applications and access data directly from the server's local hard drive.

As a Terminal Server administrator, you need to be meticulous when implementing your server's file security, otherwise users could inadvertently destroy critical system files. This starts with the decision to use an NTFS partition during server installation, rather than FAT or FAT32. NTFS is the only partition type that supports the advanced level of security needed for your local drives on Terminal Server.

Reliability

Server reliability is also critical in a multiuser environment. In a plain Windows 2000 Server environment, if your server goes down, your users might still be able to work locally with their documents still in memory on their local PCs.

With Terminal Server, the computing environment is more like that of a mainframe. If the mainframe goes down, everyone's terminal goes dark and no one can work. Imagine how frustrated you would be if you were typing in a large document when all of a sudden your Windows Terminal screen went black and your document was lost.

Throughout this chapter, you learn many tips that will help ensure the reliability of your Terminal Server, starting with documenting your server installation carefully.

Performance

You should take a close look at the hardware resources you will need to support your users. Because all application processing occurs at the server, Terminal Server normally requires more server resources per user than standard Windows 2000 Server does. Also a slowdown on the server affects all the users on the server. If one user is able to monopolize the resources, all the other users will suffer. The first step in ensuring good performance on your servers is sizing your servers correctly.

Sizing Your Terminal Servers

Sizing your Terminal Servers correctly is very important for the success of your Terminal Server solution. Before you can put together a cost of the solution, you need to first determine how many servers you need and how big they each should be. Unfortunately, this can be a tricky process because there are few comprehensive benchmarks to follow.

In this section, you will learn some ballpark techniques for sizing your Terminal Server solution. However, what will be presented here will require some guesswork on your part and is only a rough estimation. If you intend to deploy large numbers of servers, it is highly recommended to set up a performance-testing lab to accurately size your servers and establish your own benchmarks and baselines. In Chapter 21, "Performance Tuning and Resource Management," this is exactly what you will learn how to do.

Classifying Application Processor Usage

Processing power is most often the biggest bottleneck with Terminal Server performance, assuming applications do not run out of memory. Having enough processing power for your users is critical for ensuring that they have adequate performance. How much processing power and how many systems you will need varies greatly depending mainly on what applications your users use and how actively they use them.

To achieve a rough estimate of how many users you can fit on one box, you need to first rank your user's application and system processing usage on the *Application Processor Usage scale* (APU scale) shown in Table 7.1.

This scale is based on processor usage during active use of the application. This is a measurement of how heavy the application tasks your processor only during typical *active* usage; this does not take into account how long users typically use the application or how many use it simultaneously.

The column titled "Concurrent Active Users" gives you a better idea of what each level means in terms of concurrent users. This is the number of *active* users possible on a single 500MHz processor Terminal Server before application response time begins to degrade to an unacceptable level. This normally begins to happen on a server after processor utilization exceeds 80 percent. Unless typical active application processor usage is extremely light, you will rarely find that you will be able to fit more than 65 active users on a single processor 500MHz server.

Author's Note

Although processor speeds today go well past 1GHz, a 500 MHz processor is a good place to start for this discussion. You will learn how to adjust for actual processor speed in the "Sizing the Server" section later in this chapter.

It also is important to emphasize that the APU scale is a measurement of active usage. This type of usage can easily be simulated using macros and other automation technology, as you will see in Chapter 21. Because it can be simulated, you should be able to generate good estimates of this number.

How often your users are active is a different measurement. This measurement is much more subjective, but can play a big role in sizing your servers.

Table 7.1   Application Processor Usage (APU) Scale

Level	Concurrent Active Users Possible with 1000MHz CPU	Typical Applications
1	45 to 65	*Light processor usage* Typical usage on word processing applications, help desk packages, light data entry, and terminal emulation.

Level	Concurrent Active Users Possible with 1000MHz CPU	Typical Applications
2	25 to 45	*Medium processor usage* Typical usage on more processor-intensive applications, such as accounting applications, spreadsheets used for calculations, ERP applications, normal use of development tools and compilation, web browsers, and image retrieval.
3	5 to 25	*Heavy processor usage* Heavy use of processor-intensive applications, such as CAD, nationwide or large data ware house reporting applications, scientific and mathematical analysis, high-end graphics or multimedia applications, or heavy use of development tools. Applications that involve animation, change the screen rapidly, use sound heavily, or where users print large amounts often also fall into this category.

Level 1 Application Usage

Level 1 application usage is typically the level where task-oriented users use their applications. If you are typing at an average rate into a word processing application, for example, you are probably at Level 1 on the APU scale. Most usage of data entry and task-oriented applications fall into this category.

Level 2 Applications

Level 2 application usage is where during normal, active use the processor is taxed more heavily due to frequent calculations, extraordinarily heavy user interaction, or frequent screen updates, such as with web browsing.

Where an application falls on the APU scale depends not only on the application, but also on what your users typically use it for.

If your users are all in the accounting department and typically use Microsoft Excel for reporting and data calculations when they are actively using it, for instance, their usage of the application will be at Level 2 on the APU Scale. If they use Microsoft Excel just for data entry or table updates, however, their processor usage will likely be at Level 1.

Level 3 Applications

Level 3 applications are typically applications that use extraordinary amounts of processing time and system resources during normal, active usage.

The majority of applications that are run on Terminal Server fall into Level 1 or 2. Only classify an application as Level 3 if you know that during normal usage users are constantly performing calculations with the application, using the application in ways that generate significant processor utilization, or the application itself continually taxes the processor, such as with multimedia or animation.

For example, a reporting application such as Crystal Reports could be either a Level 2 or Level 3 application depending on typical active usage. If your users work with smaller or summarized datasets and can generate reports in very little time with short periods of heavy processor usage, your application usage is generally at Level 2. If Crystal is being used to report off of large datasets or is most often used to generate complex reports that take significant time to run and tax the processor heavily, however, the application usage is at Level 3.

Remember that with Terminal Server, significant processing and resources usage can be taken up just with screen updates. If your application constantly changes large portions of the screen, such as with a multimedia application or a graphical monitoring utility, this can add additional overhead on Terminal Server. Take this into account when assessing what level your active application usage is at.

Level 3 Applications

Be careful with using Terminal Server to deploy these types of applications because their heavy processor usage will restrict the number of users you can put on a box. These types of applications, especially applications that use animation, are often avoided in the Terminal Server world.

Sometimes, however, using Terminal Server to deploy Level 3 applications can really pay off for a business. One big advantage of using Terminal Server with these types of applications is that a high-performance Terminal Server will be able to generate results for these applications much quicker than running the applications on a typical workstation. In addition, you will be able to upgrade processing power much easier centrally than if you had to upgrade processing power at the workstations.

For applications such as nationwide reporting, scientific analysis, mathematical analysis, and development, you can typically provide wider access and better performance than running these types of applications locally.

Assessing Application Usage

Often as an administrator you might be taxed with having to install an application you are not familiar with on the server farm. It is very important in a Terminal Server environment that you become *intimately* familiar with *every* application that needs to be installed. You need to not only understand the technical details of how the application is installed and what it requires, but also how users normally use the application.

When assessing whether an application is normally used at Level 1, 2, or 3, it pays to meet with the most experienced users of the application and have them show you typical use of the application. During this meeting, while they are using the application, keep a close eye on the application for the following:

- **Heavy calculations**   Watch for tasks that require heavy calculations such as generating a report.

- **Slow response**   One definite indicator of heavy processor usage is the hourglass. If your user has to wait for the machine before he can go on to the next task, it is likely that the machine is heavily using the processor at that point.

- **Animations and screen changes**   Look for any animations within an application or frequent changes of the screen. Often these animations can be shut off; however, some are an integral part of the application, such as moving graphs displayed by monitoring programs. If only a fraction of the screen changes at a time, the application usage will be lower on the APU scale than if large portions of the screen change rapidly, such as if a user has to quickly page through an electronic document or images.

- **Heavy file system or network usage**   Every time a user or application has to pull information from either the hard drive or network, the CPU has to work hard to bring that information into memory and help handle the I/O. The larger the amount of data that the user has to pull in and work with, the more CPU time the application will take.

- **Printing needs**   Be especially aware of the size of print jobs that are typical with the application. You can watch the print queues as the person prints out typical reports, and you can see the size of the documents. Remember that this document needs to be streamed back across the network to the remote user. This is especially important in a WAN environment. Typical text documents are between 50 and 300KB in size, depending on their length. However, even small graphically rich documents can be well over 1MB in size. This can quickly take up a lot of network bandwidth.

Using Task Manager Effectively

While you are watching application usage, one quick and easy technique to assess what tasks within an application labor the processor the most is using Task Manager. Task Manager is only available on Windows NT, Windows

2000, and Windows XP workstations. Get to know it well! It provides a ton of very important information for a Terminal Server administrator and enables you to quickly assess the status of your server.

To bring it up, just go to the Start menu, click Run, enter **TASKMGR.EXE**, and click OK. If you are at the console of the server, press Ctrl+Shift+Esc to bring it up quickly. In the Task Manager window that appears, click the Performance tab to view a graph of processor utilization.

By arranging the windows, so that Task Manager is on the screen at the same time as the application, you can watch for peaks in processor usage as the user walks through typical tasks in the application. Ideally, you should watch Task Manager at the server console while the user is logged on and using the application through a Terminal Server session. The more often you see heavy processor usage during normal application usage, the higher on the APU scale the application usage will be.

Experimenting with Task Manager

To get a better feel for application processor usage on your own, bring up Wordpad and type in a short passage. Unless you are typing well above 60 words per minute or you have a very slow processor, your average processor usage will be less than 5 percent.

This is definitely Level 1 application usage, which is typical for data entry or word processing applications. If you want to see what a Level 3 application looks like, try bringing up a multimedia application or game, such as Microsoft Pinball. You will likely find average processor utilization above 50 percent while the application is active.

A Level 2 application will fall somewhere in between. It might have low utilization while the user is entering information or navigating the application. However, often during typical use there will be significant spikes in processor usage as the application processes data or pulls up necessary information. On average this will use up significantly more processor time than a Level 1 application.

Assessing Multiple-Application Usage

The chapter so far has been focused on assessing the APU level of a single application. This assumes your users will mainly be running that application on the servers you are trying to size. If your users will be running multiple applications, you need to take a little bit of a different approach. Your goal is still to find a single number on the APU scale. However, this needs to be a weighted average of the APU for the primary applications the users will run.

To get this average, estimate the percentage of time that each of the primary applications will be used when your users are actively using the server. This number is referred to as *PercUse(n)*, representing the percentage of time application *n* is used by your user versus the other primary applications.

The following formula shows you how you can come up with an overall APU value for your server if users are running multiple applications on the server:

APU for all applications = (PercUse(1) * ProcUse(1)... + PercUse(n)*ProcUse(n)) / 100

Suppose, for example, that you are deploying Microsoft Word and Excel to your users. You estimate that 80 percent of the time they will be using Word at APU Level 1. However, the users also need to run several reports from Excel as part of their daily tasks. You therefore estimate that 20 percent of the time they will be using Excel at Level 2. Your overall weighted APU level is calculated as follows:

APU for all applications = (80 * 1 + 20 * 2) / 100 = 1.2

Determining the Maximum Active User Percentage

After you have found the correct APU level for active use of the application, you need to figure out how often your users actively use it in order to correctly size your server. To do this you need to estimate the maximum number of *active* concurrent users you expect to have. This is the maximum number you expect across all the new servers that you will be purchasing for this solution. Take this number and divide by the total number of users this solution is for. This percentage is referred to as the *maximum active user percentage* (MAUP). If you need to roll out this application to 50 users, and you estimate that at most only 25 will be active at one time, for example, your MAUP is 50 percent.

Although the total number of users is very easy to determine, determining the MAUP can be more challenging. To do this, you need to consider the following:

- How long users typically interact with the application
- How often users need access to the application
- What the peak usage times for the application will be

This MAUP is important to determine as accurately as possible because it will have a great effect on the final cost of your solution and on the perceived system performance by the users.

This number is different from the number of maximum concurrent users you expect on your system, because even though users might be on the system, they are not necessarily active.

To determine this number, one of the key factors you need to look at is how much of a user's job function involves using the application. Suppose, for example, that you intend to deploy Microsoft Outlook to 25 office workers. You estimate that even though everyone will stay connected to the server with Outlook open all day long, only 10 percent of the users will be actively using Outlook actively at one time. The MAUP would then be 10 percent.

On the other hand, suppose you are deploying Outlook via Terminal Server to an email customer service group. Because Outlook is a main part of their job function, they are in Outlook and using it actively a good part of the day when responding to messages. In this case, your MAUP percentage would be significantly more than 10 percent.

MAUP is a measure of active concurrent users but not just concurrent users. For example, even though everyone might keep Microsoft Outlook open during the day, only a small percentage might actively be using it at the same time. It is the percentage of active use of the application that counts in your estimate of the MAUP, whether the user is interacting with the application causing processor utilization or the application is running a batch process and performing calculations.

Sizing the Server

Now its time to put these numbers together to figure out the number of servers and processors you need for your Terminal Server solution. Assuming you will be rolling out the application on identical servers, first figure out how many concurrent active users one of your servers will handle.

Use the following formula to estimate the maximum number of *active users on a single processor* (AUSP). This is directly related to the APU and can be estimated as follows:

Active users on a single processor or AUSP = $(85 - 20 * \text{APU})$

If you estimate that your users will be running applications at Level 1 APU, for example, the maximum number of AUSP will be $65 - 20 * 1$ (or 45). As with all the estimates in this chapter, this is a conservative estimate. You may actually be able to fit up to 65 users. When sizing Terminal Server, however, always estimate conservatively to ensure you have enough hardware. Remember that this estimate is for a server with a single 500MHz processor.

You might think that you can just take this number and multiply by the number of processors to get the total number of users. However, the problem with this is that you would be assuming that each processor you add will increase your performance equally. In the real world, this is almost never the case. You can normally expect 10 to 25 percent fewer users per processor as each processor is added.

If your users are running an application at Level 2 APU, for example, you calculate that you can safely run about $65 - 20 \star 2$ (25) concurrent users on the first 500MHz processor. You might expect that if you have a dual-processor server, and each processor is 500MHz, that you could run double the number of concurrent users (or 50 users) on the server. This is definitely not the case. In reality, you could expect between 40 and 50 users to be able to fit on the server because of the overhead of having 2 processors in the system.

This percentage tends to increase as more processors are added. This means that the more processors you add, the less of an effect they have on the number of concurrent users that the server can support. This is mainly due to the extra processor overhead caused by managing the split up of the processor load and by application inefficiencies over multiple processors. The exact percentage is very difficult to determine except in a controlled lab environment. However, the following formulas assume a linear reduction of 25 percent of AUSP, for each processor added, and will help you put together a good rough estimate. Choose the appropriate formula, based on the number of processors in your server:

Active users per server (1 processor) = AUSP

Active users per server (2 processors) = AUSP + (.75) $\star$ AUSP

Active users per server (3 processors) = AUSP + (.75) $\star$ AUSP + (.50) $\star$ AUSP

Active users per server (4 processors) = AUSP + (.75) $\star$ AUSP + (.50) $\star$ AUSP + (.25) $\star$ AUSP

Suppose, for example, that you calculated that the maximum number of AUSP is 45. You want to get a rough estimate of how many users you can fit on your server if you install 2 processors. So, you use the second formula to come up with $45 + (.75) \star 45 = 45 + 33.75 = 78.75$ or 79 concurrent users rounded off.

To save you the hassle of calculating these estimates yourself, just look up the rough estimate in Table 7.2 based on the APU of the applications that your users are running and how many processors are on your server.

Table 7.2 Users per Server

APU	1 × 500MHz	2 × 500MHz	3 × 500MHz	4 × 500MHz
1	45	79	101	112
2	25	44	56	62
3	5	9	11	13

Author's Note

If you have not guessed it by now, server sizing can be anything but an exact science. One of the goals of this chapter is to give you a simple rough estimate of how many users you can fit on a server and provide you with a better understanding of the various factors that can affect this number. If this is a large project and you need a better estimate, however, you should set up a test lab with the actual servers you will be using. You can then install the applications that you need to deploy onto these servers and do more advanced performance testing to get a significantly more accurate estimate of the number of users you can fit on one server. Chapter 21 covers this technique in detail.

Practical Limits on the Number of Users per Server

Now you have a pretty good rough estimate of the number of users your server will support. However, you must consider some other very important things before generating your server quote.

First, this formula does not take into account increases in the number of active users possible per processor due to increases in processor speed or performance, such as with modern Intel Xeon processors. The estimation for AUSP is based on what you could typically expect to be able to handle on a server-class system with a single 500MHz processor. However, processing speeds today are significantly higher. You can expect significantly more users per processor as your processor speeds increase. In reality, you will not see double the number of users per processor if you double the processing speed; but to be safe, you could expect up to 50 percent more users to be active on a single-processor box, if you were to double the processor speed.

Suppose, for example, that you are putting 1GHz processors in your servers. Because a 1GHz processor is twice the speed of a 500MHz processor, you can expect about a 50 percent increase in the number of concurrent users that this box will hold. To make your rough estimate, just look up the concurrent user estimate for your processor configuration and APU in Table 7.2 and then add 50 percent.

The second major item to realize is that the formula assumes that the main bottleneck for users is solely processing speed. Although this is normally the case with Terminal Servers with relatively small numbers of concurrent users, as you begin to exceed 100 concurrent users, other system bottlenecks become more apparent. Even with application processor usage at APU Level 1 on a high-end, four 1GHz processor server, you can expect to start running into significant system bottlenecks when attempting to run more than 150 users concurrently.

Typical bottlenecks at this level of usage can be memory limitations, lack of PTEs available, lack of open file handles, networking card bottlenecks, bottlenecks on the system bus, and especially bottlenecks caused by heavy paging file usage. If you intend to use your servers this heavily, it is imperative to do thorough performance testing beforehand and tuning (as discussed in Chapter 20, "Advanced Printing Techniques").

Memory

Memory is the next most important part of your server's performance. Memory normally will not cause a bottleneck with the server if you plan your memory requirements well. As with processor requirements, the amount of memory your server needs depends greatly on the applications your users use. It also depends on how many applications your users normally have open at the same time, and how much data they are working with. For single-application, task-oriented users, the memory requirements are much less than for power users who might have several applications open simultaneously on their desktops.

You can typically expect each user session to use somewhere between 5MB and 25MB on average for running most office applications. Estimating memory usage is much easier than estimating processor usage. To obtain a rough estimate of how much you need, perform the following steps on any Windows 2000 Terminal Server on which you have installed the application:

1. Open one instance of the application at the console of the Terminal Server. This will load the application and its common components into memory. When second instances of this application are loaded, they often share some of the components already loaded in memory.

2. Open Task Manager on the console of the server by running TASKMGR.EXE from the Start menu, Run dialog box. Note the Mem Usage number on the Performance tab.

3. Now using either the ICA or RDP client, whichever you intend to use in the actual deployment, connect to the Terminal Server and run the application. If users normally work with documents in the application, open a typical-sized document.

4. Note what the increase is in the Mem Usage.

Now keep repeating steps 3 and 4, while leaving your existing sessions connected. The additional memory usage as you open up each new session will normally be about the same. If you average these increases, you can come up with a good estimate of the amount of memory that will be needed per user (MemPerUsr).

In addition, make sure to test differences in memory usage caused by opening up documents and doing other memory-intensive tasks in an application. If users regularly open up large documents, their memory requirements will be greater.

Besides the per–user memory requirements, the base operating system itself takes up quite a bit of memory. Windows 2000 Server alone can take anywhere from 100 to 150MB of memory by itself, depending on what services are loaded. To be safe, assume that the operating system is using up 150MB.

Now, to calculate your memory requirements, use the following formula: Memory needed = 150 + MemPerUsr ★ maximum number of concurrent users

Remember that the maximum number of concurrent users is different from the maximum active users. If your users typically log on to the server and open an application and then leave it open throughout the day, they count as a concurrent user even though they are not actively using the application.

Now you can see why the 4GB limitation is so important in the Terminal Server world. Theoretically, with multiple GHz processors your servers should be able to run hundreds of users. In practice, however, the closer you get to 4GB, the more the system will have to rely on virtual memory to handle fluctuations in application memory usage. This basically means that your paging file activity will increase dramatically as you approach this limit. Users who have to wait for their applications to pull up information from the paging file will quickly start complaining of poor system performance. This is where the placement of your paging file on the fastest drives possible makes a big difference in Terminal Server performance.

Fewer Big Servers or More Smaller Ones?

Now that you know how many users you can fit on a single server and how much memory you need, you need to decide how many servers you will purchase.

There are basically two approaches to server sizing. The first approach is to buy a small number of large servers with multiple processors and to fit as many users as you can on each server, but leaving some room for growth.

The second approach is to purchase a large number of smaller servers to handle the same number of users and spread your users across them. Which approach you should take depends a lot on how much you have budgeted for the project and how much growth you expect.

Choosing to go with a smaller number of larger servers is normally the most economic choice. You will be able to fit more users on a single box and have to purchase only additional processors and memory, rather than a whole new system. When deciding how many users you want to fit on one server, always take into account expected growth. If you expect significant growth, and you intend to purchase four-processor-capable systems, estimate the number of servers you need based on each server having only two processors. That way, as your capacity requirements grow you can just add more processors and memory instead of having to install a brand new server every time. On the other hand, if this will be it for users for a long time, buy four processor boxes with enough memory.

Although choosing to purchase a small number of large servers might be the most economic choice, you need to be concerned about the reliability and scalability problems you can run into by putting too many users on the same system. For these reasons and more, it is highly recommended to purchase as many servers as you can afford for your solution.

By using load sharing or load balancing, you can distribute the user load across the servers. If one server fails, you do not lose as much overall capacity as if you were using larger servers. In a load-sharing situation, the remaining servers will be able to quickly pick up the load of the failed server. Because the servers will generally be running fewer than 100 users, you will not likely have to deal with any bottleneck beyond processor usage.

Having a large number of redundant servers also makes maintenance a lot easier. You can normally bring down one server for maintenance or upgrades while the other servers pick up the user load. You also can quickly bring down a server that is having problems to be able to do more extensive troubleshooting. If you have to reboot a server to make a problem go away, you will be able to do so without affecting as large a number of users as you would affect on a larger box.

Network

Planning your network is a very important part of Terminal Server installation. Without adequate planning your Terminal Server, users might suffer dismal performance due to lack of network capacity.

Network planning is especially important for WAN access to Terminal Server. In general, you can expect an average of anywhere between 10Kbps and 25Kbps of network bandwidth utilization per user. This will vary depending mainly on the graphical activity of your users' applications, how often they print, and how often they transfer files. To get a rough guess of how many concurrent users you can handle across a WAN connection, just divide the connection speed by 20Kbps. Suppose you have a 128Kbps connection to a small remote office. You could expect up to six active users to be able to concurrently access your Terminal Server across the connection at a respectable speed, assuming there wasn't significant other WAN traffic at the same time. Although more than six users could be handled, the more users simultaneously access the server, the slower the response time for each user.

One important new feature with MetaFrame XP is that printing band-width usage can now be controlled at the server. This is a welcome improve-ment for users with large deployments over the WAN because printing traffic can take up a significant portion of WAN usage. Printer bandwidth usage is controlled in the Citrix Management Console.

On a local area network, 15Kbps is a trivial amount of bandwidth com-pared to the 100Mbps and 1000Mbps capabilities of modern network cards. Even so, your choice of network card is a critical component of your server performance and reliability. Make sure to choose the highest performance network card available for your server and ensure that it is running at the fastest speed when connected to your network switch. It is not uncommon to find 100Mbps cards running at 10Mbps or half-duplex because they did not auto-negotiate their speed correctly with the switch. Manually setting the speed and duplex on both your server and the switch can ensure this will not happen to you.

Using a gigabit connection to a switch is highly recommended, if you can support it in your environment. This is especially the case if the majority of the users will be accessing the server via the local area network. Besides the additional bandwidth available with gigabit connection speeds, the latency (or in other words, the response time) is greatly improved.

Understanding Terminal Server Installation Choices

One of your main concerns when first installing Terminal Server should be file security. The main decision you need to make on file security at this point is the format you want to use for your operating system partition. You basically have three choices during the installation with Windows 2000: FAT, FAT32, or NTFS. It is strongly recommended that you install the operating system on an NTFS-formatted partition. When Terminal Server is installed on NTFS, the install program applies important default security rights to the partition, which helps prevent future users from damaging critical system files. The following sections explain the main differences between FAT and NTFS and the reason why choosing NTFS during installation is important.

Choosing NTFS, FAT, or FAT32

There are many differences between NTFS and FAT. The most important overall difference is that NTFS is an object-oriented file system. Although this might not immediately seem important, NTFS's object-oriented design is what makes its robust file security possible. Important security features such as auditing, file-level security, and directory-level security are not available with FAT because it is not an object-oriented file system. Although you can apply share-level security to a FAT partition, this offers scant security for Terminal Server users, who have the same access to the partition as if they were sitting at the server console.

The following are some of the many features that are supported only on NTFS partitions. You will likely find many of the features to be very useful with Terminal Server:

- **Disk quotas**   Disk quotas will help you gain control over the space usage on your Terminal Server. With disk quotas you can ensure that users on your server are allowed only a given amount of storage space on your volumes.

- **Auditing**   Auditing enables you to track file usage, modification, and deletion in detail on your server. This is not only an important security feature, but also can be used as a troubleshooting tool.

- **Encryption**   Now with Windows 2000 you have the ability to encrypt files on your system. Users on your server might want to do this to secure their files.

- **Compression**   Only with NTFS can you enable compression of your server files in a particular folder or on a particular volume.

Another important advantage of NTFS is that it is extensible. Developers can add additional properties to the file system to support new types of access. For Terminal Server administrators who have Macintosh users on their network, this is especially important. Microsoft's Macintosh Services for NT extends NTFS by adding additional properties that support Macintosh files. In this way, your Macintosh users not only can run Windows sessions off your Terminal Server, but they also can save and retrieve files from it by using AppleTalk.

NTFS Default Security Settings

Some administrators choose FAT rather than NTFS during installation because a FAT partition can always be converted later to NTFS using the `convert [drive] /fs:ntfs` command. Although you can convert a FAT partition to NTFS later, a large number of file security settings will not be applied. This file security is only applied if you choose NTFS as the partition type during the initial installation of the Windows 2000 operating system.

NTFS Performance Versus FAT

FAT is generally considered slightly faster than NTFS on partitions smaller than 1000MB because of the additional overhead imposed by the NTFS disk structures. For this reason, Windows 2000 administrators might choose to make a small FAT system partition and a large NTFS data partition.

With Terminal Server, this is definitely not recommended. The difference in performance, if any, is minimal compared to the security problems that could occur by not having file- and directory-level security on your system partition.

In addition, several things on Terminal Server, such as profiles, can take up significant space on the system drive. Normally, you are better off making a system partition significantly larger than 1000MB and formatting it by using NTFS.

Maximum Drive Sizes

FAT partitions on Terminal Server can currently be up to only 4GB in size. Although you can now go up to 32GB with a FAT32 partition on Windows 2000, NTFS is still strongly recommended for Terminal Server. With NTFS you can create drives that are up to 32TB in size.

In addition, Windows 2000 has gotten rid of a significant drive size limitation of Windows NT 4.0 Terminal Server. With Windows NT 4.0, even though NTFS supported drives up to 32TB, you could perform the installation only on a partition that was less than 4GB in size. This limitation no longer exists in Windows 2000. You can create as large a system partition as you need when you first install the operating system.

Running Applications on NTFS

Some administrators choose FAT just because they are most familiar with it. They also might have had experiences in the past in which applications did not seem to run correctly on NTFS. If you find that you have a problem running a particular application on NTFS, it is much more likely that the user does not have sufficient rights to run the application than that application just will not run on NTFS. Application problems due to NTFS are very rare.

To isolate the cause of an application problem, first try running the application as an Administrator equivalent with full rights to the applications and operating system directories. If this works, NTFS is definitely not the culprit.

Take a closer look at the files your application needs access to. You can use Table 7.1 to isolate the rights your application needs to the operating system directories, if this is where the problem is occurring.

Another possibility is that you tested the application on a compressed NTFS partition. Some timing-sensitive applications might not work on compressed drives. Try testing the application again on an uncompressed NTFS directory or partition. Also give the software publishers a call and see whether they have had similar problems and know of a better solution. If you still find that your application will not run on NTFS or runs better on FAT, leave space during installation for a 500MB or smaller FAT partition from which you can run this application. Make sure you still install your operating system on an NTFS partition to maintain its security.

Emergency Recovery on FAT Versus NTFS

With Terminal Server, if one of the critical boot files is missing or you have a corrupted driver, you might not be able to start the operating system. Because FAT is not as secure as NTFS, you can boot from a floppy disk and have full access to the system partition files. The administrator can then replace missing or corrupted files by copying them from the installation CD.

With NTFS, you can still replace any missing files by booting from the install floppy disks or CD and selecting Emergency Recovery from the main installation menu. The emergency recovery process scans your hard drive for any missing files and prompts you for their replacement.

Windows 2000 also has a new feature that works with NFTS partitions: the *Recovery Console*. The Recovery Console provides a command-line interface where you can run simple DOS commands to do things such as enable and disable services, replace system files, and format and repartition drives. This utility is available from the Emergency Recovery menu when you boot from the installation CD. It also can be installed as a menu option during bootup by installing the operating system using the `WINNT32.EXE /CMDCONS` switch.

Selecting Terminal Server Hardware

You need to be very careful when selecting hardware for Terminal Server. Hardware drivers are written in the kernel mode, and thus have direct access to many of the operating systems resources. If you have ever experienced the *blue screen of death*—a blue-colored error dump screen produced after an unrecoverable error—you know how helpless you can feel with hardware related problems.

Hardware problems can often become manifest as intermittent lockups. Your server will be working fine all day with no problems, and suddenly your phone lights up with calls from users complaining that they can no longer access the server. When you take a look at the server, you see the blue screen or a server lockup and are forced to reboot to bring your server back up. To prevent this from happening with Terminal Server, you must make some important decisions before installation even begins.

Before installing Terminal Server, always make sure that the hardware you choose for Terminal Server is on the Windows NT Hardware Compatibility List (HCL). You can find the HCL at www.microsoft.com/hcl.

To get their products on this list, hardware manufacturers must subject their equipment to rigorous testing by using Microsoft's own testing utilities. Although this testing does not completely guarantee that you will have no problems with the hardware, it is definitely a good start. It is also important to note that only servers whose hardware is in the HCL are fully supported by Microsoft.

If a driver for the device you have chosen was not included on the original Terminal Server CD-ROM, you might be able to find the driver that was tested with the device on this web site. Do a search from this web site for your hardware. If the driver is available, you will see a hyperlink for downloading it.

It is highly recommended that you start here before any Terminal Server installation. Do a search for all of the hardware you plan to use for your Windows Terminal Server, including the following:

- **Server model**   The HCL includes compatible, tested server models from a wide variety of server manufacturers. There are often important notes on BIOS levels and their compatibilities on the HCL list. If you are using a multiprocessor system, make sure that you have the correct HAL for your system.

- **Video adapters**   Video adapters are a frequent cause of blue screens of death. Make sure your adapter is on the list. Many video driver adapters, which you will need during installation, are available from the HCL web site.

- **Network cards**   During installation, it is important to have the correct network card drivers. You cannot finish the install process without loading drivers and having them available for at least one network card.

- **Storage devices**   Ensure that your hard drive controller is on the compatibility list and that the driver is included with the standard Windows NT installation. If it is not, you must download it and have it available for the installation process.

- **Modems**   If you are using MetaFrame with dial-in client access or Terminal Server with RAS, make sure your server modems and communications card are on the HCL. If the modem is not on the list, you must obtain the latest MODEM.INF file from the manufacturer and merge it with the [`term server dir`] `\system32\ras\modem.inf` file after Terminal Server is installed.

Choosing Your Drive Technology

One of the most critical installation choices is how you decide to set up your storage system. In general, *redundant array of inexpensive disks* (RAID) storage systems can provide the highest level of reliability if you choose the correct RAID level. Most administrators choose either RAID level 1 (mirroring) or 5 (disk striping with parity).

RAID 1—Mirroring

RAID can be implemented with either software or hardware. The Windows 2000 operating system innately supports two levels of RAID software: RAID level 1, or mirroring; and RAID level 5. With RAID 1, you need two drives or partitions of equal size to establish the mirror. After the mirror has been established using the built-in Disk Management utility in Windows 2000, all data written to the first drive in the mirror also gets copied to the second. If either drive fails, Windows 2000 automatically switches over to the working drive. Although RAID 1 is a good option for your system drives, realize that you need twice as many drives to reach your storage requirements. If you need a 9GB mirrored system partition, you need to purchase two 9GB drives (or 18GB total).

RAID 5—Striping with Parity

With RAID 5, your data is striped equally across all the drives in the array rather than mirrored. In addition, data parity is calculated and written to the drive array. If any drive in the array fails, the server can use the parity information on the remaining drives to reconstruct the data on the failed drive. You need a minimum of three drives to implement RAID 5. Because of the extra processing power and time required for calculating the parity while writing information to disk, RAID 5 tends to be slower than RAID 1 when writing data. For this reason, RAID 5 tends to be a good choice for your data and application volume.

Choosing Hardware-Based Versus Software-Based RAID

Even though Windows 2000 supports both RAID 1 and RAID 5 inherently, most server manufacturers sell RAID controller cards that can provide RAID technology at a hardware level. This dedicated hardware RAID solution offers significantly better performance than using the operating system to handle your RAID array. It is strongly recommended to go with a hardware-based RAID solution for Terminal Server. This is especially true of RAID level 5, in which the parity of every block written to the hard drive has to be calculated.

RAID 0+1 in Hardware-Based Solutions

In addition, with hardware-level RAID solutions you will likely find additional features, such as additional RAID levels, and the ability to expand RAID arrays on-the-fly without having to back up and restore your data. One significant alternative RAID level offered with most hardware-based RAID solutions is RAID 0+1. RAID 0+1 combines the best of both worlds, striping and mirroring, to offer the highest level of RAID performance available.

With RAID 0+1, each pair of drives in the array is mirrored. Data is striped across mirrored pairs of drives when data is written to the drives. In this way, multiple mirrored sets can be written to at the same time, increasing performance. The disadvantage of RAID 0+1, like mirroring, is that you need double the number of drives for a given amount of required storage space. If you have multiple drives available, however, RAID 0+1 can be a good choice for either your system or your application and data logical drives.

Author's Note

You can learn more about RAID technology by visiting the Adaptec web site at www.adaptec.com. Adaptec is a leading vendor of RAID technology and offers several innovative RAID and storage technology solutions. In addition, be sure to visit the web site for your server's manufacturer. Many server manufacturers offer their own hardware-based RAID solution optimized for use on their systems.

Storage Area Networks

In recent years, companies such as EMC and Compaq have led in the development of a new breed of storage technology called a *storage area network* (SAN). SANs are a powerful storage solution that enables you to consolidate and centralize your network storage needs. This new technology has important implications for Terminal Server administrators and should be considered when planning any Terminal Server solution.

Most SAN solutions consist of a central set of storage devices often referred to in the industry by the acronym, JBOD, or *just a bunch of disks*. In Compaq's RA4100 low-end SAN solution, the JBOD is contained within a rack-mounted drive array cabinet that can hold up to 12 hot-pluggable SCSI drives. The array cabinet includes it own built-in controller that handles drive communication and RAID-level processing. Other manufacturers offer similar centralized storage enclosures that are normally designed to house large numbers of SCSI drives and their associated RAID controllers.

For this information to be useful, there must be some way to connect it to the servers. Traditionally, external storage solutions relied on external SCSI cable connections and could be used only by a single server. With a SAN solution, you build a special storage network, so that multiple servers can have access to a central collection of storage drives.

This network is conceptually similar to a local area network, however it relies on a completely different fiber-based communication technology called *Fibre Channel*. Fibre Channel is highly optimized for storage needs and can transfer file information with significantly less overhead than other communication protocols such as TCP/IP.

With a SAN solution, you install Fibre Channel cards in your servers and attach them to a Fibre Channel switch or hub using a fiber cable. You then attach all of your storage arrays to this same Fibre Channel switch or hub, thus creating a storage area network. Just like you would connect your computers together on a local area network using a network hub or switch, a SAN enables you to connect your storage devices and servers together using a Fibre Channel hub or switch.

After you have attached your servers to the central JBOD using Fibre Channel, the drives in the SAN appear as local drives on your server. In other words, to your server it appears as if all the drives in the SAN array are attached via a SCSI cable! Most SAN solutions support the same RAID technologies that you would find in a high-end SCSI controller. However, SANs most often come with advanced storage management software that can do things that cannot normally be done in the SCSI world of storage.

The following are some of the many reasons you might want to consider using a SAN in your Terminal Server solution:

- **Many SANs are supported as boot drives.** This means you do not even need to install drives in your Terminal Servers. Just attach them to the SAN array via Fibre Channel and have them boot off of a drive on the array. If the server fails, just replace it and have the new one boot off of the array instead.

- **SANs allow for easy server replication.**   With most advanced SAN software solutions, you can take clones or snapshots of your logical drives quickly and easily. This can enable you to clone all the server's drives in a matter of minutes. You could then assign the cloned drives to another server, change the name and other machine-specific information (that is, SIDs), and you would have yourself a new Terminal Server, identical to the old one.

- **SANs allow for easy backups.**   Some SANs enable you to take an online snapshot of a drive within a matter of seconds. You can then do a backup of this snapshot instead of having to back up a live server. With this technique, you no longer have to worry about open files or incomplete backups of your servers. Your backup will contain an exact snapshot of that server at the moment in time you took the snapshot. Many SANs now also support direct-to-tape technologies where you connect a tape drive to the SAN and set up backups to happen directly to tape without having to have an intermediary backup server.

- **SANs support "growing drives."**   Many SANs support seamless drive additions. Unlike other solutions where you often have to restore your data after a hard drive upgrade, with a SAN, you can add hard drives as you please, and it will appear to your server just as a larger drive, without losing data or having to reboot!

SANs can be an excellent solution for ASPs and large corporate environments because they greatly simplify storage management. For companies that have hundreds or thousands of servers, this technology can be a huge time saver. Also, its advanced features, such as cloning and snapshots, provide a lot of flexibility.

Data Storage on the Terminal Server

Storing application data on your Terminal Server should normally be avoided. However, in some situations, such as with reporting applications, you can realize great speed improvements by giving local access to data rather than access data across a network. If you have an application for which fast access to data is critical, consider storing the data on a SAN and provide Fibre Channel access to the data from your Terminal Servers.

If you need to access the same set of data from multiple Terminal Servers, consider using cloning technology to clone the data to a separate set of drives in the SAN. In this way, each server can access it's own "clone" of the original data. If any server fails, the other servers will be able to easily pick up where it left off.

Drive Types and Speeds

When choosing the drives for your server, always favor performance over capacity in a Terminal Server environment. As covered in the "Deciding on the Drive Arrangement" section that follows, one tenet of good Terminal

Server solution design is to avoid putting application data on the Terminal Server itself or at least separate it from the system partition. You should focus on ensuring your Terminal Server is a highly optimized platform that will easily support multiple users and multiple applications simultaneously.

Generally, when choosing drives for your server, you should choose the highest RPM drives you can afford. The higher the drive RPM, the higher the performance of the drive. This makes a significant difference for Terminal Server performance, especially with drives that contain the paging file.

You also should choose higher performance drive technologies, such as SCSI or Fibre Channel, rather than IDE/ATA. Nearly all server manufacturers today choose SCSI or Fibre Channel technology for their high-performance server solutions. Most also invest significant time to tune their systems for optimal performance with SCSI and Fibre Channel solutions and their related controller technologies.

Deciding On the Drive Arrangement

Proper drive arrangement and sizing are very important for optimal Terminal Server performance. There are many different ways of setting up the drive arrangements on your servers. However, not setting up your drives in a consistent manner across your servers will cause you numerous headaches in the long run. Consistent setup becomes even more important with the more servers you have. If you intend to deploy more than 10 servers, it pays to do performance tests on different drive arrangements as you will be shown how to do in Chapter 21. Whether your deployment is large or small, you need to decide on the drive arrangement philosophy you will follow, document it in your Terminal Server Setup Guide, and use the same philosophy on all of your servers.

For the best performance and reliability, you should use a minimum of three logical, and ideally physically separate, drives for your Terminal Server: a system drive, application and data drive, and a dedicated paging file drive.

System Drive

The system drive is your main drive and the one on which you install your operating system. Both reliability and performance are critical with the system drive. For the best combination of reliability and performance, the following is recommended:

- **Use RAID 1.** Use RAID 1, or 0+1, rather than RAID 5. RAID 1 offers better write performance than RAID 5 offers.

- **Use the highest RPM drives available.**   As covered in the preceding section, drive RPM has a big impact on performance.
- **Format the partition for a minimum of 4GB or 9GB in environments with more than 500 users.**   It is very important for server reliability that you provide plenty of room on your system partition. You will be surprised at how quickly you can run out of space on a system partition with Terminal Server.

Drive Size Formula

Drive space can be a big issue on Terminal Server if you do not plan ahead. Drive space usage is very different with Terminal Server than with a regular Windows 2000 server. Remember Terminal Server is like a workstation for your users. Because of this, you will need to install their application on the Terminal Server itself. Even though it is recommended to install your applications on a different partition than the system partition, their DLLs and other components still reside on the system drive. In addition, each user who logs on to the box stores a local copy of his profile on the system partition. This can quickly add up to hundreds of megabytes in large Terminal Server deployments. Printing queues, system logs, backup logs, and many other items can all add up to significant storage space usage on Terminal Server.

It is highly recommended to create a system partition of at least 9GB on any Terminal Server deployment and even more for larger environments. Space is relatively inexpensive compared to the reliability problems you can run into if you run out of it. If you intend to put your paging file on the system drive, which is not recommended, add two times the amount of memory to the minimum system drive size. Here is a simple formula you can use to help you estimate the right size:

Minimum drive size = 3000MB for system files and growth + 20 MB * # total users + 2 * amount of system memory (for the paging file)

Application Drive

The application drive is a separate logical drive that you dedicate for use for your application installations. You also can use this drive for the storage of the I386 directory, hardware drivers, system-specific application data, and other miscellaneous static storage needs. This separation of system and applications is very important in a Terminal Server environment. You need to think of the two as two separate entities. By keeping them separate, you avoid problems such as causing system problems by running out of space during an application install. You also want to be careful to use the same drive letter across all of your servers for your application drive. This makes it much simpler for publishing applications and for automating application installation.

For the application drive, performance is important; however, so is capacity. If you have three or more drives remaining for your application logical drive, you will realize more capacity by configuring them for RAID 5 rather than for a RAID 1 solution. Also because data will normally be read from an application drive far more often than written, you will not suffer from the performance effects of RAID 5's slower write speeds.

Paging Drive

If you have five or more drives available in your system, it is recommended to dedicate one of those drives for the paging file.

The system paging file is used by the system to create a virtual memory area for your applications. As your applications become more heavily used, so does your paging file. Putting the paging file on a separate drive than the operating system can result in significant performance improvements, especially on heavily used Terminal Servers.

Recommended Drive Configurations

The following are the recommended drive arrangements based on the number of drives you can put in your system. Always choose the highest performance drives available for your system:

- **Two drives**   With two drives, you have very few choices. Mirror the two drives and split the drive into two partitions. Put your system on partition one and put your applications and paging file on partition two.

- **Three drives**   With three drives, you can realize much better performance by mirroring drives one and two and dedicating the third drive for paging use only. Create two partitions on the mirrored drives. Install your system on partition one and your applications on partition two.

- **Four drives**   With four drives, mirror drives one and two, and mirror drives three and four. Put the system on mirrored drives one and two and the applications and paging file on mirrored drives three and four.

- **Five drives**   With five drives, mirror drives one and two, and mirror drives three and four. Dedicate drive five for paging use only. Use drives one and two for the system and drives three and four for applications. If you do not think you will have enough capacity for applications, you can instead opt to make drives three, four, and five a RAID 5 partition. However, you will need to move the paging file to this partition, which will decrease performance.

If you have additional drives available, you can create multiple drives for your paging file and span the file across them. Windows 2000 will automatically determine write paging file updates to the least busy drive. You also might find in your environment that you get better performance by splitting the paging file across your paging drive and application drive.

Other Important Planning Decisions

You need to make several other important decisions while planning to install and configure your server, but they all boil down to one thing: simplicity. The simpler you make your server and the fewer features and services you install, the easier you will be able to troubleshoot it and the better it will perform. A key tenet of Terminal Server configuration is to run only what is absolutely needed and nothing more.

Here are the main points to remember:

- **Make it a member server.**   Windows 2000 Server is such a feature-rich operating system that it is tempting to load several services onto it at one time. On any production Terminal Server, especially one that will be supporting a large number of users simultaneously, however, run it only as a member server and not a domain controller. Significant extra processing is necessary with a domain controller for handling logons and Active Directory updates. This will rob processing time from your Terminal Server users. In addition, if you intend to use MetaFrame XP realize that it is not supported on a domain controller, only member servers.

- **Do not install unnecessary services or BackOffice products.** Reliability and performance are both good reasons not to load multiple services on top of Terminal Server. The more services you load, the greater the chance that a software bug will either down your server with the dreaded blue screen of death, cause a memory leak, or hoard your processing resources. When installing your server, only install the minimum number of operating system components that you need installed. Unless absolutely necessary do not install BackOffice products, such as Exchange or SQL on your Terminal Server.

- **Back up remotely.**   In general, it is best to back up your server remotely across a high-speed link instead of loading complicated and bulky backup software locally. If you do load backup software locally, go with a tape drive and SCSI card that have been tested to work with your choice of backup software. Because tape and SCSI card drivers are kernel-level software, they are a potential source of serious problems. The built-in NT Backup utility is an excellent choice for simple local backup.

   One of the biggest concerns with running backup software locally is the amount of processing and memory resources that backup software tends to need during backups and restores. Backups should be done at off-peak times, such as at night. If you have to do a restore of a set of files for a user, also try to do the restore during off-peak times. With some backup software, even a small restore can rob significant processing power and memory from the rest of the applications running on your server.

- **Store data centrally.** Try not to store too much data on the server itself. This results in a large backup and restore window. In case of hardware failure, you want to be able to bring up your server as quickly as possible. It is recommended that you save space for only your applications, operating systems, and user settings directories. Data should be stored on other servers and accessed with shares. Of course, with databases and other data-intensive applications, it might be necessary to keep the data locally.

Overall it is very important to keep in mind the concept of simplicity. The simpler your setup, the easier it will be to troubleshoot and often the better it will perform.

Choosing the Mode for Terminal Services

During the installation of Terminal Services, you will need to decide whether to run Terminal Services in Remote Administration mode or Application Server mode. The following sections provide you with more information on the exact effects of each choice.

The Effects of Choosing Remote Administration Mode

Remote Administration mode is provided to allow for remote control of your server using the Terminal Services client. With Remote Administration mode, you can have up to two concurrent users remote controlling the server at the same time. Because Terminal Services are available on all Windows 2000 servers, adding Terminal Services and enabling it in Remote Administration mode is a convenient, and *free* way to enable remote access to your server.

Remote Administration mode is also very useful for testing. Because no licenses are used up or required for Remote Administration mode, you can set up a test Terminal Server in this mode and use it for testing applications or for running administrative tools remotely. Citrix MetaFrame XP also can be installed on a Terminal Server in Remote Administration mode. This means you can use the server to test your applications with Citrix.

It is important to realize that there are also security differences between Remote Administration mode and Application Server mode. Remote Administration mode is designed for use by administrative-level users. You do not have the option to make permissions compatible with Windows NT 4.0, as you will see in the next section. Although performance testing can be done in Remote Administration mode, do not choose this mode for user security testing.

Author's Note

Be sure you are certain before you choose the mode in which you intend to run your Terminal Server. If you later change your mind and switch modes or uninstall Terminal Services, this can cause some applications that you have installed to fail. Be prepared to reinstall your applications on the server if you need to switch modes.

The Effects of Choosing Application Server Mode

Application Server mode is the mode you need to choose for your production Terminal Servers that will be handling connections for multiple users. In Application Server mode, when a client connects to the server, it checks the following:

1. **Is the client already licensed?** The first thing the server checks is to see whether the client is already licensed. If it is, it skips the rest of the steps.

2. **Is there a Terminal Server License server available?** If the client does not have a license, the Terminal Server will query the network to determine whether there is a special Terminal Server License server available. If not, it will assign a "90-day temporary pass" to the client. This will allow the client to connect for up to 90 days for free. If on day 91 the client tries to connect and a Terminal Server License server still can't be found, its connection will be rejected. If a license server is found, whether on day 1 or day 91, it will go on to step 3.

3. **Terminal Server License server issues a license.** The Terminal Server License server will now issue a permanent license to the client. The client stores the license number in its local Registry. The next time it connects, it will show that it is already licensed in step 1. If no licenses are available, however, the Terminal Server License server will not return anything to the client. If the client still has a valid 90-day temporary pass, they will still be able to connect; if it is past 90 days, however, the connection attempt will be rejected.

Permissions Compatible with Windows NT 4.0 or Windows 2000

During the installation of Terminal Server, you also have to decide whether you want permissions compatible with Windows NT 4.0 or with Windows 2000. The difference between these two permission modes is not documented at the level of detail you might need to understand. The sections that follow explain why.

The Way Security Was in Windows NT 4.0 Terminal Server

In Windows NT 4.0, the Everyone group was used extensively on both the server files and in the directories for granting rights. The problem with doing this was that the Everyone group included *everyone*, including a special type of user called an *anonymous user*, which does not require a username or password to make a network connection to a Windows NT 4.0 server. This anonymous user was used for various security exploits in Windows NT 4.0, which could be resolved only by applying the latest service pack.

The Everyone group was also, by default, given read/write access to the HKLM\Software key in the Registry. For those who are not familiar with the Registry, this key is a very important part of the Registry where software settings are written when applications are first installed. This area of the Registry is shared by all users. Any changes to the Registry keys in this area can affect all the users on the system.

In a single-user environment, this is not much of a problem. Changes made to the system area of the Registry will affect only one user. In a Terminal Server multiuser environment, however, there is the potential for one user to make a change to this part of the Registry that will affect all users on the system. For example, a user might change an application setting such as changing the background color. If the application writes this to the system area of the Registry, the background color will be changed for all users who use the application on the system.

The Changes to Security in Windows 2000

Because of this and other security issues, the default security was radically revamped in Windows 2000. Although things might appear the same to the casual user, several important changes have taken place under the hood.

The first change is that the Everyone group has been removed from most default file and Registry security settings and replaced by the local Users group, including on the HKLM\Software key.

Second, the local Users group now includes two special built-in groups called NT Authority\Interactive and NT Authority\Authenticated Users by default. This basically means that if you are logged on interactively, meaning at the console or through Terminal Server, or if you have logged on to the server across the network but are not anonymous, you are a member of the local User group on the server.

Instead of granting the local User group read/write access to the HKLM\Software key, it now only has read access by default. However, Administrators and Power Users are still given read/write access, so that they can install applications, because nearly all applications write changes to this key when they are first installed.

With this default security setup, applications will *not* be able to record settings in the HKLM\Software key when run by a *regular user*. If the applications need to record settings, such as a change to the background color, they need to write to an area of the Registry dedicated to just that user, rather than the system area. That way, any setting changes in the application will affect only that user and not everyone in the system.

How the Permission Modes Work

Although this is a much better security setup than before, some older applications were not written to work this way. They might require that a user can make changes to the system area of the Registry. If you are logged on as a regular user to Windows 2000, these applications might fail to run or error out when the user attempts some particular operation. Although applications should not be written to modify the system area of memory during normal use, you might be stuck with one that does and you have to make it work!

To enable you to fix this problem, Microsoft created a simple solution. There is a new built-in group in Windows 2000 Server called the *TERMINAL SERVER USER* group. This group is given read/write access to the HKLM\Software key and to other important areas of the Registry and file system.

If you are running Windows 2000 Terminal Server in Permissions Compatible with Windows NT 4.0 mode, you are automatically made a member of the TERMINAL SERVER USER group when you log on to Terminal Server or interactively through the console. This grants you read/write access to the HKLM\Software key along with added access to other select areas of the Registry and file system. If you are running an older application that needs read/write access to HKLM\Software, it should work fine.

If you chose to run Terminal Server in Permissions Compatible with Windows 2000, you are *not* made a member of the TERMINAL SERVER USER group when you log on. Because you are a member of the local User group, you will at least have read access to the HKLM\Software key, but you will *not* have write access unless you are an Administrator or Power User. This means that older applications that need to write to the HKLM\Software key will not work correctly.

Choosing the Appropriate Permissions Mode

So how do you choose which mode to run in? The recommended choice is always to run in the more secure Permissions Compatible with Windows 2000 mode. This will work with nearly all modern applications without a problem. If, during initial user testing on the system, you find an application that is having an unusual problem with a setting change or errors out unexpectedly, try switching back to Window NT 4.0 Compatibility mode and see whether the problem goes away. You can switch back and forth between these modes very easily by doing the following (also see Figure 7.1):

1. Run the Terminal Services Configuration application, located in the Administrative Tools folder.

2. Open the Server Settings folder on the left by clicking it.

3. Change the Permissions Settings to either Windows 2000 or Windows NT 4.0 Compatibility as needed.

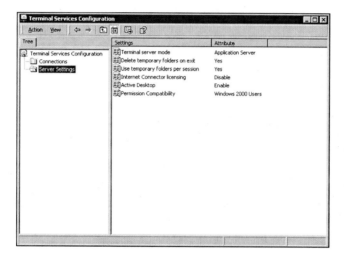

Figure 7.1 Terminal Services configuration tool.

One final note is that if you are running your Terminal Server in Remote Administration mode for testing purposes, you will not have a choice of the permissions' compatibility mode. You will be forced to use Permissions Compatible with Windows 2000. To test your applications, it is recommended to run in Application Server mode, so that you can switch between compatibility modes if an issue arises. Take advantage of the 90-day grace period to do your testing. Past the 90 days, you will start using up TS CALs on your test machines.

Documentation During the Planning and Testing Stage

Documentation is a very important factor in your server's reliability. Your server documentation should start before you begin the initial work with the server. Documentation is important in every part of a server's life, including the initial planning stages, installation, and maintenance.

Basic Server Documentation

When you first begin to plan and test your Terminal Server network, you should document the many decisions that need to be made and the criteria by which you made them. Planning and testing involves several important steps. From each step, you should create a document to record what was decided during that step. Although the particular steps might vary depending on your environment, here are some suggested documents for common planning and testing steps:

- **Network design document**   Having both physical and logical network design documents is important for making future network troubleshooting easier.

- **Performance testing and baseline documents**   One of the most important parts of planning and testing is ensuring that the performance of your Terminal Server is adequate. Chapter 21 covers performance testing in detail. Before putting your server into production, be sure to read that chapter and perform adequate performance testing.

- **Application installation document**   The steps necessary to install an application onto Terminal Server can differ significantly from normal application installation. It is very important to document your application installations thoroughly. Chapter 13, "Installing Applications," covers application installation in detail. It is easiest to create this document before you install your first application.

- **Naming standards document**   As you create your Terminal Server and its users, groups, and printers, it is important to follow a naming standard. The best time to produce a naming standards document is before setting up the servers.

- **Server log**   In environments where there is significant change or more than one administrator, keeping a server log is very important. This can be just a text document on the drive or a logbook kept next to the server. You need to keep track of any hardware or software change to the server other than simple configuration changes.

Setting Up a Periodic Maintenance and Monitoring Program

For those who come from a military background, you will recognize the importance of periodic maintenance and monitoring for keeping critical systems running smoothly. Of all the things you can do to keep your server environment running as smoothly as possible, this step is the most critical. Even in small shops, you can squeeze out that extra "9" of reliability by following these simple procedures.

In larger shops, these procedures are essential. Because you likely have more than one person who supports your Terminal Servers, it is recommended to divide your Terminal Server support people up into a morning shift and evening shift. The morning shift comes in early enough that they are there at least an hour before users normally arrive. They are responsible for recording server information into a server log and running simple system tests to ensure that servers are ready to handle the daily load. They need to be proactive in identifying problems before they occur and take quick action if necessary.

The evening team is responsible for planned server updates and hardware upgrades. They typically stay at least three hours past when users normally leave. They also are responsible for periodic maintenance that might affect server usage.

Daily Monitoring

To start your own period maintenance program, you need to create two documents. The first is a Terminal Server System Log Sheet. You can create this document in Excel. Use at least 11" × 17" paper for the log sheet. This log normally will have a list of days on the left and a list of system checks across the top. The following are some of the system checks you should record in this log every day:

- **Record system and application drive space for every server.** You can easily gather this type of information centrally. One of my favorite tools to do this is Hyena, by Adkins Resources, available at www.systemtools.com. Using the graphical interface on this tool, you can quickly view drive statistics for your servers. Vendor-specific server monitoring tools, such as Compaq Insight Manager, are also a good choice for this need.

- **Record unusual errors in the System, Security, and Application event logs.**   Check the event logs on each server for unusual errors. I recommend briefly checking the event logs once a day and addressing any critical or unusual problems that day. On your monthly periodic maintenance, print out the logs or centrally archive them, so that they can easily be searched.

- **Check all published apps.**   Make sure you can get into each of your published applications and can do a simple function, such as print a document. Watch the logon process closely for unusual errors. In large environments, this might be impractical, so focus on critical, widely used applications. Be sure to do these tests with a test user account and not an administrative account to verify that possible security changes from the night before did not affect your user. For Terminal Server administrators, use Connection Manager and create connections to either your server applications or desktops, depending on how your typical users are set up.

- **Record number of hung users.**   Check for users whose accounts are locked in the system or who are in a disconnected state since the preceding day. You might have to manually reset them. If you see this situation frequently, look into adjusting your timeouts as shown in Chapter 9, "Setting Up Terminal Server Users."

- **Record memory usage.**   Check memory usage on each of your servers. Look for unusual amounts of memory usage caused by leaky applications.

- **Record Terminal Server and MetaFrame licensing.**   Make sure your Terminal Services Licensing server has sufficient TS CALs available and that the service is running. Also check that the licensing on your MetaFrame server farm is reported correctly in the CMC.

- **Schedule virus scans and check virus logs.**   Always schedule for a daily virus scan on all of your servers and check the virus logs daily. Viruses can wreak havoc on your environment and are more likely in a multiuser situation.

- **Check drive status.**   Check your drives for failure indicators on all your servers. In addition, if you have an LCD panel that records errors, check it for unusual errors during the night.

- **Check network monitoring logs.**   If you have a network monitoring system, make sure to check the logs to see whether the server rebooted itself or any connection errors occurred during the evening.

- **Check SNMP logs.**   If you have MetaFrame XPe, you can now monitor your servers even more closely using an SNMP management package. Check for traps or unusual events in SNMP.

Setting Up Automated Monitoring

If you have MetaFrame XPe, it is highly recommended to set up monitoring of your servers using SNMP. This is covered in detail in Chapter 24, "Advanced Network Management and Monitoring." With XPe, you also can set up Resource Monitoring to a central database. You will find out how to do this in Chapter 21. Whether you monitor via SNMP or Resource Monitoring, checking these monitoring logs should be a part of your daily routine.

Even if you do not have these resources available, you can follow some simple steps in Performance Monitor to help increase your system reliability. Performance Monitor in Windows 2000 is significantly more advanced than in Windows NT 4.0.

To set up Performance Monitor, so that you can record the server's performance during the day, follow these steps:

1. Open Performance Monitor from Control Panel, Administrative Tools. You can put a shortcut to open Performance Monitor automatically every time the server starts by creating a shortcut in the Startup folder for PERFMON.EXE.

2. Click System Monitor.

3. On the right, click the plus sign (+) to add the following performance counters for your server:

   - *Processor / % Processor Time*   Either total or for each processor.

   - *Processor / Processor Queue Length*   Either total or for each processor.

   - *Terminal Server / Inactive Session*   This will give you an idea as to whether people leave their sessions logged on for long periods of time.

   - *Terminal Server / Total Sessions*   The total number of sessions. This is a very good counter for tracking server usage during the day.

   - *Paging File / % Usage*   Percentage usage of the paging file. This gives you a good idea of whether you need to adjust your paging file size.

   - *Print Queue / Jobs*   This will give you a better idea of how often your users print.

   - *Print Queue / Bytes Printed per Sec*   This is important for determining the size of documents that your users print in general.

   - *Server / Bytes Total per Sec*   Indicates how many bytes per second are being sent and received by your servers. This is a good indicator of how busy your server and network card are.

   - *Memory / Pages per Sec*   Indicates the number of pages per second where your system needed to retrieve information from the paging file on the hard drive. The greater this number, the less effective your system is at keeping what is needed the most in memory. This is usually due to a lack of memory, but also can be caused by heavy server usage.

If this number is always high and you know you have enough memory, make sure that your paging file is on the highest performance drives possible and does not share the system drive.

- *Logical Disk / % Free Space* Put a counter up for every drive in the system. Making sure there is enough space is critical with Terminal Server.

You also can select to add performance counters from remote servers if this is the central Performance Monitoring workstation.

4. Now that your counters are all up, click the System Monitor Properties button shown in Figure 7.2 with an arrow next to it.

5. In the System Monitors Properties window, click the General tab. Change the Update Automatically Interval to a larger interval, because you will be looking at this only once a day. I recommend either 900 (15 minutes), 1800 (30 minutes), or 3600 (1 hour).

6. Click the Graph tab and change the Title, Graphs, and Scale if needed, and then click OK.

You can record this information on your daily rounds and use it to determine whether there are any problems you should be looking at. You can either run Performance Monitor on the console of each server or, better yet, run it on a central network monitoring workstation and set it up to record performance information from each of your servers remotely.

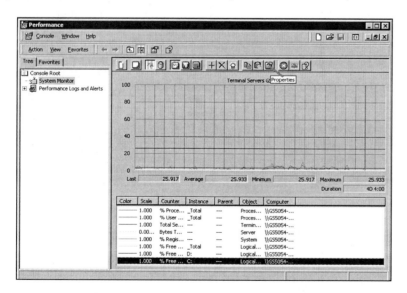

Figure 7.2 Setting up Performance Monitor.

Now that Performance Monitor is set up properly to monitor the critical parameters of your server, add a check of Performance Monitor and the recording of the statistics to your daily rounds. It would be a good idea to record the following numbers in the daily log:

- Maximum number of sessions
- Maximum paging file usage
- Percentage of free space on each drive
- Maximum pages per sec
- Maximum inactive sessions

Saving Your Performance Monitor Settings

Setting up Performance Monitor in this fashion can be very useful and an inexpensive way to help ensure the reliability of your Terminal Server systems. However, it is a major pain to have to set up this stuff all over every time you run Performance Monitor. Now in Performance Monitor for Windows 2000, there is an easy way to save your settings. Here is how:

1. Set up Performance Monitor with all the counters you need from all the servers you intend to monitor.

2. Click the Copy Properties button in Performance Monitor. It is located just to the left of the Properties button, which is pointed to in Figure 7.2.

3. Go into Notepad and select Edit, Paste (or press Ctrl+V).

4. Save the Notepad document to the desktop as Performance SETTINGS.TXT.

Next time you want to set up Performance Monitor, just open it up and paste in the contents of the Performance SETTINGS.TXT file from your desktop. To paste in the settings, follow these steps:

1. Open the Performance SETTINGS.TXT document in Notepad.

2. Press Ctrl+A to select all and then Ctrl+C to copy it to the Clipboard.

3. Open Performance Monitor and click the Paste Counter List button. The button is located to the right of the Copy button you pressed earlier.

You should now see all the performance counters set up just the way you had them before! If you want to automate this process even further, you could install a macro utility to record the keystrokes and mouse movements necessary to do this. Then you would play them back when the computer was started.

Monthly and Quarterly Maintenance

Besides the daily monitoring, you should do a few things on a monthly or quarterly basis. These tasks are somewhat involved but should be put on a schedule and done regularly.

The following items should be done at least once per month:

- **Defragment the drives.** Run a defragmentation utility that has the capability of defragmenting both the drive and the paging file. The one built in to Windows 2000 can be scheduled for a weekly defrag on the weekends. However, you should ensure that all drives, including the paging file, are defragmented once a month. The free utility Page Defrag, from www.sysinternals.com, can handle defragmenting your paging file on reboot, whereas you can use the built-in defragmenter for the rest.

- **Archive the event logs.** Set up the event logs so that they do not overwrite information for 45 days. Then, once a month, archive the event logs to a central location. Several third-party tools will do this automatically for you. The Event Log Manager at www.systemtools.com is an excellent utility for doing this.

- **Review the logs for patterns.** Review the daily logs you collected for unusual patterns or patterns that might lead to system problems, such as a gradual increase in concurrent users or drive space usage.

- **Reboot the server.** Your Terminal Servers should be rebooted at least once per month. Depending on the applications you run, you might want to even schedule a weekly or daily reboot. Rebooting the server clears the memory and the temp files out.

- **Do a test restore.** Verifying that your backups are working properly and that you can restore information is a very good choice. Make especially sure that central user information areas, such as profile directories and data directories, are being backed up properly and can be restored quickly.

- **Verify performance settings.** Several Registry tweaks and other performance settings can help your servers under heavy loads. Be sure to record the performance changes you make on your servers and verify that these performance changes are in place on all of your servers using this checklist.

The following items are more involved and should be done once per quarter:

- **Do a planned failure test to verify load balancing.** If you use load balancing for failover to a set of emergency backup servers, you need to test that this failover works at least once a quarter. This needs to be planned in advance with your users.

- **Practice a rebuild from an image.** On a test server, practice rebuilding the server from scratch using imaging technology. Make sure everyone on your team knows how to do this quickly and efficiently.

Top-Ten Installation Planning Tips

This chapter discussed many of the decisions you need to make when installing Terminal Server. Now it's time to summarize those decisions in a top ten list:

1. **Per 500MHz processor, 10 to 65 users; 150MB minimum plus 10 to 30MB memory per user.** These are good rough guidelines to start with, but they do not supplant proper performance testing. In addition, add another 64MB to your calculations if you intend to run Citrix MetaFrame XP.

2. **Use only hardware that is on the HCL.** It is important to verify that your hardware is on the HCL. The list is also a good starting point for collecting the drivers you need for installation.

3. **Gather together the drivers for your hard drive adapter card, NIC card, video card, and HAL prior to installation.** The install process forces you to load a hard drive adapter, network card, video card, and HAL. If the drivers are not included with Windows NT's base set of drivers, you will need to have the driver disks in hand.

4. **Make sure all processors and other hardware, such as NIC cards, are installed prior to installing the operating system.** Prior to installation, check in your BIOS to ensure that the system has detected all installed hardware and that the interrupt levels do not conflict.

5. **Use NTFS for system partition. Do not use FAT and then convert to NTFS later.** At the end of the installation process, a default security setup is applied to your NTFS partition. If you choose FAT for your system partition, this security is not applied, even if you later convert the partition to NTFS.

6. **Documentation starts here.** Start documenting your server during the initial installation.

7. **Use hardware level RAID 1 or RAID 5.** Using RAID greatly improves your server's reliability. Using the software-level RAID that comes with Windows NT can tax your processing power.

8. **Simplify the server.** Do not run unnecessary applications or services on your Terminal Server.

9. **Use a high-speed network adapter and lock your speed, transceiver, and duplex options.**   A slow network adapter can easily become a bottleneck. Manually force your speed, transceiver, and duplex options instead of having the card auto-detect them.

10. **Prepare for fast recovery.**   Keep together your installation documentation and driver disks near the server to speed disaster recovery.

Implementing a Windows Terminal Server and Citrix MetaFrame Solution

8

Installing Windows 2000 Terminal Server and Citrix MetaFrame

CHAPTER 7, "PLANNING FOR THE INSTALLATION of Terminal Server and Citrix MetaFrame," focused on the many decisions that you need to make both prior to and during the install of Terminal Server. It is time to cover the installation itself. If you are already very familiar with the installation of Windows 2000 Server and Terminal Services, skip to the "Installing Terminal Services Licensing" section. For those who are not, however, you will learn a lot of Terminal Server installation tips that are good to know about.

Installing Terminal Server

This section discusses the general steps and decisions you need to make during the install of Windows 2000 Server in preparation for it to become a Terminal Server. Remember that a Windows 2000 Terminal Server is just a Windows 2000 server with Terminal Services installed. You can add Terminal Services at any time to your Windows 2000 server to make it into a Terminal Server.

Windows NT 4.0 and Windows .NET Terminal Server Administrators

In the Windows NT 4.0 world, you had to buy a separate Windows NT 4.0 Terminal Server product to get Terminal Services. However, starting with Windows 2000 and also now available in Windows .NET, Terminal Services is an add-on service rather than a separate product. This is a big difference. As an administrator, this means you can turn any of your Windows 2000 or Windows .NET servers into Terminal Servers at any time or you can remove Terminal Services at any time, just like any other installable service for the Windows Server platforms.

Although the instructions in this chapter are geared specifically toward the installation of Windows 2000 Server, you will find that many of the concepts covered and general steps apply to all versions of Terminal Server, including the new Windows .NET Terminal Server.

Minimum Requirements

For the sake of completeness, the following is a list of the minimum requirements for Windows 2000 Server and Windows 2000 Advanced Server from Microsoft:

- Minimum of an Intel Pentium 133 MHz
- Minimum of 256MB recommended (128MB is the absolute minimum, and the maximum is 4GB for Windows 2000 Server, 8GB for Advanced Server, and 32GB for DataCenter Server)
- 1GB of hard drive space

Even though these are the printed minimums, I would not recommend building a production server with any less than the following:

- **Minimum of Intel Pentium 733MHz**   System should be at least dual-processor capable for future expandability.
- **Minimum of 512MB**   However, you need to calculate your memory requirements carefully, as shown in Chapter 7, based on the number of maximum concurrent users and the memory usage of the applications they run.
- **Minimum of 4GB on system drive**   Never build a production Terminal Server with less than 4GB. Terminal Server has special space requirements, as covered in Chapter 7, which go beyond normal space usage of a Windows 2000 operating system.
- **Separate partition or preferably drive for the paging file**   This should be more than twice the size of installed memory.

Installation Options

If you will be installing Terminal Server in production, a fresh install is the only recommended choice. Starting with a fresh install onto a formatted hard drive is the best bet for a successful installation and a reliable server.

To set up a Windows 2000 Terminal Server, you must first install Windows 2000 Server. If you are already familiar with this process, skip ahead to the "Installing Terminal Services" section.

The first step of the install process begins with deciding what media will be used to install Terminal Server. You can choose from several different installation methods available: CD-ROM, network installation, and server imaging.

Terminal Server CD-ROM

The simplest installation method by far is booting off the operating system CD-ROM. This method is supported on most major servers today that support booting off of the CD drive. However, this feature might need to be enabled in the BIOS of your server. The procedures for doing this depend on the make and model of your system. Refer to your manufacturer for information on whether your server supports bootable CD-ROMs and how to enable them.

If your server does not support bootable CD-ROMs, you can use the boot floppy disks instead. Creating the boot floppy disks under Windows 2000 is different from Windows NT 4.0. With Windows 2000 Server, you need to run the MAKEBT32.EXE program from the [cd]:\bootdisk directory on the operating system install CD. You will need a set of four blank, formatted disks. Be aware that this method takes quite a bit of time to create the floppy disks and boot off of them. Only use this method if your server does not support bootable CDs and you do not have a Windows operating system installed where you can access the install files from the CD.

If you do have an older version of Windows installed, it will be easier to do the upgrade by running the WINNT32.EXE program from the [cd]:\i386 directory on the CD. This procedure will work from any 32-bit version of Windows. When you run WINNT32.EXE and follow the wizard, it will copy a set of install files to the local machine automatically and reboot the system. When running WINNT32.EXE, it is recommended to use the /makelocalsource command switch. This will copy the full set of operating system files to the hard drive of the machine, so that you will not need the CD after the install is complete. Make sure you have room. You should never install Terminal Server on any partition less than 4GB in size, unless of course for testing, so you should have plenty of space.

Windows 2000 and Service Pack Slipstream Installs

Windows 2000 comes with a very useful feature referred to as *Service Pack Slipstream Installs*. In Window NT 4.0 Terminal Server, you would always have to install the operating system off of the CD first and then install the latest service pack from another CD. In addition, if you installed any new system components from the operating system CD, you would have to reinstall the service pack to get the latest fixes for that component.

Now with Windows 2000 Server, you can update your install files with the service pack before installing! This makes installs much quicker and easier and gives you an updated source that you can use to install additional operating system components without having to reinstall the service pack.

The easiest way to get the version of the server operating system CDs is to be a member of a Microsoft program such as MSDN, Select, or TechNet—which entitle you to receive automatically a new set of operating system CDs with the service packs already included when new service packs are released. If you do not have access to CDs through one of these programs, however, you can perform the following steps to update your install source with a service pack:

1. Download the network installation files for the latest service pack to a folder on your network and expand the files.

2. Run update.exe –s:[OS path] from the service pack directory, where OS path is the drive path to the install files for Windows 2000 Server that you want to update.

Network Installation

An alternative method for larger rollouts is doing a network installation. With a network installation, you have a lot of control over the automation of your Windows 2000 Server installation. If you are rolling out several Terminal Servers or would like to have a means of quick recovery, network installation is a good choice.

To perform a network installation, follow these three steps:

1. You must copy the install CD to one of the servers on your network. Because the install CD is large, you must have around 400MB of space available to copy down the entire CD. If you are short on space on the network, you can just copy down the \i386, \bootdisk, and \clients directory.

2. You need to create a network boot disk. The network boot disk is a bootable DOS or Win98 disk that contains FORMAT.EXE, FDISK.EXE, and enough drivers to attach to the network server on which you have the copy of the CD.

3. You must perform the install. This involves booting from the disk, mapping a local drive to the server on the network that has the install files, and running WINNT.EXE from the \i386 directory, the 16-bit version

of the install program. If you are good with batch files, create a batch file that will walk through the format automatically, copy the contents of the \i386 directory to an \i386 directory on the hard drive, and then run the WINNT.EXE setup program.

Creating a Network Boot Disk

The methods of making a network boot disk have almost become an arcane science in today's world of bootable CDs and imaging software. Depending on your environment, however, network boot discs can be a great solution for you for installing not only Windows 2000 Server but also other workstation and server operating systems.

Novell NetWare has always been one of the most "network boot disk"–friendly operating systems around. Novell fully supports their DOS client and most network card manufacturers make DOS versions of their network cards drives that will work with Novell. If you have NetWare 5, go to http://support.novell.com and search for article number 2957107. This Novell Technical Information Document will walk you through in detail all the steps you need to know about for creating a network boot disk that will enable you to boot up and connect to a NetWare 5 server via TCP/IP and map a drive to it to get to the Windows 2000 Server install files.

Microsoft, on the other hand, has not included the boot disk creator in Windows 2000. If you want to make a Microsoft network boot disk, you need to find your Windows NT 4.0 Server CD. Under the \clients\msclient\ netsetup directory, run SETUP from DOS. This setup program will help you create a network boot disk, but is limited to only a handful of drivers. However, many manufacturers still make DOS-based drivers for Microsoft, referred to as NDIS drivers, which you can use to create the boot disk for your operating system.

Server Imaging

Over the past few years, server imaging has grown from a seldom-used and troublesome technique to a widely accepted and supported means of deploying large numbers of servers. Server imaging using programs such as Symantec Ghost is a top choice for large enterprise Terminal Server rollouts. Without too much effort, you can create a bootable server image CD that you can use to install any new server in less than a half hour with almost no user intervention!

The biggest difference with Windows 2000 that makes imaging more feasible is the new Plug-and-Play technology. You can easily create a base system image and install it on all of your servers, even if the hardware varies. This is because Windows 2000 will automatically detect hardware changes and install the correct drivers for you, even if the original image did not have them installed.

The first step for creating your bootable CD is to set up the server the way you need it and then use Microsoft's free SYSPREP utility to prepare it for imaging. You will find the SYSPREP utility in the compressed

DEPLOY.CAB file located on your operating system CD under `[cd]:\`
`support\tools`. You can run the following command from the command
prompt to extract the files from DEPLOY.CAB:

```
expand deploy.cab [destination] -f:*
```

This will expand the entire contents of the DEPLOY.CAB file to the
`[destination]` directory. Read through the information on SYSPREP
located in the DEPLOY.CHM help file to get more familiar with how the
utility works. You will also find detailed instructions on how to create your
own unattended installation file in the UNATTEND.DOC.

In short, SYSPREP.EXE is a utility that you run on a server when it is
ready to be imaged. What SYSPREP does is clean out the system-specific
information on the server, such as the SID information, and prepares it to be
imaged. It then installs a special mini-setup bootup wizard. At this point, the
server is ready to be imaged.

After you restore the image onto a new server and boot the new system
for the first time, you will be brought directly to the mini-setup wizard. This
wizard will quickly walk you through the machine-specific choices you need
to make for this machine, such as time zone, server name, domain membership, and administrator password. When finished, your imaged server is ready
for use! Even though the server name is different and this is a different
machine, you will be able to run all the applications that were on the original image.

In addition, as you can read about in the UNATTEND.DOC, there is a
simple procedure for making an answer file that will enable you to answer
many of the questions in the mini-setup in advance, such as the server time
zone, and even run other applications after the mini-setup has finished. In
this way, you can speed the imaging process even further.

To create your own Terminal Server SYSPREP image, follow these steps:

1. Install Windows 2000 Server and Terminal Services as shown in this section on a test server.

2. Apply the latest service pack if you are not using a slipstream install.

3. Create a `\tech` directory on the root of the server drive and copy the
   install files for any system specific hardware drivers that you might need
   locally on the systems you intend to install the image on, such as video
   drivers, network drivers, or drive array utilities.

4. Install any basic applications or utilities you want on all of your servers. If
   you will be using MetaFrame XPe, use MetaFrame XPe's application
   packaging and installation technologies to install applications instead of
   installing the applications on your image.

5. If this is a MetaFrame server, at this point, you need to go through the special procedures under the sidebar that follows, "Imaging a MetaFrame XP Server."

6. Copy SYSPREP.EXE to the server from where you expanded the DEPLOY.EXE file and run it from the command prompt of the server.

7. If you have created an unattended install file, save it as SYSPREP.INF under the `c:\sysprep` directory on the server.

8. Image the server using your preferred imaging software.

9. Reformat the server and restore the image to the server.

10. Boot the server and go through the mini-setup process.

11. Make sure that the server and all the applications work.

12. When your image is set the way you want it, create a bootable CD or some other easy process for distributing the image to new servers.

One gotcha to be aware of is to make sure that the *Hardware Application Layer* (HAL) driver you use in your image is the same as the one that will be used on your servers. The HAL driver is the one that directly interacts with your system processor. Different system processor types have different HALS. If the HAL on your image differs from the HAL needed by the system you are trying to put the image onto, the imaging process still might work, however you will likely have to manually switch to the correct HAL. You can check what HAL is being used on your server by doing the following:

1. Go into Control Panel.

2. Double-click System.

3. From the System window that appears, click the Hardware tab.

4. Click Device Manager, under the Hardware tab, to open the Device Manager for the server.

5. Double-click Computer.

Underneath the Computer folder, you will see the name of the HAL. Make sure this is the same HAL as is on your image. If not, you will need to test whether this image will work for your servers.

Imaging a MetaFrame XP Server

Imaging a MetaFrame XP server is very possible. However, you will not be able to image the *data store* (DS) server or a server where there is an SSL certificate installed. The following steps are recommended for the preparation of your server:

1. Stop the IMA Service on the server and delete the follow values from the Registry. These will be re-created from the DS when you restart the service later:

   - `HKLM\Software\Citrix\IMA\Runtime\HostId`

   - `HKLM\Software\Citrix\IMA\Runtime\ImaPort`

   - `HKLM\Software\Citrix\IMA\Runtime\MasterRanking`

   - `HKLM\Software\Citrix\IMA\Runtime\PSRequired`

   - `HKLM\Software\Citrix\IMA\Runtime\RassPort`

   - `HKLM\Software\Citrix\IMA\Runtime\ZoneName`

2. Set the IMA Service to start manually.

3. Now continue with the imaging of the server.

When your image is done, set the IMA Service back to automatically start and restart the service.

After you image a new server, you will need to do the following for it to join the server farm correctly:

1. Make sure the machine name is different from the first server and the SIDs have been replaced. Using the SYSPREP technique shown previously, this will be automatically taken care of.

2. Do a search for the WFCNAME.INI file and change the server name in the file to the new server name.

3. If you are using a SQL or Oracle DS, do a search for the MF20.DSN file. This is normally located under the installation directory for Citrix MetaFrame: `%program files%\citrix\independent` management architecture.

4. Edit the file and remove the `WSID` parameter, which contains the name of the old server.

5. Change the old server host name under the following Registry key to the new one:

   `HKLM\Software\Citrix\IMA\ServerHost`

6. Now start the IMA Service.

Verify that the server connects correctly to the farm by running the `qfarm` command from the command line. Go into the Citrix Management Console and ensure the server is displayed. Right-click the server, select Properties, click the Information tab, and ensure the product code is correct. If not, change it by right-clicking the server, selecting Set MetaFrame Product Code, and entering the product code that you need.

Installing Windows 2000 Server

The first part of installing Windows 2000 Terminal Server is installing the Windows 2000 Server itself. For those who are already intimately familiar with this process, or whose server is already set up, skip ahead to the "Installing Terminal Services" section. For those who are not as familiar with it, however, you will be guided through the process and the important decisions you need to make during the install for a server that will become a Terminal Server.

For those who have installed Windows NT before, the process for installing Windows 2000 Server is nearly identical. The install is still started by using either WINNT.EXE or WINNT32.EXE, booting from the Terminal Server CD-ROM, or with the install floppy disks. This leads you to the character-based portion of the install. During this part, your initial hardware is detected and an initial set of files is copied to your server. The server then reboots into the graphical portion of the setup, where the installation is finished. The next few sections cover this installation process in detail.

Starting the Install

The installation process can be started in any of three ways. The first way is to run `winnt` or `winnt32` from the command prompt of your server. This is the option you would normally take if you were upgrading from Windows NT 4.0 Terminal Server to Windows 2000. The install program will load the Windows 2000 boot sector on the machine and some startup installation files, and then reboot the server.

The second and simplest option is to just boot off of the CD. You also can boot off of floppy disks, but Windows 2000 now takes four boot floppy disks, not three like in Windows NT 4.0. This means if you choose to boot off of floppy disks, be prepared to wait about 15 minutes in front of the server console while you have to manually load each floppy disk. This is not a good option unless a bootable CD-ROM drive is not available.

Character-Based Stage

Upon booting into the install process, you will be taken to the initial character-based stage of the setup. During the character-based stage, the drivers for the critical components of your server, which are necessary for the GUI portion of the install, are loaded. This includes components such as the hard drive adapter, keyboard, video adapter, CPU type, and mouse.

During the character-based stage, you need to select or create the partition on the hard drive where Terminal Server is to be installed. You also need to choose whether you will format it and what file system you will use for the format. It is highly recommended to use NTFS.

The following list briefly covers the steps involved in the character-based setup:

1. At the Windows 2000 Setup screen, press Enter to begin the install.

2. The install program attempts to detect your storage devices and lists them. Make sure it detects all of your drive controllers correctly. Press s to specify additional devices or Enter to accept those listed and continue.

Author's Note

If the SCSI controller for your boot drive is not detected, you will likely have to load it before entering the installation. To do this, reboot the system and press F6 when you see the blue screen, before you get to the main install menu. You will then be able to add the driver for your hard driver controller from a floppy disk.

3. Read the Microsoft License Agreement and press F8 to accept.

4. The install program performs a search for previous Windows NT Server or Windows 2000 installations and lists them. Highlight the installation you want to upgrade, and press Enter or press N for a new install.

5. Select the partition in which Windows 2000 is to be installed from the list shown and press Enter. You also can press D at this point to delete a partition or press C to create a new one if necessary.

At this point, the install program copies an initial set of operating system files to the hard drive. After the copy is finished, you are prompted to remove any floppy disks and reboot. You are now ready to move on to the next stage of the installation process.

GUI-Based Setup

After rebooting the machine, you are taken to the graphical portion of the setup. All the devices you detected in the character-based portion of the setup should now be working, including your mouse, keyboard, video adapter, and processors. In the GUI-based portion of the setup, you are finishing up the installation. The following instructions guide you through this part of the process:

1. Click Next at the initial Windows 2000 Server Setup screens. On newer versions of the of the Windows 2000 Server CD, the system will automatically skip past nonessential intro pages and the Plug-and-Play detection.

2. Select your Locale and Keyboard Layout at the Regional Settings page, and then click Next.

3. Enter your Name and Organization at the Personalize Your Software page and click Next.

4. Select Per Seat licensing at the Licensing Modes page. Terminal Server does not legally support per-server client access licenses.

5. Enter the computer name and administrator password, then click next.

6. At the Windows 2000 Components screen, make sure that only the following items are checked. If you absolutely need other services such as IIS, check them to install. However, you should install only what is needed and no more. The following items are the minimal options required:

   - Accessories and Utilities.

   - Terminal Services.

   - If this is going to be a Terminal Services Licensing server, also select Terminal Services Licensing.

7. Enter your area code and other Modem Dialing Information, and then click Next.

8. Enter the correct date, time, and time zone, and then click Next.

9. If you selected Terminal Services, you will now be asked whether you want to run in Application Server mode or Remote Administration mode. If this server will be used as a productions server, select Application Server mode. If you will be using it only for testing and will not exceed two concurrent users, select Remote Administration mode. See the section, "Choosing the Mode for Termianl Services,"on these two modes in Chapter 7.

10. If you selected Application Server mode, you will be asked whether your users should have access permissions compatible with Windows NT 4.0 or Windows 2000. Select the one appropriate for the applications you will be running. It is highly recommended to choose Windows 2000, unless you know of an application that does not work on Windows 2000. You can easily change this later using the Terminal Services Configuration utility available in the Administrative Tools folder. For more information, see the section on these two modes in Chapter 7.

Installing the Network

At this point, the installation process will vary depending on what Windows components you selected to be installed. If your server detects that networking components are installed, the installation will attempt to automatically detect and install the network components. You will have the option of using Typical Settings or Custom Settings. Select Custom Settings, and then select Properties for TCP/IP and enter the static IP address for the server and other static networking information. Never use DHCP to obtain IP address information automatically on a production Terminal Server.

The last networking-related choice you need to make is whether to join a domain or workgroup. Enter the domain name you want to join, if this will be a member server; otherwise enter the workgroup name.

Finishing Up

After the network components have been installed and the network has been started, the install process will finish up the final steps of the install process on its own and reboot the server.

When you reboot the server, you are asked to log on for the first time to Windows 2000. If you did not install with a Windows 2000 CD that included the latest service pack, you should download and install the latest service pack now. Service packs can be found by doing a search at www.microsoft.com/downloads.

If you did not choose to install Terminal Services, you will need to follow the procedure under the "Installing Terminal Services" section. Otherwise, if you will be installing MetaFrame, skip ahead to the "Installing MetaFrame XP" section.

Installing Terminal Services

If you did not choose to install Terminal Services when initially installing Windows 2000 Server, it is very easy to add it afterward. Because of the manner in which Terminal Server needs to record application Registry changes, however, you will have to reinstall any applications that your Terminal Server users will need to run after you install Terminal Services.

The following short set of steps is all it takes to make your Windows 2000 server into a Windows 2000 Terminal Server:

1. Double-click the Add/Remove Programs icon in Control Panel.

2. From the Add/Remove Programs window, scroll down and check the box next to Terminal Services, and then click Next.

3. You will now be asked whether you want to run in Application Server mode or Remote Administration mode. Select the mode as appropriate. If this server will be used as a productions server, select Application Server mode. If you will be using it only for testing and will not exceed two concurrent users, select Remote Administration mode.

4. If you selected Application Server mode, you will be asked whether your users should have access permissions compatible with Windows NT 4.0 or Windows 2000. Select the one appropriate for the applications you will be running. Windows 2000 Compatibility mode is highly recommended, unless you know of an application that does not work on Windows 2000.

The Terminal Services software will now install on your machine. After you reboot, your Terminal Server will be ready for use.

At this point you should review some of the many Registry tweaks and performance tips in Chapter 21, "Performance Tuning and Resource Management." You should decide which performance tips to implement in your environment. Remember to make a checklist of the ones you install and verify that they have been applied on each of your servers once a month as part of your monthly maintenance.

Author's Note

You will find the 16-bit and 32-bit install files for the Terminal Services client under the %systemroot%\ system32\tsclient directory on your Terminal Server. You can run the setup program from the correct directory to install the client for testing.

Installing Service Packs

At this point, you should install the latest service pack for Windows 2000 on your Terminal Server. These service packs are very important to ensure the highest level of reliability, security, and performance of your Terminal Server solution. In addition, be very careful to ensure that the service pack level you install is the same across all the Terminal Servers. This is especially important if you intend to install Citrix MetaFrame XP on top of these servers.

As of this writing, the latest service pack for Windows 2000 Server is Service Pack 2. However, several important security-related hotfixes have been released by Microsoft that fix vulnerabilities in the RDP protocol. Be sure that you also install at least the following hotfixes from Microsoft by going to these web sites, downloading the hotfix, and installing it:

www.microsoft.com/technet/treeview/default.asp?url=/technet/security/bulletin/ MS01-052.asp

www.microsoft.com/technet/treeview/default.asp?url=/technet/security/bulletin/ MS01-040.asp

To obtain a list of all of the latest hotfixes available for your Terminal Server, go to http://windowsupdate.microsoft.com from the console of your Terminal Server.

Security Patches for Windows NT 4.0 Terminal Server Administrators

In addition to the security vulnerabilities in Windows 2000 Terminal Server, several vulnerabilities in Windows NT 4.0 Terminal Server have important patches. If you are installing a Windows NT 4.0 Terminal Server, first ensure you are running the latest service pack. Service Pack 6a is the last service pack released for Windows NT 4.0 Terminal Server. Next go to http://windowsupdate.microsoft.com from the console of the Terminal Server. From this web site, you will be able to see what additional hotfixes are available for your Terminal Server.

Installing Terminal Services Licensing

After installing Terminal Services in Application Server mode, you have 90 days to do your testing before it will start verifying licensing with a Terminal Services Licensing server on the network. Use these 90 days wisely to ensure that your solution will work as you expect it to.

After a Terminal Services Licensing server has been installed, you need to activate the server before it can start giving out Terminal Server CALs. This is done by contacting the Microsoft Licensing Clearinghouse to obtain an activation code for your server. After your server has been activated, you will need to add licenses to it, so that it can respond to license requests.

Installing the Terminal Services Licensing Service

To install a licensing server, follow these steps:

1. Go into Control Panel, Add/Remove Programs, and click Add/Remove Windows Components.

2. In the Add/Remove Windows Component window, put a check next Terminal Services Licensing and click OK.

3. Select the scope for this licensing server as either Your Entire Enterprise or Your Domain or Workgroup, enter the location for the licensing database, and click Next. Note that you will be able to select only Your Entire Enterprise if this server is set up as a domain controller. For more information on the impact of this choice, see Chapter 5, "Licensing Terminal Server and Citrix MetaFrame".

Activating the Terminal Services Licensing Server

The Terminal Services Licensing server will now begin installing. When the installation is finished, you need to go into the Terminal Services Licensing tool, which is located in the Administrative Tools folder in the Start menu, and do the following:

1. Right-click the licensing server you want to activate, and select Activate Server. If you do not see your server in the list, select Connect from the Action menu, and enter the name of the server to which you want to attach. You need to be able to ping it by name to attach through this utility.

2. Click Next at the welcome screen.

3. From the drop-down list, select Phone, Fax, Web, or Internet and click Next.

At this point, the procedure will vary depending on what you selected. Activating your server across the Internet is the easiest procedure. You do not need any codes to do this, just fill in your contact information and email address. Microsoft will send a PIN number to the email address you entered to verify that it is correct. Enter this PIN number in at the licensing server and the server will be activated.

Activating it via the web is also very easy. Just go to `https://activate.microsoft.com`. Make sure you enter the **https** in front to establish a secure channel with the activation servers. From this web page, you will be able to activate your server or add licenses for your server. You will need to enter contact information and the product code for your server. In return, you will receive a license activation code to activate your servers or add licenses.

If you choose Use Fax For Activation, you will need to select your country first. In the case of faxing your codes, you will be guided through entering your contact information. At the end of the process, you will be able to print out a sheet that includes your contact information and the product code for your server. You will receive a license code back via fax to the fax from which you called.

The final alternative is just to call the Microsoft Licensing Clearinghouse and do the process over the phone. There are different phone numbers for the clearinghouse depending on the country from which you are calling. You will be asked what your country is and then shown the phone number to call. The phone number for the United States is 888-571-2048. As of this writing the phone center is open 8 a.m. to 10 p.m. EST, Monday through Friday. This means if you will be activating a licensing server by phone, make sure to plan ahead and do it during the week. You will need to provide your contact information and server product code. In return, you will receive the activation code.

Adding Licenses to the Licensing Server

The final step before your server will be ready to serve licenses is to add them into its license pool. Adding licenses into the pool also can be done via the Internet, web, phone, or fax. The method that will be used will by default be the same method you used to activate the server. If you want to change the method for activating the licenses, follow these steps:

1. Right-click the server and select Properties.
2. Under the Connection Method tab, change the connection method to the method you want and click OK.

To add licenses you will need one of the following three codes:

- **Enrollment agreement number**   This number is provided as part of a Microsoft Select or Enterprise Licensing Agreement. These are special high-volume licensing programs available from Microsoft.
- **License code**   If you purchase a retail version of Terminal Server client access licenses, you should see a license code on a sticker on the licensing paperwork inside the product package.
- **Microsoft Open License confirmation**   In the case of licenses purchased through the Open Licensing program, you should receive an authorization number and license number from your reseller.

After you have this license code, right-click the licensing server and select Install Licenses. Depending on which connection method you chose, the procedure will vary. However, you will normally need to enter or provide the license codes you received. In return, the license will be activated or you will receive an activation code.

When the licenses are entered, Terminal Server users will be immediately able to retrieve them via the network. To monitor your license usage, just highlight the server in the Terminal Services Licensing tool. On the right you will see how many Windows 2000 Terminal Server CALs remain.

Installing MetaFrame XP

MetaFrame XP installs as an add-on option for both Windows NT 4.0 and 2000 Terminal Server. Unlike MetaFrame 1.8, where the NT 4.0 and Windows 2000 version were sold separately, MetaFrame XP's install CD has a version of MetaFrame for both operating systems. It will automatically detect during the install which type of server it is running on.

If you are installing MetaFrame XP on Windows 2000, you need to first ensure that the server has Terminal Services already installed and working. Also on either Windows NT 4.0 Terminal Server or Windows 2000 Terminal Server, make sure the latest service pack has been applied.

Setting Up the Data Store

Before you can start the install of the product itself, you need to decide where the DS will be held. If you will be using a local Microsoft Access DS, the database will automatically be configured for you on the first server you install. Skip ahead to the section, "Installing the First MetaFrame XP Server." If you intend to use a SQL or Oracle DS, follow the steps in the following two sections.

Using Microsoft Access as a Data Store

Again, remember that using Microsoft Access for a DS is not recommended except in testing environments. Even though documentation from Citrix indicates an Access database can handle up to 100 servers, Access is not an enterprise-class database system. You will find that SQL and Oracle databases, even though more expensive to set up, are by far the best choice for ensuring the highest level of reliability and performance for your MetaFrame XP Citrix server farm.

Setting Up a Microsoft SQL Database for a Data Store

For those familiar with SQL Server administration, the setup is very simple. Just create a new database and grant DB_Owner access to the database to either a Windows NT account or a SQL Server account. You will need to set up an *Open Database Connector* (ODBC) connector to this database on each MetaFrame XP server you install.

If you are not familiar with setting up databases on SQL, here are the step-by-step instructions to get you started:

1. Open up the Enterprise Manager from the SQL Server 7.0 folder in the Start menu.

2. In Enterprise Manager, right-click the Databases folder underneath the server you want to install the DS on, and select New Database.

3. In the Database Properties screen, enter the database name.

4. Double-check that the location where the database will be stored (shown under the Location column) has plenty of available space and then click OK to create the database. The database will take roughly 20MB per 100 servers in the farm.

5. Click the Security folder on the left to expand the options underneath.

6. Right-click the Logins folder under Security and select New Login.

7. Enter the username, and then select either Windows NT Authentication or SQL Authentication. If you select Windows NT Authentication, you will need to select what domain the username is from. If you select SQL Authentication, you need to enter the password for the username.

8. Click the Database tab and put a check next to the Citrix DS database you created. The database roles that the user has permission for will appear underneath.

9. Put a check next to the DB_OWNER role to make the user an owner of the database and click OK.

The database is now set up correctly and ready for use by your first MetaFrame XP server. When setting up the connection to the database, you need to use the username you set up in step 7.

Choosing SQL Server or Windows NT Authentication

Whether you choose SQL Server or Windows NT Authentication depends mainly on your environment and security requirements. SQL Server Authentication is a simpler means of database access. The username and password are kept on the SQL Server, so the only thing you need is a good connection.

Windows NT Authentication relies on being able to authenticate against an external domain controller to access the SQL database. The advantage of this approach is security is centralized on the domain controller. However, the disadvantage is that if the SQL Server cannot reach the domain controller, your database and the Citrix server farm would fail.

Setting Up Oracle as a Data Store

Setting up a database on Oracle is not for the faint of heart. If you have a production Oracle database in-house, however, your database administrator should be able to create one in a flash. Here are the recommended parameters needed for the database:

- **Initial size**   20,000K

- **Auto-extend**   On

- **Maxsize**   Unlimited (You can limit the size to #servers ⋆ 400K + 20000K if necessary.)

You will need to have the database administrator set up an account with read/write access to the database that you will use when you make the ODBC connection.

Creating the ODBC Connection

Those who are already intimately familiar with setting up databases will undoubtedly be familiar with creating an ODBC connection. For those who are not as familiar with ODBC, this section will walk you through setting up an ODBC connection.

Most database applications designed to run on Windows use ODBC connections to connect to the database(s) that they need. ODBC drivers for most common databases, including Oracle and SQL, are included in Windows 2000. The advantage of these drivers is that they provide a layer of separation between applications and the databases. Applications can be written once to communicate with an ODBC driver that in turn can communicate with most any database.

To set up an ODBC connector for a SQL-based DS, follow these steps:

1. Double-click the Data Sources icon in Control Panel, Administrative Tools.

2. From the ODBC Data Source Administrator window, click the System DSN tab and select Add.

3. Select the SQL Server as the data source and click OK.

4. Enter the Name you want to use for the data source and the server name of the SQL server. If the server is not on the local network, you need to enter the name because the drop-down box will not pull up any names.

5. At the authentication page, select whether the SQL database you had created requires Windows NT Authentication or SQL Server Authentication and fill in the information, and then click Next.

6. Change the default database to be the Citrix DS database on the SQL Server, and click Next.

7. Leave the defaults on the last screen and click Finish. A dialog box will appear. Click Test Data Source. If it comes back successful, the database is set up properly.

To set up an ODBC connector for an Oracle-based DS, you first need to install the client and networking components from Oracle. This will install the latest ODBC driver for Oracle on your system, which you can set up for connection to the database. Refer to Oracles' product documentation for more information.

Installing the First MetaFrame XP Server

Installing your first MetaFrame XP server in a farm is a little different from the installation process for the rest of the servers. If you will be using a local Access DS, that DS will reside on the first server you install. Also during the first server installation will be the only time you need to enter the product license. This product license determines whether the farm will be an XPe, XPa, or XPs server farm. When the remaining servers asks for a license code during installation, you can add more connection licenses; however, you will not need to enter the product license again.

If you are upgrading from MetaFrame 1.8, the install process will automatically import your existing published applications into MetaFrame XP. Do not uninstall MetaFrame 1.8 before installing MetaFrame XP if you want this to happen.

Before running the setup for MetaFrame XP, make sure that all your applications are closed. If you are upgrading a MetaFrame 1.8 server, make sure that no users are logged on. You might want to disable logons for the period of time you are upgrading the server through the MetaFrame Administer Tool.

Also if you intend to make this server an NFuse web server, you need to install Internet Information Server v4.0 or above. It is not recommended to make your Citrix servers NFuse servers unless you have an environment with three or less servers. It is better to install NFuse on a separate server at a later point.

Here are the steps for the installation:

1. Insert the CD into the CD drive.

2. From the Citrix MetaFrame CD-ROM window that appears, click the MetaFrame XP Setup icon. If this screen does not appear, run the `[cd]:\autoroot.exe` executable.

3. If you did not install IIS, as recommended, you will receive an NFuse Requirements Not Met screen. Click Yes to continue.

4. Click I Agree at the license statement, and then click Next at the Welcome and Data Store Configuration screens.

5. At the Data Store Setup screen, because this is the first server in a new farm, select Create a New Farm. This is also the correct option to select if you will be running MetaFrame XP in mixed mode with an existing farm.

6. At the Data Store Configuration screen, select Use a Local Database to set up a local Access DS, or select Use a Third Party Database for connecting to a SQL- or Oracle-based DS and click Next.

7. At the Zone Name screen, normally on the first server, just leave the box checked next to Use Default Zone Name. Your server's default zone name will be the subnet address of the network. If you intend to set up multiple zones, however, you might want to enter a zone name here. Click Next.

8. If you selected Use a Third Party Database in step 6, you will now be shown a list of compatible ODBC connections. Select the correct ODBC driver for the Citrix DS. If you have not yet set up the ODBC drivers, you will find instructions in the preceding section. Click Next.

9. You will now be prompted for the username and password for the database. Enter the username and password you set up when the database was first created and click Next. The user ID needs read/write access to the database.

10. At the Server Farm screen, enter the name for your server farm. If you need to run in mixed mode, you will need to enter the exact same farm name as the existing MetaFrame 1.8 farm. Click Next, and then click Next again to confirm the creation of the DS.

11. At the MetaFrame Interoperability screen, select to run this farm in either native IMA mode or mixed mode and click Next.

12. Now enter the username and domain for the initial farm administrator. This is the only user who will initially be able to log on to the Citrix Management Console and manage the farm. You will need to add more users using the CMC once the farm is up.

13. If you have more than one protocol loaded on the server, you will be able to select for which protocols connections will be configured. Select the protocols needed for Citrix and click Next. A connection configuration is needed for every protocol you intend to use to connect to the Citrix server using the ICA client.

14. At the TAPI Modem Setup screen, you can add a new modem by clicking Add Modems and then clicking Next. If you have modems available, you will be able to select which ones that Citrix will configure connections for at this screen. You need to configure a connection for every modem to which you want users to be able to dial in.

15. At the Shadowing Setup screen, select to either allow or not allow shadowing of ICA sessions on this server and click Next twice. This only applies to this server and not the farm.

16. At the Server Drive Reassignment screen, you have the option to remap your drive letters.

Author's Note

This is highly recommended. By remapping your drive letters, when users log on, their local drives will appear as C: and D: on their Citrix server desktop. If you do not remap the server drives, users' local drives will be mapped higher in the alphabet because C: and D: are taken by the server. This can be very confusing for users and leads to unnecessary support calls.

17. At the Citrix XML Service screen, enter the port you want to use for XML. The default is 80. All the servers in the farm will run this service with MetaFrame XP. It is the protocol used to communicate both with NFuse and Citrix clients that use TCP/IP and HTTP.

18. The wizard will now begin the install of Citrix MetaFrame XP. On the Client Distribution Wizard screen that appears, click Next to install the latest client software on your server for automated downloads to the users and follow the wizard. Click Cancel if you want to install client software at a later point.

Author's Note

Citrix MetaFrame has the capability to automatically update client software when users connect to the server. This is a great feature; however, use it carefully. If you have a large server farm, you should do updates one server at a time before proceeding to the next. Also, if you are upgrading from MetaFrame 1.8, remember that the next time your users log on, they will likely receive a message to update their client. It is usually better to handle this by telling your users what to expect and who to call if there are any download problems instead of just rolling it out without warning. Chapter 12, "Installing and Deploying ICA Clients," covers how to use the ICA Client Update Configuration tool to control the roll out of updated versions of the client.

Licensing the First MetaFrame XP Server

The install is nearing completion. There are two more important things to enter: the product license and the product code. Both of these should be found on a sticker on the install CD for MetaFrame XP.

The following instructions show you how to license your server during the installation of MetaFrame:

1. At the MetaFrame XP 1.0 Licensing screen, click the Add button and enter the product license for either MetaFrame XPe, XPa, or XPs as appropriate. You only need to enter a product license once for a farm.

2. At the MetaFrame Product Code screen, click the Use Suggested Product Code button. Verify that this product code matches the one on the CD. This product code indicates that when users connect to this server they will take an XPe, XPa, or XPs license from the license pool. It also indicates what product features this server will support.

When you restart the server, you will be up and running on MetaFrame XP!

Installing the Service Pack and Feature Release

Before doing anything else, you should always install the latest service pack and any appropriate hotfixes for Citrix MetaFrame XP. This is a critical step for the proper functioning of your farm. You should install at least Service Pack 1 for MetaFrame XP, because there are some *very* important hotfixes bundled in this service pack that will help improve the stability of your MetaFrame XP solution.

As of this writing, Service Pack 1 for Citrix MetaFrame XP is bundled with Feature Release 1 for the product. You can download the bundled install package from the Citrix web site at www.citrix.com.

Install the service pack in accordance with the directions provided by Citrix. Although Feature Release 1 also is included, it is not enabled by default. You must enter the license code for the feature release in the licensing section of the Citrix Management Console in the same way you add connection licenses to your farm. The steps for adding licenses are covered in the "Adding Connection Licenses" section.

Keeping Service Pack Levels the Same

Whether you choose to install a service pack or a combination of a service pack and particular hotfixes is up to you for your environment. However, it is critical in the world of Citrix MetaFrame to always keep the same service packs and hotfixes across your server farm.

If you want to resolve a particular problem by installing a particular hotfix, make sure you plan a time after hours to install that hotfix on every server in the farm. Many hotfixes and service packs make significant changes in the way in which servers in a farm communicate with each other. If you install a hotfix on one server in the farm, but not the others, you stand the chance of running into serious communication problems between servers that can affect the reliability of the entire farm.

In the same way, you should always ensure that the service pack level you apply on Windows 2000 or Windows NT 4.0 Terminal Server is the same across all servers.

Adding Connection Licenses

Citrix tightly controls the licensing of the MetaFrame product. When you add any MetaFrame license to the server farm, you have up to 35 days to activate the license. This gives you a lot of time to test your servers and applications, so use the time wisely. If you activate the product too early and then have to reinstall it, reactivating the license can sometimes be difficult.

After you have finished the installation of your first MetaFrame server, it is a good time to add all of your connection licenses to the farm. Here is how:

1. Run the Citrix Management Console from the Citrix folder in the Start menu.

2. Enter the username, password, and domain that you had entered during the MetaFrame setup for the MetaFrame administrator.

3. At the Citrix Management Console screen, shown in Figure 8.1, click Licenses and then click the License Numbers tab. In this window, you will see a list of every license you have entered into your farm, including both product and connection licenses.

4. Right-click in the area underneath License Numbers and select Add License.

5. Enter the license serial number in the Add License window that appears and click OK.

Your license will now appear in the License Numbers window as shown in Figure 8.1. Now that you can see in this window the number of grace days left on a license and whether a license has been activated.

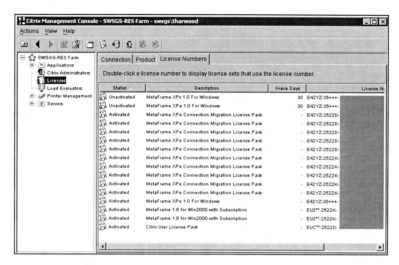

Figure 8.1 Adding and reviewing licenses.

Author's Notes

Remember that if you will be installing upgrade licenses, you need to make sure the license code for the preceding version of MetaFrame is added under the license numbers. Normally, when you upgrade a MetaFrame 1.8 server, it will automatically add its license number into the MetaFrame XP farm. If you do a clean install, however, you will need to add the license code for MetaFrame 1.8 to MetaFrame XP. If you do not, your users will receive license warnings when they log on to the server.

Activating Licenses

After you have entered all the licenses and done the testing that you need to, it is time to activate the licenses. Activating a license involves registering the license and machine codes with Citrix. In return, you will receive an eight-digit activation code that you can use to activate the license.

Notice that when you add a license number to the Citrix server, it appends and eight-digit code onto the back of the number. This eight-digit code is called the *machine code* and is a specially generated code unique to your machine and the time you installed it. If you remove this license and then add it again, the machine code on the end will change.

What this means is that when you register the license and machine code with Citrix, you will receive a unique activation code in return. This activation code can be used only to activate this particular instance of the license. If you delete the license and reinstall it or install the same license on a different server, the machine code will be different and you will not be able to activate it with the same activation code.

Getting an activation code or reactivating an existing license can now be done simply and easily through a web-based interface called the *Citrix Activation System*. This system is integrated with the SAMRI system for Subscription Advantage members.

To activate your license, do the following:

1. From the Citrix Management Console, select Licenses, and then click License Numbers on the right.

2. Right-click the license you want to activate, and select Copy to Clipboard to copy the license code to the Clipboard of the computer. If this server does not have access to the Internet, write the number down. Remember that you will need both the license code that you initially entered and the machine code. These are both displayed as one long number under the license numbers in the CMC.

3. Go to www.citrix.com/activate and follow the instructions. You will likely need to log on to the Citrix Activation portal. If you do not have an ID already, you will have the option to create one.

4. At some point during the activation process, you will be asked for the license code. Because a copy of it is on the Clipboard, just press Ctrl+V to paste it to the window. You should receive an eight-digit activation code in return.

5. Now go back into the CMC and right-click the license and select Activate. Enter the activation code in the window and click OK.

Your license should now show a status of Activated in the CMC window under license numbers.

Installing the Remaining Servers

The installation process for the rest of the servers is much the same as the first with the following exceptions:

- Instead of selecting to Create a New Farm, select Join Existing One.
- If you are using an Access DS, select Indirect Access and enter the server name that contains the DS. This will establish the connection to the DS for your server.
- If you are using a SQL or Oracle DS, select Direct Access and select the ODBC connection to the database. If one has not been created yet, follow the instruction under the Creating an ODBC Connection section.

- Skip past the Add License screen. You should have all the licenses already entered into the farm by this point.

- Use the same product code as the first server you installed. This is very important or licensing will not work correctly. You should normally use the same product code on all the servers in the farm.

Setting Up Terminal Server Users

9

AFTER YOU HAVE YOUR SERVERS INSTALLED, you need to create your users and the connections to which they will attach.

For those who are already familiar with the creation of users and groups in a domain with Windows NT Server 4.0 and Windows 2000, you will find that the basics of user and group creation have not changed with Terminal Server. Users and groups are created using either the User Manager for Domains for Windows NT 4.0 domains or the Active Directory Users and Computers tool for Windows 2000.

However, several additional per-user properties, such as initial program, client drive mappings, and timeouts, apply only when a user logs on to a Terminal Server. In Windows NT 4.0 domains, these properties can be set using only the special version of User Manager that comes with Terminal Server. In Windows 2000, however, these properties are now part of the default schema of Active Directory and can be modified from any domain controller using the Active Directory Users and Computers tool.

In addition to setting up your users, you need to ensure that the connections at the server that they will attach to also are set up properly. Many of the same properties that you can set at a user level, such as timeouts and initial drive mappings, you also can set at a connection level.

This chapter starts with a basic discussion of users and groups on Terminal Server. Then the focus turns to showing you how to create users and groups in Terminal Server and describing all the user properties that you can set.

Terminal Server Users and Groups

This section discusses the general concepts of users and groups in a Windows networking environment and how these concepts are applied with Terminal Server.

You can set up your Terminal Server users and groups in many different places. You can set them up locally on each server, on a central domain, or through trust relationships, on multiple domains in the enterprise. In this section you will learn where best to set up your users and groups depending on your particular situation.

Local User Accounts and Groups

Every Windows 2000 server and workstation on the network, including a Windows 2000 Terminal Server, has a local user account database. This database by default contains The Local Administrator account, Administrators group, Power Users group, Users group, and a handful of additional user accounts and groups. You can "log on locally" to a Windows 2000 Terminal Server just as you would with a Windows 2000 server or workstation, by entering the username and password of the local account and selecting the server name from the domain drop-down box at the logon prompt.

To view the members of your Terminal Server's local account database, right-click My Computer on the server desktop and select Manage. Under Local Users and Groups, you will see the list of user accounts and groups. From here you can modify user properties and reset the users' passwords.

Although you can set up local user accounts on your Terminal Servers for users to log on with, this approach has several limitations. If you use local user accounts, and you have several servers, you will have to administer the user account on each server separately. Suppose, for example, that you have a user named John Doe who needs access to applications on three different Terminal Servers. You would have to set up a separate John Doe user account on each of the servers for John Doe to log on with. To do simple administrative tasks such as renaming his account or resetting his password, you would have to rename it or reset the account on each server separately. In anything but the smallest of environments, using local accounts for logon to Terminal Server quickly becomes impractical.

Securing Local Accounts

Even if you intend to use domain accounts and not local accounts for logon to your servers, it is very important that you realize that they exist and the potential security problems they can cause. Remember that your Terminal Server users have, in essence, local access to the system. They are basically able to log on as if they were standing at the console of your server from wherever they can connect to the server using the Terminal Services client.

By default, all servers are set up with a Local Administrator account. If you are able to log on with this account through Terminal Server, you will have full access to the server. If you use the same Local Administrator password or a weak administrator password on your servers, a potential hacker can gain administrative access to your server farm by just guessing the password. For this reason, it is very important to ensure that your administrator password is secure.

If you allow users to transfer files from your system back to their local drive, be very careful to ensure that users only have User-level access and not Power User access to the system. Double-check that they do not have the ability to copy the Registry files in the `%systemroot%\repair`. Using these files and readily available cracking tools, such as L0phtcrack, a rogue user could crack the Local Administrator password for your machine. If you use the same administrative password for all of your servers, the hacker would now have local access to every one of them!

To prevent this type of problem, take the following security precautions:

- Rename your administrative account on your server.

- Use a minimum of a 10-character alphanumeric password for your local administrative accounts, preferably with upper- and lowercase letters, and one or more special characters such as "~,@,!,#" . One password combination that works well (and is relatively easy to remember) is a combination of a secret password and the server's serial number. Even if you knew the secret, you would need physical access to the servers to know the password.

- Do not use the same administrative password on all of your Terminal Servers.

- If you provide access to the desktop, lock it down tightly using policies.

In Chapter 22, "Securing Your Server," you will learn several more security tips for securing your server properly.

Anonymous Users in Terminal Server

On Windows 2000 Terminal Server and Citrix MetaFrame, some important new local users are automatically created during the install; these are used for anonymous access to the server.

The first user that will be discussed is the TSInternetUser. The TSInternetUser is a special user account created during the installation of Terminal Services. It is intended for use by those who have purchased an Internet Connector License for their server.

The Internet Connector License is a per-server license that allows for up to 200 users to connect anonymously to your server at the same time. This license must be installed on your Terminal Services Licensing server, and you must enable Internet Connector Licensing using the Terminal Services Configuration tool for this process to work.

Once enabled, when users connect to your server via the Terminal Services client, they will be logged on to the server automatically using the TSInternetUser account. The password for this account is changed daily (automatically by your server) and set to never expire. By default the account is only a member of the local Guests group. However, this account can be administered just like any other account, and you can change group membership or other user properties.

Anonymous Users in MetaFrame

If you have installed Citrix MetaFrame on your server, you will notice several new anonymous local users named Anon000 to Anon014 that were created during the installation. These users are made to be a member of both the local Guests group and a new group called Anonymous. The users are set up with random passwords, set to not expire, and a 10-minute idle timeout by default.

Like Terminal Server, Citrix MetaFrame supports anonymous access to the server. With MetaFrame, however, you need to publish an application or a desktop using anonymous access to grant anonymous access to your server. When a user sets up a connection to this anonymously published application, the user will be logged on automatically using the next available anonymous user account. If all anonymous user accounts are taken, the server will dynamically create new user accounts, starting with Anon015.

Anonymous accounts are very useful for many situations. The following list identifies a few times you could use anonymous accounts with Citrix MetaFrame effectively:

- **Application demonstrations and trade shows** Setting up anonymous access to applications for demo purposes is a great way to show off both the application and server-based technology. For example, you could use Citrix NFuse and anonymous applications to demo an application being run through a web browser either at a trade show or on a product demo web site. Because it is anonymous, users are brought directly to the application without having to log on.

- **Kiosks and information portals**   If you need to set up public access to an application at a kiosk or an information portal, anonymous published applications are a great way to do this. You could set up an application such as an information lookup application, product catalog, or even a library catalog.

- **Terminals in a secured area**   If you already have a secured area and network that your users will be attaching to Terminal Server from, you might want to consider anonymous access. For example, you might need to set up a student lab at a school with access to a few applications through Terminal Server. The students are already given magnetic cards to gain access to the lab. Instead of having to do double-administration by also creating Terminal Server user accounts, you might just want to publish the applications anonymously or set up an Internet Connector License.

- **Training**   You might find it easier to publish an application anonymously for training, instead of setting up new accounts. This is especially the case in large training centers where there is a constant influx of new users.

Maximum Anonymous Users

MetaFrame will keep on creating new anonymous users on a server up to the Maximum Anonymous User count in the Registry. By default this maximum count is 99 users. You can change this maximum by using REGEDIT to edit the value at the following Registry key:

`HKLM\SYSTEM\CurrentControlSet\Control\Citrix\MaxAnonymousUsers`

Also the idle timeout for anonymous connection is set by default to 10 minutes for all of the anonymous users. You can change this manually on each anonymous account; however as new anonymous accounts are dynamically created, their idle timeout will again be the default value of 10 minutes. To change this default value, edit the following key (value in minutes):

`HKLM\SYSTEM\CurrentControlSet\Control\Citrix\AnonymousUserIdleTime`

Windows NT 4.0 and 2000 Domain Users and Groups

Although local accounts and groups can be used for user logon, most administrators use domain accounts instead. Both MetaFrame 1.8 and XP support logons from accounts on either Windows NT 4.0 or Windows 2000 domains.

The account database for a Windows NT 4.0 domain resides on the primary domain controller and is replicated to the backup domain controllers for that domain. By default this account database does not contain any Terminal Server–specific user properties. However, Windows NT 4.0 Terminal Server comes with a special version of the User Manager for Domains. This version of the utility enables you to extend the user properties that are available to include Terminal Server–specific user properties, such as Terminal Server profile, Terminal Server timeouts, and more.

On Windows 2000, the account database is stored in the Active Directory database and is replicated to all Windows 2000 domain controllers that are a member of the same tree. Windows 2000 enables you to divide out your users in the Active Directory tree into one or more domains.

In Active Directory, all items in the tree, such as users, groups, and computers, are referred to as *objects*. Each object has certain properties. In the case of users, typical properties would be username, address, and phone number. The definition of the objects that are available in Active Directory and their properties are referred to as the *schema*. The schema can be extended by software when it is installed. When you install Exchange 2000, for instance, it extends the Active Directory schema to include user's email properties.

The default schema in Active Directory includes Terminal Server–specific user properties. This is a welcome feature to Windows NT 4.0 administrators because you no longer have to have a special version of the user administration tool to administer Terminal Server–specific properties. In Windows 2000, the user administration tool is called *Active Directory Users and Computers* and is available in the Administrative Tools folder. This is the only tool you need to manage your Windows 2000 users and to set their Terminal Server–related properties.

Terminal Server–Specific User Properties

Besides username, password, and other default user properties, each Terminal Server user has the following other settable Terminal Server–specific properties:

- **Startup Program**   You can define a certain program to start every time a user logs on to Terminal Server.

- **Client Devices**   Enables you to select whether printers are automatically mapped when the user logs on.

- **Terminal Server Home Directory and Profile**   Enables you to specify a different home directory and profile than your normal one when you log on to Terminal Server.

- **Remote Control** For setting whether this user's session can be remote controlled and whether the user is notified.
- **Session Settings** You can define many session settings, including idle timeout, maximum session time, and how long to keep disconnected sessions running.

Although each of these settings can be controlled at a user level, you also have the option of controlling many of them at a server level using the connection settings. You will be shown how you can control each of these settings at both a user and server level later.

Publishing Administrative Tools

Make sure to take advantage of the capabilities of your Terminal Servers to make remote administration easier. In large distributed environments, for example, it is often the case that you will need to grant access for users on remote domains to your Terminal Servers or MetaFrame server farm. Both of these products can easily be set up so that accounts from multiple domains are able to run applications off of the same box. If you need to modify Terminal Server–specific properties for these accounts, however, you would have to send out a copy of the User Manager (USRMGR.EXE) that comes with either Windows NT 4.0 TS or Windows 2000 with Terminal Services to every remote administrator.

A better way to do this would be to publish the User Manager tool through published applications in MetaFrame or through the web. Other tools, such as the Citrix Management Console, Connection Configuration tool, Terminal Services Configuration tool, and Terminal Services Administrator are some of the many tools that could be published for easy, secure remote use.

Taking this idea a step further, you can use NFuse technology in conjunction with MetaFrame or the TSAC technology in Terminal Server to create your own support web site. Not only could you publish all the support tools your remote administrators would need, but also you could put important support information, downloads, and even system maintenance notices on the site.

Terminal Server Groups

Each user can be made a member of one or more groups. Groups are the best means to provide access for or identify categories of users. Like users, groups can be granted access to your domain's resources. Granting access to the resources using groups is generally more efficient and more easily tracked than granting access to individual users.

Imagine having to grant 10 users access to 5 different directories. For each of the 5 resources, you would have to individually select and grant access for each of the 10 users. This would take at least 50 steps.

By adding the 10 users to a group, however, you only have to select the group and add the group once to the access list for each of the 5 resources. If in the future you need to revoke a user's access or grant access to a new user, you can just delete or add that user from or to the group.

Groups in Windows NT 4.0

In a Windows NT 4.0 domain, the following two types of groups can be created using User Manager for Domains:

- **Local groups** Local groups are server-specific. Each server has its own set of local groups. These local groups reside in its local account database. Local groups can be used only to assign rights to resources on that server. Local groups can contain either users or global groups.

- **Domain global groups** Global groups can be assigned rights throughout the domain. Through trust relationships to other domains, global groups also can be given rights to resources on remote domains. Global groups reside in the domain's account database on the primary domain controller. You can administer global groups and their membership from any server by using the User Manager for Domains and selecting the domain for which you want to manage its global groups. Global groups can contain only domain users; they cannot contain other groups.

Groups in Windows 2000

Windows 2000 comes with the group types available with Windows NT 4.0. However, two additional group types have been added:

- **Domain local groups** Domain local groups are just like domain global groups in Windows NT 4.0, with one exception: They cannot be granted rights to resources outside of the domain.

- **Universal groups** Universal groups are available only in native mode on Windows 2000. They are very similar to domain global groups in Windows NT 4.0. However, universal groups can contain not only users, but also domain global groups. Universal groups are ideal for consolidating group membership and security across Windows 2000 domains.

Using Groups Effectively

With all the different types of available groups, it can be confusing to set up an easy-to-use group membership standard that scales well. You can follow several different recommended techniques, depending on your environment.

Using Groups in a Windows NT 4.0 or Mixed NT 4.0/2000 Environment

The main deciding factor is whether your users authenticate to a Windows 2000 domain controller. If they do not authenticate against a Windows 2000 domain controller, they will not receive the access tokens for any domain local groups or universal groups of which they might be a member. In other words, unless you are in a pure Windows 2000 environment, do not use domain local groups and universal groups.

If your users might still authenticate against Windows NT 4.0 domain controllers, the following is recommended for group setup:

1. Create one domain global application group for each application you run on your servers named App-[Application Name]

2. Grant this domain global group either read or read/write access to the application directory on each server the application runs on.

3. If you are using MetaFrame from Citrix, publish the application to this domain global group.

4. Add the users who need access to the application to this domain global group.

If you are in a large environment with multiple domains and users on those domains need access to applications on a central set of servers, follow these steps for each domain. Be sure to create a naming standard before deploying so that you use a standard set of group names for applications. By establishing a naming standard early, it makes administration much easier in the long run. You will see in the next section how to set up your own naming standard.

Suppose, for example, that you need to publish Microsoft Outlook through MetaFrame for users at your main domain CORPORATE and two branch domains, BRANCH1 and BRANCH2. You would first create an App-Outlook domain global group in each domain. Then you would grant these groups access to the application files by granting them read or read/write access to the application directory and its subdirectories on each server that they needed. If you were using MetaFrame to publish the application, you would publish the application to all three domain global application groups. Finally, you would add the users in each domain who needed the application to that domain's application group.

Using Groups in a Pure Windows 2000 Single Domain Environment

In a pure Windows 2000 environment, you have a lot of leeway in choosing which types of groups to use. Because all the domain controllers are Windows 2000, when users on those domains authenticate, all the groups that they are a member of will be listed in their access. This includes universal groups and domain local groups. Although the extra choice is beneficial, it is even more important to set standards early on as to how you will use groups in your Windows 2000 domain.

If you are running in a single domain Windows 2000 environment and all of your IS administration is centralized, your choices are very simple. In this situation, the following is recommended:

1. Create an MF-Apps or TS-Apps organizational unit in the appropriate location in your tree.

2. Create a domain global group under this organizational unit for each application named App-[Application Name].

3. Grant this domain global group either read or read/write access to the application's folders on each server the application runs on.

4. If you are using MetaFrame, publish the application to this domain global group.

5. Add the users who need access to the application to this domain global group.

This simple solution scales well, and you will be able to search for your application groups very easily in the tree by looking for groups starting with "App." In addition, you can secure access to the MF-Apps or TS-Apps organizational unit to only those administrators who need to manage application access to Terminal Server.

Although this solution works well for a completely centralized IS department, many of us can only dream of this level of consolidation. For those who work for companies where administration is delegated out geographically or by department, you must consider some additional complexities when planning how you want to set up your groups.

If you have a single Windows 2000 domain and administration is delegated, you are likely using organizational units extensively to help divide out that administration. Suppose, for example, that your top-level organizational units are based on geographical location. Their names are Mia, Atl, and NY. Each of these organizational units has a designated administrator who handles the administration of users, groups, and computers in their respective organizational unit. New York is the corporate headquarters, and the administrators there manage most of the MetaFrame servers. However, the administrators in New York want to ensure that the administrators in Miami and Atlanta are responsible for handling day-to-day administration, such as password resets, adding new users, and deleting users who have left. If this sounds a little bit closer to your work environment, here are some recommendations:

1. Create a TS-Apps organizational unit under the Mia, Atl, and NY top-level organizational units.

2. Create a universal organizational unit under NY. This organizational unit will be for your universal groups.

3. For each application used throughout the enterprise, create a Mia-App-[Application], Atl-App-[Application], and NY-App-[Application] domain global group under each of the respective TS-Apps organizational units for the locations.

4. Create a single App-[Application] universal group for the application and put it in the universal organizational unit.

5. Add the Mia-App-[Application], Atl-App-[Application], and NY-App-[Application] domain global groups to this universal group.

6. Grant the universal group read or read/write rights to the application's folders on each server the application runs on.

7. If you are using Citrix MetaFrame, publish the application to the universal group.

8. Add users to either the Mia-App-[Application], Atl-App-[Application], and NY-App-[Application] domain global groups to give them rights to the application.

Although more complicated than the preceding solution, this solution is very flexible. The administrators for each organizational unit will be able to manage their own users, controlling who has access to the applications on the central farm. If a new user needs to be set up, they just create the user in their organizational unit and add them to the appropriate App global groups in their organizational unit.

This solution takes advantage of the ability to consolidate global groups by nesting them into a single universal group. If the New York administrators do not want a particular site to have control of the user membership for an application, they would just not add that site's App global group into the central App universal group.

On a single Windows 2000 domain, you cannot create two groups with the same name, even if they are in different organizational units. For this reason, prefixing the organizational unit name to the group name is a good way to keep a naming standard across your organization. The problem with this technique is that the group names can become very long, very quickly. For this reason and more, always try to keep your organizational unit names as short and abbreviated as possible, especially the top-level organizational units.

Additional Group Types for MetaFrame Deployments

Although the App-[Application] groups are very useful and highly recommended to set up for your Citrix MetaFrame server users, you might want to consider a couple of other groups types.

The first recommendation is to set up a Desktop-[Server Name] group for every server in your server farm. Publish the desktop for that server to this group using the Citrix Management Console. Rather than set up a Custom ICA connection for your users or administrators who need access to a MetaFrame server desktop, just add them to this group and have them refresh their published applications for the farm. This is a highly recommended step because it gives you easy central control over who gets access to desktops.

In addition, this technique can be very useful for troubleshooting such things as user printer problems. If a user is having a difficult printer issue with a published application, have your help desk publish the desktop to them temporarily. They then can remote control the desktop and troubleshoot the printing from the desktop rather than from within the published application (where fewer options are available).

The second recommendation is to set up Doc-[Document Name] groups for commonly used documents and then publish the document itself rather than the application. This proves especially useful for granting central access to shared or commonly accessed documents. You also can use this technique to publish instructional documents for your users.

As long as the file association is working, you should be able to enter the path for the document when specifying the command line for the published application. If that does not work, you might have to specify the path for the application and then put the document path next to it.

Content Publishing with Feature Release 1

If you have purchased and installed Feature Release 1 on your MetaFrame XP server, you can take advantage of an additional related feature called *Content Publishing*. Using Content Publishing, you can publish various types of content such as streaming media and documents from a MetaFrame server, just like you publish applications. However, the content is viewed locally rather than remotely on the server itself.

Suppose, for example, that you use Content Publishing to publish a streaming media file. Instead of displaying the streaming media file from Windows Media Player running on the server, which would greatly tax the processing power of the server, the file is streamed to you and Windows Media Player is launched locally.

The advantage of this technique is in the obvious processor time savings you achieve by running the "viewer" application locally rather than on your Citrix MetaFrame server.

Specific instructions for publishing applications is provided in Chapter 15, "Application Publishing and Load Management with Citrix MetaFrame."

Groups in a Pure Windows 2000 Multidomain Environment

The last type of environment you might have is a pure Windows 2000 multidomain or multitree environment. In this situation you normally will have domains divided geographically. Instead of assigning an organizational unit for each geographic location, you have a separate domain.

Suppose, for example, that you have locations in Paris, Tokyo, and New York for a fictional Acme Corporation. There is a separate domain for each location, called Acme_Paris, Acme_Tokyo, and Acme_NY. These domains are all part of the same Acme corporate tree. Users in all locations need access to a server farm located in Tokyo and managed by the Tokyo IS staff. The Tokyo IS staff wants to ensure that basic user administration is handled by each location, whereas farm administration is handled in Tokyo. In this situation the following is recommended:

1. Create a TS-Apps organizational unit under the Acme_Paris, Acme_Tokyo, and Acme_NY domains.
2. Create a universal organizational unit under Acme_Tokyo. This organizational unit will be for your universal groups.
3. For each application used throughout the enterprise, create a Par-App-[Application], Tky-App-[Application], and NY-App-[Application] domain global group under each of the respective TS-Apps organizational units for the locations.
4. Create a single App-[Application] universal group for the application and put it in the universal organizational unit in the Acme_Tokyo domain.
5. Add the Par-App-[Application], Tky-App-[Application], and NY-App-[Application] domain global groups to this universal group.
6. Grant the universal group read or read/write rights to the application's folders on each server the application runs on.
7. If you are using MetaFrame, publish the application to the universal group.
8. Add users to either the Par-App-[Application], Tky-App-[Application], and NY-App-[Application] domain global groups to give them rights to the application.

Universal groups also can be leveraged in multitree environments by using them to consolidate application publishing groups from the domains in each tree.

Creating a TSUsers Group

Now that you have a better idea how your application groups should be set up, there are a couple more groups you will likely want to consider setting up, a TSUsers and TSAdmins group.

In both Windows NT 4.0 and Windows 2000, you need to have the Log On Locally user right to log on to a Terminal Server. On a Windows NT 4.0 member server, this right, by default, is granted to the local Users group, which in turn contains the domain Users group. This means that everyone who has an account on the domain has the ability to log on to the Terminal Server. To allow users from other domains access to your Terminal Server, you would have to set up a trust relationship and then add them to the local Users group on the Terminal Servers.

In Windows 2000, the default rights were changed. On a Windows 2000 member server, a special purpose Authenticated Users group is now a member of the local Users for every server. The Authenticated Users group includes any user who is able to authenticate to any domain trusted by the server. This, in effect, gives any Authenticated User the right to log on locally to your Terminal Servers. In a large, multidomain environment this could easily mean thousands of users, most of which do not even need access to the Terminal Server!

In addition to the Log On Locally right, each type of protocol connection you can make to your server also can be assigned particular rights. If you use the ICA protocol over TCP, for instance, you can ensure that only certain users and groups have the right to connect with just this protocol. This security is controlled using either the Terminal Services Configuration utility for RDP connections or the Citrix Connection Configuration utility for ICA connections. By default on both Windows NT 4.0 and Windows 2000 Terminal Server, the Everyone group is granted logon access.

For these reasons and more, it is more secure to do the following:

1. Create a TSUsers global group on each of your NT 4.0 or Windows 2000 domains on which there are users who need access to your Terminal Servers.

2. Add all of these TSUsers global groups to each local Users group on all of your Terminal Servers.

3. Remove either the domain Users or Authenticated Users groups as appropriate.

4. Go into the Terminal Services Configuration utility or Citrix Connection Configuration utility as appropriate.

5. Right-click the connection entries and select either Properties or Permissions.

6. Grant all the TSUsers global groups User-level access to the connection.

7. Remove the Everyone and the local Users group from the Connection Permissions.

8. For each domain, add all of your Terminal Server users to the TSUsers group.

Only users who are made a member of the TSUser's group for their domain will have access to the central servers. As you can imagine, in a large multidomain environment this can add some complexities. If you are fortunate enough to have a pure Windows 2000 Server environment with Active Directory, you can set up a single universal TSUser's group and then add your App-[Application] groups to it. In this way, when you add your users to any App group, they will automatically be able to log on to your Terminal Servers, making administration simpler.

Creating a TSAdmins Group

A final and important tip is to create a TSAdmins group on the domain where your Terminal Server administrators are, as follows:

1. Create a global TSAdmins group on your Windows NT 4.0 or Windows 2000 domain.

2. Add the TSAdmins group to the Local Administrators group on each of the servers.

3. Grant the TSAdmins group full control permissions to your ICA and RDP connections using either the Terminal Services Configuration utility or the Citrix Connection Configuration utility. This will grant them the ability to reset sessions, shadow sessions, and more.

4. If you are using Citrix MetaFrame, go into the Citrix Management Console, right-click Citrix Administrators and select Add Citrix Administrator. Add the TSAdmins group and grant it read/write permissions.

Using this group you can grant administrative access to your Terminal Servers without having to grant them full domain admin access. In addition, you can grant this group special Terminal Server and MetaFrame permissions, such as the ability to shadow other sessions.

In larger environments you will likely find that you will have to divide administration duties out further than just creating a TSAdmins group. The following tips are suggested:

- **Create a TSOperators group.** Grant this group the ability to reset sessions and shadow sessions. However, do not grant the group Local Administrator access to the Terminal Servers. You can add your operators

or first-level help desk staff to this group and give them access to either
the Terminal Server Administration utility for RDP sessions or the Citrix
Management Console for ICA session so that they can reset stuck sessions
and shadow.

- **Create TSAdmins-[Server Group] groups.** You might want to
  divide your servers into separate groups for administration. Grant members of the TSAdmins-[Server Group] administrative access to just the
  servers in their group.

- **Create a TSEntAdmins group.** The TSEntAdmins Group is for the
  top-level administrators and should be granted administrative access to all
  the Terminal Servers in the enterprise. Using a single TSEntAdmins group
  and several TSAdmins-[Server Groups], you can easily divide out administrative duties, even on the largest of farms.

Creating a Naming Standard

Having a naming standard for your users and groups makes administration
significantly easier. When assigning rights to files, connections, or other
Terminal Server resources, you need to list the users by domain. In large
domains it is easy for them to become "lost in the list." By establishing and
adhering to a naming standard, it is much easier to keep track of them,
because their names are organized in an understandable fashion. Even in
smaller domains, the purpose of every user and group can be difficult to
keep track of if a naming standard is not followed.

Naming standards also make the setup of your server farm much easier to
understand. This simplicity will make it easier for you to train people who
support the farm. In large server farm environments where administration is
highly delegated, an easy-to-follow naming standard is critical for helping to
ensure that administrative mistakes are not made.

Finally, naming standards are especially important for good security.
Security in a Terminal Server environment can be complicated. Unlike most
other servers where you need to be concerned only with their security from
the network, with a Terminal Server you need to carefully look at local file
security. Naming standards, especially for groups, make it easier to assign
NTFS rights correctly to applications and directories on the server.

To create your own naming standard, just create a document titled
`Terminal Server Naming Standards`. For each type of Terminal Services
resource on your network, make a section in the naming standards document. In that section use a table to show how the resource should be named.

Be sure to cover how to handle possible duplicate names. If you have two people on your network named John Smith, for example, how will you differentiate between the two? Also cover the character set that is available for naming and give some examples of the use of the standard. Some resources that you should include naming standards on are usernames, group names, server names, published application names, and farm names.

Naming Users

When you create a user, you need to enter the username, description, and full name in the New User dialog box in a Windows NT 4.0 domain. On Windows 2000, you have far more choices, including the user's phone number, address, and title. How you assign these values and what conventions you follow will have a great effect on the ease of future administration of your domain and Terminal Server.

In general, try to avoid the following when creating usernames:

- **Creating usernames by using different techniques**   This can quickly lead to confusion.

- **Letting users assign their own usernames**   This again can lead to confusion because it is not likely the users will create usernames in a consistent manner.

- **Using spaces between first and last names**   This is a common standard, but it can cause difficulties when setting up an email system. You must make aliases for the usernames because spaces are not allowed in Internet email addresses. It is best to plan for the future by using Internet-compatible usernames.

- **Using just first names or last names**   You will quickly run into issues with duplicate usernames if you adopt this standard.

Another suggestion is to put an @ or some other symbol at the start of the full name for special accounts, such as service and test accounts. In this way, when you sort by full name, you can easily differentiate between normal users and special-purpose users. This technique works well for large networks where service accounts can get lost easily.

Table 9.1 shows some different naming standards for different types of users.

Table 9.1 **Username Naming Standards**

Standard	Description
First Initial, Last Name, [#] (JDOE or JDOE1)	Probably the most common, this standard works well because the Last Name names are short and tend to be unique. If there are duplicate names, either add a number at the end or use the people's middle initials to differentiate the names.
First Name, Last Initial,[#] (JOHND)	Also a very common standard, but is less likely to generate unique names on large networks. For small networks, it is good because first names are generally easier to remember and spell.
First Name.Last Name,[#] (JOHN.DOE)	This standard is easy to remember and is compatible with most email systems. The disadvantage is that usernames are significantly longer.
Hash Codes (JD6771)	In corporations where security is critical, such as financial or government institutions, often a cryptic hash code is generated for users. For example, [the user's initials]+[the user number]. This makes the username very difficult to guess and makes it more difficult for the potential cracker to break into the network.

Naming Groups

As with users, it is a good idea to come up with a naming standard for your groups. Naming standards for groups are very important because they are often used for assigning security on a domain. In addition, in a MetaFrame environment groups can be used for application publishing.

Table 9.2 contains some suggested naming standards for the different types of groups.

Table 9.2 **Group Naming Standards**

Name	Description
APPLICATION GROUPS App - [App Name]	Create a group for every application that you publish on your server farm or use with Terminal Server. Use this group to assign rights to the application directory. If in a Citrix MetaFrame environment, also publish the application to this group.

Name	Description
[Location]-App- [App Name]	Use this standard for larger organizations where administration is delegated. At each location where there is an administrator, the administrator can have control of the membership to his [Location]-App-[App Name] group. The central administrators then add the [Location]-App-[App Name] group to all the central App - [App Name] universal group. The central group is then used for granting file rights to the application and for publishing the application to Citrix MetaFrame users.
TERMINAL SERVICES RIGHTS	
TSUser or [Location]-TSUser	Members of these groups have user access to your Terminal Servers, meaning that they have the ability to log on, assign logon rights, and grant the appropriate TSUsers groups logon access through the connection permissions.
TSAdmins or [Location] - TSAdmin	This group is used to provide administrative access to the Terminal Servers, such as the ability to remotely control or reset sessions. Add this group to the Local Administrator group on all of your Terminal Servers. Also grant them full control through the connection permissions.
TSUserAdmin	In larger environments you might want to divide out administration further by creating a TSUserAdmin group. This group would not be granted administrative rights to the servers; however, they would be granted full control through the connection permissions on each server. This means they would have the ability to reset sessions and remote control, but would not be given administrative level access to the system.
ORGANIZATIONAL UNIT ADMINS	
[OU]-Admin	If you have a Windows 2000 environment with multiple organizational units (OUs), you can create an [OU]-Admin group for each top-level OU and assign object administration rights for that OU to it. In this way each administrator for a particular OU has the rights to manage all the users, computers, printers, and other objects in his OU. If these administrators also need to manage Terminal Server users from their OU, you can assign the [OU]-Admin group TSUserAdmin rights to the Terminal Servers so that they have the ability to reset sessions and shadow other sessions.

Naming Servers

The last naming standard that you need to document for your Terminal Servers is how you intend to name the servers. In smaller environments of fewer than 10 servers, you might just number your servers sequentially. If your company name is Acme and location is New York, for example, you might choose to name each of your servers AcmeNY-TS[#], where # is replaced by the server number.

Although this simple naming standard works well for fewer than 10 servers, you will likely want to consider a different naming standard for larger environments. Part of deciding on the naming standard depends greatly on how you will set up your server farm. The following are some recommended ways to organize and name large numbers of servers.

Primary and Disaster Recovery Groupings

In large load-balanced or load-sharing environments, group your servers into a primary group and one or more secondary groups. When naming your servers, be sure the naming standard reflects which group they are a part of. Suppose, for example, that you have 10 servers, each of which is load balanced with an identically configured server at a disaster recovery location. You might then choose to name your primary servers AcmeNY-TS[1 to 10] and your disaster recovery servers AcmeDR[#]-TS[1 to 10].

Application Groupings

It is often beneficial in large farms to group servers into general application groups. The servers in each application group are dedicated to serving the applications in that group or category only. This technique works well for ASPs that have a shared server farm used by several customers. This technique also works very well for corporations setting up their own internal ASP for various lines of business applications.

The applications are generally load balanced across the servers in the application group. Some example application groups would be Office applications, Reporting applications, and Accounting applications. For example, say your servers were divided into three different application groups: Office, Reporting, and Accounting. You might then choose to name your servers AcmeTS-Off[1 to n], AcmeTS-Rep[1 to n], and AcmeTS-Act[1 to n].

You could divide out your administration groups similarly by adding Off, Rep, or Act to the group name. For example, you could have a global TSAdmins group that had administrative rights to every server, but also TSOffAdmins, TSRepAdmins, and TSActAdmins groups, which were granted administrative rights just for the servers in that application group.

Geographical or Organizational Groupings

The last administrative grouping is used in large farms that are either spread across several locations or where it is very important to create a high level of administrative isolation between server groups. In this case you might want to label your servers by either geographical location or organizational grouping. Suppose, for example, that you have servers at your Tokyo, New York, and Paris locations. You might then choose to name the servers just AcmeTky-TS[1 to 10], AcmeNY-TS[1 to 10], and AcmePar-TS[1 to 10]. If servers at the New York location are further divided out and managed by administrators in different departments, such as Sales and Accounting, you might name the servers AcmeNY-Sl-TS[1 to 10] and AcmeNY-Ac-[1 to 10].

Creating Users

The process for creating users is very different for Windows 2000 than it is for Windows NT 4.0. Instead of using the User Manager for Domains, you now have a new tool called the Active Directory Users and Computers tool. Although the process might be different, the special Terminal Server–specific properties available are much the same.

This section is written for administrators who are already familiar with creating users using either the User Manager for Domains or the Active Directory Users and Computers tool, but who are not familiar with the Terminal Server–specific properties that these tools can set. The differences between standard user creation and creating a user who will be using Terminal Server is covered in detail.

In addition, you will learn about the important aspects of user properties such as user home directories, profiles, and logon scripts.

Terminal Server's User Manager for Domains

The User Manager for Domains that comes with Windows NT 4.0 Terminal Server differs from the one available on your Windows NT 4.0 servers. Although the look and feel are much the same, several Terminal Server–specific properties can be set only from the User Manager that comes with Terminal Server. The following is a list of the main ones:

- **Config Settings** Terminal Server has an additional group of settings called the *Config Settings*. These include many per-user settings related to some of the per-connection settings, such as client device mappings, initial program, and timeouts.

- **Terminal Server Home Directory** Under profile settings, the TS User Manager has an additional field for you to define a home directory used only when logging on to Terminal Server.

- **Terminal Server Profile Path** You also can define a profile path that is used only when logging on to Terminal Server. In this way, your workstation's profile and TS profile are kept separate.

If you have a mixed Windows 2000 and Windows NT 4.0 environment, you also can find a copy of the Terminal Server User Manager for Domains on your Windows 2000 servers. To access this copy, just run USRMGR.EXE from the Start, Run window.

Creating users using the Terminal Server User Manager for Domains (TS User Manager) does not mean that they can log on only to Terminal Server. A user created with the TS User Manager is identical to one created with the standard User Manager, with the exception that a handful of Terminal Server–specific properties are added to the user's account.

You will find Terminal Server's User Manager for Domains in the Administrative Tools folder by selecting Properties from the Start menu. If you have a mixed Windows 2000 and Windows NT 4.0 environment, you also can find a copy of the Terminal Server User Manager for Domains on your Windows 2000 servers. To access this copy, just run USRMGR.EXE from the Start, Run window.

The first difference that you are likely to see between the TS User Manager and that included with Windows NT Server 4.0 is the addition of the Config button in the User Properties window. You can get to the User Properties window for any user by double-clicking that user from the main window of the TS User Manager. Figure 9.1 shows the properties settable from within the Config window.

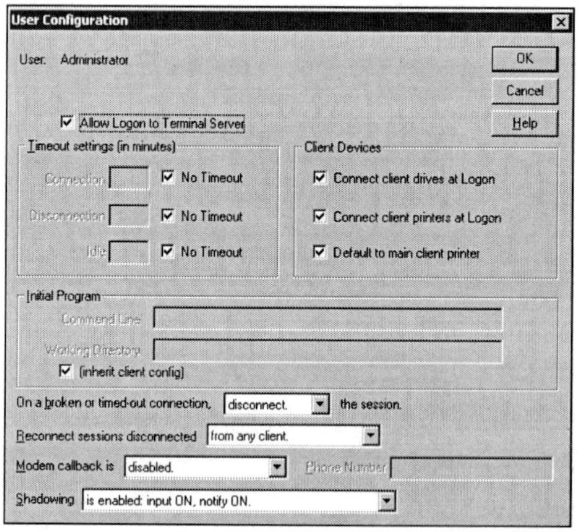

Figure 9.1 User config settings.

Additional Terminal Server–specific settings can be seen by clicking the Profiles button in the User Properties window. In the Profiles dialog box, you will see such additional settings, such as the Terminal Server Home Directory and Profile Path (see Figure 9.2).

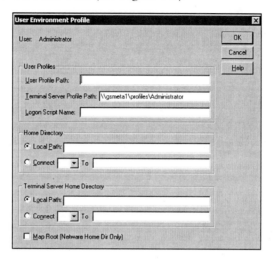

Figure 9.2   User profile settings.

These two windows are the only two areas in Terminal Server User Manager where you can change Terminal Server–specific properties. Other than these, the rest of the user settings are identical to those that can be set with the regular User Manager for Domains.

Creating a Terminal Server User on a Windows NT 4.0 Domain

The following is a basic overview of the steps necessary to create a user through the TS User Manager. Following this overview is a discussion of each group of user properties that you can set in detail. You will learn what they are for and how to set them.

To create a new user, follow these steps:

1. Open the User Manager for Domains from the Terminal Server Start menu under Programs, Administrative Tools.

2. Select New User from the User menu to create a new user. The New User dialog box appears.

3. Fill in the Username, Full Name, Description, and Password. For ease of administration, it is important that you follow a naming standard when setting these properties, as discussed previously in the "Naming Users" section.

4. Check any of the boxes that are appropriate, such as the User Must Change Password at Next Logon box.

5. Set the user properties as appropriate, such as the Groups, Config, and Profiles, by clicking the corresponding buttons, filling in the properties in the dialog box that appears, and clicking OK. These properties are discussed in detail in the following sections.

6. Select Add to add the new user to the user list.

The user is now created in the domain's user database as the *primary domain controller* (PDC). The user can log on to any Terminal Server or Windows workstation that is a member of that domain or is trusted by that domain by using the username and password that you have set.

User Configuration

To set the user's User Configuration properties, click the Config button in the New User window. The User Configuration dialog box, shown in Figure 9.1, contains many Terminal Server per-user settings such as timeouts, initial program, and client devices.

You will notice from the discussion of connection settings in Chapter 10, "Setting Up Terminal Server Connections," that many of these options also can be set per connection. By default, connections will inherit whatever you set per user. If you change the setting at the connection, however, it overrides what is set for the users.

Take, for example, the initial program setting. To set the Initial Program, uncheck Inherit Client Config and enter the Command Line and Working Directory of the program you want the user to run. The next time the user logs on, Terminal Server takes the user directly to this application rather than to a Terminal Server desktop. Now if you set an initial program on the connection the user is logging on to the server with, as shown in Chapter 10, this setting overrides the initial program setting that you set per user.

User Environment Profile

The User Environment Profile window, shown in Figure 9.2, can be accessed by clicking the Profile button in the New User dialog box. In this window, you will find the following settings:

- **User Profiles**   In this area you will find fields in which to set the Terminal Server profile path, standard profile paths, and logon script filename. The profile path is mainly used to store the user's desktop settings and the user Registry settings. The logon script is a batch file run when the user first logs on.

- **Home Directory**   In this area you can set the standard home directory to either the user's local drive (Local Path) or to a UNC path (Connect) on the network. Home directories are normally used to store user's personal files. As you will learn shortly, home directories have additional special purposes with Terminal Server.

- **Terminal Server Home Directory**   This home directory is used only when the user logs on to the domain from the Terminal Server.

- **Map Root**   The ability to map root a home directory to a NetWare server is important for businesses whose primary network servers are NetWare.

Because of the special importance of the user profile and home directory settings with Terminal Server, these settings are discussed in detail in this section.

Active Directory Users and Computers Tool

The Active Directory Users and Computers tool is the utility that comes with your Windows 2000 servers for administering your users, computers, groups, printers, and other objects in the Windows 2000 Active Directory. Unlike the User Manager for Domains, for which there is a special version for Terminal Server, there is only one version of the Active Directory Users and Computers tool. This version enables you to easily manage both your standard user properties and all of your Terminal Server–specific user properties.

To view the Terminal Server properties available in the Active Directory Users and Computers tool, open the utility from the Start menu, Programs, Administrative Tools folder, and right-click any user and select Properties. There are four tabs under which you will find Terminal Server–related properties: Environment, Sessions, Remote Control, and Terminal Services Profile.

Under the Environment tab shown in Figure 9.3, you will find user-level environment controls such as whether various client devices are connected during logon or what program is started up for the user.

Within the Sessions tab shown in Figure 9.4, you can control several user-level sessions related to session idle times and active session limits. Using these settings, you can control how long a user can remain connected to a server and whether the user's session is kept in a disconnect state, or it is reset when a connection is broken. Because these are user-level settings, they apply to whatever server the user logs on to.

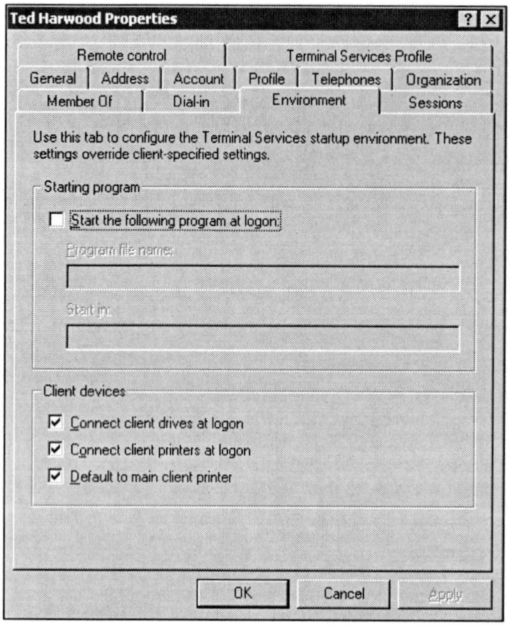

Figure 9.3   Environment tab.

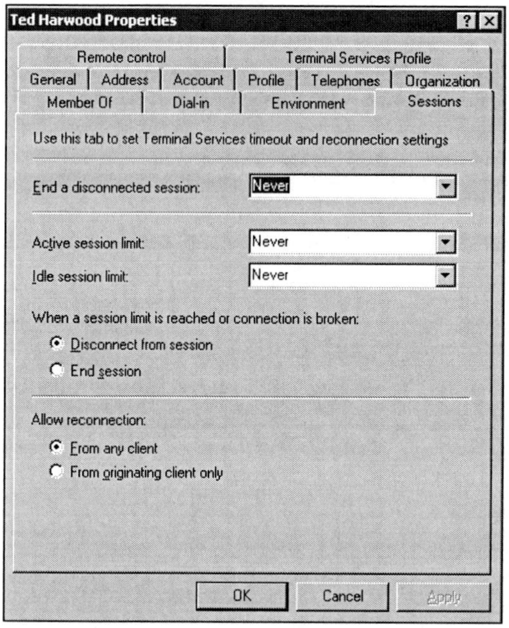

Figure 9.4   Sessions tab.

The Remote Control tab has several settings used for manipulating permissions to remote control a session as shown in Figure 9.5. The ability to remote control a user is enabled for all users by default. Although only an administrative-level user has the ability to remote control other user's sessions, you might want to restrict which users can have their sessions remote controlled.

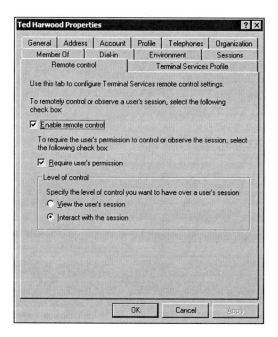

Figure 9.5   Remote Control tab.

The last group of settings can be found under the Terminal Services Profile tab shown in Figure 9.6. Here you can control such things as the location of the user's profile and home directory when logged on to Terminal Server. You also can deny users the ability to log on to any Terminal Server using the settings in here.

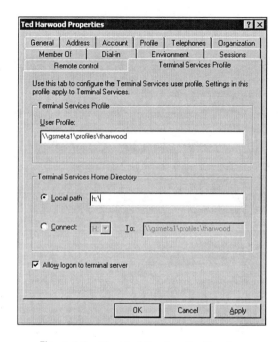

Figure 9.6   Terminal Services Profile tab.

Creating a Windows 2000 Terminal Server User

To create a Windows 2000 Terminal Server, follow these steps:

1. Open the Active Directory Users and Computers tool from the Start menu, Programs, Administrative Tools folder on your Windows 2000 domain controller.

2. Right-click the OU folder in which you want to create the user and select New User.

3. Enter the first name, last name, full name, and user logon name in accordance with your naming standards document and click Next.

4. Enter and confirm the password, and then click Next.

5. Right-click the new user and select Properties.

6. Change the user properties as appropriate under each tab.

Using Alternative User Management Tools

The built-in tool in Windows 2000 is not an efficient user management tool in large enterprise environments. Unlike its predecessor, the User Manager for Domains, you cannot select multiple users at the same time and change their properties together. This simple limitation makes administrative tasks very tedious for large numbers of users.

One of my favorite user administration tools is Hyena from Adkins Resources (www.systemtools.com/hyena). Hyena enables you to modify multiple users at the same time in both Windows NT 4.0 and 2000 domains. In addition, the enterprise version enables you to modify both Terminal Server and Exchange properties for these users.

By just publishing Hyena using MetaFrame or making it available in Terminal Server, you can greatly ease the administrative burden of managing several domains and thousands of users.

One very useful feature of Hyena is its reporting capabilities. Producing a comma-delimited list of all groups, groups members, users, servers, space on all drives, services, and other information on a domain can be done in one step.

Finally, Hyena helps centralize server management by providing capabilities such as the ability to start/stop services, view event logs, share drives, view connected users, and more.

User Home Directories and My Documents

Under both NT Server 4.0 and Windows 2000, the main purpose of home directories is that they are used by some programs as the default location for retrieving and saving user data files. The idea of the home directory is that it is a place for your users to store their personal files.

With the release of Windows 2000, Microsoft has minimized the role of the home directory by giving each user a My Documents directory. This directory is actually stored in the user's profile as you will see in the next section. It is now becoming more common that software is written so that the user's My Documents directory is the default location for user file storage, making it in essence a replacement for the role of the home directory in Windows NT 4.0. This storage location is required by Microsoft for developers to use as the default for their application's user data file storage, if they want to meet the Windows 2000 Logo Standards.

So with the diminishing importance of home directories in Windows 2000, what role do they play in a Terminal Server environment? The answer is that they play a very important one. In addition to users needing a place to store their files, so do many applications. Unfortunately, these applications are in many cases not designed with a Terminal Server environment in mind. Instead of storing their data in a separate location for each user, such as the user's profile directory, some applications store data in only one directory. When two users try to use the same application at the same time, conflicts occur.

For example, an application might need a working directory location where it can store data files for whoever is using the application. Instead of putting the data file in a user-specific directory, such as the user's profile directory, the application instead is written to store the data files under the application folder. When one user runs the application, it works fine. When two users try to run the application on the same machine using Terminal Server, however, the application tries to write to the same location for both users causing a conflict and likely an application error.

Windows 2000 and XP Logo Standards

Microsoft has put together a set of standards that Windows 2000/.NET application developers must meet for them to use the Windows 2000 or .NET compatible logo. These standards are referred to as the *Windows Logo Standards*.

These standards are very important to understand for Windows Terminal Server administrators. Applications that meet these requirements will most often run in a Terminal Server environment without need for special modifications or Registry changes. The main reason why is that Windows 2000 or .NET logo applications are required to store user-specific information in a user-specific area rather than a common area. Applications that meet the requirements for either the Windows 2000 or Windows .NET Logo must store their data as follows:

- User-specific settings should be stored in the user's Registry.

- If there is need to store more than 64K of user settings or other user-specific information, it needs to be stored in the user's profile directory under the Application Data folder.

- Any user-specific application data, which does not need to roam with the user, should be stored in the user's local profile directory under the Local Settings, Application Data folder.

For more detailed information on the logo requirements, you can go to www.microsoft.com/winlogo.

Understanding Home Directories and Application Compatibility Scripts

In response to the problem of applications not storing data in the correct location, Microsoft created a set of scripts called the *application compatibility scripts*. You will find these scripts under the `%systemroot%\application compatibility scripts` directory on both your Windows NT 4.0 and 2000 Terminal Servers. These scripts are designed to eliminate problems with the following applications running on Terminal Server:

- Microsoft Office 4.3 and 97
- Lotus Smart Suite 97

- PeachTree Accounting 6
- Microsoft Outlook 98
- Power Builder 6
- SNA Client 4.0
- Visio 5.0
- ODBC (log directory)
- Netscape Communicator 4.0
- Corel Office 7.0 and 8.0
- Eudora 4.0
- Microsoft Visual Studio 6.0

The scripts work for the most part by using utilities to make changes to the parts of the Registry or .INI files on which the application depends. The scripts search for specific user settings directories used by the application and replaces them with the home drive letter for the user.

Suppose, for example, that the user working directory for the fictional Acme Office was incorrectly set by the application developer underneath the application directory `%programfiles%\acmeoffice\workdir`. When multiple people try to run this application on Terminal Server, the application crashes because more than one user tries to share the same user working directory.

To fix this problem, you would run an application compatibility script for Acme Office, which replaced the `%programfiles%\acmeoffice\workdir` entry in the Registry with the user's home directory. In this way because each user's home directory is mapped to a different location, the application is able to run for multiple users. The application compatibility scripts also can be designed to run every time a user logs on so that Registry changes that need to be propagated to each user's own Registry area can be done at logon.

A Sample Application Compatibility Script

To better understand how this process works, take a look at one of the application compatibility scripts located under the `%systemroot%\application compatibility scripts\install` directory. Listing 9.1 is a condensed version of the ODBC.CMD application compatibility script for ODBC.

Listing 9.1 **Sample Application Compatibility Script**

```
@Echo Off

Call "%SystemRoot%\Application Compatibility Scripts\ChkRoot.Cmd"
If "%_CHKROOT%" == "FAIL" Goto Done

Set __OrigMode=Install
ChgUsr /query > Nul:
if Not ErrorLevel 101 Goto Begin
Set __OrigMode=Exec
Change User /Install > Nul:
:Begin

..\acsr "#ROOTDRIVE#" "%RootDrive%" Template\NetNav30.Key NetNav30.Key
regini netnav30.key > Nul:

Rem If original mode was execute, change back to Execute Mode.
If "%__OrigMode%" == "Exec" Change User /Execute > Nul:
Set __OrigMode=

FindStr /I Nav30Usr %SystemRoot%\System32\UsrLogn2.Cmd >Nul: 2>&1
If Not ErrorLevel 1 Goto Skip1
Echo Call Nav30Usr.Cmd >> %SystemRoot%\System32\UsrLogn2.Cmd
```

Notice that the first thing the script does is run the CHKROOT.CMD batch file. This batch file does the following:

1. Checks whether a home directory has been defined for the user in the ROOTDRV2.CMD file.

2. If not, it creates a new ROOTDRV2.CMD file, brings it up in Notepad, and instructs you to set the root drive and save the file, as shown in Figure 9.7.

The root drive is the drive letter mapped to the root of your home directory every time you log on. This is done by the local %systemroot%\system32\ usrlogon.cmd file when the user logs on, as you will see in the next section.

When this step is complete, the ODBC.CMD file changes to install mode and then runs the ACSR utility. The ACSR utility is a search-and-replace utility that first makes the Registry changes defined in the NETNAV30.KEY file, and then scans the Registry for every instance of #ROOTDRIVE# and replaces it with whatever you set the root drive to in the ROOTDRV2.CMD file.

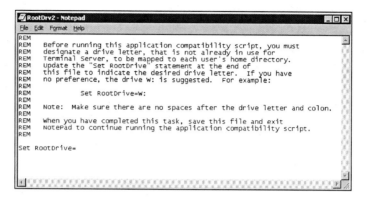

Figure 9.7 Setting the root drive.

Finally, the ODBC.CMD file appends a special startup script to the USLOGN2.CMD file in the `%systemroot%\system32` directory. This script is run when each user logs on and creates the application directories for that user underneath his root drive.

The effect of this rather convoluted process is that now the application will run correctly in a multi-user environment.

Most of the remaining application compatibility scripts under the `install` directory work in much the same way as ODBC.CMD. They basically do the following:

1. Ensure that the root drive or home directory is set and defined in the ROOTDRV2.CMD command file. If not, it brings up the command file in Notepad so that you can define it as shown in Figure 9.7.

2. Replace any user-specific directory entry in the Registry or .INI files that the application uses with `%root drive%\[application directory name]`.

3. Add their own scripts to the USRLOGN2.CMD batch file that need to be run when every user logs on. Usually these scripts create any necessary application directories for the user under his root drive.

Home Directories and the USRLOGON.CMD

The last piece missing in this puzzle is the understanding of how the root drive gets mapped to the home directory using the USRLOGON.CMD file. Unlike standard Windows NT 4.0 and 2000 Server, every person who logs on to a Windows NT 4.0 or 2000 Terminal Server runs the local `%systemroot%\system32\usrlogon.cmd` batch file. This script is run for every user right after his personal logon script is run.

The USRLOGON.CMD file does the following:

1. Sets the several environment variables equal to certain user settings such as the directory location of the user's Start menu. These environment variables are used by certain application compatibility scripts.

2. Runs the USRLOGN1.CMD command file if it exists. Some application compatibility scripts create this batch file to be run at every logon.

3. Runs the following commands to map the root drive to the root of the user's home directory:

```
net use %rootdrive% /d >nul: 2>&1
subst %rootdrive% "%homedrive%%homepath%"
```

4. Runs the USRLOGN2.CMD command file if it exists.

Notice in step 3 how the USRLOGON.CMD file uses the subst command to map the root drive to the root of the user home directory. This step is taken only if the root drive is defined in the ROOTDRV2.CMD batch file in the application compatibility scripts directory. If it is not, this part of the script is skipped.

The %homedrive% and %homepath% are set by the operating system to whatever you defined as the user's Terminal Server home directory using either the User Manager for Domains or the Active Directory Users and Computers tool. If you set your user's Terminal Server home directory to h:\jsmith, when that user logs on to Terminal Server his %homedrive% will equal "H" and his %homepath% will equal "\jsmith". If you defined the root drive to be W:, the USRLOGON.CMD batch file will use the subst command to map W: to the root of h:\jsmith.

If you do not set a home directory for Terminal Server, when the user logs on, %homedrive% and %homepath% will be set to the regular user home directory. If neither the Terminal Server nor regular user home directory is set for the user, the home directory is set by default to the user's profile directory.

Local Versus Connect for Home Directory

When setting up the home directory in User Manager or Active Directory Users and Computers, you can specify one of two paths: either a local path or a drive letter connected to a UNC path (\\[Server Name]\[Share Name]).

Local paths are useful with Terminal Server if your user logs on only to Terminal Server and does not log on to any other machine in the domain. Because users log on to Terminal Server as if they were locally logging on, the local path refers to a folder on the local hard drive of the Terminal

Server. If you set the local path to c:\users\[username], when the user logs on to the domain from Terminal Server, his home directory is set to c:\user\[username] on the c: drive of the Terminal Server.

Entering a UNC path next to Connect is a better option if your users want to keep their home directories in the same location no matter where they log on to the domain from. To set up the home directory using a UNC path, you must first share your user directory on the network. Next, enter the UNC path \\server name] \[user directory share name] for the Connect path and select a drive letter to connect it to. Now when the user logs on to the domain from Terminal Server or from any workstation, his home directory path is set to the UNC path you entered.

Map Rooting in Windows 2000

One very nice and seldom noticed new feature in Windows 2000 is the built-in capability to map root to folders underneath shares on the network. This is a very important feature to understand for Terminal Server administrators who need to ensure that user home directories are map rooted to the root of the user's folder on a user share.

To understand what the difference is, set up a Users share somewhere on the network and put a JSMITH folder underneath it. Now go to your Windows NT 4.0 Terminal Server or any Windows NT 4.0 workstation or server and run the following command:

```
net use x: \\[server]\users\jsmith
```

Next go to a Windows 2000 Terminal server or any Windows 2000 Server or workstation and run the following command:

```
net use x: \\[server]\users\jsmith
```

You will find that on Windows NT 4.0, instead of mapping X: to the root of \\[server]\users\jsmith folder, X: was mapped to the root of the \\[server]\users share. To get to the user directory, you need to go down one level to x:\jsmith.

On the Windows 2000 machine you will find that the X: drive was properly connected to the root of the JSMITH folder.

This problem in Windows NT 4.0 is what led to the use of the subst statement in logon scripts such as the USR-LOGON.CMD to map to the root of the user directory. If you run the following command on Windows NT 4.0, the H: drive would map properly to the root of the x:\jsmith home directory:

```
subst h: x:\jsmith
```

In other words, if your Terminal Servers are all Windows 2000, there is no need to use a subst statement anymore in the logon script to map the home directory!

In addition, say your home directory in your user settings is set to Connect X: to \\[server]\users\jsmith. When you log on to the domain from a Windows 2000 Terminal Server, it will now map X: to the root of the JSMITH folder.

Home Directory Setup Recommendations

Now that you have a better idea of the many aspects of home directory usage, the following are some specific recommendations on how to set up home directories for your environment. Although there are other methods of setting up home directories, the technique shown in the following sections is simple and works well for most small to large environments.

Create a Central User Share for Home Directories

One key tenet of Terminal Server setup is to avoid putting data on your Terminal Servers. User data should always be kept on a central share. In large environments, consider using server clustering on the central share.

The main reason for this is that if any Terminal Server fails, you can more quickly recover from the failure if you do not also have to deal with user data restoration. In addition, in a load-balanced MetaFrame environment, storing user data centrally makes it very easy to load balance your users between servers.

The following are the basic steps to do this:

1. Create a share on your main file server for Terminal Server home directories.

2. Remove any default share security, and then grant read/write access to the share to the TSUsers group (if you created one) and full control to TSAdmins.

3. Grant read-only file rights to the root of the share to TSUsers and full control to TSAdmins.

4. As each new user is added, create a user folder for him by his logon name and grant his read/write access to the folder; grant TSAdmins full control.

Choose a Home Directory Drive Letter and Map Root to It

First you need to choose the home directory drive letter that all of your users will use. h: for home directory is an easy-to-understand and common choice.

In either your central domain logon script, container logon script, or local USRLOGON.CMD script, map root the home directory drive letter to the user's home directory when she logs on. The following is an example statement to do this. For more examples of how to do this and which logon script to use, see the "User Logon Scripts" section later in this chapter.

```
subst h: \\[server]\tsusers\%username%
```

Set the User's Terminal Server Home Directory

Using either User Manager or the Active Directory Users and Computers tool, ensure that the local drive setting for the user's Terminal Server home directory is set for the home directory drive letter. Let the logon script take care of mapping the drive letter to the directory. Even though it is possible to map the drive letter to the user share using the connect option, if the user logs on from Windows NT 4.0, this does not map to the root of the share. For consistent mapping of the home directory, it is best to control it through the logon script.

Point User-Specific Data to the Home Drive

After installing your applications, you need to ensure that the applications save their user-specific data to the user's home drive. If an application compatibility script is available for your application, run it. Ensure the root drive is set to the drive letter of your user's home directory. These scripts will automatically replace any user specific data setting in the Registry or .INI files to the root drive.

The application compatibility scripts generally rely on the USR LOGON.CMD file being run. Make sure that you run the scripts on each server on which you have the application installed, making sure to set the root drive to the same letter. You will likely need to change the USR LOGON.CMD file to map the home directory correctly.

If there is not an application compatibility script for your application, as part of your application compatibility testing, you will need to search the Registry and settings files for file storage locations and replace any user-specific file storage location with the home directory. For more information on how to do this see Chapter 13, "Installing Applications."

Encourage Users to Save Documents to Their Home Drive

It is important to encourage users to save documents to their home drive and never to the server or to their My Documents directory. If they save it to the Terminal Server or MetaFrame server, this will greatly complicate the restoration process if you need to recover from a server outage, because you will have to determine whether there were any user documents on the server.

Dealing with the My Documents Folder

By default, most new applications default to saving their documents in the My Documents folder. The My Documents folder is kept in the user's profile. If you centralize your profiles, as recommended in this chapter, that means the My Documents folder for your users is actually kept in the central profile location for your users. When users log on and log off, a copy of the profile is sent to and from the central location.

If users save a lot of documents to their My Documents folder, it can significantly lengthen logon and logoff times as the folder is copied to and from the central profile location. In addition, if profiles are not centralized, users will have a different profile on each server and different My Documents folders, which can quickly lead to confusion.

The easiest solution is to just discourage your users from storing documents in their My Documents folder.

If you are in a pure Windows 2000 environment, you have another option referred to as *My Documents redirection*. Using group policies you can enforce a policy so that your user's My Documents folder are kept in a central network location and not in their profile directory. This is a very good policy to implement with Terminal Server.

Understanding Profiles and Profile Settings

The next user settings that need to be discussed are profiles. The role of user profiles in a Terminal Server environment is critical to understand. All Terminal Server users, whether on Windows NT 4.0 or 2000, have their own profile. On Windows NT 4.0 Terminal Servers, you will find the profile located under the `%systemroot%\profiles\[username]` directory. On Windows NT 2000 the location has moved to `%systemdrive%\documents and settings\[username]`. Under this directory you will find the following user-specific information:

- **User Registry settings**   This includes user Registry settings for applications such as application user preferences. This also includes user desktop preferences, mapped drives, printers, and any other setting included in the HKEY Local User area of the Registry. The file that contains the user Registry is NTUSER.DAT and is located in the root of the profile.

- **My Documents and My Pictures (Windows 2000 only)**   In Windows 2000, your profile also includes the My Documents and My Pictures folders intended for the storage of personal documents and pictures. It is highly discouraged to use these folders.

- **Application data (Windows 2000 only)**   To meet Windows 2000 and XP Logo Standards, applications should store their user-specific application data in this directory.

- **Local settings**   Contains user-specific application data that does not need to roam with the user. This directory is not replicated with a central roaming profile if one is set up.

- **Templates**   Contains legacy user templates from various applications.

- **NetHood** Network neighborhood favorites and links.
- **Start menu** Start menu shortcuts for the user.
- **Windows settings** The Windows folder will appear only in a Terminal Server user's profile. It is used for maintaining user-specific .INI files and other Windows components that are normally kept only in the central Windows directory. In this way each user has a separate copy of an application's .INI files and does not share a central one.

In addition to these folders and files, various applications will put their own information in the user profile directory when the application is run.

Roaming Profiles and Terminal Server

By default with Terminal Server, your profile is stored locally on whatever server that you log on to. If you normally log on to just one server, this technique works fine because your user settings will be stored on that server in a local profile directory.

If you access applications on multiple servers, however, which is often the case with Terminal Server, things can quickly get complicated. Because your profiles are stored locally on each server, you will have a different user profile on every server you log on to—this means a different desktop, application settings, My Documents directory, and more. If you run an application that is load balanced across servers, the application settings will differ depending on which server you log on to.

Suppose, for example, that you run an application that is load balanced across two servers. The first time you log on, you are sent to server one. You make a change to an application setting while logged on to the server, such as changing the view of the application. When you log on the next day, you are sent to server two instead. Because the setting change was stored in your profile on server one, you do not see the change while logged on to server two. You then need to make the same change again.

In addition, disaster recovery is made much more difficult with local profiles. If a server fails or you need to move users to another server, you will have to deal with restoring the user profile directory. If you do not, your users will lose any application and desktop setting changes that they made. If they stored any documents in their My Documents folder or anywhere else in their profile directory, they would lose them when the switch is made.

For these reasons and more, it is highly recommended to centralize your profile using the roaming profile capability with Terminal Server. Much like centralizing your user home directories, centralizing profiles allows users to freely move between Terminal Servers while their central profile settings follow them.

To centralize the profiles, you create a share on one of your file servers. Then in either User Manager or Active Directory User and Computers, change the Terminal Server User Profile setting to point to the share for the user's profile.

Roaming Profiles and Space Usage

Because applications reference files in the user profile directory often during use, if those profiles were accessed centrally by hundreds of people, it could quickly cause performance issues with both your network and with your applications. For this reason, both in Windows NT 4.0 and 2000 your roaming profile is copied to a local profile directory when you log on. While you are using the application on that server, you are using the settings in the local copy of the roaming profile. When you log off, any profile changes you have made are uploaded to the central roaming profile directory.

Although roaming profiles can be a big help with Terminal Server, they also can be the source of several issues, especially if they become too large. Profiles are generally somewhere between 500K and 5MB in size for average use. If users save large files to their My Documents directory, or if a user's applications save large amounts of data to the profile, however, they can quickly grow to 25MB or more in size.

Profiles allowed to grow this large can quickly fill up system drive space. It is not unusual to see profile directories that by themselves are 500MB to 1GB in size in large environments. Unfortunately, the only place that profiles can be stored is on the system drive. This is one of the main reasons why planning for a minimum of 4GB for your system drive is important with Terminal Server (even though the operating system will take only around 1GB). When you add 500MB to 1GB in profiles and another 500MB to 1GB in application DLLs and other system files, you can quickly reach 3 to 4GB.

Large profiles also can slow down logon and logoff times as the profile is downloaded from and uploaded to the central profile location. You can view the size of all the profiles on a single server by doing the following on Windows 2000:

1. Right-click the My Computer icon and select Properties.

2. In the System Properties window, click the User Profiles tab.
   You will see a list of profiles and their size similar to that shown in Figure 9.8. It is a good idea to periodically review the size of the profiles on your Terminal Servers to determine whether any are growing unnecessarily large.

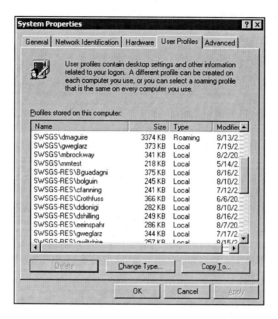

Figure 9.8 Roaming profiles.

Windows 2000 Profile Merging

When you log on to a Windows NT 4.0 Terminal Server and are using a roaming profile, the server first checks the time stamp on the local profile to determine whether it is newer than the roaming one. If so, it will prompt you as to which one to use. If not, the operating system just overwrites the local profile with the roaming one. When you log off, the opposite process occurs. Any changes you made to the local profile, while you were logged on, are now written to the roaming profile as you log off.

Although this simple method works well in most cases, in some situations problems can occur. Suppose, for example, that you are logged on to two servers at the same time, each server having a copy of your central profile. You make a change to something in your profile, such as deleting a file on one of the servers then logoff. As you log off, the changes you made to the profile are uploaded centrally and the file you deleted is deleted on the central profile. Next you log off of the second server. Because the second server still has a copy of the file you had deleted on the first, it uploads it back to the central profile! Although this is likely not a frequent event, issues like this would occur more often in a multiuser, multiserver Terminal Server environment.

With Windows 2000, Microsoft has implemented a more advanced profile merging algorithm rather than just a profile copy. As you log on Windows 2000, the following happens:

1. The time you logged on to the server is recorded locally.

2. Your central profile is synchronized with your local profile at a file level. File date and time stamps are com pared to ensure that newer files are not overwritten on your local profile.

3. If there are any newer files on your local profile, you do *not* get the Your local profile is newer than your roaming, do you want to use the local profile? prompt as you would in NT 4.0.

4. After you have finished your work and log off, your local files are again synchronized with your central profile. Any changes you made to files on your local profile are written to the central one.

5. If you delete a file from your local profile, it is normally deleted from your central profile during the synchronization. However, the system first compares the logon time recorded in step 1 to the file date and time stamp on the central profile that it is about to delete.

6. If they are the same, it knows that the file was the one you brought down during logon and deletes the file.

7. If the file on the central profile is newer than the time you logged on, this file likely was updated on another server and is *not* deleted.

Roaming Profiles Versus Local Profiles

Because of the heavy use of profiles with Terminal Server, it is important to thoroughly understand how they work. The flowchart shown in Figure 9.9 shows the process that Windows 2000 goes through every time someone logs on to ensure that her profile is set up correctly.

Note the following important points in Figure 9.9:

- No More Use local or remote profile prompt. Unlike Windows NT 4.0, Windows 2000 will never prompt users whether they should use the local profile or the roaming profile if it detects files on the local profile are newer. Instead it just synchronizes the local profile with the roaming one at logon, overwriting only older files on the local profile with newer ones from the roaming profile.

- If the roaming profile is set, but the profile cannot be accessed, it will use the local. If you have set your user to use a roaming profile, but the server it is on is down or the share is inaccessible, the system will warn the user and then use the local profile. This is good to know. If you need to take the central profile server down during the day, users will still be able to work off of their local profile.

- If the roaming profile is set but cannot be accessed and there is no local profile, it will create a temp profile. This is a new feature with Windows 2000. If no local profile or accessible roaming profile is available, it will create a temporary profile for the user to work with, instead of denying the user the ability to log on.

- If a roaming profile directory does not exist, it is created automatically. This is a very handy feature as you will see in the following section on migrating local profiles to roaming ones. If there is no roaming profile folder set up for the user, but the profile server is accessible, a new roaming profile directory will be created automatically for the user. The default rights for the directory grant full access to it for the user and for SYSTEM.

- The local default user profile is used as the initial profile. If there is no local profile, the system will create one using a copy of the hidden default user profile. This also can be handy because you can add files to the default user profile that you want every new user on that server to have.

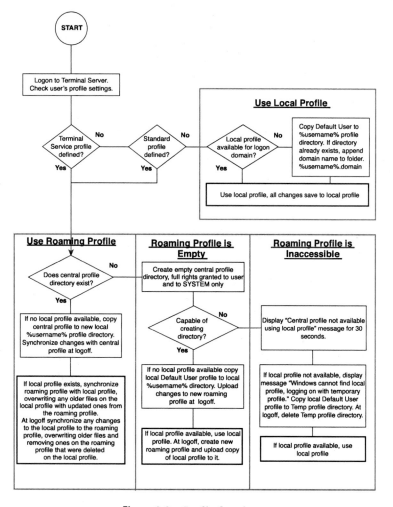

Figure 9.9 Profile flowchart.

Migrating from Local to Roaming Profiles

Often administrators might need to migrate existing users and their local profiles to roaming ones without losing any of the settings in the local profile. This is very easy to do by taking advantage of the auto-profile creation feature of Windows 2000. However, you need to follow these instructions exactly:

1. Create a central profile share on one of your file servers.

2. Grant either the domain Users or TSUser's group read/write access to the share.

3. Grant either the domain Users or TSUser's group full control file rights to the root of the share so that they can create new profile folders.

4. Change the Terminal Server Profile setting for each user to point to `\\[profile server]` `\profiles\[username]`. Make sure that the profile directory for `[username]` does not already exist.

5. Log on each user to the server that you want to upload the user's profile from (you can pick only one server) and then log the user off.

As each user logs on to the network, the server will realize that the central profile directory does not exist for the user and will create it. When the user logs off the server, it will copy his local profile from that server up to the new roaming profile directory. From this point forward the user will always use his roaming profile on other servers.

One thing to be aware of with this technique is that as each profile directory is created, the profile user and the SYSTEM user are granted full rights, but not the administrator. After all the profiles are created, you will have to take ownership of the profile directories and manually add other permissions, such as given access to the profile directories for domain admins or TSAdmins.

Profile Best Practices

So now that you understand the many different aspects of profiles, it is time to discuss how to best implement them in your environment. The following are some general best practices for implementing profiles with Terminal Server:

- **Use roaming profiles.**   Even if you only have a few servers, use roaming profiles rather than local profiles. There are many advantages to using roaming profiles in a Terminal Server environment, including ease of movement between servers and quicker recovery times.

- **Set profile location using Terminal Server profile.**   Although you can set the profile location using the standard profile location, it is almost always best to use the Terminal Server Profile location instead. This way your local desktop and settings are not confused with your Terminal Server roaming desktop and settings.

- **Use a share on a reliable server for profiles.** Set up a share on your most reliable file servers. Although Terminal Server can handle not having the share available, it is not recommended. They should be on a reliable and fast server. If you have a large server farm, consider clustering the server that contains the profile share.

- **Back up the profile share.** If you lose the profile share, your users lose a lot of setup information that can be tedious for them to re-create. Make sure you are taking backups of the central profile directory so that it can be restored quickly in case of problems.

Understanding Logon Scripts

Logon scripts can be nearly any type of program that you want to run when users first log on to the domain. Logon scripts are normally written as batch files that do such things as setting environment variables, mapping drive letters, and connecting LPT ports to printers. By assigning a single logon script to several users, you can easily centrally control your user's environment and desktop settings. More advanced logon scripts can centrally control user Registry changes, assign drive mappings based on groups, and even deploy software.

User Logon Scripts

In a Terminal Server environment, several different logon scripts can be run when a user logs on. The first logon script, is the one you define for each user using either the User Manager for Domains or the Active Directory Users and Computers tool in the user's properties.

When logging on to either a Windows NT 4.0 or Windows 2000 domain, this logon script is run from the NETLOGON share off the domain controller with which you authenticated. On a Windows NT 4.0 domain, the domain controller can be either primary domain controller (PDC) or backup domain controller (BDC) for the domain and the NETLOGON share is located in that server's %systemroot%\system32\repl\import\scripts directory. On a Windows 2000 domain controller, you will find the NET LOGON share underneath the [sysvol]\[domain name]\scripts folder. By default, the SYSVOL folder is located under the %systemroot% folder on a Windows 2000 domain controller.

Users can log on to either a PDC or BDC in Windows NT 4.0. Because the logon script that is run is run from whatever domain controller they logged on to, you need to manually replicate the logon script between the PDC and all BDCs. You also can set up a replication service for automated replication.

With Windows 2000, the logon scripts are kept under the SYSVOL folder that is replicated by default with all Windows 2000 domain controllers on that domain. As with Windows NT 4.0, the user will run the logon script from the local Windows 2000 domain controller.

Group Policy Logon Scripts

The second logon script that can be set to run for users is the group policy logon script. This logon script is run only by users who log on to a Windows 2000 domain from a Windows 2000 Terminal Server. The logon script must first be defined as a policy for the Active Directory container of which the user is a member. Any user in that container or its subcontainers will run the defined logon scripts at the point of logon. Like user logon scripts, these logon scripts can be pretty much any executable program or script file; however, they are normally batch files. They reside in the appropriate policy folder in the SYSVOL folder of the Windows 2000 domain controller and are replicated to other domain controllers for that domain.

In addition to logon scripts per user, you also can define system startup and shutdown scripts, and user logoff scripts.

To set up a group policy logon script for your users, follow these steps:

1. Open the Active Directory Users and Computers tool.

2. Right-click the organizational unit you want to set up logon scripts for and select Properties.

3. Click the Group Policy tab and click the New button.

4. Enter the name of the new policy and then click Edit to edit it.

5. Under the User Configuration, Windows Settings, Scripts (Logon/Logoff) folder, right-click the Logon icon and select Properties.

6. Click the Show Files button. The folder that contains the Logon Scripts for this organizational unit will be shown. Click the down arrow next to the Address bar to see the full path to the folder.

7. Cut and paste your logon scripts to this folder.

8. Close the window and click the Add button from the Logon Properties window.

9. Select the logon script you copied to this folder in step 7 and click OK. Then click OK again from the Logon Properties window.

If you are interested in setting up a system startup or shutdown script, go under the Computer Configuration, Windows Settings, Scripts (Startup/Shutdown Folder) in step 5 instead.

Using Windows 2000 Group Policy Scripts Effectively

The new ability to run logoff and system startup/shutdown scripts in Windows 2000 can be very beneficial to Terminal Server administrators, especially for handling periodic maintenance and user setting cleanup. The following are just some of the types of scripts you can set up:

- **Profile cleanup** You might want to delete certain folders under the user local profile folders that can take up unnecessary space at logoff such as the NetHood and My Documents folder. Create a small batch file logoff script to delete these from the %userprofile% folder.

- **Application cleanup** You might want to clean up certain user-specific application working files depending on the applications you have installed at the point of logoff.

- **Registry changes and file distribution** You can enforce certain Registry changes across your server farm or the distribution of a common set of files by putting all your Terminal Servers under a single OU and applying a startup script to that OU. The startup script would copy files from a central location to a local directory on the server and make any necessary Registry changes.

- **Server cleanup** A server shutdown script is a good place to put commands to clean up various directories on the server, especially directories that tend to grow over time. You might set up a periodic server restart program and use a shutdown script to archive log files, such as event logs to a central location.

USRLOGON.CMD Logon Script

All Terminal Server users run the local USRLOGON.CMD batch file every time they log on to the Terminal Server. This batch file is located in the %systemroot%\system32 directory. This special-purpose logon script file's main purpose is for use by the application compatibility scripts that come with Terminal Server. However, this file also can be used for other purposes as well. Because this logon script is run locally and not across the network, it runs faster (especially if your logon scripts are lengthy or rely on large executables). In addition, you can use this logon script for Terminal Serve–specific settings that do not need to be included in your main logon script.

For these reasons, some administrators choose to skip the main logon script and run the USRLOGON.CMD script instead. Using a batch file, you can easily set up a central USRLOGON.CMD file and push a copy of that file out to all the servers in your farm. Listing 9.2 is an example of such a script.

Listing 9.2   **Logon Script Propagation Batch File**

```
@echo off
echo Copying master logon script to server farm...
echo Updating [Server name]...
copy \\[servername]\m$\windows\system32\usrlogon.bk1
\\[servername]\m$\windows\system32\usrlogon.bk2
copy \\[servername]\m$\windows\system32\usrlogon.cmd
\\[servername]\m$\windows\system32\usrlogon.bk1
copy o:\tech\@scripts\usrlogon.cmd
\\[servername]\m$\windows\system32\usrlogon.cmd
copy o:\tech\@scripts\kx*.* \\[servername]\m$\windows\system32\
copy o:\tech\@scripts\kix*.* \\[servername]\m$\windows\system32\
copy o:\tech\@scripts\*.scr \\[servername]\m$\windows\system32\
copy o:\tech\@scripts\*.pol \\[servername]\m$\windows\system32\
....
```

In addition, Listing 9.2 will copy down any necessary KiXtart files and logon scripts if you use them in your environment. Just copy and paste the original script, for every server that you have in your environment, replacing [servername] with the name of the server to which you need to send a copy of the USRLOGON.CMD file. In this example, the system directory on the server is m:\windows\system32. This might also vary in your environment.

Using this script you would make modifications to the central USR LOGON.CMD batch file located in the o:\tech\@scripts directory on your primary Terminal Server. You would then run the UPDATE.BAT batch file to push this updated logon script to all of your Terminal Servers.

In addition, you could put the following command (see Listing 9.3) at the top of your user or group policy logon scripts to ensure that they were skipped in the case a user was logging on to a Terminal Server. The user would then run only the USRLOGON.CMD file on the Terminal Server.

Listing 9.3   **Skipping the Main Logon Script for Terminal Server Users**

```
@echo off
if exist %systemroot%\system32\usrlogon.cmd goto the_end
[body of the User or Group Policy Logon Script]
...
...
:the_end
```

Sample Logon Scripts

The following are some tips and some sample logon scripts that you can use in your environment.

- **Set up a single logon script for your location.**   Managing multiple logon scripts can get very complex, very quickly. You are best off setting up a single logon script. Divide out the logon script into a global section that applies settings for all users and a group specific section that applies settings only for certain groups. You can either use the Resource Kit's `ingroup` command or KiXtart to run code based on what groups the users are part of.

- **Report what the script is doing to the user.**   Report what the script is doing to the user using `@echo` commands. Let the user know whom to contact in case the script freezes or has some type of problem. On Windows 2000, the logon script will run minimized; however, it is possible for the logon script to hang or take significant time depending on what it is trying to do. See Listing 9.4 for an example.

Listing 9.4   **Displaying Logon Script Progress to the User**

```
@echo off    <- Disables command echoing
echo Acme Corporation Main Logon Script
echo.  <- Sends a linefeed to the console
echo Welcome to the Acme Corporate Network, if you encounter any
echo problems with this logon script please contact our help
echo desk at 757-HELP.
echo.
echo Mapping global drives
[Statements for global drive mappings]
echo Mapping user drives...
[Statements for user drive mappings]
echo Mapping group drives...
[Statements for group drive mappings]
echo Done!
```

- **Use the `subst` Command for Windows NT 4.0 and the `net use` command for Windows 2000 to map a home directory for the user.**   You should use the `subst` or `net use` command to map a home directory for the user. Map the home directory drive letter to the root of the user's home directory. Optionally you can have the script create the home directory if the user does not already exist. However, the user would need read/write access to the root of the home directory share. Listing 9.5 shows these techniques.

Listing 9.5   **Mapping Home Directories**

```
echo Mapping user home drive (H:)
subst h: /d > nul
net use h: /d > nul
if exist \\[home dir server]\users\%username%\. Goto MapHome
md \\[home dir server]\users\%username% > nul


:MapHome
if exist %systemroot%\system32\compmgmt.msc goto Win2K
subst h: \\gsmeta1\data\%username%
goto continue

:Win2K
net use h: \\gsmeta1\data\%USERNAME% > nul

:continue
```

Using KiXtart for Logon Scripts

Although everyone has her own preference for logon script languages, KiXtart is definitely worth taking a look at. Even if you have looked at it in the past, many things have changed in recent versions, adding important functionality and now the ability to debug your logon scripts. This freely available scripting language has several powerful and useful features, including the following capabilities:

- Run commands based on what group a user is a member of.
- Map drive letters.
- Set user wallpaper.
- Add, delete, and check for the existence of particular Registry keys.
- Receive user input and process it.

To implement a KiXtart logon script, follow these steps:

1. Download the latest version of KiXtart from `www.kixtart.org`.
2. Expand the files and copy them to your logon script directory. The KIX32.EXE executable is the core interpreter program and should be in the same directory as your logon script.
3. Create a script using KiXtart and add the following command to your logon script to run it:

```
%0\..\kix32.exe [kix script].scr
```

The `%0\..\` nomenclature is required for running the Kix logon script from the `netlogon` directory. For more information, refer to Microsoft article Q121387.

The following are some sample logon and other scripts that you can use in your Terminal Server environment:

- **Map drives based on group membership.** Often you need to map drives based on what group a user is a member of. Listing 9.6 shows you how. The first `ingroup` statement shows how to map the x: drive to a network share if the user is a member of [group name]. The second `ingroup` statement shows the use of the `shell` command for running regular DOS commands from within a KiXtart script.

Listing 9.6 **Mapping Drives Based on Group Membership**

```
IF INGROUP("[Group Name]")=1
USE X: "\\SERVER\SHARE"
ENDIF

IF (INGROUP("[Group Name]")=1 and @WKSTA="[Server Name]")
SHELL "SUBST W: O:\[Directory]"
ENDIF
```

- **Set wallpaper to none.** One handy feature of KiXtart is the ability to set the wallpaper. By using the following command, you can force the wallpaper to be set to none or to particular wallpaper at logon:

```
setwallpaper ("")  <-sets the wallpaper to none
or
setwallpaper ("[wallpaper].bmp")
```

This is a good idea in a Terminal Server environment, where graphically intense wallpaper slows the system down. Even more creatively you could use Paintbrush to create a message for your users, save it to a .BMP file in the `system` directory, and use this command to display it on the desktop as wallpaper. Another idea would be to create a .BMP file with the server name called SERVER.BMP and use this command to display the SERVER.BMP server name on all servers as the default wallpaper.

- **Check for the existence of applications or Registry keys.** Often it is handy to check for the existence of certain applications or Registry keys upon logon and then run commands based on the application found. Suppose, for example, you want to run an automated profile generator for Outlook, but only if Outlook is installed on the machine. The easiest way to do this is to check for the existence of the application keys underneath

HKLM\Software\Classes. Most applications, when they are installed, will create a subkey under here to report their existence to the operating system. The following script uses the existkey command to check for the existence of Outlook:

```
IF EXISTKEY ("HKEY_LOCAL_MACHINE\SOFTWARE\Classes\Outlook.Application") = 0
[Commands to run upon logon if Outlook is installed]
ENDIF
```

- **Add a Registry entry upon logon.** If you need to propagate a certain Registry entry to all of your users, the easiest way is through a logon script command. The following sample script creates a test Registry key and a string value:

```
ADDKEY ("HKEY_CURRENT_USER\SOFTWARE\Test")
WRITEVALUE ("HKEY_LOCAL_MACHINE\SOFTWARE\TEST","Test Variable","Test Value","REG_SZ")
```

Using the Resource Kit Utilities for Logon Scripts

For those who are familiar with batch files and do not want to learn another scripting language such as KiXtart, you can find a wealth of useful utilities you can use in your logon scripts in the Windows 2000 Server Resource Kit. The following are just a handful of the many utilities that you can use.

- **ifmember [group name]**   Checks whether the user is a member of the specified group. If Error Level is returned as 0, the user is a member of the group. You can use this in a batch file instead of using KiXtart's ingroup command.

- **drmapsrv**   A very useful tool for those who use only Terminal Server. This tool will automatically map drives on Terminal Server to client drives on the Terminal Services client. Much like the automatic drive-mapping feature in MetaFrame.

- **rdpclip**   Another useful tool for Terminal Server administrators. This one, when installed on both the client and the server, will enable you to cut and paste files from the server to the client and vice versa using the Clipboard.

- **sleep [seconds]**   Pauses a batch file for the specified number of seconds, and then resumes.

- **timeout [seconds]**   Pauses a batch file for the specified number of seconds, and then resumes. However, unlike SLEEP.EXE it will continue if a user presses a key.

- **gettype**   You can use this utility in a batch file to determine whether the server the user is logging on to is a Windows 2000 server or a Windows NT 4.0 Terminal Server.

- **usrstat**   Displays user's name and last logon date.

- **associate**   Associates a particular file extension with a particular file.

- **setx**   Enables you to set environment variables for a user. This can be very useful if you are running older applications that require environment variables.

- **delprof** A very handy tool in a Terminal Server environment that enables you to delete profiles, even remotely. Several command-line options are available.

For more information on the Resource Kit and how to get your own copy, go to www.microsoft.com/ windows2000/techinfo/reskit/default.asp. You also will find free tool downloads here.

Top-Ten User and Group Setup Tips

As a conclusion to all you have learned about setting up users, following are the top ten user and group setup tips:

1. **Standardize your naming conventions.** Always standardize your naming conventions as a first step when setting up new domains. Written naming conventions help make administration much easier in the long run.

2. **Create a TSUsers and TSAdmins group.** The TSUsers should have user-level access to your Terminal Servers, and TSAdmins should have administrator access by adding them to the local Users and Administrators groups. Do not allow users who are not members of the TSUsers group to log on to your Terminal Servers.

3. **Select a home directory drive.** Select a drive that you will use as the home directory for all of your users. Normally h: is a good choice. This is the drive letter you will use for your application compatibility scripts root drive and for any user-specific folder setting in your applications.

4. **Create a home directory folder for each user under the home directory share.** Create a central home directory share and create a home directory for each user under the share. Grant only rights for that user to their home directory.

5. **Map root the home directory drive to the home directory folder using logon scripts.** Using either a personal, group policy or local USRLOGON.CMD logon script, map the home directory drive letter to the root of the user's home directory folder using either the subst or net use commands.

6. **Use the same logon script for all Terminal Server users.** Set all of your Terminal Server users to use the same logon script so that you have central control of their logon settings.

7. **Create a roaming profile share and a folder for each user's profile under the share.** Create a central roaming share for user profiles. It should be a separate share from the user's home directories, unless you are certain users will not store significant data there. Remember that the entire profile directory gets copied down to the local servers as they log on. Lock the user folders so that only they, and administrators, have access.

8. **Point the Terminal Server profile path to the user's profile folder.** Using either User Manager or Active Directory Users and Computers, point the Terminal Server Profile Path to the user's profile folder under the profile share. Do not set the standard profile path, only the Terminal Server profile path.

9. **Set up App-[App Name], Desktop-[Server Name], and Doc-[Document Name] global or universal groups.** Set up these groups and grant them access to the application directory in the case of the App group, the desktop using group policies in the case of the Desktop group, and the document in case of the Doc group. If using MetaFrame, publish the application, desktop, or document to users in these groups.

10. **Delegate administration by embedding global App, Desktop, and Doc groups into universal groups.** If you are in a pure Windows 2000 environment, set up global App, Desktop, and Doc Universal groups for each container or domain. Embed all the global groups for a particular application, desktop, or document into a centrally controlled universal group. In this way, you can delegate control of who has access to applications, desktops, and documents on your Terminal Servers to administrators of these containers or domains.

10

Setting Up Terminal Server Connections

AFTER YOU HAVE SET UP YOUR USERS, the next step is to ensure that they have connections available at the server to connect to. You can make two main types of connection: RDP and ICA connections. RDP connections support connections to the Terminal Server by the Terminal Services client. ICA connections support connections by the Citrix ICA client.

Connections are defined by making connection entries using either the Terminal Services Configuration Tool or the Citrix Connection Configuration Tool depending on whether you have Citrix installed on your system. In this chapter, you will learn how to create connection entries using both tools.

Creating RDP and ICA Connections

For those already familiar with connection configuration under MetaFrame 1.8 or under Windows NT 4.0 Terminal Server, you will find that connection configuration has changed very little in MetaFrame XP and Windows 2000 Terminal Server. This is one of the few functions not handled by the Citrix Management Console in MetaFrame XP, because this is a per-server, locally controlled setting.

Using the appropriate connection configuration tool, you will need to define one connection entry for every protocol combination with which you want your users to be able to connect. With Terminal Server alone, only one protocol combination is possible, RDP over TCP, and thus only one type of connection entry. This entry is set up by default when you install Terminal Services. So unless you need to change a connection setting, you should be able to connect automatically to your Terminal Server as soon as you install Terminal Services.

With MetaFrame XP you also get the ICA protocol, which runs on top of many different protocol transports, such as TCP, IPX, SPX, direct serial connections (asynchronous), dial-in modem connections (asynchronous), and NetBEUI (NetBIOS). For every ICA protocol combination you need, such as ICA over TCP, or ICA over IPX, there must be a connection entry defined using the Citrix Connection Configuration Tool. By default, Citrix will create a connection entry for every protocol you have installed when you first install MetaFrame XP. If you need additional protocol combinations, you will need to add them manually later.

The following sections discuss the basics that you need to know to set up a new connection on your server and covers the many connection options you might want to modify for your connection. Many of the options you can set at a connection level are the same as those you can set on a user level. By setting them at a connection level, however, you can control the setting for any user who logs on to the server, regardless of what his user level setting is. In addition, you can set many important security options at a connection level that can greatly increase the security of your Terminal Servers.

Connection Configuration Tools

To work with the connections and connection entries on your Terminal Server, you need to use the Terminal Services Connection Configuration Tool, which is located in the Start menu under Programs, Administrative Tools. If you have Citrix MetaFrame installed, you should use the Citrix Connection Configuration Tool instead, located in the Programs, Citrix, MetaFrame XP folder. Both programs have a very similar user interface for connection modification. When you first start either of the tools, they will list the connection entries that have currently been created for your server. With both tools you can create, delete, modify, and rename connection entries.

During the installation of Terminal Server and MetaFrame, the respective install programs will automatically create the initial RDP and ICA connection entries that your clients must have to connect to the server. Take a look at Figure 10.1. This snapshot was taken from a MetaFrame server loaded with TCP/IP and IPX/SPX, right after the initial installation of Terminal

Server and MetaFrame. Notice that several connection entries have been defined automatically: ICA over IPX, ICA over TCP, and RDP over TCP. One initial connection entry has been created for each protocol combination currently available on the server, by their respective install programs.

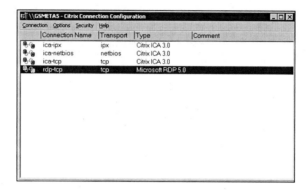

Figure 10.1   Citrix Connection Configuration Tool.

This initial setup will at least enable users to connect to the server. Because the initial connection entries are set for unlimited connections, you do not have to worry about manually increasing the number of connections if you add more Citrix or TS CAL licenses. The following, however, is a list of several reasons why you will likely want to modify the default settings:

- **Adding or deleting upper-layer (ICA or RDP) protocols**
  Generally for both reasons of performance and security, you should have connection entries set up only for the protocols you are going to use. If you intend to use ICA but not RDP, you should delete the default RDP connection entry.

- **Adding or deleting lower-layer protocols (IPX, TCP, async)**   If you add or delete protocols from the server, you must add or delete the related connection entries within the Citrix or TS Connection Configuration Tool.

- **Changing options**   You might want to change many options such as idle times, what devices are mapped, and initial startup programs for each connection entry. These options are covered in detail in the "Connection Options" section later in the chapter.

- **Adding/removing modems from your server (MetaFrame only)**
  Although network connection entries are defined once for every protocol combination, you need to define connection entries individually for each modem with which you want your remote clients to be able to directly dial into MetaFrame.

Only Define Connections You Need

It is very important for reasons of security, reliability, and performance to define connection entries only for those protocols that you intend to use. If you have installed Citrix and will be setting up ICA clients only, there is no need for RDP. You can delete or disable the RDP connection entry using the Terminal Services Configuration Tool.

Already, as of this writing, at least two known vulnerabilities exist in the Microsoft RDP protocol (search for article MS01-040 and MS01-052 at www.microsoft.com/security). Hotfixes are available at http://windowsupdate.microsoft.com to fix these vulnerabilities. Because both ICA and RDP are network services, however, it is very important to ensure your servers are patched with the latest service packs and applicable hotfixes, and that you do not enable connection entries unnecessarily.

Creating RDP Connections

Creating connections is a relatively easy process. This short subsection covers how to set up a basic RDP connection entry by using the Terminal Server Connection Configuration Tool. The many more advanced options that you can set are covered in the "Advanced Options" section later in the chapter. To set up the entry, follow these steps:

1. Open the TS Connection Configuration Tool from the Programs, Administrative Tools folder.

2. From the Terminal Services Connection Configuration window, select Create New Connection from the Action menu.

3. From the Terminal Services Connection Wizard that appears, click Next, and then select RDP 5.0 from the drop-down list and click Next again.

4. Select the Encryption menu and click Next again.

5. At the Remote Control screen, select whether users who use this connection can have their session remote controlled and click Next.

6. Enter the name of the session and click Next.

7. At the Network Adapter window, select whether all adapters have this protocol bound to it or just one of the adapters. Also select what the maximum number of connections will be, click Next, and then click Finish.

After the RDP connection is created, you are immediately able to attach to your server by using RDP clients, up to the maximum number of connections you defined or for which you are licensed.

Creating ICA Connections

Because of the additional protocol transports available with ICA, the decisions involved in creating ICA connections are a little more complex. This subsection covers the setup of a basic ICA connection entry and the advantages and disadvantages of the many transports available for ICA connections. To set up an ICA connection entry, follow these steps:

1. Open the Citrix Connection Configuration Tool from the Programs, Citrix, MetaFrame XP folder.

2. Select New from the Connections menu.

3. From the New Connection window that appears, enter the connection name.

4. Select Citrix ICA 3.0 for the Type from the drop-down list.

5. Select the Transport type that you want for the connection. Your choices are async, IPX, SPX, NetBIOS, or TCP, depending on which protocols are loaded on your server.

6. If you selected async, you need to select the communication port for this connection. You need to create a connection entry for every communication port on your server. If the modem is not yet installed on this port, you can click the Install Modem button.

7. Click either the Advanced, Client Settings or ICA Settings buttons to set additional options for this connection. These options are covered in detail later in this section.

8. Click OK when finished to create the connection.

After you have created your ICA connection, you can use it immediately.

ICA Protocol Transport Choices

Because of the many protocol transport choices with ICA, it can be difficult to choose which one you need to use. The following is a list of each of the choices available and their advantages and disadvantages:

- **TCP**   This is the most widely supported protocol and the recommended choice for most network configurations. You will find that nearly all possible client types support TCP for connections to a MetaFrame server. This protocol is well designed for WANs, is routable, and is the only protocol that will enable you to provide access to your Citrix farm across the Internet.

- **Async (asynchronous protocol)**   Using an async connection you can dial directly into your server using a standard dial-up modem or null modem cable. This protocol supports all types of asynchronous access to the server through standard asynchronous communications ports, such as COM1 or COM2, or multiport communications cards, such as a Digiboard.

- **NetBIOS**   The version of NetBIOS referred to with Terminal Server connections is the one that rides on top of NetBEUI (NetBIOS Extended User Interface). It is a very simple protocol with low overhead. NetBIOS is not routable and is a good choice only for small networks or test environments.

- **IPX**   This is a routable protocol commonly found on Novell networks. IPX is an ideal choice if your clients currently use only IPX.

- **SPX**   SPX works at the session layer, above IPX. Because with SPX a session is established between clients and server, the link tends to be more stable than IPX alone. It also means that extra protocol overhead can degrade performance. SPX is routable. Generally IPX is a better choice for connection to a Citrix server in a Novell environment unless you are having lost connection or timeout problems.

Connection Options

The real power of connections is the many connection options available. To see the different options, double-click one of your connection entries. When the New Connections dialog box appears, you will see buttons for Advanced, Client Settings, and, if you have MetaFrame installed, ICA Settings. You can click any of these buttons to open a dialog box from which you can select the related options. Connection options apply to all users that connect using a particular connection entry.

The following sections describe the different connection options. Because these options can often be controlled on different levels, the first part of this section considers the differences between configuring these options at a connection, user, and client level. The subsections that follow describe the purpose of the options available after clicking the Advanced, Client Settings, and ICA Settings buttons.

Configuring Options at Different Levels

To understand how options are set, you must first understand the difference between setting options at a connection, user, and client level.

Options set at the connection level are global options for a connection type. They are what this chapter is all about. If you want to set an option that affects all users who connect to the server using a particular protocol combination, setting them at the connection level is the way to do it. Connection options can override whatever has been set on either a user or client level.

Many of the same options that can be set on a connection level, such as Timeouts and Initial Program, also can be set on a user level. User-level options are set by using the User Manager for Domains administrative tool. These options apply only to the user from whom you set them.

Many of the connection-level options also can be set at the client level. Client configuration options are set by using the client software. Client configuration options enable you to set up AutoLogon or to run a particular application when the session is first started (Initial Program setting). Just as with user-level options, client options can be overridden by connection-level options.

Consider, for example, the Disable Logon setting. If you wanted to disable logons to Terminal Server for a particular user, you would disable their ability to log on by unchecking the Allow Logon to Terminal Server button in the user's properties under the Terminal Services Profile tab in Active Directory Users and Computers. If you wanted to disable logon for a particular connection on a server, however, you would disable logon by clicking the Logons Disabled radio button in the Advanced settings window for the connection. This would disable the ability for all users who attempted to attach to the server from using this connection type.

Table 10.1 shows all the connection options that will be covered in this section that also can be set at a user and/or client level. This table applies for both Terminal Server and MetaFrame, except as noted.

Table 10.1 **Terminal Server and MetaFrame Connection, User-and Client-Level Options**

Option	Connection Level	User Level	Client Level
INITIAL PROGRAM	X	X	X
Encryption Level	X		X (Citrix MetaFrame only)
AutoLogon	X		X
Logon Disabled or Enabled	X	X	
Idle Time Limit	X	X	
Disconnect Time Limit	X	X	

continues ▶

Table 10.1 **Continued**

Option	Connection Level	User Level	Client Level
Active Time Limit	X	X	
Connect to Client Printers and Set Default Printer	X	X	
Disable User Wallpaper	X		
Disable Printer, LPT, COM, and Clipboard Mapping Overrides	X		
CITRIX METAFRAME-ONLY SETTINGS			
Sound Quality	X		X
Connect Client Drives	X		X
Disable Audio Mapping	X		X
Only Run Published Applications	X		
Disable Drive Mapping	X		

Advanced Options

You can get to the advanced options by double-clicking the connection entry you want to modify and then clicking the Advanced button in the Edit Connection dialog box. The Advanced Connection Settings dialog box, shown in Figure 10.2, appears with its wide variety of advanced options. Advanced options are settable for both RDP- and ICA-based connection entries.

The following list briefly describes the different advanced options available:

- **Logon** Allows you to enable or disable the ability to log on to the connection.

- **AutoLogon** Enables you to define a username and password by which all users of this connection automatically log on.

- **Timeout Settings** Lets you define idle, active, and disconnect timeouts for all users who attach to this connection.

- **Security** Allows you to select the level of encryption enforced for users of this connection.

- **Initial Program** Launches a particular application for all users of this connection.

- **User Profile** Provides the ability to disable user wallpaper.
- **Other Settings** Finally, other noncategorized settings are available for controlling shadowing and disconnect behavior.

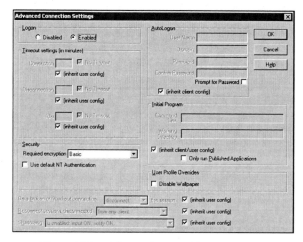

Figure 10.2 Advanced options for connections.

Initial Program Option

The Initial Program option defines the command line and working directory for an application that will run every time users attach to this connection and log on. By default, the initial program is inherited from either the client-level or the user-level settings.

Setting the Initial Program option at a connection level is a good option for environments in which all users need to run only a single application. Be aware, however, that this option also forces administrators who attach using this connection to run that application.

One good use for this option is for asynchronous connections. Suppose you were to set up a bank of modems with an asynchronous connection for each modem that has the Initial Program option set. Any user dialing into this modem bank would be able to run only the application you set. This improves server security by providing remote users access to a single application versus providing them access to an entire Windows desktop.

Encryption

Encryption is enabled by default with both RDP and ICA connections. With RDP, encryption can be controlled only at a connection level.

Three levels of encryption security are available: Low, Medium, and High. RDP encryption security is initially set to Medium, which is adequate for most internal security needs. Use the High setting in situations in which the extra processing time taken by encrypting packets is warranted to reduce the security risk. Here are the different RDP encryption levels and what they do:

- **Low**   All data from client to server is encrypted using a 40-bit key. All encryption is done using the RC4 encryption algorithm.

- **Medium**   Data both from client to server and from server to client is encrypted using a 40-bit key.

- **High**   Data going both ways is encrypted using a 128-bit key (40-bit key for exported versions of Terminal Server).

With ICA, encryption levels can be set at either the connection level or at the ICA client. The setting at the client level will override the setting at the connection level for just that client.

Since MetaFrame 1.8, much has changed with the encryption levels available with ICA. All the encryption levels that used to be available only by purchasing the now obsolete SecureICA package are available in both Feature Release 1 for MetaFrame 1.8 and in MetaFrame XP. These include the following levels:

- **None**   No encryption at all. There is rarely a reason to choose this option because basic encryption requires little overhead.

- **Basic**   A simple scrambling of the transmissions between client and server.

- **RC5 128-bit Logon Only**   Encrypts all parts of the logon sequence with 128-bit encryption.

- **RC5 40, 56 or 128-bit**   Encrypts all traffic, including logon traffic with either RC5 40-, 56-, or 128-bit encryption.

Basic encryption is the default option, but really is only a scrambling of parts of the traffic between client and server. If your traffic needs to travel across an unsecure network, such as the Internet, set the connection encryption to a minimum of RC5 40-bit if you have no other means of encrypting the traffic available. It is preferred in most cases to use other means to encrypt your traffic besides having the server do the encryption for you. Two highly recommended solutions are either the Citrix Extranet product or using a VPN product to establish a secure tunnel for the Citrix MetaFrame traffic. Both of these options are discussed in Chapter 17, "Firewalls and SSL Relay."

Encryption is the only option that also can be set at a published application level. By setting this option when you publish an application using the CMC, you can enforce that just this application needs to be connected with using a higher level of encryption. This can be a very useful option for ensuring the security of certain sensitive applications.

AutoLogon

By default, the connection inherits whatever AutoLogon option has been set up at the client level. If you override this option and fill in the AutoLogon information at the connection level, all clients who use this connection will automatically log on using the username, domain, and password you entered.

Although this defeats the logon security of the Terminal Server, it can be very useful in several situations. If your clients are running a client/server or a terminal emulation application from Terminal Server that requires them to log on to a remote host, you can use this option to prevent them from having to log on twice. Set up AutoLogon to Terminal Server at the connection. They will be brought directly to the desktop where they can run the terminal emulation application and log on.

Another good application for the AutoLogon feature is for a publicly accessible Windows-based terminal, such as in a kiosk. You can set up the kiosk's thin client terminal to either automatically dial in or connect across a WAN link to a central Terminal Server. You would then set up the connection entry on the server to log on automatically using the AutoLogon username and password.

Logon Enabled or Disabled

Logon ability for all users using this connection entry can be enabled or disabled with this option. This is a good way to disable the logon ability of users while doing maintenance. If you need to disable the logon ability of a single user, you should use the option in either User Manager for Domains or Active Directory Users and Computers instead.

For Citrix MetaFrame administrators, this is the only setting that also can be set at a serverwide level using the Citrix Management Console. If you want to disable logon for an entire server and all of its connections, you can right-click the server, select Properties, click the MetaFrame Settings button, and deselect the Enable Logons to This Server check box.

Timeout Settings Options

Timeout settings are very important in a Terminal Server environment. By default, there are no timeout limits. This means that if a user disconnects his session, that session could stay running in a disconnected state until the next time the server is rebooted or the next time the user logs back on. Because disconnected sessions take up valuable server resources, it is highly recommended to set up appropriate timeout limits on every Terminal Server you set up.

Timeout limits can be set at either a user level or a connection level. By default, the connection timeout settings inherit their configuration from what is set for each user in either User Manager or Active Directory Users and Computers. By unchecking the Inherit Client Config check box in the Advanced Connections Settings window, you can set your own timeout values. The following are the three timeout settings you can set and what they are for:

- **Connection**   The connection timeout refers to the maximum amount of time a user can be connected before the session is disconnected or reset. This timeout applies even if a user is actively working with the application. This option might be useful for public access terminals for which you want to restrict the amount of time a person can use the terminal.

- **Idle**   Idle timeout is the number of minutes of inactivity before a session is either disconnected or reset. The Idle option is very useful for conserving both network bandwidth and server resources. If the application is heavily used throughout the day, set your idle timeout for a large number of minutes, such as 240. If the application is generally used for brief amounts of time, set the idle timeout lower to 120 minutes. In this way, sessions will be disconnected or reset when they are not using the Terminal Server, freeing up valuable resources for other users.

- **Disconnection**   The disconnection timeout refers to how long a session can remain in a disconnected state before it is reset automatically. Because resetting a disconnected session causes users to lose data, if your users will be working with documents, such as with a word processing application, you might not want to set this setting too low. If, instead, users are accessing data remotely, such as through a client/server application, resetting the session will not likely cause problems.

Notice that when either the Connection or Idle timers expire, the user's session will be either reset or disconnected. What determines whether it is reset or disconnected depends on what the On Broken or Timed-Out Session [Reset/Disconnect] the User setting. This setting can be set at either a connection or user level. If you set it for reset, when either the idle timer or connection timer expires the session will be reset and any open documents will be lost.

If you set it for disconnect, then when either of these timers expire or if the network connection is lost, the session will go into a disconnected state. While in a disconnected state, the session remains running on the server even though the user is not connected to it. This means that any open documents remain open at the server. When the user attempts to reconnect to the session, she is brought back to exactly where she left off! This is a very handy feature and is highly recommended. Even a momentary network outage can cause your users to lose connection to your servers. By having the sessions go into a disconnected state instead of resetting them, your users can return to where they left off when the connection is reestablished.

At the point the session goes into a disconnected state, the disconnect timer starts. When the disconnect timer has expired the session will be reset. It is normally a good idea to set this timer so that sessions that are left in a disconnected state, by such incidents as a user shutting off her computer, do not stay running for too long.

Whether you set your timeouts at a connection level or a user level depends a lot on how you loaded your applications on the servers. Generally it is easiest if you load applications that will have similar timeout values on the same server if possible. What timeout values you should set depends on your users' typical use of the applications on a server. Table 10.2 details some suggested timeout values for different uses.

Table 10.2   **Suggested Idle and Disconnect Timeouts**

Application Usage	Idle Timeout	Disconnection Timeout
Light application usage Users are in application for only short periods of time.	30	15
Medium application usage User gets into application once or twice a day to pull information and then gets out.	120	30
Heavy application usage Users use application throughout the data and work on documents and other data while in the application.	240	120

Use Default NT Authentication Option

With Windows NT and 2000, a developer can replace the default logon prompt with a custom logon to provide additional logon features. The Use Default NT Authentication option in the Security section forces clients to use the Windows NT default GINA (MSGINA.DLL) or logon program.

A malicious developer could write a logon screen that looks like the standard Microsoft logon but that secretly captures users' passwords to a log file. By checking the Use Default NT Authentication option, you can help prevent security breaches such as these.

This setting is not recommended with MetaFrame XP, which installs its own GINA, or if you are using Novell's Client 32. In a pure Microsoft Terminal Server environment, where no additional GINA is needed, this setting can help increase server security.

To determine whether your server is using a third-party GINA, check the value of GinaDLL in the following Registry key:

```
HKLM\Microsoft\Windows NT\Current Version\WinLogon
```

Only Run Published Applications

The Only Run Published Applications option applies only to ICA clients. With MetaFrame, applications can be published using the Application Configuration Tool. If you want to force users to use just these published applications, check this box. This setting applies to all users who log on to the server, including administrators. If anyone attempts to gain access through a custom ICA connection to the desktop, he will receive the following rather cryptic error message: `The system cannot log you on (52E)`.

Despite the cryptic error and the fact it locks out even administrators, this setting is highly recommended for securing your server environment. For environments that have users who access the server desktop, you can now very easily publish desktops to the user using the CMC. Although you could do this before with MetaFrame 1.8 by just creating a published application with no command line, now with MetaFrame XP you can specify during initial setup of a published application whether you want to publish the server desktop, application, or content.

To lock down your Citrix server environment, follow these steps:

1. Publish a desktop for each one of your servers to a Desktop-[Server Name] group.

2. Add users who currently get desktops through custom ICA connections to these groups.

3. Set up their ICA clients to connect to the server farm and retrieve their published applications.

4. Have them switch to using the published desktop rather than the custom ICA desktop.

5. Change all the connection entries on your servers to run only published applications.

6. Remove or disable RDP on all your servers.

After you have completed these steps, users will be able to run only applications published to them. This gives you complete central control over who has access to what on your servers. Although you will still need to take the appropriate steps to lock down any published desktops using group policies, you now have control over exactly who can get to a desktop and who cannot.

Accessing the Server Desktop

Even though you have published desktops you still might want to have a remote "back door" into your server in the rare case that application publishing is not working correctly. By running remote-control software on the console of your server, you can gain access to the server desktop from wherever you are, regardless of whether published applications are working.

Several remote-control packages work without any problems for providing remote access to the server console. One highly recommended one is *Virtual Network Computing* (VNC). Although remote control software is a bit on the slow side, it is small, secure, and best of all, free! It can prove very useful in a pinch for getting access to your server console. You can easily and quickly install it as a standalone application or as a service. Access is locked through a password. You can download a copy of VNC at www.uk.research.att.com/vnc.

Disable Wallpaper

The Disable Wallpaper option is recommended for any Terminal Server connection. Graphically complex wallpapers can eat up large amounts of bandwidth when being sent across the wire to clients. Preventing the use of wallpaper can save precious server resources and will increase access speed over dial-up lines.

Reconnect Sessions Disconnected

When a session is disconnected, you have two choices for reestablishing the connection. You can allow a disconnected user to reconnect his session from any client (the default), or you can require a disconnected user to connect from the original client only. Here is what the options mean:

- **From Any Client**   When you select this option, the next time a disconnected user logs on from any client, he will return to his disconnected session.

- **This Connection Only**   If you select this option, the only way a user can return to a disconnected session is by logging on again at the station from which the connection was lost. This option is good for high-security environments.

Getting Rid of Wallpaper and Screen Savers

Both wallpaper and especially animated screen savers can cause serious performance issues with both Terminal Server and Citrix MetaFrame. To ensure that they are not available for use in your environment, it is highly recommended to just delete them from your servers. You can easily create a central script that will do the work for you, using Listing 10.1.

Just copy and paste the Listing 10.1 statements for each server you have into the same batch file, changing the drive letter and system directory as needed. In the example, the server's system directory is under m:\winnt. Be careful that you do not have any KiXtart logon scripts in these directories that end with the .SCR extension, because this script will delete them. Just rename the script to *.KIX instead.

You also might consider creating code for removing the sample screen saver located in the default User profile area and the read-only LOGON.SCR in the system32 directory on Windows 2000 servers.

Listing 10.1 **Removing Wallpaper from the Server**

```
@echo off
echo Removing wallpaper and screen savers from [servername]...
del \\[servername]\m$\winnt\*.bmp
del \\[servername]\m$\winnt\web\wallpaper\*.* /Q
del \\[servername]\m$\winnt\system32\*.scr
...
```

Shadowing and Remote Control

Shadowing and remote control are two different names for the same thing. *Shadowing* is the Citrix name for Terminal Server's remote-control capability. You will see this feature referred to by both names, depending on which utility you are using to manage the settings.

You can remote control a Terminal Server session only from another Terminal Server session. You cannot remote control a Terminal Server session if you are logged on to the server console, unless you run either the Terminal Server or ICA client at the console.

Remote control is great for quick user assistance. If a user calls you to complain of trouble doing something in an application, you can remote control his session and see what he is seeing.

The ability to remote control a user's session can be controlled at either a connection or a user level. Although by default these options are controlled at a user level, controlling them at a connection level is generally easier. In addition, with MetaFrame XP there is the option during server installation to disable completely the ability to shadow on a server.

In the Advanced Connection Configuration window within the Citrix Connection Configuration Tool, you have the options to control whether shadowing is enabled, whether you can control the cursor and keyboard of the users when shadowing them (Input ON), and whether users are notified when you try to shadow them (Notify ON).

For your RDP connection, you can control similar settings using the Terminal Services Configuration Tool, selecting properties for the RDP connection entry, and changing the settings available under the Remote Control tab.

Client Settings

With both MetaFrame and Terminal Server, you have some additional options available that you can set at a connection level. To view these options, click the Client Settings button in the Edit Connection dialog box. This brings up the Client Settings dialog box, shown in Figure 10.3.

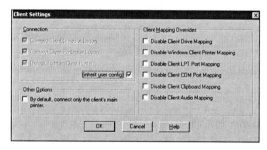

Figure 10.3 Client Settings dialog box.

Client settings control whether the client's local resources, such as hard drives and printers, are automatically connected to and available within a Terminal Server session. With the release of RDP 5.0 in Windows 2000 Terminal Server, Terminal Server can now connect to every local device type automatically with the exception of audio and client drives. Only with ICA can sounds from an application on Terminal Server be redirected to a user's local speaker system. In addition, client drives are automatically made available with a Terminal Server session only when using the ICA client and Citrix MetaFrame. Although you can access a user's local devices from an RDP session, that user must share them on the network first.

The following sections cover the different options you have available within the Client Settings dialog box.

Connection Settings

The settings under the Connection area match up with a similar set of settings available at a user level. The following settings control whether the client's local drives and printers are automatically added to their Windows Terminal desktop when they log on:

- **Connect Client Drives at Logon**   Makes the client's local drives available in the Windows Terminal session. When the user opens up Explorer, for example, he will see his local drives along with all the Terminal Server mappings and local drives.

- **Connect Client Printers at Logon**   Makes the client's local Windows-based printers available to applications running in the Terminal Server session. This option is very useful if the user wants to be able to print to his local printer from an application running on Terminal Server.

- **Default to Main Client Printer**   Changes the default printer for the client's Terminal Server session to the user's local default printer.

When a client tries to print a document to one of their local printers defined within their Terminal Server session, Terminal Server redirects this print job across the network to the client's printer. In the same way, when they try to save to one of their local drives, Terminal Server will encapsulate the traffic in ICA and send it back across the network to the client.

Client Mapping Overrides

By default, all local resources that can be mapped are mapped. Because mapping is done during logon, however, it can quickly slow down logon times if large numbers of devices need to be mapped. For this reason it is important to consider disabling the mappings for any device types you do not need.

Under the Client Mapping Overrides section, you can disable device mappings at a connection level, which can greatly decrease the logon times for your server. The following mappings can be disabled:

- **Disable Windows Client Printer Mapping**   Disables the capability for Terminal Server to auto-create printers during logon.

- **Disable Client LPT Port Mapping**   Disables the capability for Terminal Server to give applications, such as DOS applications, access to the client's LPT ports.

- **Disable Client COM Port Mapping**   Disables the capability for applications running on Terminal Server to obtain access to the client's local COM ports.

- **Disable Client Clipboard Mapping**   Disables the capability for clients to cut and paste data to and from Terminal Server applications by using their clipboards.
- **Disable Client Drive Mapping (Citrix MetaFrame only)**   Disables the capability for Terminal Server to map drives to the client's local drives. Out of all the settings, this one can save the most time. Definitely disable drive mappings if you do not need them.
- **Disable Client Audio Mapping (Citrix MetaFrame only)**   Disables the ability for Terminal Server to play sounds through the client's audio system. If you do not need sound on your systems then you should disable this setting.

ICA Settings (MetaFrame Only)

The final option available in the Edit Connection dialog box for ICA connections is the ICA Settings button. When you click this button, the ICA Settings dialog box opens, as shown in Figure 10.4. This dialog box contains only one setting: Client Audio Quality.

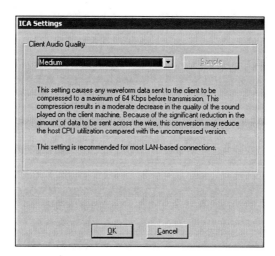

Figure 10.4   ICA Settings dialog box.

Recall that one of the features of ICA connections is the ability to receive audio at the client from audio-enabled applications running off the Terminal Server. Perhaps you want to run an application at the server that records and plays users' voice mail. Using the ICA client, users can play their voice mail off the Terminal Server and hear the messages at their terminals.

For this feature to work, the audio must be packaged and sent across the wire. With the Client Audio Quality option, you can control how much bandwidth this will take. The Audio Quality option basically controls the level of compression and the sampling rate of the audio. By default, this option is set to Medium quality. Giving your clients the ability to use audio is not recommended unless they are attaching to Terminal Server across a LAN.

Connection Permissions

Connection permissions are settable for both RDP and ICA connections and are an important way to secure your server from unwanted users. Terminal Server gives you a large amount of control over the security of your connections. You have control over the connection permissions granted to different users and groups, by connection.

To see how these permissions are controlled, right-click the connection and select Permissions from either the Citrix Connection Configuration Tool or the Terminal Services Connection Configuration Tool. From the Permissions dialog that appears, you can add or delete users and groups from the access control list for the connection. For each user or group, you can grant either full control, user, or guest access to the connection.

For more granular control of the connection permissions, click the Advanced button. You can select any user or group, click View/Edit, and set the following permissions:

- **Query Information** Allows clients to query information about their settings with the Connection Configuration Tool.

- **Set Information** Allows clients to set various options using the Connection Configuration Tool.

- **Reset** Allows clients to reset other sessions.

- **Shadow** Allows clients to shadow other clients.

- **Logon** Gives clients the ability to log on to the server. This option is useful for restricting which groups can or cannot log on to Terminal Server.

- **Logoff** Gives clients the ability to log off another session.

- **Message** Allows the selected users or groups to send messages to other users.

- **Connect** Allows the clients the ability to reconnect to a disconnected session.

- **Disconnect**   Allows clients to disconnect their sessions.
- **Virtual Channels**   Lets the client establish additional virtual channels to the server.

By default the local Users group, which normally includes all Authenticated Users, has user access to the server. In addition, the local Administrator group, which includes the domain Administrator group for the domain that the server is a member of, has full control access to the connection. This basically means that anyone who can authenticate to any domain from your Terminal Server will be able to get to the desktop of the server!

The following is recommended when setting up connections to your server:

1. Right-click the connection whose permissions you want to modify and select Permissions. In the Terminal Services Connection Configuration Tool, you will find permission settings under the Permissions tab, after selecting Properties for the connection.
2. In the Connection Permissions dialog box, remove all but the SYSTEM group from the access control list.
3. Add in the TSUsers group for every domain that has users who need access to this server and grant the group User rights.
4. Add in the TSAdmins group and grant it full control.

After you create new users who you want to use the Terminal Server, make sure you make them members of the TSUsers group.

Anyone who needs administrative access to the Citrix MetaFrame servers needs to be added to the TSAdmins group.

Creating a TSOperators Group

In large environments, you might want to allow some users to remote control and to reset sessions, but not give them administrative access to your servers. In this case it is recommended to create a TSOperators group and add these users to it.

To ensure that this group has appropriate rights, follow these steps:

1. Add the TSOperators group to the local Users or Power Users group on all of your servers, depending on whether you want to give them Power User access.
2. Grant the TSOperators group all advanced rights except Set Information for each ICA connection on all servers you want them to help manage. This includes the following: Reset, Shadow/Remote Control, Message, Query Information, Connect, Disconnect, Logon, and Logoff.

Using Multiple Network Cards

In some situations you might want to set up multiple network cards in your server. By default, connection entries apply for all cards in your server. However, you can set up connection entries for each card separately or for just one of the cards by changing the LAN Adapter setting in the Edit Connections window from All Network Adapters to just one of the listed ones.

The following are some scenarios in which this might prove useful:

- **Multihoming your server**   If you multihome your server with the cards on separate networks, you can make connection entries for the card on only one of the segments. In this way, users on the other segment do not have access to your server. Users from the first segment, however, can access the server and run applications that need access to either segment.

- **Management segment**   Many large corporations set up a separate management VLAN to which only network administrators have access. Using this technique you could put a separate card and connection entry that is attached to the management segment. On this connection entry, you would grant full access to the administrators.

- **Controlling the number of users per card**   In some situations, you might want to restrict the number of users that can simultaneously attach to your server or to a particular card on your server. You can control the number of users under the Edit Connections screen.

- **VPN access**   If your server also is a VPN server, you can have one card on the Internet that only handles the VPN connection and does not have any connection entries. You would then set up your internal card with the connection entries for Citrix MetaFrame or Terminal Server to which your VPN clients would connect.

Top-Ten Connection Setup Tips

Now it is time for the top ten list of connection setup tips. The following are the ten most important tips you should consider when setting up connections for your servers:

1. **Set up only the connections you need.**   Connections are set up automatically for every protocol you have loaded on your server with MetaFrame. Be sure to delete connection entries for those protocols you do not intend to have users connect with. Also delete or disable the RDP protocol if you intend to use only ICA.

2. **Grant TSUsers User rights to the connection.**   Add all of your users to a TSUsers global group and grant them access to the connection. Remove the default Users group. Because the default Users group contains Authenticated Users, granting it rights to the connection can essentially grant access to your Terminal Server for anyone in the enterprise on a trusted domain.

3. **Grant TSAdmins full control rights to the connection.**   Add your Terminal Server administrators to a TSAdmins global group and grant them full control access to the connection. Remove the Administrators group. It is better to control administrative access through a separate TSAdmins group.

4. **Review the timeout settings.**   Make sure to review the timeout settings. The default option of no timeouts will likely leave sessions hung on your server for long periods of time. Review the information under the "Timeout Settings Options" section for more specific advice on what timeouts should be set.

5. **Disable mapping any unnecessary device types.**   Always be sure to disable the automatic mapping of any unnecessary device types. The automatic mapping of device types at logon can slow down the logon process considerably. Especially make sure to disable audio mapping, drive mapping, and printer mapping if not needed.

6. **Set as many possible options at a connection level rather than a user level.**   Setting options at a connection level is generally a better choice than at a user or client level because you have central control over the settings. If you must set options at a user level, be sure to document those options and why they are set.

7. **Leave encryption set to default and use external encryption instead.**   Even though encryption can be set up for Citrix MetaFrame and Terminal Server, the encryption process can significantly degrade the performance of the server, especially for higher levels of encryption. Instead of having the server handle encryption, use a device such as a VPN that is heavily optimized and dedicated to establishing an encrypted, secure tunnel between a client and a server.

8. **Only run published apps (Citrix MetaFrame only).**   Even if you use desktops in your environment, publish them instead of letting users create custom ICA connections for them. After they have been published, shut off the ability for users to run anything but published applications. This gives you central control over who has access to the desktops of your servers.

9. **Disable wallpaper.** This is an easy way to ensure good performance over slow network connections. In addition, you might want to consider creating a script that deletes the wallpaper and screen saver files for all of your servers.

10. **Create a TSOperators group with rights to reset and shadow sessions.** In large environments, create a TSOperators group. Add this group to the local Users group on your servers. Instead of giving them only User access to the connection, however, grant them either full control or all advanced rights except Set Information. In this way, members of this group can help manage users on the server without having to have full administrative rights to the server.

11

Installing RDP Clients
for Windows

U P TO NOW YOU HAVE LEARNED HOW to install both Terminal Server and
MetaFrame, set up users and groups, and create the necessary connections.
The last piece that needs to be covered before your users will be able to
connect and use Terminal Server is how to set up the client software.

Although the installation of the software itself is rather simple, you might
be surprised at the number of different ways you can make the installation
easier and more automated for large client rollouts.

In this chapter, you will learn the basics of how to install and use the
Microsoft Terminal Services client. You will be shown some of the many
ways of customizing the installation of the client. This chapter also
discusses ways to automate the deployment.

Basic RDP Client Installation

Terminal Server provides clients for the following versions of the Windows
operating system:

- Windows 95/98 (32-bit client)
- Windows NT 3.51/4.0/2000/XP (32-bit client)
- Windows for Workgroups 3.11 (16-bit client)
- Internet Explorer 4.x, 5.x and 6.x (downloadable ActiveX client)
- Windows CE (downloadable CE client)

The Microsoft Terminal Server client uses the RDP protocol to communicate with the server. Because RDP runs only on top of TCP/IP, you need to have that protocol set up on your clients before installing Terminal Server. This section covers the different Microsoft Terminal Server clients available, what their minimum hardware requirements are, and how to install and use them.

In addition, with the release of the Terminal Services Advanced Client, Microsoft also has made available a new version of the 32-bit client that includes a Microsoft Installer Package (.MSI file). This important new release is a boon for Terminal Server administrators faced with large deployments of the Terminal Server client. Not only will this MSI package make the automation of the installation easier, but you also can easily customize the installation and set up a web site for automated client deployment.

For administrators unfamiliar with the basic installation process of the RDP client, this section will walk you through the installation for all the versions currently available. For those who want to learn more advanced techniques for automating the installation of the client, skip ahead to the "Automating the RDP Client Installation" section.

Microsoft Terminal Server Client Hardware Requirements

One of the main advantages of Terminal Server is that the clients do not need to have a lot of processing power. This makes it very easy to integrate Terminal Server into networks that still consist of many legacy PCs. If you are on a very tight budget and/or have a lot of legacy PCs still around, you can easily run a Microsoft Terminal Server client on as little as a 386 PC or 486 PC with 8MB of RAM running Windows for Workgroups! For companies with a little larger budget, thin client terminals are a good alternative. They are less expensive than new, full-blown PCs; are very easy to install and configure; and normally come preloaded with either the Microsoft or Citrix client, or both.

If you are deploying a Terminal Server–only solution, be sure to check with the thin client vendor to see whether they support a version of the RDP client. Many vendors have their own Windows CE version of this client that they make available for their thin client terminals. The last option is to run the Terminal Server client on the desktops of your existing PCs, just as if it were another application. The 32-bit client can be run on every 32-bit version of Windows available from Windows 95 all the way to Windows XP Professional.

Table 11.1 covers the minimum hardware requirements for the Microsoft Terminal Server clients and which Microsoft Terminal Server client (RDP client) you need for each operating system.

Table 11.1 **Terminal Server Client's Minimum Requirements**

Operating System	Processor	RAM	Hard Drive
Windows 3.11	386	8MB	4MB
Windows 95/98	386	16MB	4MB
Windows NT	486	16MB	4MB

Remember that these requirements are minimums. If you don't find that they provide acceptable performance, you might need to increase the amount of RAM or processing speed. In addition, the RDP 5.0 version of the Terminal Server client now supports caching bitmaps to the local hard drive, which can greatly enhance performance. Caching bitmaps, however, will increase the hard drive requirements by a few megabytes.

Even so, notice how meager the requirements are. The Microsoft Terminal Server client has to have only enough processing power to receive, process, and send screen updates and user interface commands. The real processing power occurs at the server. The beauty of the server-based solution is that clients are merely a window to applications running at the server. The applications run with the performance and power of a server, regardless of the capabilities of the client. As you will see in a little while, the "thinness" of the clients also makes them incredibly simple and quick to install.

Installing the 32–bit Microsoft Terminal Server Client

During the installation of Terminal Services on Windows 2000 Server, the Terminal Services client installation software is copied underneath the `%systemroot%\system32\clients\tsclients` folder. Within this folder you will find the following subfolders:

- **`win32\disks\disk[1-2]`** Contains the disk images used by the Terminal Services Client Creator program for creating client install disks.

- **`win16\disks\disk[1-4]`** Contains disk images for the 16-bit Terminal Services client.

- **`net\win16 and win32`** Contains the full installation for either the Windows 16-bit or 32-bit Terminal Services client, designed for installation across a network.

You can install the software on the client workstations manually in several ways. Using the Terminal Services Client Creator utility, located in the Administrative Tools folder on the server, you can create client install disks, which you can use to install the client on the workstations as follows:

1. Open the Terminal Services Client Creator utility from the Administrative Tools folder.

2. Select either the Terminal Services 16-bit or Terminal Services 32-bit client, as shown in Figure 11.1, insert the first formatted disk in the drive, and then click OK. It will prompt you to insert the disks in sequence until all the disks have been created.

3. To install the client software, run SETUP.EXE from the first disk. The installation process is very simple. There are few choices except for what folder you want to install the client into and what Start menu folder the icons for the client software should be put in.

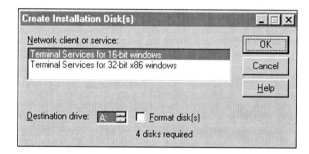

Figure 11.1 Terminal Services Client Creator utility.

The second way to install the client is to install across the network, as follows.

1. Share the `%systemroot%\system32\clients\tsclient` folder as TSClients on the network. Alternatively, you can copy the contents of this folder to a central application install share.

2. From the workstation, browse the network for the TSClient share and run SETUP.EXE from the `\net\win32` directory.

The installation process is short and simple. After the install program has finished, you will see several shortcuts to new applications listed inside the Terminal Services Client folder located at Start menu, Programs.

The first shortcut is for the Client Connection Manager. The Client Connection Manager enables you to set up and save connection entries for multiple Terminal Servers and access them from a single consolidated view. In addition, you can set what application is run, the initial screen size, and other options for each connection entry.

The second icon created is for the Terminal Services client. The Terminal Services client enables you to browse the network for Terminal Servers and quickly connect to them. Unlike the Client Connection Manager, the Terminal Services client is intended for more immediate use and does not enable you to save connection settings.

Installing the 16–Bit Microsoft Terminal Server Client

Some companies still have *Windows for Workgroups* (WFW) stations on their network or have a significant number of WFW licenses. Using the 16–bit Microsoft Terminal Server client, your WFW stations can run today's 32–bit applications with ease. Remember that you need Windows for Workgroups, not Windows 3.1. Windows for Workgroups includes the capability to attach to Microsoft networks and can run the TCP/IP protocol. If you need a Terminal Server client for Windows 3.1, you need to purchase the MetaFrame add-on from Citrix.

The 16–bit client is located on the Terminal Server CD under `%systemroot%\system32\clients\tsclient\net\win16` folder.

Installing the WFW TCP/IP Stack

Because Microsoft's Terminal Server client for WFW uses RDP over TCP, you must first have TCP/IP installed in WFW. To install TCP/IP on WFW, follow these steps:

1. From the WFW workstation, install Microsoft Networking by running Network Setup from the Network program group in the Program Manager.

2. Make sure Microsoft Windows Network is listed to the left of the Network button in the Network Setup window. If not, click Networks, select it from the list, and add it.

3. Install your network adapter and the TCP/IP adapter by clicking Drivers from the Network Setup window, selecting your network adapter from the list, and adding it. If you don't have one of the network adapters in the list, you will need the NDIS driver for WFW from your network adapter manufacturer.

4. After you have installed the network adapter, select Protocol from the Network Setup window. Because the TCP/IP protocol is not included with the base set of WFW files, you will need to click the Unlisted Protocol button and enter the directory where the TCP/IP protocol install files are located.

5. After you have installed the Microsoft client, network adapter, and TCP/IP protocol, return to the main Network Setup screen. Click OK to bind the protocols and complete the installation.

6. Exit and reboot to complete the installation and start the networking components.

7. Test connectivity to Terminal Server by pinging either its IP address or name from the DOS command prompt.

Installing the 16-bit Client on WFW

Up to this point, you have been setting up the networking components that the Terminal Server client needs; now it is time to install the client itself. Share the `%systemroot%\system32\clients\tsclient` folder on your Terminal Server and map a drive to the share from the Windows for Workgroups workstation. Run SETUP.EXE from the `\net\win16` folder on the share. You also can run it from Disk1, if you have created the client disks using the Terminal Services Client Creator utility.

You do not have many options during the installation other than the directory that the client will be installed into (`c:\tsc`, by default). The client installation will create a TS Client group in Program Manager. Inside this group you will find icons for the following applications:

- **TS Client**   The main Terminal Server client

- **TS Connection Manager**   Enables you to create automated connections for connecting to Terminal Server

Installing the Windows CE Client for Terminal Server

Microsoft has made available a Windows CE client for Terminal Server on its web site at `www.microsoft.com/technet/downloads/exe/hpcrdp.exe`.

This client enables you to connect to your Terminal Server and run applications from a Windows CE device. Currently the only supported version of Windows CE is the Windows CE, Handheld PC Edition v3.0 with a core operating system version of 2.11. Verify with the manufacturer of your handheld whether it comes with this version of Windows CE.

To install the Windows CE client download the HPCRDP.EXE file to your local workstation and run it. During the installation, you will need to specify the folder on your workstation where the install files will be extracted. The installation program will copy the following .CAB files into this directory, RDP.HPC_SH3.CAB, RDP.HPC_SA1100.CAB, RDP.HPC_MIPS.CAB, and RDP.HPC_SH4.CAB. Each of these .CAB files contains the installation files for the handheld RDP client, compiled for a different processor type. In addition, it will copy an HDCRDP.INI file and a README.TXT file.

To install the software on your handheld PC, you need to use the application installation feature of Windows CE Services. The software and instructions for installing applications varies from one handheld to another. Therefore you will need to refer to your manufacturer's instructions for the exact procedure.

When installed, you will be able to run the Terminal Services Client from the desktop of your handheld. You will need to make some type of connection to your Terminal Server first to use the client. With most handhelds, this involves either dialing up to the Internet and accessing your Terminal Server across the Internet or dialing into your corporate remote access server and accessing the Terminal Server through it.

Automating the RDP Client Installation

Installing a single client is a rather simple process. For large enterprise deployments, however, these simple steps can become very tedious when multiplied by hundreds of machines. In addition, the installation of the client does not include the many extra steps required for the setup of the client and the connections.

In this section, you will learn some very important techniques that can be used to automate the installation of the client itself. You also will learn how you can customize the client installation, controlling which icons and files get installed on the user's workstation.

Automating the Terminal Server Client Installation from the Command Line

By using the quiet (/q) command-line option, you can automate the install of your Microsoft Terminal Server client. This is the simplest of RDP client installation automation techniques. Although it does not address the issue of setting up the client connections, it does help greatly with the automation of the client installation itself.

The following is a list of the command-line options you can use when running the 32-bit client's SETUP.EXE from the command prompt:

- **/q** Installs the 32-bit client with default options and displays the exit prompt when finished.

- **/q1** Suppresses the exit prompt at the end of the installation. The user will still see the file install "blue bar."

- **/qt** Suppresses all user interaction and screens; the installation will run in the background without the user knowing it.

Using these command-line options, you can easily set up scripts—using either a simple logon script, Microsoft's SMS package, or NetWare's NAL—that will roll out the 32-bit Terminal Server clients for you automatically.

Listing 11.1 is a sample logon script that you can use to automate the deployment of the Terminal Server 32-bit client to your environment. This logon script assumes that your users have Power User rights to their local workstations so that they can install software. If this is not the case, see the next section on using the Windows Installer service to install the RDP client.

Listing 11.1 **Automating Client Deployment**

```
@echo off
REM Automatic RDP Client Distribution Batch File
REM
REM This batch file will silently install the Terminal
REM Services Client to users who are a member of the App-RDP
REM Global Group. A log of installed users and problems
REM during installation is recorded in the \\[servername]\
REM [sharename]\logs\rdpinst.log file.
REM
REM In order to use this batch file you need to copy
REM the following utilities from the Windows 2000 Resource
REM Kit to the logon script directory: NOW.EXE, IFMEMBER.EXE,
REM and FREEDISK.EXE. In addition, you need to copy the contents
REM of the %SystemRoot%\system32\clients\tsclient\net\win32
REM directory to a RDP subdirectory of the logon script directory.
REM


REM Skip script if logging onto a Terminal Server
if exist %SystemRoot%\system32\usrlogon.cmd goto the_end

echo Checking for applications to install...

:RDP
ifmember "App-TS Client"
if not errorlevel 1 goto NextApp
REM Check if application is already on system, if not start log
if exist "%SystemDrive%\program files\Terminal Services Client\mstsc.exe" goto NextApp
if not exist \\[log server]\[log share]\logs\rdpinst.log md \\[log server]\[log share]\logs
now >> \\[log server]\[log share]\logs\rdpinst.log
```

```
echo User %username%  PC %computername% >> \\[log server]\[log share]\logs\rdpinst.log

REM Check if free space is sufficient, then silently install
freedisk c: 15000000
if errorlevel 1 goto RDPErr

echo Installing the Terminal Services Client...
%0%\..\RDP\setup /Q1
echo Client Installed >> \\[log server]\[log share]\logs\rdpinst.log
goto NextApp

:RDPErr
echo Insufficient space >> \\[log server]\[log share]\logs\rdpinst.log

:NextApp
REM Put more code here for additional app installs if needed


:The_End
```

To use this logon script, you need to use some of the utilities that come with the Windows 2000 Server Resource Kit. This kit is available for purchase at www.microsoft.com/windows2000/techinfo/reskit/default.asp. These utilities also should be available in the Windows NT 4.0 Server Resource Kit if you do not have the newer one. The cost of the Resource Kit is a very worthwhile investment for any Terminal Server administrator. You will find a plethora of utilities in addition to very detailed information on Windows 2000 functionality.

To implement this logon script, follow these steps:

1. Write these commands to an RDP.BAT logon script batch file or incorporate them into your existing logon script file.

2. Copy the script to the NETLOGON share (also referred to as the logon script folder) of your domain controllers. (On a Windows NT 4.0 PDC and BDCs, this is the %systemroot%\system32\repl\import\scripts folder.)

3. Create a subfolder called RDP in the logon script folder and copy the contents of the %systemroot%\system32\clients\tsclient\net\win32 folder from one of your Terminal Servers to it.

4. Create a share on one of your servers for holding the log file and replace any references to [Log Server]\[Log Share] in the sample script with the actual log server and share names.

5. Create an App-TS Client global group on the users' logon domain and add any users to it that you need to install the TS client for. You can add just one user and test the script first, and then gradually add more users to roll out the RDP client.

6. Make sure the users are set to run this logon script by setting their logon script property using User Manager or Active Directory for Users and Computers to be RDP.BAT.

Packaging the Application Using WinZip Self-Extractor

The problem with the techniques so far is that you have to either build a script or give your users instructions on how to run the setup. Wouldn't it be easier if you could just package the application into a self-extracting executable and either send it to your users through email or make it available on the web? Well, by purchasing a relatively inexpensive product called the WinZip Self-Extractor from WinZip Computing, you can make an unlimited amount of royalty-free, self-extracting, and self-installing versions of your Terminal Services client. Here's how to do it using version 2.2 of the WinZip Self-Extractor:

1. Zip the contents of the `%systemroot%\system32\clients\tsclient\net\win32` folder into a TSCLIENT.ZIP compressed Zip file.

2. Download and install WinZip Self-Extractor from `www.winzip.com`.

3. Double-click the WinZip Self-Extractor shortcut and then click Next at the introductory window that appears.

4. Select Self-Extracting Zip for Software Installation and click Next. Click Next again at the screen asking about using multiple disks.

5. At the next screen, click the Browse button and select the TSCLIENT.ZIP file you created in step 1, and then click Next.

6. If you want to display a message to the user before the software extracts, enter the message at the next screen and the title for the window, and then click Next. Note that for the installation process to stop, the user must respond to this message.

7. Check the Unzip Automatically check box and click Next.

8. Type in `setup.exe` `/q` for the command to issue when the unzip operation completes and click Next.

9. Enter a message such as `Installing the Terminal Services Client on Your Workstation` in the Software Installation dialog window and click Finish.

At this point, you will have an opportunity to test the installation. If you specified a message box in step 5, it will appear asking for a response. After this message box, the installation should self-extract and run successfully without any user intervention.

A TSCLIENT.EXE self-extracting and installing executable will now be created for you in the same folder as the TSCLIENT.ZIP. If you have a support web site available, just publish the executable to the web server and update the web page so that users can go to the support web site and download it themselves. Alternatively, just send this executable to your users and instruct them to double-click it. Using standard Zip compression the executable will likely be around 650KB in size.

Automating the Client Install Using .MSI Files

As part of the release of the Terminal Server Advanced Client, Microsoft has made available an enhanced version of the Terminal Services Windows 32-bit client that includes a *Microsoft Installer file* or .MSI file. As you will see in this section, the .MSI file adds a great deal of flexibility to your installation options. You can download this new client from `www.microsoft.com/WINDOWS 2000/downloads/recommended/TSAC/tsmsi.asp`.

To extract the .MSI client install files just download and run the TSIMSISETUP.EXE executable from this web site and select the folder where you want the install files to be extracted. By default, the files are extracted to the `%programfiles%\terminal services client msi` folder. In this folder you will find the new Terminal Services CLIENT.MSI install file.

Installing the Installer Services

To install the application using the .MSI installer file, you must have the Windows Installer service on your workstation. By default, both Windows 2000 and Windows XP have the Installer service loaded and running. If you have Windows NT 4.0 clients, you can download a version of the installer service for them from `http://msdn.microsoft.com/downloads/default.asp?URL=/code/sample.asp?url=/MSDN-FILES/027/001/456/msdncompositedoc.xml`.

For Windows 95, 98, or ME clients, you can find the Installer service for them at `http://msdn.microsoft.com/downloads/default.asp?URL=/code/sample.asp?url=/MSDN-FILES/027/001/455/msdncompositedoc`.

After you have installed it, you should be able to run the MSIEXEC.EXE installer program file from the Run prompt. If you do not use any command-line parameters, a dialog box will appear showing the version of the Installer service you are running.

Installing Terminal Services Client Using .MSI

To install the Terminal Services client from the .MSI file, you can just double-click the .MSI file. An installation wizard will appear that will walk you through the steps for installing the client. Instead of just running the .MSI file itself, however, you can run the MSIEXEC.EXE installer application and take advantage of the many command-line options available. They include the following:

- **/i [msi file name and path]**   Installs the application based on the information in the specified .MSI file.
- **/x [msi file name and path]**   Uninstalls the application based on the information in the specified .MSI file.
- **/q**   Installs in quiet mode with no user interaction.
- **/q+**   Installs quietly, and then displays a message at the end that the software was installed successfully.
- **/qb**   Installs without user intervention, showing a progress bar as the files are copied.
- **/qb+**   Installs without user intervention, and then displays a confirmation message at the end stating software was installed.
- **/fa**   Refreshes installation by reinstalling all files.

To use a quiet install to install the Terminal Services client, for example, you could put the following line in a batch file, such as a logon script:

```
msiexec /i "terminal services client.msi" /qb
```

To uninstall the client from a script quietly, you would use the following command:

```
msiexec /x "terminal services client.msi" /q
```

For a list of additional available command-line options, see Microsoft Article Q254099.

Additional MSI Benefits

One additional beneficial feature of .MSI files is that many of the command-line features can be accessed by just right-clicking the .MSI file. When you right-click the file, you will be able to select to Install, Uninstall, or Refresh the installation.

Also with Windows 2000, you can now deploy applications using a group policy and MSI objects. For more information on how you can use group policies in Windows 2000 to deploy applications, such as the Terminal Services client, refer to Chapter 14, "Policies and Desktop Management." One of the big advantages to using policies and the Installer service to install application is that the service runs in the security context of the SYSTEM. This means that you can install the application even if you only have User-level access to the workstation.

Customizing the Installation Using WinINSTALL LE

One of the many advantages of using .MSI files for installing your Terminal Services client is that you can easily customize the installation. Included with Windows 2000 Server is a lightweight version of Veritas's WinINSTALL product called *WinINSTALL LE*. Using this free version of their software, you can easily customize the .MSI file and control such things as what files are copied to the workstation and what shortcuts are created. Here is how to use it:

1. Install WinINSTALL LE by running the SWIADMLE.MSI file from the `\valueadd\3rdparty\mgmt\winstle` folder on your Windows 2000 Server CD.

2. From the Veritas Software folder that it creates in your Start menu, select the Veritas Software Console.

3. Add the Terminal Services client .MSI file to the console for editing by right-clicking the Windows Installer Package Editor icon, selecting Open, and then browsing to the location of the Terminal Services CLIENT.MSI file. This file is normally located in the `%programfiles%\ terminal services client msi` folder after extracting the MSI package as shown previously in this section.

At this point your screen should look like that shown in Figure 11.2. Note under the Title window that you can modify several different aspects of the .MSI file. They are as follows:

- **General** Enables you to modify general properties such as the application description and whether the install is per-user or per-machine.

- **Files** Enables you to specify which files will be copied to the users hard drive as part of the install. You can add files to or delete files from the installation using this option.

- **Shortcuts**   Enables you to control what shortcut entries are made, what folder they are made in, what their title is, and any command-line options for the entries.
- **Registry**   Enables you to change the Registry entries created during the installation.
- **Services**   Enables you install Windows NT services as part of the installation.
- **.INI Edits**   For older Windows applications, you can control what .INI files are created and what they contain.
- **Advertising**   This takes advantage of the new application advertising feature available with IntelliMirror technology, where you can advertise an application to your users. If they want to install it, they can select it from with Add/Remove programs.

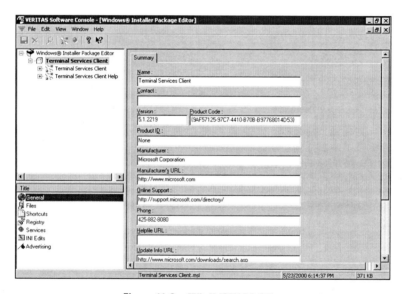

Figure 11.2   WinINSTALL LE.

The following sections give you an idea of some of the many useful things you can do by modifying the .MSI file.

Customizing Shortcuts by Modifying the .MSI File

Many advantages of the MSI version of the Terminal Services client result from some new command-line options for the MSTSC.EXE executable. The following list identifies these new options:

- **-v:[server address or name]**   Connects the user directly to the server specified.

- **-f**   Specifies full-screen mode.

- **-h:[height] -w:[width]**   Enables you to specify the window height and width that will be uses. Values are in pixels.

By creating shortcuts with these command-line options in your .MSI file, you can avoid having to have your users manually enter the address for your servers. The following is how to do this using WinINSTALL LE. (Before doing this, make sure you make a backup of the original .MSI file, in case you run into problems or need it in the future.)

1. Right-click the Terminal Services CLIENT.MSI file in Explorer and select edit with WinINSTALL LE. If this option is not available, you can manually open the .MSI file as shown in the previous section, "Customizing the Installation using WinINSTALL LE."

2. Highlight the Terminal Services client under the Windows Installer Package Editor folder.

3. Click Shortcuts in the Titles section. You will see the current list of the shortcuts that will be installed as part of the installation. By default, this list includes the shortcut for the Connection Manager and for the Terminal Services client.

4. Click the green New button on the right side of the screen to add a new shortcut. The Shortcut window displays (see Figure 11.3).

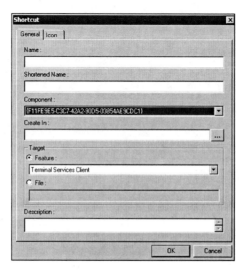

Figure 11.3   General properties in the Shortcut window.

5. Enter the name for the shortcut. This is the name that will appear in the Start menu or wherever you decide to put the shortcut.

6. Select the {F11FE9E5... GUID from the Component drop-down list. This is the *globally unique identification number* for the Terminal Services client.

7. Click the button next to the Create In entry. Select [ProgramMenuFolder] to place the shortcut in the Program menu and click OK. You also can select [DesktopFolder] to put the icon on the desktop, [StartMenuFolder] to put it at the top of the Start menu, or [Startupfolder] to have the shortcut run every time the machine is started.

8. Add the name of the program menu folder you want to put the shortcut in, next to [ProgramMenuFolder]\. For example[ProgramMenuFolder]\Terminal Services Client.

9. Select Terminal Services Client from the Feature area to indicate that this shortcut will be running the Terminal Services client. Alternatively, you could click the file button and enter the path to the file you want this shortcut to run.

10. Enter a description for the shortcut. This description appears after a few seconds when users keep their cursor on the shortcut.

11. Click the Icon tab at the top of the Shortcut window. The options shown in Figure 11.4 will appear.

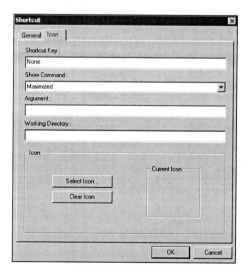

Figure 11.4 Icon properties in the Shortcut window.

12. Change Show Command to Normal so that the application starts normally.

13. Enter `-v:[server name or ip address] -f` for the Argument entry. This will set up this shortcut to automatically connect to the server specified in full-screen mode when this shortcut is run.

14. Select an icon for the shortcut, and then click OK.

15. Select Save from the File menu to save the new .MSI file.

To test your new installation file, just uninstall the existing version of the client and then double-click the new .MSI file. The shortcut you created will now be automatically installed. If you double-click the shortcut, it will connect to the server you specified in full-screen mode.

Customizing Files Copied by Modifying the .MSI File

Customizing which files are installed is a little more complicated. However, it might be worth it for you if you want to either add new files as part of the installation, or if you want to ensure that only certain utilities are copied to the user. If you want your user to run only the Connection Manager, for instance, you might want to delete the MSTSC.EXE client from the installation and from the shortcuts. Another possible use would be to copy a custom connection file for your users.

To modify the .MSI file correctly, you need to first understand a little about how .MSI files are constructed. An .MSI file is first broken down into features. When you do a custom install of an application, you normally have the ability to select which features of the application are installed. In the case of the Terminal Services client, there are two features: the client itself and the Terminal Services client help.

Each of these features is broken down into components. Components identify individual registered application components, each assigned its own GUID. This GUID identifies this component to the operating system and is recorded in the Registry so that applications running on the system can identify which other application components are currently installed. You can view the MSTSC.EXE component installed with the Terminal Services client by editing the .MSI file and clicking Terminal Services Client, Terminal Services Client, {F11FE9E5... as shown in Figure 11.5.

Notice in this figure that the source folder for the MSTSC.EXE component is set to `[sourcedir]\system32\`. This is important to note because any files that need to be installed as part of this component need to be placed in the `system32` directory under the directory of the .MSI file.

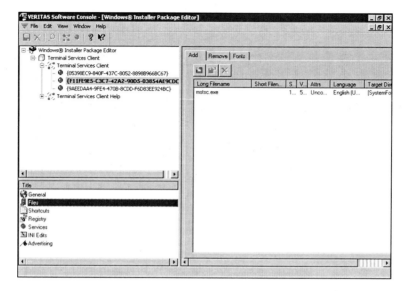

Figure 11.5   Terminal Services client component.

If you now click Files in the lower right with the {F11FE9E5... component highlighted, you will see that this component consists of only a single file, MSTSC.EXE. To add another component to the installation at this point, follow these steps:

1. Copy the file to the [sourcedir]\system32 folder.

2. From the Veritas Software Console, with the {F11FE9E5... component highlighted, click Files.

3. Click the green Add button in the upper right and select the file from the [sourcedir]\system32 folder that needs to be added to the installation.

4. Select Save from the File menu to save the installation.

Now when you run the .MSI file, it will install the file you selected to the same folder into which the other files in the component were copied.

Packaging .MSI Files

Just like you can package a standard installation as shown previously using the WinZip Self-Extractor, you also can package your custom .MSI file. Realize, however, that the users must have the installer services installed on their workstation for the installation package to work. To package the .MSI file for self-extraction and self-installation, follow these steps:

1. Zip the contents of the Terminal Services MSI directory and all subdirectories into a Zip file. Make sure to save directory information so that when the file is unzipped, the subdirectories are created.

2. Use the WinZip Self-Extractor utility to package the application into a self-extracting executable.

3. Set up the executable to run the modified .MSI file with the /q option at the end for a quiet install (that is, `terminal services client.msi /q`).

Centrally Deploying RDP Connection Entries

Now that you have the client on the workstation, the user still has to manually create custom connection entries to run applications on your servers. However, there is actually an easy and free technique for centrally deploying new connection entries to your clients using .MSI files. Much like the application publishing ability in Citrix MetaFrame, by using this technique you can centrally push out new applications to your users using only the Terminal Services Connection Manager. Although you will not be able to take advantage of the many more advanced Citrix MetaFrame application publishing features such as Seamless Windows, this simple technique will at least allow you to deploy Terminal Server applications and desktops without having to visit individual workstations. This section shows you how.

Setting Up the Environment for Connection Deployment

For this technique to work, you must ensure the following steps are taken for every machine in your environment:

- **Install the installer services.**   Every machine must be capable of running .MSI files to set up the new connection entries. Windows 2000 and Windows XP both include installer services. If you have Windows 95, 98, or NT 4.0 workstations, you will need to download and install the installer services on them. The address to download the service from is covered in the section, "Installing the Installer Services."

- **Ensure Terminal Services client version is the same.**   You need to ensure that the version of the Terminal Services client is the same on all workstations. Make sure to upgrade any older versions to version 5.x.

- **Ensure users have local Administrator access to their workstations.** Unless you intend to use group policies and the Installer service to install the applications, users must have the security rights necessary to install applications on their workstation. Depending on the Registry keys that need to be changed, they will likely need local Administrator access to their machine. On Windows NT and 2000, this is done by adding the user ID to the local Administrator group on the workstation.

Application Publishing in Terminal Server Using Third-Party Tools

For those who would rather purchase a third-party tool to handle application publishing with Terminal Server, you can find a highly recommended tool at www.99point9.com, called *EOL App Portal*. Using this tool, you can publish applications to your Terminal Server users. A screen shot from the configuration utility for this tool is shown in Figure 11.6. The disadvantage of using a tool like this of course is cost, whereas the techniques shown in this section are free.

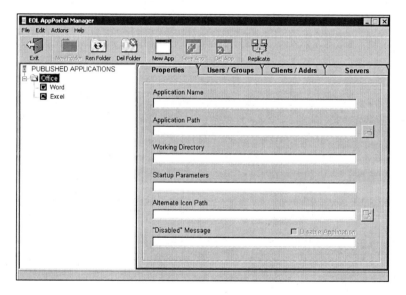

Figure 11.6   EOL App Portal.

You also might want to make a desktop shortcut for the Client Connection Manager. Because this technique relies on creating new connection entries within the Connection Manager, users will have to go into the Connection Manager frequently to access their Terminal Server.

For a more polished approach, you can use the techniques outlined in the "Customizing Shortcuts by Modifying the .MSI File" section to build your own custom client installation .MSI file that puts the shortcut on the desktop for you.

Granting Local Administrator Access

This requirement alone can be a reason not to use this technique. In many environments, administrators do not give users local Administrator rights to their machines so that users cannot install their own applications. If this is the case in your environment, you can still use this technique. You, however, will need to use Windows 2000 Group Policies to deploy the install files.

Using Group Policies, the local Installer service is the one that actually installs applications. This service runs in the SYSTEM security context, which means it has full rights to install the application.

To test whether a user can use an .MSI file, just try to run the Terminal Services .MSI file from that user's workstation, logged on as that user. You will receive an error message if the user does not have sufficient rights to install the application.

Creating the Connection .MSI File

The idea behind this technique is to use the freely available WinINSTALL LE utility to create individual .MSI files that will install individual connection entries into the Connection Manager. When you add a connection entry to the Connection Manager, your entry settings are recorded in the following user Registry key in version 5.0 of the RDP client:

```
HKEY_CURRENT_USER\SOFTWARE\Microsoft\Terminal Services Client\[Connection Name]
```

Under this key you will find some rather cryptic values that represent the settings you chose when you created the connection entry. Instead of trying to interpret the values and create your own Registry modification script, let the Discover utility of WinINSTALL LE do the work for you. Using the Discover utility, you can create a snapshot of your machine before and after any installation to create a custom .MSI file with the installation changes that the application makes. You can then use this .MSI file to install the application on other machines:

1. Install the Terminal Services client and WinINSTALL LE, preferably on a clean workstation.

2. Stop any unnecessary services, items running in the taskbar, and close all programs running on the workstation.

3. Open and then close both the Connection Manager and the Terminal Services client. This will write any default entries to the Registry that they make upon first opening.

4. Run the Discover utility from the Veritas Software folder in the Start menu. Click Next at the main window.

5. Enter the name that you want to save the .MSI file as and the location and click Next.

6. Select the drive to store working files on and click Next. You should have several megabytes available on this drive.

7. Select your system drive and click Add and then Next. This is normally your C: drive.

8. Add the \program files, \winnt (%systemroot%), and any other directories you do not need to scan to the list of files and directories to exclude and click Next. This will save a great deal of time during the discovery process because these directories will not have to be scanned for changes. Modifying connection entries does not change files on the system-only Registry entries.

After doing this the initial scan of your system will commence. At this point WinINSTALL is creating a list of the versions of all the files currently on the system and a list of the Registry entries. After the scan is complete, you will be prompted to run the setup program. Because you need to create a connection entry only and not set up a new application, click Cancel and continue with the following instructions:

1. Open the Client Connection Manager from the Terminal Services Client folder in the Start menu.

2. Select New Connection from the File menu and click Next at the main screen of the wizard.

3. Enter the connection name and the address or name of the Terminal Server you want the connection to connect to, and then click Next.

4. If you want the connection entry to automatically log on to the server, click the Log On Automatically check box and enter the username, password, and domain. Then click Next.

5. At the Screen Options window, select the initial screen size and click Next. Full Screen is recommended. Remember that this setting must work across all the clients to which you want to deploy it. If the setting you choose is too high for the client, they will be brought to the Terminal Services client screen when they attempt to connect so that they can change the video mode.

6. At the Connection Properties window, check the box next to Enable Data Compression and Cache Bitmaps, and then click Next. Cache Bitmaps is always recommended. However, only use data compression if you will be deploying this connection for users across a WAN or through dial up.

7. At the Starting a Program window, click the Start the Following check box and enter the path and working directory of the application you want them to run on the server. Then click Next. Remember that the idea is to create a connection entry for each application that you want to deploy from your Terminal Servers. If you would rather use this connection entry for the user to reach the desktop, leave this setting empty.

8. Change the icon and program group that the icon will be put into. Then click Next and Finish.

9. Close the Connection Manager. Avoid testing the connection until the "after" snapshot has been taken.

10. Run the Discover utility from Veritas Software folder in the Start menu.

11. Select to take the "after" snapshot and click Next.

At this point WinINSTALL will scan your workstation for the Registry changes that were made by creating a new connection entry and record them to a .MSI file. To test this new .MSI file, just delete the connection entry from the Connection Manager, close the Connection Manager, and then run the new .MSI file. If you open the Connection Manager, you should see the connection entry re-created. If you close the Connection Manager, right-click the .MSI file, and select Uninstall. It should uninstall the connection from the Connection Manager.

Author's Note

If you run into any problems, be sure that the workstation you used to make the .MSI file is as clean a load of the operating system as possible. Ideally, use a clean install of Windows 2000 Workstation with the latest service pack. Remember to ensure that no applications or unnecessary services (for instance, virus protection) are running at the time you are doing the discovery. Applications running in the background can make Registry and file changes that will be captured by the discovery process and can cause problems with the .MSI file.

Packaging and Distributing the .MSI File

You can distribute the .MSI file in several ways. Remember, however, that you not only need to send the .MSI file, you also need to send any other associated files, such as the .REG file. Remember that your users must have local administrative access to their workstations for these techniques to work. If they do not, the only method that will work is using Group Policies to deploy the application.

Using the WinZip Self-Extractor utility, as shown in the "Packaging the Application Using WinZip Self-Extractor" section, you can package the .MSI file and any associated files up into a self-extracting executable. After you have this executable created, just email it to your users when you need to deploy a new connection entry. When they double-click the .MSI file, it will automatically install the new connection entry.

You also could easily set up a small web site on which you put a collection of the self-extracting executables for download and installation by your users.

Using Group Policies, with Windows 2000 and Active Directory, you can deploy these .MSI files in a very controlled and automated fashion. For more information on how to use Group Policies to deploy .MSI files, see Chapter 14.

Using the RDP Client

For experience administrators, using the Terminal Services RDP client is fairly self-explanatory. However, a few things might not be immediately obvious, such as useful shortcut keys, how users can disconnect from a session versus logoff, and how to access local client drives from within a session. This section briefly covers these topics.

Microsoft Terminal Server Client Shortcut Keys

The Microsoft Terminal Server client acts just like any another application running on your desktop; you can minimize the window and work on other applications while the client runs in the background. When the Terminal Server window is active, several shortcut keys will affect your Terminal Server desktop. The following is a list of the available shortcut keys:

- **Alt+Home**   Displays the Start menu on the Terminal Server desktop.
- **Alt+Ins**   Switches running tasks.
- **Alt+PgUp/PgDn**   Brings up a small window with icons representing the running applications and enables you to switch between them. This is equivalent to the Alt+Tab hotkey used with Windows NT.
- **Ctrl+Alt+End**   Displays the Windows NT Security dialog box. From the Security dialog box, you can change your password, launch Task Manager, log off, and more.
- **Ctrl+Alt+Break**   Switches the Terminal Server client between full-screen and window mode. In window mode, you can adjust the window size or minimize it.

- **Ctrl+Alt+Minus**   Takes a snapshot of the currently active window with the Terminal Server session and copies it to the Clipboard.
- **Ctrl+Alt+Plus**   Takes a snapshot of just the Terminal Services Session window and copies it to the Clipboard. This can be very useful for creating instructional documents for your Terminal Server users.

Changing Passwords and Logging Off

The easiest method for users to perform tasks such as changing their password and logging off is to show them how to use the Ctrl+Alt+End keyboard shortcut to bring up the Windows Security window from within their Terminal Server session.

From the Windows Security window, shown in Figure 11.7, administrators can do many things. The following are the most important options available:

- **Change Password**   This is quickest way for users to change their password. When you change the password from the Windows NT Security dialog box, you also will be prompted to change the passwords for the other systems to which you are currently logged on. If you are logged on to a NetWare server inside a Terminal Server session, for example, you will be prompted to change both your Terminal Server and NetWare passwords.

- **Logoff**   This enables you to log off the system. You also can log off by selecting Logoff from the Start menu. Logging off will close all running applications and end their session on the server. This is preferred over just closing the window, because just closing the session window leaves the session in a disconnected state.

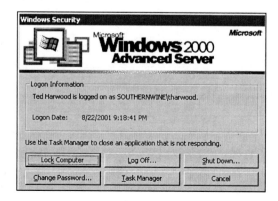

Figure 11.7   Windows Security dialog box.

Accessing Local Drives from a Microsoft Client Session

Although Microsoft has made significant strides in version 5.0 of the RDP client for the automatic mapping of client devices, the one big piece still missing is the ability to automatically map to users' local drives. This feature is currently slated to be included in version 5.1 of the RDP client that will be released with Windows .NET Terminal Server. For now, however, you must either use manual techniques for giving your users access to their local drive or purchase Citrix MetaFrame.

Most techniques for granting access for your users to their local drives involve sharing the drives or a folder within the drives on the network first. If they are shared, the users will be able to establish a connection to them from within their Terminal Server session.

The following are some different methods you can use to establish this connection:

- Just have users browse for their workstation in Network Neighborhood and connect a drive to the workstation's shared folder.

- Provide a batch file for your users that uses the net use [drive letter]: \\[workstation name]\[share name] command from the command prompt to connect a drive letter to their workstation share.

- Use a central logon script that maps a particular drive letter to a share on the user's workstation. For this to work, you need to ensure that the shares are named consistently across the workstations. Using the IFMEMBER utility in the Resource Kit, you also can check whether this user is a member of a drive mapping group before mapping the drive. Listing 11.2 demos this technique.

Listing 11.2 **Mapping a Drive**

```
IFMEMBER "[Domain Name]\TS-Map Usr Drv"
IF ERRORLEVEL 1 GOTO THE_END
NET USE [User drive]: \\%ClientName%\[Share name]
:THE_END
```

Make sure that if you use this technique, you only grant that particular user access to her own share and remove the default Everyone group from the access list. It is also highly recommended to share only a particular sub-directory on the workstation rather than the entire system drive. You can make a shortcut for this directory on the user's desktop for easy access.

The problem with the shared drive techniques is that setting up shares for several workstations on your network can quickly lead to administrative headaches. You should do this only in moderation. By allowing users to share their hard drives and printers, you are basically decentralizing your control of the network and putting it into the hands of users who are likely unfamiliar with proper network administration. Each workstation essentially becomes its own file and print server on a peer-to-peer network with Terminal Server. This increases the number of servers you have to manage.

In addition, certain viruses (such as the SIRCAM virus) are written to target user shares, making your network more vulnerable to attack.

Using Third-Party Utilities to Control User Shares

Controlling user shares from a central location can be very difficult with the utilities available from Microsoft. One highly recommended shareware utility is Hyena. Using this utility you can view all the workstations on your network and drill down to view the shares on those workstations (see Figure 11.8). In addition, you can create new shares remotely and control share security. This utility is available from www.systemtools.com.

Hyena also has an Enterprise version that enables you to control Terminal Server–specific user settings such as Terminal Server Profile location. This tool is well worth an evaluation for any Terminal Server administrator.

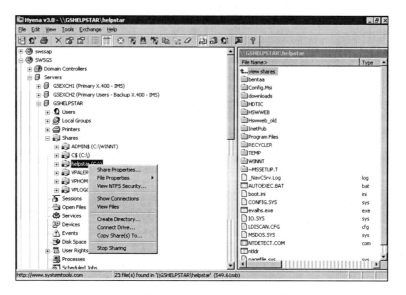

Figure 11.8   Managing shares with Hyena.

Mapping Local Drives Using the Drive Share Utility

Included in the Windows 2000 Resource Kit is a set of application components, including DRMAPSRV.EXE and DRMAPCLT.DLL, that you can use to map local drives automatically for Terminal Server users. Unfortunately, these components will work only with your Windows 2000 or Windows NT clients and involve making Registry changes to both the server and workstation. The following are the procedures to make this work:

1. On your Windows Terminal Server, use REGEDIT to create a new Drive Map Service subkey under the following Registry location:

HKEY_LOCAL_MACHINE\SYSTEM\CurrentControlSet\Control\Terminal Server\AddIns

2. Within this key, create a REG_SZ value called NAME with a value of DRMAPSRV.

3. Also create a REG_DWORD value within this key named TYPE with a value of 3.

4. Add drmapsrv to the Startup Programs value under the following Registry key:

HKEY_LOCAL_MACHINE\SYSTEM\CurrentControlSet\Control\Terminal Server\Wds\rdpwd

If there is a value in this key, then separate the value by commas (for example, "fxrdpclp,drmapsrv").

5. Copy DRVMAPSRV.EXE to the %systemroot%\system32 folder on your server.

6. On each Windows 2000 or NT 4.0 client, use REGEDIT to create a drmapclt subkey under both of the following Registry keys:

HKEY_CURRENT_USER\Software\Microsoft\Terminal Server Client\Default\Addins

HKEY_LOCAL_MACHINE\Software\Microsoft\Terminal Server Client\Default\AddIns

7. Copy the DRMAPCLT.DLL file from the Windows 2000 Resource Kit to the local %systemroot%\system32 directory.

If you intend to deploy this capability to a large number of Windows 2000 or NT workstations, you can use the same techniques outlined in the "Creating the Connection .MSI File" section to create your own .MSI file that makes these changes for you. By doing a discover before making these changes and then after, you can easily create an .MSI file that will automatically make the necessary Registry and file changes. Alternatively, you can use

WinINSTALL LE to modify the Terminal Services client .MSI file to include these Registry changes and push out the DRMAPCLT.DLL to the client.

Letting Users Cut and Paste Files from Terminal Server

In addition to Drive Share, Microsoft has made available another useful add-in for Terminal Server in the Windows 2000 Resource Kit called the File Copy tool. This tool allows your Windows 95, 98, NT 4.0, and 2000 Terminal Server clients to cut and paste files to their local workstations using the Terminal Server Clipboard. Like the installation of the Drive Share tool, installing the File Copy tool involves Registry changes on both the client and the server. Also the version of the File Copy tool included with the Windows 2000 Resource Kit is missing files. For specific instructions on how to install this feature, including how to find and apply the necessary hotfix, refer to Microsoft Article Q244732.

12

Installing and Deploying ICA Clients

IN THE PRECEDING CHAPTER, YOU LEARNED all about installing and deploying the RDP client. In this chapter, you will learn the same for the Citrix ICA client. Although the majority of the deployment methods you used in the preceding chapter will work just as well for the ICA client, the features you can set up on the ICA client differ significantly. This chapter discusses both the details of the client deployment and client setup that you need to know for your Citrix MetaFrame users.

Installing the Citrix ICA Client

The Citrix ICA client has more features and has been ported to a much wider variety of operating systems than has the Microsoft Terminal Server client. Although you will learn how to install the ICA client only on Windows 32-bit and 16-bit operating systems in this section, the client is available and can be run on all the following operating systems:

- Windows NT 3.51, NT 4.0, 2000 and XP
- Windows 95/98/Me
- Windows for Workgroups 3.11
- Windows CE (built in to many thin client terminals)
- Internet Explorer using the ActiveX-based Terminal Services Advanced Client
- Macintosh Client 68030/040 and Power PC-based systems

- Most flavors of UNIX including HP-UX, Sun Solaris/x86 and Solaris/Sparc, SunOS, Compaq Tru64, HP/UX, SGI, SCO, IBM AIX, and Linux
- DOS 4.0 and above
- OS/2 v2.1/3.0/4.0
- EPOC/Symbian OS
- Java applet version, which will run on any platform that supports the Java SDK 1.1 and above
- Netscape Navigator and Communicator using a downloadable plug-in
- Microsoft Internet Explorer using an ActiveX client

Author's Note

For administrators who are already familiar with the basic installation process, skip ahead to the "Customizing the Installation of the ICA Client" section.

Choosing and Installing the Network Protocol

If you are connecting to MetaFrame across a network, you should make sure the correct protocol is loaded and functional before you begin installing the ICA client. Because the ICA client supports more protocols than the Microsoft Terminal Server client does, you have a lot of choices to make in terms of which protocol is best for your clients.

Both the 32-bit and 16-bit ICA clients support TCP/IP, IPX, SPX, and NETBIOS. Your choice of protocol depends mainly on your network and your clients. Most often the best protocol to use will be TCP/IP. TCP/IP is routable and is therefore an excellent choice for both large and small networks. Most routers support TCP/IP out of the box, making WAN connections relatively easy. TCP is also the most widely supported protocol across the various Terminal Server clients. It is also the only protocol supported by the Macintosh, Microsoft RDP, UNIX, and web clients.

If you have a network that consists mainly of Novell NetWare servers running IPX/SPX, and if most of your clients already have IPX/SPX loaded, it might be better for you to stick with the IPX/SPX protocol set for your ICA clients. This is the case especially if you intend to install the ICA client on your DOS or Windows 3.x workstations that already have the IPX/SPX protocol stack set up. Whereas it is relatively easy to add new protocols to Windows 95/NT, adding new protocols to DOS or Windows 3.x clients can be tedious. Like TCP, IPX/SPX is routable.

NetBIOS is the simplest of the protocol choices. NetBIOS can run on top of other protocol transports, such as TCP/IP and IPX/SPX; however, with the Citrix ICA clients, NetBIOS runs only on top of NetBEUI. NetBIOS over NetBEUI has very little overhead, in part because NetBEUI is not routable. Because of the simplicity and low overhead of NetBIOS, you might find that it has a slight performance advantage over the other protocols. NetBIOS over NetBEUI can be a good choice on small networks, test networks, or on other networks where the inability to route the NetBEUI protocol is not an issue.

32-Bit Windows Protocol Setup

No matter what protocol you will be using to connect to the server, the steps to setting it up are very simple with Windows 32-bit platforms. All the listed protocols are included on the installation CD for Windows 95, 98, Me, NT, and 2000. To install the desired protocol, add the protocol through the network Control Panel for your operating system.

Windows for Workgroups Protocol Setup

With Windows for Workgroups, support for both IPX and NetBEUI protocols is included; however, TCP/IP support is not included. To get TCP/IP you need to install it from the Windows NT 4.0 Terminal Server CD-ROM. (You can find it in the `d:\clients\tcp32wfw` directory.) The network driver and protocol software are installed through the Network Setup program. For further instructions, refer to the "Installing the WFW TCP/IP Stack" section in Chapter 11, "Installing RDP Clients for Windows."

The steps for installing the NetBEUI and IPX protocols are similar to the steps for installing TCP/IP. Instead of selecting Unlisted Protocol, as you would with TCP/IP, just select either NWLink IPX/SPX or NetBEUI from the protocol list when adding the protocol.

Obtaining the Client Install Files

Now that the protocol has been installed, it is time to install the client. The first thing you need to do when installing the client is to get access to the installation files. One of the simplest methods is to use the Client Install CD that comes with MetaFrame XP. This CD contains the following client versions:

- ICA Win32 Client Version 6.01
- ICA Win16 Client Version 6.01
- ICA UNIX Client Version 6.0

- ICA Macintosh Client Version 6.0
- ICA Java Client Version 6.0
- ICA WinCE Client Version 6.0
- ICA DOS32 Client Version 4.21

You will find a copy of the full 32-bit ICA client install under [cd]:\ icainst\en\ica32.

Like Terminal Server, there is an alternative way to obtain the client install files on disk by using the ICA Client Creator utility. You will find this utility in the Program menu under the Citrix MetaFrame XP folder. Just run the utility, select the client type you want to install, and click OK. You will need to have three disks available to hold the Windows 95/98 and NT version (32-bit version) of the client.

The next option is to just use the ICA client install source on the server. If you select to install ICA clients during the installation of MetaFrame XP, it will create an ICA folder under the %systemroot%\system32\clients folder, which contains installation folders for all the listed clients on the Client Install CD. You might want to share this folder on the network and access the client install from it.

The final and most up-to-date source of client install files is from the Citrix web site. From their web site, you can download the latest client files and use them to update your clients. If this is a new install, it is highly recommended to download the latest version of the clients and deploy them to your workstations instead of using those available on the CD. You can access the Citrix download site at www.citrix.com/download.

MSI Version of the ICA Client

In the preceding chapter on installing the RDP client, there was much discussion about the MSI (Microsoft Installer) version of the Terminal Services client. Using an .MSI file, you can more easily automate the deployment of a piece of software using the automated installation functionality that is built in to Windows 2000 and Windows XP Professional.

Starting with version 6.2 of the 32-bit ICA client, Citrix now makes an MSI version available of the client. One big reason why this is important is that using the .MSI file, you can easily deploy the client using Windows 2000 policies. For more information on how to use policies to deploy applications, see Chapter 14, "Policies and Desktop Management." You also can refer to Microsoft Technical Article Q236573.

Web Version of the ICA Client

In addition to the full client install, Citrix has now made available a version optimized for the web. This version of the client includes only the files necessary to run an ICA settings file from a web page or to work with an NFuse web site. It does not include the Citrix Program Neighborhood. The download size is much smaller than the full-featured ICA client and, therefore, takes much less time to download across slow connections. You will learn more about this version of the client in Chapter 19, "Deploying Applications over the Web Using NFuse and Wireless Technologies." In this chapter, and for most of the book, the focus is on the full-featured client.

Installing the ICA 32-Bit Client (.EXE Version)

The installation of the 32-bit client is very simple. To install it, just follow these steps:

1. Run SETUP.EXE from the install directory for the client.

2. Click Next past the Intro screen and license agreement.

3. Browse to the location where you want to install the client and click Next.

4. Select the program folder for the shortcuts for the ICA client and click Next.

5. Select the client name and click Next. By default this is the workstation name that is the recommended setting.

6. Select whether you want to use the local username and password and then click Next.

After the client files are copied to your computer, the installation program will create shortcuts for the client in the Citrix ICA Client folder in the Program menu.

Using Pass-Thru Authentication with Citrix

Version 6.01 of the ICA client now has the capability to pass-thru a user's initial logon credentials to the Citrix server. This is a very welcome feature for both users and administrators. By enabling the client for pass-thru authentication in step 6, users no longer have to enter their username and password when logging on to Citrix. Having to enter the username and password once during logon to the workstation and then again every time users connect to Citrix was tedious for many. As an administrator this feature is very beneficial because you can easily standardize your user authentication scheme for your enterprise, instead of having to manage a separate authentication scheme for Citrix. In addition, users do not have to enter their password twice, which reduces calls to the help desk for incorrect passwords or locked accounts. This is a feature that can be turned on or off for an organization depending on their security needs.

Installing the 16-Bit ICA Client on WFW

You can find the 16-bit client on the MetaFrame CD in `d:\icaclient\ ica16`. As with the 32-bit client, you will find two disk images under this directory. These can be copied to a location on your network or to two formatted high-density floppy disks. The simple installation of the client itself can be done as follows:

1. Run SETUP.EXE from the installation source.

2. Follow the onscreen instructions. The client installs into the `c:\ica16` directory by default.

3. When you are prompted for a connection name, enter something unique.

The install program will copy the client files to your computer and create an icon for the Citrix Program Neighborhood in Program Manager.

Customizing the Installation of the ICA Client

Although the installation of the RDP client can be greatly automated, you need to develop custom techniques to deploy the client settings you need to your clients. With the ICA client, however, Citrix has taken many steps to ensure that not only the installation is easy but also the deployment of a standardized setup to all of your users. Using the customizable client .INI settings file, you can control all aspects of the client configuration, including the following:

- **Creation of custom ICA connections and application sets**   You can specify certain custom ICA connections and application sets that will automatically be set up during the client install.

- **Locking down the client**   You can lock down portions of the client, such as preventing users from creating custom ICA connections on their own.

- **Standardize ICA settings**   ICA settings, such as whether the user's local username and password are used can be standardized for your clients.

- **Disaster recovery**   You can set up the connection information your clients need to connect to a disaster recovery server farm and then deploy these settings in a standardized fashion, instead of relying on the manual entry of these settings for every client.

In this section you will learn how to create your own customized installation of the ICA client and how to best deploy the customized application to your users using web and other technologies.

The APPSRV.INI and PN.INI Files

The first step in building an easily deployable customized ICA client involves installing the Windows 32-bit ICA client on a test workstation and customizing the settings. Most settings changes for the ICA client are recorded in one of the following .INI files:

- **PN.INI** Contains your application set connection entries and all associated settings for each published application set you created in the client. The PN.ini is generally changed for user settings only.

- **APPSRV.INI** Contains general ICA client settings that are found under the ICA Settings dialog box which is under the Tools menu. In addition, all the custom ICA connection you set up and their associated settings are found in this .INI file. The APPSRV.INI is changed for administrator settings only as custom ICA connections are generally made to desktops.

Because every user on a workstation can have her own settings, these settings are normally found in the user's profile folder on the local workstation under the hidden `%userprofile%\application data\ica client` folder.

After you have set up the client the way you want it for your users, you would need to overwrite the PN.SRC and APPSRV.SRC files on the installation source with your customized PN.INI and APPSRV.INI settings files. When you now install the client using these source files, it will install every time with your customized settings.

The following instructions walk you through this process step by step:

1. Make a copy of the source ICA client install files found either on the client CD or under the `%systemroot%\system32\clients\ica\ica32\disks` folder.

2. Install the client from this folder onto a test workstation.

3. Set up the custom ICA sessions and application sets that you want for your users. Change any ICA settings that you need changed. Test the settings and then close Program Neighborhood.

4. Overwrite the PN.SRC and APPSRV.SRC files in your installation source with a copy of the PN.INI and APPSRV.INI files from your `%userprofile%\application data\ica client` folder. This is a hidden folder.

5. Install and test the client from the customized install source on another workstation.

6. Verify that all the connection entries and other settings you created in step 3 exist and work.

You can make a separate set of install source files for every different set of settings your users need. To deploy these clients, you can either share these install folders on the network and install them from the network onto your workstations or follow one of the many more automated deployment techniques.

Special Settings in APPSRV.INI

Although nearly all settings in the PN.INI file can be set through the GUI, several settings in the APPSRV.INI file can be modified only within the .INI file itself. Here you will learn the most important additional settings available and how to set them properly.

While reviewing these settings, take a look at your APPSRV.INI file on your workstation. You will find it under the `%userprofile%\application data\ica client` folder. You will notice that the APPSRV.INI is broken down into several subsections. The subsection title and the settings for those settings that cannot be controlled from the GUI are as follows:

- **Browser Retry ([WFClient] Setting)**   Indicates the number of times the client attempts to contact the master browser. By default this is set to 3. If users are having problems contacting the master browser or any MetaFrame server in an XP environment from the client, you might want to increase this setting and the relate BrowserTimeout setting. On faster networks you might want to reduce the default values.

- **BrowserTimeout ([WFClient] Setting)**   Number of milliseconds waited for a response from the master browser or any MetaFrame server in an XP environment. The default is 1000 or 1 second.

- **ApplicationSetManagerIconOff ([WFClient] Setting)**   This is a very useful setting if you want to remove the ability for your users to go into the Application Set Manager and change their settings. You would use this setting if you publish applications to your clients and do not want them to make changes to the setting. The client will be able to access the published application icons for their default server farm only, and no other farm. They will not be able to set up new custom ICA connections, new application sets, or change any of their default application set settings. This is highly recommended because you can set up the client the way you want and then lock down the settings for your users.

- **CustomConnectionsIconOff ([WFClient] Setting)**   Removes the custom ICA connections icon, so that they cannot access and create new custom ICA connections. This setting and the following one are recommended together if you have multiple farms that users need access to, yet you do not want them to be able to make their own custom ICA connections.

- **FindNewApplicationSetIconOff ([WFClient] Settings)**   Removes the Find New Application Set icon on the client so that users cannot connect to new application sets.
- **AddICAOff ([WFClient] Settings)**   Prevents users from creating new custom ICA connections.
- **DragoutOff ([WFClient] Settings)**   Prevents users from dragging an icon from Program Neighborhood to the desktop.
- **MouseTimer ([Connection] Settings)**   Amount of time in milliseconds that mouse movements are queued. By default this is set to 0, when you set that mouse movements are to be queued for a connection in the connection entry's properties it changes this value to 100 milliseconds. You can adjust this value as needed to achieve the response time you want with the mouse over slow connections.
- **KeyboardTimer ([Connection] Settings)**   Amount of time in milliseconds that keystrokes are queued. This is set to 0 by default and is set to 50 if you enable keyboard queuing. Like the MouseTimer setting, you can change this setting if needed to get the keyboard responsiveness you want.

Figure 12.1 shows an example of a completely locked down Program Neighborhood. In this example, the following was done:

1. Status bar and large buttons were removed using the options under the View menu.
2. A connection to the default server farm was set up.
3. Folders were created for certain applications.
4. The Application Set Manager setting was removed using the ApplicationSetManagerIconOff setting in the APPSRV.INI.

Figure 12.1   Locked down Program Neighborhood.

Note how simple and clean the interface is. The simplicity of the interface means it is easier for your users to use and means less calls for your help desk. By standardizing your interface to something similar to that in Figure 12.1 and then making this customized client widely available for download from an internal web site or other means of deployment, you can ensure that client settings are standardized across the enterprise.

After you have added the connections that you want to the client and customized the interface as desired, it is time to "package" the custom client settings for deployment. To do this, just overwrite the .SRC files in the source folder for the client install with the APPSERV.INI and PN.INI files from your profile folder, as shown in the preceding section.

Automating the Initial Deployment

After you have a customized installation available for deployment, there are many methods of automating the initial deployment. You can create a self-extracting executable that contains the source files and email it to your users. You also can make such a file available on an internal support web site. The best way to automate the deployment, however, probably is to download and install the freely available software for creating a web-based ICA client installation. Because this is part of the NFuse package, you will find the steps for doing this in Chapter 19.

Another option you might want to experiment with for deployment is using the WinINSTALL LE tool to modify the MSI version of the Citrix ICA client. Many command-line options are available with .MSI files, such as the ability to do a silent install. For a list of the command-line options for MSI installs, see Chapter 11.

Author's Note

One problem with the MSI technique is that the client name will be the same for all stations. To get around this problem, one trick you might try is to leave the client name blank in the WFCNAME.INI file in the source files for the MSI. When you log on to the server, the server will automatically set your client name to the name of your workstation.

Using Client Update to Deploy

After your Citrix MetaFrame users have an initial version of the ICA client installed and can make a connection to your server, future updates to their client installs are very easy to do centrally using the Citrix Client Update feature. To update the client version for all the clients that connect to a particular server, follow these steps:

1. Download the latest client installs from the Citrix web site and expand them to an empty directory. Normally you should download the CAB version of the files and use the `expand [filename].cab [destination folder] -f:*` command to expand them.

2. Run the ICA Client Update utility from the Program menu, Citrix MetaFrame XP folder.

3. Select New from the Client menu.

4. From the Description dialog box that appears, click the Browse button and browse for the location where you expanded the client install files. There should be an UPDATE.INI update definition file that was included with the client installation. When you find it, click Open, and then click Next.

5. At the Update Option screen, you have several options available on how the client will install. Select the options you need and then click Next.

6. At the Event Logging window, check the box next to the type of event logging you want for the client installs and click Next.

7. Click the Enable check box to enable the client and then click Finish.

At this point, the client install files will be added to the client update database. When users log on to the server, by default their client version number will be compared to the client version you installed in the database on the server. If the version on the server is newer, they will be prompted as to whether they should download the newer version of the client to their workstations. This process can occur in the background while the user is working. After the download has completed, the users will be prompted as to whether they want to disconnect, finish the update, and then reconnect to the server.

This automatic update process happens for every user who attaches to the server. For users across dial-up lines, the download times can be tedious, so be sure to warn users in advance of the upcoming client update. This process makes life much easier for the administrator, however, because all client updates can be deployed automatically.

Setting Up the Program Neighborhood

The steps for setting up a connection to the MetaFrame server are similar for most all versions the ICA clients. On some versions of the ICA client, such as those typically included with thin client terminals, however, your connection type choices are limited to just custom ICA connections. With the full version of the Citrix ICA client, you also get Program Neighborhood functionality. The Citrix Program Neighborhood enables you to make a connection to a published application set, in addition to making custom ICA connections. The following list describes these two types of connections in more detail:

- **Custom ICA desktop or application**   With this connection type, the user connects to the Citrix server and receives either a full desktop on the server or runs a particular published application. You would create a desktop connection normally for users who run most or all of their applications from Citrix MetaFrame, rather than their local desktop, such as thin client terminal users. This can be a good option for thin client terminals to connect to an application on the farm that might not have the capability to connect to the entire published application set.

- **Published application set**   By setting up an application set, your users are shown a set of application icons based on what applications you published to them. This application set is refreshed every time you start Program Neighborhood. This configuration is one of the most flexible for administrators because you have complete central control over the applications that your users have. You can easily deploy or remove applications for hundreds of users at a time by just adding them or removing them from the associated application publishing group. In addition, you can publish full desktops to your users, just like you would publish an application.

Connection Methods

During the creation of the connection entries, you need to make several choices common to both custom ICA connections and published application sets. One of the most important choices is what method of connection that you will use. The following are the methods available with the Windows 32-bit ICA client:

- **LAN connection**   Use this connection method over a high-speed local area network. This type of connection will not use a local cache for bitmaps.

- **WAN connection**   Use this connection method over a low-speed connection, such as a wide area network connection. By default, this type of connection will use a local disk cache for bitmaps.

- **Dial-up (PPP/RAS)** When users attempt to use this method of connection, Program Neighborhood will first attempt to establish the selected dial-up PPP or RAS connection, before making the connection with the server. Use this connection method if your users need to dial up to the Internet to connect to your server, or if they dial in remotely to a RAS server, and then connect to the Citrix server.
- **ICA Dial-In** ICA Dial-In is a feature that enables remote Citrix MetaFrame users to dial into a modem or modems attached directly to the Citrix server. This is an excellent way to enable easy remote administration and offers the highest level of performance over a dial-up line for a Citrix MetaFrame connection.

Seamless Windows

During the setup of either a custom ICA application or an application set, you can specify whether the application will run in a remote desktop window or use Seamless Windows. For those who are not familiar with the Seamless Windows feature, the choice might not be obvious.

The main difference is in how functions such as resizing the application window and minimizing and maximizing the application are handled. With Seamless Windows, the Citrix client makes the application look and feel as any other application running on your desktop, even though it is actually running on the Citrix server. This is the preferred choice for most situations because it is the most seamless connection setup for your users.

Using a remote desktop window, the window itself normally has a title bar that identifies it as a Citrix application. In addition, you can resize two windows, the one around your application and the application itself. With Seamless Windows, your users see only the application window itself, making the choice less confusing. Seamless Windows is a feature available only with Citrix MetaFrame. You can use this feature through the regular 32-bit client or through the web client with NFuse.

Listing Servers, Applications, and Server Farms

During the creation of either a custom ICA or application set, you will need to select from a list of servers, applications, or server farms as shown in Figure 12.2. The process by which this list is generated is important to understand, because unless your network environment is set up correctly, users will not be able to browse servers, applications, and farms from this list and will need to manually enter the IP address or name of your servers every time they need to set up a connection to the server farm.

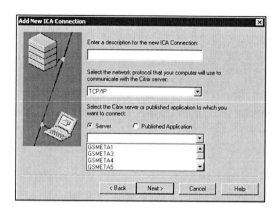

Figure 12.2   Browsing for servers during custom ICA connection creation.

Citrix Service Browsing Using Broadcasts

At the point you click the drop-down list under servers, as shown in Figure 12.2, your client sends out a broadcast message for any server in an XP environment or master browser in a MetaFrame 1.x environment on your network to retrieve the server list. Under MetaFrame 1.8, the master browser automatically responds by sending the list.

Under MetaFrame XP the data collector, by default, will *not* respond, unless they have the Microsoft *Remote Access Service* (RAS) loaded. This same process applies for users who are trying to browse for applications while making a custom ICA application connection or for server farms, when setting up a connection to an application set.

You can easily change this setting in MetaFrame XP using the Citrix Management Console by doing the following:

1. Log on to the Citrix Management Console with read/write access.
2. Right-click the farm name at the top of the screen.
3. Click the MetaFrame Settings tab shown in Figure 12.3.
4. Put a check next to Data Collectors Respond to ICA Client Broadcast Messages.
5. Click OK and close the CMC.

This can be a very beneficial setting for ease of connection setup for MetaFrame XP and is highly recommended if you have a MetaFrame XP-only environment. If you have a mix of MetaFrame 1.8 or XP servers in different farms on the same network, you should leave this setting unchecked because unpredictable behavior might result when users attempt to browse for Citrix services.

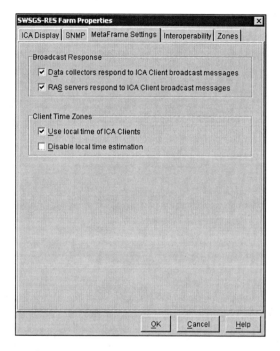

Figure 12.3   MetaFrame settings on a farm.

Citrix Service Browsing and Wide Area Networks

Broadcasts only go as far as your broadcast domain, which in most cases is your local area network. This means that if you enable this setting, users on the local area network will now be able to browse for Citrix services using broadcasts, however users on the remote sites will not. With MetaFrame XP, there are three methods around this issue, which are covered in the following sections.

Use TCP/IP + HTTP for Browsing

The first method is to take advantage of the new browsing capabilities of the TCP/IP + HTTP protocol. When you select TCP/IP + HTTP from the protocol list and click the down arrow to browse for Citrix services, the client sends out a directed packet to `ica` by default. If `ica` or `ica.[workstation domain name]` resolves to the address of one of your Citrix servers, the client will retrieve the list of services from that server. As long as you set up name resolution correctly using WINS and/or DNS across your enterprise, clients from anywhere on your network will easily be able to browse for Citrix services using the TCP/IP + HTTP protocol.

Author's Note

With the version 6.2, release 985, of the 32-bit ICA client, Citrix now refers to the TCP/IP + HTTP protocol as HTTP/HTTPS instead. This is due to the inclusion of SSL encryption capabilities in the Citrix ICA client.

Although a detailed discussion of naming service set up is beyond the scope of this book, the basic goal is to make `ica` or `ica.[workstation domain name]` pingable from all workstations in your enterprise. If the domain name for your company is acme.com, for example, you should make an entry on your DNS servers for **ica.acme.com**. You also need to ensure your workstations are set to acme.com through DHCP. The following short instructions show you how to do this. (These instructions assume you have already set up enterprise-wide WINS replication and DNS replication for the domains of which your workstations are set to be a member.)

1. Enter a new static entry for `ica` in your WINS server. Set it for the IP address of your primary data collector.

2. Make sure you are setting the domain name for your workstations to the correct domain name using DHCP. Just like there is an entry on DHCP for what DNS servers your workstations will use, you also can set their member domain.

3. Enter a new host entry for `ica.[your workstation's domain name]` on your primary internal DNS server for each domain name you use on your workstations at all locations. Set the new host entry to the IP address of your primary data collector.

4. Make sure your workstations are set to use either a WINS server and/or a DNS server for name resolution. DNS is the preferred choice for name resolution.

5. Try pinging `ica` from a couple of test workstations on the network to verify that name resolution is working correctly. It should resolve to the IP address of your primary data collector.

Although you can set the IP address that `ica` resolves to, to any server in your farm, it is recommended to set it to the address of the data collector. In larger environments, as discussed in Chapter 6, "Planning a Terminal Server and Citrix MetaFrame XP Solution," it is recommended to dedicate one of your servers as the farm data collector to handle requests such as service browsing requests. Remember, this is easy to do now with MetaFrame XP because Citrix does not require the 15-user base license anymore.

Changes in the ICA Client Version 6.2 (Release 985)

Citrix made a significant change in the search order for a MetaFrame server farm in the ICA client version 6.2, release 985. When setting up an application set in previous versions of the 32-bit ICA client, the client would default to sending a TCP/IP broadcast message to try and find the farms that are on the local area network. With release 985, however, the default protocol is HTTP/HTTPS and the default server address is ica or ica.[domain name]. This change makes it even more useful and important to make sure that ica or ica.[domain name] is a resolvable hostname on your network that points to the address of the data collector for your MetaFrame XP farm.

Set Up a Local Citrix MetaFrame XP Server

Another option is to set up a Citrix MetaFrame XP server on the local network to handle browse list requests. Unlike MetaFrame 1.8, Citrix MetaFrame XP does not need an ICA gateway setup for browse lists to be shared between servers across a wide area network.

By default, a data collector is elected for every local network. All the data collectors on a farm replicate a common browse list of all Citrix services available across the farm. This means that if a client on the remote network sends out a broadcast, and there is a Citrix MetaFrame XP server on that network, it will respond to the broadcast with a list of services. For this technique to work, you need to enable Citrix server browsing using broadcasts as shown in the "Citrix Service Browsing Using Broadcasts" section.

This is a highly recommended option where you have two or more large data centers with numerous Citrix clients at each data center. Unlike MetaFrame 1.8, MetaFrame XP can be installed on as many servers as needed without incurring the cost of a base license. For this reason, you could choose one of your Windows 2000 servers on the remote site, load Terminal Services and XP, and then enable Citrix service browsing using broadcasts. At that point, any clients on the remote LAN should be able to browse for Citrix services using broadcasts.

Manually Entering Server Locations

The final alternative for locating servers across a wide area network, or on a local area network if service browsing using broadcasts is disabled, is to click the Server Location button during connection setup and enter an address for your Citrix server. This is also the only way to attach to a Citrix server through a reverse proxy setup or using an alternate address across a firewall connection. For more information on using clients through a firewall or proxy server, refer to Chapter 17, "Firewalls and SSL Relay."

The window that appears when you click the Server Location button is shown in Figure 12.4. In this window, you have several options for manually specifying the location of your Citrix server farm. By default, for all protocols except TCP + HTTP, the address is set for (Auto-Locate). If the client is using the Auto-Locate feature to browse for Citrix services, it is using broadcast packets and must be on the same local area network as the Citrix servers. If the client is across a wide area network, you would set up the ability to browse for Citrix services by doing the following:

1. Click the Add button.

2. Enter the appropriate address type. If using TCP/IP, you can specify a server name, IP address, or DNS address for the server you want to connect to, and then click OK.

3. Go back to step 1 to continue adding addresses.

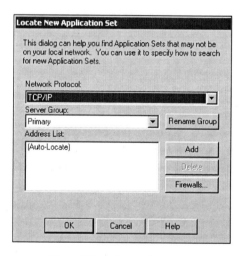

Figure 12.4 Server location.

When you browse for Citrix services, the client will send a packet to every server in the list. The client will display the list of services from the first server that responds. Generally you should put the address of your data collector server or servers in this list, otherwise any server that responds might have to respond with the address of the data collector, causing your client to have to send out another discovery packet.

As a means of disaster recovery, you also can specify up to two backup groups of servers from which the client can obtain a list of services. For more information on disaster recovery techniques, refer to Chapter 26, "Disaster Recovery Techniques and Enhancing Reliability."

Setting an IPX/SPX or NetBEUI Server Location Address

If you are using IPX/SPX, enter the **network:node** address (for example, 101:0877789f4509) in the Server Location window. You can determine the network address and node address by using the `ipxroute config` command on your Terminal Server console. Remember that the network number is unique not only for a segment, but also for a frame type. Make sure your client and the server are using the same IPX/SPX frame type. For NetBIOS over NetBEUI, your only choice is to enter the server name.

Setting Up a Custom ICA Connection

The following instructions show how to set up a custom ICA connection for either a desktop or an application using a full Windows 32-bit ICA client:

1. Run the Citrix Program Neighborhood from the user's desktop or from the Citrix ICA Client folder in the Program menu.

2. Double-click Application Set Manager from the main window and then click Custom ICA Connections.

3. Double-click Add ICA Connection.

4. At the Add New ICA Connection window that appears, select whether the connection method will be using a LAN, WAN, Dial-up, or ICA Dial-In, and click Next.

5. Enter the name for the custom ICA connection entry.

6. Select the appropriate protocol, and then select whether the connection will be to a desktop or a published application. If the connection is to a desktop, you will need to either select the server from the drop-down list, or enter the pingable name or address of the server. If it is to an application, you will need to select the application from the drop-down list. Click Next.

7. If the connection is to a published application, select whether to run in a Seamless Window or remote desktop.

8. Select the encryption level or use default, and then click Next.

9. If you want the have the user log on automatically, enter the user's name, password, and domain, and then click Next.

10. Select the number of colors used by the connection or use the server default and click Next.

11. If the connection is to a desktop, you will be prompted for an application to start when the connection is made. If you want an application started automatically for this connection, enter the application name and working directory, and then click Next.

12. Click Finish to create the connection.

The custom ICA connection entry you just created will now appear in the Program Neighborhood. If you want to change any properties for the connection in the future, right-click the connection and select Properties. The following options can be set only after the connection is made, by right-clicking the custom ICA connection entry and clicking the Options tab:

- **Use Data Compression**   This option is set by default for all custom ICA connection entries. It has a minimal effect on system performance versus the network bandwidth it can save. However, you might want to disable it when all your users have high-speed local area network connections to the server.

- **Use Disk Cache for Bitmaps**   Controls whether bitmaps are cached to disk from a Citrix session. This option can greatly improve screen-paint times on slow connections and is enabled by default when you select WAN as the connection method.

- **Queue Mouse Movements and Keystrokes**   If users complain that they are losing keystrokes or having to click twice to make actions happen within applications, you might try having them set this setting. However, the newer SpeedScreen Latency Reduction technology is generally a better choice for resolving these type of issues.

- **SpeedScreen Latency Reduction**   You can force SpeedScreen latency reduction to be on, off, or auto. The default is auto. For more information on this setting, see the section on SpeedScreen Latency Reduction in Chapter 21, "Performance Tuning and Resource Management."

- **Sound Quality**   You can disable sounds or override the server sound quality settings by changing this selection. Sound is generally easier to control at a connection level. You might want to do it at a user level window, however, if you have a few users who need sound and the rest do not.

- **Window Size**   You can control the screen size or use the server default using this setting.

These options are shown in Figure 12.5.

Setting Up an Application Set Connection

The following instructions cover setting up a connection to a published application set from your Citrix server farm. Users prefer this method over a custom ICA connection.

1. Open Citrix Program Neighborhood.

2. Double-click the Application Set Manager and then Find New Application Set.

3. Select WAN, LAN, or Dial-Up Networking from the Connection Method drop-down list and click Next.

4. Click the down arrow next to Browse for the Application Set to Add. At this point the client will send out a broadcast to attempt to find a list of server farms available on the local network. If no servers respond, you will need to click the Server Location button and enter an IP address for one of the servers in the farm.

5. On the next screen, select to enable sound, override the server default for the number of colors, and specify the window's size, if necessary, and then click Next and then Finish.

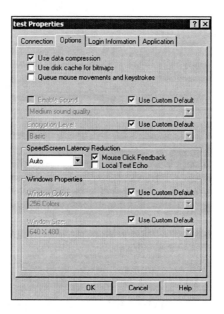

Figure 12.5 ICA options.

An icon for the application set you just created should now appear in the Citrix Program Neighborhood. Like with a custom ICA connection, you can right-click the application set, select Application Set Settings, and access several settings not available during the initial setup of the connections. The available settings are identical to those listed previously for custom ICA connection with the exception of the ability to control desktop integration.

Under the Options tab, you will find the additional option of turning off desktop integration. This can be handy for users or administrators who do not want shortcuts automatically created on their desktop or Start menu for published applications. When desktop integration is disabled, any icons that have been published to the desktop or Start menu will be removed and will appear only within the Citrix Program Neighborhood.

Changing ICA Settings

You will find that several different general settings can be modified for the Program Neighborhood by selecting ICA Settings under the Tools menu. The following sections cover the various settings available under each of the tabs within the ICA Settings window.

General Settings

From the General tab under the ICA Settings window shown in Figure 12.6, you can change the following settings:

- **Client Name**   This is the client name reported to the Citrix server when the client logs on. This is the main identifier for the client when you use Citrix administrations tools, so you want to be sure that the client name used is consistent. If you need to remote control a client, for example, you will need to know their client name first. Generally set this for either the workstation name or username. By default, it gets set to the workstation name during client setup.

- **Serial Number**   Only necessary for licensing purposes, if you use a special version of the client from the Client PC Pack.

- **Keyboard Layout and Keyboard Type**   Enables you to change the keyboard settings from within the Citrix session. This is an important feature for international deployments of Citrix solutions.

- **Display Connect to Screen Before Making Dial-In Connections**
  Enables you to verify connection settings before dialing in.

- **Display Terminal Window When Making Dial-In Connections**
  Provides more information to the user on the status of the progress of the dial up. Normally used for troubleshooting dial-up connection problems.

- **Allow Automatic Client Updates**   Allows for the automatic download of client updates to the user during logon.

- **Pass-Through Authentication**   This is an important option to know about. If during the initial setup you selected to not enable the ability to use pass-through authentication, you can re-enable it here. Pass-through authentication allows a user's initial workstation logon credentials to be passed through to their Citrix logon seamlessly. In this way they do not have to enter their credentials twice, once at logon and once again when going into Citrix.

- **Use Local Username and Password for Logon**   Overrides the logon username and password specified for any connection by using the user's local username and password, unless the check box within the connection saying Don't Use Local Username And Password is checked. This is a good option to set for companies that want to enforce the use of single sign-ons. This also means that users do not have to bother with setting up logon credentials during the initial setup.

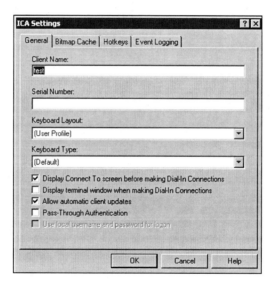

Figure 12.6   General tab.

Bitmap Cache

The bitmap cache is used to cache commonly viewed screen bitmaps locally. Instead of sending the entire window across the line to the client, Citrix SpeedScreen technology will determine whether it can just send a reference to a portion of the screen that has already been cached in the client's bitmap cache. This technology is most beneficial over slow-speed connections, such as dial-up connections.

You can change the following three settings:

- **Amount of Disk Space to Use** This is the percentage of the disk drive used for bitmap caching. By default, it is set for 1 percent of the user's drive space. With the size of modern hard drives, 1 percent of the drive space is normally plenty. If you want to adjust it, however, you can do it with this setting.

- **Bitmap Cache Directory** By default, on Windows 2000, this is set for the Application Data folder under the user's profile folder. This is normally the best location.

- **Minimum Size of Bitmap to Cache** This is the minimum size of a bitmap before SpeedScreen technology will consider it for caching. The size of 8K was determined through extensive testing and is optimal for most situations. If you find that your users are using applications that have a lot of repeated small graphics and these graphics are not being cached, however, you might want to decrease this setting to 6K or 4K.

Event Logging

Under the Event Logging tab, you can specify several options for creating an event log that logs user session information. The following settings are available:

- **Event Log File** The folder and filename where the event log will be stored. By default, this is under the user's profile in the Application Data folder. You can set the log to overwrite every time or append to the log.

- **Connections/Disconnections** Logs connection and disconnections from the Citrix servers.

- **Errors** Logs any error messages that occur during logon or during the session.

- **Data Transmitted and Data Received** Logs data packets transmitted or received.

- **Keyboard and Mouse Data** Logs keyboard and mouse movements.

The last three settings can greatly slow down session performance and generate very cryptic entries in the log. These settings are generally not recommended unless you are requested to set them by Citrix to help resolve a problem.

On the other hand, logging the error messages can be very handy. If your users are having an intermittent problem logging on to Citrix, or random disconnects, you might try setting the log to be appended rather than overwritten and make sure that the Errors box is checked. After a couple of days, you can check the log to see whether you can gather any additional information on the problem.

Hotkeys

The hotkeys or shortcut keys used in the Citrix ICA client are different from the keys used by the Terminal Server client. You can define the hotkeys used in a Citrix session within Citrix Program Neighborhood by selecting ICA Settings from the Tools menu and then clicking the Hotkeys tab. The hotkeys you can set under this tab are shown in Figure 12.7. As you can see, you can easily redefine the keys as you need them.

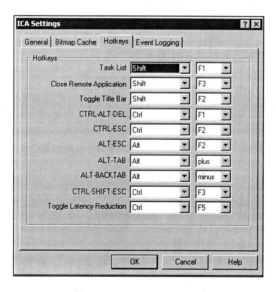

Figure 12.7   Hotkeys tab.

One of the most useful shortcuts to teach users is Ctrl+F1. This is equivalent to the Ctrl+Alt+End keystroke with Microsoft's client. Ctrl+F1 brings you to the Windows NT Security window, where you can change your password, log off, or disconnect.

Using the ICA Client

After you have created the connections you need, it is time to use them. Whether you have set up a custom ICA or application set connection, when you are connected into a Citrix server many of the same concepts apply. In this section you will learn more about the important concepts and procedures that you need to understand after you make a connection.

Access to Local Hard Drives

It is very easy to access your local resources with the Citrix ICA client. By default, when you log on, your local drives will become part of your Citrix MetaFrame desktop. With the Microsoft Terminal Server client, you need to first share your local drives and then connect to them in Terminal Server to access them.

If you remapped the Citrix system drives higher in the alphabet during installation, when your client connects their drive letters within Citrix, they will be the same as their local drives. In other words, if the user needs to save a document to his local C: drive from within an application running on Citrix, he just saves it to the C: drive on Citrix. Citrix has already taken care of mapping this C: drive to the user's local C: drive during logon.

If instead, the Citrix system drives were not remapped and start with the letter C:, when the user logs on his local drives will be available higher in the alphabet, usually starting with the letter V. You need to instruct your users that if they need to save their documents to their local C: drive from within Citrix, they need to save it to the V: drive, not C: drive. This can be very confusing for users, so it is highly recommended to remap drives during installation if your users will need to save documents to their local drives.

Mapping to a Single-User Drive

By default, when you log on to Citrix, all of your local drives will be brought into your Citrix server setting. Not only is this not always necessary, but it also takes additional time during logon to scan for your local drives. You can have the Citrix server attach to the user's C: drive and nothing more during logon by doing the following:

1. Open either your central user logon script or the individual USRLOGON.CMD scripts for each server and add the following line, replacing drive letter with the drive letter in Citrix that you want your users to use for their local C: drive.

```
net use [drive letter]: \\client\c$
```

2. Go into the connection settings for the ICA connections on the box and remove the check next to Disable Client Drive Mappings.

For environments where some users also need access to their D: drive, or you want to control who has access to their local drive in Citrix, you can create a ctx-map c and ctx-map d command. Using the KiXtart logon script techniques shown in Chapter 9, "Setting Up Terminal Server Users," you can easily create a logon script that checks whether they are members of the respective groups and then map the appropriate drive.

ICA Connection Center

One very important feature of the Citrix Program Neighborhood client that is often not fully utilized is the ICA Connection Center. The ICA Connection Center is accessible by clicking the small ICA icon that appears in your taskbar tray after you establish a session to Citrix. The ICA Connection Center is shown in Figure 12.8.

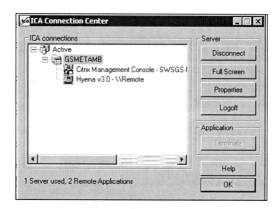

Figure 12.8 ICA Connection Center.

Using the ICA Connection Center, you can do the following:

- **Disconnect** Enables you to disconnect from a server but leave your session still running on it.
- **Full Screen** Enables you to switch to full-screen mode for a particular application running at the server. This option is available only when you select a server that you are running an application on using Seamless Windows.
- **Properties** Enables you to gather statistics, such as number of packets sent and received, for a particular session.
- **Logoff** Enables you to log off of an application running on a server.
- **Terminate** Enables you to terminate or reset an application you are running on the server. This option is available only when you are running the published application in Seamless Windows mode.

Training Users on the ICA Connection Center

It is very useful to train your users about how to take advantage of the features of the ICA Connection Center. When they initially make a connection to Citrix MetaFrame server, the red dot on top of the *I* in ICA, on the icon will bounce while the connection is being established. When the connection is made, it will be listed in the ICA Connection Center.

Sometimes applications error out and get stuck on the server. This might prevent the user from reconnecting, because she reconnects to the application in an errored state. To get around this issue, first you need to be using published applications and Seamless Windows. Then train your users to go into the ICA Connection Center, select the application, and then click Terminate. In this way the application is terminated on the server, and they should be able to reconnect without a problem.

Top-Ten ICA Client Setup Tips

As a summary to the information provided in this chapter, the following is a list of the most important tips related to the setup and deployment of the ICA client:

1. **Do not use custom ICA connections for users.**   Because of the flexibility of published applications, it is highly recommended to set up application sets for the clients rather than custom ICA connections. You can easily add or remove applications centrally from an application set. If you deploy ICA clients using custom ICA connections to applications and servers, however, you must manually go to each workstation to make a change.

2. **Use the new .MSI version of the Citrix ICA client for client deployment.**   More and more companies are starting to deploy their applications using .MSI files. .MSI files can make application deployment very easy, especially for companies that have Windows 2000 workstations and Active Directory. Many third-party vendors also make tools that can help you customize .MSI files, such as Veritas WinINSTALL.

3. **Use the web version of the client for NFuse.**   The web version of the client is a much smaller version that includes the majority of the features of the full version but is designed for accessing Citrix applications through a web browser. For the greatest ease of client deployment, set up a Citrix NFuse server and deploy the web version of the ICA client to the users through the web.

4. **Train users to use the Connection Center.**   The Connection Center is a very useful tool on which it is important to train your users. Using the Connection Center, they can better manage the connection they have to the server and help themselves out of connection issues instead of having to call the help desk.

5. **Enter a Static WINS entry for the ICA hostname.** Make sure you make a static WINS entry on your WINS servers for ICA. Point the address to your MetaFrame XP data collector. This is the default hostname that the ICA client will attempt to query to list the MetaFrame XP farms on the network.

6. **Set domain names for your workstations using DHCP.** Using DHCP you can push down a DNS domain name to your workstations. When your workstations attempt to ping an address, they will automatically add this domain name to the end of the hostname. If your domain name is yahoo.com and your workstations are set to this domain name, for instance, when you try to ping a hostname, such as ica, from your workstations, they will attempt to add the yahoo.com domain name to the host name (that is, ica.yahoo.com).

7. **Enter a static DNS entry for the ICA hostname.** After you have made sure your workstations are set to the correct domain name, go to your internal DNS servers and add an address entry for the ICA hostname that points to your primary data collectors.

8. **Download the latest client.** Many important changes have been made to the ICA client over the years. Version 6.2 release 985 of the ICA client has several significant changes, including an MSI version and a switch in search order for farms so that the client searches for the ica hostname first to retrieve the list of farms.

9. **Use the settings in the APPSRV.INI file to lock down your Program Neighborhood.** Using settings in the APPSRV.INI, you can restrict access to certain sections of the Program Neighborhood, making it easier to set up and support the client.

10. **Use DNS names for server locations.** Set up a primary and secondary DNS server on your internal network and then use DNS hostnames for your server locations that you use on the ICA clients.

13

Installing Applications

INSTALLING APPLICATIONS AND GETTING THEM to work smoothly and
efficiently can be one of the most challenging aspects of Terminal Server
administration. Although most applications will run without a problem, you
will find that there are often ways of making applications run better in
Terminal Server's multiuser environment. To make this happen, you must
seek to gain a deep understanding of the applications that run on your
Terminal Server. You need to know where they store their files, how they
are typically used, and especially where and how they store their settings.

This chapter discusses in detail what it takes to get your applications up
and running on Terminal Server and how to resolve any application problems that might come up.

Basic Application Installation and Tuning

Installing and running applications on Terminal Server might seem deceptively similar to installing and running them on a workstation; however,
there are some important differences. One of the main differences to running applications successfully on Terminal Server is the need to understand
the concept of application competition. Applications running on the
Terminal Server compete with other applications and users for limited
system resources. This means that if one application is taking more than its
share of resources, this inequity will quickly start affecting all applications
being run by all users on the system.

The second key concept is application isolation. In a multiuser environment, each instance of an application must run separately and use its own set of resources. Because you can have multiple applications running on the same server at the same time in a multiuser environment, making sure these applications are isolated from each other might take some special tweaking of their settings. Whether this tweaking is necessary depends mainly on how the application is designed, what resources it uses, and where it stores its settings.

This section discusses the basic steps required to install an application on Terminal Server, how to test whether the application is working properly, and how to tune the application for the best performance and multiuser use.

Install and Execute Modes

When you first bring up a Terminal Server, it comes up in what is referred to as execute mode. In this mode, the server is prepared to run applications and is the normal mode of Terminal Server operation.

Before you install an application on Terminal Server, however, you need to switch the server into another mode referred to as *install mode*. To do this you can either run the `change user /install` command from a command prompt and then run the application setup program, or add the application through the Add/Remove Programs dialog box in Control Panel. Either method switches the server into install mode during the installation of the application.

Install mode is a mode that helps applications work correctly in a multiuser environment. When an application is installed in install mode, certain user-specific application settings, such as user Registry settings and .INI files are "captured" by the server. When you change back to execute mode, using the `change user /execute` command, users are able log on and use the application. In execute mode, the recorded user Registry changes captured during the installation are propagated to each user's Registry. User-specific application setting files, such as .INI files, are copied to the user's personal Windows directory in the user's profile. By installing applications in install mode, you help ensure that user-specific application settings will be kept separate for each user, which is critical in Terminal Server's multiuser environment.

Applications installed in install mode need to be installed only once for all your users because the user-specific changes that the application makes will be propagated to each user as the user logs on and runs the applications.

Planning an Application Installation

Even though application installation is most often a very easy process, it is important to realize that the installation of an application can cause problems with other applications running on the server. For example, an application might install a newer version of a .DLL that is relied on by other applications on the system. If this newer .DLL has a bug in it, it is possible that it could cause problems with the other applications. If you are in the process of testing your servers, installing additional applications should be easy. If you need to install or update an application on heavily used production servers, however, you need to plan the installation carefully.

Grouping Servers by Applications

The first part of planning for an application installation is choosing the best server to run the application. In smaller environments, the choice might be obvious. In larger environments, however, you must consider many factors.

Generally, when your server farm exceeds 10 servers or the number of different production applications you need to run grows considerably, you need to start considering dividing your servers into application groups. Suppose you start out with 3 servers supporting a reporting application for your users. Before you know it you are up to 10 servers and now support the reporting application, an email application, an accounting application, and administrative tools. As your farm grows even larger, trying to ensure that all these applications work together well and are installed on all your servers correctly will become very tedious to manage. Taking this approach you will more likely run into application problems such as .DLL conflicts, possible memory issues, and installation failure.

Instead of installing all applications on all servers, it is often better to start dividing your servers into application groups. The servers in each application group are responsible for running only a certain category or set of applications, rather than all applications in the group. Ideally, servers that are part of a particular application group should have a server name that indicates in which group they belong. The following are some of the many possible application groups you could divide your servers into and suggested naming standards:

- **Office Apps (Server name: TSOffice[1-n])** These servers would be responsible for running your office application, such as word processing, spreadsheet, and email.

- **Accounting Apps (Server name: TSAcct[1-n])** These servers would be responsible for running client/server accounting applications such as Great Plains or accounting-related applications such as SAP.

- **Reporting Apps (Server name: TSRept[1-n])** On these servers you would install reporting tools and multidimensional analysis tools, such as Hyperion, Brio, or Crystal.

- **Point of Sale (Server name: TSPOS[1-n])** Custom-developed or prepackaged point-of-sales application would run on these servers.

- **Administrative Applications (Server name: TSAdmin[1-n])** These servers are used for administrative applications, such as publishing the Citrix Management Console, User Manager, Exchange Admin, or other system administration tools.

- **Test Servers (Server name: TSTest[1-n])** Used for testing your applications and server setup before rolling them into production.

When deciding on what groups you will be setting up for your servers, try to group applications together not only by type, but also by hardware requirements. For example, applications that require large amounts of processing power, such as reporting- or analysis-type applications, are best put onto their own servers. In this way you can better focus on their particular hardware needs, by purchasing a smaller number of higher performance servers for this application group, rather than a larger number of lower performance servers, as might be appropriate for office applications.

If you run 16-bit or DOS applications on your server farm, another recommended way to group your applications is by this type. DOS and 16-bit applications behave very differently than 32-bit applications behave when running under Windows NT 4.0 or 2000 Terminal Server. They rely on a simulated 16-bit command shell environment called the *NT Virtual DOS Machine* (NTVDM). The NTVDM is an actual executable that is run on the system that handles the setup of this environment. You can see the NTVDM process by running the old DOS Edit program from the %systemroot%\system32 folder on your Terminal Server. If you take a look in Task Manager (TASKMGR.EXE) you will see the NTVDM.EXE process running.

Dividing Out Security First and Then Applications

If you are setting up servers for an application service provider, or for a corporation that consists of multiple independent entities, such as a conglomerate, before grouping servers into application groups, you might have first have to group them into separate security groups or farms. This extra layer of security isolation is often necessary in organizations such as this to meet the security requirements of service level agreements, or to match the administrative structure of the corporation.

The best way to handle the separation of security is by separating the means for authentication. Instead of having all your servers as part of the same domain, for example, you might want to consider creating separate domains for each large security group. Using Windows 2000 and the Active Directory, you also could consider dividing out the security by creating separate organizational units and putting the servers under the appropriate one. This solution can be both very flexible and very secure.

If you are using Citrix, in addition to either domain or organizational separation, you might want to consider farm separation. Farm separation not only means better administrative separation, but also separation for the sake of redundancy. Even though the farms are separate, you can still provide a single point of access using NFuse as you will be shown in Chapter 19, "Deploying Applications over the Web Using NFuse and Wireless Technologies."

Understanding and Testing the Application

If this is a first time install of the application, your focus should be on learning the ins and outs of how the application works and testing to make sure it works properly on Terminal Server. Before installing it on the farm, install the application on your workstation and test it. While you are testing it, keep an eye out for the following:

- **Where settings are set** Keep an eye out for where you can set settings for the application, such as application property pages. As you will see in more detail in the "Where Applications Store Settings" section, these settings must be stored somewhere on the system. Storing user-specific settings in the same area is a common mistake that developers make and needs to be watched out for.

- **Heavy graphics use or animation** Look for the unnecessary use of heavy graphics or animation. On some applications, such as Visio, the use of graphics is what the application is all about. For other applications, however, there are ways to minimize the amount of graphics used. This improves performance time. Also, many applications have splash screens that you can disable. This is very important if you intend to deploy the application across slow connections, such as dial-up lines.

- **Links into other applications**   Be especially aware of necessary links into other applications or the use of other application components. For example, you might have an application that requires that Adobe Acrobat be installed for the user to bring up the application documents. Another example is an application that has an export button to another application, such as Excel or Word. Finally, you might have an application such as a document viewer that has the capability to send a document directly to someone else by using the installed email package. If your applications use other applications, you need to ensure that all applications on the system are installed correctly and tested.

- **Where files are stored**   On Windows 2000, the application should normally default to storing documents in the My Documents folder. You also might find some applications that store documents by default in the home directory folder. As long as both your profiles and home directories are centralized, either of these techniques will work. Be careful, however, of applications where you can set the default location for documents, especially if this location is somewhere central, such as under the application directory. You will likely need to repoint the application to the root of the user's home drive for this setting by making either a Registry or .INI file change.

- **Temporary files**   Many applications need to be able to have their own area to create temporary files. Normally application developers choose the temp directory that is pointed to a different location for each user automatically through Terminal Server. In some applications, however, you can manually set where the temporary files should be kept. This should be set to point to the user's home drive using either a Registry change or .INI change.

- **Printing**   How your application handles printing is very important. Most Windows applications print to printers installed on the Windows desktop. Using Terminal Server's printer auto-creation capabilities, applications like this should easily be able to print when used on a Terminal Server session. However, some applications, especially older DOS and Windows 16-bit applications, have their own method of handling printing. Make sure you understand all the methods with which an application prints and that printing is set up to work successfully for all cases.

- **Use of communication ports**   Certain applications, such as the synchronizer for Palm Pilot, and LPT1, and COM port printing, rely on Terminal Server's capability to redirect communication port traffic to the local workstation. Although the redirection of communications for printing generally works very well, be careful of other communication applications that might be more sensitive to timing issues. Be sure to set up a test group to pound the communications functionality to ensure it will perform well in production.

- **Multiuser use**   Make sure to test an application on a single server with multiple users. Try changing application settings from one user to ensure those setting changes do not occur for all users. If they do, you might need to lock down these settings by changing the security on either the Registry keys or .INI files that the settings are in to read-only. Have at least two people concurrently go through normal application functions running the application in different sessions on the same server. Make sure no unusual errors occur. Ideally, set up a test user group of power application users who can pound the application while on a test server and will report any problems encountered to you.

In addition to these items, reviewing the application product manual is a good step. Make sure you also have a test user ID and password setup if the application has its own security. You will need this ID for testing the application if there are any changes that need to be made on the system or if you need to duplicate a problem that a user is having.

Installation Techniques

The next part of planning an application installation is deciding on the best approach to the installation process. You can choose from several different approaches, depending on your environment and your specific goals. The overall goal is to ensure the application installation goes without a hitch and without any downtime for your users. Following are some possible approaches.

If the server you will be installing the application on is not currently in production, you do not need to worry about some of the extra precautions you need to take for installing new applications on production servers. You can just install the application, perform application testing, have some users test it, and then roll it into production.

If you are installing a new application on a production server, you could choose a downtime window and install the application then. Make sure to not only test the application you install, but also all other applications running on that server to ensure that they were not affected by the installation. If you do not have the ability to load balance or load share your servers, this is the recommended choice.

If absolutely no downtime is acceptable, you are using Citrix with load balancing, and you have the resources, install the application as follows:

1. First make sure that all the production applications on the server you will be installing the new application on are load balanced. There should be enough server resources in the load-balanced pool that the other servers can handle the load if this server needs to be taken down.

2. Adjust the load-balancing parameters to ensure this server is the least preferred.

3. Install and test the application after hours. Make sure to test all the other applications on the server that are in production, in addition to the application you install.

4. Publish an icon for the new application to a test group of users. Be sure to choose users who you know will use the application heavily and have time to test it well.

5. After a week or more of solid testing, document the application install and include any Registry or application settings tweaking that was necessary.

6. Install the applications on the rest of the servers in the load-balanced pool and even out the load balancing.

The last approach is to use application-imaging technologies to install the application. By taking an image of your application, tweaking that image as necessary, and then rolling out the image one server at a time, you can ensure that the application is installed consistently across all your servers. If you are using Terminal Server alone, consider products such as Veritas's WinINSTALL to make the application images you need. You will find a free version of the limited WinINSTALL LE on the Windows 2000 Server CD under the `[cd]:\valueadd\3rdparty\mgmt\winstle` folder.

If you use the imaging technologies to make .MSI installation files of the application, you can then use Group Policies within Windows 2000 to deploy those applications to your servers. You would need to set up a machine policy, rather than a user policy, and add the application image files to the policy. For more information on how to do this, see the information in Chapter 14, "Policies and Desktop Management".

If you are using Citrix MetaFrame XPe, you can install and use the Citrix Installation Management product. These services enable you to create an application package that you can deploy across your server farm using application-packaging technology. This powerful and tightly integrated service can be managed from within the Citrix Management Console. For more information on how to use this technology refer to Chapter 23, "Advanced Application Installation and Installation Management."

Application Upgrade Techniques

The approaches you can take for an application upgrade are different than those you would use for a new install. Following are some ideas.

If you are upgrading a production application on Terminal Server, unless you are using Network Load Balancing, your main choice will be to upgrade the application after hours. Be sure to set aside enough time to test the application and all other production applications on the server, after the upgrade. Be especially aware of possible application problems caused by the upgrade. Some applications install better by doing a clean uninstall of the previous application first. Other applications require an upgrade install to bring in the previous application's settings.

If you are using Citrix and you are upgrading an existing application, the best approach is to use the dual-icon approach. For this approach to work you must have the existing application load balanced across servers in such a way that you can take one server down and still support the users on the rest of the servers. If this is the case, do the following. (In this example, the application is SAP GUI and the original version is 4.6D. The SAP GUI is a graphical accounting application used by companies that have deployed SAP's accounting system. You are upgrading to version 4.6E of the GUI. The version 4.6D of the SAP GUI is currently published to the users as SAP GUI.)

1. Choose a server in the load-balanced pool for the application installation.
2. Take this server out of the load-balanced pool for the original application and make it the least preferred for other applications that might be running on the server.
3. Upgrade or do a fresh install of the new application to the server.
4. Publish a second icon to a test group of users for the new application, call it **SAP GUI 4.6E - Test**. This test group should consist of application power users who understand the application very well and are willing to test it thoroughly.

5. After a week or more of testing of the new application, roll out the application to the other servers in the farm.

6. Point the original published application icon, SAP GUI, to the new version of the application and take away the test icon, SAP GUI 4.6E - Test. After you have finished, users should see only one icon for the application: SAP GUI. This is the one they had used before the upgrade.

Application Installation and Upgrade for Large Server Farms

Although the techniques described so far will work well for most environments, when you begin to exceed around 100 servers, many additional factors start to come into play for application installation. Here are some ideas on handling application installation properly for the largest of environments, including ASPs.

First, there should be a dedicated application-testing group. They would be responsible for testing all new applications and application upgrades on a dedicated pool of test servers. On these servers the applications are tested thoroughly before deployment into the production environment. During the testing, this team would be responsible for the following:

- **Documenting the application installation thoroughly** Every detail of the application installation should be documented thoroughly. Details such as how the application is installed, where the application settings are kept, what settings might need to be tweaked, how the application is imaged, and how the application is used should be recorded in an application installation document.

- **Testing the application thoroughly** The application should go through an intense period of testing that is handled by the combined efforts of the testing team and a select group of application power users.

- **Benchmarking the application** Using scripts, this team would benchmark the application, simulating typical single- and multiuser usage. During these benchmarks, processor and memory usage would be closely monitored and recorded for various application functions. In addition, other performance parameters, such as network usage, paging file use, and drive space use, especially with user profiles, would be monitored. The goal would be to more accurately determine the hardware requirements necessary to support the application. These techniques are covered in more detail in Chapter 21, "Performance Tuning and Resource Management."

- **Application imaging**   Using imaging technologies, the application testing group would create images of new applications and tweak them and then test their installation. This would ensure that applications are installed in a standardized fashion across the servers.

Instead of using the load-balancing techniques described earlier to test the application, the application would be thoroughly tested, documented, and imaged on the test servers. After the completion of the testing process, the application would be rolled into production. For environments where absolutely no downtime is acceptable, the rollout into production should leverage load-balancing capabilities to gradually move the application into production instead of moving it into production to all production servers at once.

Application Data Storage

Where applications store data and how they access data is a critical issue to plan carefully and plan well. In general, the larger your environment, the more important it is to centralize the data that your Citrix MetaFrame or Terminal Servers access. In other words, the role of your Terminal Servers is to serve applications to your users. This concept of putting applications only on your Terminal Servers and not data is important for the following reasons:

- **Disaster recovery**   If one of your Terminal Servers fails, you can easily and quickly rebuild it by installing the operating system and the applications, without having to worry about the additional step of restoring the data. Because the data is centralized, when the server is rebuilt, users will immediately be able to access the data.

- **Load balancing and load sharing**   Unless your data is centralized, there is no effective way to load balance your servers. If you store data on one of the servers in the load-balanced pool and that server fails, all the servers in the load-balanced pool fail. If you store it centrally and a server fails, however, users will still be able to access the data and applications from the other load-balanced servers.

- **Data administrative isolation**   By centralizing your data, you also can better focus on proper data management and disaster recovery. You will be able to take advantage of enterprise-class data-focused solutions, such as *storage area network* (SAN) arrays, dedicated database servers, and data warehousing software. The extra reliability, scalability, performance, and disaster recovery capabilities offered by these data-focused solutions are critical for large deployments. In addition, you will be able to dedicate data experts to managing and monitoring the data solution.

The planning of the data centralization not only includes centralization of application data, but also should include the centralization of home directories, profiles, and other user data. In larger environments you will likely want to consider using clustering technologies or SAN solutions to hold this critical user data. All these decisions are a very important part of the planning process.

Planning the Installation Location

It is generally a very good idea to standardize the installation location of your application across the server farm. This makes troubleshooting much easier and enables you to make global changes to the application using scripting technologies.

In addition, it is very important to create a drive or separate volume on your server dedicated for applications. This common and best practice helps ensure the reliability of your servers. Instead of filling up the system drive with applications, and risk crashing the server, it is much preferred to use the application drive. Generally, the best folder to user is `[app drive]:\program files\[app name]`. For more information on creating a dedicated application drive, Chapter 8, "Installing Windows 2000 Terminal Server and Citrix MetaFrame."

Although it might seem obvious, it also is important to check across your farm to ensure that you have adequate drive space to handle the new application. As part of the testing and documentation process, you should find out how much space an application takes on both the system and application drives and add it to your application install document.

Installing the Application

The actual installation of the application is relatively easy compared to the planning considerations necessary before application installation. The following instructions cover how to install an application on Terminal Server:

1. From the Control Panel, double-click Add/Remove Programs.
2. Click the Add New Programs button.
3. Insert the application install CD or floppy disk into the server.
4. Click CD or Floppy and then follow the wizard to start the install. If the install files are on the network, you will have the opportunity to browse for the setup program after the scan of the floppy disk and CD drives is complete.
5. After the installation has finished, click Next and then click Finish. Only do this after the entire installation has finished.

Terminal Server will automatically take care of switching the server between install mode and execute mode for you during the installation, if you use this process. If you would rather switch this mode manually, use the following instructions instead:

1. Select Run from the Start menu and enter the following command to change the server into install mode: `change user /install`.

2. Open the Run window again and browse for the application setup program by clicking the Browse button.

3. Install the application by clicking OK to run the setup program.

4. After the install has finished, open the Run window and enter the following command to change the server back into execute mode: `change user /execute`.

In some cases you might want to open the application and change settings before changing the server back to execute mode.

How Terminal Server Keeps Applications Separate

When you run applications on Terminal Server, a fair amount of magic goes on in the background to keep applications isolated from affecting one another. In addition, as a Terminal Server administrator you might need to take some of your own steps to ensure the applications running in a multiuser environment have their own isolated space in which to work. This section discusses how Terminal Server keeps applications separate and some of the steps you might need to take to help this process out.

Separating Temporary Folders

Many applications rely on the use of temporary folders to store temporary application components. By default on Windows 2000 and Windows NT 4.0 Server, however, the temporary directory is the same for all users who log on. In a multiuser environment where two users can be using the same application at the same time, one user's temporary files can conflict with another's because they are stored in the same folder.

To circumvent this problem, both Windows NT 4.0 and 2000 Terminal Server setup separate temporary directories for each user who logs on. In Windows NT 4.0 Terminal Server, each user is given his own temporary folder upon logon under the `%systemrootdrive%\temp\[session id]` folder. Under Windows 2000, this location has changed to below the user's profile directory by default. This location is now `%userprofile%\localsettings\temp\[session id]`.

Separating Application Objects

Windows NT is an object-oriented environment. When an application needs to accomplish a task, it often has to reference certain system and application objects. This task is handled by the Object Manager component of the operating system. In a multiuser environment, there needs to be some method of differentiating between global objects that all users have access to and local objects that only a single user can see. To handle this need, Microsoft has written a special \sessions\[session id] namespace. In this namespace the operating system automatically writes all user-specific, session-related objects.

Viewing Session Objects

You can actually view a hierarchical layout of all the system objects currently in use on your Terminal Server using a freely available utility called WinObj from SysInternals web site. To download this utility, go to www.sysinternals.com and look for the WinObj program under the Windows NT / 2K monitoring tools section of the web site.

When you run this utility, you will be presented with a list of all the object types on the system. To view the \session objects that are currently created for each session on the server, just click the \session\ [session id] folder of choice.

Separating .INI Files and Windows Files

If you have ever had any experience with Windows 16-bit applications, you undoubtedly have encountered .INI files. These files are text-based settings files that contain application settings for various applications that run on your system. Although Microsoft has been pushing developers for the past several years to move their settings to the Registry, many applications out there still use .INI files.

Traditionally, an application's .INI files are stored in the %systemroot% folder, normally using the name of the application (for instance, ACROREAD.INI) for the .INI file. In addition to application specific .INI files, there are also two system .INI files: the WIN.INI and SYSTEM.INI. The WIN.INI file traditionally contained such Windows-related settings as fonts, file associations, and startup programs. The SYSTEM.INI contained more system-related settings, such as drivers that needed to be loaded upon startup.

The problem with .INI files in a multiuser environment is that by default only a single set of .INI files is on a server. If multiple users try to make changes to the same .INI file, each user's change will overwrite the last user's change. This will lead to such problems as one user changing an application setting that changes that setting for all users.

To avoid this problem, Terminal Server does the following:

1. Intercepts any read or write request to .INI files that exist in the `%systemroot%`.

2. Makes a copy of the .INI file that the user's application is attempting to read or write and places the copy in the user's `%userprofile%\windows` folder.

3. Performs the read or write request on the user's personal copy of the .INI file.

In addition to .INI files under the user's `%userprofile%\windows` folder, you also will find many other files that a user's application might install during its initial setup in the `windows` or `windows\system` folders, such as application-specific .DLLs.

Editing .INI Files

Although you do not have the need as often today to edit .INI files in a multiuser environment, the proper way to do it is to edit the central .INI file with Terminal Server. When the user first runs the application, he will get a copy of this .INI file sent down to his personal `%userprofile%\windows` folder.

Separating Registry Changes

When the Windows Registry was initially created, it was designed with a multiple users in mind. There is both a global portion of the Registry, referred to as the `HKEY_LOCAL_MACHINE`, and a user-specific portion of the Registry, referred to as `HKEY_LOCAL_USER`. Each user has her own copy of the user-specific portion of the Registry, whereas all users share the global portion.

Because the Registry is already divided out so that it will work well in a multiuser environment, Terminal Server does not do any further magic in the background to keep settings separate. Instead it is the job of the application developers to write their applications so that user-specific settings are written in the user's Registry, and global settings are put in the global area.

Unfortunately, this simple rule is often not followed by many application developers. This alone is the cause of some of the most difficult issues with Terminal Server.

Separating Printers

Normally, with Windows 2000 and NT 4.0 Server you can define only one set of printers on the server. In a multiuser environment, this can be a serious problem because everyone would have to share the same list of printers. To get around this issue, Terminal Server does the following:

1. By default, as a user logs on, her local printers are auto-created as `[workstation name]#[printer name]` on Terminal Server.

2. Her default local printer becomes her default printer on Terminal Server.

3. Printer security is automatically set up by Terminal Server so that unless the user has administrative privileges, she will be able to see only her own printers and no one else's that have been auto-created on the server.

When users browse for their printers, they are listed as the following:
`[workstation name]#[printer name]`.

Separating Other Devices

Many other devices that an application can use are redirected automatically on Terminal Server with Citrix MetaFrame to the associated local device for each user. The following is a list of all these devices:

- **Communication ports** If an application on Terminal Server with Citrix MetaFrame attempts to use a local COM port, Terminal Server with Citrix MetaFrame will by default redirect the read or write request to the user's local COM port on his workstation.

- **LPT printer ports** If an application attempts to send a print job directly to an LPT port on the Terminal Server with Citrix MetaFrame, it will redirect the job to the user's local LPT port by default. This is normally an issue with older 16-bit or DOS applications that do not take advantage of the Windows 32-bit printing capabilities.

- **Local drives (MetaFrame only)** On Citrix MetaFrame a user's local drives are made available in his Citrix session as a drive letter on the Citrix server. When the user reads or writes to this drive, his request is automatically redirected to the associated local drive on the user's workstation.

- **Audio redirection (MetaFrame only)** If an application uses audio, that audio can be redirected to the user's local audio system using Citrix MetaFrame.

Where Applications Store Settings

Knowing how to find out where applications keep their settings is one of the most important skills to learn with Terminal Server. You should not only understand where your applications store their settings, but also add this information into your application installation document.

Applications generally store their settings in one of three places: the Registry, .INI files, or custom settings files stored in either the application directory or user profile directory. In this section you will learn more about each of these storage locations for settings and how to determine which one(s) your applications use.

Searching for Recently Changed Files

One of the easiest ways of finding exactly what files your application installs or changes is to use the built-in search capabilities in Windows 2000. The Search function enables you to search the entire hard drive for files that have changed recently. If you make a change in an application and then do a search for recently changed files, you'll find the file in which the application makes those changes.

You can either run the search command directly after the application install to determine the files that the application installed or modified, or you can run the command after changing a particular application setting to see what file that setting is stored in. Usually the latter choice is a better method of determining where application settings are stored.

Here are the steps you need to follow:

1. Close all other running applications, including any applications running in the taskbar.

2. Stop as many unnecessary services as possible.

3. Run the application you are investigating and make a change to one or more application settings, such as changing the background color.

4. Select to Look In your Local Hard Drives.

5. Select the For Files and Folders from the Start, Search menu on your Windows 2000 Terminal Server.

6. Click the Date check box, and then select In the Last 1 Days.

This will produce a list of files that have changed over the past day. You can order this list by modified date by clicking on the Modified column. You will find that because several files are modified by your system and background services on a regular basis, it might be difficult to determine which files were modified by the application and not the system. You normally should look for files that are in one of the following folders, however, because these are the most common places that application settings are stored.

- Application install folder
- Underneath the user's profile folder
- Under the `%systemroot%` folder

This technique works very well for finding .INI files where application settings are written. You can quickly see which .INI files have changed recently because of the application change you made.

Using an Application Image

If you want to obtain a list of all the files that your application installs onto a system, the easiest way to do this is to use application-imaging technology. Using a product such as Veritas' WinINSTALL, you can take a before-and-after discovery of your system. Not only will you be able to see all the files that an application changes, but you also will see a list of all the Registry changes. This is a highly recommended first step for any application investigation. Here is how to do it:

1. Make sure that the system you are installing is clean of any of the application components, by uninstalling any unnecessary loaded application. Ideally start with a fresh load of Windows 2000 Server on a test server.

2. Install the limited-edition WinINSTALL LE, located on the Windows 2000 Server CD under `[cd]:\support\3rdparty\ mgmt\winstall`.

3. Run the Veritas Discovery application from the Veritas Software folder in the Program menu and take the before snapshot of your system.

4. Do a clean install of your application.

5. Run the Veritas Discovery application again to take the after snapshot.

6. Open the Veritas Software Console from the Veritas Software folder in the Program menu.

7. Right-click Windows Installer Package Editor and select Open.

8. Browse for the .MSI file you created in step 3 and click OK.

9. Highlight the name of the application and look in the Registry, Files, INI Edits, and Services folders to see what components the application installs.

If you are using MetaFrame XPe, you also can use the discovery tools available in the Installation Management Services to create a list of all the components your application installs. For more information, see Chapter 23.

Checking for Registry Changes

Often an application makes certain changes to the Registry to record application settings. Normally, how your application uses the Registry for the storage of settings can be very difficult to determine. However, there is a freely available tool from SysInternal's web site called *Regmon*, which will open a window into how your application is using the Registry. To download this tool, go to www.sysinternals.com and download the freeware REMON.EXE utility.

Using Regmon, you can watch all the Registry changes an application makes while it's running. To use this utility, follow these steps:

1. Open your application.

2. While the application is open, open Regmon.

3. Make a settings change somewhere in the application that you suspect is saved in the Registry.

4. Use Alt+Tab to switch to the Regmon screen to view the log of changes and to look for the change you just made.

If the application records the changes in the Registry, you'll see exactly where it puts them. Generally you will find that an application will store settings in one of the following two places:

- **HKEY_LOCAL_MACHINE\SOFTWARE\[Publisher or Software Name]**   This is the global key, so this is where the application should store changes that will affect all users.

- **HKEY_CURRENT_USER\SOFTWARE\[Publisher or Software Name]**   This user-specific key is where applications normally store user-specific application settings.

If you find that the application improperly stores the important user settings in HKEY_LOCAL_MACHINE rather than in HKEY_CURRENT_USER during normal use, you can use Registry security to restrict who is able to change them. However, this technique might or might not work with your particular application depending on how it reacts to an inability to change a Registry setting.

Note that Regmon is also a very useful learning tool, especially during application installation. The next time you install an application, use Regmon to monitor the installation to see what changes your application makes to the Registry.

Author's Note

Tools such as Regmon are powerful but are meant for use during low activity or off-peak hours. Ideally, these type of tools should be used only in a test environment and not on a production server. If you attempt to use Regmon on a heavily active server, you will greatly affect its performance because every Registry change has to be captured and displayed on the Regmon log screen.

Understanding the Registry

To effectively administer Terminal Server, especially on a large scale, you need to gain an intimate knowledge of the inner workings of the Registry. What you really need to understand is how your applications use the Registry.

For those unfamiliar with the Registry, it's just a central database for keeping operating system and application settings. Every time you change the wallpaper on your desktop, install a new piece of hardware, or change a setting in a control panel, you are saving your changes in the Registry. The Registry is mainly used by Windows 32-bit applications, although some Windows 16-bit applications are able to write to it.

Basic Registry Organization

For the information in this section to really sink in, open up the Registry on your Terminal Server using REGEDT32.EXE and follow along.

When you first open the Registry on Windows NT using REGEDT32.EXE, the following five Registry keys pop up:

- **HKEY_LOCAL_MACHINE** Settings that apply globally.

- **HKEY_CURRENT_USER** Current user's user-specific settings.

- **HKEY_USERS** The currently cached user keys, including the .DEFAULT user key. The .DEFAULT user key is also called the *system default profile*. This key controls the settings, such as the wallpaper and colors, you see when you first log on to Terminal Server.

- **HKEY_CURRENT_CONFIG** Alias to a location in HKEY_LOCAL_MACHINE (hardware profiles).

- **HKEY_CLASSES_ROOT** Alias to another location in HKEY_LOCAL_MACHINE (file extensions).

Out of these five keys, the two that are of the most importance to you when you are administering Terminal Server are `HKEY_LOCAL_MACHINE` and `HKEY_CURENT_USER`. The rest of the keys are merely pointers (or aliases) to sections of these two main keys. Because they are aliases, they do not contain anything new. To avoid confusion, minimize all the keys except `HKEY_LOCAL_MACHINE` and `HKEY_CURRENT_USER`.

The settings in the Registry are organized in a hierarchical fashion. Browsing through it is a lot like browsing through a file system. Instead of the folders being called directories, they are called *keys*. Under the keys are subkeys. Both subkeys and keys can contain values. Values can be anything from strings to binary numbers. These values are used by the operating system and applications to store their settings.

HKEY_LOCAL_MACHINE

`HKEY_LOCAL_MACHINE` is the most critical system Registry key. This key contains configuration data for the system as a whole. If a setting applies to all the users and not just one, it belongs in `HKEY_LOCAL_MACHINE`. You'll find information about device drivers, hardware resources, file extensions, network settings such as machine name, and much more. A complete coverage of all the keys in `HKEY_LOCAL_MACHINE` could fill a book on its own! Only the most relevant ones are covered here.

The most important thing to remember about `HKEY_LOCAL_MACHINE` is that any settings in here affect all your users. If your application stores any settings in `HKEY_LOCAL_MACHINE`, they will apply for everyone who uses the application. Properly written applications put only global parameters under this key. One of the problems you might encounter with Terminal Server is applications that store user-specific settings under here and not global settings.

If you have an application that stores its color scheme in `HKEY_LOCAL_MACHINE`, for example, every time someone changes his colors, it will affect all the users of the application. Luckily there are ways to detect and prevent problems like this (as discussed later in this chapter in the troubleshooting sections).

With Terminal Server, you need to be concerned mainly about the settings under a single key: the `SOFTWARE` key. Under this key you'll find several subkeys. The following subsections cover the most important ones.

HKLM\SOFTWARE\Classes

`HKLM\SOFTWARE\Classes` is a critical application key that contains file extension associations and registered application components. Nearly every application installed on the system will make some type of change under this key.

When you install Excel, for instance, it will add a key under `Classes` for .XLS, the extension for Excel spreadsheets. When you double-click an .XLS file, it will open in Excel. Because this is a global key, when new applications extensions are installed under `Classes`, they are available to all users.

Common problems that can occur with `Classes` are extension conflicts. Graphic file extensions are a common culprit. Suppose, for example, that you install automated fax software that registers itself as the default viewer for several graphic formats (.GIF, .TIF, .PCX) so that users can view and save their incoming faxes in electronic form. A couple of months later you install a web browser for a couple of users, which also registers itself as a viewer for graphics formats. A day after installing it, you start getting calls from your users saying that their faxes now open up in the browser rather than the fax viewer! For this reason, it is important to be careful of which extensions your applications install.

HKLM\SOFTWARE\Microsoft

Under the `HKLM\SOFTWARE\Microsoft` subkey are some of the most important keys on the system. These keys control important aspects of the behavior of all Microsoft software on your system, including the operating system itself.

Any Microsoft product will store its global settings under here. Many useful ones can be found under `microsoft\windows nt\current version`.

HKLM\SOFTWARE\Citrix

`HKLM\SOFTWARE\Citrix`, of course, is where Citrix stores its global settings for the server. If you browse under this key, you will find numerous subkeys for such settings as for the IMA Service, SNMP settings, and the Installation Manager.

HKEY_CURRENT_USER

`HKEY_CURRENT_USER` contains settings that apply only to the user who is currently logged on. If an application needs to maintain a setting for this user only, such as the location of her document's directory or preferred text colors, that setting belongs here.

The file that holds the `HKEY_CURRENT_USER` key is actually stored in the user's profile directory, in a file called NTUSER.DAT. By default, the user profile directories are under `c:\documents and settings`, under the user's name. The NTUSER.DAT file is stored in the root of the user's profile directory.

Several keys under HKEY_CURRENT_USER are important to know about, but like HKEY_LOCAL_MACHINE the primary one of concern is the SOFTWARE key. The following is a list of the main keys under HKEY_CURRENT_USER and what they're for:

- **AppEvents** This one sounds more important than it really is. This key keeps the associations between sounds and Windows events. When Windows starts up and you hear a startup sound, for example, it's because of a value in a subkey here.

- **Console** This key holds the default options for the DOS command console. You can change these settings by going into Control Panel and selecting Console. Remember that these settings affect the current user only. This is also the area that options for the NTVDM console are stored.

- **Control Panel** Just about every user-specific setting you can change with Control Panel is under this key, including color scheme, mouse settings, international settings, cursors, accessibility settings, and more.

- **Environment** Here's where the user's environment variables, such as the PATH variable, are kept. You can control these variables by going into Control Panel and selecting System, Environment. Environment variables also can be set with AUTOEXEC.BAT and AUTOEXEC.NT.

- **Keyboard Layout** This controls which input locales and keyboard layouts are currently loaded. You can control these through Control Panel by selecting Keyboard, Input Locales.

- **Network and UNICODE program groups** The Network key was used to store persistent connections. Neither of these keys is used any longer with Window NT 4.0.

- **Printers** Under this key, you'll find the settings for the user's currently installed printers.

- **SOFTWARE** Out of all the branches, this is where you will probably spend most of your time. The SOFTWARE branch is where your applications keep their user-specific settings. You'll often find a key for a particular piece of software by looking for the name of the application's publisher under this branch. Under this key you will find the application's user-specific settings.

Where the Registry Is Stored

The Registry actually consists of several files located on the hard drive of your system. You will find the HKEY_LOCAL_USER Registry key in the NTUSER.DAT file in each user's profile directory. The HKEY_LOCAL_MACHINE system Registry files are located under the %systemroot%\system32\config folder.

Backing Up the Registry

With Windows 2000 Server, it has always been a good idea to back up the Registry before any installation. With Terminal Server, it's even more important. The installation of one poorly written application can affect all your users. By backing up the Registry, you create a back door through which you can get back to a working system.

You can back up the Registry in several different ways. Because the Registry files are open when Terminal Server is running, you cannot use the copy or xcopy commands to back up the files. You need a program that's specially written to back it up.

The first and simplest is to use RDISK.EXE. This program is included with Windows 2000 and can be run from the run command in the Start menu. With this utility, you can either back up the Registry files to the %systemroot%\repair folder by clicking Update Repair Info or create a floppy disk with the Registry info on it by clicking Create Repair Disk.

Another option is to use a utility called REGBACK.EXE, which is included with the Windows NT Resource Kit. This utility is like xcopy for the Registry. You can back up the Registry files into any directory you want.

Understanding Install and Execute Modes

Now that you understand what HKEY_LOCAL_MACHINE and HKEY_CURRENT_USER are for, it is time to discuss the unique changes to the Registry that occur on Terminal Server when the server is in install mode versus execute mode. Recall that you need to place the server in install mode using the change user /install command before you install any application on the server. Normally, however, the server is run in execute mode, which can be manually switched to using the change user /execute command.

When you put your server in install mode, the first and most important difference is that any changes to the user Registry by the application will now be copied under the following Registry key:

```
HKEY_LOCAL_MACHINE\SOFTWARE\Microsoft\Windows NT\Current Version\ Terminal
Server\Install
```

All changes that an application makes to `HKEY_CURRENT_USER\` `SOFTWARE` key are put under the `\SOFTWARE` subkey in this location. Some changes to the `HKEY_LOCAL_MACHINE` also are captured here and placed under the `MACHINE` subkey.

The second difference between execute and install modes is that in install mode any files that are written to `%systemroot%` or `%systemroot%\system32` are not redirected to the user's `%userprofile%\windows` directory. In execute mode, however, they are written to the user's profile folder so that each user has his own copy of any settings files, such as .INI files, which are used by the application.

After the application is installed and the Registry changes are captured, the administrator uses the `change user /execute` command to switch the server back into execute mode so that users can run the application.

When a user first runs the application while in execute mode, Terminal Server will propagate the user Registry changes recorded during installation to the user. It normally copies changes from the central location only when the application attempts to access that key.

Suppose, for example, that you had installed Adobe Acrobat Reader on your system while in install mode. During the installation, Terminal Server made a copy of changes to any user software keys under the central Registry location (`HKLM\SOFTWARE\Microsoft\ TerminalServer\Install`). After the installation, you switched the system back to execute mode. You then logged off and logged back in as a test user and opened Adobe Acrobat Reader. At the point the Adobe Reader application attempted to retrieve any user key, Terminal Server intercepts the request while in execute mode. If that key does not exist already, Terminal Server copies it down from the central Registry location so that the user starts with the copy of the key as it was originally installed.

In this way each user is given a fresh copy of the application's user-specific keys when he runs the application.

Troubleshooting Application Problems

As you can see, a lot is going on under the surface to help applications run correctly in a multiuser environment. Even so, sometimes an application just doesn't want to run correctly on Terminal Server. The following sections give you the tools and guidance you need to start troubleshooting and resolving application problems.

Troubleshooting DOS Applications

So far, you've learned mainly about running Windows 32- and Windows 16-bit applications with Citrix MetaFrame. Many of you might have to support DOS legacy applications in addition. Because of their lack of interface into the Windows 32-bit API, DOS applications can be some of the most challenging types of applications to get running well. The following sections discuss some of the most useful ways to tweak your DOS applications to run well on your Terminal Servers.

Memory over Utilization

If your server slows to a crawl every time your users try running DOS applications, there's a good chance that they are using too much memory. Certain DOS applications, such as some versions of FoxPro for DOS, will use up all available server memory by default.

To check whether this is the problem, bring up Windows Task Manager by running TASKMGR.EXE (from Start, Run, and click the Performance tab). Watch the physical memory available and memory utilization as you run your DOS application. If the amount drastically changes, your DOS application is the culprit.

You can try adjusting the .PIF settings as shown in the section "Using .PIF Files for DOS Applications." Also refer to your application's developers for tips on limiting the amount of memory.

For example, with FoxPro for DOS, you can solve this problem by adding `MEMLIMIT=60,4096,6144` to the CONFIG.FP file found in the FOXPROxx directory.

Processor over Utilization

DOS applications were never designed for a multitasking environment. Many DOS applications will overutilize the processor with idle processes. There are several ways to control this problem. Under Windows NT 4.0 Terminal Server, the recommended method is to use the DOSKBD utility. The DOSKBD utility prevents a DOS application from overutilizing the processor by polling constantly for user input. To use the utility, just add `doskbd` to your AUTOEXEC.NT file under `%systemroot%\system32` file. DOSKBD is included by default with Windows NT 4.0 Terminal Server.

DOSKBD has many special settings that you can adjust to optimize response time for DOS applications. The default settings should be adequate for most situations. However, compare the processor utilization of the application, with and without DOSKBD, using the Windows Task Manager, especially when the application is in an idle state waiting for input. If you find you need to further adjust the settings, type **doskbd /?** for an explanation of the settings available.

In Windows 2000 Terminal Server, DOSKBD is no longer available and the version on Windows 4.0 Terminal Server will not work. Your only choice is to try adjusting the idle sensitivity using .PIF files or to only use the application on Windows NT 4.0 Terminal Servers. See the "Using .PIF Files for DOS .COM Applications" section.

Using the Tame Application

For those who have to frequently deal with making DOS applications behave well on Terminal Server, one shareware application that is definitely worth looking at is Tame. Tame is available for evaluation at www.tamedos.com. This application is much like the DOSKBD utility in that it helps control keyboard polling by DOS applications. Unlike DOSKBD, however, it works with Windows 2000 Terminal Services and has several more features.

Blinking Cursors and Text Animations

If your DOS application uses blinking or spinning cursors or any other type of animation, such as scrolling banners, make sure you turn them off when possible. These animations will use up tremendous amounts of processing power and network bandwidth to handle the screen updates necessary to display them.

Using .PIF Files for DOS .COM Applications

If you use DOS applications that use a .COM extension, you might want to create a Program Information Files (.PIF) file to control the DOS application's settings. These files are a way to control environment settings for DOS applications that comes from the days of Windows 3.1 and Windows 3.11.

To create a .PIF for your DOS application, just right-click the application executable in Windows Explorer and select Properties. You will see several tabs containing both standard application settings and additional settings that specifically control the DOS environment. By changing any of these settings and applying them, Windows Explorer will automatically create a .PIF file for your application in the current directory using the same name as the application, [APPLICATION].PIF. The next time you run the DOS application, Terminal Server will set up the DOS environment in accordance with the associated .PIF before running the application.

The following settings are some of the most important of these DOS-specific settings that you can set:

- **AUTOEXEC.BAT and CONFIG.SYS** By default, DOS applications use the `%systemroot\system32\autoexec.nt` AUTOEXC file and the `%systemroot%\system32\config.nt` CONFIG file when they start up. If you want to change this, click the Program tab, click the Advanced button, and then enter the AUTOEXEC and CONFIG files you want to use instead.

- **Total conventional memory and initial memory**   Under the Memory tab, you can change several different DOS environment settings related to memory. There are several settings under here to control the memory environment for your DOS application. The first setting under Conventional Memory enables you to specify both the initial memory given to a DOS application and the total memory that it can use. If you are getting out of memory errors in your DOS applications, you might try these settings. However, the default setting of Auto for both is normally adequate.

- **Expanded memory and XMS memory**   The concepts of expanded memory and XMS memory go back a long way. However, the basic idea was that these two types of memory were two different methods for DOS applications to break through the 640K memory barrier. A DOS application can be written to be able to use either of these memory technologies. If you are getting out of memory errors with your application and you have maxed out the conventional memory settings, you might try one of these settings to increase the memory available for your application.

- **Foreground and background**   Under the Misc tab, there are several important settings. The first is the Foreground, Allow Screen Saver check box. Uncheck this box if the screen saver is causing your DOS applications to lock up. Screen savers should not be run on a Terminal Server, so this check box is rarely used. The second setting is the Background, Always Suspend setting. By default, when a user switches windows on a Terminal Server and a DOS application is put into the background, it will be suspended rather than allowed to continue running. This can cause problems with some DOS applications, so you might need to uncheck this box.

- **Idle Sensitivity**   Another important setting under the Misc tab is Idle Sensitivity. Idle Sensitivity enables you to adjust the processor utilization by your DOS application when the application is in an idle state awaiting user input. This is the only way to control processor utilization in Windows 2000 Terminal Server for DOS applications, because the DOSKB utility is no longer available. If you find your DOS applications are using too much processor time, adjust this setting higher. If they are running sluggishly, try lowering this setting.

CPU Prioritization in Feature Release 1

One interesting new feature to note, available only with Feature Release 1 for MetaFrame XP, is the ability to control the CPU priority of published applications. When publishing applications, you can set the priority that the published application will start in on the server. This can help in certain situations where some applications tend to monopolize the CPU time on a server.

Using DOS Window Settings

The problem with .PIF files is that they apply only to DOS applications that end with .COM. In addition, you will find that several of the settings in .PIF files do not behave as expected; especially those that have to do with the display of the DOS application.

To better control the display properties of a DOS application, you need to get to the DOS window settings by doing the following:

1. Open the application on Terminal Server, logged on as an administrative user.
2. Right-click the C:\ prompt in the upper-left corner and select Properties.
3. Change the DOS window properties as needed under the Options, Fonts, Layout, and Colors tabs; then click OK.
4. Select to Save Changes for All Windows with the Same Title.

Note that this change will affect every DOS application that this user attempts to run, with the exception of CMD.COM itself. The reason for this is that all DOS applications run under a single system application (the NTVDM). The NTVDM is responsible for simulating the DOS environment on which your DOS application runs. When you modify the properties for a DOS application and save the changes for all windows of the same title, you are actually saving those changes for the NTVDM window. In other words, any changes you make using the preceding instructions will affect every DOS application that is run for that user.

Terminal Server records these DOS windows setting changes under the following user key:

```
HKLU\Console\%SystemRoot%_System32_ntvdm.exe
```

Because this is a user key and not a machine key, you would normally have to log on as each user and adjust his or her DOS windows settings manually to propagate the changes you need. However, using either policies or group policy objects you can automatically propagate these changes to all the users on a particular Terminal Server. For more information on how to propagate a Registry change using a custom policy, see Chapter 14.

Troubleshooting Windows 16- and 32-Bit Application Problems

The following are some solutions to common problems running Windows 16- and Windows 32-bit applications on Terminal Server.

Application Does Not Run at All

If the application does not run at all, you need to step back and do a couple of tests. First, try running the application on a Windows 2000 workstation. If it does not work on the workstation, it will not work on Windows 2000 Terminal Server. You might try running it on Windows NT 4.0 Terminal Server to see if it works. However, the first requirement for any application is that it will run on Windows NT. You also could try running it from the console of your server versus from a session. If this works, you might have a video issue with the application, and you will need to contact the application developers to see if a fix is available.

Strange Behavior or Lockups

If you are experiencing strange behavior or lockups, double-check that the user is running the application in execute mode and that the home directory is set up correctly. This might seem simple, but this is where a lot of problems occur. Type **change user /query** while logged on as the user to ensure that the user is in execute or user-specific mode. Next, type **set** to check the environment-setting variables. The HOMEDRIVE and HOMEPATH variables should point to the correct location for the user's home directory.

"File Missing" Errors

"File missing" errors are a common problem. More often than not they are due to either a faulty installation or files are not being copied over in install mode. Many times the errors are related to incorrectly registered .DLLs.

To solve this problem, try uninstalling the application, closing all unnecessary applications, shutting down all unnecessary servers, and then installing the application again. Never install an application while other users are using the system. They will likely have files locked open that the installation program needs to replace. To get users off and install the application, follow these steps:

1. Send a message to users to log off using the **msg * "[message]"** command.

2. Reset any sessions that are still open from either the Terminal Services Administration Tool or the Citrix Management Console.

3. Disable new logons using the **change logon /disable** command.

4. Change to install mode and install the application.

5. Change back to execute mode and use the **change logon /enable** command to re-enable logons to the server.

"Access Denied" Errors

Often on new installations, you run into security issues. It is very important to always test your applications with a user ID that is a member of only the local user group and is not an administrator. This will help you determine whether there are any issues related to security in running the application.

If you encounter this type of issue, you will normally need to adjust the security of a file, a directory, or a Registry key using the appropriate utility. If it is not obvious which file or Registry key is the issue, try running either SysInternals Filemon or the Regmon utility. These utilities are available for free at www.sysinternals.com. Filemon enables you to watch and log all file activity on a system, whereas Regmon enables you to watch Registry activity. By using these utilities while you duplicate the security error, you can determine which file or Registry entry the application was trying to write to or read from.

Application Requires a Temp Directory

Application requires a temp directory is a very common need and is one of the main reasons why map-rooting home directories is so important. Many times an application keeps the setting for its default temporary directory a machine Registry key. The challenge becomes how to enter a single path for an application temporary directory that will be unique for all your users.

Suppose, for example, that you have an application called Acme-Organizer that has a setting for the directory for the user's organizer files. Unfortunately, the developer put this setting in HKEY_LOCAL_MACHINE. You need to distribute this application to 50 users, all of whom will need their own location for their Organizer file. How do you do it?

Specify the location for the Organizer files as [home drive]:\, where [home drive] is your standardized user home drive letter. When users log on, [home drive] will be map-rooted to their personal home directory. Their personal Organizer files will be put under \.

You could take this a step further and lock the Organizer data path in the Registry using Registry security. This way, one user could not change the setting and thus disable everyone's Organizer.

Users Complain That Their Settings Keep Changing

If your users complain that their settings keep changing, after installing an application in install mode, log on as one of the users and run the application. Change as many of the user-specific default settings as possible, such as those under a Properties section of the application (text colors, server names, cache parameters). Now log on as another user and run the application. Do you see the default settings or do you see the one user's settings?

If you see user one's settings, the application is storing user-specific settings in HKEY_LOCAL_MACHINE. Remember that HKEY_LOCAL_MACHINE is only for global settings, and HKEY_CURRENT_USER is for user settings. If this is the case, you can either warn your users about the problem and request that they not change their settings or you can research where the Registry settings are, set them to a single value, and use Registry security to prevent users from changing them in the future. Regmon is a good tool to use to discover the Registry keys that change when you change an application's settings.

If your application stores its settings in .INI files and you're having this problem, check to make sure that the user has his own copy of the .INI file in his home directory. If not, make sure you are in execute mode and that the home directory settings are correct.

Advanced Application Troubleshooting

If you absolutely have to get a particular application to run with Terminal Server and have completely run out of options, there's one more possibility to look into, the Compatibility keys. These are a set of three keys you can use to help solve application Registry, .INI, and performance problems.

You will find the Compatibility keys located under the following machine Registry location:

```
HKLM\SOFTWARE\Microsoft\WindowsNT\CurrentVersion\TerminalServer\
Compatibility
```

Underneath this key you will find the following subkeys:

- **Applications** This key and its subkeys are used for tuning the performance of your applications. This key is covered in more detail in Chapter 21.

- **IniFiles** This Registry key controls how the .INI files located in the system directory are synchronized with the files in the users' home directories. The .INI name with a REG_DWORD of x44 means that changes to that .INI file will be merged with the user's .INI file of the same name. Notice that the SYSTEM and WIN.INI files are, by default, included in this Registry. If, for example, you edit the SYSTEM.INI files using SYSEDIT while in user global mode and then log on as a user, the changes you made to the central SYSTEM.INI file will be merged with the user's SYSTEM.INI file.

- **Registry entries**   This Registry key controls how and whether the Registry keys under `HKEY_LOCAL_MACHINE\SOFTWARE\Microsoft\WindowsNT\CurrentVersion\TerminalServer\Software` are synchronized with the user's Registry keys. A value in here with a DWORD of x108 means that that particular key under `HKLM\SOFTWARE` and its subkeys will not be synchronized with the user's keys.

For additional information on advanced troubleshooting and tuning techniques, refer to Citrix technical article CTX846521.

Making the Most of Your Resources

Many, many troubleshooting resources are available to you for resolving application and other Citrix MetaFrame issues. It is important that you make the best use of them.

Using Citrix Resources

After trying the basics to resolve a problem with an application, try searching the Citrix web site for implementation tips (`www.citrix.com`). Citrix maintains an excellent online database of application installation tips.

Another important resource is the Citrix Solution Tools program. You will find more information about this program at `www.citrix.com/services/soltools`. This is a yearly subscription-based program that gives you access to the latest Citrix support tools and information. This currently includes access to a special Solution Tools web site and a quarterly CD with technical information, presentations, and other information.

Citrix SouthEast Group on Yahoo!

Citrix has several online forums available on Yahoo! These online forums are an outstanding resource because they give you direct access to a large community of highly experienced people who can likely help you through problems implementing and supporting Citrix products. There are currently more than 2000 members on this online forum and membership is free. To join, go to `http://groups.yahoo.com/group/citrixse`.

Using Microsoft Resources

Microsoft also maintains an excellent knowledge database on its web site located at www.microsoft.com under the Support section. In addition, Microsoft offers a TechNet subscription-based program that is similar to the Citrix Solution Tools program. In this program you get monthly CDs sent to you that are loaded with important technical information, beta software, utilities, and operating system patches. For more information on this program, go to www.microsoft.com/technet.

Online Forums and Third-Party Web Sites

Online forums and third-party web sites are an excellent way to communicate with your peers and use their experience to help with your problems. You can find the answers to many commonly encountered problems by searching these forums or web sites. For a list of the most widely used web sites and forums, see Appendix C, "Web Sites, Newsgroups, and Other Resources."

The Thin.net Online Forum

Of the many Citrix-related online forums available at Yahoo!, perhaps the most well-known and widely used is the one run by Jim Kenzig of Thin.net. This forum has nearly 4000 members and is highly active and loaded with good tips. You can join this free online forum by going to http://groups.yahoo.com/group/thin.

Service Providers

Citrix has one of the largest service provider channels of any software product. This basically means to you that there are a lot of knowledgeable and highly qualified people that you can contract onsite to help you with you Citrix MetaFrame and Terminal Server implementation issues. To find a reseller near you, contact your local Citrix sales representative.

Terminal Server Application Development

On some occasions, getting an application to run properly on Terminal Server will require the assistance of the developers. If you're going to develop applications for Terminal Server or you desire a developer-level understanding of what's required, this section is for you. If you can understand how Terminal Server is designed, you can understand how it can be fixed.

You need to follow these basic guidelines when developing applications for Terminal Server:

- **Applications need to be able to work with Windows NT.**   This is by far the most important rule. An application that cannot run on standard Windows NT or 2000 workstation will not run on Terminal Server.

- **Applications need to make use of standard Windows API calls.** Terminal Server captures several Windows API calls for Windows applications to be able to work correctly in the multiuser environment. Applications that do not adhere to Microsoft guidelines on writing them to the Windows API might not run well on Terminal Server. If your application uses custom code, especially machine-coded sections for additional speed, it will not run well or run at all on Terminal Server.

  One very important point on this topic is how an application makes changes to .INI files or the Registry. It needs to do so through the Windows API for Terminal Server to keep these changes separate. If one application running on Terminal Server records something in the Registry or an .INI file, you do not want this to affect all users of the application.

- **Do not write directly to the hardware.**   Examples of these types of applications are DOS graphics applications, Windows applications that use VxDs, and many games. Because they write directly to the hardware and do not work through the Windows APIs, there's no way for Terminal Server to capture these calls. Typical DOS applications that use graphics are desktop publishing applications, spreadsheets with graphs, graphing programs, and games. Typical Windows applications that use VxDs are communication programs that use VxDs for the COM ports, hard drive caching programs, and games. Typically, the DOS and Win16 applications you need to worry about are applications you wouldn't want to run on Terminal Server anyway.

- **Do not rely on a network address to identify users.**   If an application uses the IP address, MAC address, or network name of the client workstation to identify users, it might not work correctly on Terminal Server. This rule applies mainly for client/server or terminal applications.

  In a Terminal Server environment, the MAC address, IP address, and network name are that of the Terminal Server for all users. If you want to run a mainframe client through a gateway that identified the user by MAC address, for example, you would be able to allow only one user through the gateway. The software needs to be able to support some other means of identifying the user, such as a workstation ID setting, to work.

- **Applications need to return control to the OS.** When an application is idle or waiting for a response, it should return control to the OS. Applications that constantly poll the user, have time animations (such as blinking or spinning cursors), or that have any other constant activity during idle time will slow application performance significantly and tax the processor. If there's any way to turn the animations off, you should do so.

- **Do not store user-specific information in global areas.** This is probably the most often-abused rule and also one of the most important. Applications should not store user-specific information in global areas. This guideline is very important for proper application function on Terminal Server.

  Global settings belong under HKEY_LOCAL_MACHINE. User-specific settings belong under HKEY_CURRENT_USER. Global data files belong in a central folder, and user data files belong in the user's home or profile folder.

- **Avoid animations or complicated graphics.** Animations and complicated graphics take extra processing power to be compressed and sent across the line to the users' terminals. You should use simple graphics. Also stay away from bitmaps, and use vector graphics when possible. If the animations and graphics are needed for the presentation of the application, be sure to allow for a way for them to be disabled using a global Registry setting.

  The same goes for splash screens for applications. Splash screens increase application load times and can especially slow down performance across slow dial-up lines.

- **Design the application with the concept of resource competition in mind.** If your application uses resources unfairly, it robs resources from the rest of the applications running on the server. Remember that your application is always in competition for the limited resources of the Terminal Server.

- **Conform to Windows Logo Standards.** You can find most of the preceding application tips and more in the Windows Logo Standards documents available at www.microsoft.com. Even if you are developing an in-house application, closely following the Windows Logo Standards will help ensure that your application will run properly on Terminal Server.

Top-Ten Tips for Installing and Running Applications on Terminal Server

The following tips go over some of the key points regarding application installation on Terminal Server:

1. **The application must work on a Windows NT or 2000 workstation.**   If your application does not work on a Windows NT 4.0 or 2000 workstation, it will not work on Terminal Server. Always purchase the NT-compatible version of an application, if available.

2. **Use 32-bit applications for the Best Performance.**   DOS or Windows 16-bit applications will suffer up to a 25 percent drop in performance when run on Terminal Server. This is due mainly to the fact that a 16-bit-to-32-bit API translation needs to occur for nearly every system call the application makes. This 16-bit translation is handled by the NTVDM. Because each session must load its own NTVDM, the NTVDMs can take up a significant amount of memory when multiple users run multiple DOS applications. DOS applications that use polling can also further decrease performance and have to be specially tuned. In other words, if you can avoid 16-bit or DOS applications, do so.

3. **Standardize on a home directory drive letter.**   Standardizing on a home directory drive letter makes it much easier to resolve application problems in a multiuser environment. If an application needs to store user-specific data, point it to the user's home directory. Because the drive letter is the same for all users, this will always be a unique location for each user using the application.

   The home directory needs to be mapped to the root of the user directory using the `subst` or `net use` command in the logon script, as shown in Chapter 9, "Setting Up Terminal Server Users."

4. **Replace global locations with user-specific ones.**   After installing the application, be on the lookout for application settings that put user-specific data in a common location. Change the setting to the user's home directory rather than the common location so that each user has his own data. If there is a setting for the temporary folder for an application, for instance, make sure this points to the home directory drive letter rather than a common location such as `c:\temp`.

5. **Install application on the application, not system drive.**   During the installation of the server, be sure to assign a separate partition or set of drives as an application drive. On every server in your server farm, make sure to install applications on the application drive and not system drive. Also be sure to install applications into the same directory structure across your servers. Generally, the best place to install applications is [app drive]:\ program files\[app name] on each server. Make sure you document this location so that this is used consistently for new application installs.

   The main reason it to separate your applications from the system drive is just for the sake of storage space. It is bad practice to add things to the system drive unnecessarily because you risk filling up the system drive and crashing the system. Remember, even though there might be hundreds of megabytes free on the system drive, it can quickly fill up in a Terminal Server environment with things such as user profiles and print jobs.

6. **Keep data and applications separate.**   This is a general guideline that's a good idea for most operating systems. Keeping data and applications separate helps simplify backups, drive storage arrangement, and security. Application programs are generally static, but the user data is generally dynamic. Because user data is changing all the time, it needs to be backed up daily. Applications, on the other hand, might need to be backed up only weekly. Also, in general, user data requires read/write access, and applications require only read access. If a user is given read/write access to a directory that contains both applications and data, she can delete or overwrite critical application files. By keeping user data and applications in separate directories, you can more easily address the different backup and security requirements for these two types of information. Also keeping user data on a separate server works well for load balancing, because users will have access to their data no matter which load-balanced server they're using.

7. **Perform a clean install.**   When possible, always perform a clean install of an application instead of doing an application upgrade. This helps ensure that the application installation will go smoothly.

8. **Use application-imaging technology.**   Using application-imaging technology to install your applications, instead of manually installing them, is the best way to ensure the consistency of application installations across the farm. The images also generally provide detailed information on the components your application installs and the Registry changes it makes. This information proves very useful for application troubleshooting.

9. **Test, test, and then test some more.** *Always* test your applications thoroughly before implementing them widely. A good idea is to create two application test users. Make them a member of the same groups as the users who will be using the application. After installing the application as administrator in global mode, log on as the application test user.

10. **Document what you found.** One of the most often overlooked aspects of Terminal Server administration is proper documentation. You should create an application install document and thoroughly document the application installation. Be sure to include at least the following in the document:

   - Basic information, such as the application name, version, publisher, and phone number for application support
   - Application installation location
   - Installation instructions
   - Location of an application image or possibly a list of Registry setting changes and file changes made by the application
   - Any special Registry or settings changes that need to be made to make the application run properly
   - Application data location and required drive mappings
   - Free drive space needed on system and application drives

14

Policies and Desktop Management

FOR A TERMINAL SERVER ADMINISTRATOR, the ability to both manage and properly secure a user's Terminal Server desktop is of great importance. Policies are the tools that you need to do this.

Besides the ability to lock down desktops, policies also can be used for many other purposes, especially the group policy objects available with Windows 2000 and Active Directory. Using group policy objects, an administrator can control such things as event log parameters, account policies, auditing, logon scripts, application settings, and even application installations.

In this chapter, you first learn how to manage users' desktops so that the users have access to what they need, but are prevented from doing things that could cause problems on Terminal Server. The main tool you will learn about to do this are policies. However, you also will learn several other techniques for managing user desktops, such as mandatory profiles and third-party tools.

The chapter ends with a detailed discussion of the many other things you can do with policies besides desktop administration that are important to know about as a Terminal Server administrator. You will be shown examples of such things as how to use policies to install applications, control logon scripts, and distribute Registry changes to your Terminal Servers.

Basic Terminal Server Desktop Management

What you decide to put on user desktops and how you secure them has a direct effect on the reliability, security, and administrative cost of your Terminal Server solution. Remember that a user who runs applications from a Terminal Server desktop is essentially running the application as if standing in front of the server in your server room, accessing the server console. Whatever the user could do to the server while logged on to the server at the console, he could do while sitting hundreds of miles away remote controlling a desktop on your Terminal Server. When you multiply this concept by hundreds or even thousands of users, you can see how the concept of securing your servers, and especially your user desktops, is so important.

One of the primary goals of desktop management is to give the users access to only what they need by removing nonessential items from the desktop. The more nonessential items that users have access to, the more you will have to support and the more likely you will have problems with your server. In other words, a simple and secure desktop is a supportable desktop.

Take a look at the problems of the "complex desktop" and some of the risks that it presents in a multiuser Terminal Server environment. Refer to Figure 14.1 for an example of a complex desktop in Terminal Server. Although this desktop might look similar to what you are familiar with on a Windows workstation, the extraneous items on this desktop can lead to serious problems in a multiuser environment. Using a combination of profiles, policies, and other techniques, which you will learn about later in this chapter, you can easily bring order to this desktop and simplify it considerably.

The following sections cover what is wrong with the desktop shown in Figure 14.1 and what problems it could cause in a Terminal Server environment and how to solve them.

Disabling Access to the Control Panel, *Run* Command, and Command Prompt

When users have access to the Control Panel, it is possible for them to cause serverwide problems. Although many of the items in Control Panel are usable by administrators only, it is best practice to restrict user access to Control Panel. In addition, granting access to the command prompt and run command from the desktop can be very dangerous because it enables a user, or even a potential hacker, to run any command on the system. Access to the Control Panel, run command, command prompt, and more can be easily restricted through the use of policies.

Figure 14.1   The complex desktop.

Policies in Windows NT 4.0 versus Windows 2000

Many aspects of policies are greatly improved in Windows 2000 Active Directory with group policy objects. In addition, you can now control hundreds of more settings. You can take advantage of Windows 2000 system-related policies, however, only if you have Windows 2000 Terminal Servers that are a member of a Windows 2000 domain. Also to use the Windows 2000 user-related policies, such as desktop control, your user accounts must reside on Windows 2000.

If you have not yet moved your environment to pure Windows 2000, and need better justification, the improvements in policies are one of the most important feature enhancements that Windows 2000 provides. You can use the information in this chapter to help justify that purchase to management.

Removing Desktop Shortcuts, Wallpaper, and Screen Savers

Remember that users' desktops must be compressed and sent across the wire to them. Desktop wallpaper and patterns should not be used, and should be made inaccessible. The same goes for screen savers. Animated screen savers can be huge resource hogs and can slow your server to a crawl if your users choose to use them. Also desktop shortcuts should be kept to a minimum, if possible. The fewer shortcuts there are on the desktop, the quicker the desktop can "repaint."

You can simplify your user desktops in several automated ways. The first is to use policies. Using policies, you can hide unnecessary system shortcut icons on the desktop, such as the Network Neighborhood and My Computer. Remember, however, that you need to be careful of the shortcuts you hide. If you hide the Network Neighborhood from the desktop, the users will not only not see it on their desktops, but they also will not have access to it from their applications. This might be an undesired effect for environments that solely use published applications.

Next, both wallpaper files and screen saver files should just be deleted from your server. As is recommended several times in this book, it is a very good idea to set up a central administrative batch file for your server farm on one of your servers. You can use this batch file to perform file changes to all the servers in your server farm, such as updating the USRLOGON.CMD, distributing a set of command-line utilities to a tech directory on each server, and, in this case, getting rid of unneeded wallpaper and screen savers. Listing 14.1 can be included in this batch file to clean the wallpaper and screen saver files from your servers. You will need to repeat this code in the batch file for every server in your server farm. This example assumes the %systemroot% folder is m:\winnt.

Listing 14.1 **Removing Screen Savers**

```
...
@echo off
echo Removing wallpaper and screen savers from [servername]...
del \\[servername]\m$\winnt\*.bmp
del \\[servername]\m$\winnt\web\wallpaper\*.* /Q
del \\[servername]\m$\winnt\system32\*.scr
...
```

If you want to disable wallpaper only, you can use several techniques besides just deleting the wallpaper files. The first is to set the Disable Wallpaper setting at a connection level. For more information on this technique, see Chapter 10, "Setting Up Terminal Server Connections." Another technique is to use the KiXtart setwallpaper ("") command to set the wallpaper to none in your KiXtart logon script.

Managing Start Menu Shortcuts

Two types of folders make up the Start menu on a Terminal Server: All Users folders and user-specific folders. Shortcuts in the All Users folders are seen by all users on your Terminal Server when they go into their Start menus.

Shortcuts in the user-specific folders are stored in a user's profile and are seen only by that particular user. In Windows NT 4.0 Terminal Server, the shortcuts that were seen by all users were shown at the top of the Program menu, then there was a dividing line and at the bottom was a list of user-specific shortcuts. In Windows 2000, this dividing line does not exist; shortcuts for all users and user-specific shortcuts are presented to the user as a single consolidated Program menu.

Whether you are using Windows 2000 or Windows NT 4.0 Terminal Server, the issue is the same. You should strive to simplify your users' Start and Program menus.

Most applications install shortcuts for themselves in the All Users folders and not user-specific folders. What this means to you as a Terminal Server administrator is that after you installed a particular application, that application's shortcuts will appear for all the users on the system regardless of whether they need the application.

Cleaning Up Shortcuts Manually

To resolve this issue and simplify users' Program menus, it is highly recommended to remove any shortcuts for applications or application components that are not needed by all users from the All Users menu. To do so, follow these steps:

1. Log on as an administrator on your Terminal Server.

2. Right-click the Start menu and select Explore All Users. You will be brought into Windows Explorer and to the Start Menu folder within the All Users profile.

3. Browse under the Start menu and remove the shortcuts that do not need to be displayed for all users on the system, such as the Uninstall [Application] type shortcuts.

4. Move the most commonly used shortcuts to either the root of the Programs folder (the Program menu) or the root of the Start Menu folder, depending on how you want the shortcuts displayed for your users.

As you saw with the All Users shortcuts, they are actually just a collection of shortcuts that reside in a folder on your Terminal Server. User-specific shortcuts are the same way. The following is a list of the folder locations for shortcuts on your system, depending on what operating system you are using:

- Windows 2000 All Users shortcuts are under `%systemrootdrive%\ documents and settings\all users`.

- Windows NT 4.0 All Users shortcuts are under `%systemroot%\profiles\`
  `all users`.

- Windows 2000 user-specific shortcuts are under `%systemrootdrive%\`
  `documents and settings\[username].[domain name]`.

- Windows NT 4.0 user-specific shortcuts are under `%systemroot%\`
  `profiles\[username][#]`.

Instead of right-clicking the Start menu and selecting Explore, you also can
just open the listed folders in Windows Explorer and make the changes you
need there.

Cleaning Up Shortcuts with the Central Admin Batch File

In addition to cleaning up wallpaper and screen savers, you also can use the
central administrative batch file for cleaning up and moving shortcut entries
across your server farm. It is highly recommended to handle shortcut management in this way because it helps ensure consistency across your server
farm. Listing 14.2 is a sample subsection in a batch file that can be used to
clean shortcuts across your farm. In this batch file, the `%systemrootdrive%` is
M:, it is a Windows 2000 server, and the file is set to remove the unneeded
Microsoft Office Tools folder and the link for Internet Explorer.

Listing 14.2 **Cleaning Up Shortcuts**

```
...
@echo off
echo Cleaning up shortcuts on [servername]...
del "\\[servername]\m$\Documents and Users\All Users\Start Menu\Internet Explorer.lnk"
rmdir "\\[servername]\m$\Documents and Settings\All Users\Start Menu\Microsoft Office Tools"
/s/q
...
```

Creating All Users Shortcut Templates

Although this type of batch file does a good job of cleanup, in larger farms
you will likely want to create a standard All Users folder for your servers.
For this approach to work, you need to be able to divide your servers cleanly
into application groups. For example, you might have a server application
group for Office applications. These servers run nothing but Office applications. You also need to make sure that the drive letters used and the
application installation locations are standardized. If you can cleanly divide
your servers into application groups and your drive letters and application

installation locations have been standardized, the following instructions will show you how to take complete central control of your servers All Users folders:

1. Choose a central server or admin server where you will create the administrative batch file.

2. Make a folder to contain the batch file and subfolders for each application grouping in your server farm. For example, ..\office, ..\reporting, ..\reportingII, ..\accounting.

3. Share this central batch file folder as Batch.

4. Go to one server in each of the server application groups and copy the current All Users\Start Menu shortcuts folder to the appropriate central \\[servername]\batch\[application grouping] folder.

5. In addition, make a backup copy of the All Users\Start Menu folder for each server under \\[servername]\batch\backup\[application grouping].

6. Modify the All Users shortcuts folder at the central location. Simplify the All Users\Start Menu folder as much as possible, by taking out the shortcuts you do not want and moving shortcuts out of Program Menu folders into the root of the Start menu or Program menu, as needed.

7. Push this All Users shortcuts folder down to all the servers in the application group using a batch file similar to Listing 14.3.

Listing 14.3 **Pushing Down All Users Shortcuts Folder**

```
...
rmdir "\\[servername]\m$\Documents and Settings\All Users\Start Menu" /s/q
xcopy "\\[central servername]\batch\[application grouping]\*.* \\[servername]\m$\Documents and
Settings\All Users\Start Menu" /s/e
[repeat these statements for every server in the application group]
...
```

What this technique does in effect is replaces the All Users shortcut folder for every server in an application group with the central All Users shortcut folder. Suppose, for example, that you have 10 servers that are members of a Microsoft Office application group and therefore are used for nothing but Microsoft Office. Microsoft Office has been installed in the same location on all servers and all servers have their C: drives remapped to M:. Instead of having a Start menu cluttered with additional icons that are not needed, you would use this technique to create a central All Users shortcuts template for this application group. This template would have only icons for Word, Excel,

PowerPoint, and other needed Office applications. You would then replace the existing All Users\Start Menu folder on all the servers with the simplified version using the previous batch file snippet.

If you use this technique, you need to make sure that you have taken a backup of the original Start Menu folder somewhere underneath the central \\[servername]\batch share, as shown in step 5. Remember that this technique will replace folders such as the Administrative Tools and Accessory folders on your servers with the central All Users shortcuts and folders. For this reason, if you use this technique, you will have to control your administration from a central server instead of relying on the shortcuts being available for administrative tools on each server you log on to. If you are using Citrix, it is highly recommended to make all the administrative tools your administrators need available to them using published applications. In this way, they will not need to rely on the shortcuts available on the server.

Even though the shortcut might not exist for a particular tool, this does not mean that it cannot be run. Just browse for the executable and run it from the Run section of the Start menu. For your users, however, you can disable the Run option in the Start menu, and they will not be able to run anything but those shortcuts that you provide them from their desktop.

By default, members of the local Users group, which includes all Domain Users, only have read access to the shortcuts in the All Users folder. Members of the local Administrators group and in Windows 2000, the Power Users local group are the only ones who have full access, and thus the ability to add or change shortcuts. As part of your batch file testing, you should make sure that this is the case after you push out standardized All Users templates.

One final note is that you also can use this technique to control All Users\Desktop folder shortcuts. Any shortcut installed in the All Users\Desktop folder is seen by all users on the Terminal Server. Unfortunately, many applications install a shortcut for themselves in the All Users\Desktop folder. This can cause the same problem that installing shortcuts in the All Users\Start Menu folder causes; basically it complicates the user desktops and provides an option that all users might not need. Just like you created a central template for the Start menu under the \\[servername]\batch\[application grouping]\start menu folder, you could create a central template for the users' Desktop folder under \\[servername]\batch\[application grouping]\desktop. You would then modify the administrative batch file to push out this folder in addition to the central Start Menu folder to all servers in the application grouping.

Application Publishing with Terminal Server

The technique just described not only is good for managing user desktops, but also can be used as a rudimentary form of application publishing for your Terminal Server users who do not use Citrix. Suppose, for example, that you set up a central Terminal Server server farm and divide it into application groups. You then set up connections to the server desktops for each of your users. When they log on, they will see the shortcuts for the applications that were pushed out from the central All Users\Start Menu folder that you control, and not other shortcuts. If you want to publish a new application for your users, just do the following:

1. Install the application on all the servers in a particular Terminal Server application group.

2. Make sure you install the application in the same folder on each server and document the installation location and install instructions in your application installation document.

3. Copy the shortcut for the application to the central All Users\Start Menu folder.

4. Run the central administrative batch file to push out a fresh copy of the central All Users\Start Menu folder to all servers in the application group.

You can do this while users are logged on, without causing any interruption. The next time they click their Start menus, they will see the icon for the new application.

More advanced Terminal Server administrators might want to use Network Load Balancing to load share users across the servers in a particular application grouping. For more details on this technique, see Chapter 27, "Network Load Balancing for NFuse and Terminal Servers."

Using Profiles for User Desktop Management

As you saw with the All Users profile, profiles can be a powerful way to manage user desktop environments. However, the problem with the All Users profile is that changes to it affect all users simultaneously. If you have more users in your environment who use desktops than published applications, the need for more granular desktop administration capabilities will surely arise. For example, you might want to add a shortcut to just a few user desktops or Start menus rather than All Users. In addition, for some users, you might want to lock down their desktop so that they cannot make any changes using mandatory profiles. In this section, you learn how to do both of these things and more by using profiles.

Profiles Explained

User profiles primarily contain user-specific Registry settings and the shortcuts that make up each user's desktop and Start menu. In addition, user profiles also can contain user-specific application data, shortcuts to recently used documents, a user's My Documents folder, and more.

Each user has his own profile, which, by default, is stored under `%systemroot%\profiles\[username][#]` for Windows NT 4.0 and `%systemrootdrive%\documents and settings\[username].[domain]` for Windows 2000.

You can break a profile down into two basic components: the user Registry and the user's personal folders. The user Registry is contained in the NTUSER.DAT file located at the root of the user's profile directory. The second part of a user's profile is the user's personal folders. The personal folders are all located under the root directory of each user's profile (see Figure 14.2).

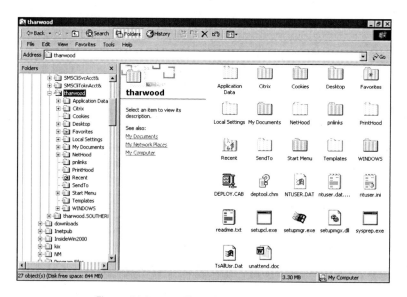

Figure 14.2   Locally cached profiles folder.

Although there are several folders in a user's profile, the following folders are the ones of the most interest when it comes to managing a user's environment.

- **Desktop (hidden directory)**   This folder contains the shortcuts displayed on a user's desktop. Although shortcuts for system-related icons such as My Documents and Network Neighborhood can be controlled only through policies, you can control most other user desktop shortcuts by adding or deleting the shortcuts in this folder.

- **Favorites**   This folder is used by Internet Explorer to store a user's favorite URLs. You could publish a URL for a corporate web site to one or more of your users by putting it in here.

- **Start Menu**   The Start Menu folder contains all the user's personal shortcuts and folders in the Start menu. This is where you could publish application shortcuts to one or more of your users.
- **My Documents**   The My Documents folder is the user's personal documents folder. As an administrator, you might want to transfer a document to a particular user. You can do this by putting it in the My Documents folder.

Types of Profiles

There are three types of profiles: local, roaming, and mandatory. Because of the great importance of profiles with Terminal Server, it is important to understand these three types. The following sections describe each type of profile and cover how to manage your user's environment with each.

Local Profiles

A Terminal Server user will use local profiles only if no profile location has been set up for the user by setting the profile property for the user through User Manager or the Active Directory Users and Computers tool. Local profiles are stored locally on the Terminal Server the user logged on to. Because the user is using local profiles and not roaming profiles, this user will get a different profile for every server she logs on to.

By default, when a user logs on to a Terminal Server for the first time, the following steps happen:

1. The Terminal Server checks to see whether the user's profile exists under either `%systemroot%\profiles` for NT 4.0 or `%systemrootdrive%\documents and settings` for Windows 2000.

2. If not, it creates a new user profile folder under the server's profile area and copies the contents of the Default User profile to it.

This process is important to understand for two reasons. First, because every user's profile starts as a copy of the Default User's profile on a server, you can use this to your advantage. If you wanted to ensure that a certain personal Start menu shortcut, desktop shortcut, or file is copied to every users' profile folder on a new server, just do the following:

1. Copy the file or shortcut to either the `%systemroot%\profiles\default user` on NT 4.0 or the `%systemrootdrive%\documents and settings\default user` profile.

2. Log on to the system with a test user who has not logged on to the system before.

3. Verify that the file or shortcut has been copied down to the test user's profile folder.

Another technique involves the central administration batch file again. You could put a line in the batch file to copy a particular file or shortcut to all Default User folders for all your servers or just for particular servers.

The second reason why the Default User process is important to understand is that the Default User folder is your "fresh copy." In other words, if you want to clean up a person's profile or you are having other problems with a profile, just have the user log off and then delete it as follows:

1. Make sure the user is logged off of the server.

2. Right-click My Computer, select Properties, and then click the User Profiles tab.

3. Select the user's profile from the list and click Delete.

If you want to add a shortcut or file to a user's profile that already exists, just copy the file or shortcut to the user's profile folder on whatever server(s) that user normally logs on to.

Roaming Profiles

Whereas local profiles are stored locally on the machine the user is working on, roaming profiles are stored centrally on a share on the network. Because they are stored in a central location rather than locally, they follow, or roam, with you.

In larger environments, roaming profiles are highly recommended to set up for Terminal Server solutions. The problem with local profiles is that if a user logs on to several different servers, she gets several different desktops. There is no way, in a large environment that uses local profiles, to easily manage a user's environment using profiles because there are so many profiles to manage. If you use roaming profiles instead, however, it is very easy to manage them because you can manage them from one location.

Suppose, for example, you want to add a desktop or Start menu shortcut for one of your users and that user is using roaming profiles. To add the shortcut, follow these steps:

1. Have the user log off of the system.

2. Copy the shortcut to the user's central profile under either the Start Menu or Desktop folder as appropriate.

3. Have the user log back on to the server.

As the user logs on, the Terminal Server will compare the roaming profile to the local profile. Because you added the shortcut to the roaming profile, it will now be copied down to the user's local profile. The user will then see the shortcut on her desktop or Start menu. Remember that even if the user has roaming profiles set up, she always works off of a local copy of the roaming profile and not the roaming profile itself.

Always be aware how profiles use network bandwidth and space on the local hard drive. A typical profile is between 500KB and 1MB, but can vary considerably depending on the size of your personal folders and the number of Registry entries that you have. If you have roaming profiles set up, when you log on to a server or a workstation that you have not logged on to previously, your entire profile is downloaded across the network from the central location and cached locally on that system's hard drive. The next time you log on to the system, your locally cached profile will be synchronized with your roaming profile. Only the updates will have to travel across the network.

Mandatory Profiles

The third and last type of profile is a mandatory profile. Mandatory profiles work in both Windows NT 4.0 and 2000. They enable an administrator to prevent users from making permanent changes to any setting contained in their profile. This includes their desktop settings, such the wallpaper, screen saver, and colors. In addition, this includes other items held in their profile, such as their desktop and Start menu shortcuts.

To change a user's profile to a mandatory profile, follow these steps:

1. Have the user log off.

2. Using either User Manager or Active Directory for Domains, add `.man` to the end of the path for the user's profile. For example, if their profile is `\\[server name]\profiles\[username]`, change it to `\\[server name]\profiles\[username].man`.

3. Rename either the user's roaming profile folder or whatever profile folder you point her to in step 2, to `[foldername].man`.

Now when the user logs on, the profile will be set as a mandatory profile. To verify that it is a mandatory profile, right-click My Computer from the user's desktop, select Properties, click User Profiles, and look for the user profile. It should indicate that it is a mandatory profile (see Figure 14.3).

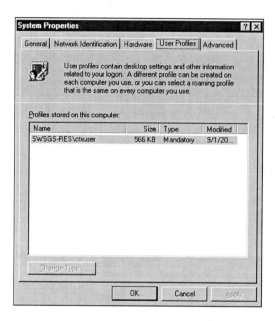

Figure 14.3   Verifying a mandatory profile.

Note that setting a mandatory profile for a user does not prevent her from making changes to her desktop settings; it prevents her from making permanent changes. In other words, a user can change the color of her desktop, delete or add shortcuts, or modify the Start menu. When she logs off of the server, however, her changes will not be saved.

One of the big benefits of mandatory profiles is that multiple users can use the same profile. In other words, you can create a small collection of mandatory profiles and point all of your users to them. Because users cannot overwrite mandatory profiles, these profiles will never change. This is a nice feature because you no longer have to worry about bloated profiles taking up too much drive space. Not only do you have fewer and smaller central profiles, but also a fresh copy is copied down every time the user logs on, erasing anything that was changed from the last logon.

Another big advantage of mandatory profiles is that they can save significant space on your server. Over time, most user profiles will grow greatly in size. If your profiles are centralized, the central profile has to be synchronized with the local profile at every logon. If your profiles grow large, this can greatly slow down logon times, as well as take up significant space both at the central profile location and at each server's profile location. By setting up mandatory profiles, you ensure that your profiles always remain the same size.

Using Only Mandatory Profiles

Some administrators prefer to use only mandatory profiles for their users. If you find mandatory profiles to be useful and you do not want to bother with implementing similar lockdown capabilities available by using policies, set up and distribute a central collection of mandatory profiles by doing the following:

1. Log on as a test user to your system.

2. Change the desktop settings, desktop shortcuts, and personal Start menu shortcuts the way you want them for this mandatory profile.

3. Right-click My Computer, select Properties, and then click the User Profile tab.

4. Highlight the profile and click the Copy to button.

5. Enter the UNC of the central profile location and mandatory profile name to which you want to copy this profile.

6. Point the users that you want to use this profile to this central mandatory profile folder by changing their Terminal Server profile setting.

Most administrators who implement mandatory profiles will use a handful of central mandatory profiles for all of their users.

Policies

Policies are some of the most powerful tools at your disposal for administering user desktops. Policies can be used to control a user's environment and the system environment through a specific set of Registry settings. You can control many things with policies, including the following:

- The ability for the user to view the Control Panel, Network Neighborhood, My Computer, Find, and Run buttons
- Users' colors and wallpaper
- Drive letters available to a user
- The ability to use the Registry Editor
- Whether common program folders are shown

With policies you can lock down a desktop very tightly and provide access only to the applications and settings that users absolutely need to perform their daily work.

Although the goals of policies are the same for Windows NT 4.0 and Windows 2000, the implementation significantly differs. This section explains how policies work for both operating systems and how to implement them in your environment.

Understanding Windows NT 4.0 Policies

Policies are implemented in Windows NT 4.0 by using the System Policy Editor included with Windows 4.0 Terminal Server. With the System Policy Editor, you create a policy file that contains all the restrictions you want to apply for users. Restrictions can be applied to groups and users. When a user logs on, the system reads the settings in the policy file and applies the restrictions to his Registry.

To implement the policy on a Windows NT 4.0 domain, you need to save it as NTCONFIG.POL. This file should be copied to the \\[pdc or bdc name]\$repl share on your domain controllers; this folder is the same folder that is shared with read-only access to the Domain Users as \\[pdc or bdc name]\netlogon.

When you log on to a Windows NT 4.0 domain from either a Windows 2000 or Windows NT 4.0 Terminal Server, the Terminal Server looks in the NETLOGON directory of the domain controller it is validating against for the NTCONFIG.POL file. This process is shown in Figure 14.4. If the file is there, Terminal Server applies the policy settings in that file to its Registry.

It is important to emphasize that Windows NT 4.0 domain policies will work even if you are logging on to the Windows NT 4.0 domain from a Windows 2000 Terminal Server. As an administrator, this enables you to upgrade your Terminal Servers to Windows 2000 and still use the same policies that you had before.

In addition, if you log on to a Windows 2000 domain from a Windows NT 4.0 server, you can still use Windows NT 4.0 policies. The technique is the same as under Windows NT 4.0. You need to copy the NTCONFIG.POL file to the \\[windows 2000 domain controller]\$repl share (NETLOGON). As you log on to the Windows 2000 domain, the Windows NT 4.0 Terminal Server will look for the NTCONFIG.POL file in the NETLOGON share and apply its policy settings.

It is important to realize that the only time policy settings are applied in Windows NT 4.0 is at the point of logon. As policies are applied, changes are made in the Registry to reflect the policy. When the user logs off, these changes still remain. To remove the policy, you must clear the policy setting in the System Policy Editor and have the user log back on to the Terminal Server. Only when the user logs on will the policy be cleared.

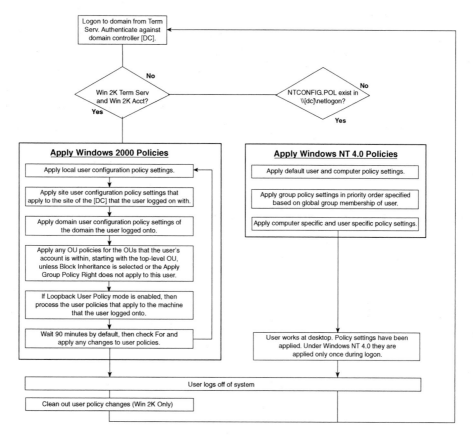

Figure 14.4 Applying Windows NT 4.0 policies.

System Policy Editor and Policy Template Files

The first step in setting up policies for your Windows NT 4.0 Terminal Server is to create them using the System Policy Editor. The System Policy Editor is located in the Administrative Tools folder in the Program menu.

System policies are based on policy template files; these files end with the .ADM extension. The policy template files are customizable text files that contain instructions for changing various system and user Registry settings. You can load as many policy template files as you want to have the settings you need to create your NTCONFIG.POL policy file. Windows NT 4.0 comes with three policy template files by default:

- **COMMON.ADM**   Contains both machine Registry and user Registry settings that can be used with Windows 95 or Windows NT
- **WINNT.ADM**   Contains Windows NT-specific user and machine settings, such as the ability to make customized Windows NT program folders and logon banners
- **WINDOWS.ADM**   Contains Windows 95-specific user and machine settings

When you first run System Policy Editor, it loads the WINNT.ADM and COMMON.ADM policy files by default. These files are located under the `%systemroot%\inf` folder. You can view the files that are loaded by selecting Policy Template from the Options menu. In the Policy Template Options window, you see all the currently loaded template files. At this point, you can add or remove template files as necessary to have the settings you need for users.

Creating Your Own Admin Templates

The reason why admin templates are mentioned in such detail is that many administrators create their own to be able to push out custom Registry changes via policies. Any change you need to make to a user's Registry or a system Registry you can do through policies. This makes them a very powerful tool for not only managing a user environment, but also for changing application settings, applying Registry changes to improve system performance, and more.

Although creating your own admin templates will not be covered in detail in this book, if you are interested, the basic steps are as follows:

1. Open one of the admin templates, such as WINNT.ADM, in Notepad and review the format.

2. Make a copy of the admin template into your own TEST.ADM admin template file.

3. Modify the template file to create your own set of Registry changes. Basically, modification involves editing the template file in a text editor, such as Notepad.

4. Run the System Policy Editor and add the TEST.ADM template to the policy.

5. Check the boxes for the policies you want to apply that you just created in the TEST.ADM template file.

For more detailed information, see Microsoft article Q185589.

Many larger shops have their own set of server- and application-tuning template files. For example, they might create an application-tuning template file that disables the splash screen for commonly deployed applications.

Using Third-Party Tools for Registry Changes

You can use several freely available third-party tools to apply custom Registry changes, just like you can by creating your own admin templates. However, the advantage of using the third-party tools rather than custom admin templates is that there are much more detailed instructions available on how to create your own custom Registry changes than are available with administrative templates. One of the best is X-Setup by XTeq. You will find this free powerful utility at www.xteq.com.

Using XTeq, you can easily create your own Registry-tweaking templates. In addition, XTeq comes with a plethora of tweaks on its own that go far beyond those already available using just policies.

Creating Your Own Policies

After you have loaded the policy templates you want, it is time to create the policy file. Go into the System Policy Editor and select New Policy from the File menu.

In the System Policy Editor window, you will see two icons: Default User and Default Computer. The Default User settings are Registry settings that change keys in the user's HKEY_CURRENT_USER hive (NTUSER.DAT). The Default Computer settings change keys in the system Registry or HKEY_LOCAL_MACHINE of the user. Because all users on Terminal Server share the same machine, any setting changed under Default Computer affects all users on Terminal Server, including the administrator! This is a very important distinction to remember. For the most part, you will want to make changes only to the Default User settings.

Author's Note

Even though you usually want to stay away from making setting changes to the Default Computer key, sometimes it just makes good sense. You can enable or disable many performance and system reliability-related settings that use policies, such as Dr. Watson error logging. For more information on some of these types of Registry changes, refer to Chapter 21, "Performance Tuning and Resource Management." Beware, however, that for you to set up these types of policies, you will have to create your own custom administrative policy templates.

Creating the policy is fairly simple to do. For this example, double-click the Default User icon. In the Default User Properties screen, you will see a hierarchical list of all the different policy categories from the loaded policy template files. This is an all-in-one view of all user policies that are available. As you load more policy template files, you will see additional categories and settings in this list, depending on which template file you add.

Each policy can have one of three settings: checked, unchecked, or grayed out. Knowing the difference between these three settings is very important for implementing policies properly. Although reading the differences between the three, it is important to remember that each policy actually represents a specific change that will occur to a key in the Registry during user logon:

- **Checked**   Enforces the policy and applies the necessary change to the Registry as the user logs on
- **Unchecked**   Removes the effects of the policy by resetting the policy Registry key to its default setting
- **Grayed out**   Makes no changes to the policy's Registry key

Suppose, for example, that you checked the box for Restrict Display of the Control Panel and Remove Taskbar from Settings on Start Menu in the System Policy Editor. Next, you unchecked the box next to Remove Run Command. Leaving the remainder of the settings in a grayed-out state, you saved the config file to the \\[pdc and bdc]\$repl (NETLOGON) share as NTCONFIG.POL on your primary and any backup domain controllers.

When the user logs on to the Terminal Server, the Terminal Server reads the policy from the NTCONFIG.POL file located in the NETLOGON share of the authenticating domain controller. Because the options Restrict Display of the Control Panel and Remove Taskbar from Settings on Start Menu are checked on the Default User policy, the system applies these Registry settings to the appropriate policy keys in the user's Registry. After the user logs on, she will not be able to access the Control Panel or taskbar settings. Next, the Terminal Server returns the policy key for the Remove Run Command from Start Menu policy to its original setting, thus enabling the user to see the run command. Because the rest of the settings are grayed out, the system skips over them.

It is important to remember that after you have set a policy for a user and that user logs on, that policy is saved in his Registry. The only way to reverse a policy is to clear the policy by unchecking it and having the user log out and then log back on.

ZAK Policy Template Files

The *Zero Administration Kit* (ZAK) is a freely available set of administration tools that you can download from Microsoft at www.microsoft.com/windows/zak/default.htm. If you are already familiar with using the ZAK on

Windows NT 4.0 Workstation, you might be wondering how you can use the ZAK with Terminal Server. To answer that question, you should understand what is included with the kit and for what it was intended.

The ZAK is a specially designed set of policy template files and techniques that can be used to simplify the administration of multiple Windows machines. One of the primary needs addressed by the ZAK is application distribution. Using custom scripts and system difference files, the ZAK enables you to distribute applications automatically to machines as they log on to the system. With Terminal Server, the ability to distribute applications is built in.

Because the ZAK is designed for use on multiple machines and not for a Terminal Server, you must be careful about implementing some of the techniques included with the kit. One of the most useful pieces of the ZAK that can be used with Terminal Server is the set of policy template files. The ZAK includes the following policy template files, which you can add to your System Policy Editor:

- **ACCESS97.ADM**   Access 97-specific user and machine settings, such as the default database directory and screen settings.

- **IEAK.ADM**   Internet Explorer-specific user and machine settings, such as proxy server settings and start pages. These are very useful for controlling user access to browsers.

- **OFF97NT4.ADM**   Office 97-specific user and machine settings, such as default directories and shared tools settings.

- **OUTLK97.ADM**   Outlook 97 user and machine settings that control things such as screen settings and folder locations.

- **QUERY97.ADM**   Query 97 user settings.

- **ZAKWINNT.ADM**   Windows NT-specific user settings such as user folder locations and hiding drive letters. The drive letter hiding technique can be very useful in a Terminal Server environment to hide the server's system drives.

With the combination of the default policy files and the ZAK policy files, you can do everything—in terms of desktop administration—that you can do with the ZAK by just using the System Policy Editor with Terminal Server.

In addition to the policy files, the ZAK comes with several useful utilities that you can incorporate into your Terminal Server logon scripts, such as CON2PRT.EXE, which enables you to connect to Windows printers through a logon script.

Useful Windows NT 4.0 Computer Policies

The majority of the most useful policies for Terminal Server are listed under Default User. Even so, you might consider implementing several policies under Default Computer. Remember that with Terminal Server, any policy you implement under Default Computer will affect everyone who logs on to the server.

To set the Default Computer policies for users, you must first get to the Default Computer window:

1. Double-click the Default Computer from the main System Policy Editor window.

2. From the Default Computer Properties window, go to the policy setting in the order shown for the bulleted item.

To get to the Remote Update policy, for instance, from the Default User Properties window click Network, and then click System Policies. You will see the Remote Update Policy check box, underneath System Policies Update. If you put a check mark in the Remote Update Policy check box, that policy will be in effect for users the next time they log on. If you remove the check mark, that policy will be "reset" or cleared the next time users log on.

To put a policy into effect, you always need to put a check mark in the policy's check box. This policy will be in effect until you remove the check mark from the check box. The following sections describe many of the most useful default computer policies.

Remote Update Policy

You will find the Remote Update policy under Network, System Policies in the Policy Editor. The Remote Update policy controls from what directory the policy file is retrieved. One problem with policies is that they affect everyone in the domain. If your Terminal Server is on the same domain as standard Windows NT or Windows 95 workstations, any policies that you implement also affect those workstations. The reason is that you are required to store the NTCONFIG.POL file in the NETLOGON directory of your authenticating servers.

If you want a policy that applies only to your Terminal Server, this Remote Update policy key is the answer. By checking this policy and setting Manual Update, you can specify the UNC path to your Terminal Server-specific policy file (\\[server]\[share]\ [filename]). To implement the policy, you must save it to NTCONFIG.POL and place it into the NETLOGON directory.

The next time someone logs on to the Terminal Server, the change is made to the Registry. From then on, the policy file is retrieved by the Terminal Server from the directory you specified. To reset the setting, you must set the Update Mode back to Automatic.

This setting is also great for environments where users from multiple domains log on to your Terminal Servers. Suppose, for example, that you have a single Terminal Server, but it is used by users from three different domains. If you want to make a change to a policy, you would need to change the NTCONFIG.POL file in the \\[pdc or bdc]\$repl folder for every domain controller in all three of the domains. Not only is this tedious to do, but you might not have full administrative control of all the domains. Instead of going through this hassle, you should follow these steps:

1. Set up a read-only share for the policy file on a server on the local area network.

2. Create the policy file.

3. Use the Remote Update policy to set the policy retrieval location for your servers to the new location.

Manually Setting the Policy File Location

If you want to set the location for the policy file manually rather than through a policy, follow these steps:

1. Run REGEDIT.EXE from the server whose policy location you want to change.

2. Browse to the following key:

HKEY_LOCAL_MACHINE\SYSTEM\CurrentControlSet\Control\Update

3. Add a REG_SZ value with the name "**NetworkPath**" and a value of the path to the new profile file. For example, "\\[servername]\policy\termserv.pol".

Logon Banner Policy

You will find the Logon Banner policy under Windows NT System, Logon in the Policy Editor. With this policy, you can create a logon banner that users see when they log on to the system. This is a good technique for some types of system notices. However, realize that users will have to acknowledge the banner every time they log on to the server, even if they are running only a published application.

Run Logon Scripts Synchronously Policy

You will find the Run Logon Scripts Synchronously policy under the Windows NT System, Logon section of the Policy Editor. By default, logon scripts run as a thread and do not have to finish before your desktop comes up. By setting logon scripts to run synchronously, however, they must finish before any other programs are run. If you have settings in the logon script that your applications require to run, such as drive mappings, it is a good idea to have the logon script finish before any applications can be run.

Types of Windows NT 4.0 User Policies

Now that you have learned about some useful computer policies, it is time to discuss user policies. You can implement three types of user policies:

- **Default user policies**   Affect all users on the Window Terminal Server
- **Group policies**   Affect all users in a particular Windows NT global group
- **Single-user policies**   Are settings for a specific user on the system

Group and single-user policies are implemented in a similar way to computer-specific policies. To implement a group policy, select Add Group from the Edit menu in the System Policy Editor main window and select the global group for which you want to set policies. To implement a single user policy, select Add User from the Edit menu in the System Policy Editor main window and select the user for whom you want to create specific policies. Because group policies are implemented globally, they apply for global groups only.

   Because the policies implemented under Default User take effect for every user on the domain, they are a rather blunt administrative tool. The best way to control policies is through groups. One of the better ways to do this is through job function groups.

   Suppose you have 10 remote users who need access to corporate email and an accounting application. You could create an ACCT_USERS group that has a group policy assigned to it. In the group policy you could set up several controls on the accounting users' desktops, including a shared read-only directory for Program menu items. In this way, all the accounting users would have the same desktop and icons and the same level of control over their desktops.

   Distributing new applications to this group would just be a matter of installing the new application in install mode and putting the icon for the application in their shared Program menu item directory.

Useful Windows NT 4.0 User Policies

The following list describes some of the many useful user policies. The listed policies are set in the same manner as described previously for default computer policies. To understand the user policies and how to set them, open the System Policy Editor on your server and follow along. The System Policy Editor is located in the Administrative Tools folder in Start menu, Programs. In the System Policy Editor, click the Default User icon. In the Default User Properties window that appears, open the policy settings as shown for each policy covered in the following list:

- **Control Panel, Display, Restrict Display**   Checking this policy prevents the user from seeing the Control Panel. This setting is highly recommended for regular users.

- **Desktop, Wallpaper**   This policy restricts the user to a particular wallpaper for the desktop. Because of the extra network bandwidth that could be taken up by transmitting complex desktops to the user, you might want to consider using this policy. This policy is especially useful for remote sites, where network bandwidth is at a premium. A single-color, blank desktop is the easiest to compress and send across the wire.

- **Desktop, Color**   This policy restricts the user to a particular color scheme. This is a good policy to implement for public access Windows Terminals, where user color preference is not important.

- **Shell, Restrictions**   Under shell restrictions there are several very useful policies for controlling user desktops. One of the most useful is Hide All Items on the Desktop. By hiding all the items on the desktop, you greatly reduce desktop clutter and force the user to use only the items under the Start menu. This restriction significantly improves network performance because very few graphically complex icons must be transmitted across the wire.

  Two other recommended restrictive policies are removing the run command and removing the folders under Settings. With the run command, users have complete access to any executable or document on any drive to which they have read has access. This can be a potential security problem. With the run command, users also might attempt to install their own applications.

- **System, Restrictions**   Under System, Restrictions, there are two policies: Disable Registry Editing Tools and Run Only Allowed Windows Applications. Disable Registry Editing Tools prevents the user from running the Registry Editor (REGEDT32.EXE), even from the command line. This restriction is highly recommended. The Run Only Allowed Windows Applications tool enables you to enter a list of applications that a user can run. In general, it is easier to control the applications a user can run by disabling the run command and removing all icons except for the ones a user needs.

- **Windows NT Shell, Custom User Interface, Custom Shell** With Custom Shell, you can make any application the user's default shell. If a user runs only a single application off Terminal Server, this setting might work well for you. The user is taken directly into the application when she logs on, and is logged off when she exits. This prevents the user from doing anything other than running the application she needs.

  The same restriction can be enabled by setting the Initial Program setting in the user's Config in User Manager to this application. The advantage of using Custom Shell is that your administration is centralized with policies, instead of having to keep track of both User Manager and policy settings for a particular group.

- **Windows NT Shell, Custom Folders** This is one of the most powerful and useful set of policies. With these policies, you can define custom folders that contain the shortcuts you want to appear in the user's Program menu, on the user's desktop, in the Startup folder or in the Network Neighborhood.

  To use this policy to set up the user's program items, make a folder on your Terminal Server that contains the program items you want the group to have. Make the folder read-only. Enter the path to the folder in the policy for the group. When members of the group log on they receive the program folder you just created. If you need to distribute applications to the members of the group in the future, just add the shortcuts to the group's program folder.

- **Windows NT Shell, Restrictions** There are several useful policies under here for restricting user actions in the NT shell. One of the most useful is the Remove Common Program Group from the Start Menu option. A common security problem with Citrix is applications that leave their icons in the common program group or folder after they are installed. This makes the application available to all users on the server, which often is not desirable. To control the proliferation of common folder icons, it is recommended to disable the ability for users to see common program group icons. Use group policies and custom shared folders to distribute application icons instead.

- **Windows NT System**   The Run Logon Scripts Synchronously option is one of the most useful policies under this folder. By setting this option on a user or group level, you have more control than if you set it system wide using the equivalent Default Computer policy.

Understanding Windows 2000 Group Policies

If you already have or are intending to move toward a pure Windows 2000 environment for your Windows 2000 Terminal Servers, you need to know about Windows 2000 group policies. Group policies in Windows 2000 is one of the most important reasons for moving to Windows 2000. They give you an unprecedented level of control over the security and administration of your Windows 2000 Terminal Servers and have significant improvements over the policy capabilities that were available in Windows NT 4.0. This section explains how they work and how they are applied.

Categories of Group Policies

When you talked about policies under Windows NT 4.0, you were really talking about Registry changes. For every Windows NT 4.0 computer or user policy that was applied, there was a corresponding change that was made to a Registry entry on the workstation or server that the user logged on to. Although Windows 2000 Group Policies do include a subset of user and computer policies implemented through Registry changes, several brand new categories of policies do not involve the Registry at all.

Before you learn about specific policies, it is important to start getting used to the Group Policy Editor. To open the Group Policy Editor, go to your Windows 2000 domain controller and open the Active Directory Users and Computers tool from the Administrative Tools folder in the Program menu. Right-click your domain name and select Properties, and then click Group Policy. You should see the Default Domain Policy listed. Highlight it and select Edit. The Group Policy Editor tool will open (see Figure 14.5). As each group policy category is covered, you will be able to browse to it within the Group Policy Editor to see the specific policies that it contains.

The following is a list of all the major categories of policies available in Windows 2000:

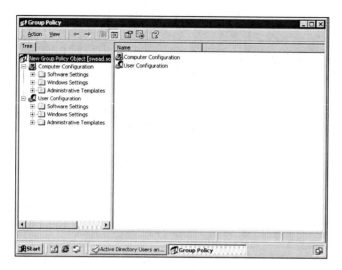

Figure 14.5   Group Policy Editor.

- **Computer Configuration**   Under Computer Configuration, you will find policies that are applied to every computer that the group policy object is for.

- **Computer Configuration, Software Settings**   Under here you will find the Software Installation policy folder. This policy is one of the most powerful and useful new policies available with Windows 2000. Any software .MSI packages that you add reference to under this policy will automatically be installed on all the computers to which this policy applies. Using this policy you could theoretically deploy an application to hundreds or even thousands of computers just by adding a reference to the .MSI file for the installation here.

- **Computer Configuration, Windows Settings**   In this policy folder, you will find subfolders for startup/shutdown scripts and security settings. Startup/shutdown scripts are a new feature with Windows 2000. This policy enables you to define either a script to be run at shutdown or startup for any computer to which the policy applies. Under the Security Settings Policy folder is an extensive selection of policy subfolders that contain settings for such things as the event logs, password policy, account lockout policy, audit policy, and security options. In addition, you can define how common system services are started, specify Registry values to be deployed, and even define a set of files to be copied to all computers.

- **Computer Configuration, Administrative Templates** Much like system policies in Windows NT 4.0, the policies under Computer Configuration - Administrative Templates are based solely on changes to the Registry. In addition you can add custom administrative templates as needed under here. By default, you will find the ability to change such settings as disabling NetMeeting Desktop Sharing, controlling how startup and shutdown scripts are run, controlling printers, and controlling offline files, among many others. Remember that because these are all computer configuration policies, they make changes under HKEY_LOCAL_MACHINE on all the computers to which the group policy object applies.

- **User Configuration, Software Settings** Under here you will find the Software Installation policy. Unlike the Software Installation policy under Computer Configuration - Software Settings, which is applied to every system the policy applies to, this policy applies only to the users to which the policy applies. In other words, if you want to distribute an application to a particular set of users, rather than particular set of computers, this is the policy to use. Under the Software Installation policy, you can add application packages. Each application package is an .MSI file that defines the application installation you need to deploy.

- **User Configuration, Windows Settings** In this policy folder, you will find several very useful user policies, such as the policy you need to use to define logon or logoff scripts, folder redirection (such as the redirection of a user's My Documents folder to the network), and the ability to change Internet Explorer settings.

- **User Configuration, Administrative Templates** Much like Windows NT 4.0 user policies, the policies under this folder are all based on Registry changes to the HKEY_LOCAL_USER Registry. You will find the ability to change a plethora of user settings. This is the main policy folder you will use for desktop lockdown. This policy folder enables you to control what sections of the Start menu display, control what system icons are shown on the desktop, disable the ability to use Control Panel, and disable Task Manager, among many other settings.

How Policies are Created and Applied in Windows 2000

In Windows 2000, policies are stored in the Active Directory as group policy objects. You create group policy objects using the Group Policy Editor tool. This tool is not a standalone application like the Policy Editor in Windows

NT 4.0; instead, it is accessible as a plug-in to the Microsoft Management Console. You also can access the Group Policy Editor by editing the Domain or Organization Unit policies within the Active Directory Users and Computers tool or by editing the site policies within the Active Directory Sites and Services tools.

Group policy objects (GPOs) can be defined for a site, domain, and organizational unit or locally on each server or workstation. Because they can be defined in so many locations, one computer or one user can have multiple GPOs that apply to it. To understand the net effect of GPOs, you need to understand the order in which they are applied. The following list shows that order starting with the first applied:

1. **Local**   The local policy is always applied first. Every Windows 2000 workstation and server has its own local policy. You can access the security-related subset of this policy through the Local Security Policy shortcut in the Administrative Tools folder; however, to access the entire policy, you need to open the Microsoft Management Console in admin mode and add the plug-in for the Group Policy Editor, with the local policy.

2. **Site**   In Windows 2000, sites can be thought of as collections of Windows 2000 domain controllers. Generally, you create a site for each local area network in the enterprise that contains Windows 2000 domain controllers. For each site, you can define one or more group policies using the Active Directory Sites and Services tool. You can open and edit the policy for a site by going into the tool, right-clicking the site you want to edit, and clicking the Group Policies tab. The site policy that will apply to you, depends on what site the Windows 2000 domain controller you authenticate with is a member of. In other words, if you make all the domain controller at Acme Corporation's main headquarters, a member of the Acme Corporation site, anyone at the headquarters who authenticates against one of these domain controllers will have the Acme Corporation's site policy applied to him.

3. **Domain**   Domain policies are defined using the Active Directory Users and Computer tool by right-clicking the domain, selecting Properties, and then clicking the Group Policies tab. You can define one or more policies for the domain, and you can define the order in which they are applied. Any policy defined at a domain level will affect all computers and users in that domain.

4. **Organizational unit** For every organizational unit in Active Directory, you can define one or more GPOs. Although policy inheritance can be blocked, by default, policies applied at higher organizational units will apply for all computers and users below it. Like domain policies, organizational unit policies also are defined using the Active Directory Users and Computers tool.

As each policy is applied, it will overwrite any changes made by the last policy. Because organizational unit policies are applied last, they have the highest priority and will override any policy applied at a local, domain, or site level.

Using Third-Party Tools for Policy Management

If you have not guessed by now, policy management can become very complex in the enterprise. This section explains how to simplify the complexity and use policies to their fullest; however, you might be interested in investing in one of the many third-party policy management tools now available.

One big piece missing from the policy management tools provided by Microsoft is a simple way to view what policies are in effect for a particular computer or user. Tools such as FAZAM, by Full Armor, enables you to more easily manage your policies at an enterprise level and provide you with a consolidated view of the net effect of your policies. To download a trial version of FAZAM 2000, go to www.fullarmor.com.

Through Microsoft, Full Armor also has released a reduced-functionality version of FAZAM 2000 on the Microsoft web site. This version is freely available and intended for organizations with fewer than 500 computers to manage. It is highly recommended to download this tool. Not only is it free, but it might be all you need! You can find this version at www.microsoft.com/windows2000/techinfo/reskit/tools/existing/fazam2000-o.asp.

How to Apply User Policies for Terminal Server Users

With all these different types of policies available, it can be very confusing to decide how to apply policies effectively to your Windows 2000 Terminal Servers and their users. What is most important is to come up with an intelligent methodology and apply that methodology consistently across all your Terminal Servers. This section discusses a couple of different methodologies that work well in a Terminal Server environment.

The methodology you choose depends a lot on who logs on to your servers and what domains they are a member of. The biggest problem that you can run into with Terminal Server is that you might not want the policies that you apply to Terminal Server to affect the user's local desktop environment. By default, however, any user policies you set for your users will affect any system that they log on to, including their local workstation and their Terminal Server session.

Suppose, for example, that you set a user policy for the Accounting organizational unit. In this policy you restrict access to the command line, restrict access to the Control Panel, and enforce that only certain programs can be run, because your Accounting users mainly run their accounting applications from Terminal Server. When these users log on to Terminal Server, the user policy goes into effect and restricts access on their Terminal Server desktop. However, when they log off Terminal Server and try to run another application, or access the Control Panel, from their local desktop, they are denied. This is because the user policies follow the user and not the computer. In other words, the same policies that apply to a user on Terminal Server, will apply to that user on his local desktop.

One option to get around this problem is to set up dual-user IDs. Create an *organizational unit* (OU) in your Active Directory called TS Users (see Figure 14.6). In this OU create a new user ID for every user on the network who needs access to Terminal Server. If the user's original ID is in the same Active Directory tree, name the ID something slightly different from the original. If John Doe's original ID is jdoe, for instance, create a Terminal Server ID for John Doe as jdoe.ts. When John Doe logs on to a Terminal Server, he would use the jdoe.ts ID and not the jdoe ID. You could then apply OU policies to the TS User's OU that will affect only these users.

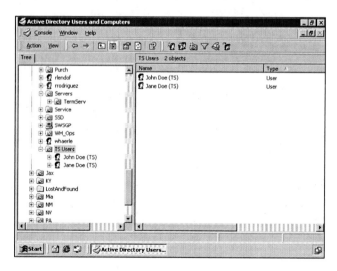

Figure 14.6 The dual-user methodology.

This technique works well in situations where you intend to keep your Terminal Server security as isolated as possible for the foreseeable future. For example, you might want an entirely separate domain for Terminal Server users, even though users normally use an ID on another domain to log on to their workstation. In large enterprises that do not intend to move soon to Windows 2000, this enables you to take advantage of Windows 2000 policies for your Terminal Server users without having to move all the domains to Windows 2000. This technique also works well for ASPs, which nearly always provide their own user IDs and passwords to customers instead of trying to integrate with a customer's domain security. This is also a good technique for setting up external web access to Terminal Server, because it is often very important to isolate your external security from your internal security.

For corporations that want users to use the same ID on their workstation that they use on Terminal Server, but do not want their policies for Terminal Server to affect their local workstation, a solution exists: a special technique called *loopback processing mode*. Loopback processing mode is a computer policy that forces the computer's user-related policies to apply to every user who logs on to the server.

Suppose, for example, that your Terminal Servers are in a TS Servers OU off of your main Active Directory domain. Your users who use Terminal Server exist in a different OU, called the TS Users OU. You define a policy for the TS Servers OU that restricts access to the Control Panel underneath the user configuration part of the policy. However, when your users log on to Terminal Server, access to Control Panel is not restricted. The reason is that the only policies that normally make a difference to a Terminal Server are the computer configuration policies, not the user configuration policies. The Control Panel policy is a user configuration policy ignored by the Terminal Servers. Instead, the users will use the user policies defined in the OU in which their user ID resides.

Remember from our previous discussion of group policy categories that when you define a policy, you can define both user configuration and computer configuration settings. If you define a policy that makes changes to both user and computer configurations for a particular OU, the users under that OU will apply the user policies for themselves when they log on and the computers will apply the computer policies when they start up.

In some situations, such as with Terminal Server, you want the policy you defined for the TS Servers OU, in the example, to apply to all the users of those servers. To make this happen you need to set the user group policy loopback processing mode in the policy for the TS Servers OU as follows:

1. Open the Active Directory Users and Computers tool from the Program menu, Administrative Tools folder.

2. Browse to the OU that contains your Terminal Servers. For this technique to work, you should put all of your Terminal Servers into the same OU. In the example, this was the TS Servers OU.

3. Right-click the OU and select Properties, and then click the Group Policy tab (see Figure 14.7).

4. Either click the Add button to add a new policy or the Edit button to edit an existing one. At this point the Group Policy Editor will launch to enable you to edit the policy.

5. Browse down to Computer Configuration, Administrative Templates, Systems, Group Policy, and double-click User Group Policy Loopback Processing Mode.

6. Select Enabled, and then select Replace for the Mode.

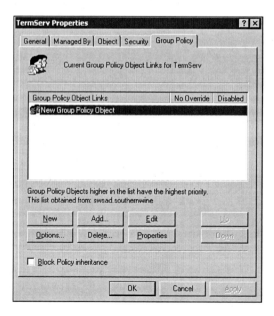

Figure 14.7 Group Policy tab.

Now when users log on, no matter what policies apply normally to their user ID, they will be replaced with those policies that apply to the Terminal Server itself.

Creating a Server Organizational Unit

In larger enterprise environments, one idea you might want to consider is creating a separate OU that is just for servers, both Terminal Servers and other servers in the enterprise. This OU might contain servers only at one location if your administration is highly distributed or it might contain all the servers for the enterprise if administration is completely centralized.

With this scheme you would group your servers by type, as shown in Figure 14.8. Underneath this OU, you would put separate OUs for each server grouping or purpose. For example, you might create a TermServ OU, SQL OU, Exchange OU, and WebSrv OU.

Now that your servers are well organized in the directory, you could easily apply computer policies as needed for your servers. For example, at the Servers OU level, you would define a policy with settings that would apply to all of your servers. This policy might contain such things as event log settings and common startup and shutdown scripts.

At each subordinate OU, you would define more specific policies that applied to just that OU's servers. In the TermServ OU policy, for instance, you would set up user loopback mode processing and change the user policies to control the Terminal Server desktop.

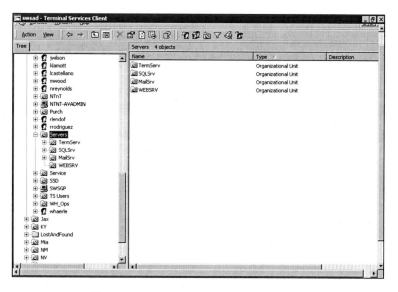

Figure 14.8   Grouping servers in OUs by type.

Installing Applications Using Policies

One of the more useful policies features is the ability to install applications using policies. In a Terminal Server environment, you can use this to automate the installation of an application across your server farm. Using application packaging and distribution programs such as Veritas WinINSTALL, you can create your own set of customized application images in the form of .MSI files. By making a computer policy for your Terminal Servers, you can push the application out automatically to all Terminal Servers in a farm. The following instructions cover how to do this:

1. Open the Active Directory Users and Computers tool.

2. Put all your Terminal Servers into the same TermServ OU in the Active Directory.

3. Right-click the TermServ OU and select Properties. Then click the Group Policy tab.

4. Browse down to Computer Configuration, Software Settings.

5. Right-click Software Installation and select New Package.

6. Browse to the .MSI file on the network for the installation.

7. Make sure the Windows Installer service is started on all the servers.

Useful Windows 2000 User Policies for Terminal Server

The following is a list of some of the most useful Windows 2000 policies for Terminal Server. These are user policies, so you will find them under the User Configuration folder when editing the policy. For these policies to be effective, you need to either create a GPO with them in it for the OU that contains your Terminal Server users, or as shown in the preceding section apply them to a TermServ OU where your Terminal Servers are, but use loopback mode.

- **Windows Settings, Folder Redirection, Desktop**   Using this policy you can define a single set of desktop icons for your users by pointing them to a folder on the network that contains the icons. By defining separate policies for different groups, you can set a standardized desktop for a particular group of users.

- **Windows Settings, Folder Redirection, My Documents**   With Terminal Server it is bad practice to let users use their My Documents folder for document storage. They instead should use their home directory. However, by default users have full access to their My Documents folder in their home directory, and it is the default storage location for many applications. Using this policy, you could instead point all your Terminal Server users to a single My Documents folder on the network. If you want to prevent users from saving in the My Documents folder, just make this folder read-only.

- **Windows Settings, Folder Redirection, Start Menu** Instead of using a central administration script to push out a common Start menu, one highly recommended method is to point all your users to a Start menu on the network. You could create different policies for different user groups and then assign the users to those groups. Each group would be pointed to a different common Start menu on the network.

- **Administrative Templates, Windows Components, Internet Explorer** Under here you will find more than 20 different Internet Explorer settings that you can change. This is a very important key for Terminal Server administrators who intend to deploy Internet Explorer. You can use the settings under here to make Internet Explorer more secure and perform better on Terminal Server.

- **Administrative Templates, Start Menu & Taskbar** This is where you can control what is in the Start menu. You can do such things as remove options in the Start menu or show only user or common Program menu items. Removing the Search and Run options from the Start menu is highly recommended because they can be used to run most any program on your server. In addition, disable changes to the taskbar and Start menu, adding Logoff to the Start menu, and disabling shutdown are recommended.

- **Administrative Templates, Desktop** Under here you can control the user's desktop. Removing Network Places is highly recommended so long as users need only mapped drives and do not need to browse the network. However, realize that this setting also will remove Network Places from all applications that they run, including published applications. Removing the Internet Explorer icon also is recommended. For the cleanest setup, set the Remove All Desktop Icons setting and let users access programs only through the Start menu. Users who have access to My Documents will be able to easily run their own applications from the desktop, so removing all icons will help prevent this security hole.

- **Administrative Templates, Control Panel** In this section you can control what is accessible in the Control Panel for your users. Generally, it is just best to select to Disable Control Panel. If you want to disable only portions of the Control Panel functionality, however, you have the option to do that with the settings under here.

- **Administrative Templates, Network, Offline Files** Allowing your users to create offline files could potentially fill up large amounts of your server drive space. Because Terminal Servers will always remain connected to the network, you are best off just disabling this functionality for your users. To disable it, enable the setting for Disable User Configuration of Offline Files.

- **Administrative Templates, System** Under here are many very important security settings. The following are the recommended ones to set: Disable Registry Editing Tools, Disable the Command Prompt, Disable AutoPlay, and Don't Display Welcome Screen at Logon. These settings, along with disabling the Run and Search options in the Start menu, as shown previously, will prevent your users from running anything but those applications for which you provide shortcuts. To completely lock access to applications, you might want to set the Run Only Allowed Windows Applications policy. This policy setting is highly recommended to set up for kiosk or Internet-accessible Terminal Servers.

Useful Windows 2000 Computer Policies for Terminal Server

The following is a list of the most useful Windows 2000 computer policies. These are the policies you would set under the Computer Configuration section of the GPO. Because this is a computer policy, you would create a GPO for this policy and apply it to the dedicated OU that held your Terminal Servers (that is, TermServ OU).

- **Software Settings, Software Installation** Under here you could add packages for applications you wanted to install across your server farm.

- **Windows Settings, Startup/Shutdown Scripts** In here you can define scripts that are run at startup or shutdown on all your servers. Often Terminal Server administrators reboot their servers on a periodic basis. You could use a startup or shutdown script to clean out any application settings that were not needed or remove old log and temp files.

- **Windows Settings, Security Settings, Event Logs** It is highly recommended to standardize on log settings and apply them through policies. The default settings are generally inadequate. It is recommended to set all three logs to a minimum of 9984KB and overwrite as needed through this policy.

- **Windows Settings, Security Settings, Account Policy** The Account policy applies only to local accounts on the machine. However, remember in a Terminal Server environment anyone on the network can get access to the logon prompt. This means that not only do you need to be careful about domain account access, but also local account access. For example, a potential hacker would likely try to guess the local administrator account password. For this reason and more it is highly recommended to at least set the following under here: Account Lockout Duration (15 minutes), Account Lockout Threshold (3 times), Reset Account Lockout (15 minutes), and Minimum Password Length (8 characters). For even greater security enable the Passwords Must Meet Complexity Requirements setting. This ensures that passwords must be at least six characters, contain characters from three of four different categories (uppercase, lowercase, numbers, symbols), and do not contain portions of the username.

- **Windows Settings, Security Settings, Local Policies, Audit Policy** It is recommended to enable auditing for account logon. This will enable you to see when users attempt to log on locally to your server. Remember that this is only local logons; domain logons are audited at the domain controller.

- **Windows Settings, Security Settings, Local Policies, User Rights Assignment** One of the most important security settings under here is the Log On Locally setting. By using policies to change this setting across your Terminal Servers, you can easily and centrally control who can log on to your Terminal Servers. By default this is set de facto to authenticated users on the servers, which means any user who authenticates to any domain also can log on to your Terminal Servers. As covered in Chapter 9, "Setting Up Terminal Server Users," it is recommended instead to create a TS Users group and allow access only to your Terminal Servers for this group. You can enforce this easily by adding the TS Users group to the Log On Locally setting in this policy. In addition, you might want to review the default security rights settings for your servers for any other security issue and then change the settings for all your servers at once by doing it here with a policy.

- **Windows Settings, Security Settings, Local Policies, Security Options** You will find a plethora of miscellaneous security settings under here. One setting of interest to a Terminal Server administrator is the amount of idle time before disconnecting a session. You can use this to centrally change this setting. However, this is not a complete set of connection settings, so you are likely better off changing connection settings at each server. A more useful setting is the Message Text for Users Logging In. Using this setting, you can display system messages, such as warnings about upcoming maintenance. You also can post legal disclaimer messages.

- **Windows Settings, Security Settings, Registry** This is an incredibly useful policy for Terminal Server administrators. You will likely find many Registry tweaks and settings to improve the performance of your Terminal Servers or the applications that run on them. You can define these machine Registry keys in this setting and they will automatically be pushed out to your Terminal Servers.

- **Windows Settings, Security Settings, System Services** You might want to centrally control how certain services are set. However, the only services you can control are the ones that normally come with Windows 2000. You might want to use this policy to make sure the Windows Installer service is set to start automatically if you intend to push out applications to your servers using group policies.

- **Administrative Templates, System, Logon** Under here you will find a couple of important settings. The Delete Cached Copies of Roaming Profiles is an often-recommended setting that helps conserve drive space. If you have hundreds of users who log on to the server, this setting is recommended; otherwise the cached profiles alone can easily take up hundreds of megabytes. Also the Run Logon Scripts Synchronously setting is recommended for applications that require drive mappings. Often an application is started with a particular data file in a particular directory, such as the user's home directory. By default, logon scripts run concurrently, which means that the logon script might not have completed before the application starts. If this is the case, the drive mapping will not have finished and the application will not be able to start up with the file. By setting logon scripts to run synchronously, you can avoid this problem by ensuring all the mappings are finished before the applications run. If you set this setting, you should also set the Maximum Wait Time for Group Policy Scripts to Run. If your logon script hangs, it will prevent users from logging on. By setting a maximum wait time, you can ensure that at least users can get past the logon script.

- **Administrative Templates, System, Group Policy** The most important setting under here is the User Group Policy Loopback Processing Mode setting discussed earlier in detail. This setting enables you to apply your Terminal Server's user policies to every user who logs on, overriding their own user policies. Besides this setting, you might want to disable some of the policy processing that your servers do (to increase logon speeds). In addition you might want to experiment with the Apply Group Policy for Users Asynchronously During Logon setting to see whether logon speeds improve. By default, it is applied synchronously, that users need to wait for the policy to be applied before they get to the desktop.

Getting More Information on Policies

The coverage here has only been of policies that would be used most often by Terminal Server administrators. However, hundreds of other policy settings are available. One thing that is not widely known is that you can find extensive documentation on each policy setting in the Windows 2000 Server Resource Kit. When you install the Resource Kit, it will install a shortcut in the Program menu for a group policy help file. This help file is organized in the same manner as the policies are organized in the Group Policy Editor tool. For each policy, you will find a detailed write up on what that policy does.

Windows 2000 Policy Tips and Tricks

Many aspects to administering group policies are not obvious on the surface. This section covers some tips and tricks for administering policies effectively and deploying them efficiently.

Building a Custom Policy Console

Although you can use the Active Directory Users and Computers tool to administer your policies, you have to manually browse down to the correct OU for each policy you want to edit and then go into the Properties for the OU to edit it. Using the customization capabilities of the Microsoft Management Console, however, you can create a console that has a single consolidated view of all the policies for all of your Terminal Servers, as follows:

1. From the Start menu, Run option, run **mmc** **/a**. (mmc is the executable for the Microsoft Management Console, and the /a option puts it into administrative mode so that you can edit it.)

2. Under the Console menu, select Add/Remove Snap-In.

3. Click the Add button, and then select Group Policy from the snap-in list.

4. By default, you will add the group policy for the local computer. To select a particular site, domain, OU, or computer policy, click the Browse button and select the policy from the Browse for a Group Policy Object window, and then click OK and Finish.

You will be brought back to the Microsoft Management Console, and the policy you just selected will appear. Repeat steps 1 to 4 until all the computer policies for your Terminal Servers are shown in the console, along with any site, domain, or OU policies that apply to your Terminal Servers. After you have built your Terminal Server policy administration console, select Save As from the Console menu and save the console as TS.MSC.

If you save the TS.MSC on the network in a central Admin Consoles folder, you will be able to just double-click it in the future to manage all the policies that affect your Terminal Servers! For a more advanced solution, you could use application publishing to publish the console as an application for your administrators. The command line you need to run in the published application is `"mmc \\[servername]\console\ts.msc"`, assuming you stored the custom consoles in a central console share on your network.

Creating Other Admin Consoles

This technique is not only useful for policies, but also can be useful for creating many other types of custom administrative consoles. Be sure to take full advantage of your Terminal Servers capabilities to run applications remotely to provide access to these consoles. The following are some of the many types of consoles you could make:

- **System Information Console**   By adding in the system information for all your servers, you can create one consolidated view of general system information such as memory, processor speed, and much more.

- **Event Viewer Console**   You can add an Event Viewer snap-in for each of your Terminal Servers to provide you with a consolidated view of the entire event logs of all your servers.

- **Computer Management Console**   By adding the Computer Management snap-in for all your Terminal Servers, you can create a single console from which you can defragment drives, administer local users and groups, monitor performance, and more for all your servers.

- **Terminal Server Connections Console**   This is a really useful type of MMC console that not a lot of people are aware of. This MMC console comes with the Terminal Server Advanced Client. To install it, run the TSMM-CSETUP.EXE file that can be downloaded from www.microsoft.com/WINDOWS2000/downloads/recommended/TSAC. This will install a new snap-in called the *Terminal Services Connection snap-in*. Using this snap-in you can create a console with connection entries for all of your Terminal Servers (see Figure 14.9).

To get more ideas, see the list of snap-ins available when you select Add/Remove Snap-In.

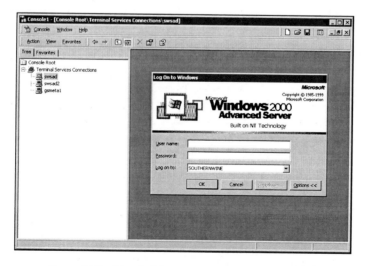

Figure 14.9   Terminal Server MMC Connection Console.

Reducing Policy Processing Time

In large enterprises you might have hundreds of policies in the Active Directory. When a user logs on, the Terminal Server needs to process both the user and computer configuration portions of each policy that applies to the user. This can take a significant amount of time if there are several policies. The first recommendation is to try to limit the number of policies that apply to a user. Using the FAZAM 2000 tool mentioned earlier, you could easily generate a list of all the user and computer policies applied to a user when he logs on to Terminal Server. Generally no more than five policies should ever apply for a particular user.

In addition, for a particular policy you can disable the user configuration or computer configuration portion of it if it is not needed. This also can speed up processing time. Here is how:

1. Open Active Directory Users and Computers tool from your domain controller's Administrative Tools folder.

2. Browse to the location in the Active Directory for the policy.

3. Right-click the OU and select Properties, and then click the Group Policy tab.

4. Highlight the policy you want to change and select Properties.

5. From the Properties window shown in Figure 14.10, select to disable either Computer Configuration Settings or User Configuration Settings as appropriate, and then click OK.

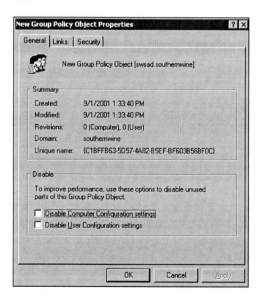

Figure 14.10   Disabling processing of user or computer configuration.

Applying Policies to Particular Groups

So far you have been shown how to make a policy for your Terminal Servers and Terminal Server users. If you are creating a GPO for an OU, however, the policy applies for every computer and user under that OU. If you want to restrict the application of the policy to a particular user or group of users, you need to set up group policy filtering. To do so, follow these steps:

1. Open Active Directory Users and Computers tool from your domain controller's Administrative Tools folder.

2. Browse to the location in the Active Directory for the policy.

3. Right-click the OU and select Properties, and then click the Group Policy tab.

4. Highlight the policy you want to set up filtering for and select Properties.

5. Click the Security tab (see Figure 14.11).

6. Remove the Authenticated Users group by highlighting it and clicking the Remove button. By default, policies are applied for all authenticated users.

7. Click the Add button and add the group or user to which you want the policy to apply.

8. Make sure the Read and Apply Group Policy boxes are checked for this group or user under the Allow column.

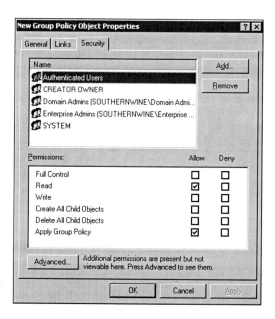

Figure 14.11   Filtering group policies.

Applying Policy Changes Manually

In Windows 2000, policies are applied by default every 90 minutes. If you make a change to a policy and you want to view the effect without having to wait 90 minutes, you can use the following command to refresh the policy for computer configuration:

```
secedit /refreshpolicy machine_policy /enforce
```

To refresh a user configuration policy, use the following command:

```
secedit /refreshpolicy user_policy /enforce
```

Author's Note

A final tip for this section is group policy troubleshooting. How group policies work in Windows 2000 is a surprisingly complex topic, the details of which are beyond the scope of this book. If you are having problems getting group policies to work as you expect them to, Microsoft has a very informative and useful troubleshooting article available that you should read. Refer to article Q250842.

Restricting Applications That Can Be Run

In certain high-security environments or where your Terminal Server clients are accessed publicly, it is highly recommended to lock down the list of applications that can be run from your Terminal Server. You can do this in a couple of different ways.

The first method is to use the APPSEC, an application security application in Windows NT 4.0. You can run this application from the run command in the Start menu. With this application you can define a list of applications that can be run on your Terminal Server. Those applications, and only those applications, can be run on this server. Because this is such a heavy restriction on your server, you need to be careful to include the following applications as a minimum in this list:

- **EXPLORER.EXE**   Explorer is the applications that handles the display of the desktop. Unless you intend to run a different desktop shell, you need to include EXPLORER.EXE in the allowed application list; otherwise, you will not be able to get to the desktop at all.

- **SYSTRAY.EXE**   Systray is the application responsible for the display of the taskbar. Both this application and EXPLORER.EXE need to be in the allowed application list for the desktop to be displayed.

- **CMD.EXE**   This is the DOS command shell. You need this application to run any batch file from the command prompt. It also is needed to run the logon script. Use the restrict access to the command-prompt policy to restrict users from getting to the command prompt, but allowing the system access to it.

- **USRLOGON.CMD**   The local logon script should be part of the allowed applications.

- **USERINIT.EXE**   This utility initializes the desktop and is run when the user first logs on to the desktop.

- **CMSTART.EXE**   This is another initialization utility that runs during logon.

- **UPDATDRV.EXE**   This utility runs during logon and handles updating changes to the drive letter if you chose to change the drive letter during the installation of Citrix MetaFrame.

The second method is to use group policies. This method works in both Windows NT 4.0 and 2000. In Windows 2000 you will find the policy to Run Only Allowed Windows Applications under User Configuration, Administrative Templates, System in the Group Policy Editor. In this policy, you can define a list of applications allowed for this particular user. Be sure to include the previously listed applications in addition to any other applications that your user needs to run. In addition, with Windows 2000, instead of only defining a list of allowed applications, you also can define a list of applications that are not allowed if you so choose.

Remember that these applications are restricted only if they are launched from the command or desktop shell. Applications launched from within other applications, such as through the use of OLE, are not restricted by this policy. If you find this to be a problem, you might try restricting access to that particular application executable using file security instead.

Top-Ten Tips for Setting Up Desktops

Now that you have an understanding of what policies and profiles are and how to implement them, take a look at this summary of the top-ten recommended tips on using them to lock down user desktops:

1. **Simplify, simplify, simplify.**   Simplicity is the most important aspect of any well-managed desktop. Put on the desktop only the icons or Start menu items that the user absolutely needs to perform his job. The best approach is to first imagine a blank slate: a Windows NT 4.0 or 2000

desktop with no icons, a Start button, and no shortcuts in the Start menu. Now think about the icons you need to add for the user to perform his job. This is the desktop design you want.

2. **Deny access to the `run` command, `Find/Search` commands, and command prompt.**   A user who has access to the `run` command, find command, command prompt, and/or Explorer can cause a lot of damage very easily. By using user policies, deny access to these commands if they are not necessary for users to do their work.

3. **Restrict drive and network access.**   If users absolutely need access to Explorer or the command prompt to perform their jobs, you can still limit the drives to which they have access. To control what is available to users on the network, try setting a policy to hide the entire network and work-group contents. Now when they go into Network Neighborhood, they see only the servers you defined. If you want to restrict the drive letters users can see, use the ZAKWINNT.ADM policy template. This template can be used with both Windows NT 4.0 and 2000. With this template, you can define a 26-bit binary number that controls which drive letters the user can and cannot see.

4. **Create a custom Start menu for each group of users.**   Group users by application needs. Create custom read-only folders that contain shortcuts to the applications they need and set a group policy that points the group to this program folder or Start menu.

5. **Hide desktop icons and have the user use the Start menu to launch applications.**   With Terminal Server, users can launch applications either from the desktop or from their Start menu by default. Because you have shortcuts in two places, this adds to the desktop clutter and increases the administrative burden. There are also several desktop icons that are difficult, if not impossible, to remove that you might not want users to have access to. Enable the Hide All Items desktop user policy. You can completely clean up the desktop, prevent users from going places where they do not belong with My Computer or Network Neighborhood, and make the client run faster because there is less desktop clutter to send across the wire.

6. **Restrict display of the Control Panel.**   There's rarely a need for users to access items in the Control Panel. To restrict access, select the Restrict Display user policy under Control Panel, Display in the User Policy window.

7. **Disable use of Registry editing.**   Remember that even on a secure system, the user necessarily has to have read/write access to several keys in the Registry. Giving the user direct access to tools that can edit or delete these keys, especially the systemwide keys, is a potential security risk. To reduce this risk, check the Disable Registry Editing Tools user policy under System, Restrictions in the User Policy window.

8. **Be careful of common folders.**   Unless you specifically restrict their display with a user policy, the common folder icons can be seen by all users. These icons are actually stored in the All Users folder under the system profile directory. Common folders can be useful in situations where all users on the system need access to certain applications. By putting the shortcuts to the applications in the All Users folder, you basically have distributed the application to all the users. If you decide to use common folders, you must first clean out the shortcuts to which users do not need access. For example, you will definitely want to get rid of any shortcuts for uninstalling an application.

9. **Use policies to deploy Registry changes.**   By creating a custom administrative template, you can use policies to deploy Registry changes to your Terminal Servers. This is often a very important need for such things as application and server tuning through Registry settings. In addition, with Windows 2000 there is a Registry policy available where you can just add the Registry entry you want to deploy without having to build a custom administrative template.

10. **Delete wallpaper and screen savers.**   Complicated backgrounds can take up large amounts of network bandwidth to transmit. In addition, certain screen savers can take up enormous amounts of processing power. Neither of these are necessary on a Terminal Server. To get rid of them, create a central administrative batch file that goes out to each server and deletes the wallpaper and screen saver files as shown in this chapter.

15

Application Publishing and Load Management with Citrix MetaFrame

THIS CHAPTER COVERS TWO VERY POWERFUL features of Citrix MetaFrame: application publishing and load balancing. When it comes down to it, serving up applications is what server-based computing is all about. With application publishing, you set up your servers to publish a set of applications to your users. If you are using Citrix MetaFrame, publishing applications is the preferred approach instead of providing your users with a desktop on your server and having to worry about locking their desktops down.

With published applications and Seamless Windows in Citrix MetaFrame, their applications on Citrix MetaFrame appear to the user as just another application running on their desktop. Not only is this a more secure approach to providing applications to your users, but it also is less confusing for users. They do not have to deal with two desktops. They only have to deal with their local desktop and the applications that they run from their Citrix MetaFrame servers.

If you purchased either Citrix MetaFrame XPs or XPe, you will definitely want to take advantage of the load-management features that those packages provide. Load management enables you to evenly and automatically spread your published application users across a select group of servers in your Citrix MetaFrame server farm. When a user attempts to run a particular load-managed published application, the server farm will decide which server is being used the least and will connect the user to it.

In this chapter, you will first learn how to use the *Citrix Management Console* (CMC) on MetaFrame XP to publish applications in your server farm. For those who are using MetaFrame 1.8, the options available using the Published Application Manager tool are nearly identical to those in the CMC, so you will be able to benefit from many of the tips in this chapter.

Finally, you will learn how to load manage your applications and the differences in load balancing found in Citrix MetaFrame 1.8 and load management found in Citrix MetaFrame XPa and XPe.

Advantages of Desktop-Centric, Application-Centric, Document-Centric, and Content-Centric Approaches

There are four basic approaches to deploying applications to your Terminal Server users: either a desktop-centric, application-centric, document-centric or content-centric approach. The following sections discuss the advantages and disadvantages of each approach, so that you can better decide how you want to set up access to your server-based applications in your environment.

Desktop-Centric Approach

A *desktop-centric approach* means that your users are each provided a desktop on Terminal Server, and from that desktop they run their applications. If you are using Terminal Server alone, that means you create connection entries to connect to the server with the Terminal Services client. If you are using Citrix MetaFrame, this means you create custom ICA connection entries on the clients to connect to a desktop on the server.

Although you can run all of your applications off the desktop with the desktop-centric approach, this approach is not recommended. The main reason is for security. After you give users access to a full desktop, you need to ensure that that desktop is completely locked down using policies. For more information on locking down desktops, see Chapter 14, "Policies and Desktop Management."

Application-Centric Approach

The second approach is the *application-centric approach*. In a Terminal Server-only environment, this means you set up connection entries that run a particular application on startup for the user. If you are using Citrix MetaFrame, that means that the clients run Program Neighborhood, the Program Neighborhood Agent, or NFuse to access their applications on Citrix MetaFrame.

With the application-centric approach on MetaFrame, an administrator can centrally publish new applications to users using the CMC. An administrator can publish applications to either particular users or groups. In addition, applications can be published anonymously for access by all. If you want everyone in the Accounting global group to be able to run Microsoft Great Plains accounting from your Citrix MetaFrame servers, for example, you can just publish the Great Plains application to that group.

One of the big advantages of published applications is that as an administrator you can publish or unpublish applications for your users just by adding or removing them from the global groups on the domain. This gives you the ability to quickly deploy hundreds of applications in a fraction of the time it would take if you had to go out and install the applications locally on the workstations.

Users see the applications published to them using either Program Neighborhood, an NFuse web site, or the Program Neighborhood Agent. With Program Neighborhood, you set up a connection for the user to a particular Citrix MetaFrame farm's applications, called an *application set*. When that user logs on to the farm through the application set, he sees icons for all the applications that have been published to him.

By setting up an NFuse web site, as you will be shown in Chapter 19, "Deploying Applications over the Web using NFuse and Wireless Technologies," your users will be able to run all the applications you publish to them through their web browser. Because web browsers are readily available on most every operating system, this means you can deploy applications to users without first having to manually install the Citrix MetaFrame Program Neighborhood for them. Instead, with NFuse, the web browser itself becomes a "virtual" Program Neighborhood. When users go to the NFuse web site that you set up, they are prompted for their username, password, and domain. NFuse then authenticates the user to the Citrix MetaFrame server farm and displays a list of the icons for the applications published to the user. To run the applications, the user needs a small plug-in or component for their browsers. If they do not have the plug-in installed, they will automatically be prompted to download it. Once installed, the user can then click any application icon to launch the application over either the Internet or corporate intranet.

One other big advantage of NFuse is that it can be set up to enable you to see all the applications that have been published to you from multiple Citrix MetaFrame farms. This can be advantageous in a number of situations. If you are migrating from a MetaFrame 1.8 farm to a MetaFrame XP farm and you do not want to run in mixed mode, for example, you could instead set up an NFuse web site that shows users the applications published to them from both farms. You can then easily move applications from the old MetaFrame 1.8 farm to the new MetaFrame XP farm. This technique is covered in more detail in Chapter 19. This also can be useful for disaster recovery. You can set up a primary server farm at one location and a disaster recovery server farm at another; users will receive icons for applications published from both farms in their web browser. This technique is covered in more detail in Chapter 26, "Disaster Recovery Techniques and Enhancing Reliability."

With MetaFrame Feature Release 1, there have been many improvements to application publishing. One incredibly useful and powerful new feature is called the *Program Neighborhood Agent*. The Program Neighborhood Agent is available for most Windows platforms and runs in the background on the client workstation. With the Program Neighborhood Agent, you can take advantage of the following features, and more:

- **Ability to publish application icons to users' desktops, Start menu, and system tray**   Although you can push icons down with standard Program Neighborhood to the desktop, the Program Neighborhood Agent is specifically designed for this feature. In addition, icons can be pushed to the system tray.

- **Ability to centrally control Program Neighborhood settings** Settings such as display settings and the Start menu or desktop folder name that application icons are published to can now be configured centrally.

- **Automatic periodic publish application refresh**   This is a huge benefit for administrators who want to push icons down to the desktop. Standard Program Neighborhood refreshed icons only when Program Neighborhood was run. If you unpublished an application, the now inactive icons for the application would still be on the user's desktop until Program Neighborhood was run again. If you use the Program Neighborhood Agent instead, however, it runs in the background and periodically connects to the Citrix MetaFrame server farm to refresh the published application icons automatically.

The agent itself is available for free download for most Windows platforms from the Citrix web site (www.citrix.com/download). However, the agent currently works only with Citrix MetaFrame XP with Service Pack 1 and Feature Release 1. In addition, you must set up an NFuse 1.6 web site that the agent can connect to in order to download the list of published applications. For more detailed information on setting up NFuse and the Program Neighborhood Agent, see Chapter 19.

Program Neighborhood Lite on Windows CE

For those considering providing access to applications on Citrix MetaFrame XP from a handheld, one useful feature to know about is Program Neighborhood Lite. Unlike the Win32 ICA Program Neighborhood, you do not have the ability to set up a connection to an application set with the WinCE client. However, using the Program Neighborhood Lite feature, you can set up the WinCE device to obtain a list of applications that have been published to the user. Much like the Program Neighborhood Agent, you configure Program Neighborhood Lite to download the list of applications from an NFuse 1.6 web server on the network.

By setting up an Internet accessible NFuse 1.6 web server and wireless access to the Internet for your handhelds, you can provide complete wireless access to all your corporate applications running on Citrix MetaFrame XP!

Document-Centric Approach

The next approach is a *document-centric approach*. This is very similar to an application-centric approach, except that when you publish the application, you also specify a particular document to bring up in the command line. When the user clicks the icon, it not only brings up the application, but also brings up the document along with it. Suppose, for example, that you want everyone on a project team to be able to easily access a central Microsoft Project document. Instead of publishing just Microsoft Project to the team and showing them how to manually bring up the document, you could publish Microsoft Project with the command-line option to bring up the needed project. That way, when they double-click the icon for the published application, the project would be brought up automatically. In other words, you publish the document to the users rather than the application.

Content-Centric Approach

The last approach is a *content-centric approach*. With MetaFrame XP and Feature Release 1, you can now publish "content" just like you can publish any application. Unlike application publishing, however, users view the content locally rather than by running an application on your MetaFrame servers to view the content. Content publishing is really a fancy name for pushing out shortcuts to documents and files on your network using UNC paths (`\\[server name]\[sharename]\[filename]`).

Suppose, for example, that you want to publish a Microsoft Project document to all the members of the project team, however unlike the last example, you know all the people in the project team have Microsoft Project installed on their workstations. By publishing the document as content, users will bring up the document from the network and view it *locally*, instead of viewing it from Microsoft Project running on your Citrix MetaFrame XP server farm. This approach has several advantages, including the following:

- **You do not take up resources on your Citrix MetaFrame servers.**
  Hardware resources on your servers are expensive. By publishing content, rather than documents or applications, users view the content locally and do not use up resources on your server farm.

- **All applications and documents are in one interface.**   Using NFuse you can give users one complete portal for all their applications and documents. Users do not need to flip back and forth between NFuse and local applications because the links to commonly used documents are published as content to their NFuse "virtual" desktop.

- **Forms and common documents are easy to publish.**
  Corporations can easily create an NFuse application portal where they can publish the most commonly used forms and documents using content publishing and the most commonly used applications using application publishing.

It is important to realize that for content publishing to work, all people who need to be able to view the content need to have the "viewer" application installed locally. If you publish a Word document using the content-publishing technique, for example, all users who need to view the document must have Microsoft Word. Content publishing basically publishes only a UNC link to a particular file. When users click the link, the file is downloaded and viewed locally. If your users are accessing content across a slow connection, remember that users must download the file first. This can take several minutes for large documents over slow connections and can take up significant bandwidth. Although content publishing is a great feature, it is best used over fast connections or when the file size is small.

You can publish pretty much any type of file as long as the users have the viewer locally. Some examples of file types you can publish using content publishing are common forms, logos, audio and video feeds, spreadsheets, projects, and even hyperlinks to web pages.

Comparing Approaches

Using a combination of application, document, and content publishing, instead of providing remote desktops for users, is highly recommended for the following reasons:

- **Security**   When you set up published applications, you can control which groups or users can use them. This is a very simple and easy way to secure access to your server's applications. If you set up access to applications from the desktop, you have to manually control what icons they have access to on the desktop, and you must take the many steps necessary to properly lock down their desktops.

- **Seamless windows**   This is a great but often misunderstood feature of Citrix MetaFrame, which is intended for published applications. When you run a published application in a seamless window, it appears as just another application on the user's local desktop. The user can minimize, maximize, and resize the application window, just as he could with any other local desktop application. This seamless integration into the user's desktop is a boon to the administrator and to the user. With a desktop-centric approach, a user has two different desktops: his desktop and the MetaFrame desktop. This doubles the work of administrators, because they have two desktops to administer, and makes things more complicated for the user.

- **Load management**   Citrix MetaFrame makes it very easy to publish applications and load manage them across multiple servers. This can greatly increase the reliability and ease of maintenance for your server farm. Remember that load management is a feature that is available only in MetaFrame XPa or XPe, not XPs.

- **Publishing applications on the Internet**   If you want to make applications available through a web browser, application publishing is the way to go. Using NFuse technology, a user's web browser becomes his "virtual desktop." He will be able to log on to your NFuse web page, see all the icons for the applications that you have published to him, and be able to run them by just double-clicking the icon. You will learn a lot more about this approach in Chapter 19.

Publishing Desktops

One additional approach possible with Citrix MetaFrame and very useful in many situations is publishing desktops. Instead of publishing a particular application or document using the CMC, you publish a desktop of one your Citrix MetaFrame servers. The user then will see the server desktops that they are assigned in their Program Neighborhood. This approach is useful in many situations, including the following:

- Providing temporary access to the desktop   Often you might need to provide temporary access to the desktop for a user to resolve an issue, such as a printing issue. You can publish the desktop to the user and then remote control her session to resolve the problem. After you have finished, just take the user out of the desktop publishing group, and the user again will be able to only use her assigned published applications and documents.

- Desktop load management   If you want to use a desktop-centric approach, and give desktops to your users, consider providing the desktops by publishing them to the users instead of manually creating a custom ICA connection. By publishing it to the users, you maintain central control of the desktop. If one server goes down, you can publish a desktop for your users on another server. You also could load manage a desktop across servers for reliability as long as you were careful to kept your users profiles centrally and the application installations exactly the same across servers.

- **Thin client terminal deployments** Because many thin client terminals, with the exception of those that use embedded NT, do not have their own customizable desktop, you could publish desktops to your thin client terminal users, instead of creating connection entries for your servers. In this way you have central control over what servers your thin clients connect to. If you need to switch the terminal users over to another server, you can switch it by changing the published application parameters using the CMC, instead of having to create new connection entries on all the thin client terminals.

Publishing Applications

If you choose to take either an application- or content-centric approach in your deployment, this section is for you. In this section you will learn about the many options you have for publishing applications and exactly how to publish them using the CMC. For those who are using MetaFrame 1.8, the minor differences between the way you publish an application in 1.8 versus the way you publish an application in XP are covered.

Setting Up the Citrix Management Console

All application publishing is now handled in the CMC in MetaFrame XP, rather than the Published Application Manager tool as it was in MetaFrame 1.8. The CMC is a Java-based application accessible from the Program Menu, Citrix folder on your Citrix MetaFrame servers. Just like any application running on your Citrix MetaFrame server, you can publish the CMC to your administrators for easy access to the console. This is by far the recommended approach for providing access to the management of your Citrix MetaFrame servers. Using this approach, you can even manage your Citrix MetaFrame servers from the web by using the CMC as a published application through NFuse.

Although not highly recommended, you also can access the CMC by installing it on your local workstation. The following are the hardware and software requirements necessary:

- Windows 2000 or NT 4.0 Workstation
- Java Runtime Environment 1.3 (installed with the console)
- 25MB of drive space
- 64MB of RAM

To install the CMC on your local workstation, follow these steps:

1. Insert the MetaFrame XP CD.
2. From the splash screen that appears, click MetaFrame XP Setup. If the splash screen does not appear, run `[cd]:\autoroot.exe` from the CD.

3. Follow the instructions provided from the wizard interface. During the setup you will need to specify an administrative account that you will use initially for administration through the CMC.

Author's Note

One of the many reasons why it is better to run the CMC as a published application, rather than as a local application on a workstation, is due to the many changes made to the CMC by products and patches installed on your Citrix MetaFrame servers. If you install Installation Management, for example, it makes changes to the CMC. It is much easier to install this once on your servers, instead of having to install it on all of your servers and all the workstations that run the CMC locally. In addition, Service Pack 1 makes significant changes to the CMC. To manage a server farm where Service Pack 1 has been applied using a local installation of the CMC, you must apply Service Pack 1 to your workstation first.

When you run the CMC, whether from a Citrix MetaFrame server or from your local workstation, you will see the logon screen shown in Figure 15.1. You need to enter the server name for one of the servers in the server farm you want to administer, your logon name, password, and the domain name for your account. This account must be one that has been specifically granted either read or read-write access within the Citrix Management console.

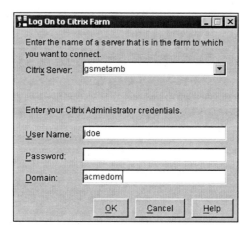

Figure 15.1   Citrix Management Console logon.

During the setup of the CMC, you are asked to specify an administrator account. When you log on to the CMC for the first time, use this administrative account. To grant access to additional accounts, follow these steps:

1. Log on to the CMC using the administrative account.

2. Under the farm name on the left, select Citrix Administrators. A list of the current accounts that have been granted access will be shown on the right.

3. Right-click Citrix Administrators and select Add Citrix Administrator.

4. Select the Domain for the account or group that you want to grant access to (see Figure 15.2).

5. If you want to grant access to a particular user and not a group, check the Show Users box.

6. Select to grant the user or group either Read Only or Read-Write Access, and then click OK.

The user or group will need read-write access to publish applications using the CMC.

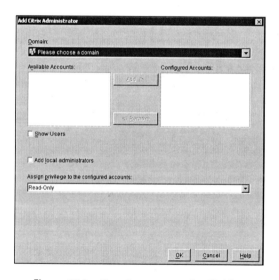

Figure 15.2 Granting access to the CMC.

Publishing the Citrix Management Console

If you are using Citrix MetaFrame, why install the CMC locally on a workstation when you can publish it instead? Several times throughout this book, using Citrix MetaFrame to publish your administrative tools is highly recommended. Not only can you use Citrix MetaFrame to publish the CMC, but you also can publish other administrative tools, such as the Citrix Connection Configuration tool, User Manager, Active Directory Users and Computers tool, and even the Citrix MetaFrame documentation. By using Citrix MetaFrame to deploy your administrative tools, you can easily and quickly provide remote administration capabilities to your key administers and the help desk staff.

To publish the CMC using Citrix MetaFrame, publish the following executable:

`%systemrootdrive%\program files\citrix\administration\ctxload.exe`

Publishing an Application with the Citrix Management Console

After the CMC has been set up, it is time to publish an application. The basics of application publishing are fairly easy. However, you need to understand many options. The following instructions provide example of how to publish a simple application without load balancing:

1. Open the CMC, which is normally located in the Program Menu, Citrix folder on your Citrix MetaFrame XP server.

2. Right-click the Applications folder and select Publish Application, or press Ctrl+P.

3. From the Publish Application window that appears, enter the published application name and description, and then click Next.

4. Enter the command line and working directory for the application and click Next. If you want to publish the desktop of your server instead, click the Publish Desktop radio button. If you want to publish content, choose the Content button.

5. At the Program Neighborhood Settings screen, change the icon if needed, specify the program folder to which the application should be published (and whether an icon should be published to the user's Start menu or desktop), and then click Next. For more information on this decision, see the following subsection on shortcut placement.

6. Select the window size and colors, and then click Next.

7. Select to turn Audio On or Off and the default encryption level, and then click Next.

8. In the Specify Servers window, highlight and add the servers to the Configured Servers list that will be running the application and click Next. If you will not be load balancing the application, select only one server. If the application is in a different location on one of the servers, highlight that server in the Configured Servers list and click the Edit Configuration button to change the command line for that server.

9. In the Specify Users window, select the domain from the drop-down list and then select the group in that domain that you want to publish the application to and click Finish. If you want to publish it to a particular user, check the Show Individual User Accounts check box. If this is an anonymous application, click the Allow Anonymous Connections check box.

Changes in Feature Release 1

For those who have installed Feature Release 1 on their MetaFrame XP servers, you will have the following additional options available during the publication of applications:

- **Application Priority**   With Feature Release 1, you can now control the CPU priority at which your applications run. This will enable you to better control CPU utilization on your servers by applications.

- **SSL**   You can set whether an application can be connected to via the SSL protocol while publishing it. This means all communication will happen over port 443 and can be encrypted with 128-bit key encryption.

- **Parameter Passing**   You can now pass command-line parameters from a client to an application running on Citrix MetaFrame. This is useful in certain situations, such as where shortcuts for applications need to be emailed out to users with command-line parameters. For more information on how to set this up see the "Passing Parameters to Publish Applications" section later in this chapter.

- **Content Publishing**   When you select to publish an application with Feature Release 1, the Application Publishing Wizard will ask whether you want to publish an application or content. If you select content, you will then be prompted to enter the UNC for the content data file. Once published, users will now see the icon for the published content in their Program Neighborhoods. When they click the icon, the content will be shown in their local viewer application, just as if they had clicked the same file in the file Explorer.

- **Instance or Connection Limits**   You can now limit the maximum number of instances of an application that users can run. Because each instance of an application takes up additional resources on the server farm, limiting the number of instances of an application can help control resource utilization on your servers.

The application will now appear under the Applications folder in the CMC. When the users who you published the application to click the Refresh button in their Citrix Program Neighborhood client, they will receive the icon for the new application you just published. By double-clicking the icon, they will be able to run the application.

Organizing Published Applications in the CMC

One very handy new feature in the CMC, not possible in MetaFrame 1.8's Published Application Manager, is the ability to organize your published applications in folders. For companies with hundreds of published applications, this makes administration much easier than before. If you had hundreds of published applications in the Published Application Manager (PAM), not only would you have to scroll through the list to find the application you needed to manage, but the process of enumerating the published applications during the startup of the PAM would take a significant amount of time.

To organize your application in the CMC for easier administration, follow these steps:

1. Open the CMC

2. Right-click the Applications folder and select New Folder.

3. Enter the name of the new folder for grouping your published applications, and then click OK.

4. Right-click the newly created folder and select Publish Application to put a new published application in that folder.

Some suggested folder names are Documents, Desktops, Administration, Reporting, Accounting, and Office.

In the following sections, you will learn the details and recommendations for the many advanced application publishing features that you can take advantage of.

Published Application Options

The following are some of the many options that you can set for published applications and recommendations on how and when to set those options. To access these options, right-click the published application you want to modify in the CMC and select Properties. The window shown in Figure 15.3 will appear.

Application Name

Under the Application Name tab, you can set the following parameters:

- **Display Name**   This is the name of the application displayed to the client. Try to keep this name as short as possible.

- **Application Name**   This can be a more descriptive name for the application. Clients will see this name in the list of available applications if they try to create a custom ICA connection entry for the application. By default, the application name and display name are set the same.

- **Application Description**   For the application description, you can enter a more detailed description of the application, such as the version number or other information. This description is displayed to the clients if they choose to view detailed information in their Program Neighborhood.

- **Disable Application** If you select this box, users will still see the published application in their Program Neighborhood; however, if they choose to run the application, they will get a message saying that it has been disabled.

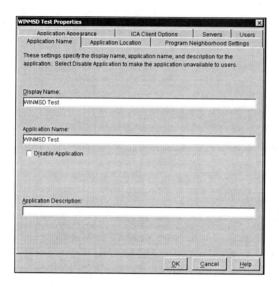

Figure 15.3 Application's Properties window.

The most important setting here is the Display Name. The Display Name is the name shown in the client's Program Neighborhood when he connects to the published application. If you choose to push the published application icon out to the desktop or Start menu, the display name is what is used for the icon title. The following are some tips to consider when choosing a display name:

- **Be consistent.** As your farm grows, it is especially important to be consistent in your application naming standards. Whatever standard you decide on, make sure to document it and use it consistently for all of your applications.

- **Use [app name][version] for applications.** If you are publishing an application, this simple naming standard works for most cases. It is important to include the version number, because in the future you might want to publish a new version to your clients, and they will need to differentiate between the two.

- **Use doc-[doc name] for documents or content.**   If you are publishing documents, this is a simple and effective naming standard. The benefit of this standard is that applications that bring up documents are clearly identified and will appear together in client's Program Neighborhoods.

- **Abbreviate as much as possible.**   There is not enough room under an icon for a lengthy application name. If you make the name much past 10 characters, it will just be cut off when displayed under an icon. Try to keep the name under 10 characters by abbreviating the application name heavily. For example, you might choose to use PwrPnt 2K, rather than Microsoft PowerPoint 2000 for the application name.

Problems with Changing Application Names

One big gotcha to be aware of are the problems that can occur if you decide to change an application name after you publish it. After you change an application name, your users *must* refresh their published application icons by clicking the Refresh button in Program Neighborhood before they can use the application. The old icon for the application with the old name will still exist in the users' Program Neighborhood until they refresh their application list. If you change the name in the middle of the day and then a user clicks the icon for the old application, the user will get an error message unless she refreshes her applications first.

Although the newer versions of the Citrix ICA client refresh their published application icons periodically, during startup of the Program Neighborhood and during the launch of any application, it is still important to ensure that your users understand how to refresh their icons. Normally it is recommended to send a message to users, warning them of an application name change before it occurs.

One way to get around this problem is using the Program Neighborhood Agent, rather than Program Neighborhood. As mentioned previously in this chapter, you must have MetaFrame XP with Feature Release 1 and an NFuse 1.6 web site set up to use the Program Neighborhood Agent. After these are set up, however, user's published icons will be refreshed automatically in the background every six hours by default. You can modify this refresh rate centrally, along with many other important Program Neighborhood parameters.

Application Location

Under the Application Location tab, you will find the following settable properties:

- **Command Line**   The command line for the published application.
- **Working Directory**   The directory in which the application is started.
- **Publish Desktop**   If you select this radio button, the desktop of the server is published to the user, rather than an application.

The main thing to be aware of with these settings is how to handle command-line options. If you have command-line options you need to specify, such as a document that needs to be opened, enclose the command in quotes and put the command-line options next to it, as follows:

```
"c:\winnt\notepad.exe" c:\document.txt
```

Program Neighborhood Settings

Under the Program Neighborhood Settings tab, the following options are available:

- **Program Neighborhood Folder**   You can specify a folder here that the icon will be contained in for your published application. When users connect to the application set, they will see the folders for the applications first and then be able to click them to access the applications within. You can specify multiple folder levels by separating the folder names with backslashes. For example, to push an application out to your client in an accounting\great plains folder, you would specify "accounting\great plains" for the Program Neighborhood folder.

- **Add to the Clients Start Menu**   Adds the icon for the application to the user's Start menu. Only applies to the Windows 32-bit ICA client.

- **Add Shortcut to the Client's Desktop**   Adds the icon for the application to the user's desktop. Only applies to the Windows 32-bit ICA client.

- **Application Icon**   Enables you to change the icon that appears to the client for the application.

Generally, unless your clients commonly run more than 10 different applications from your Citrix MetaFrame server farm, it is not recommended to make Program Neighborhood folders for the applications. Overuse of the Program Neighborhood folder, and especially using multiple levels of these folders, can make it more difficult for users to access their applications. If you choose a document-centric approach for your environment, however, you might choose to use a Program Neighborhood folder to separate the documents from the applications.

For example, you could specify a Documents Program Neighborhood folder for all of your published documents. In that way you would not have to name the documents Doc-[Document Name], as recommended earlier. You could instead just name the published document by the [Document Name] and specify that it goes into the Documents Program Neighborhood folder.

Another recommendation is to avoid adding icons to the user's desktop or Start menu, unless users are running the Program Neighborhood Agent and not the Program Neighborhood. If your users have the Program Neighborhood, encourage and train users to go into it and use it instead of using an icon published to the desktop. If your users use the Program Neighborhood Agent, however, the agent is specifically designed to push application icons out to the user's desktop, Start menu, or system tray. Unlike the standard Program Neighborhood, which needs to be manually refreshed for users to see changes to their published applications, the Program Neighborhood Agent automatically refreshes applications once every six hours by default.

Application Appearance

The following options are available under the Application Appearance tab in the Application Settings window:

- **Session Window Size** You can specify the default session window size from this drop-down list. This does not apply for Seamless Windows sessions.

- **Colors** You can specify the number of colors used for application display to the client. The default is 256.

- **Hide Application Title Bar** If you are not using Seamless Windows, this setting will hide the application title bar.

- **Maximize Application at Startup** This setting maximizes the application at startup. Like the title bar setting, it applies only for application sets not using Seamless Windows.

Most of these settings apply only if you do not use Seamless Windows. There are very few cases where you would not want to use Seamless Windows on your clients. Seamless Windows make the application look and feel as if it is running locally for your user.

By default when you set up an application set on your ICA clients, as shown in Chapter 12, "Installing and Deploying ICA Clients," the application set is set up to use Seamless Windows. To check whether this is the case for your clients, go into Citrix MetaFrame Program Neighborhood, right-click the application set name, and select Properties. Under the Default Options tab, shown in Figure 15.4, look at the setting for Window Size. If this setting shows Seamless Windows or a particular window size, the published application settings will be ignored. If instead the Use Server Default check box is checked, the applications in the application set will be displayed as specified in the published application settings.

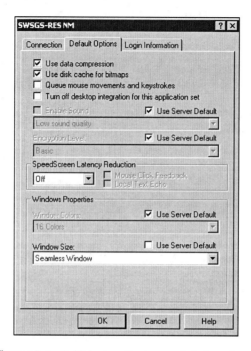

Figure 15.4 Published application set default options.

The one setting that will affect the default options for your client's Program Neighborhoods is the Color option. By default, this is set to 256 colors in the published application settings. As shown in Figure 15.4, the default setting for Windows Colors in the client's application set settings is to Use the Server Default. What this means is that by default, you have complete control of how many colors are used by your applications from the published application set settings at the server.

This is an important and often over-looked performance-tuning tip. If you can reduce the number of colors used for display of your application, they will display significantly faster across slow connections. For this reason it is highly recommended to always set the Colors setting for published applications to the lowest number of colors necessary. In many cases you will find that you do not need 256 colors to display a particular application and that 16 colors is adequate for normal usage. By decreasing the Colors setting for this application to 16, you will greatly increase the screen response time for the application across slow connections. However, there are options to use high color and true color if needed with an application.

ICA Client Options

The following options are available under the ICA Client Options tab:

- **Audio**   You can either set the Audio Off or On, depending on whether the application requires audio. By default, this setting is on. Best practice is to turn this off if your application does not need it.

- **Encryption**   You have several different encryption options under this drop-down list. By default the encryption is set to Basic, which means that application traffic is just "scrambled" and not encrypted.

For performance reasons it is highly recommended to disable audio by turning it off unless it is absolutely needed. By default, Citrix MetaFrame Program Neighborhood clients will use whatever is set at the server. If you do not disable audio at a connection level, audio will be enabled for your applications. Because of the large amount of bandwidth that audio can take, you should normally disable it both at an application level by changing this setting to Off and at a connection level if not needed. It does not have to be disabled in both locations, but to be certain it remains off, this is recommended.

One way to control the encryption used by your applications is by setting it here. By default, Citrix MetaFrame Program Neighborhood and other versions of the ICA client are set to use the server defaults for encryption. By specifying the encryption level using the published application settings, you can enforce a certain encryption level for your applications. Encryption is important if your session traffic needs to travel across untrusted networks, such as the Internet. Beware of the extra processing overhead required for encryption. During your application testing and server sizing, you should take into account what encryption level you intend to run your applications at and test the application's processor usage at this level. For more information on proper performance testing see Chapter 21, "Performance Tuning and Resource Management."

Author's Note

With Feature Release 1, you now have the ability to encrypt traffic by establishing an SSL tunnel between the client and the Citrix MetaFrame or NFuse server. For more information on this important security feature, see Chapter 17, "Firewalls and SSL Relay."

The Encryption Enigma

The fact that you can change encryption settings at a client, connection, and application level makes it somewhat complicated to understand how best to set up encryption for your environment. The following are some tips:

- **Keep the connection encryption setting at Basic.**   The connection encryption setting represents the minimum encryption level needed for connection to any application running on the server through that connection. However, this is *not* a server default. In other words, if you change the connection encryption setting to a minimum of 128-bit encryption, you will have to manually change each of your Program Neighborhood client's application sets to 128-bit encryption, otherwise users will receive the encryption warning message when they attempt to log on.

- **Keep the encryption settings for clients at Use Server Default.**   The default encryption setting for your Citrix MetaFrame Program Neighborhood clients is to Use Server Defaults (see Figure 15.4). It is normally best to keep it this way and to control encryption centrally at the server.

- **Control the encryption by changing the encryption for the application.**   Enforce the encryption that you need by changing the encryption level using the published application settings in the CMC. If you want to be certain that even older clients connect to the application at the required encryption level or their connection is not allowed, check the box next to Minimum Requirement.

These tips work well for most environments. If you ever want to see what encryption level a published application will run at, there are two ways to find out. The first and easiest method is to just right-click the published application icon in the Citrix MetaFrame Program Neighborhood's application set, and then select Properties. A window similar to the one shown in Figure 15.5 will appear. Note the encryption setting for this application shown in this window.

The second method is to have the user run the application and then to go into the CMC, browse to the application under the Applications folder, and highlight it. You will see a list of all the users currently running the application displayed on the right side of the screen. Right-click the user you want to check and select Session Information, and then click the Session Information button. You will see a window with information similar to that in Figure 15.5.

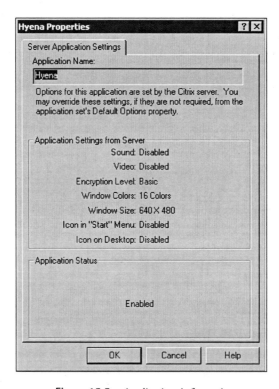

Figure 15.5   Application information.

Servers

Under the Servers tab, you can select the servers from which the application will be available. If you select more than one server from the list, the application will automatically be load managed across those servers. Load management is covered in greater detail in the "Load Managing Applications" section later in this chapter.

By default, the application is run using the Command Line and Working Directory that you specified under the Application Location tab. If the application was installed in a different folder on a particular server, you can highlight that server in the Configured Servers list and click the Edit Configuration button. From the dialog box that appears, you can set a different location for the application executable (see Figure 15.6).

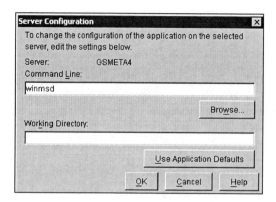

Figure 15.6   Server configuration.

Application Limits

The Application Limits tab appears only if you have installed Feature Release 1 on your MetaFrame XP servers. Under the Application Limits tab, you have the following options:

- **Concurrent Instances**   In this small dialog box area, you can specify the maximum number of instances that a particular user can open of this application. This is very useful to help control situations where users tend to open up numerous instances of the same application, causing excessive server utilization.

- **CPU Priority**   Using this dialog box, you can select what priority your applications are started in on the server. Be very careful with this option, especially when assigning applications a higher than normal priority. Excessive use of these high-priority applications can quickly monopolize CPU time, causing other lower priority sessions to appear frozen or to slow down considerably.

User

The last tab available is the Users tab. Under this tab you can specify the users or groups that this application is published to. You can publish applications to the following users and groups:

- **Active Directory universal groups, global groups, domain local groups, and users**   Any Active Directory domain will display in green in the domain list. Universal groups in the Active Directory will display in red, and domain local groups will display in yellow.

- **Windows NT 4.0 domain global groups and users** You can publish an application to any Windows NT 4.0 domain global group or user.

- **Machine local groups and users** You also can publish applications to particular users and groups in the local user database for whatever computer you are running the CMC on.

- **Built-in** A special set of groups used for Novell environments. For more information on this option, see Chapter 25, "Terminal Server and NetWare".

- **Anonymous connections** If you want to publish this application for anonymous use, you would check the Allow Anonymous Connections check box. Anonymous use of an application means that anyone who had a network connection to the Citrix MetaFrame server and an ICA client could create a custom ICA connection for the published application and run the application.

- **NetWare NDS groups and users** If you are using Feature Release 1, you can now select users and groups to publish applications to, from your NetWare directory. This is an important new feature for Novell shops.

Using the *start* Command for Running Published Applications

One technique that can be useful in certain situations is to use the built-in `start.exe` command to start your applications. You can use the `start` command to do the following:

- **Start applications with a different priority** Applications are normally started with Normal priority. If you want to start an application with increased or decreased priority, use the following command:

```
start [/low | /normal | /high | /abovenormal | /realtime] [application path]
```

Author's Note

Although this technique works great for MetaFrame 1.8 and MetaFrame XP administrators, for those who have MetaFrame XP with Feature Release 1 this technique is not needed. You can now set the application priority using a drop-down menu within the published application settings.

- **Start a 16-bit application in its own memory space** If you run 16-bit applications on your servers and they share the same memory space, if one application crashes it will crash the rest. For this reason it is often recommended to run 16-bit applications in their own memory space. To do this, use the following command line to run the application:

```
start /separate [application path]
```

- **Start an application either minimized or maximized** In some cases you might want to start an application either minimized or maximized. To do this, use the following command line:

```
start [/min | /max] [application path]
```

Running Applications from Batch Files

In some cases, especially with 16-bit or DOS applications, you might want to run an application from a batch file instead of running it directly. If you run it from a batch file, it gives you the opportunity to prepare the environment for the application before the user runs it. You also can clean up the environment after the application is run.

Suppose, for example, that you want to replace an application data file with a fresh copy for each user who runs the application. The application is set to retrieve the application data file from the user's home directory, which in this example is h:\. The following sample batch file could be published, rather than the application itself:

```
@echo off
copy \\[server]\[share]\appdata.txt h:\ /y
[application path]
```

Using the **runh** Command to Run a Batch File Hidden

One problem with running this batch file is that the user will be able to see it run. To hide the fact that a batch file is run, but to bring up the application that it launches, you can use the freely available RUNH.EXE utility from www.scripthorizon.com. To use this utility, download it and extract it to the %systemroot%\system32 directory on your Citrix MetaFrame servers. When you publish the batch file, publish it using the following command line:

```
runh [batch file path]
```

The batch file will run in the background and will not be visible to the user. However, any application that the batch file launches will appear in the foreground.

Some administrators also use the RUNH.EXE utility to hide the command window that appears when the USRLOGON.CMD file is run during logon. To implement this trick, you need to modify the Registry value that specifies the files run at logon. You will find this value in the following Registry key:

```
HKLM\SOFTWARE\Microsoft\Windows NT\Current Version\WinLogon
```

The value you need to change is the AppSetup value. On a Windows 2000 Terminal Server, this value normally contains the following text: usrlogon.cmd,cmstart.exe,updatdrv.exe. To run the USRLOGON.CMD hidden, change the value to: "runh usrlogon.cmd,cmstart.exe,updatdrv.exe". The RUNH.EXE should be in the %systemroot%\system32 folder for this to work.

Be careful with this setting change because it affects every person who logs on to the console of the server. While you are still connected to the server, open up another session to it to ensure that you can log on and that the USRLOGON.CMD was hidden properly. If you have a problem logging on to the server, you can use REGEDIT remotely to change the value back to the original value.

Publishing the Printer Control Panel

If you are like most Citrix MetaFrame and Terminal Server administrators, a good deal of the issues that you will face will be in some way related to printing. Many times you might want to give a user access to the Printer Control Panel, so that she can change her default printer, change printer settings, or add a new printer if necessary, without giving them access to the full desktop. You also might want to be able to publish the Printer Control Panel to them temporarily, so that you can shadow them and manually add a printer or resolve a printing issue. The problem is that the Printer Control Panel is not a standard application that you can just publish, it is actually a part of a DLL on your system. Luckily there is a trick to publish it. Here is how:

1. Log on to the server whose Printer Control Panel you want to publish.

2. Copy the `\%systemroot%\explorer.exe` file to `\%systemroot%\expl-prt.exe`.

3. Publish this folder by using the following command line:

```
c:\winnt\expl-prt.exe /n,/root,::{2227a280-3aea-1069-a2de-08002b30309d}
```

   Make sure to use the double-colons (`::`) exactly as shown in the example.

4. Use `printers-[server name]` for the Display Name for the application and publish it to whatever groups or users need to see the Printer Control Panel on this server.

At this point your users should be able to double-click the Printers-[Server Name] published application icon and be brought into their view of the server's Printer Control Panel. From this view they can change their printer settings or you can shadow them and see what printers they have.

Published Applications and License Pooling

Suppose you're running two published applications on your workstation: Application A and Application B. Because these are published applications, you have two connections opened with your MetaFrame server, one for each application. How many MetaFrame licenses are you taking? The answer is only one.

Changing Passwords Through a Published Application

In many situations you might want to publish an application to your users so that they can change their own passwords. This is especially the case in environments that use only published applications or that use older versions of NFuse (prior to 1.6) for application deployment. The easiest way to do this is to publish a password-changing utility. As of this writing, there is a freely available password-changing utility that you can publish for your users at Emergent Online's web site, www.99point9.com. The utility is called EOL SetPassword. Just download this small application and publish it to your users so that they can change their password as needed.

With NFuse 1.6, there is now a small web application to change your password. To use NFuse 1.6, however, you must have MetaFrame XP with Service Pack/Feature Release 1 installed.

One thing that is important to realize with MetaFrame is that connection licenses are pooled. Citrix has gone to great lengths by implementing improvements on both the client and server side to ensure that only one license is taken up, no matter how many connections a user makes to a single server farm.

Passing Parameters to Published Applications

When you install many applications on a desktop, they make changes to the file associations so that they are launched automatically when the user attempts to open a particular file type. When you install Microsoft Word, for example, it automatically makes a file association so that whenever you attempt to open a document whose filename ends with the .DOC extension, Word is launched with that document. However, because applications on the Citrix MetaFrame servers are not installed locally, there is no link between local file types and the Citrix MetaFrame applications.

In some environments, this can cause problems. For this reason and more, Citrix MetaFrame has included the ability to pass command-line parameters to Citrix MetaFrame applications in Feature Release 1. You can now launch applications on Citrix MetaFrame servers using local file type associations and command-line parameters. One good example of the usefulness of this feature is with the SAP accounting application. Using command-line parameters, you can start the application in a particular transaction. In a transaction-oriented system, such as SAP, this is a very useful feature. Before Feature Release 1, there was no way to launch SAP in a particular transaction unless you published an icon for that particular transaction. Now with Feature Release 1, however, you can pass the command-line parameter for the particular transaction needed to get the SAP GUI application running on Citrix MetaFrame.

To set up this functionality, you need to do two things. First, on the server follow these steps when publishing the application:

1. Right-click the application in the CMC and select Properties.

2. Click the Command Line tab.

3. Add `%` to the command line for the application. For example, if the command line is currently `m:\winnt\notepad.exe`, change it to `m:\winnt\ notepad.exe %`.

The `%` is the placeholder for the command-line parameters that will be passed to the application from the client. Now at each client that needs to pass command-line parameters to the Citrix MetaFrame application, change the file association for the desired file type to use the `pn.exe /app:[pub lished application name]` Program Neighborhood application. If you want to launch the Ctx – Notepad application from the ProdFarm application set on the client with command-line parameters, for instance, you would change the local file open association for `*`.TXT files to point to `pn.exe % /pn: prodfarm /app:ctx - notepad /param:%1`.

On a Windows 2000 machine, you would do this as follows:

1. Right-click the Start menu and select Explore.

2. Select Folder Options under the Tools menu.

3. Click the File Types tab.

4. Highlight the .TXT file type in the list and click the Advanced button.

5. Select Open and then click Edit.

6. Change the open file association to `c:\program files\citrix\ica client\pn.exe /pn:prodfarm /app:ctx - notepad /param:%1`.

The new `/param:` command-line parameter for the Program Neighborhood executable (`pn.exe`) is available only in the 6.20.985 ICA client and later. Whatever text you put after `/param:` will be passed as a command-line parameter to the application running on the Citrix MetaFrame server.

Author's Note

Although these instructions apply only to running a published application from an application set with command-line parameters, you also can pass command-line parameters to custom ICA connections using the `pn.exe /app:[custom ica connection name] /param:%1` format for the pn.exe command. For a list of additional parameters available for pn.exe, run `c:\program files\citrix\ica client\pn.exe /?`.

Load Managing Applications

Load managing is perhaps the most powerful feature available in MetaFrame XP and is one of the most convincing reasons for the purchase of Citrix MetaFrame over Terminal Server alone.

Using load management, you can manage the load on your servers very easily by controlling which server users use when they attempt to run a published application. In addition, load management provides a high level of fault tolerance. If one of the load-managed servers is taken down for maintenance or fails for any reason, users will be able to reconnect to the application running on one of the remaining servers.

With MetaFrame 1.8, load management was referred to as load balancing. Load balancing was a separately purchased service that you could enable by purchasing and entering the license code for Load Balancing Services. Once enabled, you could manage the load balancing of your servers using the Load Balancing administrative tool.

In MetaFrame XP, load management is built into both MetaFrame XPe and MetaFrame XPa. If you are using either of these versions, you can manage the load from the CMC, instead of using a separate administrative tool as was the case with MetaFrame 1.8. In addition, MetaFrame XP offers both server load management and application load management. This is a significant enhancement over the server load balancing alone that was available in MetaFrame 1.8 and provides you with more granular control over how both applications and server usage are balanced in your farm.

In this section you will learn all about how load management works and how to set up load management for your applications.

Planning for Load Management

The first step for setting up load management is to publish your applications to the load-managed server group. The load-managed server group is the set of servers that the application will be load balanced across. There are currently no stated limits on the number of servers you can load balance a single application across. With MetaFrame XP, you can even load balance applications across servers that are on different subnets or that are connected across a WAN. The only key requirement is that all the servers in the load-balanced server group need to be part of the same server farm.

Choosing and Grouping the Servers

Ideally when you choose which servers to load manage your applications across, those servers should have identical hardware and software setups. This is not a requirement, but it makes load managing much easier because the hardware capabilities are the same on each server and the software is installed in the same location on each. Even if your hardware is not identical, Citrix MetaFrame provides plenty of ways to balance your users properly between the boxes, as you will see in this section. If the software is not installed in the same folder on each server, you can manually specify the location when publishing the application.

In addition to choosing servers with identical hardware and software, it is normally best, especially for large enterprise deployments, to choose servers in the same application grouping. The concept of grouping your servers by application type goes back to previous planning discussions in this book. The concept of application grouping is very important, especially in large Citrix MetaFrame server deployments. Instead of trying to run all of your applications on all of your servers, you should instead choose to group your applications in a logical manner and put that group of applications on a particular group of servers.

For example, you might have a particular internal line of business order entry application that is updated frequently and requires that the server be set up in a certain fashion with certain .DLLs. Instead of trying to install this application on the same server you are using for deployment of Office applications, such as Microsoft Office, you could choose to create an order entry server grouping and an office server grouping. The servers in the order entry and office application groupings would follow the same naming standards, such as ctx-order[#] for the order entry servers and ctx-offc[#] for the office servers. You would then install the order entry application on the order entry servers and load balance the application across them. Next you would install the Office application on the Office servers and load balance the Office applications across them.

Although this is the ideal setup, reality is that this is not possible for all environments. Even if you can head toward this ideal as your Citrix MetaFrame environment grows, it will make administration easier in the long run and increase the reliability of your server farm.

Centralizing Profiles

After you know which servers you will be load managing the application across, you need to make sure that your users' profiles and home directories are centralized. If they are not centralized, your users will have different application settings depending on which server they connect to.

Suppose, for example, that user profiles were not centralized, you bought a new server, and you then attempted to load manage an accounting application across the new server and the old one. The accounting application kept many settings, such as the file location for accounting files and number formats, in the user's Registry. This application had been in use for more than a year by users on the old server before you attempted to load manage it, so by this point users had made several changes to their own application settings. When you now load manage this application across the old server and the new one, you will likely start to get complaints from users that their settings keep changing. Whenever they are sent to the old server, they have their old application settings. When they connect and are sent to the new server, however, all their old settings are gone.

To avoid this problem, you need to ensure that your profiles are centralized before load managing an application. If you are going from a single server environment to a load-managed environment, you also will need to copy the user profiles from that server to the central location. Otherwise, if this is a new install, you can just ensure that profiles are centralized before users first log on.

In addition to centralizing profiles, it also is important to choose a home drive directory letter for your users and make sure that the logon script maps the letter to the root of their home directory during logon. This is the letter that you need to ensure the application uses as a storage location for all user specific files. If your home directory drive letter is H:, for example, you need to ensure by looking through the application's Registry keys and menu settings that any user-specific file location, such as the location for document backups, goes into the user's h:\ folder.

For more information on how to centralize profiles for your users, see Chapter 9, "Setting Up Terminal Server Users." You also will find information in this chapter on how to set up the logon script to map a letter to the root of a user's home directory.

Publishing an Application for Load Management

After you have chosen the servers you want in your load-managed pool, and your profiles are centralized, the next step is to publish the application across them. This is actually a very simple process, because all you need to do is to select all the servers in the load-managed group when publishing the application.

If you are load managing an existing application currently only running on a single server, however, you might want to take a different approach. If this is the case, one recommended approach is to leave the existing published application alone and instead create a new published application by a different name. You can then have a select group of application power users test the new application to ensure that the load management is working properly, before removing the old published application.

Suppose, for example, that users were using PeopleSoft on a single server for the past year. The number of users has now grown to the point where you need to load manage the application to a new server. The safest and recommended approach would be to select a small group of application power users who are capable of testing the application thoroughly or who use the application extensively. Then publish a new version of the PeopleSoft application called PeopleSoft - LM to these power users, which you load balance across the old and new server. After they have tested it thoroughly and load management is working properly, send a message out to users informing them of the change. At the planned time, publish the PeopleSoft - LM application to all the users and delete the old published application. Remember that the users will need to refresh their icons in Program Neighborhood for the icon switch out to occur.

Author's Note

This is one of the many reasons why it is important that users know the basics of how to use Program Neighborhood, instead of having them know how to run published applications only from icons on their desktop or Start menu.

Publishing an application to be load managed is nearly identical to publishing a single server application. You need to open the CMC, right-click the Applications folder, and select New Application. The exception is when you come to the step of choosing the servers on which the application can be run. When you get to this step during the setup of the published application, you need to move all the servers on the left, that are part of the application's load-managed group, over to the configured servers on the right. If the application is installed in a different location on any of the configured servers, highlight that server, click the Edit Configuration button, and change the command-line path.

If you need to load balance an existing application, right-click the application in the CMC under Applications and select Properties. Click the Servers tab and add all the servers in the load-managed server group into the list of configured servers.

Understanding Load Evaluators

After you have published the application to your load-managed server group, the next step is to set up the load management. Load management in MetaFrame XP is handled very differently than load balancing was in MetaFrame 1.8. In MetaFrame 1.8, you could change load balancing evaluation rules only at a server level. This means that new users were routed to servers solely based on the reported server load. New users would be sent to the server that reported the least server load.

In MetaFrame XP, you can assign load evaluators to both servers and applications. A load evaluator is customizable sets of load evaluation rules. Every server is assigned one load evaluator rule. By default, all servers are assigned the default load evaluator rule. The default rule evaluates the load of a server based on the number of users connected to it. The more users on a server, the higher the value of the load reported by that server. If you use server load evaluators only, load management becomes load balancing as it was in MetaFrame 1.8. New users who try to connect will be routed to the server that reports the least server load, based on whatever load evaluator is assigned to that server.

In MetaFrame XP, however, you also can assign a load evaluator to a particular application on a particular server. This more granular level of load management control can be important for controlling the usage of a particular application on a particular server or across a load-managed server pool. For example, you might want to restrict the times of access for only one application running on a server, but not the other applications. In MetaFrame 1.8, there was no way to do this. In MetaFrame XP, however, you can set up a scheduling load evaluator and assign it to an application.

If both an application load evaluator is assigned to the application a user is trying to connect to and a server evaluator is assigned to the server, the highest reported load of both evaluators is considered the load for that server. If the application load evaluator reports a load of 200 and the server load evaluator reports a load of 100, however, that server's load is considered to be 200. When a new user attempts to connect to this application, this load value is compared to the load value of the rest of the servers in the load-balanced pool and the user is routed to the server with the smallest current load.

Load Evaluator Rules

Load evaluators can be set up that calculate a server's load based on the following adjustable rules. Although you can use the listed load evaluation rules for either a server or application load evaluation, some rules are better suited for either one or the other. The intended use for each rule is shown in parentheses.

- **Application user load (application load only)** Instead of calculating load based on the number of total users connected to a particular server, you can calculate it on the number of total users for a particular server using a particular application.

- **Context switches (server load only)**   Load can be calculated on the number of CPU context switches. You can set a low and high value for the range. If the context switches are at or below the low value, load is reported as none. If context switches are at or above the high value, the server reports that it is fully loaded.

- **CPU utilization (server load only)**   You can create a load evaluator for a server that reports load based on a server's CPU utilization. As with context switches, you can set a low percentage that means no load and a high percentage that means full load. For applications that are very processor-intensive, you might want to use this as a load evaluator. Realize that processor usage tends to spike frequently however, so this might not be a solid indicator of server utilization.

- **Disk data I/O (server load only)**   This type of load evaluator will report a server's load based on the overall throughput in kilobytes for a server. This is an indicator of disk activity on a server. For servers used for very disk-intensive applications, this can be a good measurement for server load.

- **Disk data operations (server load only)**   As opposed to disk data I/O, which reports load based on the amount of data transferred, this parameter reports load based on the number of data transactions that occur over a one-second period.

- **IP range (server or application load)**   This is an interesting and new way to control the load of your servers. Using IP range, you can specify whether a certain IP range can or cannot have access to a particular application running on a particular server. If the client is outside of the IP range specified for the application for a particular server, the client is denied access to that server. If the IP range specified for the application for every server is the same, the client will not be able to connect to that application. If you set up a different IP range for different servers in the same load-balanced server group, you can ensure that only users in certain subnets access certain servers. Because this is an all-or-nothing type of load evaluator rule, you should combine this rule with a standard load evaluator rule such as user load, to balance the application properly.

- **License threshold (server load only)**   You can use this load evaluator to ensure that a certain application does not take up too many licenses on a server farm. With this load evaluator you can specify the number of pooled licenses that must be available before a user can connect to an application.

- **Memory usage (server load only)**   This is a good load evaluator to use for memory-intensive applications or where memory is becoming a bottleneck with one or more of your servers. Using this load evaluator, you can specify a certain percentage of memory that must be left for a user to be able to connect to the application on a particular server.

- **Page fault (server load only)**   Page faults occur when an application tries to achieve a section of code from memory, but has to be redirected to the paging file because that code has been swapped out to paging file. This tends to occur during heavy server usage or during low memory situations and can be a good indicator of server load. Using this load evaluator you can have a server report its load based on the current usage of the paging file.

- **Page swap (server load only)**   This load evaluator is similar to the page fault load evaluator except that it measures how often a server is swapping out memory to the paging file, rather than when an application has to use the paging file.

- **Schedule (server or application load)**   This is another new and interesting type of load evaluator that you will not find in MetaFrame 1.8. Using this load evaluator you can make an application available only on a particular server during certain times of the day or week. Realize, however, that this counts only for new connections; existing users will not be kicked off outside of those times. Because this is an all-or-nothing type of rule, you should use it in combination with a standard load evaluator rule, such as server user load for proper load balancing.

- **Server user load (server load only)**   The server user load is the most commonly used means of evaluating a server's load and is what is used by the default load evaluator. This load evaluator will report a server's load based on the number of currently connected users to the server.

As you can see from the list, the only rules appropriate to apply to applications are schedule, IP range, and application user load. When applying schedule or IP range to an application, however, you should combine it with one of the other rules for proper load balancing, such as server user load. Remember when planning how you will deploy your load evaluators that the highest load is the one that counts between a server and an application load evaluator.

Understanding Load Balancing

When a user attempts to connect to a load-managed application, the farm's data collector goes through the following basic process to decide which server to direct the user to:

1. The client contacts the server that it is configured to contact in the application set's properties, and requests to connect to a particular application.

2. If that server is not the local data collector, the server passes the request onto the data collector.

3. The data collector first checks the published application's parameters to determine what servers are in the application's load-balanced server group.

4. Next, it checks the current load of all of those servers. The calculated load for each server depends on what load evaluator you have assigned to that server. This reported load is then compared to the calculated load for whatever load evaluators you have assigned to the application the user is trying to run. Whichever value is greater is considered the reported load for the server for this application.

5. The data collector then sends the name of the server with the least load back to the client.

6. The client establishes a connection with the application on that server.

7. The server now sends an update on the change in server load to the data collector to keep the data collector up-to-date.

It is important to reinforce the difference between the evaluation of a server load evaluator and an application load evaluator. As you will see in the following section, a load evaluator can be assigned to either a server or to an application. Servers always have a load evaluator assigned to them. Applications can optionally have a load evaluator assigned. When the server farm needs to decide where to route an incoming request for an application, it needs to calculate the load for every server in the load-managed group and route the request to the server with the least load. For each server in the load-managed group, it first checks what the reported load is by that server's load evaluator. It then checks the reported load by any application load evaluators that have been assigned to the application the user is trying to use. The greater of these two numbers is considered the actual load of that server.

Setting Up Load Balancing

After you have decided on what load evaluators to use for your published application, it is time to load manage the application. The first step is to create the load evaluators that you will be using for the application. If you will be evaluating server load based on the number of users connected to the server, you can use the default load evaluator. If you want to base load on a combination of CPU usage, memory usage, and page swapping, you can use the advanced load evaluator. These load evaluators are built into MetaFrame XP and cannot be adjusted. If you want to base load on a different set of load parameters, you need to follow these steps to create the load evaluator:

1. Open the CMC from the Program Menu, Citrix folder on one of your Citrix MetaFrame servers in the farm.

2. Log on to it with an administrative account that has read–write access to the farm.

3. Right-click Load Evaluators under the farm name and select New Load Evaluator.

4. Enter the name and description for the load evaluator. Try to enter a name that describes the load parameters used. If you will be setting up a load evaluator to report full load if memory usage is more than 80 percent, for instance, you might call the load evaluator memory usage < 80.

5. Add the load parameters or rules that you want to the Assigned Rules list by selecting them and clicking the Add button. Remember that you can add multiple rules to a single load evaluator. If you intend to use the IP range or scheduling load evaluator, be sure to include another load evaluator such as server user load for proper load balancing. IP range and scheduling are restrictive rules that by themselves do not load balance.

6. Highlight each load rule and change the options as needed for that rule; click OK when you are done.

You should now see the new load evaluator listed in the CMC window. The next step is to assign the load evaluator to either the servers in the load-managed pool or to the application itself. The following instructions cover how to do this:

1. Open and log on to the CMC.

2. To assign a load evaluator to a server, follow these steps:

   1. Click the Servers folder to open it.
   2. Right-click each server in the load-balanced pool and select Load Manage Server.
   3. Highlight the load evaluator you want to use for that server, and then click OK.

3. To assign a load evaluator to an application, follow these steps:

1. Click the Applications folder to open it.

2. Right-click the application you want to load balance and select Load Manage Application.

3. For each server in the load-balanced pool that you want to assign a load evaluator to, select the load evaluator, select the server and click Add, and then click Apply. This applies that application load evaluator to that server. If you want to remove a particular load evaluator, assign the <none> evaluator to the server. By default, all servers will be set to <none>.

4. Click OK when finished.

Testing, Monitoring, and Troubleshooting Load Balancing

After you have set up load balancing, you will likely want to monitor it carefully to ensure that it is working properly. If you are using only server evaluators in your load balancing, you can monitor the server load through the CMC. To view a graphical display of a servers current load, follow these steps:

1. Open and log on to the CMC.

2. Right-click the server you want to monitor under the Servers folder and select Load Manager Monitor.

A screen similar to that shown in Figure 15.7 will display. In this screen you will see the overall reported load on the top and then the effect of each rule in the load evaluator listed below.

For a more detailed view, which includes the calculated application load and server load, the best command to use is the Query Farm /App command. This command can be run from the command prompt of any server in the farm. It will produce a list of all the applications currently running on the farm, what their application load currently is, and what the server load is. Listing 15.1 is the sample output from this command.

Listing 15.1   **Sample Output from** *query_farm_/app* **Command**

Application Name	Server Name	App Load	Serv Load
WINMSD Test	GSMETA1	10000	200
WINMSD Test	GSMETA3	10000	600
WINMSD Test	GSMETA5	0	400
WINMSD Test	GSMETA6	99999	200
WINMSD Test	GSMETA4	400	400

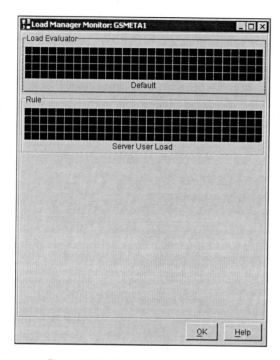

Figure 15.7   Load Manager Monitor.

When MetaFrame calculates the load of an application or server, it calculates it on a scale from 0 to 10000. Ten thousand means that the application or server is fully loaded and is not ready to accept any additional connections. A load of 0 means that there is no load on the application or server. The special load value of 99999 is used for the application load for applications to which you have not assigned a load evaluator. Table 15.1 shows some additional load values that might displayed and their meaning.

Table 15.1   **Load Values for App or Server Loads**

Load Value	Description
0–9999	These are valid reported server or application load values.
10000	This value means that the server or application is fully loaded.
99999	This value is reported by an application if you have not assigned it a load evaluator. This value will not be used in the load calculation.

Load Value	Description
20000	This is a special-purpose value that means that licensing is not set up correctly for load balancing. You will usually see this code if you have not assigned the correct or a valid product code to your MetaFrame XP servers. Find the XPe or XPa product code and assign it to the server reporting 20000, by right-clicking it in the CMC and selecting Set MetaFrame Product Code.
99990	This can indicate a serious system problem with load management, such as a corrupted local host cache file. Hopefully, you will not run into this one. If you do, try stopping and starting the IMA service or rebuilding the local host cache.
10000!	This indicates the application is disabled.

Remember that when a new user attempts to connect to a particular application, the load used for a particular server is the greater value between either the app load or server load. For example, the load used for the WINMSD Test application on GSMETA1 is 10000, not 200. However, the load used for WINMSD Test on GSMETA5 is the server load of 400, and not the app load of 0. On GSMETA6 the app load of 99999 is ignored because it indicates that no application load evaluator was assigned to this server. Instead, the server load of 200 is used.

When a user tries to connect to WINMSD Test at this point, he will be assigned to the GSMETA6 server. This is because the load is 200 and is the smallest used load of all the servers.

After you have load managed an application and you want to see which servers that users are using the application on, the best way to do this is using the CMC. In this CMC, follow these steps:

1. Open the Applications folder and browse for the load-balanced application.

2. Highlight the application.

You will see a list of the current users for the application across the server farm. Next to each user's connection name, you will see the server to which each user is connecting. If your intention is to load manage users equally across your servers, make sure that the users currently logged on to the application are split equally between the servers in the load-managed pool.

Top-Ten Application Publishing Tips

Now it's time to summarize the tips in this chapter with the top ten application publishing tips list, which follows:

1. **Name applications consistently.**   Choose a naming standard and stick to it, early in the farm setup. As your farm grows larger, naming standards become very important. Remember that an application name must be unique across your farm.

2. **Use short display names and long descriptions.**   Always use as short of a display name for an application as possible. This name should be heavily abbreviated and ideally fewer than 10 characters. For example, use Pwpt 2K rather than Microsoft Power Point 2000. In large environments you might need to use larger names to differentiate similar applications.

3. **Publish the CMC.**   Take advantage of the fact that you can publish applications by publishing the CMC and other useful administrative tools. When publishing the CMC, publish it from the data collector for the main zone.

4. **Divide your servers into application groups.**   This is a common theme throughout this book that is especially important in large environments. Dividing servers into application groupings makes load balancing applications much easier and helps better organize the farm.

5. **Use identical hardware and software configurations in each application grouping.**   Ideally you should use the same hardware across an application grouping. In addition, you should install the applications in the same folder, using the same directions. Record these directions in your application install document. If the hardware and software is the same across the application grouping, load balancing applications is much simpler.

6. **Use centralized profiles.**   Centralizing your profiles is an important step, even if you are not currently load balancing your applications. If you ever need to load balance the application in the future, you just need to add an extra server and load balance it. Otherwise, you will have to deal with centralizing the old profiles before you load balance the application.

7. **Use the Program Neighborhood Agent.** If you are using MetaFrame XP with Feature Release 1 and have an NFuse 1.6 web site, you should definitely look into using the Program Neighborhood Agent, rather than the standard Program Neighborhood. With the agent you gain much better central control over the deployment of Citrix MetaFrame applications than with Program Neighborhood. In addition, the auto-refresh feature alone makes it worth the switch. If you still intend to use Program Neighborhood alone, however, make sure that users are trained on simple procedures, such as how to refresh their application list.

8. **Reduce published application colors if not needed.** By default, published applications are set to use 256 colors. You should reduce this to 16 colors if your application does not need all 256 colors. This can significantly improve application performance over slow connections.

9. **Use application load evaluators only for special purposes.** Generally it is much easier to just use server load evaluators when load balancing your applications. Application load evaluators should be used only when you need to modify the schedule that a particular application can be run (scheduling), control the IP range that can access a particular application (IP range), or control the number of users that can use an application (application user load).

10. **Publish everything, including desktops.** As a Citrix MetaFrame administrator, try to take full advantage of the central control that application publishing provides by publishing everything. Do not use custom ICA connections for your users. If a user needs an application, publish the application. If he needs a document, publish the document. If the user must have a desktop, such as for thin client terminal users, publish the desktop instead of creating a custom ICA connection for it.

16

Dial-In and VPN Access

ONE OF THE MORE POPULAR USES FOR Terminal Server is to provide secure remote access to networked applications through either dial-up connections or a *virtual private network* (VPN). The problem with many remote control products on the market today, such as pcAnywhere, is that they put the control of network security in the hands of the users. By using a dial-up connection or VPN to access Terminal Server, however, network security is centralized at the server, and in the hands of those who have the experience and training to set it up properly.

Centralizing remote access can help eliminate the modem proliferation that occurs at many corporations as modems are installed on desktops for both dial-in and dial-out applications. Terminal Server also helps make the best use of the analog lines you have available by sharing them between remote users.

In addition, using VPNs for remote access to your Terminal Servers is a compelling solution for many corporations. Instead of having to maintain a modem bank for analog or ISDN dial-in access, with a VPN you need only a network connection to the Internet. The VPN enables a user at home to establish a secure, encrypted connection across the Internet to your network. Through this connection, the user can access any Terminal Server to which you give him access.

This chapter covers some of the many ways you can set up remote dial-in access to both Terminal Server and Citrix MetaFrame servers.

First, you will see an overview of the three main remote access options: Microsoft *Remote Access Service* (RAS), dial-in ICA, and the Microsoft implementation of a VPN. Next, you learn details of how to set up and use RAS, dial-in ICA, and VPN access for every client situation you are likely to encounter. The chapter ends with examples of some of the many types of hardware remote access solutions available.

Remote Access Solutions for MetaFrame and Terminal Server

The remote access solutions you have available depend on whether you have MetaFrame. MetaFrame supports all means of remote access supported by Terminal Server. In addition, MetaFrame offers a special type of remote access called *dial-in ICA*. The following sections describe the remote access options you have available and the advantages and disadvantages of those options.

Remote Access Service Dial-In

Microsoft RAS is one of the most commonly used remote access dial-in solutions. RAS is a service included in both Windows NT 4.0 and Windows 2000 Server. Using RAS, a remote user can dial in to either an analog, ISDN modem, or modem bank; or logon and establish a connection into the corporate network. You can access nearly any server on the network by dialing in remotely using RAS, including your Terminal Server and MetaFrame servers. Like most remote access solutions, after the remote connection has been established, you can connect to services on the network as if you were locally connected to the network.

RAS Security

Security must be carefully implemented with RAS. Although your remote users need to authenticate using their domain name and password to gain access, after they have authenticated, the users have the same level of access as a workstation connected locally to the network. This might be more access than you want to give. You might want to consider restricting their access to just a single subnet or IP address.

RAS Solutions

RAS allows for remote access from a large variety of operating systems and devices. All modern Windows platforms have the built-in capability through Dial-Up Networking to establish a connection to a Microsoft RAS server. In addition, most handhelds and even some thin client terminals can easily be set up for remote access to a RAS server. Besides Windows, you also will find that you can make dial-up connections to RAS using many other operating systems, such as Linux and Macintosh. Therefore, the universal nature of RAS makes it an excellent solution for remote access beyond just for use with Terminal Server alone.

One reason many smaller companies choose Microsoft RAS is that it is inexpensive. For environments that have only one or two Windows servers, RAS is a good solution for providing remote access. The RAS software comes with Windows NT 4.0 Server, Windows NT 4.0 Terminal Server, and Windows 2000 Server out of the box. Setting it up is relatively easy and at a minimum requires only the purchase of a single modem and a phone line connection. Also because there is a large base of RAS users and because it is a Microsoft product, support for RAS is easy to find.

RAS also can be a good solution in situations in which users need access to more than just Terminal Server. As a node on your network, your remote users can do anything that a person on the network can do. They can access hosts directly through Telnet, check their corporate email, print directly to printers on the network, and access any other type of network resource your local network users can, providing they have the correct software on their remote machines. For more restrictive environments, you could just provide remote access only to Terminal Server through RAS, and only allow access to internal services by having the user run the client software on the Terminal Server.

Suppose a network administrator wants to access the network remotely. With RAS, after the administrator establishes the connection, he is actually a node on the network. At that point, he can run any software on his desktop that he would normally run at work, including the ICA MetaFrame client, MS Terminal Server client, terminal emulation software, network administration tools, and even network monitoring software. This is a great means for an administrator to check on the status of the network or resolve problems remotely while traveling or at home.

RAS and Handhelds

In addition, many administrators and users now make extensive use of handheld devices. Nearly all business-class handhelds, such as the Compaq iPAQ and HP Jornada, can connect to the corporate network through a RAS server. By using either the Citrix MetaFrame or Terminal Services client on the handheld, you can provide remote access to nearly any Windows application running on the Terminal Server. As an administrator this means you could remotely resolve problems with a device you could carry in your pocket. For remote users, they can basically carry their corporate desktop in their pocket and be able to access all of their core applications remotely.

RAS Drawbacks

One of the big drawbacks of RAS, and any dial-in solution, is the cost of phone services. Although RAS is an ideal solution for remote access to a network while you are in the area, if your users travel out of the area frequently, they will start racking up the long-distance costs dialing in remotely to the server's modem bank. For this reason many administrators tend to use RAS for remote access to people in the area, such as a local sales force or dial-in access from employees homes. For globetrotting users, the best choice for an easy and inexpensive means of remote access is setting up a VPN.

Remote Access Devices

Very similar to Microsoft RAS, remote access devices are network devices made by other vendors dedicated to providing dial-in access to your network. After remote users have dialed in to and authenticated with a remote access device, the device connects them to the network, where they can access Terminal Server or MetaFrame as if they were locally connected.

The disadvantage of these devices, just as with RAS, is that after remote users are on your network, they also can access other devices on your network as if they were connected locally. Again you need to be careful to choose a secure solution. Many remote access devices enable you to restrict a remote user's access to a single IP address, such as that of the Terminal Server.

Another disadvantage is that the security system used for authentication is often separate from any current security system on the network, such as the Windows NT user domain database. There are ways around this, using authentication methods such as RADIUS, but keep this possible limitation in mind when looking at these types of solutions. Users will need not only a username and password to access the network, but also another username and password for the Windows NT domain. For more information on authentication methods, see the "Remote Access Authentication" section later in this chapter.

On the client side, most vendors' remote access solutions work with standard Windows Dial-Up Networking. That means that you normally do not need to install a special client on your remote Windows workstations for them to connect. Instead you just need to set up Dial-Up Networking.

Virtual Private Networks

The Internet is quickly becoming the best, least expensive, and most widely available means for remote access to corporations. However, its global, ubiquitous nature also means that so many people from so many countries have access to the Internet, and that providing remote access for your corporation through the Internet presents many security concerns. To address the need for a secure means of remote access across an unsecured network, VPN technology was created. VPN technology is a secure tunneling technology. In other words, using a VPN client your users can establish a secure, encrypted "tunnel" into your network through a VPN server.

How a VPN Works

Figure 16.1 shows a conceptual picture of how a VPN works. Establishing a VPN connection starts with installing a VPN client on your users' remote workstations, laptops, or handhelds. Depending on what vendor's VPN solution you choose, you can normally find VPN clients for most versions of Windows and other operating systems, such as Linux or Solaris.

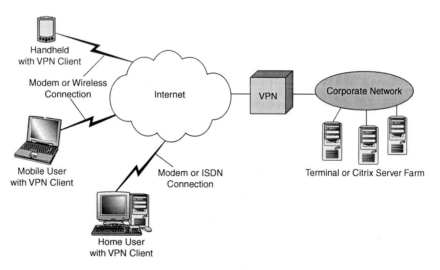

Figure 16.1 VPN for secure remote access.

The user first needs to make some type of connection to the untrusted network. In most cases this is a dial-in connection to the Internet through an Internet service provider. This is the connection that the VPN tunnel will "ride" on, so it needs to be established first.

The next step is that the user needs to run the VPN client. Normally the VPN client will ask them for their username, password, and the address of the corporate VPN server on the Internet. After a user enters this information, the client authenticates with the VPN server across the Internet, and then establishes a secure, encrypted "tunnel" between the client and the VPN server. At this point, the client is remotely connected to the corporate network in much the same way as a user would be connected to the network remotely using RAS. The difference is that all network traffic between the client and the corporate network is encrypted.

You can imagine a VPN as a secure tunnel that travels between the client and the corporate network. Any traffic destined for the corporate network gets put into this tunnel, where it is automatically encrypted and sent to the VPN server at the other end. When it reaches the VPN server, the VPN server decrypts the traffic and places it on the corporate network. Any return traffic is sent to the VPN server where it is encrypted and sent back through the tunnel to the client.

IPSec and PPTP

VPNs can be a complex technology because of the many different VPN solutions available today and the choices you can make with each solution as to how you will implement the tunnel. The first choice you need to make is to choose the protocol that you will be using for the VPN tunnel. Many different choices are available today, but the most prevalent choices are either the *IP Security* (IPSec) or *Point-to-Point Tunneling Protocol* (PPTP). Nearly all vendor VPN solutions available today implement their solution using either the IPSec or PPTP protocol, or give you the choice to use either one.

IPSec is an internationally supported protocol found in nearly every VPN solution on the market today. In an ideal world, one vendor's IPSec VPN client could connect to another vendor's IPSec VPN. In reality, however, this is not often the case. Normally during the configuration of the VPN server, you will need to choose the protocol that the server will support. If you choose IPSec, you will need to deploy that vendor's IPSec-based client to your users.

Microsoft offers IPSec in its VPN solution, but the protocol is not fully implemented according to the standard and is used only as the method of encrypting the traffic. The actual establishment of the tunnel is handled by another protocol entirely, called *Layer 2 Tunneling Protocol* (L2TP). This non-standard approach means that the Microsoft IPSec/L2TP solution is currently useful only for the establishment of a VPN tunnel between Microsoft servers. Nearly all IPSec VPN clients on the market today will not work with their IPSec/L2TP solution. Also Microsoft does not make an IPSec client for any version of its operating system. In reality, Microsoft supports only PPTP for remote access.

On the other hand, many other vendors' implementation of the IPSec protocol is closer to the standards; and in many cases, one vendor's IPSec implementation in an IPSec client that will work with another vendor's IPSec VPN server. All of these vendors offer their own IPSec-based VPN client and often offer many features in these clients that you will not find in other types of VPN clients.

PPTP can be an excellent choice for providing remote access for Windows-based clients. Microsoft makes PPTP connections possible on nearly all Windows Workstation platforms, including Windows 95, 98, Me, NT, 2000, and XP. Although you need to install a freely available patch for PPTP to work with Windows 95, every other operating system has the capability to establish a PPTP tunnel built in. PPTP of course is fully supported in the Microsoft VPN solution, which is covered in this chapter and is the protocol of choice for providing remote access for users using their VPN solution. You also will, in most cases, be able to establish a PPTP tunnel from a Windows client to any vendor that supports the PPTP protocol without having to install a special client from that vendor.

One disadvantage of using the Microsoft PPTP VPN solution, rather than other vendors' solutions, is its lack of robust client-side features commonly found in other vendor's IPSec VPN clients. When deciding on which solution you will implement in your enterprise, be sure to compare both the server and client components of the VPN solution between vendors.

Although detailed coverage of the technical details of PPTP and IPSec protocols is beyond the scope of this book, both protocols have robust encryption schemes and are excellent choices for securing traffic across un-secured networks. For more detailed information on these protocols, see *Windows 2000 Virtual Private Networking*, by Thaddeus Fortenberry (New Riders Publishing, 2001), ISBN: 1578702461.

VPNs Versus RAS for Remote Access

One of the main reasons why VPNs are becoming such a popular remote access solution is cost. You can make a connection to the Internet from most anywhere in the world and connect to your corporate network remotely. The cost of an Internet connection is often significantly cheaper than the long-distance charges incurred if users have to dial in remotely.

Suppose, for example, that you were an international company with sales representatives around the world. As the network administrator, you have been tasked with providing remote access to key business applications for traveling employees. You set up these applications on Terminal Server and then set up a VPN server to provide remote access to them across the Internet. From a business standpoint, the only recurring costs of this solution are the relatively inexpensive charges for the Internet service provider accounts that you will need to set up for these employees. Compared to the likely enormous costs of users dialing in to the corporate network with international long-distance fees, the monthly costs of providing an ISP account for employees would be relatively cheap.

Using VPNs Internally

In some cases, such as with multinational corporations, conglomerates, or highly secure organizations, you might want to treat parts of your internal network as unsecured or untrusted. In other words, using a VPN tunnel you cannot only provide secure access across the Internet, but also within an organization. Suppose, for example, that you have a special Terminal Server farm set up for highly sensitive applications, such as payroll applications. Instead of putting these servers directly on your internal network, you could put a VPN server in between the servers and your internal network. In that way, users throughout the company could access the servers through their network connection. However, they would be able to access them only by establishing a secure VPN tunnel into the Terminal Server subnet first. Figure 16.2 diagrams this solution.

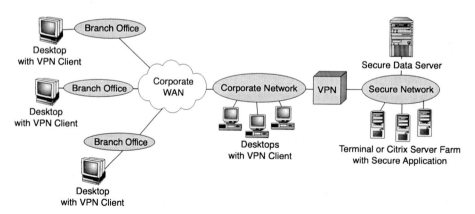

Figure 16.2   VPN for secure internal access.

Using VPNs for Branch Office Connections

An increasingly common use of VPNs is for network connections to small branch offices. With the high cost of Frame Relay and other common remote office WAN connections, many corporations are turning to the Internet as an inexpensive alternative. Instead of installing a leased line for a remote location, which points directly to the corporate network, you make a connection to the Internet for the branch office.

Across this local Internet connection, the users in the remote branch office can establish a VPN tunnel into the corporate network. This can be done by either using VPN clients on the branch office's workstations, or preferably and as shown in Figure 16.3, by using a VPN server or router with VPN software to establish the secure tunnel into the corporate network.

Often the recurring fees for a local Internet connection for a small office are significantly less than the fees for a leased Frame Relay or point-to-point WAN connection back to corporate. This is especially the case for international offices, where international WAN fees can become exorbitant very quickly. Figure 16.3 shows this VPN solution.

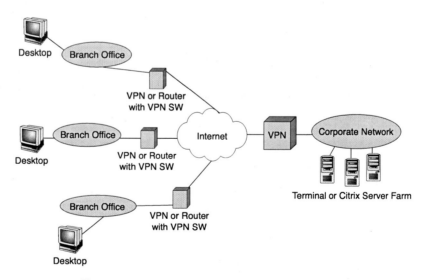

Figure 16.3 Branch office connections using VPNs.

Using VPNs for Business Partner Connections

Finally, the speed with which you can set up a VPN connection is definitely worth mention. In today's quickly changing corporate world, you are likely often tasked with the need to establish connections to new partners or other organizations very quickly. In the past, this was often done using either dial-up connections or WAN connections, such as Frame Relay. The problems with dial-up connections were lack of speed and long-distance charges. The problem with Frame Relay and other WAN solutions is both cost and speed. Frame Relay is expensive to set up and has high recurring costs. In addition, it can take several weeks, if not months, for a connection to be established. If both organizations use VPN technologies instead, however, you can quickly establish a secure connection between your organization and the other by setting up a VPN tunnel. Figure 16.4 shows this solution.

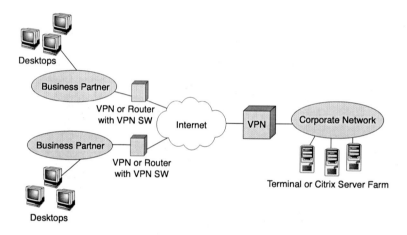

Figure 16.4   Business partner connections with VPNs.

VPN Versus a Firewall

You might have noticed in many of the diagrams that firewalls are missing. The reason for this is that you are starting to see firewall-like features in many of the VPN offerings today. Not only will you find VPN technology available in many firewall offerings, such as CheckPoint, but you also will find traditional firewall features, such as NAT, firewall policy lists, on many VPN products. In larger corporations, you may likely choose to have a separate firewall from the VPN. In small to medium-size businesses, however, a VPN might be all you need to secure your network from the Internet and also provide VPN access for remote users, business partners, and branch offices.

VPN Solutions

This chapter covers the specifics of how to set up remote access using the Microsoft VPN solution. In your quest for the best VPN solution, however, you also should consider some of the many other vendors that make VPN servers. You will find excellent VPN solutions from the following vendors and more:

- **Cisco** Cisco offers VPN technology in their core IOS software, which is available for most all of their routers. Using a Cisco router, you can establish remote access for users using the Cisco VPN client. Because of Cisco's large market share in routers, Cisco's are also an ideal solution for setting up branch office–to–corporate VPN tunnels across the Internet and for setting up secure business partner–to–business partner VPN tunnels.

- **Nortel** Nortel makes a highly regarded line of VPN servers called the *Contivity* switches. Be sure to check out their VPN solutions at www.nortel.com.

- **CheckPoint and other firewalls** Often you will find that your firewall vendor offers a VPN solution. In the case of CheckPoint, you can use your corporate CheckPoint firewall not only for secure access to the Internet, but also for secure remote access to your internal network using CheckPoint's VPN client. Like most VPN products, you can establish a secure tunnel to another corporation's or branch office's CheckPoint firewall across the Internet.

  - **Citrix Extranet** Citrix makes its own brand of VPN solution specially customized to provide secure remote access to a Citrix server farm or to any network. One thing that makes this solution appealing is the Java VPN client. This client can be run from most any operating system as long as it has a Java Virtual Machine. For more information on the Citrix solution, go to www.citrix.com.

There are plenty of other VPN solutions besides just these four. Be sure to check out periodic reviews in networking-related magazines, such as *Network Computing*. Also another good starting point is the ICSA Labs. Many vendors have the ICSA Labs put their VPN and security-related products through a rigorous set of security tests to achieve the coveted ICSA Labs Certification. For a list of devices that have achieved this certification, go to www.icsalabs.com.

Dial-In ICA Connection (MetaFrame Only)

Dial-in ICA works only with MetaFrame. Dial-in ICA enables you to put a communications board, such as a Digiboard, inside your Citrix MetaFrame server for incoming calls. You then set up MetaFrame connections to receive them. For smaller implementations, you also can use the server's built-in serial ports. For this solution to work, you will either need modems to plug into the Digiboard's serial ports or purchase a solution that has the modems built in.

All the following ICA clients can dial-in remotely to the MetaFrame server: DOS ICA, 16-bit ICA (Windows 3.1/3.11), and 32-bit ICA.

Although RAS is a good solution when you need a remote node solution in addition to remote control, dial-in ICA is a simpler solution than RAS. Establishing a RAS connection requires two steps: establishing the connection and then running the client. Dial-in ICA, on the other hand, requires only setting up the connection once.

This solution also has some strong security advantages. Instead of connecting to your network first and then connecting to your server, users can access the network only through the server. This means that network security is controllable through server security.

Dial-in ICA has been highly optimized for speed and efficiency with remote connections. It does not have the overhead of the networking protocol (TCP/IP); instead, it just uses straight ICA. This is important in bandwidth-limited, remote access solutions. Although the Dial-in ICA has been highly optimized, it is not guaranteed to be the fastest solution for your hardware setup. As always, make sure you test the different remote access solutions available to ensure that performance is adequate for your needs.

Remote Access Authentication

As part of the decision-making process of what remote access solution you will use for your environment, you also should carefully evaluate how you will provide authentication. The means of authentication for remote access solutions varies widely. What authentication options your vendor supports and how authentication is handled is very important for ensuring both the security and scalability of your remote access solution. Although most means of authentication are secure, you will find that many means of authentication do not scale well for large enterprise deployments. The following sections cover the most common means available today.

Local Authentication

Most remote access solutions offer some type of local user database that can be authenticated against. For example, one option you can choose for authentication with the Nortel VPN Contivity switch is to use a local LDAP database. Although other options are available, if you choose to use the local database, that means that you need to manually set up the user IDs on that VPN switch.

The advantage of this approach is simplicity. You just use the tools provided by the vendor to create the accounts on the local device. Remote users authenticate against this local account database using a username and password.

The biggest disadvantage of this solution is scalability. Because the accounts reside in a single remote access device, if you need to scale your remote access solution using multiple remote access servers or VPNs, you will have to now centralize your authentication and reset all your current users' passwords.

Generally, local authentication is a good choice for small to medium-size businesses that do not anticipate significant growth in remote access in the future.

Windows Domain Authentication

For large Microsoft shops, having remote access devices that support Windows Domain Authentication makes administration much easier. In most cases, users will be able to log on to the network remotely using the same name and password that they use when at work. Microsoft Remote Access Service is a commonly used solution that uses Windows Domain Authentication as its primary means of authentication.

You will find that some other devices made by different vendors also will support Windows Domain Authentication.

The disadvantage of Windows Domain Authentication is that it also can lead to vulnerabilities. You might not want users to be able to use the same password that they use at work to log on remotely. If you are considering using Windows Domain Authentication for remote access, be sure to implement a written security policy before the implementation. As part of this policy, you should ensure that passwords expire after a given number of days and are required to be of a certain length. If you do not do this before the implementation of the remote access solution, you can open up easy access for hackers into your network; hackers can use readily available tools to quickly crack simple passwords.

RADIUS

RADIUS is a commonly deployed means for authentication for large enterprises and Internet or application service providers. With a RADIUS solution, you set up a collection of one or more central RADIUS servers that share a common account database. When users attempt to connect to your remote access solution, the device redirects the authentication request to the central RADIUS servers. After the user has been authenticated, the device will check what the user is authorized to do and allow them authorized access to the network.

The advantage of a RADIUS solution is scalability. Not only can you have multiple RADIUS servers that handle authentication, located at different points in your network, but you also can deploy multiple remote access devices that use these RADIUS servers for authentication. For ISPs, this is an excellent solution because they generally have access points throughout the country, yet need to be able to authenticate users against a single, replicated account database. By replicating an account database across multiple RADIUS servers, ISPs and other companies that use RADIUS, can build significant redundancy and reliability into their authentication solution.

RADIUS services are freely available in Windows 2000 Server and can be used for centralized authentication for either a Microsoft VPN or Remote Access Service solution. This is an excellent way to provide a high-level of scalability to your Microsoft remote access solution. As with IPSec, however, the Microsoft implementation of RADIUS is proprietary enough that you might have difficulty making it work with other vendors' remote access solution. Be sure to check with your remote access vendor as to what RADIUS solutions they support for authentication.

Access Cards and Digital Keys

One of the big disadvantages of all the solutions covered so far is that they all provide access through a username and password. In many cases, this can be a huge vulnerability, because all a potential hacker needs are the username and password of only one individual in the corporation, and he has access to the entire network remotely. Using social engineering or password cracking, many advanced hackers have little difficulty in purloining at least one user's password and user ID. Also users, even when told not to, often let others know their password or come across the passwords of other users. If such a user leaves the company and you lock out her account, she can still gain access using other users' passwords that she learned while she was there. This makes it not only difficult to lock users out, but also difficult to determine the source of an attack, because the potential hacker is impersonating another user.

For this reason, many large corporations or businesses where security is of high concern have turned toward access cards and digital keys as a solution for remote access. If you use one of these solutions, a user must have the card or digital key in his possession to access the company's network remotely. In most cases, the user also must remember a short pin or password in addition to using the card or key to gain access.

One commonly used solution like this is RSA's SecurID cards and keys. These specially designed cards and keys have a small LCD display that displays a number that changes periodically. For a user to gain remote access to a VPN that uses SecurID for authentication, the user must enter the number currently displayed on the card or key and then enter a small pin or password. The VPN then checks that this number is a valid number for that user against an internal RSA SecurID access server. Locking out a user is as simple as disabling his SecurID account. After disablement, his key will no longer work.

If a user loses her key or card, a potential hacker would still have to know the pin or password to gain access. If you choose to use this type of solution, however, users must be informed to report lost or stolen keys or cards immediately, so that they can be disabled. For more information on RSA's authentication solutions, go to www.securid.com.

Besides the authentication solutions mentioned, several other means of authentication are available depending on what your remote access device vendor supports. Be sure to contact the vendor to go over the advantages and disadvantages of all the means of authentication they support before purchasing the device.

Author's Note

One other means of remote access not mentioned in this chapter is just poking a hole in the firewall to your Citrix servers and using ICA client encryption to help provide a secure connection. Although you need to be very careful with security if you choose this approach, this is a simple approach that many companies choose to use. You do not need to worry about setting up a VPN client for your remote users; they only need an Internet connection and a Citrix client. This is also a choice commonly used with NFuse technology. For more information on how to do this and what ports you need to open see Chapter 17, "Firewalls and SSL Relay."

Installing and Using Microsoft RAS on Windows NT 4.0 Server

If you have Windows NT 4.0 servers in your environment that you are not intending to move anytime soon to Windows 2000, they can still make for excellent remote access servers using Microsoft RAS. You can install RAS on either Microsoft Windows NT 4.0 Server or Microsoft Windows NT 4.0

Terminal Server. The steps are the same. Realize, however, that Windows NT 4.0 Server will support only domain or local authentication with RAS, and not more advanced means of authentication, such as RADIUS, that are available in Windows 2000.

Installing the RAS Service

On Windows NT 4.0 Server, RAS can be installed either during the initial install of the server or later through the Network Control Panel. RAS installs as a standard network service in the Network Control Panel. Before installing RAS, make sure all the communications devices that you want to use are installed and working.

Most communications adapters, such as Digiboards, install as network adapters and create COM ports in the system for each new communication port they add. To install an eight-port Digiboard, for example, you would normally get the network adapter driver for the board from Digi. After you install this, it adds eight additional COM ports to your system. These COM ports can be configured through RAS to send and receive calls.

After you have installed your communications equipment, including all modems, installing RAS is a breeze. To install RAS on the server, follow these steps:

1. Install the Remote Access Service by selecting Network from Control Panel. From the Network window, select the Services tab and click Add. Choose Remote Access Service from the list in the Select Network Service window.

2. The RAS installation process lists any modems already defined on the system in the Add RAS Device window. Select the device you want to add for RAS from the drop-down list and click OK. If no modems are installed, you are asked whether you want to launch the Install New Modem Wizard. Modems are installed into the system using the standard Windows NT 4.0 TAPI method for installing modems into the system (by selecting Modems in Control Panel). Remember that you need to have first installed your communications card and drivers. If not, the COM ports will not be there to assign the modems to.

3. After you have selected your first modem for RAS, you are taken to the Remote Access Setup window, where all the modems currently enabled for RAS access are listed. At this point, you have the options of adding more modems for RAS by clicking Add; configuring the modems for dial out, dial in, or both dial out and dial in, by clicking Configure; or setting the network parameters for your RAS connections, by clicking Network. After you have finished, click OK.

4. If you have not set the network configuration parameters for your RAS connection by clicking Network, you are prompted for the parameters for each protocol as it is bound to RAS. After RAS has finished installing, you return to the Services tab in the Network window.

5. Click Close from the Network window and restart the system when prompted.

By default, no users have been granted access to dial in. Although the RAS service might be started if users tried to dial in, they would be given a message that they do not have dial-in permission. See the "Administering RAS" section for instructions on how to enable dial in.

Author's Note

For your reference, Table 16.1 shows the hexadecimal port values and IRQ values. This information can still be useful in some situations when configuring COM ports on Intel-based systems.

Table 16.1 **Common I/O Ports and IRQs**

COM Port	Base I/O Port	IRQ
COM1	3F8	4
COM2	2F8	3
COM3	3E8	4
COM4	2E8	3

Configuring the RAS Network Parameters

In step 3 of the RAS installation process, you had the option of configuring the network parameters. Although most steps of the RAS installation process are simple, configuring the network parameters correctly can be challenging. In this section, you learn how to set these parameters correctly for your network.

To configure the network parameters, click Network from the Remote Access Setup window in step 3. You can get back to the Remote Access Setup window after RAS has been installed by doing the following:

1. Select Network from Control Panel.

2. Click the Services tab.

3. Highlight Remote Access Service and click Properties.

From the Network Configuration window (select Network from the Remote Access Setup window), you have several options that affect how the remote clients will be communicating with the server. These options apply for all the modems that you have configured in the Remote Access Setup window.

You can use three protocols across a RAS communication line: IPX/SPX, TCP/IP, and NetBEUI. TCP/IP is by far the most commonly used protocol today for remote access and is the one you will learn about in this chapter.

By clicking the Configure button, you can configure each protocol's RAS settings independently. All protocols enable you to specify whether the remote client has access to just this server or the entire network. This is an important security setting. By default, the remote client will have access to the entire network, including your Terminal Server. This means she could directly log on to any host on your network, which can be a big security risk.

It is recommended to always set up RAS connections for access to the Terminal Server only. From a Terminal Server session, the user can still access hosts on the network, but will have to log on to the Terminal Server first. This makes your Terminal Server the first line of security.

Configuring TCP/IP

To configure TCP/IP options, click the Configure button next to TCP/IP in the Network Configuration window. The RAS Server TCP/IP window will appear.

With TCP/IP, addresses are assigned to dial-in clients in one of three ways: through DHCP, through an address range, or manual assignment. By default DHCP is used, which of course requires a DHCP server on the network. If you do not have a DHCP server, your clients do not receive any IP address when they log on. Although they do not have IP addresses, your clients can still access the Terminal Server using IP because the server knows which connection the client is coming in from.

For better control of IP addresses, you can assign an address range by selecting the Use Static Address Pool option button and assigning a range.

Your clients also can manually assign their own IP addresses in their Dial-Up Networking window. Because this option puts the control of the IP addresses in the hands of the clients, this could easily cause you security problems. Suppose a client accidentally uses an IP address that conflicts with one of your mission-critical servers; this mishap could cause communication problems with that server. In general, it is best to uncheck the Allow Remote Clients to Request a Predetermined IP Address box and to assign addresses solely through DHCP or an address range.

Administering RAS

The main tool for administering your RAS server is the Remote Access Admin tool. Located under the Administrative Tools group, this tool enable you to perform the following tasks:

- Start, stop, and pause the RAS service
- Set dial-in and callback options for users
- View port statistics
- View current users and send messages

In the following sections, you learn about each of these capabilities in detail.

Starting and Stopping the RAS Service

By default, the RAS service is set to automatically start when you start up your server. If you want RAS enabled only for occasional remote access use, you can set the service to manually start by going into Control Panel and selecting Services. Highlight Remote Access Service and select the Startup button. Change the Startup type to Manual. The next time you reboot your server, you must start the Remote Access Service manually. The Remote Access Service can be started, stopped, and paused using the Remote Access Admin tool. These options are all under the Server menu on the main window.

Setting Dial-In Permissions and Callback Options

By default, no user has dial-in permission. Dial-in permission can be granted in one of two places: either in the Remote Access Admin tool or in User Manager. In the Remote Access Admin tool, select Permissions from the Users menu. In the Remote Access Permissions window that appears, you can enable dial-in access for anyone in the domain.

Another important RAS feature is callback, which is good for both security and for lowering the telephone bills of users who have to dial in remotely from long-distance sites. You will find the callback settings in the Remote Access Permissions window along with the ability to grant dial-in access. There are two types of callback options:

- **Set by Caller**   If you set the callback options to Set by Caller, when users dial in they receive a dialog box asking for their callback number. After a user enters the number, the server hangs up the connection and calls the user back. Meanwhile, the user's RAS client goes into auto-answer mode to receive the incoming call from the server.

- **Preset** By defining a preset number, the RAS server automatically breaks the connection when the user first attaches and then calls back the preset number. This offers the highest level of security, but allows the user to call in from a single location only.

Checking Port Status

You can get a lot of good information about the connection by selecting Communications Ports from the Server menu, highlighting the port of interest, and clicking Port Status. The error counters in the Port Status window that appears in the management tool can be useful for determining the connection quality. In addition, the compression status and bytes counters can be useful for quick performance or bandwidth usage checks.

Viewing Current Users and Sending Messages

To view the users currently on the server, select Active Users from the Users menu. In the Remote Access Users window that appears, you will see a list of all active users along with the time that they connected to the system. From this window, you also can send messages to individual users. Note that this feature does not work for all types of clients; you are better off using the Send Message feature in the Terminal Server Administration tool.

Installing and Using Microsoft RAS and VPN Solutions for Windows 2000

With Windows 2000, Microsoft has added a new service called the *Routing and Remote Access Service* (RRAS). This versatile built-in product provides the following features:

- **Remote Dial-In Access Services** RRAS is the equivalent of Windows NT 4.0 RAS when it comes to remote dial-in access.

- **IPSec and PPTP virtual private networking** Using RRAS, you also can set up your Windows 2000 server as either an IPSec or PPTP VPN server, which can be accessed remotely from most Windows clients using the built-in PPTP client or can establish a secure VPN tunnel to a remote network through another RRAS server acting as either a PPTP or IPSec VPN server.

- **Network routing** By putting multiple NIC cards in your server and using RRAS, you can make your Windows 2000 server into a network router.

In this section, you learn how to set up your Windows 2000 server as either a RAS or VPN server.

Before you learn the details of installing the service, however, you need to decide which server to set up. For smaller environments, you might want to run RRAS on your Windows 2000 Terminal Server. This is a good solution to save costs, and RRAS will work fine in conjunction with Terminal Services on the same environment. However, this solution does not scale very well and will tax your Terminal Server with the extra processing and memory requirements necessary to support remote users. Therefore, for larger deployments you should set up one or more dedicated Windows 2000 RRAS servers that handle only remote access for the corporation.

RRAS in Windows NT 4.0

RRAS is freely available from Microsoft for Windows NT 4.0. Although it is not built into Windows NT 4.0 Server, you can download it from the Microsoft web site. The setup of RRAS for Windows NT 4.0 Server is much the same as for Windows 2000 and provides a similar interface and set of features. If you are interested in using one of your existing Windows NT 4.0 servers to provide remote access, rather than a Windows 2000 server, download RRAS from www.microsoft.com/NTServer/nts/downloads/winfeatures/rras/rrasdown.asp and review the concepts covered in this section.

Make sure that after you download and install RRAS, that you reinstall the latest service pack for Windows NT 4.0. There have been significant enhancements and bug-fixes to RRAS in later service packs.

Realize that there is a gap in features between RRAS for Windows NT 4.0 and that included in Windows 2000. For example, RRAS for Windows NT 4.0 does not support branch office–to–branch office-type VPN connections, only remote client connections using PPTP. For a comprehensive list of features available in Windows 2000 RRAS and a comparison to those available in RRAS for Windows NT 4.0, see the document at www.microsoft.com/ntserver/techresources/commnet/RRAS/rras.asp.

Enabling and Configuring Routing and Remote Access for Dial-In Access

The Routing and Remote Access Service is installed by default on every Windows 2000 server, but the service is disabled. To enable the service and set up routing and remote access, you need to use the Routing and Remote Access Administrative tool, which is located in the Program menu, Administrative folders. Using this tool, you can enable the service and set up dial-in access to your Windows 2000 network.

Planning Address Assignment

Before setting up RRAS, you should decide how you want to handle address assignment for remote users. Normally most administrators choose to handle address assignment using DHCP. For this to work, you must have a DHCP server on your internal network. Be careful with this approach that you have enough DHCP addresses to handle all the remote users.

For this reason and reasons of security, for large remote access deployments it is highly recommended to put your RRAS servers on a separate subnet. This subnet would be dedicated for remote access use. On this subnet, put a DHCP server or enable DHCP forwarding or services on the router to the subnet. When remote users connect to the RRAS server, they would obtain their IP address from this DHCP server. In this way you can dedicate all of your DHCP addresses for remote access use.

If you instead choose to put the RRAS servers on the same network as your users, both the local and remote users will have to share the same pool of addresses. If you have a lot of remote users and a lot of internal users, you could easily run out of addresses to assign.

By separating RRAS to a separate subnet, you can better control access from that subnet to your internal network. You could place blocking rules or firewall services on the router between that subnet and the internal network to control which devices remote users have access to and to be able to log their access.

Installing the Modems

Before you instal and set up the RRAS service, you should install your modems. Installing modems on Windows 2000 is very easy and a process you are probably already familiar with. Basically, all you need to do is plug the modem into the COM port or install the communications card on Windows 2000 and either reboot the server or select Add/Remove Hardware in Control Panel. Windows 2000 will normally auto-detect the hardware and install the correct drivers. In some cases you might need to manually install the drivers. The procedures for this vary from manufacturer to manufacturer, so you are best off referring to the manufacturer-provided instructions.

When you are finished, you should see the modem listed in Control Panel, Phone and Modem Options under the Modems tab. Make sure to test the modem to make sure both the modem and phone line are working properly.

Using ISDN

ISDN is becoming a frequently used option for remote access for telecommuters and others who need high-speed digital remote access. ISDN modems are fully supported on Windows 2000 and can be used just like an analog modem for providing remote access through RRAS.

With an ISDN solution, you will need to order an ISDN line for your remote users and one for your main office. Normally, a remote user will use a standard BRI ISDN line, which provides two 64Kbps digital communication channels on a single connection. This connection plugs directly into the ISDN modem from the wall jack. After you have attached the ISDN modem to your computer's serial port, connected the ISDN line, and entered what are referred to as the SPID numbers into your modem using the ISDN modem's configuration tool, you should be ready to go. At this point, the ISDN modem will behave just like any other modem. You can use Dial-Up Networking to establish a connection to your central RAS server. Just like a standard analog modem, you will need to enter the phone number for your central ISDN line into the Dial-Up Networking configuration before it will be able to establish a remote connection. Depending on your configuration, you will normally be able to establish either a 64Kbps connection or a bonded 128Kbps connection to the central RRAS server across the line. Contact your local telephone service provider for more information on their ISDN solutions.

On your RRAS server, you can install an ISDN modem with a single BRI line, if you need to provide only one or two 64Kbps connections at a time. If you need to provide additional connections, you can either install multiple ISDN lines and modems or purchase a PRI line and a PRI ISDN card for your RRAS server that supports it. A PRI line can handle up to 24 simultaneous 64Kbps remote connections into the RRAS server.

Installing the Service

The following instructions guide you through the installation of RRAS for remote dial in:

1. Open the RRAS Administrative tool from the Program menu, Administrative Tools folder on your Windows 2000 server.

2. From the RRAS window that appears, right-click your local server name and select Configure and Enable Routing and Remote Access. The Routing and Remote Access Setup Wizard will appear. Click Next at the intro screen.

3. Select Remote Access Server from the Common Configurations screen and click Next.

4. Verify that TCP/IP is listed in the Protocols screen and click Next. You need to have TCP/IP installed on your server for it to appear in this list.

5. From the Network Selection screen, select the network card with which the dial-in users will connect to your network. If you have a server with multiple NICs, choose the "inside" NIC. This NIC should be assigned a static address and not assigned an address through DHCP.

6. From the IP Address screen, select either Automatically, to use the DHCP server on the network for address assignment; or select From a Specified Range of Addresses, to manually assign a range of addresses that will be assigned to remote users as they dial in and connect to the RRAS server. Then click Next. Either way, remote users must be given a valid address on your internal network to be able to access internal network services.

7. From the RADIUS Server Selection screen, select whether you will be using a RADIUS server for authentication, and then click Next and then Finish. If you select Yes, on the next screen you will need to enter the address for the primary and alternate RADIUS server on the internal network, along with the shared secret key used to establish a secure encrypted tunnel to the RADIUS server for secure authentication.

At this point RRAS will be enabled and started. You will be brought back to the Routing and Remote Access Administrative tool main screen.

At this point, your server is ready to receive connections. When remote users attempt to dial your server using Dial-Up Networking, the server will answer the call and assign the user an IP address on your network. It will then attempt to authenticate the user using standard Windows Domain Authentication on the network. Once authenticated, the RRAS server will check in the user's properties whether he has been enabled for remote access. This is a setting that can be set with either User Manager for a Windows NT 4.0 or Active Directory Users and Computers for Windows 2000. As long as the user has been enabled for dial-in access, he will be able to log on. Realize, however, that this must be manually set for each user, because the default option for both Windows NT 4.0 and 2000 is that remote dial-in access is disabled.

Windows 2000 RAS Group Policies

Windows 2000 comes with a robust set of remote access policies that you can set using the Routing and Remote Access Administrative tool. By default the only policy that is set is that users must be enabled for dial-in access to connect through the RAS server. However, you will find a multitude of other policies that you can create to control remote access by right-clicking Remote Access Policies in the RRAS Administrative tool and selecting New Remote Access Policy. From the wizard that appears, you will be able to either restrict or grant access by the following parameters and many more:

- **Windows Group Memberships**   Using this policy, you can either grant access or restrict access for certain Windows groups. You also can use this policy in combination with a profile to control RRAS session parameters for a particular user. See the information that follows on what can be set through profiles.
- **Time Restrictions**   Using this policy, you can restrict the time of day that users can access the network remotely.
- **Dial-In Phone Number**   If your system supports the passing of call-in information via caller ID, you can take action based on the number of the phone with which user dialed in to the RRAS server.

After you have set the particular policy that users must match, you also can configure a profile that changes RRAS parameters for those users. You can use profiles to control such RRAS parameters as the following:

- Level of encryption
- Session idle timeouts
- IP filters for filtering access to certain networks
- Multilink bandwidth adjustment
- Authentication methods

Although full coverage of remote access policies and profiles is beyond the scope of this book, you can find out plenty of information on them in the online help file or by referring to *Windows 2000 Routing and Remote Access Service*, by Kackie Charles (New Riders Publishing, 2000), ISBN: 0735709513.

Enabling and Configuring RRAS for VPN Access

The process for enabling and configuring RRAS for VPN access is similar in many ways to that of configuring it for dial-in access. You still need to use the Routing and Remote Access Administrative tool; the process starts by right-clicking the server and selecting Configure and Enable Routing and Remote Access. However, there are a couple of significant differences. In this section, you will learn exactly how to set it up for your environment.

Setting Up the Server for VPN Access

You have many different options for setting up your VPN server, but the most common method is to just install two network cards. Plug one network card into the unsecured or untrusted network; this will be referred to as the *public network side* of the server. Plug the other network card into the secure or trusted network; this will be referred to as the *private network side* of the server. Make sure to assign a static IP address for both network cards on their respective networks.

If you are trying to provide remote access through the Internet, the public NIC card would be plugged into your Internet subnet and be assigned a public IP address. For a client to make a VPN connection to this IP address, it must be able to ping the address. You can check this by just dialing up to your ISP and trying to ping the IP address of the public NIC card. As long as you connected it properly and assigned a public IP address, you should receive a response to your ping.

For better security, it is highly recommended to put your RRAS servers behind your firewall. Many corporations create a special secure, but publicly accessible network called the *demilitarized zone* (DMZ). The DMZ is a separate subnet than your internal network, but is attached to one of the NIC cards in the firewall. Figure 16.5 shows a diagram of this configuration. To set up this more secure remote access configuration, follow these steps:

1. Install your RRAS server with its public NIC card plugged into the DMZ network segment (see Figure 16.5).

2. Plug the private NIC card into your internal network (Option 1 in Figure 16.5) or, for the highest level of security, into a dedicated RRAS remote access subnet with a DHCP server (Option 2 in Figure 16.5) in it that has another firewall between it and the internal network.

3. Open the appropriate security ports on your firewall to provide access through the firewall to the RRAS server for VPN tunneling.

For this solution to work properly, you need to ensure that devices on your DMZ use public IP addresses and not private IP addresses. Using Network Address Translation on your firewall to translate the public to private address for your VPN can cause issues with many VPN protocols, especially IPSec.

To test whether your configuration is set up properly, try pinging the public IP address of your RRAS server from a client. As long as you have pings (ICMP) enabled on the firewall to the RRAS server, you should receive a response.

The ports you need to open up to your RRAS server depend on which protocol you will be using. Table 16.2 lists the ports that you need to open. Normally you would need to open only the ports for either IPSec or PPTP to the outside world for remote access to the RRAS server. If your RRAS server uses RADIUS for authentication, however, you might need to open the RADIUS ports on any device between your RRAS server's internal NIC card and the internal network.

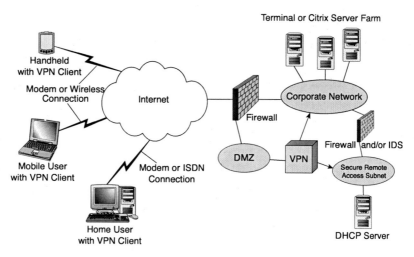

Figure 16.5 Choosing the VPN setup.

Table 16.2 VPN-Related Ports

Protocols Used	Ports That Need to Be Opened in the Firewall to and from your RRAS server
IPSec	TCP 50, TCP 51, UDP 500, UDP 1701 (L2TP), TCP 88 (only if domain controllers need to talk across link)
PPTP	UDP 1723 (PPTP), UDP 1701 (L2TP)
RADIUS	UDP 1812, UDP 1813, UDP 1645, UDP 1646

Option 1 or Option 2 in Figure 16.5?

Whether you should choose Option 1 or Option 2 in step 2 depends a lot on the security features of your VPN and what you need for your corporate network. If you choose Option 1, to plug the internal card of the VPN directly into the internal network, you are relying on the security features of the VPN to protect your network. If a hacker is able to obtain or crack a VPN user ID and password, for instance, the hacker will have full access to the internal network through the VPN. If the VPN does not have significant security logging capabilities, you might never be able to prove that an attack occurred. However, many VPNs do include firewall-like features. Therefore, you will likely be able to limit VPN users' access to particular internal networks or devices.

Choosing Option 2, plugging the internal card of the VPN into a secure remote access network, is highly recommended for large corporations or where security is of the greatest concern. The advantage of this approach is that even if a hacker is able to get into the VPN, the hacker still has to go through a firewall to get access to the internal network. This means that not only can you block the hacker's access with the firewall policies, but you also can log all access to internal resources.

Many vendors also offer *intrusion detection systems* (IDS) that can be added onto their firewall product. These systems watch network traffic for suspicious traffic patterns and can be set to alert an administrator. For this reason, it is recommended to put IDS software or an IDS device on the remote access network, so that it can watch remote users' access for suspicious traffic patterns. If a hacker gains access through the VPN, for instance, one of the first things the hacker will likely do is to do port scans on internal devices to check for vulnerabilities. An IDS system will alert on this type of scan. Refer to your firewall vendor or local security specialists for more information on this type of solution.

Enabling RRAS and VPN Services

To install RRAS for remote VPN access, follow these steps:

1. Open the RRAS Administrative tool from the Program menu, Administrative Tools folder on your Windows 2000 server.

2. From the RRAS window that appears, right-click your local server name and select Configure and Enable Routing and Remote Access. The Routing and Remote Access Setup Wizard will appear. Click Next at the intro screen.

3. Select Virtual Private Network Server from the Common Configurations screen and click Next.

4. Verify that TCP/IP is listed in the Protocols screen and click Next. You need to have TCP/IP installed on your server for it to appear in this list.

5. From the Internet Connection screen, select the network card in the list that is attached to the public network and has a public IP address assigned to it.

6. From the IP Address screen, select either Automatically, to use the DHCP server on the network for address assignment; or select from a specified range of addresses, to manually assign a range of addresses that will be assigned to remote users as they dial in and connect to the RRAS server. Then click Next. Either way, remote users must be given a valid address on your internal network to be able to access internal network services.

7. From the RADIUS Server Selection screen, select whether you will be using a RADIUS server for authentication and then click Next and then Finish. If you select Yes, on the next screen you will need to enter the address for the primary and alternate RADIUS server on the internal network, along with the shared secret key used to establish a secure encrypted tunnel to the RADIUS server for secure authentication.

At this point the RRAS will be enabled and started. By default, 128 virtual PPTP WAN ports and 128 virtual L2TP WAN ports will be created. You can view these ports by clicking the Ports folder in the main menu on the left of the RRAS administrative tool. These "virtual" ports are the ports with which your remote VPN clients or servers will establish connection. Because there are 128 default PPTP and L2TP virtual ports available, you can make up to 128 PPTP and 128 L2TP simultaneous connections to this server. If you want to change the number of ports available for a particular protocol, follow these steps:

1. Right-click ports and select Properties.

2. Select either WAN Mini-port (PPTP) or WAN Mini-port (L2TP), and then click the Configure button.

3. Change the maximum ports to the number that you need. If you want to disable this protocol completely for connections, change the value to 0.

At this point, your server is ready for remote PPTP and/or L2TP connections to the public interface. To test the server, just set up the PPTP client on a workstation on the public network. Enter the IP address of the RRAS server into the Microsoft PPTP configuration and then enter your username and password. The remote workstation should establish a connection, log on to the server, and assign itself an address on the local network. You should then be able to easily access devices on the local network.

Using WINS and DNS Effectively

For remote access to work correctly, you need to ensure that your DHCP server is set up to not only provide an IP address for your remote users, but also a WINS and DNS server if they need to access internal devices by name.

Also for ease of remote access, you might want to make a DNS entry for your RRAS server on your external DNS. That way remote PPTP clients only have to remember the DNS address for the server and not the more difficult-to-remember IP address.

Troubleshooting RAS and VPN Connections

RAS has been around for a long time and has become increasingly reliable over the years. The most difficult part of setting up RAS is the initial installation. After RAS is set up and working, you can count on long and reliable service. If you are having problems setting up RAS dial-in access, perform the following checks:

- **Make sure RAS dial-in permission is enabled.** This permission is commonly overlooked because it is disabled by default for all users. Users normally get an error message saying that they do not have dial-in permission. Just enable the permission in either User Manager or Active Directory Users and Computers.

- **Try another modem type such as one of the standard types.** Sometimes you find yourself in a situation in which RAS fails during connection with no plausible cause. You might want to try another modem type or a slower speed modem to see whether you can connect it.

- **Try to access the modem with HyperTerminal.** One good test to ensure your modem is communicating properly is to attach to it with HyperTerminal. First, you must stop the RAS service by going into the Remote Access Admin tool and selecting Stop Remote Access Service from the Server menu. Next bring up HyperTerminal, create a test connection, and attach to the COM port of your modem. Click Cancel when it tries to dial, so that you can get to the communications window. Type **at** and press Return. This is the standard Hayes Attention command. With most modems, you should see your characters echoed back from the modem and the modem should respond OK. If you have an external modem, you also can watch the send and receive data lights. They should blink rapidly as you type characters to the modem. If none of these are the case, double-check that your COM port settings are correct and the modem is cabled properly. Until you can get to the point where you can communicate with your modem, RAS will not work at all.

- **Make sure DTR is held high (on) and the modem is in Autoanswer mode.** With most modems, you need DTR held high and the modem to be in Autoanswer mode before it will answer the line. If you have a situation in which you dial, but the modem never answers, check to ensure that this is the case. You also might try a different modem type. For more information on how to set DTR high and put your modem in Autoanswer mode, refer to your modem manufacturer.

In addition to these basic troubleshooting steps, you also can take advantage of RAS and RRAS logging features.

Windows NT 4.0 RAS Logging

If you are using RAS on Windows NT 4.0 Server, the following instructions will guide you through enabling logging. The first type of log you can enable is the DEVICE.LOG. This log, when enabled, keeps track of communications between the server and the modems. You can review this file to see whether there are any problems in the modem initialization strings. To enable logging to the DEVICE.LOG file, you need to set the following Registry entry to 1:

```
HKEY_LOCAL_MACHINE\SYSTEM\CurrentControlSet\Services\RASMan Â\Parameters\
Logging
```

If the `Logging` value does not exist, you must add it (select Edit, Add Value in the REGEDT32). It is type REG_WORD and string value 1. After the `Logging` value has been added, stop and restart the RAS service by using the Remote Access Admin tool.

The second troubleshooting method is using the PPP.LOG file. This file keeps track of the PPP negotiation commands that occur during the establishment of a connection into RAS. To enable PPP logging, set the following Registry entry to 1:

```
HKEY_LOCAL_MACHINE\SYSTEM\CurrentControlSet\Services\RASMan\PPP\Logging
```

As with the DEVICE.LOG Registry entry, if the `Logging` value does not exist you need to add it. After you stop and restart the RAS service, the log should be enabled.

Windows 2000 RRAS Logging

Enabling logging in Windows 2000 is significantly easier than in Windows NT 4.0. Logging can be completely controlled through the Routing and Remote Access Administrative tool. To enable logging, follow these steps:

1. Open the Routing and Remote Access Administrative tool from the Program menu, Administrative Tools folder.
2. Open the Remote Access Logging folder.
3. Right-click the local file and select Properties.
4. From the Local File Properties window, select to enable one or more of the following logging options: Authentication Logging, Accounting Logging, or Periodic Status Logging.
5. If you want to change the log filename, location, or format, click the Local File tab and change the appropriate parameters.

Setting Up Windows Clients for Remote Dial-In Access

The following sections provide instruction for setting up a connection to a dial-in connection to a Windows RAS server from various versions of Windows.

Dialing In to a Terminal Server with RAS Using Windows 95/98/Me

Both Windows 95/98/Me and Windows NT 4.0 use Dial-Up Networking to establish a PPP connection with RAS. The procedure to set up a Dial-Up Networking connection varies between the two, but the general idea is the same. After the connection has been established, the Windows 95/98/Me or NT 4.0 client can use NetBEUI, IPX/SPX, or TCP/IP to communicate with the remote Terminal Server. Both the Terminal Server client and the Citrix ICA client can communicate with the remote Terminal Server across the established RAS connection.

Setting up a Dial-Up Networking connection with Windows 95/98/Me is relatively easy. Here is how:

1. Open the Dial-Up Networking Control Panel by going to Accessories and selecting Dial-Up Networking. If Dial-Up Networking has not been installed, add it by selecting Add/Remove Programs, Windows Setup from Control Panel, Dial-Up Networking under the Communications component.

2. In the Dial-Up Networking window, select Make New Connection. When the Make New Connection window appears, define the name of the new connection and select the modem you want to use. Click Next.

3. In the Telephone Setup screen, enter the telephone number and area code for the Terminal Server. Click Next one more time, verify the information, and click Finish to create the Dial-Up Networking entry.

Although Dial-Up Networking has several parameters that you can change, the default parameters are really all that you need to connect to a RAS server. The IP address, default gateway, DNS servers, and WINS entries are all normally assigned automatically by the RAS server after you are connected.

Before establishing the call, right-click the connection entry in the Dial-Up Networking window and select Properties. In the Properties window for the connection, select the Server Types tab. Under this tab, ensure that only the protocols you need to communicate with the Terminal Server are selected. Also make sure that the server type selected is PPP. RAS uses PPP for communication. If you will be using TCP/IP and you want to manually assign your IP address, DNS, or WINS entries, you can click the TCP/IP Settings button in this window. You are taken to a window where you have the option to manually enter these parameters. By default, the system is set to learn the parameters from the RAS server.

To establish the connection, double-click the new Dial-Up Networking entry. Enter your username and password for the Terminal Server domain and click Connect. After the connection has been established, you can start either the Citrix ICA or the Terminal Services RDP client to attach to your server.

Dialing In to RAS Using Windows NT 4.0

The procedure for setting up a Dial-Up Networking connection with Windows NT 4.0 is similar to setting up one under Windows 95. The main difference is that Dial-Up Networking is installed as part of RAS on the Windows NT workstation. For the initial part of the installation, follow the earlier instructions in the "Dialing In to a Terminal Server with RAS Using Windows 95/98/Me" section; the steps used for setting up RAS on the server are the same as on the workstation.

Be careful, however, when you are adding modems in the Remote Access Setup window; make sure to enable them for dial-out access by selecting either Dial Out Only or Dial Out and Receive Calls under Port Usage. If you already have RAS installed on your workstation, you can get to this window by selecting Network, Services from Control Panel. Double-clicking the Remote Access Service brings up the Remote Access Setup window. Double-clicking the modem you want to check brings up its Port Usage window.

After RAS has been set up on the workstation, reboot the workstation and make sure that RAS is started. The following instructions guide you through the rest of the setup:

1. In Accessories, select Dial-Up Networking. You first need to create a new phonebook entry. Because the phonebook is currently empty, it should prompt you to create a new entry and then take you to the New Phonebook Entry Wizard window.

2. You can either go through the wizard by using default options and entering the phone number for the server, or select the I Know All About Phonebook Entries button. It is recommended to select this button because a few options need to be double-checked and cannot be set through the wizard. If you select the I Know All About Phonebook Entries button, the New Phonebook Entry window appears.

3. Click the Basic tab in the New Phonebook Entry window and enter the Entry name and Phone number. Also ensure that the Dial Using parameter is set for the modem that you want to use.

4. Select the Server tab and ensure that the dial-up server type is set to PPP. Also ensure that only the protocols you need for this connection are enabled. If you will be using TCP/IP, you might want to review the options by clicking the TCP/IP Settings button. In general, it is best to leave the options at their defaults. By default, all your TCP/IP settings for the client are determined by the RAS server you dial in to.

Just as with Windows 95 Dial-Up Networking, you must establish the connection first. To establish the connection, go into Dial-Up Networking, select the phonebook entry you just created, and then select Dial. You are prompted for your username, password, and domain. After these items have been entered, the workstation attempts to dial the Terminal Server, establish a connection, and log on to the server. After the connection has been established, you can run either the Terminal Server or Citrix ICA clients across the RAS connection.

Dialing In to a RAS Server Using Windows 2000

Because of the new wizards in Windows 2000, setting up remote access is even easier than in previous Windows platforms. The following instructions cover how to do it:

1. In the Start menu, under Settings, Network and Dial-Up Connections, select Make New Connection. Click Next at the intro screen.

2. Select Dial-Up to Private Network and click Next.

3. Enter the phone number for the remote RAS server and click Next.

4. Select to create the connection for either all users on the workstation or only the current user and click Next.

5. Unless you intend to share this connection with other workstations, click Next at the next screen and then click Finish.

The Connect Dial-Up window will now appear. Enter the username and password that you use to authenticate with the RAS server, verify that the phone number is correct, and click Dial. At this point your modem should dial out to the RAS server and establish a connection. After a connection has been properly established, you should see a small blinking dual-computer icon in the task tray. This indicates your connection is established and blinks every time data is sent or received.

If you want to see what IP address you have been assigned on the corporate network, you can double-click this dual-computer icon and select the Details tab from the window that pops up. Under the Details tab, you will see your assigned IP address.

For more detailed information, including your assigned WINS and DNS server addresses on the corporate network, go to the command prompt and type **ipconfig /all**. You will see the connection's IP information under the PPP Adapter for the connection name.

After your connection is established to the corporate network, you can run either the ICA or RDP client.

ICA Client Dial-Up Features

The newer versions of the ICA 32-bit client now have the capability to let a user specify which Dial-Up Networking entry to dial before attempting to establish an ICA session. When creating a new custom ICA connection or connection to an application set, select Dial-Up Networking (PPP/RAS) from the Connection Type list at the first setup window. Next, select the Dial-Up Networking entry you want to establish before the ICA session is established and click Next.

When you use this ICA connection entry or application set, it will attempt to establish the Dial-Up Networking connection you selected before attempting the ICA connection. This is a convenient feature for users who can now connect to their Citrix MetaFrame servers and applications in a single step, instead of having to first set up the Dial-Up Networking connection and then run the Citrix Program Neighborhood.

In addition, because a PPTP connection is treated as just another Dial-Up Networking connection entry, you also can specify a PPTP VPN connection be established first, using the same technique. This makes for easy one-step remote access using a VPN tunnel to your Citrix MetaFrame servers.

Setting Up Windows 2000 Clients for Remote VPN Access

Setting up a VPN connection on a Windows 2000 workstation to a Windows 2000 or other PPTP-based VPN server involves setting up a network connection as follows:

1. In the Start menu, under Settings, Network and Dial-Up Connections, select Make New Connection. Click Next at the intro screen.

2. Select Connect to a Private Network through the Internet and click Next.

3. At the Public Network screen, you can specify a particular Dial-Up Networking connection that needs to be run first to connect you to the Internet, before the PPTP tunnel is established across the Internet connection. If you are accessing your PPTP VPN server across the Internet using a dial-up connection, select the one you need and click Next.

4. Enter the host name or IP address of your PPTP VPN server. This is public address of your VPN.

5. Select whether to create this connection for all users or just the current user and click Next.

6. Unless you intend to share this connection with other workstations, click Next at the next screen, and then click Finish.

The Connect Virtual Private Network window will now appear. Enter the username and password that you use to authenticate with the PPTP VPN server and click Connect. If you had specified that a Dial-Up Networking connection to the Internet be dialed first, the logon screen for that dial-up connection will now appear. Click Dial to establish the connection to the Internet first. After the connection has been established, Windows will automatically attempt to create the PPTP tunnel across the connection to the PPTP VPN server.

After a connection has been properly established, you should see a small blinking dual-computer icon in the task tray. This indicates your connection has been established and blinks every time data is sent or received.

If you want to see what IP address you have been assigned on the corporate network, you can double-click this dual-computer icon and select the Details tab from the window that pops up. Under the Details tab, you will see your assigned IP address.

Dial-In ICA Connections

Dial-in ICA connections, also referred to as *ICA asynchronous* or *dial-in remote control connections*, are one of the most efficient means for remotely accessing your MetaFrame server. Although you can remotely access your server by using RAS, dial-in ICA has less overhead; however, dial-in ICA can be used only for custom ICA connections. If you want to connect to an application set remotely using dial in, you must set up a Dial-Up Networking connection instead.

The steps for setting up a dial-in ICA connection are very similar to those for setting up a network connection. First you create the connection at the server to receive the call. Dial-in ICA uses a special type of connection type called *async*. Then you create a dial-in connection entry on the remote workstation's ICA client and dial in.

The following sections cover the steps for setting up dial-in access at the server and client in more detail. These sections also go over how to troubleshoot problems establishing dial-in connections.

Setting Up Dial-In ICA Access at the MetaFrame Server

The steps for setting up dial-in access are simple:

1. In the Program menu, Citrix, MetaFrame XP folder, select the Citrix Connection Configuration tool.

2. Create a new connection by selecting New from the Connection menu in the Terminal Server Connection Configuration main window.

3. From the New Connection window that appears, select transport type Async.

4. Select the modem you will be assigning the connection to from the Device list box. You can install a new modem, if it is not in the list, by clicking the Install Modem button.

5. Enter the Name for the connection and click OK to create it.

You need to create one async connection entry for every modem you have on the system that you intend to dial in to and establish an ICA session.

You can set several other options on a connection level by clicking the Client Settings, Advanced, and ICA Settings buttons in the New Connection window. Remember that these settings apply for the current modem connection only. Any user who dials in to this modem is affected by the options. In situations in which you have only one modem, changing these settings on a connection level makes sense. In general, it is better to control these settings at a user level using User Manager because the settings will apply no matter what modem the user dials in with.

Connecting the ICA 32-bit Client to MetaFrame

For a Windows 95 or Windows NT workstation to dial in to a MetaFrame server, you must first install the ICA 32-bit client. This client has the capability to establish several different types of connections to MetaFrame servers. Chapter 12, "Installing and Deploying ICA Clients," covers how to set up the ICA 32-bit client to connect to a MetaFrame server across a network. This section covers how to connect across an asynchronous phone line.

The steps to set up an ICA dial-in connection are very similar to the steps for setting up a network connection. When setting up a new custom ICA connection from the Program Neighborhood, follow these steps:

1. Specify ICA Dial-In for the connection type at the first setup window and click Next.

2. Enter the connection name and what modem you want to use, and then click Next.

3. Enter the phone number for the modem attached to the Citrix MetaFrame server and click Next.

4. Fill out the options on the remaining screens as you would during the normal setup of a Custom ICA connection.

After you create your new connection, it shows up in the list of connections in the Program Neighborhood. Double-clicking the connection starts the process for establishing it.

Deploying Applications on the Internet

17

Firewalls and SSL Relay

I F YOU ARE AN ADMINISTRATOR WHO WILL be integrating your Terminal Server with the Internet or your corporate intranet, this chapter is for you. It begins with topics that apply to both Terminal Server and MetaFrame, such as the TCP/IP ports they use and how to access them through a firewall. You also will learn some of the more common firewall configurations.

Next you will learn how to provide access both from the Internet and from your internal network to an application web server. Whether you build this web server using NFuse technology, as covered in Chapter 19, "Deploying Applications over the Web Using NFuse and Wireless Technologies," or the Terminal Server Advanced Client, as covered in Chapter 18, "Running Applications on the Web Using the Terminal Services Advanced Client," you will likely need to know how to set up access to it through the firewall.

For increased security, you also will learn about how to set up your own *Secure Sock Layer* (SSL) solution for connection to your Citrix MetaFrame servers across the Internet.

The chapter ends with coverage on proxy servers. You will learn about the many things that can be done with proxy servers and the role they can play in a network to protect and control access to your Terminal Servers.

Accessing Terminal Server and MetaFrame Across the Internet

When setting up access to your Terminal Server from the Internet, your first concern should be security. Any access that you provide needs to be carefully evaluated in terms of its security risk to your corporation. A person accessing your Terminal Server across the Internet can have the same access to your corporate network as someone sitting at a Windows NT workstation one cubicle away from you. Both access to the Terminal Server and the Terminal Server itself should be locked down tightly before opening it up to the Internet.

In this section, you will learn how to provide access to both Terminal Server and Citrix MetaFrame servers through the Internet. In addition, you will learn some of the general steps you should take to lock the servers down properly.

Understanding How Access Through a Firewall Works

Accessing internal network services through a firewall is one of the most common methods for providing access to corporate resources from across the Internet. Firewalls provide protection for internal network resources by tightly controlling which resources are made available to users on the Internet.

Most firewalls can be set up to allow either RDP access to Terminal Server or ICA access to MetaFrame from across the Internet through the firewall. Although many firewalls have additional security features, such as the capability to audit access or to control which IP addresses on the Internet can go through, you should realize that once a user is through your firewall and has access to your Terminal Server, he then has access to your network just as if he were accessing it locally.

Ports Used by Terminal Server and MetaFrame

To access Terminal Server or MetaFrame through a firewall, you first need to know which TCP/IP ports are used. Because the entire Internet is based on the TCP/IP network protocol, a good understanding of TCP/IP is very important when setting up Internet access to your Terminal Servers.

Just like TCP/IP addresses identify which device a TCP/IP packet is intended for, TCP/IP ports identify which service within that device should handle the packets. A Terminal Server can be set up to provide many network services, but when Terminal Services clients (RDP clients) need to connect to Terminal Services, they always connect on TCP/IP port number 3389.

If you are running Citrix MetaFrame XP on that Terminal Server, there are a large number of services that use different TCP/IP ports for their communications, depending how you have your server and ICA clients set up. Table 17.1 lists those services.

In addition to Terminal Services and Citrix MetaFrame XP services, particular port numbers have been reserved for use by many different types of TCP/IP network applications. You will find that there is a separate TCP/IP port for all the following network services and more: mail protocols (IMAP4 - 143, POP3 - 110, and SMTP - 25), file transfer protocols (FTP - 23 and SFTP), and Web protocols (HTML - 80, RealAudio, and VRML).

Table 17.1 **TCP/IP Ports Used by RDP and ICA**

Protocol	Port	Destination /Source	In/Out	TCP or UDP
RDP	3389	Terminal Servers	Both.	TCP
ICA	1494	Citrix MetaFrame 1.8 or XP Servers	In.	TCP
ICA Browsing and ICA gateways	1604	Citrix MetaFrame 1.8 or XP Servers	Both. (Outbound high ports >1023 must be enabled.) This port is not configurable for TCP/IP connections. However, you can have clients use TCP/IP+HTTP connections instead.	UDP
RDP and ICA	High Ports (>=1023)	Citrix MetaFrame 1.8, XP and Terminal Server to Client	Outbound only. (Note: On many firewalls, outbound high ports are enabled by default.)	TCP
ICA + HTTP	80	Citrix MetaFrame 1.8 with Feature Release 1 or XP server	Both. (This port is used if clients select TCP+HTTP when making the connection. Citrix MetaFrame server must be running XML service. Default is 80, but XML port can be set differently during installation.)	TCP
IMA Traffic	2513	Citrix Metaframe XP only	Both. (This port is used for communication between the CMC and the Citrix MF XP servers when managing them.)	TCP

continues ▶

Table 17.1 **Continued**

Protocol	Port	Destination /Source	In/Out	TCP or UDP
IMA Traffic	2512	Citrix MetaFrame XP only	Both. (This port is used for by Citrix MetaFrame XP servers to communicate updates to the data collector. This must be open between all servers in a farm.)	TCP
SQL Server	1433	Citrix MetaFrame XP only with SQL	Both. (This port is used only if you have Citrix MetaFrame XP servers, and they communicate with an MS SQL data store.)	TCP
SSL Relay	443	Citrix MetaFrame 1.8 with Feature Release 1 or XP using the SSL Relay service. Also NFuse.	Both. (This is used only if you are using Citrix MetaFrame XP with NFuse and SSL Relay. It needs to be open from the NFuse server to the internal SSL Relay server.)	TCP
Domain Logon	88, 137, 138, 139	All Citrix MetaFrame or Terminal Servers to domain controllers	Both. (If you need for users to authenticate from a Citrix MetaFrame or Terminal Server to a domain controller across a firewall, you will need to open these ports between them.)	TCP
PPTP	1723, 43 (GRE)	VPN connection to any Terminal or Citrix MetaFrame Servers	Both. (If you are setting up a connection to a Citrix MetaFrame or Terminal Server, or a dedicated VPN server using PPTP, you need to open these ports.)	TCP
GRE	Any to any	VPN to any Terminal Server or Citrix MetaFrame Server	Both. (If your VPN solution uses GRE, you need to open up this special type of protocol between VPN clients and the server. It is protocol type 47 and can ride on any port.)	47
IPSec	500, 50, 51, 1701 (L2TP)	VPN to any Terminal Server or Citrix MetaFrame Server	Both. (If you are setting up an IPSec connection to a VPN server for MetaFrame or Terminal Server access, you need to open these ports. Port 1701 L2TP is necessary if this is a Microsoft IPSec connection because it relies on L2TP.)	TCP

Understanding the Difference Between UDP and TCP

For those who are not familiar with the nitty-gritty details of network analysis and firewall security, do not worry; you do not have to be to make use of the material in this chapter. However, one important concept to understand is the difference between UDP and TCP, especially when you start learning about exactly how ICA browsing works across a firewall.

Although Citrix MetaFrame supports many more protocols than TCP/IP, TCP/IP is by far the most prevalent and is the only protocol covered in this chapter. TCP/IP is the only protocol that works across the Internet and is the only one for which you can configure most firewalls.

Without going into too much detail, you can think of TCP/IP as a protocol that can operate in two different modes: UDP or TCP. When TCP/IP is operating in UDP mode, it is referred to as *connectionless*. This means that when a client needs to communicate with a service using UDP, it sends its requests but does not verify that they made it there successfully. This type of connectionless traffic is normally used for noncritical traffic or where speed is of the essence.

TCP/IP also can operate in TCP mode or *connection-oriented* mode. In this mode, when a client needs to talk to a service, it will send its request and then wait for a verification that the request got there successfully. TCP is often used for more critical traffic or traffic where security is important.

Whether a client uses TCP or UDP is not determined by the client, but rather by whoever developed the service to which they are trying to connect. When a developer creates a protocol such as RDP or ICA, they make the choice whether it will run over TCP or UDP or a combination of both.

As a firewall administrator, you need to know the difference between these two, because you have to specify whether the traffic is riding over TCP or UDP. For well-known types of traffic, such as standard email protocols, a firewall administrator can just select the protocol name from the list. However, not all firewalls have ICA or RDP in their list of protocols. For this reason, the firewall administrator must know both the port number that ICA or RDP communicate on and whether the protocol uses TCP or UDP.

Understanding Public and Private Addresses

For you to access your Terminal Servers or Citrix MetaFrame servers from the Internet, you must assign them a valid public IP address. Because of the shortage of public IP addresses available and for other reasons such as security, however, most corporations choose to use private IP addresses internally. Private IP addresses are a range of IP addresses reserved for private internal use and are blocked by many of the Internet's routers. The following IP ranges are considered private IP addresses:

- 10.[1–254].[1–254].[1–254]
- 172.[16–30].[1–254].[1–254]
- 192.168.[1–254].[1–254]

If you are using these IP addresses for your Citrix or Terminal Servers, you are using a private IP address.

Request for Comment 1918

These rules about what address ranges are reserved for private use on the Internet are governed by a very important document called a Request for Comment. *Requests For Comments* (RFCs) are the documents that basically describe how the Internet itself works. Most often they are written by groups of academics, major business representatives, and/or researchers. Not only do RFCs govern what are considered private address ranges on the Internet, but they also cover most core Internet technologies, such as HTML, DNS, IMAP, POP3, LDAP, SMTP, and more.

Although there are hundreds of RFCs, the one that governs what address ranges are reserved for private use is RFC 1918. For those who are interested, you can find a copy of this RFC posted at www.cis.ohio-state.edu/cgi-bin/rfc/rfc1918.html.

Understanding Network Address Translation

For you to provide access to these servers from the Internet, you must use a common firewall feature called *Network Address Translation*. Using your firewall management tools, you need to assign a valid public IP address on the outside of your firewall to the internal private address of each of your Terminal Servers or Citrix MetaFrame servers (see Figure 17.1). To anyone connected to the Internet, the correct address for your Terminal Server is the public address. For anyone connected to your internal network, the correct address is the Terminal Server's internal or private address.

To connect to your Terminal Server from the Internet, just connect to the Internet and then enter the public address for your Terminal Server into the Terminal Services client. The firewall will seamlessly handle the translation of the public address to the private address of the Terminal Server and then pass the packet along to the Terminal Server, so that the connection can be established.

Remember that you will need a public address for every internal Terminal Server to which you need to provide access. You can normally purchase or lease public addresses from your Internet service provider.

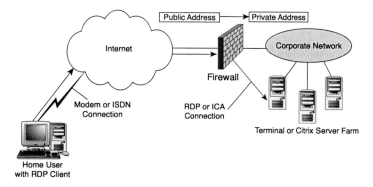

Figure 17.1 Network Address Translation.

How Terminal Server Access Works Across the Internet

To better understand how ports work and how they relate to firewalls, take a look at Figure 17.2. In this figure, you have a remote Terminal Server client attempting to open a Terminal Server session across the Internet with the corporate Terminal Server. A port has been opened in the firewall to let Terminal Server traffic through from the Internet.

When the Terminal Server client first contacts the Terminal Server, it sends out a packet whose destination port number is 3389 and whose destination IP address is the public IP address of the Terminal Server itself. If you had a network sniffer, you could view this packet and see this destination port number and destination IP address.

The firewall sees this packet and lets it through because the port for the internal Terminal Server (port 3389) has been opened on the firewall by the firewall administrator. If this port was not opened, the firewall would drop the packet, and the user would get a message on the client software saying that the server cannot be found.

When the Terminal Server receives this packet, it sees that the destination port number is 3389, so it knows that this packet should be sent internally to the Terminal Service. The Terminal Service running on the Terminal Server interprets this packet as a connection request and then sends a packet back out to the client to start the connection. After the initial "handshake" between the Terminal Server client and server, a session is now established on the server for the client. The server then sends the logon prompt display to the client, so that the logon process can begin.

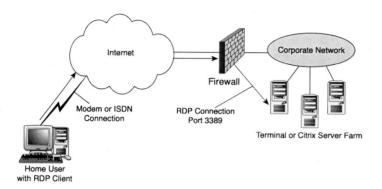

Figure 17.2 RDP connection from Internet.

In reality, even though you are going through a firewall, this connection process is almost exactly the same as the process for connecting to the Terminal Server on the LAN. You can think of the Internet as just an "extension" to your LAN. The advantage of the Internet, of course, is that this extension extends throughout the world, thus providing access to your Terminal Server from wherever your users might be.

The disadvantage of the Internet is that access is so widespread for any device you provide access to, that stringent security must be set up. As an administrator, this means that not only is it important to design the system with a high level of security, but also important security procedures must be followed, such as always ensuring you have the latest level of patches on your servers and that they are locked down properly. If you intend to open your servers to the Internet, be sure to pay close attention to the material provided in Chapter 22, "Securing Your Server." You will find a wealth of tips and procedures in this chapter for ensuring the security of your server over the long term.

Understanding the Role of a Firewall

Note in this scenario that the entire process is started by a single packet with a destination port number of 3389 and a destination IP address of the Terminal Server itself. If the Terminal Server were plugged directly into the Internet and given a public IP address, the conversation between the client and server would be established without much difficulty. However, this is a very unsecure setup because anyone on the Internet could access not only the Terminal Service on the server, but also any other service that the server was running. If there were any known vulnerability with any one of these services, a potential hacker could easily take control of the Terminal Server and gain access to everything on your internal network.

To prevent this type of security problem, most corporations put a firewall between their internal servers and the Internet. The firewall plays two roles. First, it controls access to internal services by only allowing packets through that are destined to particular ports on internal servers. In the case of Terminal Services, that port number is 3389. It will block any attempts from someone on the Internet to access any other ports or services that might be loaded on the Terminal Server. This greatly restricts what a hacker can potentially do with the Terminal Server.

The second role is that most firewalls can be set up for is intrusion detection and logging. Depending on what software you run on your firewall, many firewalls enable you to log every access or attempt at access to a device behind the firewall. If you find that someone has broken into your network, these logs are important evidence that you will need for law enforcement to be able to track the intruder down. In addition, if your firewall is running intrusion detection software, you can normally set up the software to alert you if there are suspicious patterns of access to your Terminal Server, such as attempts at cracking the password.

Using a Firewall to Control Access to the Inside

There are two approaches to providing access to your Terminal Server or Citrix MetaFrame server through a firewall. The first is to have your Terminal Server or servers directly attached to your internal network as shown previously in Figure 17.2. In this scenario, you open the appropriate ports in the firewall to each of these internal servers that you need access to from the Internet. This solution is very easy to implement; however, after a user has access to the Terminal Server, the user has unfettered access to your internal network.

The second scenario is shown in Figure 17.3. In this scenario, you put your Terminal Servers on a special secure network called a *demilitarized zone* (DMZ). Using a tertiary port on the main firewall or by setting up a second firewall between your Terminal Servers and the internal network, you can restrict what access users on the Terminal Server can have to internal network services. This setup is highly preferred for secure environments because you cannot only control what access the users on the Terminal Server will have, but also you will be able to log access and possibly alert on suspicious activities if you are using an intrusion detection system.

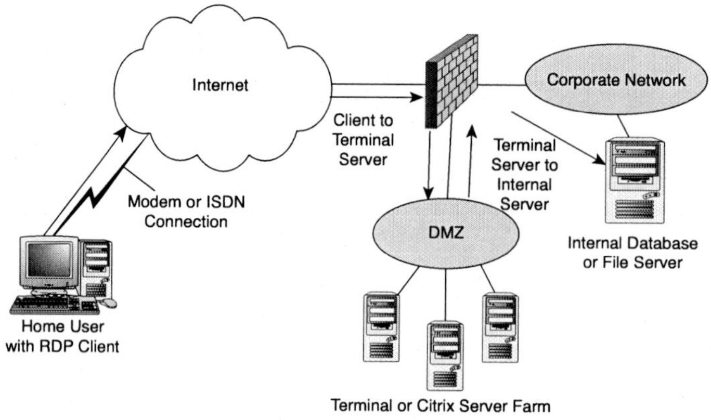

Figure 17.3   More secure access to Terminal Servers.

The disadvantages of this approach are a higher level of complexity and a higher cost. You will need to determine the port numbers and IP addresses of all the internal resources that users on the Terminal Server need access to and then lock down the firewall, so that they have access only to these resources. This can make the firewall policy list rather large and can decrease firewall performance. In addition, this solution will likely lead to higher costs because your firewall platform might need more processor resources, and you might need to purchase and install intrusion detection software.

Domain Logon Through a Firewall

In many cases, you will have your Citrix MetaFrame or Terminal Servers on one side of a firewall and the domain controllers that the users need to authenticate with on the other side of the firewall. If this is the case, you will need to open the following ports between your Terminal or Citrix Servers and the domain controllers:

- **TCP ports 137, 138, 139**   These are the standard ports used for both authentication and NetBIOS services browsing for a Windows NT 4.0 domain controller and are fully supported for backward compatibility by Windows 2000 domain controllers. If you are using any version of Terminal Server or Citrix MetaFrame and the users of the server need to authenticate with a domain controller, you need to open these ports up both ways between the domain controllers and the servers.

- **TCP port 88 Kerberos authentication**   Windows 2000 offers an alternative and more secure method of authentication called Kerberos. If you have Windows 2000 Terminal Servers and they are authenticating with a Windows 2000 domain controller, they will use Kerberos authentication by default. If you need for users of these Windows 2000 Terminal Servers to authenticate with a Windows 2000 domain across a firewall, you will need to open up this port.

Trusts and Domain Controller to Domain Controller Traffic

Although beyond the scope of what is covered in this chapter, if you need to open up communication between two domain controllers across a firewall for either trust relationship traffic or Active Directory traffic, refer to the Microsoft technical article Q179442. You can find additional, more detailed coverage of Microsoft port usage in the following technical articles: Q150543, Q174904, and Q176466.

Providing Access to Citrix MetaFrame Through a Firewall

Although Terminal Server just uses port 3389 for all communication, MetaFrame's more advanced feature set requires the use of multiple TCP/IP ports for it to work through a firewall. As an administrator, you need to thoroughly understand what these ports are, why they are necessary, and when they are used to set up the firewall security properly. In the following sections, you will learn the details of all the ports used by Citrix MetaFrame 1.8 and XP.

ICA Client Connections—TCP Port 1494

Note that the ICA protocol normally uses two TCP/IP ports for client-to-server communication. The first port is used for most standard ICA client–to–MetaFrame server communications, such as screen updates, printing, and mouse movements. This port is TCP port number 1494 and is referred to as the *ICA traffic port* in this chapter.

The second port is used by the ICA client to browse the network for ICA services, such as published applications, Citrix MetaFrame servers, and Citrix MetaFrame farms. This port is normally either UDP port 1604 or TCP port 80, depending on whether you set up the client for either TCP/IP or TCP/IP+HTTP communications respectively. It will be referred to as the *ICA browsing port* in this chapter.

When a client wants to connect to a particular Citrix MetaFrame server, after it knows the server's IP address, it will address the server on port 1494. The server will respond to the client on 1494 and assign it a port number in the "high port" range (1023–65534) for further communication. Each client that attaches to a single server is assigned a different high port number after the initial connection establishment. In this way, the Citrix MetaFrame server can differentiate between which client it is conversing with, because each client continues communication with the Citrix MetaFrame server using a different source high port number, but the destination port number will remain at 1494 throughout the conversation.

Depending on your firewall, you might have to manually open up this high port range to your Citrix MetaFrame server in addition to the standard TCP 1494 connection port for your ICA clients to be able to communicate with the Citrix MetaFrame server.

Understanding ICA Browsing

In many cases with Citrix MetaFrame, ICA clients need to browse for ICA services. This "browsing" functionality is handled on a completely different port number and in a different fashion than the normal ICA client–to–Citrix MetaFrame server traffic.

When you specify an IP address in the Server Location window of your ICA clients, such as when you set up an application set or a custom ICA connection to a published application, what you are actually specifying is the IP address that will be used for ICA browsing. This IP address is used in the following situations:

- **Servers browsing** When you are setting up an ICA client and press the down arrow to view the list of servers in the server farm, the client sends out an ICA "browser" packet to the servers you listed in the Server Location. The first server that receives the packet will respond with a list of the servers, which will be displayed to the client.

- **Published application browsing** When you are setting up a custom ICA connection for a published application and you press the down arrow to view the list of applications in the farm, the client sends out a "browser" packet to all the servers you listed in the Server Location. The first server that receives the packet will respond with a list of applications that are available in the farm. This will then be displayed to the client.

- **Farm browsing** When you are setting up an application set and need to browse for the farms available, you click the down arrow to view the farm names. The client then sends out a "browser" packet to all the servers in the Server Location list to retrieve the list of farms and display it to the client.

- **Connection setup to published application** This is a very important but often unrealized function of ICA browsing. Because the actual server location might change for a particular published application or the application might be load balanced across servers, the client must first "browse" for the correct server to connect to when attempting to run a published application. In other words, when a user double-clicks a published application in her Citrix ICA client, the client will send out a "browser" packet to find the master browser (MetaFrame 1.8) or data collector (MetaFrame XP) for the farm. Once found, the client will query the master browser or data collector to determine which server to connect to for the published application the user wants to run. The master browser or data collector will respond with the address of the correct server. At this point the client will make a standard ICA port 1494 connection to the server and run the application.

- **Connecting to a load-balanced/managed application**   Load balancing is also handled with the use of ICA browsing. When a client attempts to run an application that has been load balanced, it first must send out an ICA browser packet to either the master browser or data collector. Depending on the load-balancing rules that have been set up for that application, the master browser or data collector makes the decision on which load-balanced server to send the client to and returns the address of that server to the client.

This functionality is very important to understand, especially if there will be a firewall between the clients and the servers. For Citrix MetaFrame 1.8 or MetaFrame XP to work correctly across a firewall, you must open both the ICA traffic port, normally 1494, and the ICA browsing port.

Changes to Ports

Over the past year, Citrix has made significant additions to the ports that can be used for ICA client to MetaFrame server communications. These changes allow for better security and significantly improved ease of use over the Internet and through firewalls.

For those who are used to the old way of always using either port 1494 or 1604, pay close attention to the material that follows. You will find that there are now many more options for connecting to your Citrix MetaFrame servers. These new options are most readily apparent by taking a look at the latest Citrix ICA clients.

Your protocol choices have changed significantly in version 6.20 and later of the ICA client when setting up a connection to an application set. Notice that the default choice is now HTTP/HTTPS, and not TCP/IP, as it was in previous versions of the ICA client. This is a big change and is important to understand for those setting up access to their Citrix MetaFrame servers across the Internet.

With HTTP/HTTPS, ICA browsing is done normally on TCP port 80 or on port 443 if you have set up SSL. Citrix is moving away from using UDP port 1604 for ICA browsing. The exact reasons for this change are covered in more detail under the "ICA Browsing the Old-Fashioned Way—UDP port 1604" section that follows; however, be especially aware of this change when planning the design of your Citrix MetaFrame Internet solution.

ICA Browsing the Old-Fashioned Way—UDP Port 1604

Two different ports can be used for ICA browsing. Which port is used depends both on how you set up your servers and how you set up your clients.

The old-fashioned method of ICA browsing always used UDP port 1604. This port can be used for ICA browsing on all versions of both MetaFrame and WinFrame. It is the only port choice available for ICA browsing with WinFrame and MetaFrame 1.8 without Feature Release 1. This port number cannot be changed in any version of WinFrame or MetaFrame. This is the port used when you choose TCP/IP as the protocol when configuring the server locations within the ICA client.

By default, in older versions of the ICA client, when you browsed for an ICA service your ICA browsing occurred over port UDP 1604. Instead of sending out a packet directed at a particular server, older versions of the ICA client sent out a broadcast packet on the network to all servers in search of the master browser or data collector for the farm. Although you could manually specify a server address on older versions of the ICA client, the default was to broadcast a packet out. This is what the (Auto) setting meant in the Server Location tab in versions of the 32-bit ICA client prior to 6.20—Auto meant broadcast.

The problem with broadcasts is that every single device on a local network will receive and have to process the broadcast packet, even if it is not the type of device the broadcast was intended for. On large networks, broadcast packets can be a significant source of problems and can cause network-wide slowdowns.

Although MetaFrame 1.8 servers would always respond to UDP 1604 broadcasts, MetaFrame XP servers, by default, do not. The design changes in XP make it obvious that Citrix is beginning to discourage the use of broadcasts for ICA browsing. In fact, the use of UDP port 1604 is discouraged in general with MetaFrame XP. Even for administrators who are using MetaFrame 1.8, the use of UDP port 1604 for ICA browsing is no longer necessary so long as you have installed Feature Release 1 for MetaFrame 1.8. As you will see in the following sections, the new ports of choice for ICA browsing are ports 80 and 443.

Enabling ICA Browsing on UDP 1604 for MetaFrame XP

If you still need your MetaFrame XP servers to respond to broadcast requests from legacy clients using port 1604, you can still enable it. To enable it, go into the CMC and follow these steps:

1. Right-click the farm and select Properties.

2. Click the MetaFrame Settings tab.

3. Check the box next to Data Collectors Respond to ICA Broadcast Messages.

ICA Browsing Using TCP/IP+HTTP and XML—TCP Port 80

The main problem with using UDP 1604 across a firewall is security. Many firewall administrators balked at the concept of opening a UDP port through their firewall to an internal device. The connectionless nature of UDP makes it a less-secure choice than TCP. Because there is no "connection" established, it is easier for a potential hacker to spoof an IP address and attempt to hack into your Citrix MetaFrame servers. UDP is rarely used by large corporations for external access to important internal services from the Internet.

This problem of security and the need for a more flexible ICA browsing alternative led to Citrix's development of the XML service, on TCP port 80 by default, for ICA browsing. The XML service was first introduced in Feature Release 1 for MetaFrame 1.8 and is now included as part of the default feature set of MetaFrame XP, even without Feature Release 1 for MetaFrame XP.

On the client side, even though the ability to connect using TCP port 80 was available in earlier versions of the ICA client, you should use at least ICA client 6.20. ICA client 6.20 is the first client version that actually defaults to using TCP/IP+HTTP (also referred to as HTTP/HTTPS) to connect to your Citrix MetaFrame servers. This method of browsing is highly recommended over using UDP port 1604 for many reasons, including the following:

- **Flexibility**   As you will see later in this chapter, the default port of TCP 80 for the XML service can easily be changed. You also have the ability to change the port used during the installation of Feature Release 1 for 1.8 and during the installation of XP.

- **Security**   Browsing is now handled by a TCP connection-oriented protocol rather than UDP.

- **Elimination of broadcasts**   In MetaFrame 1.8 and WinFrame, by default when you browse for ICA services you use broadcasts, unless you manually specify server addresses in the Server Location list.
- **Future support**   Over the past several years, Citrix has taken several steps to move away from using UDP for browsing. Using TCP for browsing is significantly more secure, and as you will see in the next section, Citrix MetaFrame now supports SSL encryption over TCP. Although using UDP port 1604 for browsing is still supported for backward compatibility, going forward you should always deploy your solutions using TCP browsing.

Setting Up the ICA Client for UDP Versus TCP Browsing

Although the explanations so far explain the advantages of using TCP-based browsing over UDP browsing, it might not be clear how this is actually configured in the real world. Basically for you to deploy your Citrix MetaFrame solution using TCP for browsing, you need to make sure both the client and the server are set up correctly to use it.

If you are using MetaFrame 1.8, you will need to purchase and install Feature Release 1 for MetaFrame 1.8. During the installation of Feature Release 1, you will be prompted to choose the port used for the XML service. The default port to be used is port 80, and this is the one that you should normally choose. Although the acronyms are rather confusing, TCP browsing is supported by the XML service on MetaFrame 1.8. In other words, you must install Feature Release 1 for MetaFrame 1.8 to get the XML service. You then must ensure this service is running for clients to connect to your server using TCP for browsing. Remember that the XML services main role on MetaFrame 1.8 with Feature Release 1 (whatever port it is running on) is for TCP browsing. Standard ICA traffic still occurs over TCP port 1494 with MetaFrame 1.8.

If you are using MetaFrame XP, the XML services are included in the IMA service, which is installed by default. Although this means that there are now more acronyms that you need to remember, the most important difference you need to understand with MetaFrame XP is that TCP browsing is enabled by default. You do not need to purchase Feature Release 1 for MetaFrame XP or do any special configuration to set up TCP browsing for your XP solution. TCP browsing over port 80 is enabled by default.

After your server has been set up to handle browsing request over TCP, you need to set up the clients. Whether you use TCP for browsing or UDP is determined by your choice of protocol when you set up your application sets or custom ICA connections. With versions of the ICA client prior to 6.20, your two choices when setting up a connection were either TCP/IP or TCP/IP+HTTP. If you chose TCP/IP, that meant you were going to use UDP port 1604 for browsing for Citrix MetaFrame services. This was the default option in older versions of the client. If you instead changed the protocol choice to TCP/IP+HTTP, you would use TCP port 80 by default for browsing.

In newer versions of the ICA client, starting with 6.20, you still have the choice of using either TCP/IP or TCP/IP+HTTP for the protocol for connection to the server. However, the terms used to describe the protocols available for ICA browsing that you see when you have to specify a server location are now either HTTP/HTTPS or TCP/IP. Like the older versions of the ICA client, if you choose TCP/IP you will use UDP port 1604 for browsing. However, the default choice is now HTTP/HTTPS, not TCP/IP. If you stay with this choice, you will use TCP port 80 by default for browsing. Even though the name is different (HTTP/HTTPS versus TCP/IP+HTTP), the functionality is basically the same.

Remember that with either choice, even though ICA browsing occurs over either UDP port 1604 or TCP port 80, standard ICA traffic normally occurs only over TCP port 1494. As you will see in the "Setting Up SSL Relay" section, however, an exception applies to this rule. The new choice of SSL+HTTP for the protocol and HTTP/HTTPS for browsing now enables you to encrypt all of your ICA browsing and standard ICA traffic using SSL 128-bit encryption and send it to the server using a single TCP port, port 443!

ICA Browsing Using DNS with TCP/IP+HTTP

One additional, very important new benefit of this method of ICA browsing is its integration with DNS. By default, when you browse for ICA services from a client using TCP/IP+HTTP, it will first try to browse for list of services from whatever Citrix MetaFrame server resolves to the hostname ica. This functionality is very important to understand when you set up your Citrix MetaFrame server farm.

As an administrator, you have several options for pointing the ica hostname to a particular Citrix MetaFrame server on your network. You could set up the hostname in WINS, DNS, the local LMHOST file or a local HOST file; however, the best option for most environments is normally to set up the hostname for ica in DNS. However you set it up, the goal is simple. When the ica hostname is set up correctly on all your clients, you should be able to go to the command prompt on any of the clients, run the command `ping ica`, and be able to get a response from the Citrix MetaFrame server to which you set the ica hostname to point (see Listing 17.1). Normally you should point ica to your dedicated data collector if you have one. Otherwise, point it to one of your production MetaFrame servers.

Listing 17.1 **Pinging by the ICA Hostname**

```
E:\WINNT\system32\drivers\etc>ping ica
Pinging ica [192.168.10.251] with 32 bytes of data:
Reply from 192.168.10.251: bytes=32 time=120ms TTL=126
Reply from 192.168.10.251: bytes=32 time=110ms TTL=126
Reply from 192.168.10.251: bytes=32 time=110ms TTL=126
Reply from 192.168.10.251: bytes=32 time=110ms TTL=126
```

When you create the hostname ica on your internal or external DNS servers, it will automatically append your domain name to ica. If you put the hostname into the `acme.com` primary DNS domain, for instance, you should be able to immediately ping `ica.acme.com` from any station that has access to this DNS server. `ica.acme.com` is referred to as the *fully qualified domain name* (FQDN) for ica.

If you ping only ica and not the FQDN `ica.acme.com`, it might or might not resolve correctly depending on what domain your workstation is a member of. By default, any Windows workstation will automatically append its domain name to any hostname that you ping. That is why it is important to ensure that your DHCP servers are assigning the correct domain names to your workstations.

If in the network settings of your client's workstation or using DHCP you assign your clients to the `acme.com` domain, for example, when they attempt to browse for ICA services they will first try to retrieve the list from whatever device is assigned to `ica.acme.com`.

To see where this is set, try creating a custom ICA connection. During the setup of the connection, select TCP/IP+HTTP for the protocol and then click the Server Location button. Take the check off of Use Default, and then look at the default setting for the TCP/IP+HTTP protocol. It will be set to (ica). Remember from the previous discussion that the default setting for just TCP/IP is (Auto), meaning that if you choose TCP/IP (port 1604) you will send out a broadcast to locate your ICA services. If you choose TCP/IP+HTTP, however, you will send out a directed packet to `ica.[client domain name]` instead.

As an administrator, this makes TCP/IP+HTTP browsing very easy to set up and control for an enterprise, both for internal and external access. To set it up properly, follow these steps:

1. Assign a standard domain name to all of your workstations either manually or preferably through DHCP. You can determine what DNS domain a workstation belongs to using the `ipconfig /all` command for Windows NT 4.0/2000 and the `winipcfg` command for Windows 95/98/Me.

2. On your internal DNS server, create a host entry for ICA on this domain name. Point this entry to the internal address of your data collector or master browser. For the example, you would create a host entry for ICA in the `acme.com domain`.

3. Make sure ICA clients use TCP/IP+HTTP for establishing connections by default rather than TCP/IP.

For ease of TCP/IP+HTTP browsing from the Internet to internal Citrix MetaFrame servers, follow these steps:

1. Assign a standard domain name manually to home workstations in the Network Properties, DNS settings area.

2. On your external DNS servers, create a host entry for ICA on this domain name. Point this entry to the external address of your data collector or master browser. If the external address differs from the internal address because of Network Address Translation, you will need to use the alternate address functionality within Citrix. See the "Understanding Network Address Translation" section.

3. Make sure clients use TCP/IP+HTTP for establishing connections, not TCP/IP. Also you may need to check the "Use Alternate Address," by clicking the Firewall button when setting up the connection.

Another advantage of the TCP/IP+HTTP approach is disaster recovery. As you will see in Chapter 26, "Disaster Recovery Techniques and Enhancing Reliability," using DNS for client connection establishment has some important disaster recovery advantages.

IMA–Related Traffic and Firewalls

The final type of traffic that you will need to understand if you are intending to use Citrix MetaFrame servers behind a firewall is IMA-related traffic. The following is a list of the different ports used and when you would need to open them through your firewall. (Because the IMA service is available only in Citrix MetaFrame XP, this list is relevant only if you are using XP, not 1.8.)

- **CMC to Citrix MetaFrame server communication (TCP port 2513)**   If you need to manage your Citrix MetaFrame XP servers across a firewall, you will need to open up this port between the management station and the Citrix MetaFrame servers. TCP port 2513 is used for the establishment of a connection to your server farm by the Citrix Management Console and is used for retrieving management-related information from them, such as a list of connected users. Instead of opening this port, however, consider publishing the CMC. Using CMC as a published application on your Citrix MetaFrame servers, you would have only to open the ports necessary to access the published application (port 1494, 1603, or 80) between the management station and the server farm.

- **Citrix MetaFrame XP to data collector communication (TCP port 2512)**   This port must be open both ways between every Citrix MetaFrame XP server in the farm. This port is normally used by the Citrix MetaFrame XP servers to communicate updates to the server acting as the data collector for the zone. Data collectors on different zones in the same farm also use this port to keep each other updated on changes to the farm.

Author's Note

These port numbers can now be changed using the imaport command available with Feature Release 1 for MetaFrame XP.

- **Citrix MetaFrame XP to Microsoft SQL data store**   If your Citrix MetaFrame XP server needs to communicate with a Microsoft SQL data store, you need to open up TCP port 1433 in both directions between all the MetaFrame XP servers and the Microsoft SQL Server. If they use domain authentication and not SQL Server authentication, you also might need to open up TCP port 88/137/138/139 (domain logon and NetBIOS browsing) between the MetaFrame XP servers and the SQL Server and between the SQL Server and the domain controllers for the domain that the service authenticates against. It is recommended for the sake of simplicity to use SQL Server authentication instead when creating the ODBC connection to the database. In SQL Server 2000, you can easily change the port used using the SQL Server Network Utility.

Accessing Terminal Server Through a Virtual Private Network

For even more secure access to your Terminal Server from the Internet, you might consider a *virtual private network* (VPN) solution in addition to a firewall. Literally hundreds of different VPN solutions are available on the market from various manufacturers; there's even one included with Terminal Server that uses the PPTP protocol. For more information on VPNs, see Chapter 16, "Dial-In and VPN Access."

Using an Alternate Address Through a Firewall

If you are using Network Address Translation so that the private address of your Citrix MetaFrame server differs from the public one, you will likely need to set up your Citrix MetaFrame servers with what is referred to as an alternate address. An *alternate address* is provided to clients along with the private address when clients are browsing for ICA services. This allows the ICA client to connect to the alternate address of a server, rather than the inaccessible private address when trying to connect to the server while on the Internet. Suppose, for example, that you have two servers in your Citrix MetaFrame farm, CITRIX1 and CITRIXMB. CITRIXMB is the master browser or data collector, depending on what version of MetaFrame you are running. These servers are assigned the internal addresses of 10.10.10.100 and 10.10.10.101 respectively. You set up Network Address Translation on your firewall and assign these servers the public addresses of 150.10.10.100 and 150.10.10.101 respectively. If you make a custom ICA connection to either server's public IP address, the connection works fine. However, you now try to set up an application set to get your published applications. You enter the public IP address for CITRIX1 into the server location configuration. When you attempt to retrieve a list of your published applications, the Citrix MetaFrame client contacts CITRIX1 to retrieve the list. Because CITRIX1 is not the master browser, it sends a packet back to the client to contact GSMETAMB, providing the private address of GSMETAMB of 10.10.10.101. When the ICA client now tries to contact GSMETAMB at 10.10.10.101, the connection fails because it is using the private and not the public address.

To circumvent this problem you need to run the following command on the Citrix MetaFrame servers that you need access to from the Internet:

```
altaddr /server:[servername] /set [public ip address]
```

Remember that for published applications to work correctly, you must give every server that runs the published applications a public IP address including the master browser or data collector. You also must run the `altaddr` command for every server and set the correct public IP address for that server to report.

Besides the change on the servers that needs to be made, you also need to enable the use of the alternative address on the ICA clients. To do so, follow these steps:

1. Open the Citrix Program Neighborhood.

2. Double-click Application Set Manager.

3. To add a new application set, double-click Find New Application Set. To add a custom ICA connection, double-click Custom ICA Connections and then Add ICA Connection.

4. Click the Next button at the intro screen, and then click the Server Location button.

5. Uncheck the Use Default check box if it is checked, and then click the Firewall button.

6. Check the Use Alternate Address for Firewall Connection box.

7. Click the Add button and add the public IP address for the data collector server or master browser server in your Citrix MetaFrame server farm.

Setting Up SSL Relay

The preferred protocol choice for the best security with an Internet-connected Citrix MetaFrame server is SSL. With SSL, not only does all of your ICA browser traffic get encrypted, but so does all the standard ICA traffic. Although basic encryption is normally applied to this type of traffic by default, with SSL both your ICA browser traffic and regular ICA traffic go over the same port, TCP port 443.

From the perspective of a firewall administrator who needs to provide access from the Internet to your Citrix MetaFrame servers through the firewall, this is a much better setup. Instead of having to open a port through the firewall for both ICA browsing on port 80 and ICA traffic on port 1494, the firewall administrator needs only to open up port 443 through the firewall to the Citrix MetaFrame servers inside!

Although the SSL Relay service has been available in Citrix MetaFrame since Feature Release 1 for MetaFrame 1.8, this Relay service was mainly designed for encrypting the ICA browser traffic between an NFuse web server and the Citrix MetaFrame server with the SSL Relay service. To use SSL to encrypt all of your ICA client-to-server communication, you must have MetaFrame XP with Feature Release 1 installed and your Win32 clients must be using at least version 6.20 of the ICA client. If you do not have XP with Feature Release 1 on your servers and the latest ICA client on your workstations, your best choice for ICA client-to-server communication is TCP/IP+HTTP.

In the following sections, you will learn about what SSL is and how to set up an SSL solution for your Citrix MetaFrame server farm.

Author's Note

SSL can be a rather complicated subject. The goal of this section is to provide you enough information on SSL for you to get up and running quickly on the technology. For fuller coverage, see *Internet Information Services Administration*, by Kelli Adam (New Riders Publishing, 2000), ISBN: 0735700222.

Obtaining a Server Certificate

The first part of setting up SSL is obtaining a SSL server certificate. Without going into too much technical detail, an SSL server certificate is basically a specially formatted file that contains a unique encryption code used to encrypt traffic going between the Citrix client and the Citrix MetaFrame server. Several different file formats are used for certificates, but the file format that you need is referred to as the *.PEM format*.

When obtaining your server SSL certificate, you have two basic choices: either setting up your own certificate authority using the Certificate Services available in Windows 2000 Server or obtaining a certificate from a *Certifying Authority* (CA).

Using a Certifying Authority

If you choose to use a CA, you will need to pay them a fee to obtain the certificate. The certificate you obtain will be valid for a given period of time before the certificate expires. After it expires, SSL encryption will no longer work until you pay the fee to renew the certificate. Normally, this fee is around $100 to $200 per year.

For a client to communicate with a server using SSL, both the client and server must "trust" the same CA. This trust is established by the installation of a special type of certificate called a *root certificate* on both the client and server. Microsoft has already included the root certificate on all the latest versions of its Windows products for many CAs, including the following:

- Baltimore: www.baltimore.com
- Verisign: www.verisign.com
- Thawte: www.thawte.com

The fact that Microsoft includes the root certificate for these authorities can be a big advantage for an administrator in some ways. The most important advantage is that you do not need to install the root certificate for the authority at the client. This means your clients will be able to connect to your SSL-secured Citrix MetaFrame server without any special configuration other than having to specify that you intend to use SSL.

Using a Microsoft Certificate Server

The second option is to set up a Microsoft certificate server to provide your own certificates. The biggest advantages of this option are reduced costs and central control. Because you are setting up your own certificate server, you do not have to pay a third-party service to obtain a certificate. Instead, you just need to set up Microsoft Certificate Services on a Windows 2000 server on your network and use it to give out certificates to both the client and the server.

As is often the case with security, it comes at the cost of convenience. If you choose to set up your own Microsoft certificate server, you must not only request a server certificate to install on your server, but also each of your clients will have to retrieve the root certificate. This can make the initial setup of your SSL Relay solution somewhat tedious, because you will have to distribute this root certificate to all the clients. However, it does give you strict central control over exactly who can connect to the server.

Root Certificate Versus Server Certificate

The difference between these two types of certificates is easily confused. Without going into too much detail, just remember this: Every CA, whether you set up your own Microsoft server as a CA or you go to a third-party CA, has a root certificate that is "publicly" available; they also can assign out "private" server certificates. For SSL Relay to work, your servers must be set up with the private server certificate from a particular CA. All the clients that need to use SSL need to be set up with the public root certificate for that CA. The installation of this certificate on the client indicates that the client trusts the CA, and thus implicitly trusts any server that the CA has issued a server certificate for.

If this is still confusing, just remember that for SSL to work, your server must have a server certificate and your clients must have root certificates. Remember that out of the box, most Windows clients come preinstalled with a large selection of root certificates from vendors such as Verisign, Baltimore, and Thawte. On a Windows 2000 machine, you can actually see what root certificates you already have installed by doing the following:

1. Select Run from the Start menu.

2. Enter **mmc**, and then click OK to open up the Microsoft Management Console interface.

3. Select Add/Remove Snap-in from the Console menu.

4. Click the Add button.

5. From the Add Standalone Snap-In window that appears, select Certificates.

6. From the Certificates Snap-in window that appears, select Computer Account and click Next.

7. Select Local Computer, and then click Finish, Close, and then OK. The new Certificates snap-in should now appear in the Microsoft Management Console.

8. Browse to and open the Certificates folder under the Trusted Root Certification Authorities.

You will now see a list of all the root certificates that have been installed on your workstation by default (see Figure 17.4). This is a very important list, because it means that as a Windows 2000 client, you will trust only servers that use server certificates from one of these CAs by default.

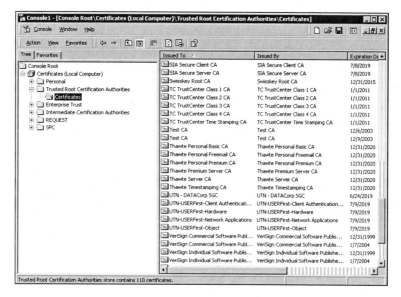

Figure 17.4   List of default CAs.

The Role of DNS with SSL

DNS plays an important role with SSL and must be set up correctly for SSL to work. When you obtain a server certificate, from either a CA or your own Microsoft certificate server, you must specify the server name during the request process. It is very important that you used the FQDN of the server when entering this name, otherwise SSL will not work. The FQDN is the hostname plus the domain name of your server. If your server name is ctxreports1 and your domain name is acme.com, for example, the FQDN for your server is ctxreports1.acme.com.

When you set up your clients to connect to a server using SSL, you must use the FQDN of the server to connect. Specifying the IP address of your server at the client is not an option, only the FQDN will work. It is important to note that the FQDN you specify when creating the connection entry in the ICA client must match the FQDN of the server's server certificate to which you are trying to connect. For this reason, how you set up your DNS is critical for SSL to work correctly.

The following are the basic rules you need to follow to set up DNS correctly for SSL:

1. Create hostnames on either your internal or external DNS server for all your Citrix MetaFrame servers.

2. Request and install server certificates into the SSL Relay service for each of your servers using its FQDN.

3. Make sure you can ping all the Citrix MetaFrame servers in the farm by FQDN from all the clients you are going to set up for SSL connections.

4. Select HTTPS as the protocol choice when setting up the connection entry at the ICA client and enter the FQDN of the appropriate server.

Making Sure DNS Address Resolution Is Enabled

One very important, but little understood, new feature in Feature Release 1 for MetaFrame is called *DNS address resolution*. This feature is critical to enable for SSL Relay to work correctly. What DNS address resolution does is return the FQDN of a server to the client, rather than just the IP address. Suppose, for example, that you have an ICA client that is trying to make a connection across the Internet to a particular Citrix MetaFrame application. The client will normally send an ICA browser message to the server it is set up for to query the address of the server that is running the application. In the past, the initial server would respond with the IP address of the server that the client needed to go to in order to run the application. With DNS address resolution enabled, however, the servers in your farm also will respond with the FQDN of the server the client needs to connect to in order to run the application.

This feature is very important for SSL, because SSL cannot make a connection unless it uses the FQDN of the server.

To enable DNS address resolution from the Citrix Management Console, follow these steps:

1. Open the Citrix Management Console from the Citrix folder in the Program menu on your server and log on.

2. Right-click the farm and select Properties.

3. Click the MetaFrame Settings tab.

4. Check the Enable DNS Resolution check box and click OK.

Installing the Server Certificate

After you have obtained the server certificate in .PEM format from either a third-party CA or your own, it is time to install it. To install it and enable SSL Relay, follow these steps on each of the servers in your server farm:

1. Copy the server certificate file to the `%systemroot%\sslrelay\keystore\certs` folder on the server you are setting up.

2. Install Feature Release 1 on your MetaFrame XP server and make sure it is enabled by right-clicking the server name in the CMC and select Set Feature Release Level.

3. Run the Citrix SSL Relay Configuration tool from the Citrix, MetaFrame XP folder in the Program menu.

4. Make sure the Key Store Location points to the correct location for your `%systemroot%\sslrelay\keystore` folder.

Author's Note

You should be aware of a rather odd little quirk in the SSL Relay utility. You must always put your certificates in a folder titled `certs`. You can create this folder anywhere on your system or on the network, but the one that is recommended to use is the one beneath the `%systemroot%\sslrelay\keystore` folder.

Even though the actual folder that contains the keys is the `\certs` folder, when you specify the Key Store Location always specify the name of the parent of this folder.

5. Click the down arrow next to server certificate. The name of the certificate you put in the `%systemroot%\sslrelay\keystore\certs` folder should appear.

6. Select this certificate, enter the password for this certificate, and then click OK.

The Citrix SSL Relay service should now be started on your server. At this point your server is ready to accept SSL connections from clients over port 443.

Retrieving a Certificate from a Microsoft Certificate Server

Although full instructions on the setup of a Microsoft certificate server are beyond the scope of this book, after you have one of these servers set up on your network, requesting a server certificate can be easily done. The following instructions guide you through how to do this:

1. Open the web browser on your Citrix MetaFrame server and go to the web address of the certificate server followed by `/certsrv` (for instance, `http://acmecert.com/certsrv`).

2. From the Welcome page that appears, select Request a Certificate and click Next.

3. Select Advanced Request and click Next.

4. Select Submit a Request to this CA and select Next.

5. Fill in the Advanced Certificate Request form that appears. Select Web Server as the Certificate Template. Make sure to use the FQDN of your server for the Name. Use a key size of 1024 and make sure to mark the key as Exportable. Click Submit.

This request for a certificate now is added to the request queue on the Microsoft certificate server. The server administrator must go into the certificate administration tool and grant this request before you can download and install the ticket. After this has been done, you will be able to go back to the `http://acmecert.com/certsrv` web site and select to Check on a Pending Ticket from the Welcome page and then retrieve it.

After you have the certificate installed on your server, you need to export the certificate to a file and then convert it to the PEM format that your Citrix SSL Relay service can understand. The following instructions guide you through how to do this:

1. Open Internet Explorer on your Citrix MetaFrame server.

2. Select Internet Options from under the Tools menu and then click the Content tab.

3. Click the Certificate button. A list of all the server certificates installed on your server will appear.

4. Highlight the server certificate you just installed and click Export.

5. Click Next at the window that appears.

6. Click Yes to select to export the private key, and then click Next.

7. Select Personal Information Exchange (.PFX), and then click Next.

8. Enter a password to protect the certificate and click Next.

9. Select the `%systemroot%\sslrelay\` folder to save the key into, and then click Next.

10. Go to the command prompt and change directory to the `%systemroot%\sslrelay` folder.

11. Run the `keytopem` command to convert the .PFX certificate to a .PEM certificate that can be used with Citrix SSL Relay using the following command format: `keytopem [pfx filename] [pem filename]`.

12. Copy the new .PEM certificate to the `%systemroot%\sslrelay\keystore\certs` folder on the server.

Now you can use this new .PEM file as the server certificate. Follow the instructions under the "Installing the Server Certificate" section to install the certificate.

Setting Up the ICA Client to Connect to an SSL Server

To connect to a Citrix MetaFrame server using SSL, you must be using at least ICA client version 6.20. Only this version and above has the capability to connect using SSL.

If you are using your own Microsoft certificate server, you must first install the root certificate on the client. When you install certificate services on your Windows 2000 server, it creates a special web site that can be used by clients to obtain the server's root certificate. This web site is located by default under the `\certsrv` folder off of the default web site. To install the root certificate on a client, follow these steps:

1. Enter the web address for your Microsoft certificate server followed by `/certsrv`. If the web server address is `http://acmecert.com`, for example, the address for the certification web page is `http://acmecert.com/certsrv`.

2. A Welcome page will appear. Select Retrieve the CA Certificate and click Next.

3. Select either Install this CA Certification Path to install the client on this particular machine or select Download CA Path to download it to a certificate file that you can distribute to all of your clients.

If you choose the second option and provide the file to all of your clients, all they should have to do once they get it is to open the file and click the Install Certificate button. This will install the root certificate on their machine and enable them to connect to the Citrix MetaFrame server.

Normally, if you chose to use a server certificate from a third-party such as Verisign, the root certificate for this third-party would already be installed on the clients and you would not need to go through these steps.

After you have the correct root certificate installed on your clients, you can set them up to connect to the server using SSL Relay. To set up an SSL custom ICA connection to your server, follow these steps:

1. Open Program Neighborhood.

2. Select Application Set Manager and then Custom ICA Connection.

3. Click the Add ICA Connections button to create a new connection.

4. In the Add New ICA Connection windows that appears, select the appropriate connection type, and then click Next.

5. Enter a description for the new connection and then select SSL+HTTPS from the protocol drop-down list.

6. Enter the FQDN (that is, `server.acme.com`) for the Citrix MetaFrame server you want to connect to under the Server Radio button, and then click Next.

Author's Note

If you are setting up a custom ICA connection for an application or an application set, the instructions are similar. However, you will need to enter the FQDN for the server in the Server Location list. By default, the clients are set up to attempt to connect to the `ica.[domain name]` server. If you set this FQDN to resolve to the IP address of one of the servers in your farm, you should not have to manually specify a FQDN.

7. Fill in the rest of the options as needed in the remaining setup windows of the wizard, and then click Finish. When you double-click this client, it should launch and then make the connection to the server.

You can verify that SSL is working by doing the following:

1. Double-click the small white ICA Connection button in the lower-right corner of the task tray after your connection to the server has been established.

2. From the ICA Connection window that appears, highlight the connection and select Properties.

In the Properties window, next to Encryption you should see an indication that SSL 128-bit is being used.

Changing Terminal Server and MetaFrame Listening Ports

For better security, some administrators choose to change the listening port numbers of their Terminal Servers to an obscure port number, rather than the standard. This makes it significantly more difficult for a casual hacker to identify the servers.

For a hacker to gain access to your network from the outside, he must first gather information about your network. One very common practice is for a hacker to do a port scan of your firewall or your Internet-exposed devices. If a hacker sees port 1494 open, he knows for sure that it is a Citrix MetaFrame server. If he sees port 3389 open, he knows that it is a Terminal Server. This is important information for the hacker. When the hacker has identified the service that is running, he can now research vulnerabilities for the service. He also could connect to the Terminal Server or Citrix MetaFrame server remotely and attempt to crack the password for one of the users.

By changing the port number used by either ICA or RDP, you make it much more difficult for the hacker to identify the server as a Citrix MetaFrame or Terminal Server. In addition, even if he were able to guess what type of server it was, he would still have to know how to modify the client so that it could connect on the different port.

In this section you will learn the techniques for changing both the server and client ports to your own port number for both Terminal Server and Citrix MetaFrame.

Checking Ports That Are Currently Open

Often you might want to check which ports are currently being used by your server, or after making a change to the port you might want to verify that the port is now open. The easiest way to do this is to use the netstat -a command. This command will provide a list of all the currently open ports on your server. Listing 17.2 is a partial output from this command. This output shows port 1494 (ICA), PPTP for VPN access, and port 3389 (RDP) are all open on the server it was run on.

Another useful command is either netstat -p udp or netstat -p tcp. This command will show you all the currently connected sessions to your server and to which TCP or UDP protocol they are attached. Listing 17.3 shows an outbound connection to a Citrix MetaFrame server and one to a web site.

Listing 17.2 **Partial Output from *netstat -a* Command**

```
TCP    gs5054:1494      gs5054:0        LISTENING
TCP    gs5054:pptp      gs5054:0        LISTENING
TCP    gs5054:3389      gs5054:0        LISTENING
```

Listing 17.3 **Citrix Connections**

```
Proto  Local Address    Foreign Address          State
TCP    gs5054:1080      gsmeta4.southernwine:1494  ESTABLISHED
TCP    gs5054:1124      12.8.192.53:http           ESTABLISHED
```

Changing the ICA Connection Port Number at the Server

Changing the ICA listening port, TCP port 1494, for a Citrix MetaFrame server is very easy. This is the port used between a client and a Citrix MetaFrame 1.8 or XP server for normal session setup. No matter how your network is set up, other than if you use proxy relay, you must open this port up to the Internet for all the Citrix MetaFrame servers to which you need to provide access.

To change the port being used by ICA at the MetaFrame server, run the following command from the command line:

```
icaport /port:[new port number]
```

After you run this command, reboot the server. At this point all ICA connections will have to use this new port number to connect to the server. To change it back to the original port of 1494, use the following command:

```
icaport /reset
```

Changing Ports on Multihomed Servers

In many cases administrators might want to multihome their server. *Multihoming* the server means putting two or more NIC cards into a single server and then plugging the NICs into different segments. For example, you might want to plug one NIC of your Citrix MetaFrame server into the DMZ and one into the internal network. If you are using this technique, you also might want to change the ICA port number on the DMZ for better security, but leave the ICA port number used on you internal NIC for internal clients the same. Unfortunately the `icaport` command will change the port number for all of your ICA connections, not just the external one. If you need to change it for just one connection, follow these steps:

1. Create a separate connection entry using the Citrix Connection Configuration tool for each NIC card and assign that connection to that NIC in the connection's Properties window. In this case, you would create a ICA-DMZ connection entry and assign it to the NIC that is plugged into the DMZ and then an ICA-Internal connection entry and assign it to the internal NIC.

2. Open up REGEDT32 from Start menu, Run, and browse to the following Registry key. Connection Name is the name of the connection entry whose port number you need to change. In this case, the Connection Name would be ICA-DMZ.

```
HKey_Local_Machine\System\CurrentControlSet\Control\TerminalServer\WinStations\
[Connection Name]\
```

3. Change the `PortNumber` value in this key from the default of 0x5D6 (port 1494 in decimal) to the hexa decimal value for the new port number that you want to assign.

4. Reboot the server.

This procedure will change the port value for just this connection entry and no other. If you need to change it back, just change this value back to 0x5D6 and reboot.

Changing the ICA Browsing Port Number for the XML Service

Changing the port number for ICA browsing is very easy to do if you are using the XML service and TCP/IP+HTTP. However, it is not possible to change if you are using TCP/IP with UDP 1604 browsing. To change the default port used for ICA browsing with the XML service from port 80 to something else, run the following command:

```
ctxxmlss /r[port number in decimal]
```

After changing this port you need to restart the server. After the server has been restarted, you will now be able to connect to this service from a client using the new port number. See the following section, "Changing the ICA Connection Port Number at the Client," for instructions on how to do this.

Make sure you change this port to the same number for all of your Citrix MetaFrame servers in the same farm; otherwise, TCP/IP+HTTP browsing will not work correctly.

NFuse uses only TCP/IP+HTTP for browsing, so if you have an NFuse server you also will need to change the port number that it is using for service browsing. For more information on NFuse and changing its port usage, see Chapter 19, "Deploying Applications over the Web using NFuse and Wireless Technologies."

XML Service and Port 80 Sharing

By default, the XML service will use port 80 during the install. You have the choice of changing this port if you need to. If you are running an IIS web server on the server you are installing the XML service on, you will be prompted as to whether you want to share the port with IIS. If you respond yes, the installation program will actually install a plug-in application component for the web server called an ISAPI plug-in. This component will ensure that any traffic going to port 80 that is destined for the IIS server will be sent to the Web service and any traffic destined for Citrix MetaFrame will be redirected to the XML service.

If you can justify the cost, you will be better off running IIS on a separate server instead of using your Citrix MetaFrame servers as web servers. NFuse does not need to run on an IIS, on a Citrix MetaFrame server to function. By keeping your Citrix MetaFrame servers separate from your web servers, you can ensure that any security vulnerabilities that might be exploited on a web server does not take down the Citrix MetaFrame servers with it.

Changing the ICA Connection Port Number at the Client

When connecting to the MetaFrame server from the client, you'll have to do one of two things to connect using the new port number:

- Append the new port number by using a colon to separate the address or server name in the Server field. If you changed your MetaFrame server to ICA connection port number 2000 and its IP address is 10.1.1.1, for example, you would need to enter either `[server name]:2000` or `10.1.1.1:2000` in the Server field when setting up the connection entry at the client.

- Add `icaportnumber=[port number]` to either individual server/application sections or to the [WFClient] section in the APPSRV.INI file of the client. You'll find the APPSRV.INI file under the user profile directory for the user running the ICA client.

For more information on the APPSRV.INI file and how to easily deploy clients with this setting already set, refer to Chapter 11, "Installing RDP Clients for Windows" and Chapter 12, "Installing and Deploying ICA Clients."

The default port for TCP/IP browsing, port 1604, cannot be changed. If you select to use TCP/IP+HTTP for browsing for your clients and you have changed the port number of the XML service on your Citrix MetaFrame servers, however, you will need to do the following when setting up client connections:

1. Open Program Neighborhood and select to create a custom ICA connection or application set.

2. Select the type of connection from the drop-down list and click Next.

3. At the Next screen, select TCP/IP+HTTP from the list of protocols, and then click the Server Location button.

4. From the Server Location screen, uncheck the check box next to Use Default and select TCP/IP+HTTP from the Protocol list to modify the server locations for that protocol.

5. Click the Add button to add a new server location to the list.

6. Enter the IP address of one of the servers in the Citrix MetaFrame server farm, preferably the data collector or master browser. Next to the address, change the default port value of 80 to the port value you set the XML service to on these servers, and then click OK. Then click OK again to accept the changes.

Now when you browse for services using the TCP/IP+HTTP protocol, it will use the port you specified, rather than the default port of 80.

Changing the Port Number on Terminal Server

The default port number for Terminal Services on Terminal Server is 3389. To change this port number, follow these steps:

1. Run REGEDT32.

2. Browse to the following Registry key:

`HKLM\System\CurrentControlSet\Control\TerminalServer\Wds\Rdpwd\Tds\Tcp`

3. Change the `PortNumber` value from the default hexadecimal value of `0xd3d` to the port number you want. You need to enter the hexadecimal value for the new port. You can convert from decimal to hexadecimal using CALC.EXE, by switching it to Scientific mode (View, Scientific). Enter the decimal value, and then click the Hex Radio button.

4. Reboot the server.

Author's Note

Although this technique should work without a problem for you, beware that changing the port value is currently not supported by Microsoft.

Changing the Port Number Used by the Terminal Services Client

Changing the port number used by the Terminal Services Client is relatively simple. Just follow these steps:

1. Open the Client Connection Manager from the Program Menu, Terminal Services Client folder.

2. Create the connections that you need for the Terminal Servers.

3. Select Export All from the File menu to export the settings to a .CNS file.

4. Open the .CNS file in Notepad.

5. Change the Server Port value for every Terminal Server that has the new port value, from the default of 3389 to the new port value in decimal.

6. Open the Client Connection Manager again.

7. Select Import from the File menu and point to the modified .CNS file to import the new settings. When prompted to overwrite, select Yes.

Your connection entries should now be updated to use the modified port numbers.

Basic Steps for Locking Down Terminal Server and Citrix MetaFrame

The following are some basic steps that you should take for locking down your Terminal Server or Citrix MetaFrame server if you intend to provide access to it from the Internet.

These initial security measures are only a start. For more complete security information and additional security tips, refer to Chapter 22.

Staying Informed of Security Vulnerabilities

With even the briefest search of readily accessible hacking sites on the Internet, you can come up with a list of numerous Windows Server vulnerabilities that are easily exploitable in servers that do not have the proper patch level or have services that have not been locked down properly. Reality is that Microsoft's huge market presence in the operating system world makes its products one of the biggest targets for malicious attacks.

This is not to say that a properly patched and locked down Windows server is not secure. The Windows platform can be a very secure platform. However, as an administrator you need to be extraordinarily diligent in keeping up with the latest security patches that are available and ensuring that your servers are locked down properly.

Consider, for example, the Red Worm vulnerability. A patch for this vulnerability was available in June 2000; however, less than a couple of months after the vulnerability was known, a hacker wrote an exploit for the vulnerability that was able to infect thousands of unpatched Microsoft web servers worldwide. This type of incident points to the fact that administrators need to make it a regular habit to check the Microsoft web site for important new security patch releases and follow common security lockdown tips.

The first step in any security lockdown should be subscribing to the Microsoft Security mailing list and checking the Microsoft Security web site for Terminal Server-related vulnerabilities. For more information on how to join the Security Patch mailing list for Microsoft, go to `www.microsoft.com/technet/treeview/default.asp?url=/technet/itsolutions/security/default.asp`.

Tenets of Good Security

There are two important tenets of good security:

- Information should be given only to those who need to know it.
- Access should be provided only for those who need to have it.

If you install your Windows server directly on the Internet without a firewall in between, you have in essence provided full, unlogged access to every service on your Terminal Server for everyone on the Internet. This is giving access to your server to those who do not need to have it.

Even providing access to just port 3389 of your Terminal Server to everyone on the Internet could be considered granting too much access. As an administrator, however, you need to balance ease of access with proper security. For highly secure environments, setting up VPN access is strongly recommended instead of poking a hole through the firewall. In this way you have full control of who on the Internet can access your Terminal Server. However, VPN access comes at the cost of convenience. Users must set up the VPN client first and establish the connection before they will be able to access your Terminal Server.

In this chapter you are shown how to access your Terminal Server and Citrix MetaFrame server without using a VPN, which is a common configuration. However, you need to assess whether this level of access is appropriate for the security of your network. Remember that once a potential hacker or even a disgruntled employee is able to break into the Terminal Server, it is as if he were sitting on a workstation locally on your network.

Applying the Latest Patches

One of the most important steps to take is to apply all the latest patches to your servers. If you are running Terminal Server alone, go to `http://windowsupdate.microsoft.com` from your servers and check for updates.

If you are also running Citrix MetaFrame XP, you should go to the Citrix web site at www.citrix.com and search for the latest service packs and security related hotfixes.

Vulnerabilities in Windows NT 4.0 Terminal Server

Windows NT 4.0 Terminal Server has a serious buffer overflow vulnerability that is very important to patch before exposing this server version to the Internet. This vulnerability and how to fix it is documented in Microsoft technical article Q277910. In addition, Microsoft is currently working on a "security rollup" for Windows Terminal Server 4.0. This will likely be available by the time this book is released. This is not an official service pack, but instead a collection of security-related hotfixes. You must first install Service Pack 6a before installing the security rollup. Microsoft has decided not to release any further service packs for the Window NT 4.0 Server platforms, beyond Service Pack 6a.

Controlling Which Users Have Access from the Internet

By default, when you open access on the Internet to your Terminal Server through a firewall, all users on the domain can log on just as if they were accessing the server on the local network. The first security measure you should take is to control which domain users have access to the available connections. To do so, follow these steps:

1. Create an INTERNET_ACCESS group (or similar group) using User Manager for Domains.

2. Add all the users to the group who you want to have access to the server from the Internet.

3. Go to the Start menu and select Programs, Administrative Tools. Then run the Terminal Server Connection Configuration tool.

4. Highlight either the RDP-TCP or ICA-TCP connection to which you'll be granting access from the Internet.

5. Select Permissions from the Security menu on the main window of the Terminal Server Configuration tool.

6. From the Connection Permission window that appears, remove all groups and users except SYSTEM, by highlighting each one and clicking the Remove button.

7. Click the Add button.

8. From the Add Users and Groups window, highlight the INTERNET_ACCESS group listed under Names.

9. Select Guest Access from the drop-down list next to Type of Access.

10. With the INTERNET_ACCESS group still highlighted, click Add, and then click OK.

The INTERNET_ACCESS group will now be added to the access list in the Connection Permissions window with guest access. Guest access gives only the members of the INTERNET_ACCESS group the ability to log on and log off the Terminal Server.

Remember that connection permissions are not related to NTFS security, user rights, or any other type of Terminal Server security. They are mainly used to control which users or groups have permission to log on using a particular connection. After logging on to your server, these users will still have access to their files just as before.

Setting Strict Security Policies

In addition to restricting who can access the Terminal Server, it is also a good idea to ensure that you have good security policies in place for their accounts. If your users are on a Windows NT 4.0 domain, you can use User Manager to change the security policy. Be aware, however, that this affects all users on the domain. If they are using Windows 2000, you can use GPOs to change the security policies for a particular group of users. For more information on policies, see Chapter 14, "Policies and Desktop Management."

The following are the minimum recommended settings for your security policy, if users are allowed access from the Internet:

- Minimum password length should be 8 characters.
- Lock out account after 3 attempts.
- Lock out account for 60 minutes before resetting it.
- Remember the last 5 passwords used.
- Require users to change passwords every 90 days.

Lock Down Local Accounts

One very important step missed by a lot of administrators is to lock down local accounts. A hacker can easily attempt to guess the local Administrator account. The following steps are highly recommended:

1. Rename the local Administrator account to something obscure.
2. Reset the password for the local Administrator account to a large, alphanumeric password, that is easy to remember but very difficult to guess. Use a different local Administrator account password on every server exposed to the Internet and do not use the same or a similar local Administrator account password to any administrator password used internally.

3. Make sure no other local accounts besides the local Administrator account have either Administrator or Power User access to the server.

4. Make sure that the Guest account is disabled and that there are no unnecessary local User accounts.

Accessing Citrix MetaFrame Servers Through a Proxy Server

For those who are not familiar with what a proxy server is, the easiest way of explaining the function of a proxy server is using the definition of the word *proxy*. Proxy means to act on behalf of another. Therefore, a *proxy server* is a server that acts on the behalf of another server. For example, instead of providing direct access to your Citrix MetaFrame servers from the Internet or from your internal network, you can place a proxy server in between. When clients attempt to make a connection to your Citrix MetaFrame server, they do it by making a special type of connection to the proxy server first called a *SOCKS proxy connection*. The proxy server then redirects their connection attempt to the appropriate Citrix MetaFrame servers behind it. Figure 17.5 shows an example of a proxy server connection.

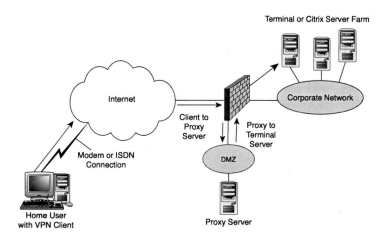

Figure 17.5 Connection to Citrix through a proxy server.

So the next question is why use a proxy server? The main reason is that most proxy servers enable you to tightly control and log access through them. In other words, you can use a proxy server, much like a firewall, to restrict access to your Citrix MetaFrame servers. One of the advantages of using a proxy server over using a firewall is that the port used by a proxy server is different from that used by your Citrix MetaFrame servers. This makes it much more difficult for a hacker to guess what lies behind the proxy server. In addition, the Citrix MetaFrame client must be specially configured to make the connection through the proxy server, which again makes it more difficult for a hacker to penetrate your network security.

Microsoft's Proxy Services

Although several different proxy server solutions are available on the market today, one of the most common is Microsoft Proxy Server. Using either Microsoft Proxy Server 2.0 or the newly available Internet Security and Acceleration Server, you can provide access to your Citrix MetaFrame server farm through what is referred to as SOCKS proxy access. For more information on these products, refer to the Microsoft web site at www.microsoft.com.

Also be ware that proxy server access is currently not supported to a Terminal Server by Microsoft. You will only be able to set up proxy server access to a Citrix MetaFrame server.

Configuring the Citrix Client for Proxy Server Access

If your Citrix MetaFrame servers exist behind a proxy server, you need to configure the Citrix Program Neighborhood specially to make the connection. By default, SOCKS proxy resides on port 1080. The following instructions guide you through how to connect:

1. Open the Citrix Program Neighborhood.
2. Double-click Application Set Manager.
3. To add a new application set, double-click Find New Application Set. To add a custom ICA connection, double-click Custom ICA Connections and then Add ICA Connection.
4. Click the Next button at the intro screen, then click the Server Location button.
5. Uncheck the Use Default check box if it is checked, and then click the Firewall button.
6. Check the Connect via SOCKS Proxy box shown in Figure 17.6.
7. Enter the address of the proxy server on the network and the port used by the server, and then click OK. Normally this is port 1080.

8. Click the Add button and add the address for the data collector server or master browser server in your Citrix MetaFrame server farm. This server must be set using the proxy server's administrative tools to be accessible through the proxy server. You also must make available any other Citrix MetaFrame server that users need to connect to through the proxy.

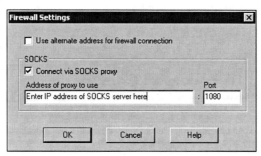

Figure 17.6 Firewall settings.

When you open this new application set or custom ICA connection, it will first establish a connection with the SOCKS proxy server that you specified. Using the SOCKS protocol, it will request access through the proxy server to the Citrix MetaFrame servers behind it.

Top-Ten List for Firewall Setup

The following are the top-ten tips you need to know about that were covered in this chapter.

1. **Use TCP/IP+HTTP rather than TCP/IP.** The TCP/IP protocol choice and browsing over UDP port 1604 is outmoded. Instead, set up your servers with the XML service and set up your clients so that the connect to your servers using TCP/IP+HTTP.

2. **Use SSL+HTTP for the best security.** For the best security across the Internet, set up SSL Relay. SSL Relay encrypts and encapsulates all of your ICA traffic, including ICA browsing, in a single port number, TCP port 443.

3. **Use VPNs for remote access.** Using a VPN for remote access is a great alternative to having to punch holes through your firewall to access your Citrix MetaFrame servers. Not only is the VPN a very secure solution, but it also offloads some of the encryption work from your Citrix MetaFrame servers. After you have connected to a network via a VPN, you have access to the entire network and not just the Citrix MetaFrame servers.

4. **Purchase and install Feature Release 1.** Feature Release 1 contains many important firewall-related improvements, including the capability for performing SSL and DNS address resolution.

5. **Use DNS effectively.** Always create hostnames for your Citrix MetaFrame servers on both your internal and external DNS servers. This is especially important if you are using SSL Relay or DNS address resolution. Make sure that the DNS hostname matches the actual host name configured for your server. You can use the `ipconfig /all` command to determine the actual hostname.

6. **Make sure your servers are fully patched.** Make sure your servers have all the latest patches and are patched consistently across the farm. This is especially critical when you are providing access to your servers across the Internet, because many patches have important security fixes.

7. **Open up only the ports needed.** Only open the ports that you need to the Internet. Opening up full access through a firewall to a Citrix MetaFrame server is a huge security risk.

8. **Be wary of installing web services on your Citrix MetaFrame servers.** There are several known vulnerabilities with IIS 4.0 and 5.0. If you install one of these web servers on your Citrix MetaFrame server, it is critical to reinstall all the latest service packs. In addition, you should go to `http://windowsupdate.microsoft.com` to download the latest hotfixes.

9. **Stay informed of security vulnerabilities.** Vendors report new vulnerabilities nearly every day. Most vendors have a security mailing list that you can join to ensure you are notified of any security-related issues in their product. Be sure to join the Microsoft Security mailing list.

10. **Secure your server.** Besides installing patches, make sure your server security is very tight before opening it up to the Internet.

18

Running Applications on the Web Using the Terminal Services Advanced Client

With the huge impact that the web is making on corporations today, many administrators are tasked with making better business use of the Internet and even creating an intranet for access to corporate information and services.

Using the ActiveX client available in the *Terminal Services Advanced Client* (TSAC), you as an administrator can create your own Terminal Server web site. Users from throughout your company, using Microsoft Internet Explorer, will be able to connect to your Terminal Servers through this web site and the ActiveX client. In addition, you can open access to this site to the Internet so that remote users can log on to your Terminal Servers across the Internet using only their web browser.

In this short chapter, you will learn the basics of how to set up your own Terminal Server web site.

Installing and Configuring the Terminal Services Advanced Client

The Terminal Services Advanced Client comes in a freely available download from the Microsoft web site at www.microsoft.com/windows2000/downloads/recommended/tsac/default.asp.

The client itself is basically an ActiveX version of the standard Terminal Services client. For those not familiar with ActiveX, it is a language that web developers can use to create applications that can be run through a web browser. ActiveX is a Microsoft language and is supported only by Microsoft Internet Explorer 4.x and above. If you want to deploy access to your Terminal Servers using other web browsers, such as Netscape, you will need to purchase Citrix MetaFrame and install the freely available Citrix NFuse product, as covered in the next chapter.

The client download comes with the following useful components:

- **TSWEBSETUP.EXE**   This component, when run, will install a sample set of web pages on any Microsoft IIS 4.x web server or above. This is the component that you will learn how to install in this chapter.

- **TSMSISETUP.EXE**   This is the Microsoft Installer or MSI version of the standard Windows 32-bit Terminal Services client. Using the provided .MSI file, you can more easily automate the deployment of your Terminal Services clients. For more information on this component, see Chapter 11, "Installing RDP Clients for Windows."

- **TSMMCSETUP.EXE**   This component is a very useful plug-in for the Microsoft Management Console that enables you to connect to your Terminal Servers from within the console. For more information on this component, see Chapter 14, "Policies and Desktop Management."

Terminal Services Web Development

One important thing to realize is that the Terminal Services Advanced Client's sample web pages are just that, sample web pages. This is a demo product, just like NFuse, and is intended as a demo of what can be done with the Terminal Services Advanced Client, rather than a full-featured solution. If you have a web development team at your corporation, be sure to demo the capabilities of the TSAC to them; they will likely be interested.

Although you can use the TSAC sample web pages as is to provide access to your Terminal Server, the true business value is gained by customizing the web pages for your own use. Toward the end of this chapter, you will learn some of the basics of how it works and how to customize the web page. With only a basic familiarity with a web page creator tool, such as FrontPage, you can modify the sample web pages into something really useful for your corporation. Be aware, however, that more advanced modifications, such as taking advantage of the object properties and methods exposed by the ActiveX client, are beyond the scope of this book and do require significant experience with web development technologies to implement. For more detailed information on the development capabilities of the TSAC, do a search for TSAC on the Microsoft Development web site at http://msdn.microsoft.com.

Installing the Sample Web Pages

The sample web pages are based on ASP technology and are designed to work on a Microsoft Internet Information Server 4.x or above. To install the sample web pages, go to the console of the server you want to install it on and follow these steps:

1. Install Internet Information Server on your intended web server. See the instructions in the following sidebar, "Installing Internet Information Server 4.x or 5.x," if you are not familiar with how to do this.

2. Download the Terminal Services Advanced Client to the server from the web site listed in the preceding section.

3. Run `tswebsetup.exe` from the console of the web server.

4. Select the location for the web site. The default location is `%systemdrive%\ inetpub\tsweb\`.

The sample web pages take only a few seconds to install onto your web server. Included in the installation is the ActiveX version of the Terminal Services client. This ActiveX version is installed on the web server in the MSTSCAX.CAB file and is set up to automatically be installed when you use the sample web page. Remember that ActiveX components act as plug-ins and work only with Internet Explorer.

Installing Internet Information Server 4.x and 5.x

For those who have not worked much with *Internet Information Server* (IIS) before, you need to know about some basic things.

Internet Information Server 4.x is the version of the Microsoft web server commonly run on the Windows NT 4.0 Server platform. However, installing it is rather tricky because Windows NT 4.0 does not come with IIS 4.0 out of the box. The basic steps for installation are as follows:

1. Install IIS 2.0.   IIS 2.0 is the version of IIS that comes with Windows NT 4.0 Server. You are given the option of installing it during the installation of Windows NT 4.0 Server. If you need to install it after the install of the server, run the `inetsetup.exe` setup program from the `[cd]:\i386\inetsrv` folder on the Windows NT 4.0 Server CD.

2. Install the Windows NT 4.0 option pack.   The option pack comes on CD with the latest service pack. The option pack contains several add-on software packages designed for Windows NT 4.0 Server, including an upgrade to IIS 4.0. By installing the option pack, you upgrade the IIS 2.0 web server on your server to 4.0. For those who do not have the CD, the option pack is available for free download at `www.microsoft.com/ ntserver/nts/downloads/recommended/NT4OptPk/default.asp`.

3. **Apply the latest service packs.** Because of the many serious vulnerabilities discovered in IIS 4.0, it is critical to not only apply the latest service pack (service pack 6a), but also to go to `http://windowsupdate.microsoft.com` after you have installed the IIS 4.0 web server and have it scan your server for any hotfixes that you need.

Installing IIS 4.0 will create a `%systemdrive%\inetpub\wwwroot` folder on your server. This folder will contain a sample set of web pages. It is a good idea to delete the contents of this folder before you install a new web site under here. Also unless needed, stop the default administrative web site using the Internet Service Manager located in the Start menu, Programs, Windows NT 4.0 Option Pack, Microsoft Internet Information Server folder on the web server. At this point, you can install the Terminal Services Advanced Client by running `tswebsetup.exe`. If you intend to install NFuse instead, the server is now ready for the installation. Instructions on installing NFuse are provided in Chapter 19, "Deploying Applications over the Web Using NFuse and Wireless Technologies."

Thankfully, the installation of IIS 5.0 is significantly easier than it is with IIS 4.0. IIS 5.0 is the web server version that comes with Windows 2000 Server. Instead of being a separately run installation, IIS 5.0 is installed just like any other Windows Server component through the Add/Remove Programs dialog box. As with IIS 4.0, however, making sure you have the latest patch levels and hotfixes installed is critical because serious vulnerabilities have been exposed in IIS 5.0 code. The following instructions cover how to install IIS 5.0 on a Windows 2000 server:

1. From the Control Panel, select Add/Remove Programs.

2. In the Add/Remove Programs window, click the Add/Remove Windows Components button.

3. Highlight Internet Information Services and the click the Details button. Select only the components you need from the list, making sure that you select at least the World Wide Web Server, and then click OK and then Next.

4. After IIS is installed, select Windows Update from the Start menu to go to the Microsoft Update web site to download and install the latest service pack and hotfixes for IIS.

Using the Web Page

Using the sample web page is very simple. You can get to the web page on your test web server by going to `http://[web server address]/tsweb/default.htm` using Internet Explorer.

The page shown in Figure 18.1 will appear. This page is the sample introduction page and can easily be modified in FrontPage or with another web page development tool to customize the look and feel. From this page, you need to enter the name or IP address of the Terminal Server you want to connect to, the screen size you want, and then click the Connect button.

After clicking Connect, you will be redirected to `http://[web server address]/tsweb/connect.asp`.

This page includes the core functionality that makes the magic of TSAC work. If you do not have the ActiveX client installed on your machine, the window shown in Figure 18.2 will appear. Click Yes at this window to download and install the ActiveX-based Terminal Services client.

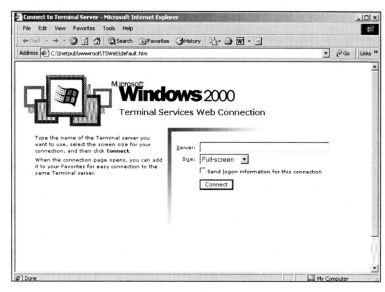

Figure 18.1   Sample introduction page.

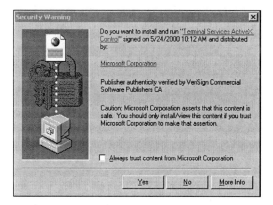

Figure 18.2   Security warning.

After the client has been installed, the logon screen for the Terminal Server
will display within the web browser window (see Figure 18.3).

The ManyServers Web Page

As a demonstration of how you could put multiple Terminal Server sessions into the same browser window,
Microsoft has provided another demo web page called the ManyServers.htm page. You can view this page by going
to http://[web server address]/tsweb/manyservers.htm.

If you enter the address for your Terminal Server, this page will make four simultaneous connections to your server
and display four separate sessions on the same page. This page is meant only as a demo of this capability and
would need to be modified to be truly useful.

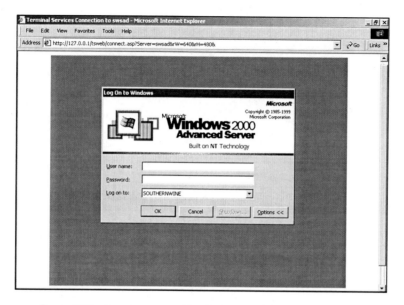

Figure 18.3   Logging on to a Terminal Server through the web.

Understanding How the Sample Web Page Works

As you can see, the sample web pages are very simple and do not include some of the many features you would likely want to make available from the web. For example, depending on exactly what you need, you easily could do the following things with the sample web page using a little knowledge of web development:

- Change the look and feel of the logon page to match other corporate pages.
- Incorporate the logon page into another web page, such as an internal technical support site.
- Provide buttons or hyperlinks to connect to each one of your Terminal Servers instead of requiring the user to type in the IP address.
- Start a particular program upon logon or make icons to launch particular applications on Terminal Server.

To provide some of these features for your users, you will first need to understand the basics of how the sample web pages work. This section assumes that you have at least a basic familiarity with web development languages such as ASP and HTML.

The Main Page—DEFAULT.HTM

The default web page is written in HTML with some embedded VBScript code. The goal of the first page is to get the IP address that the user wants to connect to, the screen size that the user wants, and then to pass this information onto the CONNECT.ASP page through the URL, where the connection to the Terminal Server will be made. The role of the HTML code is to just display the graphics on the page and gather the input. The creation of the URL and the switch to the CONNECT.ASP page is handled by the following btnLogin VBScript function (see Listing 18.1), which is embedded in the web page and called when the Connect button is pressed.

Listing 18.1   *btnLogin* **VBScript Function**

```
sub btnLogin
  'Create connection URL and redirect to login page
  conUrl = "connect.asp"

  'server
  if not Document.all.Server.value = "" then
     conUrl = conUrl + "?Server=" & Document.all.Server.value & "&"
  else
     conUrl = conUrl + "?Server=" & Document.location.hostname & "&"
  end if

  bAutoLogon = FALSE
  if Document.all.CheckBoxAutoLogon.checked then
     bAutoLogon = TRUE
  end if

  if bAutoLogon then
       conUrl = conUrl + "UserName=" & Document.all.UserName.Value & "&"
       conUrl = conUrl + "Domain=" & Document.all.Domain.Value & "&"
  end if

  'resolution width-height
  select case document.all.comboResolution.value
  case "1"
     conUrl = conUrl + "FS=" & 1 & "&"
     resWidth  = screen.width
     resHeight = screen.height
  case "2"
     resWidth  = "640"
     resHeight = "480"
  case "3"
     resWidth  = "800"
     resHeight = "600"
  case "4"
```

continues ▶

Listing 18.1 **Continued**

```
      resWidth  = "1024"
      resHeight = "768"
   case "5"
      resWidth  = "1280"
      resHeight = "1024"
   case "6"
      resWidth  = "1600"
      resHeight = "1200"
   end select

   conUrl = conUrl + "rW=" & resWidth & "&"
   conUrl = conUrl + "rH=" & resHeight & "&"
   'go to the login page
   Window.Navigate(conUrl)
end sub1.
```

The goal of this short bit of VBScript is to create a URL with the following format:

```
http://[web server IP address] /tsweb/ connect.asp?Server=[web
server IP address]&rW=[screen width in pixels]&rH=[screen height
in pixels]
```

This URL calls the CONNECT.ASP web page and passes on the value of the `Server` parameter, which specifies the IP address of the Terminal Server, the `rW` parameter, which specifies the screen width for the session, and the `rH` parameter, which specifies the screen height.

You can take advantage of this simple URL format and create your own hyperlinks or buttons that automatically call the CONNECT.ASP web page with the parameters that you want. For example, if you want to set up a web page with a button for connecting to the TSSERV1 Terminal Server using a 640×480 size session window, you could point the hyperlink for the button to `http://[web server IP address] /tsweb/ connect.asp?Server =TSSERV1&rW=640&rH=480`.

You could create separate buttons for different screen sizes if needed.

The Connect Page—CONNECT.ASP

The CONNECT.ASP page is the one that does all the actual work. The core of the page is contained in the `<OBJECT>` tag, as in Listing 18.2.

Listing 18.2   **TSAC** *<object>* **Tag in the Web Page**

```
<OBJECT language="vbscript" ID="MsTsc"
        CLASSID="CLSID:1fb464c8-09bb-4017-a2f5-eb742f04392f"
        CODEBASE="mstscax.cab#version=5,0,2221,1"
        WIDTH=<% resWidth = Request.QueryString("rW")
            if   resWidth < 200 or resWidth > 1600 then
                resWidth = 800
            end if
            Response.Write resWidth %>
        HEIGHT=<% resHeight = Request.QueryString("rH")
            if   resHeight < 200 or resHeight > 1200 then
                resHeight = 600
            end if
            Response.Write resHeight %>>
        </OBJECT>
```

For those unfamiliar with the function of the HTML <OBJECT> tag, what this tag does is to open a window for the output display of a particular object. This tag enables you to pass the height and width of the window in which the object will display to the user's web browser. In this case, the height and width are coming from the rW and rH parameters that were passed to this web page in the URL by DEFAULT.HTM.

Within the <OBJECT> tag also is specified the CLSID and CODEBASE of the object. These are two very important parameters and are what allow for the automatic download of the ActiveX client.

The CLSID parameter is the class ID for the object. The CLSID is a globally unique number that identifies a particular application component. Every application installed on a Windows-based operating system records its CLSID into the Registry of the operating system. You can find the list of CLSIDs currently installed on your system under the following key in the Registry:

```
HKLM\Software\Classes
```

When a user's web browser reads in the <OBJECT> tag, the following procedure happens:

1. The user's web browser reads the CLSID of the object.
2. If the CLSID exists in the user's local Registry, the application component has been installed. Skip to step 4.
3. The object has not been installed. Display the name of the component to the user and ask whether he wants to install it. (This is the window shown in Figure 18.2.) If so, download the component from the address specified in the CODEBASE parameter. In this case, the component is MSTSCAX.CAB and is located in the same folder as the web page.

4. Open a window, of the height and width specified, in the user's browser. Then pass control to the object.

The <OBJECT> tag works in conjunction with the following condensed bit of VBScript code (see Listing 18.3). Although the <OBJECT> tag provides the framework for the ActiveX Terminal Services client, this VBScript code is what actually makes the connection. The window_OnLoad() method means that this code is run at the point the web page is first loaded. The first thing the code does is to retrieve the value of the Server parameter that was passed to this page via the URL from DEFAULT.HTM.

Next, it assigns the value of the Server parameter to the MsTsc.Server object parameter. This sets the IP address of the server for the object. This code ends by calling the MsTsc.Connect() method, which is the method that establishes the connection to the Terminal Server.

Listing 18.3 **VBScript Code**

```
<script language="vbscript" >
...

sub window_onLoad()
     If not "<%Response.Write Request.QueryString("Server")%>" = "" then
          srvName = "<%Response.Write Request.QueryString("Server")%>"
     else
          srvName = Document.location.hostname
     end if
     MsTsc.Server        =  srvName
...
...

     MsTsc.Connect()
end sub
—>
</script>
```

Now that you understand the basics of how the page works, and with a little bit of knowledge of VBScript and HTML, you can modify this page to do what you need.

19

Deploying Applications over the Web Using NFuse and Wireless Technologies

THIS CHAPTER IS ALL ABOUT REALIZING the true application portability that Citrix MetaFrame is intended to provide by teaching you how to deploy web and wireless access to your Citrix MetaFrame 1.8 and XP server farm.

The first method of application deployment that you will learn about is how to deploy applications through the web using Citrix NFuse technology. NFuse is a freely available product from Citrix that is designed to work with your existing MetaFrame 1.8 or XP solution and help you to quickly build your own web-based application portal. With this web-based application portal, users will be able to log on to your server farm using only a web browser and run all the applications that you published to them. In effect, this product creates a virtual desktop for your users on the web, which they can access from wherever they are, through whatever connection type they choose and from whatever machine they might be on.

The second method of application deployment you will learn about in this chapter is through wireless. Wireless technology today has already become a very valuable technology for the deployment of business applications. Using Citrix MetaFrame technology and the techniques shown in this chapter, you will be able to take any corporate application and securely run it on nearly any handheld or wireless device. For example, you could run Outlook or a sales-reporting application on a color Win CE handheld via a wireless connection from wherever you have wireless connection. Although wireless connections speeds today tend to be slow, you would be surprised how fast you can run your applications and how usable they are with Citrix MetaFrame, even at speeds of less than 19.2K!

Understanding and Planning for NFuse

Before you learn the details of how NFuse works, it is important to cover the basics. NFuse has gone through several releases in the past year as more and more people have learned about this technology and demanded more features. The version of NFuse covered in this chapter is version 1.6.

NFuse started as more of an experiment by Citrix on how to bring your applications to the web. Originally, NFuse was just a set of freely available application components developed by Citrix. These applications components were intended for use by web developers to use to build their own application portal using Citrix MetaFrame technologies. There were some sample web sites included with the product, but they were intended only as demos of the capabilities of NFuse technologies and lacked many of the features important in a corporate environment.

With the release of NFuse 1.51 and NFuse 1.6, Citrix is starting to create a more turnkey product that Citrix MetaFrame administrators can use without the need for custom development. NFuse 1.6 installs with a well-designed, secure, and fully functional corporate application portal already included.

In the sections that follow, you will learn the details of how NFuse works and how to plan for your own NFuse solution.

What Is NFuse?

NFuse can be thought of as Program Neighborhood brought to your web browser. This chapter refers to this as providing a "virtual desktop" on the web for your users. Much like an application set in Program Neighborhood, NFuse enables you to easily set up a web site that users can log on to, view, and run any of the applications that you have published to them. Figure 19.1 shows the virtual desktop of a user logged on to the NFuse web site included with NFuse 1.6. From this web browser view of their applications, they can launch any of the applications, just as if it were an icon in their Program Neighborhood.

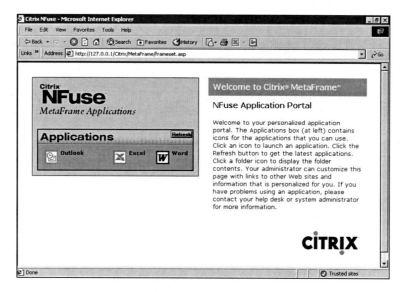

Figure 19.1   NFuse application set.

Where Can It Be Run?

NFuse is a more flexible solution than that provided by the *Terminal Services Advanced Client* (TSAC) in terms of both what clients will run with it and what servers it will run on. On the client side, TSAC will run only on Microsoft Internet Explorer browsers; however, NFuse can be used with Internet Explorer, Netscape Navigator, and pretty much any other Java-enabled web browser across multiple operating systems.

On the server side, TSAC server components work only with Microsoft IIS 4.0 and 5.0 servers. NFuse 1.6, on the other hand, has been tested on all the following web server platforms:

- Apache Server 1.3.20 on Redhat Linux 6.2/7.1 or Solaris 7/8
- iPlanet Web Server 4.1 on Solaris 7/8
- Tomcat 3.2.2 on Redhat Linux 6.2/7.1 or Solaris 7/8
- Microsoft Internet Information Server 4.0 on Windows NT 4.0 or Windows NT 4.0 Terminal Server
- Microsoft Internet Information Server 5.0 on Windows 2000 or Windows 2000 Terminal Server
- Netscape Enterprise Server 3.6 on Solaris 7/8
- IBM HTTP 1.3.12.2 on Solaris 7/8

Author's Note

In this chapter, you will learn the details of how to install NFuse on Microsoft web servers. However, much of the discussion in this chapter revolves around concepts that apply equally to deployments using any of the listed web server platforms.

It is important to note that NFuse 1.6 will work with either MetaFrame 1.8 or MetaFrame XP server farms. For it to work with a MetaFrame 1.8 server farm, however, you need to install Feature Release 1 and Service Pack 3. You also will need to make sure the following line is added to your NFUSE.CONF configuration file located in the `%systemroot%\java` folder of the NFuse server:

```
addressresolutiontype = ipv4
```

If you intend to run NFuse 1.6 with MetaFrame XP server farms, you need to have at least Service Pack 1 for MetaFrame XP installed on all the servers in the XP farm. You also will need Feature Release 1 if you intend to use any of the following features of NFuse:

- Novell NDS Authentication
- ICA over SSL
- Content Publishing

If you want to deploy an NFuse solution without Service Pack 1, you can deploy NFuse 1.51 instead. As of this writing, NFuse 1.51 is still available for download at the Citrix web site at `www.citrix.com/download`.

Where It Can Be Applied

NFuse is a very flexible product that can be deployed for many uses and customized for special purposes. The following sections discuss common and useful deployment options.

Corporate Application Portal

Probably the most common purpose for deploying NFuse is to build a corporate application portal. You likely already have or are planning to create a Citrix MetaFrame server farm to host corporate applications. Using NFuse you can bring these applications to the web for free! NFuse makes application deployment a breeze. If you deploy an application using Citrix the standard way, you still need to send out the clients and configure them correctly for the users to use them. With NFuse, you can either use a quickly downloadable "web version" of the clients or set up an automated client download site with preconfigured clients for the users.

Part of a Corporate Enterprise Portal

A big difference exists between an "application" portal and an "enterprise" portal. However, NFuse's application portal technology can easily be integrated into your existing or future enterprise portal. Many enterprise portal vendors, including PlumTree, Viador, and Yahoo!, now directly support NFuse integration.

Although NFuse alone is considered an application portal, an enterprise portal takes a product, such as NFuse to the next level. Like an application portal, users need to log on to the enterprise portal using their web browser. When users are logged on, most enterprise portals present the user with a customizable view of all their web-based applications, such as news feeds, online documents, reports, graphs, and other web content that is either subscribed to or maintained by the enterprise. Many enterprise portals include the built-in capability to integrate an NFuse application portal directly into them to provide a virtual desktop for users in addition to the other content that they provide. Figure 19.2 shows an example of this technology.

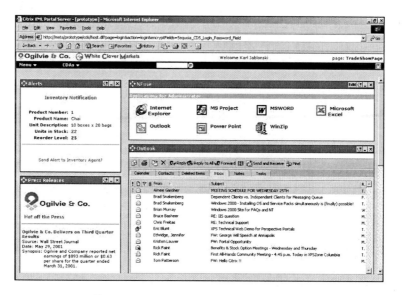

Figure 19.2   Enterprise application portal.

Most enterprise portals can provide a wealth of web-based content and applications besides just the virtual desktop application provided by NFuse alone. The following are some examples of the many different items that can be either added or subscribed to with most enterprise portal products:

- **News and weather** Companies such as iSyndicate
  (www.isyndicate.com) offer news and weather content that can integrate
  with most enterprise portal solutions; along with many other types of
  news-related feeds, such as online magazines, sports information, and
  entertainment.

- **Stocks and business news** The ability to keep track of stock information is becoming commonly available in many enterprise portal products.
  In addition, business news feeds are becoming more common; even some
  industry-specific news feeds are now available.

- **Reports and graphs** Many business-intelligence packages offer the
  ability to view reports and graphs through their own web portal, which in
  many cases can be integrated with NFuse. Some enterprise portal vendors
  are providing this functionality or at least making it very easy to build this
  functionality as a plug-in to their products.

- **Email, contact information, calendar** These are common web tools
  available in most enterprise portal offerings. Instead of taxing the resources
  of your Citrix server farm running Outlook or some other email package,
  you can have users use the web-based email tools to check their mail and
  use the NFuse applications for more line-of-business-related applications.

- **Employee news** A portal is the perfect instrument for communicating
  periodic newsletters to the company. In large companies, this can be a
  great way to communicate what various divisions within the company are
  doing.

- **Human resources information** Although not many packages on the
  market today are designed to plug in to a portal, in the future you likely
  will see more portal-friendly packages available that employees can use to
  retrieve such information as 401K contributions and status (plug-ins from
  the financial companies), employee stock options value, vacation days
  taken and left, sick days available, and more. Putting this type of information can easily save hundreds of man hours per year for the Human
  Resources department.

- **Employee forms and other documents** Many portal products offer
  what is referred to as a taxonomy. In this situation, the word *taxonomy* is
  used to refer to a hierarchical way of organizing and classifying documents
  on the web. Kind of like File Explorer for the web, this web-based
  method of document management often offers advanced features, such as
  indexing and searching capabilities, and advanced document security, so
  that employees can easily retrieve needed corporate documents and forms.

- **Online forums**   Many portal products offer the ability to easily create
  online forums that employees can use for workgroup discussions and
  online collaboration.

Of course, not all products include all of these capabilities, and these types of
products currently are very expensive. For many companies, however, the
incredible business value of combining all these features into one web interface can be well worth the investment. Citrix recently made the move into
the enterprise portal market with the purchase of Sequoia and their XPS
enterprise portal software. Although XPS is not covered in this book, you
will likely see interesting and exciting future products that take advantage of
the synergies brought about by this acquisition. As of today, NFuse integrates
easily into the XPS portal software as a "plug-in."

In addition, you will find enterprise portal offerings from companies, such
as PlumTree, Viador, and Yahoo! that do integrate easily with NFuse. These
companies are just a small sampling of the many companies that are currently
building or have built portal-like functionality into their software. One approach for researching a good enterprise portal solution for your company is
to start with a study on the players in the portal market. You can find these
types of studies available for purchase from business research and analysis
firms, such as the Gartner Group and IDC.

Multifarm Access

One very important feature of NFuse 1.6 is its capability to integrate access
to multiple farms into a single interface. By using this capability, you can
build a single NFuse web site that users can log on to and retrieve their
applications, even if those applications exist on different farms. This feature is
useful in many cases, including the following:

- **Application service providers**   ASPs that are looking for a way to
  provide a single point of access to Citrix applications, but need to divide
  their Citrix servers into separate farms for the purpose of security, can use
  this feature to create this interface for their customers.

- **Upgrading from MetaFrame 1.8 to XP**   If you are upgrading from
  MetaFrame 1.8 to XP, using NFuse's multifarm support can be an excellent choice. Instead of using mixed mode to migrate servers within the
  same farm to XP, you create a new farm in native mode that contains
  only MetaFrame XP servers. As each MetaFrame 1.8 server is upgraded, it
  is added to this new farm. You then create a multifarm NFuse web site
  that checks for user's applications in both the old farm and the new one.
  As long as users use the NFuse web page to access their Citrix servers,
  they will see a consolidated view of their applications in the old 1.8 farm
  and the new XP farm.

- **Business recovery**   One idea for a high level of business recovery capability is you could create two multifarm NFuse web sites and set them up at geographically separate locations. In addition, you could have a normal set of servers in one location and a backup set of servers with identical applications at the business recovery location.

Business Recovery

Imagine your business is in Florida and a hurricane is threatening to come inland and wipe out your data center. Even if you have a good business recovery plan in place, your key people will still need to their applications no matter where they are. In addition, users at the sites still need access to their applications.

Many corporations handle this problem by setting up a backup data center at an alternate location and replicating their data to it. If a disaster is declared, access to applications is switched over to the backup data center. However, one of the many challenges with this approach is finding easy ways to switch your applications over to the backup data center. Many companies handle this need with the "dual-icon" approach. They set up a primary and backup connection at the client to the servers to which they need access. The biggest problem with this approach is smooth coordination. It is often difficult, especially in a time of emergency, to smoothly transition all the users to use the backup systems.

By using NFuse as a disaster recovery solution, you can do this switchover centrally, without any change to the icons that the users see through the NFuse interface. To set up this approach, you would set up a backup NFuse server at your data center location and enough backup Citrix MetaFrame servers to handle running critical applications in an emergency.

Upon declaring a disaster, you would switch over your DNS servers to repoint your NFuse web site address to the NFuse servers at your business recovery center. From the user's perspective, he would still go to the same address to get his applications through NFuse; however, he would actually be logging on to an NFuse web server at your business recovery location rather than at your main data center!

This solution also has several advantages on the back end. Because your applications are published centrally through Citrix, you can easily switch the published applications over to point to the backup servers without the user seeing any difference. Suppose, for example, that you have an IBM AS/400 at your main data center named SALESORD01. You have a backup AS/400 at your business recovery center named BRCSLS1. All transactions from the primary sales order AS/400 are replicated live to the backup AS/400. Users currently know how to access the primary AS/400 through NFuse because you published Client Access terminal emulation to them with a preconfigured connection entry for the primary AS/400. The icon name in NFuse for the primary AS/400 is SALESORD01. When users click it, Client Access is run on the Citrix MetaFrame servers, and the user sees the logon screen for the AS/400.

Upon declaring a disaster, follow these steps:

1. Switch your NFuse users to the NFuse server at the business recovery center.

2. Make sure Client Access is installed and published on your backup Citrix MetaFrame servers at the business recovery center.

3. Repoint the SALESORD01 published application to point to the backup AS/400 and not the primary. You would keep the published application name the same.

Your users would still log on the same way and see the same icons. On the back end, however, you have easily and centrally switched your applications over to the backup data center!

Although this is good for recovery of your production applications, be sure to remember that Citrix MetaFrame also is an excellent place to which to publish all of your admin tools. In an emergency, as long as your administrative applications are published through Citrix, you will still have complete administrative access to your network. In an emergency, this availability of administrative applications is very important because key people will likely be scattered throughout the country (depending on individual travel situations).

Business-to-Business Web Site

The final suggested use for NFuse is for the creation or enhancement of a business-to-business web site. By creating an externally accessible application portal to selected internal applications, you can allow business partners to access important information and perform transactions. Of course in a solution such as this, security would be a paramount concern. However, using a combination of server-, application-, and data-level security, you could provide business partners with secure access to only the information to which they need access. In addition, using SSL technology included with Feature Release 1 for MetaFrame XP, you can encrypt the traffic going to and from the NFuse server.

How to Deploy NFuse

NFuse can be deployed in so many ways that it can be difficult to decide how exactly to deploy it. Although the NFuse web site included with NFuse 1.6 is ready to deploy, NFuse is a product that you can easily customize with the help of either in-house web development resources or consultants. Because it is a product that is meant to be customized, how you deploy it depends a lot on what development resources you can apply to its customization. The goal, of course, is to gain the greatest business value out of the product by integrating it with other business solutions.

Beyond just customizing the interface and integrating NFuse with other web applications and into portals, there are some important concepts to consider about the web servers themselves. This short section covers some of the common hardware deployments that you can use to deploy an NFuse solution and the advantages and disadvantages of each.

Using the Results of the Columbia Project in Your Web Site

You might have heard about the Columbia project by Citrix. However, there is a lot of confusion as to exactly what it provides and how it differs from what is included with NFuse.

Columbia is a sample NFuse web site that has been developed by Citrix. It includes several additional features not available in the sample web site included with NFuse 1.6. The latest version of Columbia as of this writing is Columbia version 6.x. Unlike NFuse 1.6, which runs on several different web server platforms, Columbia is designed to work only on Microsoft IIS 5.0 web servers.

The following are some of the many new features that you will find only in Columbia 6.x:

- Easy creation of a domain list for users to select from when they log on.

- Support for logon to multiple farms. This support combines all your applications in both farms into a single list.

- Ability to hide folders or applications.

- Support for NAT and PAT translation through firewalls.

- Ability to control the display size and number of columns for the application icons.

- Ability to have user change her password if expired.

Although instructions in this chapter are focused on the implementation of NFuse 1.6, you can download Columbia and try it out for yourself from http://apps.citrix.com/CDN/Columbia/default.asp. This web page is part of the Citrix Developer Network site. If you do not have a logon and password to this site, you can sign up for free. This is a very good site to be a member of because it contains a wealth of utilities and technical information, besides just Columbia.

Remember that Columbia is a sample product and, as of this writing, is supported by Citrix. It also is not as widely tested as the web site that comes with NFuse 1.6. If you want to try it out with your MetaFrame XP server farm, however, the general steps to set it up are as follows:

1. Install IIS on the Windows 2000 server you will be using as your NFuse server. This server does not have to have Citrix MetaFrame or Terminal Services on it, just IIS.

2. Apply the latest Microsoft service pack for your server along with all the latest hotfixes. There are many important security-related hotfixes for IIS.

3. Install Service Pack 1 on all the servers in your Citrix MetaFrame XP server farm. (This is required for NFuse 1.6 and Columbia 6.x to work.) Install Feature Release 1 if you need it for the features it provides.

4. Install NFuse 1.6 under the `%systemdrive%\inetpub\wwwroot` folder. Although you can install NFuse 1.6 and Columbia into other web folders, you might run into problems. It is best to use the default folder.

5. Download Columbia 6.x from Citrix and install it by just extracting the contents to a folder underneath the web root. For example, extract the contents to `%systemdrive%\inetpub\wwwroot\metaframe`.

In the `\config` folder off of the root of the Columbia web site, you will find a CONFIG.TXT file. This file contains all the configuration settings available for Columbia. You can edit the settings for the Columbia site very easily by opening the file in Notepad and changing them. Significant comment sections within the CONFIG.TXT file describe the settings in detail. In addition, you can find documentation online for the Columbia project at the `http://apps.citrix.com/CDN/Columbia/default.asp` web site.

Single Citrix/NFuse Server Solution

One possible deployment option is to make your Citrix server do double duty by making into an NFuse web server. For smaller environments, this can be an excellent solution because you can take the most advantage of your existing hardware investment, without having to purchase new equipment to bring your Citrix MetaFrame applications to the web.

As you will see in this chapter, setting up any Windows NT 4.0 or Windows 2000 server as a web server is very easy. In addition, NFuse is designed to integrate well with this Microsoft IIS solution by the use of a custom ISAPI from Citrix. This application component for IIS web servers allows an NFuse server to respond to NFuse requests on the same network port used for web services.

This approach offers two main disadvantages. The first is reliability. As any Windows administrator likely knows, the fewer services you run on the same server, the more reliable the server will be. In addition, if changes need to be made to the server, the changes can potentially affect both services. If you need to install a patch on the Citrix MetaFrame server and that server runs both web services and Citrix MetaFrame, for instance, it is possible that the patch can cause a problem with either the web server or Citrix MetaFrame. This increases the likelihood of server outages.

Also any work that needs to be done on the server requires both taking down the web server and the Citrix MetaFrame server. This means it could be more difficult to perform maintenance, because you would have to plan for the effects of both services being unavailable during the maintenance window. Suppose, for example, that the web services on the server were used for the company's main intranet in addition to NFuse access to applications. If you needed to do a hardware upgrade, you would have to find a time where the main intranet, Citrix MetaFrame server, and NFuse web site could be down. If they were on separate servers, only one of the services would be affected by maintenance.

The second disadvantage is security, especially if this server is to be used for external access to applications through the web. As witnessed in the recent Red Worm virus, it is very possible for a web server to be infected in a relatively short amount of time after vulnerability has been realized. A successful security attack or virus would be able to take down both the Citrix MetaFrame server and the web server components.

Dedicated NFuse Web Sever

The preferred choice for medium- to large-size business is to set up a dedicated web server for NFuse. Being dedicated, this server would not be used for any other services than NFuse browsing. This approach is very reliable and very secure.

Because the server is dedicated, it is less likely to fail, because fewer services need to work together on the same box. In addition, maintenance is easier because taking down the NFuse web server can be done without affecting the Citrix server farm. Users can still access applications directly on the farm, even though the NFuse web site is down.

Multiple NFuse Web Servers

In the largest of deployments or where reliability is a chief concern, you might consider deploying multiple NFuse web servers. You can use DNS round-robin to distribute the load of incoming users to each of the web servers. Each web server would be set up exactly the same with the same web pages. As each user tries to connect to the web farm, she is sent to the next server in sequence by DNS. However, if you choose to use DNS round-robin, realize that this is a load-sharing solution and not a load-balancing one. In addition, if one server fails, users will still be directed to that server until the server has been removed from the load-sharing list in the DNS. For more information on how to set up DNS round-robin, see Chapter 26, "Disaster Recovery Techniques and Enhancing Reliability."

Some hardware web site load-balancing solutions also might work for load balancing NFuse web sites. A hardware load-balancing device enables you to distribute incoming web server requests to multiple web sites behind it in a centrally controllable fashion. By putting a device such as this between your NFuse web servers and the users, you will have better central control over how incoming requests are distributed between servers than you would with DNS round-robin.

How NFuse Works

Now that you understand some of the many options available for deploying NFuse, it is time to learn exactly how it works. This section covers the functionality of NFuse, how it works and how it communicates over a network.

The Initial Logon

The first step in using an NFuse web site is logging on (see Figure 19.3). From the main NFuse page, a user needs to enter his username and password to log on to the page and retrieve his applications. The logon information is passed through NFuse server-side components running on the NFuse web server via port 80 or HTTP. The user can specify the domain that he wants to log on to by using the username [domain]/[username] and then entering the password. If you have a pure Windows 2000 environment and you are using MetaFrame XP, the user also can log on to the Windows 2000 domain controller using the [username]@[domain name] format.

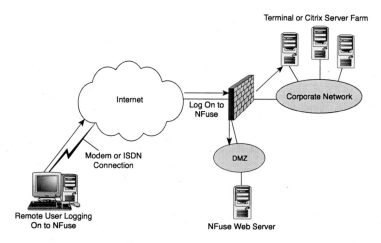

Figure 19.3   NFuse logon.

The NFuse server-side web components use this information to authenticate the user with the PDC for the domain that the NFuse server is a part of. For this portion of the communication to work, the standard ports used for either Windows 2000 or NT 4.0 logon must be open between the NFuse web server and the domain controller. For more information on these ports, see Chapter 17, "Firewalls and SSL Relay."

The XML Service and Application Enumeration

After the user has been authenticated, the NFuse server-side components running on the web server pass the user information to the XML service running on one or more servers in the Citrix MetaFrame server farm (see Figure 19.4). The XML service then uses the user information and what groups the user is a member of to generate a list of applications.

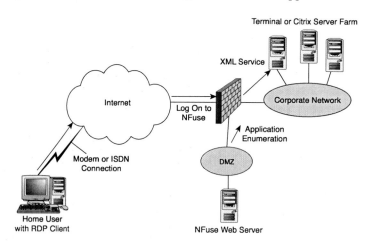

Figure 19.4   XML service and application enumeration.

If the XML service is running on a MetaFrame 1.8 server farm, this information is retrieved from the Program Neighborhood service. If it is running on a MetaFrame XP server farm, the list of applications is retrieved from the IMA service. Either way, the list of applications that a user has published to them, based on what groups she is a part of and what her user ID is, will be sent back to the NFuse web server.

The XML service is included with MetaFrame XP, and you are allowed to select the port that it uses during installation. However, the XML service is available only for a MetaFrame 1.8 server by installing Feature Release 1. Once installed, the XML service runs as a standard Windows service on whatever Terminal Server platform you installed it on, whether Windows NT 4.0 or 2000.

The port that this traffic occurs on depends on what port was assigned to the XML service when it was first installed. By default, the XML service resides on the same port used by HTTP, port 80. However, either during the installation or after the installation using the `ctxxmlss /r[port#]` command, as shown in Chapter 17, you can change the XML service's port to a port of your choosing.

During the installation of the NFuse web server components, you are asked to specify the port and IP address to be used for reaching the XML service on your Citrix MetaFrame server farm. The port specified here must match the port used on the specified Citrix MetaFrame server for NFuse to work.

Generate the HTML Code and Application Icons

After the list of applications is acquired through the XML service, this service sends the list back to the NFuse server. The NFuse server's server-side components then create the HTML code necessary to display the list of applications to the user. In addition, the graphics for each application's icon are retrieved from the Citrix server farm for display to the user.

Each application icon and name is hyperlinked in the HTML code to point to the template .ICA file at the NFuse server, with parameters specific to that application. This .ICA template file and the parameters provided are what provide the information necessary to run the application.

Creating an .ICA File

After the page has been assembled, it is displayed to the user in the user's web browser. The user basically sees a simple list of the application icons that he can click to run the particular application. When a user clicks one of the icons, this request is again sent to the NFuse server's server-side web components. These components then do the following:

1. Open the .ICA template file specified by the user's request for that particular application.

2. Create an actual .ICA file from the template using the parameter information and other user-specific information.

3. Send the .ICA file for the application back to the user, so that he can run it.

The .ICA template file is a very important part of this process. This file is located in the NFuse web directory and contains the serverwide application settings that you want to deploy for your NFuse applications. Because a user's

.ICA file is merged with the template .ICA file upon every application launch, the settings in the .ICA template file can affect all applications run from that NFuse server.

NFuse and .ICA Files

.ICA files are files that contain the settings, user IDs, and passwords that you need to make a connection to a Citrix server. If you have the ICA client on your workstation, you can double-click any .ICA file that you have access to and a connection will open with the Citrix MetaFrame server. What NFuse does is basically create an .ICA file for each of the user's applications and then sends that .ICA file to the user's ICA client when she selects that application in her browser.

Launching the Application

After the .ICA file has been put together for the application, it is passed back to the user's browser. As long as the user has the ICA client installed on his local workstation, the ICA client will run the .ICA file and make the connection to the appropriate Citrix MetaFrame server.

If the user has a problem launching the application, it is generally either a problem with the creation of the .ICA file or a problem with his local Citrix ICA client. Remember that NFuse's job is to just pass the .ICA file back to the client. The client must have some version of the ICA client installed, whether it is the web version or the full ICA client, to launch the application.

If you install the client software with NFuse 1.6, the user can download and install the necessary ICA client from the web site. The installation of the ICA client software creates an Icaweb folder off of the web root. Unless this folder is on your web site, you will not be able to automatically download clients to your users. Underneath this folder, you will find several subfolders that contain various versions of the ICA client. There is code in the NFuse 1.6 product to automatically detect the client type and present users with the correct client for them to download. If you need to update the client in the future, you can just update the appropriate ICA client install file underneath the Icaweb folder.

The connection is established directly between the ICA client and the Citrix servers. This is an important point to remember. If you need to provide access to your Citrix server farm through a firewall using NFuse, you need to open up the ports for access to both the NFuse servers (port 80) and all the Citrix servers in the farm (port 1494, 1603, and 80).

Installing NFuse and a Web-Based ICA Client Download Site

Installing NFuse involves two basic steps: installing the web server components and setting up the XML service on the Citrix MetaFrame server farm. This section outlines the steps necessary to perform both of these procedures using a Microsoft IIS server as the web server.

Setting Up the XML Service

The first step in the installation is to set up the XML service on at least one server in your Citrix MetaFrame server farm. The XML service is the service that the NFuse web server will use to communicate with the server farm. The XML service will run on either a MetaFrame 1.8 server or a MetaFrame XP server. On a MetaFrame 1.8 server farm, you need to install Feature Release 1; on MetaFrame XP, however, the XML service is included.

For a MetaFrame 1.8 server farm, follow these steps:

1. Set up either a Windows 2000 or NT 4.0 Terminal Server.

2. Purchase and install either MetaFrame 1.8 for Windows 2000 or NT 4.0 on the server.

3. Purchase and install Feature Release 1 for MetaFrame 1.8 on the server. During the installation of Feature Release 1, you have the option to specify the port to be used for the XML service. Specify to use port 80, unless you have reason to use your own port.

4. Restart the server and install the latest service pack.

5. Restart the server again and verify that the XML service is running from the server's Control Panel.

For a MetaFrame XP server, follow these steps:

1. Set up either a Windows 2000 or NT 4.0 Terminal Server.

2. Purchase and install MetaFrame XPa, XPs, or XPe. During the installation of all of these products, you are prompted for the port number to be used by the XML service (see Figure 19.5). Leave the default option of sharing port 80, unless you have reason to use another port.

3. During the installation, if the server has IIS installed, you also will be prompted as to whether NFuse should be installed (see Figure 19.6). If you want the NFuse server to be your Citrix MetaFrame server, check the appropriate boxes to install NFuse. Realize, however, that this means the server will be sharing the port used by the web server with the XML service for Citrix MetaFrame. This could cause performance problems on large farms.

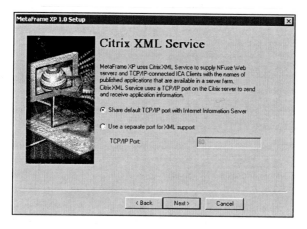

Figure 19.5   Specifying the XML port.

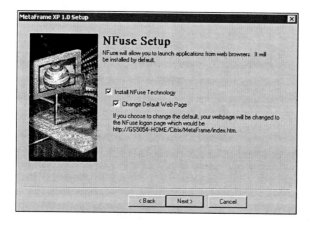

Figure 19.6   Setting up NFuse.

4. Install the latest MetaFrame XP service pack and reboot the server.

Setting Up the NFuse Web Server

NFuse can be installed on either a Microsoft IIS 4.0 or 5.0 web server, among others. Microsoft IIS 3.0 is included in the Microsoft option pack for Window NT 4.0 Server and Terminal Server. It can be upgraded to IIS 4.0 by installing the latest service pack. Microsoft IIS 5.0 is included as an installable Windows component in Windows 2000.

To set up a Microsoft IIS 4.0 web server, follow these steps:

1. Set up either a Windows NT 4.0 server or Windows NT 4.0 Terminal Server. It is preferred to use a Windows NT 4.0 Server if this is to be a dedicated NFuse web server.

2. Install the Windows NT 4.0 option pack. The option pack normally includes IIS 3.0.

3. Install Service Pack 6a.

4. Reboot the server and verify that the Web service has been started and that you can view the default web page on the server using the following web address: `http://[server name]`

To set up a Microsoft IIS 5.0 web server, follow these steps:

1. On a Windows 2000 server or Terminal Server, go into Control Panel, Add/Remove Programs.

2. Select Add/Remove Windows Components.

3. Check the box next to Internet Information Services, and then click OK.

4. Reboot the server and install the latest Windows 2000 service pack.

At this point the web server with the default web site will be set up. The next step is to set up the web site that you want to be used by the NFuse service. NFuse will normally install in a `\citrix\metaframe` subfolder of the default web site. On both IIS 4.0 and 5.0 the default web site is located in the `%systemdrive%\inetpub\wwwroot` folder. This location works fine for most situations. If you want to use another directory for the web site or if you intend to support multiple web sites on the same server, however, you need to use IIS's web site administrative tools to create the web site for NFuse in a different folder. Because NFuse puts its web folders in subfolders under the main web folder, you can have a different web site at the root of the folder and then have a hyperlink on that web site to the NFuse web site. This type of configuration is good for a corporate Internet or intranet site where NFuse is not the main purpose for which users access the main site.

Web Page Redirection and the Default Web Page

Because NFuse installs in a subfolder off of the main web site, you might want users to be brought directly to this subfolder. Suppose the NFuse location is in the `\citrix\metaframe` subdirectory and the web site name is `citrix.acme.com`. If a user needs to go to the NFuse web site, he would need to enter `http://citrix.acme.com/citrix/metaframe/default.htm`.

This is a rather complicated web address and is difficult for a user to remember. You can make it easier in couple of ways.

First, you could create a redirector web page off of the root of the web site called `default.htm`. When users enter the address `http://citrix.acme.com`, the server attempts to bring up the `http://citrix.acme.com/default.htm` web page. You can set this page to automatically redirect the user to the correct address of `http://citrix.acme.com/citrix/metaframe/default.htm` as follows:

1. Create a blank document in Notepad and save it as `%systemdrive%\inetpub\wwwroot\default.htm`.

2. Open the Internet Services Manager from the Administrative Tools folder.

3. Open the default web site.

4. Right-click the DEFAULT.HTM file and select Properties.

5. Select A Redirection to a URL and then enter the address for the NFuse web page (that is, `http://citrix.acme.com/citrix/metaframe/default.htm`).

The second option is to create a redirector web site, not a web page, with a simpler name. For example, you might want to have users be able to use the easier-to-remember `http://www.acmeapps.com` address to get to the NFuse page for acme. To do this, you have to create a redirector web site. When someone attempts to access the redirector web site, her request is redirected to the more complicated URL listed previously. To do this, follow these steps:

1. Create a new web site using the IIS administrative tools.

2. Right-click the new web site and select Properties.

3. Click the Home Directory tab and click the Radio button next to A Redirection to a URL, and then enter the full URL for your NFuse web site.

4. Click the Web Site tab and click the Advanced button next to IP Address.

5. Click the Add button and enter the Host Header Name, and then click OK twice to save. For this example, the name would be www.acmeapps.com.

6. Right-click the main NFuse web sites tab and select Properties. For the example, the main web site is `citrix.acme.com`.

7. Click the Web Site tab and click Advanced.

8. Click the Add button and enter the Host Header Name for the main web site, and then click OK twice to save. In the example, the name is `citrix.acme.com`.

9. Start both web sites and test that the redirection works properly.

This procedure does two things. First it builds a special, easy-to-remember redirector web site on the same server that holds the main NFuse web site. Second, it uses what is referred to as *host header redirection* to keep the two web pages separate. As new users attempt to connect to `http://www.acmeapps.com`, they are automatically redirected to the `http://citrix.acme.com/citrix/metaframe` NFuse web site on the same server.

Installing NFuse 1.6

Installing NFuse 1.6 is actually very easy. However, it is very important to patch your servers properly before the installation. To install NFuse 1.6 on your Microsoft web server, follow these steps:

1. Download NFuse 1.6 from www.citrix.com/download. You should see a link for NFuse on this page that will bring you to where you can download it for free.

2. If web services are running, you will be prompted to stop the Web services.

3. Select Yes to agree to the agreement, and then select the location for the IIS web components to be installed and click Next.

4. Select Typical, and then click Next.

5. Enter the name or IP address of the Citrix server that has the XML service running, enter the port number that the XML service is running on, and then click Next. This is the server that NFuse will query to retrieve the list of applications for the users.

6. Click the Browse button to browse to the NFuse web site's root folder, and then click Next. The NFuse web site will be installed under this folder.

7. You will be prompted whether you want to set up a NFuse client web site. Click Yes or No.

8. If Yes, you must enter the location of the Icaweb client folder. If you have MetaFrame XP, you will find a copy of the Icaweb folder in the root of the ICA client's CD.

This technique installs a sample set of web pages accessible at http://[web server]/metaframe. From the main page, you can log on using your network username and password. You will be presented with your application set. You can then double-click any icon in the application set to launch that particular application.

Enabling Automatic Download of ICA Clients

All versions of NFuse require users to first download and install the ICA client for them to be able to run applications. By default, NFuse automatically detects whether you have the client installed and automatically prompts you for the installation of the client. For this process to work correctly, however, you must have installed the NFuse web clients during the installation of the IIS web components as shown in step 8.

This is a very important step during the installation. If you do not install the NFuse clients during this step, users who do not have the client installed on their machine will not be able to access the web site and will have to manually find a way to install the client.

The NFuse web clients are a special version of the full ICA client that includes most everything except the Program Neighborhood. By excluding the Program Neighborhood and related components, the size of the web clients can remain small. If you want the web client to be even smaller, it is possible to take out the .DLLs of the components that you don't need (for example, audio). This is especially important now because the new web client includes the Universal Print Driver functionality. Although robust, this .DLL is more than a megabyte in size. After removing the .DLL(s) you can then repackage the client and have it auto-execute upon download to the client's machine.

Ticketing and NFuse

Ticketing is a security-related feature with NFuse that has been introduced with version NFuse 1.51. The problem that it addresses is how authentication is handled. In older versions of NFuse, the user ID and password were kept in the .ICA file on the local machine for each application that the user launched. Although the password was kept encrypted rather than in clear text, just the fact that the password was in the .ICA file meant that the .ICA file itself could be used for access to the Citrix server. For example, a potential hacker could either find and then use an .ICA file from the workstation or could intercept the transmission, record the password hash, and then use it for future entry into the Citrix MetaFrame server farm.

To address this vulnerability, Citrix created a new process for authentication called *ticketing*. With ticketing, the user's logon credentials are not recorded in the .ICA file; instead, a cryptic 30-character string called a ticket is recorded. When the user presents this .ICA file to log on to the server, the user is granted access to the application through NFuse. The key difference between this process and the preceding one is that tickets expire periodically and are valid only for a single session. Even if a hacker can retrieve the .ICA file with the ticket, he cannot establish a new session to the Citrix MetaFrame server farm. For this reason, ticketing is highly recommended to implement on your Citrix NFuse solution.

Issues with Ticketing

There have been some reports of issues with ticketing in NFuse 1.51. On some machines, users click an icon, but the application never launches. Disabling ticketing fixes this problem; however, disabling ticketing causes some security concerns because the .ICA files are now on the user's workstation with credentials that can be used to log on to the server.

Although those issues seem to have been resolved in NFuse 1.6, if you do run into the problem of applications not launching, try disabling ticketing to see whether that fixes the problem.

Customizing NFuse

On a Microsoft platform, the NFuse web sites are mostly written using standard HTML. Although they do contain some special coding for server-side processing using *Active Server Page* (ASP) commands, you do not need a full understanding of ASP to perform simple customizations of the web pages. However, you do need a good understanding of HTML to edit them, because of the special embedded ASP coding, you might not be able to easily edit the pages in a standard HTML editor without causing problems with the ASP code.

If you want to blend the NFuse web pages into your existing web sites or add additional instructions for the user, for instance, you can bring up the NFuse pages in a simple text editor such as Notepad. You can then change the background color of the page or of the tables as needed by editing the appropriate HTML tag. If you need to add additional text, you can just edit the existing text by searching in the HTML code for where the text field is that you want to edit.

The following are the main web pages used with NFuse and their basic function:

- **DEFAULT.ASP** This page presents the user with the logon prompt and gathers the user's logon information.

- **FRAMESET.ASP** This is the frame displayed to the user and contains APPLIST.ASP and BLANK.ASP.

- **APPLIST.ASP** Presents the user with a list of her applications.

In addition to editing the HTML, you can change several configuration parameters. You can find these parameters in the `%systemroot%\java\ trustlib\nfuse.conf` text file. If you open this file in Notepad, you can edit the following parameters:

- `AlternateAddress` **(default Off)** Set this parameter to On if you want the alternate address for your Citrix servers sent to the clients. You would set this to On if your Citrix servers are behind a firewall and are set up with Network Address Translation.

- `Timeout` **(default 60)** This is the session timeout value in seconds for your Citrix NFuse session. Bump this value up if users are getting disconnected from NFuse too quickly.

- `SessionField.NFuse_CitrixServerPort` **(default 80)** Set this parameter to the port used by your XML service on your Citrix MetaFrame server farm. If you changed the port number on your farm for this service using the `ctxxmlss` command, you will need to change it here on your NFuse server.

- `SessionField.NFuse_CitrixServer` **(default [server name])** This value is set to the server name of the server you specified during the installation of NFuse. If you want to change the server that your NFuse server uses, then you can change it here.

Creating a Client Download Site

Although setting up the ability to download and install ICA clients automatically is preferred, many might want to set up a web site for the manual download of ICA clients. Citrix makes this very easy with a separate, freely available set of files that you can use to create your own download site for ICA clients. The web pages from Citrix do more than just enable you to download the clients. The initial web page, shown in Figure 19.7, will detect what platform your system is running on and will automatically present a hyperlink for the correct ICA client for your platform. This makes it easier for users; you save them from having to search through a page of different ICA clients for the right one for their system. Additionally, users can download either the web version of the client that does not include the Program Neighborhood and is ideal for access to applications only through NFuse or the full version of the client that can be used for access to the Citrix MetaFrame servers even without NFuse. Note that the web-based ICA Client Install Package is available for download only from the Citrix web site and is not on the CDs included with MetaFrame XP.

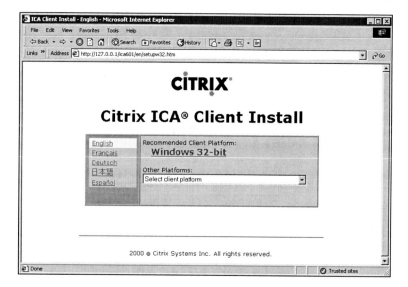

Figure 19.7   ICA client download web site.

To set up a client download web site, follow these steps:

1. Go to the product web site for NFuse, `www.citrix.com/products/nfuse` and select to download NFuse. You will need to enter marketing information to get to the download web site.

2. At the download web site, select to download the Generic Web-Based ICA Client Install Package.

3. Download the HTML front end and expand it into the default directory of `c:\ica601`.

4. Download the ICA clients for web-based ICA client installation and expand its contents into the same directory.

5. Copy this folder underneath the root folder of the web site on your server.

6. Make a hyperlink on the main page of the web site for `http://[server name]/ica601/setupen.htm` for the main page of the English client download.

The web pages are designed to reside under an Ica601 subfolder off of the main page of your web site. The client download web site is intended to be more of a sub-web site than a main web site. For example, you could create a main page for your NFuse web site and off of the main page have a link for the client download site.

Setting Up Wireless Access to Your Citrix Application

Setting up wireless access to your Citrix application is surprisingly easy to do. Although wireless access speeds today vary greatly depending on your location, before long fast wireless access will be available for everyone. Even at with today's slower wireless speeds, many applications run respectably fast using Citrix MetaFrame. At a cellular (CDPD) wireless connection speed of 14400 to 19200, applications are still very usable. Although you would not want to deploy heavily used applications, such as order entry, through this method, it is an excellent solution for remote access to business information and reporting applications, Windows administrative applications, terminal emulation, and more.

Several different types of wireless technologies are available today; however, the ones discussed in this section are CDPD and 802.11. CDPD wireless relies on cellular phone network technology to provide you wireless access to your mobile devices at speeds up to 19.2K. CDPD is available in most major metropolitan areas in the United States and is supported by several nationwide wireless providers.

The 802.11 technology is designed for wireless access within a building. With an 802.11 solution, you normally install your own wireless access points at key locations in your building and attach them to your network.

You then can connect wireless to these access points using 802.11 PCMCIA cards in your laptops or handhelds. The connection speed today for 802.11 technology is 10Mbps, and the wireless range is several hundred feet from the access point. By installing multiple access points in your building, you can provide wireless coverage throughout the entire office or warehouse area.

Usability at 19.2K

Although 19.2K is the advertised speed for CDPD, you will actually find that your connection speed will be more realistically around 14.4K. Your connection speed will vary greatly depending on the signal strength in your area.

Although 14.4K is not much for speed, you will likely be surprised at how usable your applications are at this speed using the ICA client. Although applications that demand fast response time, such as point-of-sale or sales-order entry, are not the best to run at this speed, this speed is sufficiently fast enough to be able to retrieve important business information while traveling. For example, you could deploy a sales-reporting application to your sales force so that they could pull up sales information when needed, in front of customers.

You can expect the initial connection to an application to take between one and three minutes. When the application is running, however, screen response time will be in the fractions of a second. Although a noticeable lag time will be apparent, the applications will still be very usable.

One good way to speed up logon times is to disable as many of the device mappings as you do not need. You disable device mappings at the connection level or just by editing the appropriate values in the WFCLIENT.INI file on the client device. Disable drive mappings, COM port mappings, audio mappings, and client updates, if you do not need them.

Setting Up CDPD Wireless Access

To set up a CDPD wireless solution, you need to first purchase CDPD cards for your devices. CDPD cards are available as PCMCIA cards and can be installed in most larger handhelds and nearly all laptops. Vendors such as Sierra Wireless (www.sierrawireless.com) and Novatel Wireless (www.novatelwireless.com) both make a large selection of different PCMCIA cards that you can use for your wireless solution.

After you have decided on a hardware vendor, the vendor can provide you with a list of different wireless service providers that you can use to establish the wireless service. These vendors usually provide you with your own static IP address on the Internet and the ability to use the connection for either a flat monthly fee or a per-minute charge.

After you have installed and configured the wireless PCMCIA card in your laptop or handheld and you have signed up with a wireless provider, you will basically be able to surf the Internet from wherever you have wireless connection. Although wireless coverage varies between service providers, most larger service providers have wireless CDPD coverage available in all major cities nationwide, and in some cases worldwide.

After your Internet connection has been established, the next step is to install the Citrix ICA client on your handheld or laptops. Citrix makes ICA clients for all versions of Win CE, which are compiled for all major handheld processors. You can easily run the Citrix ICA client on such handhelds as the HP Jornada, Compaq iPAQ, and NEC Mobile Pro. In addition, ICA clients are available for nearly all operating systems you would run on a laptop and for the EPOC operating system available on some cellular devices. Download the client from the Citrix web site and install it according to the specific instructions for the version of the client you need.

After the client has been installed, all you need to do is create a connection entry for your server, for a published application or for an application set. Use the public IP address for your server. You will need to assign public IP addresses for all of your Citrix MetaFrame servers in the farm. You also should create DNS hostnames for each server.

For security purposes, put a rule on the firewall to only let the IP address of the particular wireless device have access to your Citrix MetaFrame servers. The ports you need to open up vary depending on your configuration. However, normally ports TCP 80, TCP 443, UDP 1603, and TCP 1494 are the main ones. You do not need UDP port 1603 if you choose to connect using TCP/IP+HTTP or TCP/IP+SSL at the client. You also can enable encryption and even SSL on your wireless clients to encrypt the traffic going across the Internet.

If you are using NAT translation on your firewall, you will need to set the alternate address on all of your Citrix servers to the associated outside address on the firewall using the `altaddr` command from the command prompt of each server in your farm. On the client side, there will be a setting called Use Alternate Address. You must enable this setting for the client to be able to connect correctly to the outside or alternate address of your Citrix MetaFrame servers. The location of this setting varies from client to client, but you will normally find it in the Properties area of your custom ICA or application set connection entry. For more information on setting the alternate address or knowing the correct ports to open through your firewall, see the material in Chapter 17.

When all of these pieces are in place, you should be able to click the application or server icon on the client and make your connection to the Citrix MetaFrame server farm. The initial connection startup time will vary depending on your signal strength, but normally takes between one and three minutes. Once connected, you can use your applications wireless!

Running in Landscape

One problem with many of today's newer handhelds is that the screen size is very small and there is no way to run in landscape mode. However, there is actually an inexpensive third-party utility you can use to switch you handheld to landscape! This enables users to more easily view the applications on the small screen size with the ICA client. You can find this utility at www.jimmysoftware.com/Software/Landscape2. The current version of the utility works only with color screens on Compaq iPAQs and Casio Cassiopeas.

Setting up 802.11

Many of the techniques described in the preceding section about setting up CDPD are the same with 802.11 technology. You first need to find a vendor that makes an 802.11 solution. If you want to make a handheld device connect via 802.11, check with the hardware vendor for the handheld about a recommended 802.11 solution that will work with their handheld. For laptops, several vendors make 802.11 wireless solutions (for instance, Cisco and LinkSys).

After you have chosen your particular solution, you need to install the access points in your office. Access points are small devices that are basically antennas or base stations to which your wireless devices connect. The access points provide a bridge between your wireless 802.11 devices and the LAN. Many large hardware vendors work with specific contractors who have expertise in how to properly install access points. The goal is to provide wireless access from wherever you need it at your business. To meet this goal, access points need to be placed strategically throughout the building and connected into your network. If set up properly, you should be able to walk through the building with your wireless device and maintain your connection to the network.

Because the 802.11 access points are connected to your internal network, you do not have to worry about setting up access through a firewall. Instead, just install the ICA client on the laptop or handheld, along with the wireless PCMCIA card, and configure the client as you normally would.

Advanced Terminal Server and MetaFrame Topics

20

Advanced Printing Techniques

PROBABLY ONE OF THE MOST IMPORTANT yet often frustrating aspects of administering Terminal Servers is ensuring that printing works for users. When a user connects to a Terminal Server, the printers on his local workstation become printers available from his Terminal Server session. Although this is the intended goal, for various reasons this process can sometimes fail.

This chapter discusses the technical details of how this process works so that you can better troubleshoot printing problems in your environment. In addition, specific information on how to take advantage of the new printer and print driver management capabilities in MetaFrame XP are provided along with detailed information on the new Universal Printer Driver available in Feature Release 1.

How Printer Auto-Creation Works

Printer auto-creation has come a long way over the past few years in terms of robustness and capability, both in Terminal Server and in Citrix MetaFrame. In this section you will learn how printer auto-creation process works in Windows 2000 Terminal Server and how Citrix MetaFrame XP enhances it.

Printer Auto-Creation in Windows 2000 Terminal Server and MetaFrame

As you log on to a Windows 2000 Terminal Server, the server begins the printer auto-creation process by detecting the printers that you have on your local workstation. After it has a list of which printers are on your local desktop, the goal of the auto-creation process is to automatically create all of those printers on your Terminal Server desktop. Even though these printers are auto-created on the server, they are configured to redirect print jobs in the background to the client's local printers. In this way, the user can print from an application running on Terminal Server to her local printers, just like she can print from local applications. The goal of this process is to ensure that all the local printers that a user needs are available on their Terminal Server session. This is a very important goal; for without these printers being available, users could not print to any printer other than those locally defined on the Terminal Server itself. If you have 50 to 100 different users, trying to manually set up all the printers that they would need on all your Terminal Servers, this would quickly become an administrative nightmare.

The basic printer auto-creation process on a Windows 2000 Terminal Server is explained in the following sections. This process differs significantly from how printer auto-creation worked under Windows NT 4.0 Terminal Server. In addition, the process used by a Terminal Server and the one used with Citrix MetaFrame differs significantly. The points where there are differences are described in detail.

Enumerating Client Printers

The first step of the printer auto-creation process is printer enumeration. The printers available on the client's desktop are enumerated by the Terminal Server as the client logs on. The goal of this part of the process is to make those same printers available on the client's desktop on Terminal Server. To achieve this goal, the Terminal Server needs to know the name of all the printers and what the name of the printer driver is for each.

The information on which printers the client has is passed to the Terminal Server by either the ICA client or the RDP client, depending on what the user is running. This information is gathered by the client from the following Registry keys on Windows-based clients:

- **HKLM\System\CurrentControlSet\Control\Print\Printers** This key lists all the local printers currently installed on the workstation. For each local printer, there is a separate subkey under the main key. The name of the subkey is the same as the name of the printer. Within this subkey is a

`PrinterDriver` value that contains the name of the driver used for this printer. Because this is a machine key, these printers are available for all users of this workstation.

- **HKLU\Printers\Connections** Under this key is a list of all the network printers set up for this particular user. They are listed by the UNC of the printer, substituting commas for backslashes because backslashes are not allowed in key names. If the user made a connection to \\[server]\LaserJet 4, for example, the key name would be ,,[server],LaserJet 4. In the case of a network printer, the driver used depends on what is set up for the printer on the print server. This driver is downloaded to the client when the printer is installed.

For each listed printer, the printer name and the name of the driver used are determined and reported to the Terminal Server.

Mapping Client-Side Printers to Server-Side Drivers

The next step in the process is to determine what driver needs to be loaded on Terminal Server for each of the client's printers. This is the more complicated part of the process. Remember that both Citrix MetaFrame and Terminal Server support a wide variety of clients. Each one of those clients has its own operating system and printer drivers written for only that particular operating system. Although these drivers work fine for printing locally, they do not work for printing from Terminal Server. For a user to print from an application running on Terminal Server, the correct driver for the Terminal Server operating system must be loaded. The process to map the correct Terminal Server printer driver to the printers on the client is referred to as *mapping client-side printers to server-side drivers* or more simply just *printer driver mapping*.

Suppose, for example, that a user has Windows 95 and an HP LaserJet 4 printer. When that user logs on to a Windows 2000 Terminal Server, she will likely need to be able to print. For the user to print, she needs a Windows 2000 printer created on the server that points to the HP LaserJet on the client. For this to happen, some type of printer driver mapping must occur. As the client logs on, the Terminal Server sees she has a Windows 95 LaserJet 4 printer, loads the LaserJet 4 driver, and creates the LaserJet 4 printer at the server.

Although the exact method of printer driver mapping differs between Terminal Server and Citrix MetaFrame, the goal is the same. The goal is to load the correct driver for the printer on the user's Terminal Server session. This is the driver that will be used by the applications run by the user on

Terminal Server. Obtaining the correct Terminal Server printer driver is *critical* for the printing functionality of the user's applications and also for the stability of the server itself.

Author's Note

It is hard to overemphasize this point. Controlling the drivers used on Terminal Server is very important. Probably the single most common source of problems with Terminal Servers and Citrix MetaFrame is either the failure of this printer driver mapping process or the loading of an unstable or incorrect printer driver. By following the techniques outlined in this chapter, you can avoid most, if not all, of these print driver headaches.

You will see that with Citrix MetaFrame XP there is much better central control of printer drivers. By following some simple rules, however, you can still make printer management easy with just Terminal Server alone.

Although mapping drivers might seem initially to be a simple process, it is actually one of the more complicated processes that occur during client logon. This process is complicated for two main reasons. The first reason is that driver names are often not the same, even for the same printer, between operating system versions. Suppose, for example, a user prints to an HP LaserJet 4000 printer from a Windows 95 workstation. The printer name on the workstation is Accounting HP 4000 and the driver name is HP LaserJet 4000 PCL 6. If the user is to print to that printer from Terminal Server, the driver for an HP LaserJet 4000 must be loaded in the user's Terminal Server session. Because there is no strict standard for driver names by either HP or Microsoft, however, you might find the server-side driver name for an HP LaserJet 4000 to be referred to as HP LaserJet 4000, HP LaserJet 4000 PCL5, HP LaserJet 4000 PCL6, or even HP LaserJet 4000 PS. The trick is to load the correct server-side driver for the client's printer, based on the name of the driver on the client. To do this, some type of match up or mapping must be done.

The second, and most important reason that the printer driver mapping process is complicated is that not all drivers are compatible with Windows Terminal Server. Some manufacturers' printer drivers just do not work on Terminal Server. Some can even cause the dreaded blue screen of death when they are run. In addition, printer-monitoring functionality that is commonly built into many home printers does not work correctly on Terminal Server.

For this reason and more, the "Golden Rule" of Terminal Server printing is to use only those drivers included with Terminal Server, instead of attempting to install a manufacturer's drivers. Even if the exact driver is not available for your printer on Terminal Server, more often than not a compatible driver is available that will work fine for your users. If a compatible driver is not available, you can install the manufacturer's printer driver. Unless the manufacturer specifically supports Terminal Server, however, there is often a significant risk that the third-party driver might cause problems with your Terminal Server.

Between drivers whose names differ and drivers incompatible with Terminal Server, it can quickly become a challenge to make printing work smoothly on Terminal Server. To resolve these issues, you must know how to control how server-side drivers are mapped to client-side drivers. After the server has the list of client-side printer drivers and names, it begins the process documented in the following sections to determine the correct server-side driver to use. While you are learning this process, refer to Figure 20.1. Figure 20.1 diagrams this process in its entirety and is a good, simple flowchart that can be used for troubleshooting printer mapping problems.

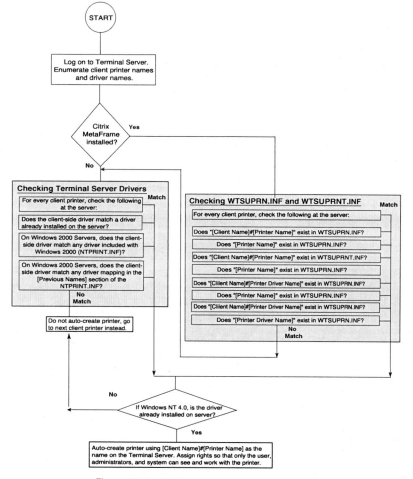

Figure 20.1 Printer auto-creation.

Matching with *%systemroot%\system32\wtsuprn.inf* and WTSPRNT.INF

If you are using Citrix MetaFrame 1.8, the first step the server will take is to check the WTSUPRN.INF and WTSPRNT.INF text files located in the `%systemroot%\system32` folder for the client's printer names or printer driver names. These files both contain a simple list of either printer driver names or printer names on a client that map to particular printer drivers on the server.

The first file referenced during the printer match up process is the WTSUPRN.INF text file located in the `%systemroot%\system32` folder. This file basically contains a simple list matching client-side drivers or printer names to server-side drivers. The WTSUPRN.INF file is the user printer file and does not exist by default. To create it, just copy the WTSUPRN.TXT template file to WTSUPRN.INF. Listing 20.1 is a sample excerpt from a WTSUPRN.INF text file.

Listing 20.1   **Sample from WTSUPRN.INF Text File**

```
...
"HP DeskJet 1200C (MS)"="HP DeskJet 1200C"
"HP DeskJet 1200C Series Printer"="HP DeskJet 550C"
"HP DeskJet 1200C/PS"="HP DeskJet 550C"
...
```

In the first line of this sample text file, you see the driver mapping for a HP DeskJet 1200C (MS) driver on the client. If a client logs on with this exact driver name, the printer is auto-created on the server using the HP DeskJet 1200C driver. When an application prints a document it uses the server's HP DeskJet 1200C printer driver to print the document and sends the formatted document down to the client to print.

The second file processed for driver mappings on MetaFrame 1.8 is the WTSPRNT.INF file. This file is also located in the `%systemroot%\system32` folder. Just like the WTSUPRN.INF file, this file is a text file that contains a simple list of client-side printer names or drivers to server-side driver mappings. Unlike the WTSUPRN.INF file, which must be created from a copy of the WTSUPRN.TXT template file, however, the WTSPRNT.INF file is always available by default on Citrix MetaFrame 1.8 servers. Table 20.1 shows the order that mappings are handled on MetaFrame 1.8.

Table 20.1 **Printer Mapping Order on MetaFrame 1.8**

Mapping in WTSUPRN.INF or WTSPRNT.INF	File
"[Client Name]#[Printer Name]" = "[Server Driver Name]"	WTSUPRN.INF
"[Printer Name]" = "[Server Driver Name]"	WTSUPRN.INF
"[Client Name]#[Printer Name]" = "[Server Driver Name]"	WTSPRNT.INF
"[Printer Name]" = "[Server Driver Name]"	WTSPRNT.INF
"[Client Name]#[Client Printer Driver Name]" = "[Server Driver Name]"	WTSUPRN.INF
"[Client Printer Driver Name]" = "[Server Driver Name]"	WTSUPRN.INF
"[Client Name]#[Client Printer Driver Name]" = "[Server Driver Name]"	WTSPRNT.INF
"[Client Printer Driver Name]" = "[Server Printer Driver Name]"	WTSPRNT.INF

When you upgrade a MetaFrame 1.8 server to MetaFrame XP, all the mappings you set up in the WTSUPRN.INF and WTSPRNT.INF files are imported into XP and made available to all the servers in the XP server farm. Under XP, instead of manually editing individual text files on each server, you manage printer mappings instead from the Citrix Management Console. Not only is manually changing the WTSUPRN.INF and WTSPRNT.INF files not recommended, even if you do manually make changes to these files, they will be overwritten automatically by the IMA service on Citrix MetaFrame XP. With Citrix MetaFrame XP, a single set of printer mappings is automatically and periodically downloaded to each server in the farm. This central control of printer mappings from the CMC makes printer management significantly easier on MetaFrame XP.

If you added a new printer mapping to one of your servers in the past with MetaFrame 1.8, for instance, you would have to copy this printer mapping change manually to every WTSUPRN.INF file on every server in the farm. Over time, different servers often began to have widely varying printer mappings as new driver mappings were added to one server, but not others. With MetaFrame XP, your printer mappings are instead consistent across the farm.

Centrally Controlling Printer Driver Mappings

Few people know why Citrix created two files for the same purpose. If you are using Citrix MetaFrame 1.8, however, the following is recommended for the sake of simplicity and ease of central printer management:

1. Put your printer driver mappings in a central WTSPRNT.INF file on one of your MetaFrame 1.8 servers on the farm.

2. Create an UPDATE.BAT batch file that copies this printer driver mapping file down to all the servers in the farm.

3. Publish the UPDATE.BAT batch file and the central WTSPRNT.INF. using Notepad to your Citrix MetaFrame farm administrators.

Using this technique, if administrators need to add printer driver mappings to the farm, they just need to open the central WTSPRNT.INF file from the published application's icon, make the changes they need, and then run the published UPDATE.BAT file to push down the changes. In this way you are ensured that all printer driver mappings are identical across your farm. This is very important for ensuring printer auto-creation consistency across the farm.

Listing 20.2 is a suggested excerpt from an UPDATE.BAT batch file. Notice that the file deletes any instance of WTSUPRN.INF. This forces Citrix MetaFrame to use the WTSPRNT.INF instead of having to process both files. It is recommended to use either WTSUPRN.INF or WTSPRNT.INF, not both.

In this sample UPDATE.BAT batch file, the central server is called mainserver and the first server in the farm is server1. Just repeat the last four statements in the batch file for each server in the farm.

Listing 20.2   **Sample UPDATE.BAT Batch File**

```
@echo off
Echo Pushing out central driver mappings to servers in the farm..
Echo Copying to SERVER1..
Del \\server1\c$\winnt\system32\wtsuprn.inf
Copy \\server1\c$\winnt\system32\wtsprnt.inf \\server1\c$\winnt\system32\wtsprnt.bak
Copy \\mainserver\c$\winnt\system32\wtsprnt.inf \\server1\c$\winnt\system32\wtsprnt.inf
.. .. ..
```

Matching with Currently Installed Drivers

The next step in the printer driver mapping process is to determine whether the drivers are already installed on the Terminal Server. If the Terminal Server does not have Citrix MetaFrame, this is where the printer mapping process begins. For a Citrix MetaFrame server, however, the WTSUPRN.INF and WTSPRNT.INF files are checked first (as described in the preceding section). This is an important difference to realize between the two systems, especially when troubleshooting problems with printer drivers not being loaded or the wrong ones being loaded.

The Terminal Server takes the information on the printer names and drivers from the client and attempts to match the drivers with currently installed drivers on the server. If the client workstation has a printer named Administration HP4, which uses a driver by the name of HP LaserJet 4, for example, Terminal Server will search in its list of currently installed drivers on the server for an HP LaserJet 4 driver. If it finds a match, the Terminal Server will set up the printer on the user's Terminal Server desktop and move on to try to match the next one.

If there is no match, the Terminal Server will check in the NTPRINT.INF file for a match as covered in the following section.

Remember that this has to be an exact name match. If the Terminal Server has a driver installed called HP LaserJet 4 PCL 5, but the driver name on the client is HP LaserJet 4, the drivers names will not match and the search for the correct driver will go on to the next step.

Where Drivers Are Stored

Every time you install a new printer on Terminal Server, a driver will be installed for that printer. Even if you later delete the printer, the driver will normally still remain. You can find a list of the drivers currently installed on your Terminal Server in the following Registry keys specified by the driver name. This is the name that Terminal Server will attempt to match to the driver name on the client:

`HKLM\System\CurrentControlSet\Print\Environments\Windows NT x86\Drivers\Version-2` and `Version-3`

The actual driver files are kept underneath the printer spooler directory on the Terminal Server. These files are normally .DLL- and .GPD-type files. The following are the folders in which they are kept by default:

`%systemroot%\system32\spool\drivers\w32x86\2` and `3`

Matching with the NTPRINT.INF File

The final file to be checked is the file that contains a list of all the drivers available on the Windows 2000 Terminal Server, the `%systemroot%\inf\ntprint.inf` file. This is a very large and specially formatted text file that contains a list of all the drivers available on the server. This list is the one where the list of drivers comes from when you add new printers to the server. This list will be checked only on Windows 2000 Terminal Servers and not Windows NT 4.0 Terminal Servers.

For Windows 2000 Terminal Server administrators who do not use Citrix, this is an important advantage of using Windows 2000, because you can now enjoy similar printer auto-creation capabilities without needing to purchase the Citrix MetaFrame add-on.

If the printer is not listed in the standard list of drivers in the NTPRINT.INF file, the server will check one more location in the file, the [Previous Names] section. Listing 20.3 is a sample of the contents of this section of an NTPRINT.INF file. Note that the format is identical to that used in the WTSPRNT.INF and WTUPRN.INF files; however, one important exception is that only printer driver name match ups are supported, printer name and client name match ups are not.

Listing 20.3 **Sample of NTPRINT.INF File**

```
[Previous Names]
"Apple LaserWriter v23.0"              =    "Apple LaserWriter"
"Apple LaserWriter II NT v47.0"        =    "Apple LaserWriter II NT"
"Apple LaserWriter II NTX v47.0"       =    "Apple LaserWriter II NTX"
"Apple LaserWriter IIf v2010.113"      =    "Apple LaserWriter IIf"
"Apple LaserWriter IIg v2010.113"      =    "Apple LaserWriter IIg"
"LaserWriter Personal NT v51.8"        =    "Apple LaserWriter Personal NT"
"Apple LaserWriter Plus v38.0"         =    "Apple LaserWriter Plus
...
```

Because this is a text file, you can add your own printer driver matchings as needed to this file.

Which One to Use?

With all the different places for matching up printer driver names, it can be very confusing to determine which one is the best to use. The choice of which one you will use mainly depends on what operating system you are using and whether you are using Citrix MetaFrame. The following are the different options and methods to use to specify printer driver match ups:

- MetaFrame XP and Windows 2000 or Windows Terminal Server 4.0   This is the easiest case because printer driver mapping is handled entirely through the CMC. Editing of text files, such as the WTSPRNT.INF, is not only not necessary, but is strongly discouraged. These files are automatically updated by the CMC.

- MetaFrame 1.8 and Windows 2000 or Windows Terminal Server 4.0   In this case, your best bet is to edit either the WTSUPRN.INF or the WTSPRNT.INF file on each server and add the needed driver matchings. To make life easier, it is highly recommended to create a central administrative batch file. Use this batch file to copy a single WTSUPRN.INF or WTSPRNT.INF file to all of your Citrix MetaFrame 1.8 servers. In this way, you can modify one central file and then run the batch file to push it out to all the servers.

- Windows 2000 Terminal Server   If you are using Windows 2000 Terminal Server without Citrix and you need to modify a printer mapping, you must put the driver mappings under the [Previous Names] section of the NTPRINT.INF file. Using a central administrative batch file also is recommended in this case for pushing out new copies of this file to your servers.

Universal Printer Driver with Feature Release 1

If you are using Citrix MetaFrame XP with Feature Release 1, a brand new option can solve many of the driver mapping headaches of the past. This option is called the *Universal Printer Driver*. One of the biggest problems with driver mapping today is that in many cases new printers need to be added manually to the driver mapping list.

In a typical scenario, a user will be set up with a new printer on his desktop. The driver is installed locally, and he can print fine from his desktop applications. When he connects to Terminal Server, however, the new printer is not found in the driver mappings, so the user cannot print from Terminal Server and has to call the help desk. The help desk then has to manually add the driver mapping for the new printer to the Terminal Server or Citrix MetaFrame server farm before the user can print.

With the Universal Printer Driver, this type of support headache goes away. You can configure the farm so that if the driver for a particular printer is not found, it will automatically use the Universal Printer Driver instead. This means that in the scenario just mentioned, because the new printer was not found in the driver mappings, the printer will be created for the user using the Universal Printer Driver instead. This enables the user to print and avoids the call to the help desk.

The Universal Printer Driver is a special driver that works in conjunction with the Citrix ICA client to handle printing. For the Universal Printer Driver to work, you must have at least version 6.20 or later of the ICA client and Feature Release 1 for MetaFrame XP installed and enabled on your server farm.

Normally when you print something from a session on Citrix MetaFrame, the print job is first sent to the printer driver on the Citrix MetaFrame server. This driver takes the print output from the application and formats it in a language that the particular printer it is designed for can understand. This specially formatted print job is then sent down to the ICA client where the client spools the job off directly to the associated printer.

With the Universal Printer Driver, the user prints the job from the server to the server's Universal Printer Driver. This special driver takes the print job and formats it in a common printer language called *PCL 4* (Printer Control Language). It then passes this job in PCL 4 format down to the ICA client. Version 6.20 and later versions of the ICA client have a built-in PCL 4 interpreter. This interpreter interprets the PCL 4 job and re-creates the original page locally on the client machine. It then "prints" this page to the associated local printer, just like any other local application would print to a local printer.

Because the job has to be converted into PCL 4 format and then reconverted locally to the correct format for the local printer by the local print driver, you need to be aware of a few limitations, including the following most important ones:

- Graphics are limited to 300 dots per inch.

- Color printing is not supported, only grayscale.

- Special printing features, such as duplex printing or printing to special printer trays, is not supported.

Even though there are these limitations, the Universal Printer Driver will work with most every printer on the market. This includes some printers that normally do not work with Terminal Server, such as the HP printers that use PPA technology (710C, 712C, and 720C)!

Creating the Printer

However the correct driver has been determined, whether through a driver mapping in the WTSUPRN.INF, WTSPRNT.INF, NTPRINT.INF, or using the Universal Printer Driver, the driver needs to be loaded and the printer has to be created for the user as he logs on to the server. Terminal Server will add the printer to the user's Terminal Server desktop with the following naming convention:

```
client\[workstation or citrix station name]#[printer name]
```

For Terminal Server clients, the workstation name is the computer name of the user's local computer. For Citrix ICA clients, the workstation name is the station name assigned during the installation of the ICA client.

When users need to print from their applications on Terminal Server, they can see the names for all the printers auto-created for them by just taking a look at the list of printers from the application's Print dialog box. If one of the printers they need to print to on their desktop was not auto-created, there was a problem detecting that printer during the auto-creation process. Normally this indicates that you need to add a new printer driver mapping for that printer to the CMC for Citrix MetaFrame XP or to the NTPRINT.INF file for Terminal Server.

One important thing to note is the difference in auto-creation between Windows NT Terminal Server Edition 4.0 and Windows 2000 Terminal Server. With a Windows NT 4.0 Terminal Server, you must have the driver already installed on the server for it to be able to auto-create the printer. On the other hand, with Windows 2000, printer drivers will be installed on-the-fly using Windows 2000's Plug-and-Play technology.

For Citrix 1.8 administrators who need printer auto-creation to work on both Windows NT 4.0 and 2000, this is a very important difference to realize. What this basically means is that you need to manually install all the drivers that will be needed by your users on the Windows NT 4.0 Terminal Server in advance. This can take a significant amount of time, but is a necessary process and should be done when setting up the server. To do this, follow these steps:

1. Print out a copy of your WTSUPRN.INF and WTSPRNT.INF files. This should be the basic list of all the drivers that you need for your farm because this is the driver matching list for the farm.

2. For each printer type in the list, create a printer on the Windows NT 4.0 Terminal Server and assign it to LPT1.

3. Delete the printer.

Because the printer driver remains even after the printer is deleted, the net effect of these steps is that all the printer drivers you need will now be available for printer auto-creation. The best bet is to install a wide variety of printers so that you do not need to install too many additional printers in the future.

As you can imagine, for large Citrix MetaFrame 1.8 server farms, these steps can become very tedious. Luckily with MetaFrame XP, Citrix came up with a good solution. Using MetaFrame XP's CMC you can now replicate printer drivers automatically, both Windows NT 4.0 and 2000 printer drivers, across all the servers in the farm. This means that instead of setting up drivers on each server locally, you need to set them up only once and then use the CMC to push them across all the servers.

For Terminal Server administrators, because printer auto-creation works only on Windows 2000, you can rely on Windows 2000's capability to auto-install the driver. The only exception to this rule is if you need to install a new driver that is not included in the base set of drivers that come with the server. Although installing after-market third-part printer drivers is strongly discouraged, sometimes no other compatible driver is available. In this case, you must manually install the driver on every server from which users need to print to that printer. You also need to add a printer driver mapping line to the NTSPRNT.INF file for the printer if it is named differently on the users' workstations.

For security reasons, only the user, the administrator, and the system are allowed access to the printer. What this means is that users will see only their own printers and not other users' printers; however, administrators will be able to see and modify all printers on the Terminal Server.

In addition, the default printer on the user's local desktop will become her default printer within her Terminal Server session.

When the user logs off, her printers will automatically be deleted from the list of printers on the Terminal Server.

Printer Security

It is important to note the effect of printer security. If you want to create a new printer on Terminal Server or if you add a new piece of software that includes a printer driver, be careful of the security for that printer. Suppose, for example, you install Adobe Acrobat, which includes a PDF writer driver. By default, any driver that you manually install will be granted access to everyone. This means that everyone on the system will now see the Adobe Acrobat PDF as part of the printers that they have available. For licensing reasons, you might want to control who has access to this type of printer, so you might want to create a group and grant only that group and administrators access to the printer through printer security.

Many software packages including imaging, faxing, terminal emulation, and other types of software include their own printer drivers upon installation. These drivers are available for all users on the system and might cause confusion when users try to select their printers.

Also if you manually add a printer for a user, make sure that only that user is granted access to that printer.

The easiest way to test which printers users see is to make a test account that has only Domain User access and not Domain Admin access. Log on as this user and view the list of printers that you have available. Look for any unexpected printers that might have been installed as part of some software package in the past.

Managing Printers with the Citrix Management Console

MetaFrame XP has a great many improvements when it comes to printer management capabilities. These improvements are all part of the new Citrix Management Console. Using the CMC, you can perform the following functions:

- **Create driver mappings**   What used to take manual editing of a printer driver matching file can now be done through the GUI interface of the CMC. You can centrally add driver matchings to the entire Citrix server farm in one step.
- **Create printer mappings for DOS and Win CE devices**   Using this new functionality, you can assign a particular printer to a DOS- or Win CE-based device and assign the port to be used.
- **Replicate print drivers**   You can select particular servers to be the source for printer drivers. These drivers can then be automatically replicated across the server farm.

- **Adjust printer bandwidth**   One problem with printer usage in large environments, especially across slow connections, is that they can monopolize network usage. Now using the CMC, you can regulate the bandwidth used by your printers.

The following sections describe how to perform each of these tasks.

Creating Driver Mappings

To create the match up list for printer drivers, you can now use the Citrix Management Console instead of manually editing the WTSUPRN.INF or WTSPRNT.INF text files on each server, as had to be done with Citrix MetaFrame 1.8. Changes made in the CMC to the driver match up list are immediately replicated to all servers in the server farm.

To set up printer mappings, follow these steps:

1. Open the CMC from the Program menu, Citrix folder and log on.

2. Right-click Drivers under the Printer Management folder and select Mappings.

3. From the Driver Mapping window shown in Figure 20.2, select either Windows 2000 or Windows NT 4.0 printer mappings.

4. Click the Add button to add a new mapping.

5. Enter the Client driver name and select the matching Server driver name from the list. Note that this list is generated from the current list of drivers on the server from which you are running the console. You also can type in the name of the server driver, if it is not listed.

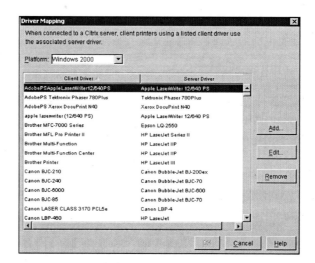

Figure 20.2   Printer mappings in the CMC.

Client Mappings for DOS or Win CE Devices

DOS and Win CE devices are a special case. Because they do not store printer mappings locally, you must define the printer mapping entirely at the server. This is a very handy feature for large thin client terminal deployments where several of the thin client terminals have printers attached locally. Using the CMC, you can match the client name you assigned to the terminal up to a printer driver and port as follows:

1. Open the CMC from the Program menu, Citrix folder and log on.

2. Right-click the Printers icon under the Printer Management folder and select New Printer.

3. Enter the Client Name, Printer Name, Driver, and the local port on the Win CE or DOS device that will be printed to.

When the user logs on to the Terminal Server from the Win CE or DOS device, this printer will automatically be added to his Terminal Server desktop. When he prints to the printer, the traffic will be redirected to the local port you specified in step 3.

Replicating Printer Drivers

Replicating printer drivers is a very valuable feature in MetaFrame XP and proves especially useful if you have a large number of Windows NT 4.0 Terminal Servers in your Citrix server farm or if you have new drivers for Windows 2000 servers that you need to deploy. To implement this feature, you should first choose a master server, referred to in this chapter as the *printer driver master* (PDM) server. This is the server whose drivers will be copied out to the rest of the servers in the server farm. This can be any server in the farm; realize, however, that if you need to manually install drivers on the server, you will need to install them on this server first. If you have a mix of Windows NT 4.0 and 2000 servers in your farm, you should choose a master server for each operating system version.

For small to medium-size environments, the first server in the server farm is a good choice for the PDM. For larger environments or environments that need to support several drivers not included in the base set of drivers with Terminal Server, it is a good idea to use a test server to test drivers first before introducing them to your production server farm.

After choosing a PDM, you need to manually install the drivers on the server that you want to distribute to the rest of the servers in the farm. Remember that Windows 2000 servers will automatically install any driver included with Windows 2000. In other words, unless the driver is not included with Windows 2000, there is no reason to install it and replicate it from the PDM. Windows NT 4.0 Terminal Servers will not automatically install drivers, however, and therefore need to have the drivers manually installed. If you have multiple Windows NT 4.0 Terminal Servers, manually install the drivers that you need replicated on the Windows NT 4.0 PDM server.

After the drivers you need to be replicated have been installed, follow this procedure to set up the replication.

1. Open the CMC from the Program menu, Citrix folder.

2. Right-click Drivers from the Printer Management folder and select Auto-Replication.

3. Select either Windows NT 2000 or Windows NT 4.0 as appropriate.

4. Click Add and select the master server from the server list.

5. Select the driver you want to replicate from this server, and then click OK. If you do not see the driver that you need, you should manually install the driver on that server.

After you have added the driver to the replication list, it will automatically be replicated to all the servers in the server farm. This process could take up to 30 minutes. Once replicated, if any user logs on to any server in the farm and needs this printer driver, it will already be installed and available.

Adjusting Printer Bandwidth

In the network world, bandwidth is a measure of the amount of the capacity of a communication circuit. Printing traffic for Citrix MetaFrame can often take up a significant amount of bandwidth, especially over slow WAN connections. By adjusting the amount of bandwidth that printing traffic takes, you can regulate the amount of traffic used for printing. In large environments and across slow network links, this ability is especially valuable.

Suppose, for example, that you have 100 users coming in across a WAN link. With normal screen updates, key strokes, and other typical Citrix ICA traffic, you find that users use between 15Kbps and 20Kbps of network bandwidth. If the network circuit speed is 128Kbps, that means you could fit roughly somewhere between 4 and 6 simultaneous users on the line before response time would suffer noticeably.

Although average Citrix ICA traffic is fairly easy to estimate and measure, printing traffic is a different story. Many documents exceed 100KB in size. Documents that include large amounts of graphics or a large number of pages can easily exceed 1MB in size. If you have only a 128Kbps connection, one user printing out a large document can quickly take up the entire line for a long period of time.

For this reason, if your users tend to frequently print large documents, it is highly recommended to adjust the amount of bandwidth allotted for use by the printer. The following procedure shows you how:

1. Open the CMC from the Program menu, Citrix folder and log on.

2. Highlight the Printer Driver Management folder.

3. Right-click the server whose printer bandwidth you want to adjust and select Edit.

4. Enter the necessary bandwidth and click OK.

It can be difficult to estimate the amount of bandwidth that should be specified. One rule of thumb to try is to enter a value that is half the speed of the WAN line. If your WAN connection is 128Kbps, for instance, enter 64Kbps for the printer bandwidth. The actual number that will work best for you depends on the number of people you expect to be printing simultaneously and the line speed.

Troubleshooting Printer Problems

Unfortunately, printing problems often make up the majority of support calls for most Citrix MetaFrame and Terminal Server administrators. However, the consistent use of some basic techniques can greatly reduce the number of calls you receive to just a trickle. This section discusses the best way to troubleshoot common printing problems and how best to set up your printing environment to prevent problems from occurring in the first place.

Printers Are Not Auto-Created

The first and most basic problem is that the printers that your users need are not auto-created during the logon process. If you find this to be the case for one or more of your users, review the following sections.

Is Printer Auto-Creation Enabled?

Printer auto-creation can be disabled at both a connection level and a user level. Ensure that both of these are enabled by doing the following:

1. Open the Citrix Connection Configuration manager from the Program menu, Citrix, MetaFrame XP folder.

2. Right-click the connection entries that users use and select Properties.

3. Click the Client Settings button. The window shown in Figure 20.3 will appear.

4. Verify that the Disable Client LPT Port Mapping, Disable Client COM Port Mapping, and Disable Windows Client Printer Mapping check boxes are not checked.

5. If the (Inherit User Config) check box is checked under Connection, check the user's settings as shown in the following procedure; otherwise make sure that the Connect Client Printers at Logon box is checked.

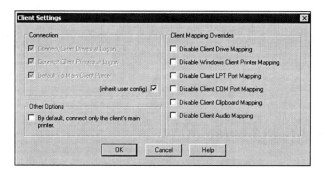

Figure 20.3 Client Settings window.

If the box (Inherit User Config) box is checked in the Connection Settings window, which is the default, you also need to check that the ability to auto-create printers is enabled for the user, as follows:

1. Open the user's properties in either User Manager for Domains or Active Directory Users and Computers.

2. If using Active Directory Users and Computers, check under the Environment tab to ensure that the Connect Client Printers at Logon box is checked.

3. If using User Manager for Domains, click the TS Config button when viewing the user's properties. Verify that the box is checked to Connect Client Printers at Logon.

Is the Driver Mapping Set Up Correctly?

The next most crucial question is whether the driver mapping is set up correctly. To do this you must first determine the driver name. When you know the driver name, you can check in either the Driver Mapping section of the CMC for MetaFrame XP administrators, in the WTSUPRN.INF and WTSPRNT.INF for MetaFrame 1.8 administrators, or in the NTPRINT.INF for Terminal Server administrators. Look for the mapping statement for the particular printer name or driver name configured on the user's desktop. Make sure that this client printer or driver name is matched to the right driver on the server. Also make sure that the printer driver being mapped to on the server has been installed on the server. If your Terminal Server is a Windows 2000 Terminal Server and the printer is not being auto-created, check for 1106 event errors in the application log. The information in the event log in Windows 2000 is all you should need to resolve your printer mapping issues. If a user logs on and the server cannot find a match for one of her printer drivers, it will record an 1106 event log error in the application log. Figure 20.4 shows an example of this error. Note in the error it gives a significant amount of information, including the client name, printer name, and printer driver name. Using this information, you can easily add the correct driver mapping statement.

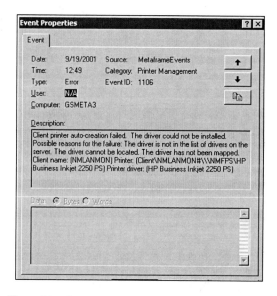

Figure 20.4   Printer error in the application error log.

If you are having problems on a Windows NT 4.0 Terminal Server, or you do not see the 1106 event errors, try the following to determine the driver name.

- **Have user check printer properties.**   Walk the user through checking the printer properties. The exact procedure for this varies from operating system to operating system. However, the exact name of the printer driver will be shown in the printer's properties on the client. This is the driver name that must match up to a driver on Terminal Server in the driver mappings.

- **Shadow the user's desktop.** One easy way to determine the correct driver for a user is to just shadow her desktop on Terminal Server. You can then go into the Printer Control Panel from the Terminal Server Desktop and attempt to add the printer manually. When adding the printer, add it from the client network. When you browse the client network, you will at least be able to see the printer name, which by default, is the same as the driver name on most systems. You can use this printer name for the driver mapping.

When you know for sure what the name of the driver is that needs to be mapped, you need to add the following line to the appropriate driver mapping file or to the driver mappings in the CMC:

```
"[client driver name]"="[server driver name]"
```

Verify the Server Driver Exists

Remember that for a driver mapping statement to work, the client driver name must exactly match the name of the driver on the client and the server driver name must exactly match the driver name on the server. If the server driver name does not match exactly or the driver does not exist on the server, the mapping will fail.

To view the exact names of the drivers currently installed on your Terminal Server, look under the following Registry key:

```
HKLM\System\CurrentControlSet\Print\Environments\Windows NT x86\Drivers\
Version-2 and Version-3
```

The sample contents of these keys are shown in Figure 20.5. When you specify the server driver name in the mapping statement, it must match the name in the Registry exactly. Suppose, for example, the client is logging on and has an HP LaserJet 2100 that he needs to print to from Terminal Server. When he logs on, however, the printer is not auto-created. You check the driver name on the client's printer and find it to be HP LaserJet 2100"; on the server (as shown in Figure 20.5), however, the driver name you need is HP LaserJet 2100 PCL 6. To resolve this problem so that the mapping occurs correctly, you would need to enter the following driver mapping statement into the appropriate driver mapping file:

```
"HP LaserJet 2100"="HP LaserJet 2100 PCL 6"
```

This statement basically means that the HP LaserJet 2100 PCL 6 Terminal Server driver will be used for any client that has a printer with the HP LaserJet 2100 driver.

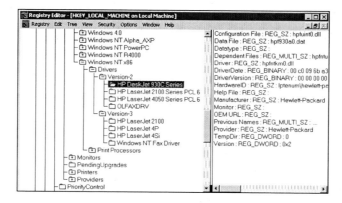

Figure 20.5 Drivers installed in the Registry.

Remember that even if the driver does not exist on Windows 2000, as long as you specify the name of one of the drivers that is included with Windows 2000, it will automatically be loaded. To obtain the exact names of the drivers included with Windows 2000, you can just browse through the list of drivers available when adding a printer. You also could browse through the NTPRINT.INF file, which contains the same list.

On a Windows NT 4.0 Terminal Server, you must either manually install all the drivers you need or use the replication feature in MetaFrame XP to replicate the drivers to all the servers. If the driver name does not exist in the HKLM key listed previously, the printer will not auto-create. This is a very important difference between Windows NT 4.0 and 2000 Terminal Server. On Windows NT 4.0 server you must have the driver installed. On Windows 2000 Server, you can specify a driver that is not currently installed and it will automatically install upon user logon. Either way the server driver name in the driver mapping statement must match exactly with the name of the driver on the server.

Use the Universal Printer Driver

If you are using MetaFrame XP with Feature Release 1, try using the Universal Printer Driver feature. To get this to work, you need to be sure Feature Release 1 is installed and licensed on your MetaFrame XP server farm. In addition, make sure that you are using at least version 6.20 of the ICA client.

To enable Universal Printer Drivers, do the following from the CMC. These options also are shown in Figure 20.6:

1. Right-click Printer Management in the CMC and choose Properties.

2. Make sure Auto-Create Client Printers is checked.

3. Select All Client Printers or Use Connection Settings for Each Server under Client Printer Connections.

4. Select Use Universal Driver Only if Native Driver Unavailable, and then click OK.

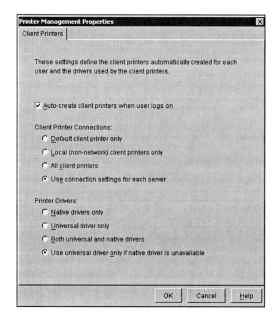

Figure 20.6 Printer Management properties with FR1.

By selecting the Use Universal Driver Only if Native Driver Unavailable in step 4, you are setting the server up so that the Universal Printer Driver will be used as a last resort. Because of the limitations of the Universal Printer Driver, this is the recommended setting. Normally it is better to use the actual driver for the printer, because the user can then take advantage of the full feature set that the driver provides. At least by making the Universal Driver available, however, even if the correct driver cannot be mapped the user can use the Universal Printer Driver to print, at least on a temporary basis until you set up the printer driver mapping for the new printer.

Other Tips for Printers Not Auto-Creating

If you are sure that printer auto-creation is enabled, the driver mapping is exact, and the driver exists, but the printer is still not auto-creating, you can try a couple of more things.

At this point it is best to start working from the user's desktop on Terminal Server. You should first try adding the printer manually from the user's desktop on Terminal Server. On Terminal Server, a user's local printers are kept in a special network grouping called the Client network. When you add a network printer in either Terminal Server 4.0 or 2000, you will have the option of either browsing the Microsoft network or the Client network. If you choose Client, you should see a listing of all the printers installed on that user's workstation. If you select one of these printers and then select the correct driver for that printer, it will add the printer to the user's Terminal Server desktop. At that point, you should be able to send a test page to the printer.

As long as you can manually add the printer, you know that the printer can be added to Terminal Server. At this point, you need to double-check that the driver name is correct in the driver mapping. Also check the entire applicable printer mapping files in the flowchart in Figure 20.1 to ensure that there is no conflicting driver mapping. Remember that in some cases one driver mapping can override another. Check for duplicate driver mappings in the driver mapping file. As a final resort, try removing the driver mapping and reentering it.

Printer Is Auto-Created, but Cannot Print

If the printer is auto-created, but when you print a test page to the printer it does not come out, review the following sections for some solutions.

Driver Compatibility Problems

The most common cause of not being able to print is selecting the wrong driver at the server. When selecting a driver, you should always use the most compatible driver available in the server's default set of drivers. Try another driver in the driver mapping and see whether that driver works.

Server-Side Manufacturer's Driver Issues

The next most common cause of not being able to print involves issues with a manufacturer's printer driver on the server. The most important rule when setting up printer drivers is to use the "most-compatible server driver." Never install a new printer driver from a manufacturer on Terminal Server if it can be avoided. There are numerous incompatibility issues with many manufacturers' printer drivers and Terminal Server.

The only true-and-tested drivers are those included with Terminal Server. Even if an exact match is not possible, you will likely find that the printer is backward compatible with a driver available on Terminal Server.

Suppose, for example, that you have a laser printer from a lesser known manufacturer. Instead of downloading and installing the driver for that printer from the manufacturer, you should check with the manufacturer as to what printers it is compatible with. You will likely find that the printer will work fine with an existing driver, such as an HP LaserJet 4 driver.

Compatible Drivers

Because of HP's dominance in the printer market, the vast majority of printers are compatible with one or more HP printer drivers. If you are having a problem locating the driver for your printer in the default list of drivers, try the following:

- LaserJet or PCL   If your printer is listed as HP LaserJet or PCL compatible, try using the HP LaserJet 4 driver in the printer mapping for the printer. If your printer is listed as compatible with PCL 5 or PCL 6, try using the HP LaserJet 4 driver.

- DeskJet Compatible   If your printer is listed as compatible with HP DeskJets, try the HP DeskJet 550C driver. This driver is a highly reliable driver that is compatible with most every DeskJet printer in the HP line of DeskJets and is compatible with many other manufacturers' color inkjet printers.

Client-Side Driver Issues

If you are certain you are using the right driver on the server, it is time to check the client. Because the client drivers are often the manufacturers' drivers, they can often be the cause of problems with Citrix MetaFrame. This is especially the case when users are using home-class and not business-class printers. These types of printers commonly come with various printer-monitoring utilities that can conflict with Terminal Server's capability to redirect the print jobs. If you suspect the client-side printer drivers, try the following:

- **Disable any printer monitoring.**   If the client is running any printer-monitoring utilities or other printer-related utilities from the manufacturer, disable them. These types of utilities often run as icons in the user's task tray and can normally be disabled by right-clicking the icon and selecting Disable. If printing works with the utility disabled, check with the manufacturer about how to remove the software.

- **Use a compatible built-in driver.**   If you are still having printing problems, try creating a new shortcut to the printer. Instead of using the manufacturer's driver, however, try using the most compatible driver available with the operating system. On the server, set up the driver mapping to this driver rather than to the manufacturer's driver. After you have verified that the printer auto-created correctly, try printing to it.

Not Compatible with Terminal Server or Citrix MetaFrame

A small number of printers will just not work with Terminal Server printer redirection. The majority of these types of printers are printers designed for home use, which require special utilities to run on the client to print to the printer. For example, HP makes a line of printers that rely on PPA or host-based technology, such as the 710C, 712C, and 720C, which are not compatible with Terminal Server.

These printers are designed for home use and include no processing capability on the printer itself. Instead, a special utility must be run on the client that handles all the printer processing. This keeps the cost of the printer itself extraordinarily low, but this utility does not work correctly with Terminal Server printer redirection. Even though the printer might be auto-created on the Terminal Server, if you send jobs to the printer, they will not go through. Other manufacturers besides HP make a similar line of inexpensive host-based printers designed for home use.

To avoid problems such as these, it is highly recommended to create a list of compatible business-class printers and publish this list to your users. Make sure to mention that host-based printers are not supported.

Author's Note

If you have MetaFrame XP with Feature Release 1, there is hope. Even though these drivers do not work on Terminal Server, you should still be able to print to these printers using the Universal Printer Driver technology. The only issue that you might encounter is that you can print only in grayscale using the Universal Printer Driver—at least you can print!

Printer Prints Garble

If the printer auto-creates, but prints garble when sending text to it, the problem is most likely related to a driver issue. Try another driver or check with the manufacturer as to what the most compatible driver is for that printer.

Using Third-Party Universal Print Drivers

Even if you do not have MetaFrame XP with Feature Release 1, you might be able to use a third-party Universal Printer Driver solution instead. Although the various solutions by third parties rely on different methods, the goal is the same. Basically they consist of a component that runs on the client and one that runs on the server. These two components work together to ensure that printing works seamlessly between the server and the client. If you continue to have printing problems, you might want to investigate using one of these drivers.

EOL's Universal Printer Driver is one such solution. This product uses the Adobe Acrobat Reader software on the client to handle print jobs coming from the Terminal Server. For more information on this solution, go to www.99point9.com.

Printer Spooler Issues

With so many people printing off of a single system, it is not uncommon to run into issues with the spooler on the Terminal Server. If you are having problems with the spooler getting hung on your Terminal Server, the first and best place to check is the event log. You will find that in Windows 2000 Server, the spooler reports status for every printed job in the event log. In addition, common spooler problems will normally cause an event in the log. You can look up these event error messages on the Microsoft web site to get ideas about how to resolve the problem.

If the printer spooler problem is seemingly intermittent, there is a way to at least alert you of a printing problem using Performance Monitor. With Windows 2000, several Performance Monitor counters are directly related to printing. These can prove incredibly useful to monitor in a Terminal Server or Citrix MetaFrame environment, especially on heavily used servers. From Performance Monitor, you can now monitor the following under the Print Queue counters:

- **Jobs** Current number of jobs in all the queues on the server (use the _Total).
- **Job Errors** Current number of job errors on the server.
- **Total Jobs Printed and Total Pages Printed** Both of these counters are good for monitoring the amount of printer usage on your servers.

To set up a Performance Monitor alert on any of these, you can run Performance Monitor on the console of your server and do the following:

1. Right-click Alerts and select New Alert Settings.
2. Enter an alert name and click OK.
3. Click the Add button and add the Performance Monitor counter that you want to alert on.
4. Change the Alert When Value to Over, and then enter the number that you want to alert on.
5. Change the sample interval to something less frequent than the default of 5 seconds.
6. Click the Action tab and specify the action you want to occur when the counter exceeds the value you entered.

With Performance Monitor you have the choice of alerting by just making a log entry, sending a message on the network, starting a performance log, or kicking off a file.

If your printer queue gets intermittently stuck all the time and you need a temporary workaround to the problem, you can try the following technique:

1. Set up a Performance Monitor alert on jobs spooling past a certain number. Normally when a spooler gets stuck, the number of jobs spooling will begin to increase significantly.

2. Have the alert kick off a RESETSPOOLER.BAT batch file.

Listing 20.4 is a sample RESETSPOOLER.BAT batch file that you can use. Note that this batch file will stop the Spooler service and delete all jobs currently printing. In a bind, this might be the most effective way to reset the spooler. However, this is not intended to be a long-term solution.

Listing 20.4   RESETSPOOLER.BAT Batch File

```
Net stop spooler
Echo y | del %SystemRoot%\system32\spooler\printers\*.*
Net start spooler
```

Monitoring Performance Variables

One nice utility to check out if you want to monitor your server's Performance Monitor counters more closely is 2MA by Quest Software. This utility enables you to not only monitor the variables, but also alert off of them. Unlike Performance Monitor alerting, which can alert only when a value exceeds a threshold, 2MA can alert when a value exceeds a given threshold for a specified amount of time. This is a very handy feature for monitoring many Performance Monitor counters that might occasionally spike and cause false alerts. You can get more information about this useful utility at www.quest.com/2ma.

Top-Ten Printing Tips

As a summary to all the tips in this chapter, the following is a list of the top-ten most important tips covered:

1. **Use the driver included with Terminal Server.**   This above all is the Golden Rule of printing using Terminal Server or Citrix MetaFrame. Because of the numerous incompatibility issues with many manufacturers' printer drivers, the best and only tested source of drivers are those that come with Terminal Server. Although some manufacturers' drivers will work with Terminal Server, and many manufacturers are now testing their drivers on Terminal Server, it is still far less likely that you will experience printer problems if you use drivers included with Terminal Server instead of downloading and installing a driver from the manufacturer.

2. **Use the most compatible driver.** If the exact driver is not available for your printer in the included driver list, check to determine whether a compatible driver is available instead of using the manufacturer's driver. If you have a printer that is LaserJet-compatible, for example, use an HP LaserJet driver instead of downloading and installing the manufacturer's driver.

3. **Set up driver mappings for printers.** If your printer does not auto-create, you will likely need to set up a driver mapping for the printer. In MetaFrame XP, this is done using the CMC. In MetaFrame 1.8, you need to add the mapping to the WTSUPRN.INF text file. For Terminal Server 2000, you need to add the mapping to the NTSPRNT.INF file.

4. **Make sure drivers are installed on all servers.** The driver mapping equates a client-side driver with a server-side driver. If the server-side driver does not exist, however, the mapping will fail. For this reason it is important to install all the drivers you will need for all the printers that your users use on all of your servers. Windows 2000 makes this process much easier, because it will auto-install any driver that is included with Windows 2000 when that driver is referenced. MetaFrame XP takes this one step further by enabling you to replicate a driver from one server to the rest of the servers in the farm. If you are using MetaFrame 1.8 and Windows NT 4.0, however, you must manually add all the print drivers you need to the server.

5. **Use built-in drivers on the client** Many times, special manufacturer printer drivers on the client-side will cause problems with printing with Terminal Server or Citrix MetaFrame. If you continue to have problems printing, the printer is being auto-created and you are certain the server-side driver is compatible, try re-creating the printer on the client using a compatible driver rather than the manufacturer's driver package.

6. **Encourage the use of business-class printers.** Many large manufacturers have both a business printer line and a line of printers designed for home use. As much as possible, encourage users to use printers in the business-class product line. Several inexpensive home-class printers are not compatible with Citrix MetaFrame or Terminal Server, especially those that use technologies such as PPA technologies where the printer processing is handled by an application on the workstation rather than on the printer itself. Your best bet is to encourage users to use business-class printers, especially printers compatible with other manufacturer's drivers, such as HP LaserJet or HP DeskJet drivers.

7. **Try Universal Printer Drivers.**   In some cases, you might need to use Universal Printer Drivers. If you have MetaFrame XP, make sure to purchase Feature Release 1, which includes Universal Printer Driver technology. If not, you can find third parties that make Universal Printer Driver solutions. Both EOL (www.99point9.com) and Tricerat (www.tricerat.com) make Universal Printer Drivers that you can use to help resolve some of the printing problems in your environment.

8. **Build an extensive driver mapping list.**   Although not covered extensively in this chapter, many administrators over time build a large driver mapping list. In this way, nearly all printer driver mappings are handled automatically instead of having to manually add a new driver mapping for each user who has a different printer. These compiled driver mapping lists can be downloaded and used for free. Citrix has one available that you can download from Citrix technical article CTX626451. You also can find a list in the http://thethin.net Download section.

9. **Upgrade a MetaFrame 1.8 Server to XP with a large mapping list.**   In MetaFrame 1.8, the driver mapping list existed just in a text file, so it was very easy to add someone else's driver mapping list to your server farm. In MetaFrame XP, there is no method yet available to import a list of driver mappings from a text file; instead you have to enter the driver mappings one by one using the CMC. If you have a large driver mapping list from MetaFrame 1.8 and you need to import it into MetaFrame XP, one trick is to just copy the WTSUPRN.INF file from that list into the %systemroot%\system32 folder of the server before you upgrade it to or install MetaFrame XP. During the installation, the list of drivers will automatically be imported into MetaFrame XP's data store.

10. **Adjust printer bandwidth over WAN connections.**   Adjusting printer bandwidth proves especially useful and is highly recommended for servers accessed across a WAN link. This new feature in MetaFrame XP can greatly help control bandwidth usage of your Citrix MetaFrame servers across slow network links.

21

Performance Tuning and Resource Management

THE LAST THING AN ADMINISTRATOR wants to hear after a deployment of Terminal Server is that it's too slow. Many things can be done to improve the performance of a Terminal Server system. Trying to improve the performance after the system is already deployed, however, is not the best time to do it. The first and most important thing you can do is proper performance testing of the system before deployment occurs.

This chapter covers how to tune your server to get the best performance possible, how to set up good performance tests, and how to use tools, such as Performance Monitor, to measure current server performance and prevent future performance problems from occurring.

Performance Testing

Planning and prototyping are critical for successful Terminal Server deployment. Because any Terminal Server's main purpose is to run Windows applications, the focus for performance testing should be on the applications that you intend to run. As part of planning and prototyping, you need to first determine what problems, if any, your application might have with Terminal Server.

After the application has been installed and any issues worked out, you need to test for acceptable performance. In the following sections, you will learn how to do this.

Performance Testing

Proper performance testing is a subject of much debate. The material in this chapter is intended to give you the tools and techniques you need to get started on performance testing of your server. Although no single perfect way exists for testing Terminal Server performance for every environment, you can improve on the accuracy of these tests in many ways in your environment by following the techniques presented in this chapter.

Understanding the Application

The first step with any prototyping is gaining an understanding of the application being tested. The best way to do this is often to just sit down with the people who use the application the most and have them show you what they do. What you are looking for are commonly used features of the applications, particularly features that take up significant processing time or memory on Terminal Server. Out of this training, you need to gain a sufficient understanding of the application so that you'll be able to accurately simulate day-to-day operations and find out which uses of the application will allow for the most use of resources on the server.

You do not need to install the application on your server to understand how it behaves. Because of the great similarities between Windows Server and Workstation, the easiest way to better understand how an application behaves is normally to just install it on your Windows NT or 2000 workstation. You can then open the Task Manager and watch processor utilization while going through different procedures in the application. While learning the application, keep a watchful eye out for the following:

- **Procedures that change large sections of the screen rapidly**
  Remember that every time the screen changes, the change needs to be sent across the wire. If large sections of the screen change rapidly during certain procedures, be sure to include these procedures in your stress testing.

- **Animations**   Be especially careful of animated graphics or cursors. By themselves, they take up large amounts of bandwidth. Before doing any testing or prototyping, find out whether these animations can be disabled. If they can, disable them and watch for the change in performance.

- **Report printing or querying**   Printing or viewing reports can take up significant processor and network time. Try to get an idea of how frequent various reports are accessed. Check with the user to determine whether there are reports you can use in your stress testing.

- **Calculations**   Any procedure that requires a significant amount of calculation will require a significant amount of processing. Examples of this are frequent spreadsheet calculations, database reports with calculations, multimedia applications, and accounting reports.

- **Heavy use of memory** If the program is displaying a large amount of data on the screen without much hard drive access, it's likely using up a large amount of memory. Using Task Manager, you can watch how much memory the program is using while you try various procedures. Some examples of large memory use are viewing large reports, queries, or tables; loading large spreadsheets or documents; and using programs that cache drive access.

Remember that many of the programs you might want to run on Terminal Server are client/server applications. Because most of the processing in a client/server application is normally done at the server, you need to mainly be concerned about how rapidly the screen will be changing at the client during typical use.

As you can probably tell, application simulation is more an art than a science. The goal of the performance testing process is to discover any potential performance problems before the application is implemented on Terminal Server.

Simulating User Interaction Using Task Sheets

When you understand how users interact with the application, you need to find a way to accurately simulate typical user interaction for performance testing purposes. Setting up this simulation can be one of the most time-consuming parts of performance testing. The first step in doing this is to generate a simulation task sheet.

While you are learning the application, you need to keep detailed notes of the most common procedures. During this learning process, create the task sheet. A task sheet is a list of typical user jobs regularly performed with the application. The idea is to generate a task sheet that will be used during simulation. Include sample data and reports that can be used during the simulation. Try to make a task sheet that is circular in nature. If the application is a hospital patient database application and the typical user is a data-entry person, for instance, you might generate the following task sheet:

1. Create a client record for user Jane Doe with the following information:

   First name: Jane

   Last name: Doe

   Address: 123 N Highway One, Boston, MA

   Phone: 343-888-1212

2. Enter the following sample health insurance information:

   [Sample insurance info]

3. Create an appointment for the patient on date [sample appointment date].

4. Print out a report of all patient appointments for that date.

5. Enter the following billing information for that appointment:

   [Sample billing info for procedures performed]

6. Generate a billing report for the day.

7. Delete the billing record, patient record, and appointment information.

Notice how the process is circular in nature. In other words, these tasks can all be repeated because the sample information that's created is deleted at the end.

Depending on the size of the implementation and the nature of the application (or applications), you might want to create additional task sheets to simulate different types of use. The idea again is to simulate what will be typical use when the server is in production.

Implementing Task Sheets Using WinBatch Scripts

Now that you know what you are going to implement and have the steps for implementation, it is time to do it. You have several ways you can perform the actual simulation. The first is to have either your coworkers or the end users run through the scripts while you watch the performance data. This works well for simple testing of the data, but repeating the tests and trying to get consistent results can be an ordeal.

A better way to implement the task sheets is to write a script that simulates user interaction. Many macro languages on the market can be used to simulate user interaction. This section shows you one of many ways to do this by demonstrating a popular third-party Windows scripting tool called *WinBatch*.

WinBatch is a shareware Windows scripting language and macro creator program, developed by Wilson Windowware. It is available for trial download and can be purchased from www.windowware.com. WinBatch will work with both 16-bit and 32-bit versions of Windows. What WinBatch does is enable you to record a series of keystrokes in Windows into a macro file. You can then play this macro file to simulate user keyboard interaction. Although WinBatch is primarily designed for automating repetitive Windows tasks, it works well for simulation.

Installing WinBatch

Installing and setting up the program is easy. Just download it and run SETUP.EXE on the workstation. Although you can install the program on the workstation or on the Terminal Server, it's important that you install it on the workstation. The reason is that you want to simulate keystrokes coming from the workstation across the network for true performance testing. If you install it on the server, instead, even though your keystrokes will be recorded from across the network, when the macro plays, it will send the keystrokes locally to the application. This will affect your network bandwidth results. The other reason to install SETUP.EXE on the workstation is that the server should not have to process the macro language, only the keystrokes.

Other Scripting Options

Another utility that many Citrix administrators use for this type of testing is the Citrix Server Test Kit. This test kit is available from the *Citrix Developer Network* (CDN) web site at `http://apps.citrix.com/cdn/SDK/ cstk_sdk.asp`. If you have not already signed up to CDN, it is very worthwhile because it comes with its own scripts and enables you to import scripts of your own such as WinBatch scripts. Not only is it free, but you also can get access to some very useful technical articles and software such as Columbia for NFuse.

You can find additional scripts and utilities from Microsoft for capacity testing at these sites:

- `www.microsoft.com/windows2000/techinfo/administration/terminal/loadscripts.asp`

- `ftp://ftp.microsoft.com/reskit/win2000/roboclient.zip`

- `www.microsoft.com/windows2000/techinfo/reskit/tools/hotfixes/tscpt-o.asp`

Setting Up the Client

After WinBatch has been installed, you should see a small owl-shaped icon in the task tray to indicate that it is active. Log on to the Terminal Server with your client of choice. Remember that many decisions you make on the client side will affect your performance results. Make sure you keep track of how the clients are set up for each test you perform. All the following settings will affect the results:

- Choice of Terminal Server protocol (either ICA or RDP)

- Choice of network protocol if using ICA (either IPX, SPX, TCP/IP, or NetBEUI)

- Choice of video resolution and colors

- Whether compression is enabled or disabled

- Level of encryption

Using the performance tests, you can determine which combination of these settings will work best for you on the client side.

Recording and Viewing the Macro

When you're logged on, bring up the application you'll be testing, and then follow these steps:

1. To begin recording the macro, click the owl icon in the task tray and select Win Macro. You also can press Ctrl+Alt+PageUp as a shortcut.

2. From the Win Macro window, under Record options, select whether you want to record keystrokes, mouse movements, or both.

3. Either click the Record button or press Ctrl+Alt+Ins to begin recording the macro.

From here on, all your keystrokes and mouse movements will be recorded. Using the task sheet you created earlier, go through the steps you want to record. Try to keep an average pace that accurately simulates typical use. If you take too long between movements, you can change the timing values later in the macro; however, it is easiest if you just record the macro as if an average user were using the application and running through the task sheet.

When you are finished with the steps in the task sheet, do the following to save the macro script:

1. Press Ctrl+Alt+End to end the recording. This will bring you back to the Win Macro window.

2. From the Win Macro window, click the Save As button.

3. Select Save Macro as WinBatch Script and enter the folder to save it in. Change the name of the macro to something meaningful, and then click OK to save.

4. When back at the Win Macro window, click the Edit Script button to edit what was recorded.

WinBatch translates your keystrokes into Wilson Windowware's *Window Interface Language* (WIL). Because these are all text commands, you can easily edit the macro file and modify timing values or keystrokes entered.

For example, try recording a simple WinBatch macro using WordPad running on Terminal Server. While recording the macro, enter a short line of text, highlight the text (Shift+Home) and then delete it by pressing the Delete key. Press Ctrl+Alt+End to end recording the macro. Save the macro with the script and then click Edit Script to edit the macro. Listing 21.1 is an example of what you might see in the WinBatch Studio window.

Listing 21.1   **Test WinBatch Script**

```
;;;;;;;;;;;;;;;;;;;;;;;;;;;;;;;;;;;;;;;;;
;
; Name: Test
;
; Description: Recorded macro translation.
;
;;;;;;;;;;;;;;;;;;;;;;;;;;;;;;;;;;;;;;;;;

TimeDelay(4.1)
SendKey("The{SPACE}quick{SPACE}b")
TimeDelay(4.0)
SendKey("rown{SPACE}fox{SPACE}jumped{SPACE}ove")
TimeDelay(4.7)
SendKey("r{SPACE}the{SPACE}lazy{SPACE}dog+{HOME}")
TimeDelay(1.5)
SendKey("{DELETE}")
```

Notice that two main commands are used in this particular macro: `timedelay` and `sendkey`. The `sendkey` command just sends keystrokes to whatever window is currently open on the desktop. Even though hundreds of macro language commands are available in the Window Interface Language, you'll probably need to know only a handful to do performance testing. `sendkey` is one of the most important because it is what you use to send keystrokes to a particular application.

The other command is `timedelay`. `timedelay` pauses the macro for the number of seconds specified. You can adjust the `timedelay` values as needed in your macros to accurately simulate normal user response times to applications.

WinBatch Studio

The new WinBatch Studio makes macro editing significantly easier. If you want to know the syntax for any displayed command just right-click the command and select Keyword Lookup or press Shift+F1.

You also can right-click anywhere in the Macro window and select Help Files from the menu. A list of all the many different help files available will display.

User Interaction and Macro Repetition Delays

Remember that users are rarely typing in the application 100 percent of the time. The amount of delay you put in the script is up to you to judge and is a very important factor for accurate server performance testing.

You can introduce two types of delay: user-interaction delay and macro-repetition delay. User-interaction delay is the delay between keystrokes and between switching screens. User-interaction delay should be set up to mimic the average typing rate of the users and the speed with which the users normally switch screens in the application when they're actively using it.

Macro-repetition delay is much more subjective and difficult to determine. Macro-repetition delay is the amount of seconds between each repetition of the macro. This delay should represent the general level of application activity of the users.

If you're going to roll out the application to a busy data center where users are typing nearly constantly into their terminals, your macro repetition delay should be very short. If you're going to roll out the application to users who will be using it only on brief occasions to gather or enter information, your usage delay could be several minutes or more. Be sure to qualify the results of your testing by the amount of macro repetition delay you put into the scripts.

Creating a Performance Testing Macro

Now that you understand the difference between user-interaction and macro-repetition delay, it is time to modify the macro that you created so that it can be used for performance testing. To do this, you must do two things: introduce the delays in a controlled fashion into the script, and also make the script loop endlessly so that you can check system performance while the script is running.

Listing 21.2 shows you how to do this. Note the use of the goto command to make the script loop endlessly.

Listing 21.2 **Repeating a WinBatch Script**

```
UsageDelay = 5
InteractionDelay = 2
:Start
SendKey(`The{SPACE}quick`)
TimeDelay (InteractionDelay)
SendKey(`{SPACE}brown{SPACE}`)
TimeDelay (InteractionDelay)
SendKey(`fox{SPACE}jumped`)
TimeDelay (InteractionDelay)
SendKey(`{SPACE}over{SPACE}the`);
TimeDelay (InteractionDelay)
SendKey(`{SPACE}lazy{SPACE}dog.`)
TimeDelay (InteractionDelay)
```

```
;Highlight the text (Shift+UpArrow) and delete it
SendKey(`+{UP}{HOME}`)
SendKey(`{DELETE}`)
TimeDelay (UsageDelay)
Goto Start
```

This script simulates a user typing rate of approximately 60 words per minute by using a user-interaction delay of 2 seconds. The script also has a macro-repetition delay of 5 seconds between repetitions.

Note how the `timedelay` (seconds) statements are evenly placed throughout the macro. This is important to simulate user interaction. If you do not space out the keystrokes using delays, they'll be sent all at once to the Terminal Server. This causes a false spike in utilization, which would not occur if an actual user were typing in the same data. By spacing things out, server utilization will more accurately reflect what it would be if an actual user were typing in the data.

Setting Up the Performance Test

When you know how to simulate user interaction and understand how your coworkers use the application, it's time for the actual performance test. For most projects, the best and easiest way to carry out a performance test is through controlled user scaling. This involves doing accurate load testing from a small number of Terminal Server stations and then scaling the results to the actual number of users who will be on the system.

The advantage of scaling is that it is quick, easy, and provides a good feel for how an application will perform on a large scale. The disadvantage is that it's more inaccurate than full-scale testing. There's an underlying assumption with scaling that performance will scale linearly. This is not always the case. (It can depend on many factors, such as how the application is written to perform under heavy use.) To help eliminate these factors, your sample group should be at least three workstations. The more workstations in your sample, the more accurate your final results will be.

Here's one way to do a scaling test:

1. Install the application on the server and create three test users (for example, apptester1, apptester2, and apptester3) who have the application icon on their desktop or Start menu.

2. Install the Terminal Server client on three or more typical workstations. Make sure you use the exact same client settings on all the workstations, such as video resolution, encryption, and compression. Try to choose workstations that will be part of the final rollout. If that's not possible, use

machines with the same operating system and basic hardware capabilities. A conference or training room is a great place to set up a performance test environment.

3. To simulate the connection, connect the machines to Terminal Server using the connection type and speed that will be used in the final rollout. If you're going to connect your clients to Terminal Server across a 100Mbps LAN in the final rollout, set up a separate 100Mbps network segment for doing the performance test. If you're going to distribute the clients across a WAN, either simulate the WAN link in your testing lab or choose a site on the WAN that's close to the main office to set up the test.

4. Prepare to capture the data. You should have utilities prepared to measure the amount of memory being used by each client, the amount of processing time, the amount of paging file use, and the amount of network bandwidth. All these parameters can be measured and recorded using Performance Monitor. Techniques for capturing this information are covered in the section "Performance Monitor."

5. Using the scripts you've created, simulate user interaction on a single workstation, on two workstations, and then on three. Record the results for each. It's normally best to run the script from the workstation, as noted earlier. If you run the script on the server, the server processing time taken to run the script will affect the results. You should see a roughly linear increase in usage at the server. If not, try the test with more workstations. Be sure all the client settings are the same. Keeping your desktop resolution setting and your client resolution, color, protocol, compression, and encryption parameters the same on all the clients is important for accurate results.

If you have the time to do a full test, rather than just an estimate, keep adding simulated users to the system. At some point the maximum capacity of the system will be reached. You will know you have reached this point when application response time has degraded significantly. Try varying one or more of the settings on the client or the hardware configuration of the server, and then run the user-scaling test again. You can use this technique to see how the change affects the results of the test.

One of the best measures of when you have reached maximum capacity on a Terminal Server is the processor queue length. You can view the processor queue length under the System counters in Performance Monitor. Processor queue length is the number of threads waiting to be processed in the processor queue. If the processor queue length exceeds 10 over a sustained period of time, this indicates significant processor congestion and that you have reached the processing capacity of the system.

You also can watch the average processor utilization. If you find that the average processor utilization scales to more than 90 percent constant utilization per processor, and you're sure the high utilization is not due to lack of memory, you'll likely need to get higher performance hardware or more processors. Make sure the usage delay parameter in your scripts is realistic for your environment. Usage delay should reflect the average use you expect in your environment. It will have a direct effect on processor utilization. Bursts of heavy processor use are normal for any environment, but constant heavy use should be avoided. Constant heavy use means that all users will get slow response times when working with their applications.

Another important factor is memory use. By looking at the memory available while adding more users to the system, you should be able to get a good feel for how much memory each user requires. Not having enough memory can bring your server to a crawl. As the server runs out of memory, it will start swapping out memory to the system paging file. This constant use of the disk is called *thrashing*, and it will slow down your server to the point that it's nearly unusable.

Note that 32-bit applications are *reentrant*. What this means is that when a 32-bit application's code and .DLLs are loaded into memory, they can be used by all users of the application on your Terminal Server. This means that with 32-bit applications, you mainly need to be concerned about how much memory each user uses. Because 16-bit and DOS applications are not re-entrant, the application's code needs to be reloaded for every user of the application. This means you need to be concerned about how much memory the application and user data take up for each user.

Measuring and Monitoring Performance

It's difficult to improve the performance of your server unless you have a way of measuring it. This section covers several techniques for measuring the performance of your server. You'll learn how to use several tools, including Performance Monitor and Task Manager, to gain insight into bottlenecks. You'll also discover how to monitor your performance over the long run to prevent problems from occurring.

Realize that performance-monitoring tools themselves can affect the results of any performance testing. Try to run your performance tests from the console and not through a remote Windows session. If you do run the tests from a remote terminal, make sure to keep the performance-monitoring window minimized during the tests. The quickly changing parameters and performance results on the screen will, by themselves, eat up large amounts of processing time and network bandwidth as they are transferred across the line.

Task Manager

Included with Terminal Server is a very simple but powerful tool called Task Manager. Task Manager can provide quick, on-the-fly answers to your server performance problems. Although you'll not get the level of detail you can get with Performance Monitor, it provides a good summary view of the state of the server. It works best when used for ongoing monitoring of the server. If you experience a performance problem, the first place to look is Task Manager. After you've assessed the nature of the problem, you can isolate it further using Performance Monitor.

While reading here about the many performance parameters you can monitor with Task Manager, bring up Task Manager on your workstation and follow along. To run Task Manager on Windows NT 4.0, select NT Security from the Start menu and click the Task Manager button. If you're at the console, you also can press Ctrl+Alt+Del and then click Task Manager.

The Performance Tab

One of the most useful parts of the Task Manager is the Performance tab (see Figure 21.1). The parameters under the Performance tab provide a global view of how your server is doing. Under Performance, you'll find a graphical view of the CPU utilization and memory usage. When you double-click the Performance tab, the CPU utilization and memory usage graphs will fill the entire window, and you can size it as you want. This window offers a quick view of the status of the server and can be kept open on the console.

Beneath the graphs in the Performance tab are several useful memory- and processor-related parameters:

- **Totals**   This gives you an idea of the workload on your processors. Totals tell you how many Handles, Threads, and Processes are currently running on the server.

- **Physical Memory**   Physical memory is just how much memory is installed in your server. It's a good idea to keep an eye on the Available count. The physical memory available is the amount of physical memory left after it has been committed to use for the applications and processes loaded on the server.

- **Commit Charge** The Commit Charge Total, Limit, and Peak are the most important memory parameters on the window. The Commit Charge Total reflects the total virtual memory that has been committed to processes running on the system. The Commit Charge is what you need to watch as you add more users onto the system to get an idea of how much memory each user is taking up. The limit reflects the total virtual memory available on the system without expanding the paging file. The final parameter is the Commit Charge Peak. The peak is the maximum memory that was committed during the session.

- **Kernel Memory** Kernel Memory parameters refer to memory available to programs running in the privileged kernel mode. Paged is the part of the total memory that can be swapped to disk.

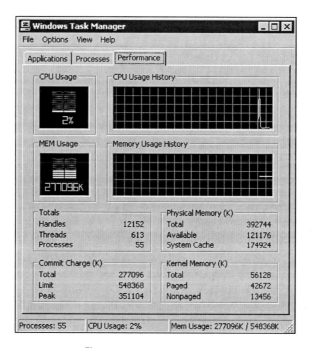

Figure 21.1 Performance tab.

With all these parameters, which is the most important one to watch? It really depends on what you're looking for. One indicator that you need more physical memory is if your committed bytes are significantly greater than your physical memory. Although this might be normal for some server situations, this normally means that your system is relying heavily on the paging file. To verify this, check the paging file usage using Performance Monitor. If it's heavily used during normal server activity, you have a good indication that you might need more memory.

You also can watch how much the Committed Bytes parameter increases as users log on and run their applications. In a controlled testing environment, you can use this parameter to get a good handle on how much memory each user and his applications will take up on the server. It's also a good idea to have the user work with the application for a while and then compare the peak committed bytes to the committed bytes before the user logged on. You might find that some applications use significantly more memory than what they started with, depending on which procedures are run with them.

Beside memory use, the utilization parameters also can be very handy. With the utilization graph, you can gain a quick understanding of the current and recent utilization of the server.

The Processes Tab

Although the parameters in the Performance tab give you a good idea how the system as a whole is running, they don't provide you with the details you need to isolate the source of any performance problems. With the information under the Processes tab, you can quickly find which processes are using up the most memory, which ones have the highest utilization, and which ones have used up the most CPU time (see Figure 21.2). This real-time information proves very valuable when troubleshooting performance problems. It's also good for periodic checking of the performance of your servers and finding out which applications and users are using up the most resources on your servers. Each process is broken down by user and image name, making it very easy to spot users who are running applications that use the most system resources.

By default, under the Processes tab, you're shown the image name, user name, ID, *process ID* (PID), CPU time, CPU utilization, and memory usage. Besides these default parameters, you can add several more by selecting Select Columns from the View menu. Table 21.1 is a list of all the process parameters you can monitor with the Task Manager.

Table 21.1 **Process Parameters**

Parameter	Description
Image Name	Name of the process. Processes usually go by the name of the application that started them.
Session ID	This is the Terminal Server Session ID of a process.
PID	Unique process ID number assigned to each process running on the system.
CPU Usage	Percentage of CPU time used by the process' threads.
CPU Time	Total processor time used by the process since the process began.
Memory Usage	Amount of system memory used by the process.
Memory Usage Delta (Windows 2000 only)	Shows the change in memory usage by a process.
Peak Memory Usage (Windows 2000 only)	Shows the peak memory usage of a process since Task Manager was started.
Page Faults	Number of instances where the disk had to be accessed to retrieve data because it was not in memory.
Page Faults Delta	Change in page faults since the last update.
User Objects	The total number of user objects in use by a process.
GDI Objects	Number of objects open in the graphical device interface by a process.
I/O Reads, Reads Bytes, Writes, Writes Bytes, Other, Other Bytes (Windows 2000 only)	The number of I/O reads and writes by a process. In addition you can display the total bytes read or written.
VM Size	Size of the section of the paging file currently in use by the process.
Mem Usage Delta	Change in memory usage.
Paged Pool	Amount of memory in use by the process that's available to being swapped out to the paging file.
Nonpaged Pool	Amount of operating system memory in use by the process. This memory is not available for paging.
Base Priority	The relative priority of the process: low, normal, or high. The priority of the process can be adjusted by right-clicking the process and selecting Set Priority.
Handle Count	The number of object handles the process has opened.
Thread Count	The number of threads the process has running.

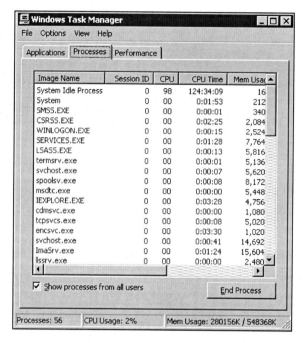

Figure 21.2   Processes tab.

Because there can easily be several hundred processes running at the same time, you need to be able to sort out which ones are which. To sort by one of the performance parameters, just click the column heading above the performance parameter.

You can find out which processes are taking up the most utilization by looking at the CPU Time and CPU Usage parameters. Sorting by CPU Usage can quickly indicate which process is currently taking up the most CPU time on the server. The CPU Time parameter is good for comparing which applications are taking up the most CPU time on the average during a given period.

Use the combination of the Mem Usage and VM Size parameters to quickly find which processes running on the system are taking up the most memory. Mem Usage represents physical memory, and VM Size represents the paging file. This is a good technique for quickly finding applications that have memory leaks or are using excessive amounts of memory.

One of the more useful but least used parameters is the Page Fault count. A page fault occurs every time a program tries to retrieve something from memory but ends up going to the paging file on the disk. Page Fault can be a very good indicator of application activity and thus processor utilization. Excessive page faults also can indicate a need for more system memory.

Performance Monitor

Performance Monitor is the premier tool included with Terminal Server for both short-term performance testing and long-term performance monitoring. With Performance Monitor, you can view performance, write performance parameters to log files for later analysis, and even run programs based on when a selected performance threshold has been exceeded.

This section shows you techniques for capacity testing your servers in a test environment and monitoring your server in the long run for performance problems.

Performance Monitor in 2000 and with Feature Release 1

Many improvements have been added to Performance Monitor in Windows 2000. Performance Monitor is now integrated with the new Microsoft Management Console technology. In addition, the counter list can now be saved out to a file and loaded automatically for easier monitoring setup. Although most of this section applies to both Performance Monitor on Windows NT 4.0 and 2000, you will find some specific information on the features of Performance Monitor in 2000 toward the end.

Although not specifically covered in this chapter, you will find several new Performance Monitor counters available if you have MetaFrame XPe with Feature Release 1 installed and activated. These new performance counters are all found under the ICA Session section of the counters. With these new counters, you can now monitor many ICA session-specific parameters such as Session Compression and Bandwidth Usage.

Even if you do not have Feature Release 1, MetaFrame XP comes with some very useful latency counters located under ICA Session. Using these counters, you can monitor the average latency or response time of sessions on your Citrix MetaFrame server.

Testing Your Server's Capacity Using Performance Monitor

During the testing stage of your server, one of the most important questions to answer is whether you have enough server power to meet the needs of the clients. Using Performance Monitor and the techniques described at the start of the chapter, you can come up with a solid answer to this question. The key is careful, methodical testing and close observation for performance bottlenecks.

The following section recommends a small set of performance parameters that you need to keep a close eye on during performance testing. Although these parameters will detect a wide range of performance problems, they will not necessarily detect all possible problems on the server. Keep in mind that you can monitor hundreds of different performance parameters with Performance Monitor. After you've identified a performance problem, you can narrow down the problem further using some of the more specific performance parameters. It's recommended that you do some of your own experimentation to determine which performance parameters you should monitor. The Performance Monitor tool is such a feature-rich and flexible tool that you'll likely find several good techniques that work for you, beyond what's suggested in this chapter.

Defining Acceptable Performance

The key to any successful performance testing is defining acceptable performance. As you go through the different tests and stress test the server, you'll see how the response times of your applications will vary. The question to be answered is what is acceptable as a response time and what is not. Remember that when you're using user-simulation scripts, you're simulating active users on the system. In the real world, your server will likely see random peaks of heavy user activity throughout the day. It's the duration of these peaks that matter. If your server cannot keep up with the average level of user activity, you will need to add more hardware or more servers.

Before implementing your server, you should assess the workload of users. Suppose you have a small office that needs to be able to enter handwritten reports into a corporate database. Before even doing the performance testing of the server, ask some of the users at the office how many reports they enter per day on average. Also find out what the maximum number of reports per day will be, and whether there are any especially busy times during the month. If you're going to roll out Windows-based terminals to several offices, make sure to ask key people at each of the offices how much time per day they spend entering information into their Windows terminal.

After you have determined the average and maximum projected use of the Terminal Server, you can set up your performance tests properly to ensure your server has the capacity to handle this use. Your user-simulation script should reflect the tasks users will perform, on average, each time they use the server. The Usage Delay parameter in the scripts should reflect the time between these task performances. If a user says he will be entering roughly 80 reports per day, that equates to 10 reports per hour, or one report every 360 seconds. For testing, you should have the user-simulation script simulate the entering of a single report and have a Usage Delay parameter of 360 seconds. Always make sure you plan for capacity and document your reasoning behind the testing. The more accurate the simulation of the worker's actual workload, the more accurate your final results will be.

One important thing to note is that even though the goal of this testing is to properly size a server based on both average and maximum use, you should always take into account future growth. If a department is projected to grow at 20 percent over the next year, their data processing needs also will grow. You should build this into your server capacity planning.

Another key to accurate performance testing is locking down the desktop. Users should have access only to the applications they need. In this way, you're aware of exactly what they will be doing with the server, and you can set up adequate performance tests to ensure the server has enough capacity.

Using Performance Monitor

The performance test is intended to gather the data you'll need to judge the performance of your server during user simulation. This performance information also will make an excellent baseline of performance for future comparison. Be sure to record exactly how the tests were set up and what parameters were measured so that in the future you'll be able to duplicate the results. In this way, when you make performance enhancements to the server, you'll be able to see the true effects of the enhancement.

Performance Monitor is available in the Administrative Tools group on both Windows NT 4.0 and 2000 servers. When you run the application, it will come up with a blank chart. If you're not familiar with Performance Monitor, add a counter, such as Processor Utilization, to the chart by clicking the button with the plus sign (+) at the top of the window. Figure 21.3 shows a snapshot of Performance Monitor in Windows 2000 after adding the Processor Utilization counter. Note the statistics at the bottom of the window. For each counter, Performance Monitor keeps track of the maximum value, minimum value, and average over the tracking period. These statistics will be important as you begin measuring Terminal Server performance.

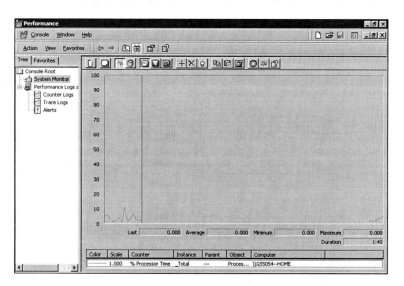

Figure 21.3   System monitor graph.

Performance Monitor comes with a plethora of counters, which are broken up into groups or objects. The following objects are some of the most useful and are the ones discussed most frequently in chapter:

- **Session or Terminal Services Session** Session is a collection of Terminal Server–specific counters. Under Session, you'll find counters such as Processor Utilization, Total Bytes, Input Errors, and Output Errors. One of the best things about the Session counters is that you can assign counters for individual or groups of connections. In this way, you can watch which users are taking up the most system resources.

- **Processor** Processor and the rest of the performance objects covered here are the same as the ones included with standard Windows NT Server 4.0. Under Processor, you'll find things such as Processor Utilization and Interrupts/Sec. You can track individual processors in the system.

- **Memory** Memory is a very important collection of counters. Under Memory, you'll find counters for things such as Pages/Sec, Page Faults/Sec, and Memory Available. One of the problems with memory counters is they only give you a picture of the memory status for the system as a whole; to understand which parts of the system are using the most memory, you'll need to use counters under Process or Session.

- **Process** Process counters provide the finest level of detail of activity and resource usage on the system. After you've determined that there's a system bottleneck using the Global Memory and Processor counters, you can narrow in on which process or processes are using the most resources. Under Process, you'll find counters for such things as Processor Utilization, Virtual Bytes, and Page Faults. You can watch these counters for individual processes by selecting the process from the instance window.

- **System** Under System are several systemwide counters, such as Processor Queue Length. The counters under System are a good place to start your search for system bottlenecks.

- **Logical Disk** Logical Disk performance counters enable you to see performance results such as Disk Bytes Read, Queue Length, and Disk Bytes Written. To record Disk performance parameters, you first need to enable them using the `diskperf -y` command from the command prompt. Disk performance parameters are disabled, by default, because they can degrade system performance. In general, you should do disk performance testing separately from your main testing. Always make sure to disable Disk performance counters (`diskperf -n`) after you have finished.

Logging Performance

So far, you've learned just how to view performance counters in real time. The power of Performance Monitor, however, is its capability to both log performance parameters and send alerts. To understand how logging works, go into Performance Monitor and select Log from the View menu for Windows NT 4.0 or click the Counters Log folder in Windows NT 2000. To start logging in Windows NT 4.0, follow these steps:

1. Select Add to Log from the Edit menu.

2. Select each of the performance counters you want to add. Note that you can add counters from other servers to monitor performance remotely.

3. Select Options from the Log menu and enter the filename and monitoring interval.

4. Select Start Log to start the logging.

To start logging in Windows 2000, follow these steps:

1. Right-click Counters Log in the Performance Monitor window and select New Log Settings.

2. Under the General tab, click Add to add the counters that you want to log. After a counter has been added, you also can change the sample interval in seconds. Note that you can add counters from other servers if you want to log performance remotely.

3. Under the Log Files tab, set the location, name, and other parameters for the log file.

4. Under the Schedule tab, either set the schedule for the log or set it to start or stop manually, and then click OK.

5. Right-click the new log entry and select Start to start logging.

The log file will begin filling with samples of the counters at the specified time intervals. After you have finished, select Stop Logging from the Log window on NT 4.0 or right-click the log entry and select Stop for Windows 2000.

Now that you have the sample information saved into a file, it's time to view it. By default, Performance Monitor is set for you to view current activity. To view this information on Windows NT 4.0, follow these steps:

1. Switch to the Chart view by selecting Chart from the View menu.

2. From the Options menu, select Data From.

3. Select Log File, and then enter the name of your log file. This prepares Performance Monitor to receive its data from the counters you recorded in the log rather than from current activity on the server.

At this point, all you need to do to see a particular counter is add it to the chart by selecting Add to Chart from the Edit menu. This will graph the values of the counter you selected for the time period you logged it.

If you want to work with a smaller section of the charted values, you can select the start and ending log times in the Input Log File Timeframe window by selecting Time Window from the Edit menu. As you change the timeframe, the average, minimum, and maximum values also will change to reflect the data in the timeframe.

For Windows 2000 users, you can view the captured log data by doing the following:

1. Click the System Monitor folder.

2. Right-click the system monitor graph area and select Properties.

3. Click the Source tab.

4. Select Log File and enter the filename for the log file you just captured.

For even better analysis of your data, you can export the data into comma- or tab-delimited format. You can then import it into programs such as Microsoft Excel or Lotus 1-2-3, to take advantage of their better analysis and graphing capabilities. To export the data from Windows NT 4.0, follow these steps:

1. Enter chart view by selecting Chart from the View menu.

2. Add all the counters to the chart that you want to export by selecting Add to Chart from the Edit menu.

3. Select the timeframe for the data you want by selecting Time Window from the Edit menu.

4. Save the data in comma-delimited (.CSV) or tab-delimited (.TSV) format by selecting Export Chart from the File menu. You can see the actual Performance Monitor data from a processor utilization test after it was imported into an Excel spreadsheet.

To export the data from Windows 2000, follow these steps:

1. Right-click the log entry you created in the Counter Logs folder and select Properties.

2. Under the Log Files tab, select .CSV or .TSV for the Log File Type, and then click OK.

3. Right-click the log entry and select Start to begin the logging to the .CSV or .TSV file.

Setting Up a Performance Test

Although this section provides some possible techniques for setting up a performance test, the exact manner in which you set up the test is up to you. In general, the steps to setting up the tests are as follows.

1. Load the Terminal Server client on three or more workstations that will be involved in the load testing of the server. Connect them to the server using the same means of communication as will be used when the project is rolled out. If most of the users will be dialing in, for example, you should set up modems and modem lines so that the test machines are dialing in to the server. The speed of the connection will definitely affect the final results of the test.

2. At the console, set up Performance Monitor logging. You should log the Session, Processor, and Memory counters. Choose your time interval for the logging. With any type of performance monitoring, you need to be careful how much the actual monitoring affects the results. Having too short a time interval can affect the results, because it will increase processor utilization. Using the console for performance monitoring is also important. If you use a Terminal Server session instead, the results can be affected because the screen will be constantly changing during logging, thus causing an increase in processor and network utilization.

3. Start the logging and then start the user-simulation script on the first machine. Let it run long enough to gather a good amount of data and then stop the logging. Change the data source to the log you just created so that you can view the logged data. Start adding the performance counters you want to look at to the chart. Set the timeframe to just the time when the user simulation occurs by selecting Timeframe from the Edit menu. Finally, export the data to a comma- or tab-delimited file.

4. While the user simulation is still running and the logging is stopped, log on to the server from another workstation. Is the performance acceptable or are there unacceptable delays? As you continue to add more simultaneous users, always check to ensure that the general performance of the server is still at an acceptable level. Ideally, you should have representatives from the user community involved in the application testing. They are the ones who can best assess application response time and likely know best how to test it.

5. Start up the user simulation on the next workstation and continue the logging process. Keep doing this until you have tested all the workstations simultaneously. You should now have a collection of log files and exported data files for at least one to three simultaneous users.

Author's Note

Note you also can set up a server to monitor the performance counters remotely using either Windows NT 4.0 or 2000 Server. This is highly recommended, especially for large performance tests. Remote monitoring will have very little noticeable effect on the performance of the server and can easily be set up to monitor several servers at the same time.

6. As a control to the testing, also take a log file of the server with no users on it. This will help you eliminate any effects that the monitoring itself is having on the performance data. An even better alternative is to run the Performance Monitor on a separate server and monitor the test server remotely.

After you've collected all this data, it's time to analyze it. Here are some of the counters you want to look at:

- **System, Processor Queue Length**   If the Processor Queue Length stays past 10 for an extended period of time, performance on the box will be sluggish at best. Watching the Processor Queue Length is one of the best indicators of application response time and system performance.

- **Processor, Processor Utilization**   If you find that your Processor Utilization is averaging more than 90 percent during the testing period, you'll likely need more processors in your server. Take a look at the difference in processor utilization as you add additional users to the server up to the maximum number of users the box will support concurrently. You can make a graph of these values. This graph can be used to predict the amount of remaining capacity in your system. Remember to make sure your Usage Delay parameter is realistic, because this will have a direct effect on the results. For a more detailed view of utilization, take a look at the Processor Utilization counters under Session. This will tell you how much processor time each session is using up.

- **Memory, Available Bytes**   The Available Bytes counter is the amount of memory, including virtual memory, available on the system. This counter will give you a good idea of how much memory each session is using. Watch this counter as you add more simultaneous users. Like processor utilization, you can scale the change in this parameter to predict how much memory you'll be using when all users are on the system. Memory Available Bytes should not increase significantly over time during a single-user simulation. If you find that the amount of memory a session takes up keeps increasing, the program might have a memory leak.

- **Memory, Pages per Second**   Pages per Second is the number of pages read from disk to resolve memory references. If this counter remains high, your system will be very slow. Try adding more memory to your system.
- **Session, Total Bytes**   Session Total Bytes is the total number of bytes a particular session is transmitting or receiving from the network. This is a good counter to check to get an idea of network utilization.

Remember that if you want to log any of the disk-related counters, you need to first enable them using `diskperf -y`. This will require a reboot of the server.

The advantage of recording your performance in this manner is that you've created a baseline. By documenting exactly how you set your tests up, what equipment was used, and what the server configuration was, and by saving all the performance results, you'll be able to repeat these tests in the future. The most powerful advantage to this is that you'll be able to see exactly how performance improves as you make improvements to the server, such as adding more processors, memory, or faster peripherals.

You can change several server parameters that will affect performance. One simple example is changing the protocol that you're using for the connections. To fine-tune performance, try changing server/workstation parameters such as the protocol, compression, and bitmap caching and then repeat the testing. If used properly, these tests can be a great tool for fine-tuning the performance of your server.

Monitoring Performance over the Long Run

After you've determined that your server is up to the job of handling all the projected users, and the system is in place and running well, you can do a couple of things to ensure it keeps running this way. One way is to just take periodic performance checks on the server and save the logs. You can review these over time and watch for any unusual rises in server usage. You also can set up constant logging at the server with a high interval rate, such as 3600 seconds (or an hour). By monitoring the server over a period of a couple weeks, you can get a good idea of what the busiest times of the day or week are.

The final technique is using alerts. Included in Performance Monitor is the Alert tool, one of the most powerful tools for long-term monitoring of your server. With the Alert tool, you can set up programs to be run if, for example, your available memory falls below 50MB. Besides running the program you set up, the Alert tool also will log the alert. When memory drops below 50MB, the server will send a message to the administrator using the `net send administrator low memory` command. To add an alert, select Add to Alert from the Edit menu and then select the counter you want to watch. On Windows 2000, you can add alerts in the Alert folder of Performance Monitor.

Tuning Tips

You can do many, many things to help ensure the best performance of your Terminal Server. Often, however, it is difficult to decide exactly what should be done. In this section you will learn the most important tuning tips and tricks for both Windows 2000 and Windows NT 4.0 Terminal Servers, and when and why they should be followed. Some of these tips require changes to the Registry, others are just guidelines for the setup and administration of your server.

One thing that is very important when applying performance tuning tips is consistency. No matter which set of tips you decide to use on your server farm, you should adhere to the same set of guidelines and tips for all of your servers. For this reason, it is highly recommended to create a Server Tuning Template spreadsheet. In this spreadsheet, just list the tuning tips that you will be applying to your servers. You can then use this template as a checklist for all your server builds.

Terminal Server Pre-Installation Tips

Even before installing your servers, you can take several steps to ensure that they will run at the top level of performance when they are put into production. These tips are summarized in the following list. These tips apply for all versions of Terminal Server. For more detailed coverage of many of these tips, see Chapter 8, "Installing Windows 2000 Terminal Server and Citrix MetaFrame."

- **Use high-performance server hardware.** Always use the highest performance server hardware available. Do not attempt to make a workstation into a Terminal Server, unless it will only be used for testing. Server-class hardware has many performance and reliability enhancements that are very important for Terminal Servers.

- **Choose a scalable server.** Choose a server that can scale to at least two processors. Even if you start with only a single processor, you can easily scale up to a second processor when usage grows. Server processing is generally the most significant bottleneck with most applications. In addition, you should choose a server that can hold up to at least 4GB of memory onboard.

- **Use only NTFS.** There is truly no good reason not to use NTFS and many, many reasons to use it. Always use NTFS for all of your partitions on Terminal Server.

- **Set up one logical drive for the system and another for the applications.** One of the golden rules of Terminal Server setup is to separate your applications from the system. This is done for both reasons of performance and reliability. From a performance standpoint, this means that users who are loading applications are not competing as heavily with the system for drive access time. From a reliability standpoint, separating the system and applications makes it less likely that you will run into drive space and other issues that could cause problems on the system partition.

- **Always make your system drive at least 4GB, if not more.** Never skimp on the drive size for your system drive; 4GB should be a minimum. Remember that on a Terminal Server, the system drives have to handle more than is usually handled on a standard Windows server. Things such as user profiles, paging files, temp files, and application .DLLs can all add up to significantly more space used than on most Windows servers. Running low on drive space can quickly lead to major performance problems.

- **Use high-performance drives.** Using high-performance, high-RPM drives can make a huge difference in performance on the busiest Terminal Servers. Drive speed is especially important on the drive used for the paging file.

- **Install only necessary components.** Never install more services or application components than are absolutely necessary. Unneeded services, such as IIS or SMTP, can take up valuable processing time and expose the server to security risks. When you are finished installing your server, check through the list of services for any services that are unnecessary or that can be disabled.

- **Do not use a Terminal Server as a domain controller.** This tip is closely related to the last. For the best performance, do not use your Terminal Server as a domain controller. Your Terminal Server users will have to compete with the processing power used for user logons and domain updates. In addition, running other major services such as Exchange, Proxy, and IIS are not recommended on your Terminal Server. Ideally, the Terminal Server should be dedicated solely for use for serving Windows applications to its users.

- **Install only needed protocols.** Only install the network protocols that are needed, preferably only TCP/IP.

Terminal Server Network Design Tip

To improve the overall performance and reliability of your terminal servers, always centralize your user profiles and user data. Although not necessarily a performance improvement tip, this can greatly enhance the reliability of your server farm. By having data and profiles centralized, you can ensure quick recovery times in case a single server fails. In addition, centralizing data and profiles makes load balancing possible. For more information on how to do this see Chapter 9, "Setting Up Terminal Server Users."

MetaFrame Farm Design Tips

MetaFrame 1.8 and XP administrators should consider a few important performance issues. These issues should be considered during the planning process for your MetaFrame 1.8 or XP server farm. For more details on planning, see Chapter 6, "Planning a Terminal Server and Citrix MetaFrame XP Solution."

- **Dedicate a server as a master browser or data collector.**   If you have more than five heavily used servers in a server farm or at a single location, you should consider dedicating one of the servers as a master browser for MetaFrame 1.8 or as a data collector for MetaFrame XP. Both of these processes can take an extraordinary amount of processing time on busy server farms. On smaller farms, the dedicated server does not have to be much more powerful than a workstation. Many server vendors make low-end, rack-mountable servers that are inexpensive and are well suited for this use. On larger farms, a multiprocessor higher end server is in order.

- **On MetaFrame XP use the dedicated server for special uses.** You can use the dedicated data collector server as the server from which you publish the Citrix Management Console, as the master server for print driver replication, and as the installation management package server.

- **Set up zones if the server farm is split across a WAN.**   If your MetaFrame XP server farm is split across a WAN, make sure to set up the servers on each side of the WAN in separate zones. Setting up a zone will help localize MetaFrame update traffic. Planning and setting up zones is covered in Chapter 6.

Post-Installation Terminal Server Tips

The following tips are some of the many things you can do after the installation of your Terminal Server to improve server performance. These tips apply for all versions of Terminal Server.

- **Use high-performance network cards and lock the network speed to the highest setting.** This performance tip is critical. Because the Terminal Server relies so heavily on the network, you need to ensure that it is using the highest performance network cards and is set to the highest performance setting possible. Never rely on the auto-negotiate process to work correctly. This process commonly fails to negotiate the best speed possible or can result in a duplex mismatch and cause a high number of network errors. Instead, work with your network administrator to manually set both the network card and the port on the network switch to the highest speed possible. Verify that no excessive errors occur when users communicate with the server.

- **Put the paging file on a separate logical drive or on the application drive.** For the absolute best performance, move the paging file to a dedicated paging drive. If this is not possible or practical, move the paging file to the application drive instead. The paging file is heavily used on busy servers, so it should be on the highest performance drives possible.

- **Set the paging file to twice the size of memory and defragment it.** Set the paging file to twice the size of physical RAM memory. On a Terminal Server, where it is common to have more than 1GB of memory, the paging files can be huge. This is normal and will result in the best performance on busy servers. It is generally best to set the paging file to the correct size and location during server setup. If you change it at a later time, you should first defragment the drives on your system before making the change. When you change the paging file location and size, use the Paging File Defragmenter available at www.sysinternals.com to defragment the paging file itself.

- **Disable paging out the Executive.** By default, Windows NT 4.0 and 2000 servers will send portions of the Executive operating system components to the paging file. This can degrade performance and is not necessary if you have plenty of memory available on your system. To disable paging out of the Executive, add/change the `DisablePagingExecutive` value to DWORD `0000001` in the `HKLM\CurrentControlSet\Control\SessionManager\Memory Management` key.

- **Disable Dr. Watson logs.** Dr. Watsons are great for troubleshooting, but with Terminal Server they can cause sessions to remain hung on the server, preventing users from being able to reconnect. To disable Dr. Watsons completely, change the `Debugger` value to blank ("") in the `HKLM\SOFTWARE\Microsoft\Windows NT\CurrentVersion\AeDebug` key. The default value is `"drwtsn32 -p %ld -e %ld -g"`.

- **Disable unnecessary device mappings.** This is a very important tuning tip that can greatly improve logon times. If you do not need audio mapping, LPT/COM port mapping, drive mapping, or printer mapping, disable them at a connection level at the server by using the Terminal Services Configuration tool. Not only will the server use less processing time monitoring these ports, but because they do not have to be connected at logon, logon times will be shorter.

- **Set the Registry to a minimum of 90MB.** The Registry can quickly grow large on Terminal Server as new users log on and user Registry hives are created. Be sure to set the Registry to a minimum of 90MB on a Terminal Server. This setting is changed at the same server performance screen used to change the location of your paging file.

- **Delete screen savers and wallpaper.** Running animated screen savers and using wallpaper can cause significant performance issues with Terminal Server. It is recommended to just delete all .SCR and .BMP files in the `%systemroot%`, either manually or using a batch file to prevent them from being used.

- **Disable debugging dumps and automatic reboot** By default, a dump of memory will be written upon a blue screen error on Windows NT and 2000. This can greatly increase reboot times. Unless you are troubleshooting a particular blue screen problem, set the server to automatically reboot upon system failure and to not write the memory dump. These settings can be controlled in Control Panel, System. In Windows 2000, you will find the settings under the Advanced tab in Startup and Recovery.

- **Change the display of operating systems to less than 5 seconds.** By default, the list of operating systems displays for either 15 or 30 seconds during bootup. To reduce bootup and thus server restart times, change this value to some value less than 5 seconds. This setting also can be found in Control Panel, System.

- **Apply latest service packs.** Service packs are critical for both the security and performance of your Terminal Server. Always apply the latest service packs to your servers, after you have thoroughly tested them in your staging area.

- **Disable Active Desktop.** On Windows NT 4.0 Terminal Server, do not install the Active Desktop with Internet Explorer. On Windows 2000 Server, you can disable the Active Desktop using the Terminal Services Configuration tool.

- **Simplify the desktop and eliminate complex graphics.** Remember that everything on the desktop needs to be compressed by the server and sent across the line. By reducing the complexity of the desktop, the compression algorithms will be able to compress the graphics much more efficiently.

- **Reduce colors.** With Terminal Server, you can use up to 256 colors simultaneously. If you can get by with 16 colors instead, use 16. The fewer colors used, the less bandwidth taken up sending your desktop across the wire. If you are using Citrix and published applications, reduce the colors used by the published applications to 16 if possible. Reducing colors can make for a huge performance improvement over slow connections. Make sure to always check the number of colors truly needed by an application.

Post-Installation MetaFrame Server Tips

The following tips apply to both MetaFrame 1.8 and XP servers, except as noted:

- **Enable SuperCache.** On MetaFrame 1.8, with the latest service packs installed, you can enable a performance feature called *SuperCache*. SuperCache helps speed up screen redraws by modifying the algorithm used for caching. This option is automatically enabled on MetaFrame XP. On Citrix MetaFrame 1.8 without Feature Release 1, however, run the following command at the command prompt: `keysync icathinwireflags /enable:2`.

- **Increase the number of idle listener sessions.** The default of two idle sessions might not be enough for large, highly active server farms. Idle listener sessions are automatically created for new users who log on. If users log on faster than idle sessions can be created, they will get error messages when attempting to connect to the Citrix server. The disadvantage of setting up more idle stations than the default of two is that they take up additional memory. However, the amount of memory taken is minimal. To bump up the number of idle sessions, change the `IdleWinStationPoolCount` value in the `HKLM\SYSTEM\CurrentControlSet\ Control\TerminalServer` key.

- **Disable audio and other client mappings if not needed.** Citrix will automatically map audio and client communication ports when the user logs on to the system. You can disable these using the Citrix Connection Configuration tool located in the Citrix, MetaFrame XP Program menu folder. Right-click the ICA connection entry and select Edit. From the Edit window, click the Client Settings button. You can check several check boxes to disable various client mappings. Remember that this affects all users who use this particular connection entry.

- **Disable ICA client updates.** If you are not using automatic ICA client updates, disable them to speed up logon times. This can be done using the ICA Client Update tool located in the Program menu, Citrix, MetaFrame XP folder. Select Properties from the Database menu and remove the check mark from the Enabled box.

- **Apply latest service packs and evaluate hotfixes.** For the best performance and security, always apply the latest MetaFrame service pack after installation and evaluate the most recently released hotfixes to determine whether they are relevant to your environment.

---

twconfig and Performance Settings in the CMC

You can now adjust many video performance-related settings from the CMC. When you adjust these settings, they affect all servers in the farm. You can change these values by going into the CMC, right-clicking the farm, selecting Properties, and then clicking the ICA Settings tab. The ICA Settings window shown will appear (see Figure 21.4). From this window, you can adjust the following:

- Discard Redundant Graphics Operations   This setting is very important for minimizing the effect of animations because only the end effect of the animation will be sent to the client, rather than each step of the animation.

- Alternate Caching Method   Uses an updated caching method for the caching of graphics.

- Maximum Memory to Use For Each Sessions Graphics   The maximum amount of memory used as a buffer for graphics being sent to the client. Only modify this parameter if the server has serious memory constraints.

- Degrade Color Depth or Resolution First   If the maximum memory is met, the server will degrade either the number of colors or the resolution depending on this setting.

- Notify User of Session Degradation   Determines whether user should be notified when this happens.

Although these settings apply for all servers in the farm, you can adjust these settings for a particular server using the `twconfig` command. To turn off the inheritance of settings from the farm, use the command `twconfig /inherit:off`. You can then change any of the settings you need manually for just that server. For a list of settings available, enter `twconfig /?`. These settings basically mirror those available in the ICA Settings window shown in Figure 21.4.

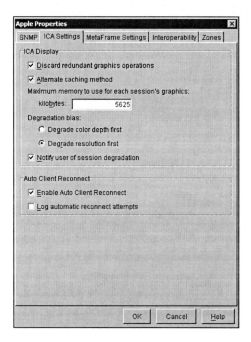

Figure 21.4   ICA Settings window.

Application Performance Tips

The following are some recommended performance and reliability tips for commonly installed applications.

- **Microsoft Office and Internet Explorer: Apply the latest Office and Internet Explorer service packs.**   Both the latest Microsoft Office and Internet Explorer service packs have vital security patches and performance enhancements that are very important in a multiuser Terminal Server environment.

- **Microsoft Word: Disable background grammar checking.**   This alone can provide huge performance improvements for Microsoft Office running on Terminal Server. To disable background grammar checking, set the `AutoGrammar` value to `0` in the `HKCU\SOFTWARE\Microsoft\Office\8.0` or `9.0\Word\Options` key. Because this is a user key, you will need to add this Registry fix to either a policy template or to the logon script to apply it to each user.

- **Internet Explorer: Remove and rename LOADWC.EXE.** If you are using Internet Explorer, remove and rename the LOADWC.EXE executable by removing the LOADWC.EXE entry in the `HKLM\SOFTWARE\Microsoft\Windows\CurrentVersion\Run` key and renaming the file to LOADWC.BAK. LOADWC.EXE is an executable that runs upon startup for every user and customizes subscription settings and other user profile information for Internet Explorer. Normally the default settings suffice, so this executable is not needed.

- **Internet Explorer 4.x and 5.x: Disable smooth scrolling.** Smooth scrolling can slow down performance by overtaxing the screen update process with too many updates. To disable smooth scrolling set the `SmoothScroll` value to `0` in the `HKCU\SOFTWARE\Microsoft\InternetExplorer\Main` key.

- **Use Windows 32-bit applications.** Terminal Server is designed to efficiently run 32-bit applications. If you are using Windows 16-bit or DOS applications, you can expect a large drop in performance. You will not be able to run as many users simultaneously using 16-bit or DOS applications as you would users who run 32-bit applications.

- **Never use animated screen savers or applications with animated graphics.** Make sure that users do not have the option of using an animated screen saver or the option of installing one from their Terminal Server desktops. You can lock down the ability to change screen savers with policies; or even simpler, do not install any screen savers on your Terminal Server except the blank screen saver. In addition, even small animated graphics within applications can take up surprisingly large amounts of network bandwidth. Many applications, such as web browsers, enable you to disable animated graphics. If you see animated graphics or cursors in any of your applications, check with the publisher to find out how to disable them.

Shortening Logon Times

A lot of times the perception of poor server performance is created while applications are run. However, one thing that is annoying for most everyone is the fact that it often takes a long time to log on to the server and just start up an application, especially over slow connections. You can take many specific steps to reduce the amount of time it takes to log on to the server and run applications. The following are some of the most highly recommended techniques:

- **Disable mapping of all client devices on a particular connection or for particular users.** Mapping various client devices takes an extraordinarily long time, especially with drive mappings. If your users do not need the mapping, make sure to disable it.

- **Disable automatic drive mappings and map needed drives manually.** You can use a simple net use command in the USRLOGON .CMD script to manually map a needed drive rather than have the server spend time during logon trying to detect the correct drive mappings.

- **Make sure users logging on to Terminal Server do not run the domain logon script.** Use the local USRLOGON.CMD logon script rather than the domain logon script and only put the commands you need in this script. You can use a batch file to push out a copy of this script to all of your servers so that they have the same logon script. This step alone often saves a large amount of time during logon, especially if your domain logon script is complex. You can put the following line at the top of your domain logon script to skip the domain logon script if the user is logging on to a Terminal Server:

```
Title : Skipping the Domain Logon Script for Terminal Server Users
if exist %systemroot%\system32\tsadmin.exe then goto End
...
[domain logon script contents]
...
```

- **Clean the startup folder.** Make sure nothing is in the Startup folder that does not absolutely need to be run.

- **Clean the Run key.** Make sure nothing is set to run from the HKLM\SOFTWARE\Microsoft\Windows\CurrentVersion\Run key that does not need to be.

- **Use mandatory profiles or take steps to reduce the size of user profiles, especially if your profiles are centralized.** Profiles can quickly become huge in size and cause extraordinarily long logon times. Taking steps to reduce the size of profiles will make a big difference in logon times.

- **Eliminate splash screens from applications.** Most applications have a Registry key you can use to disable the splash screen.

- **Disable wallpaper.** Disable desktop wallpaper using the Connection Configuration tool. This property is under a connection's Advanced connection setting.

- **Use few policies.** Make minimal use of policies. Policies are processed during logon and can take a significant amount of time.

Installing and Using Resource Manager with MetaFrame XPe

Included with MetaFrame XPe is a very important performance monitoring tool called *Resource Manager*. Using Resource Manager, you can closely monitor the resource usage of not only all the servers in your farm, but also individual applications. Much like Performance Monitor, you can use Resource Manager to monitor and log various Performance Monitor counters available on your Citrix MetaFrame server. In addition, Resource Manager enables you to receive either a pager, email, or SNMP alert when any monitored counter exceeds a settable threshold. Unlike Performance Monitor, you also can set alerts for counters when they exceed a particular threshold over a specified period of time.

For large server farms, this level of information is very important. The detailed resource utilization information provided by the Resource Manager can be used to help do the following:

- **Size servers** You can use the information provided by Resource Manager to help you size your servers properly.

- **Plan for capacity** Resource Manager can be used to gather the information needed to establish a performance baseline and to be able to plan for future capacity needs.

- **Troubleshoot performance problems** You can use many performance monitor variables to help troubleshoot performance issues.

- **Closely monitor server performance** With Resource Manager, you can monitor server performance much more closely. You can set up alerts to let you know first when the server is running slowly before the users call.

In the sections that follow, you will learn how to set up Resource Manager and use it to help monitor the servers in your Citrix MetaFrame XPe server farm.

Installing and Using Resource Manager

Resource Manager comes on the System Analysis and Monitoring CD that comes with MetaFrame XPe. Much like Installation Manager, Resource Manager is a separately installed product designed to "plug-in" to your existing MetaFrame XPe servers. Instead of providing a separate management tool, when you install Resource Manager, it adds resource management capabilities to the Citrix Management Console.

You can install Resource Manager on either a Windows NT 4.0 or 2000 Terminal Server; however, it requires that MetaFrame XP be installed and that the server be licensed for the XPe edition.

During installation, the Resource Manager install process creates a small Access database under the install location for the program. The default folder and filename for this database is `%programfiles%\citrix\citrix resource manager\rmlocaldatabase.mdb`. This database is the one that will contain all the monitored performance metrics for the server. Depending on how many performance metrics you intend to monitor, this database can grow rather large.

Once installed, the Resource Manager runs as a part of the IMA service on your Citrix MetaFrame XPe server. Every 15 seconds, a snapshot of the counter values for all the measured performance metrics is written to the local Resource Manager database. Performance metrics specific to particular applications are written to the database every 20 seconds once one instance of the application is started.

The current version of Resource Manager is designed more for short-term monitoring and alerting, rather than for long-term information gathering on performance statistics. Performance statistics are kept only for 48 hours before being purged and overwritten with new information. This means you can create graphs and reports only for at most two days back. Although this might be useful for many performance-monitoring needs, this is an important limitation to be aware of. For those used to the continual performance-gathering capabilities of Resource Management Services for MetaFrame 1.8, this is a big change to how things are done.

Because the data is kept for only 48 hours, you do not have to be too concerned with the Resource Manager database growing too large in size. On average, for each Performance Monitor counter you are keeping track of, you can expect the database to grow by 4MB in size.

In addition to the statistics gathered in the local database on each server, a few statistics, such as the number of instances a particular application runs, are gathered centrally for the farm and written to the data store. This job is handled by a specially designated Citrix MetaFrame server called the *farm metric server.* Because the farm metrics are always written to data collector first, it is best practice to designate your farm's data collector as the farm metric server. On large server farms, you should already have designated one of your servers as a dedicated data collector. Use this server as the farm metric server.

In addition to the farm metric server, you need to pick one of the servers in the farm as the server that will handle sending out SMS and email alerts. This server is referred to in this chapter as the *Resource Manager alerting server* and can be any one of the servers in the MetaFrame XPe server farm. As long as you have a dedicated data collector server, it is recommended to use the dedicated data collector as your farm's Resource Manager alerting server. This server needs to have email software installed (such as Outlook) that has a MAPI interface for the server to be able to send out email alerts. Also to send out *Simple Messaging System* (SMS) alphapage alerts to alphapagers, this server needs a dedicated modem installed.

Changes from Resource Management Services in MetaFrame 1.8

Citrix has completely revamped resource management with MetaFrame XP. For those familiar with Resource Management Services for MetaFrame 1.8, there are a significant number of major differences between the two resource management solutions:

- Resource Manager in XP is a short-term monitoring solution and only gathers 48 hours of information. Resource Management Services in MetaFrame 1.8 can gather days or even months worth of statistics.

- Resource Manager does not include resource usage accounting capabilities. This feature with Resource Management Services was mainly intended for ASPs or companies that wanted to be able to keep track of system usage by user for accounting reasons.

- Resource Manager relies on a local Access database and does not connect to an external database. With Resource Management Services in MetaFrame 1.8, you had to make an ODBC connection into some database server on the network when installing it. This server was the one that recorded the performance statistics.

- Resource Manager is mainly designed to monitor Performance Monitor counters. Resource Management Services in MetaFrame 1.8 had many of its own custom counters. Several of these are no longer available. However, you get many more things you can monitor through Performance Monitor counters.

These differences are not necessarily bad, just different. Whether you need to install and configure Resource Manager will depend on the needs of your environment.

Taking Best Advantage of Resource Manager

One important tip that might not be readily apparent is that the change in licensing policy for MetaFrame XP provides many beneficial effects. With MetaFrame 1.8, you had to purchase a base server license for every server on which you installed MetaFrame 1.8. This base license was several thousand dollars. However, with MetaFrame XP you only purchase the "base" license once for the entire farm. You can then install MetaFrame XP on as many servers as you want. In terms of Resource Manager, this licensing change is awesome. You can easily use Resource Manager to help monitor and manage the performance of servers on your network that you do not intend to even put users on!

In other words, suppose you have a production server that you have been wanting to monitor and alert off of particular Performance Monitor counters on. Your choices are to either setup Performance Monitor on the server and deal with its severe alerting limitations or purchase an expensive third-party performance-monitoring suite, such as NetIQ. If you have MetaFrame XP, however, you can just install MetaFrame XPe on the server, add it to your farm, install Resource Manager, and now not only can you monitor all the server's performance statistics, but you also can alert off of them and more easily remote control the server using the features of MetaFrame XP! Not a bad solution considering the price of most monitoring suites.

Installing Resource Manager

The Resource Manager install process is very easy. Remember that the installation process makes changes to the CMC that enable you to manage resources using the tool. It is highly recommended for this reason and more to always run the CMC from the server. Although you do have the capability to install and run the CMC from a local workstation, this is strongly discouraged. Instead, run it on your server and publish it as an application for your Citrix MetaFrame administrators.

Before installing, make sure your server has the latest Windows Server service pack installed. You should install the latest MetaFrame XP service pack after the installation of Resource Manager because there are significant updates in the service packs for Resource Manager in particular. Because the installation stops and starts the IMA service, this is not an install that you want to do during the middle of the day.

It is recommended to install Resource Manager on your farm's dedicated data collector and on only those servers that you want to monitor. Publish the CMC from the farm's data collector and use that CMC to manage your farm and its resources.

To install Resource Manager, follow these steps:

1. Insert the System Monitoring and Analysis CD into the CD drive of the server you are installing Resource Manager onto and click the Citrix Resource Manager Setup button in the window that appears. You also can manually run this install utility by running [cd]:\en\setup.exe.

2. Click Next from the main window that appears.

3. Select the folder to install Resource Manager to and click Next. Remember that the Resource Manager database gets created under this folder. You should have a good 500MB free on this drive before installing, assuming you will be monitoring up to 100 performance counters.

4. Apply or reapply the latest MetaFrame service pack. Also apply or reapply the latest feature release software if you are licensed to use it.

The install will now begin. During the install, the IMA service will be stopped and then started again. Repeat this installation on all the servers you want to manage.

Author's Note

If you ever need to uninstall MetaFrame XP, make sure you uninstall Resource Manager and Installation Manager first. Otherwise, you will likely experience problems during the uninstallation or during a possible future reinstallation of the products.

Configuring Server and Application Monitoring

During the installation of Resource Manager, several changes are made to the CMC. First, you will see a new icon for Resource Manager (see Figure 21.5). If you click this icon, you will be presented with a number of different tabs where you can change various Resource Manager configuration settings, such as SMS, email, and SNMP alerting. In addition, you can run Resource Manager reports from under the Reports tab.

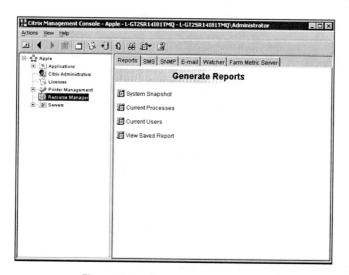

Figure 21.5   Resource Manager icon.

Besides the obvious changes to the CMC, you will find that a new Resource Manager tab has been added to the tabs available for each server and for each application. Figure 21.6 shows the window you get when you click the Server tab. Notice the number of default objects automatically monitored as soon as you install Resource Manager. By default, the following Performance Monitor counters are all monitored starting the moment you finish the install on your server:

- Percentage of Disk Time and Disk Space on all logical drives on the server
- Available Memory
- Pages per Second and Paging File Usage
- Bytes per Second on Network Interfaces
- Percentage Processor Time and Percentage Interrupt Time
- Context Switches per Second (indication of server processor congestion)
- Number of Active and Inactive Sessions

Remember these counters are recorded every 15 seconds.

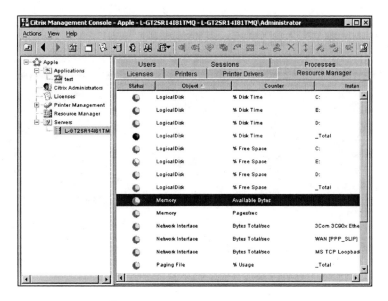

Figure 21.6   Resource Manager tab.

You can add or remove any of the counters or metrics that are being monitored for a particular server by just doing the following:

1. Select the server under the Servers folder in the CMC.

2. Click the Resource Manager tab.

3. Right-click in the Resource Manager window and select Add/Remove
   Metrics.

4. From the Add/Remove Metrics window that appears, select the object
   whose counters you want to modify under the Objects pull-down list and
   select or deselect the counters you want.

Although it is very easy to monitor a large number of metrics on your
server, remember that for each metric added it will add around 4MB to the
size of the local Resource Manager database over a period of 48 hours. Also
realize that monitoring a large number of different metrics can have a performance impact on your server. It is recommended to keep the number of
variables monitored to fewer than 20 per server.

If you want to view a graph of the recent values of any of the monitored
metrics for your server, just right-click the metric under the Resource
Manager window and select Real-Time Graph. A graph will quickly be generated showing the metric values over time (see Figure 21.7). The yellow and
red threshold values also will be shown for the metric as horizontal lines.

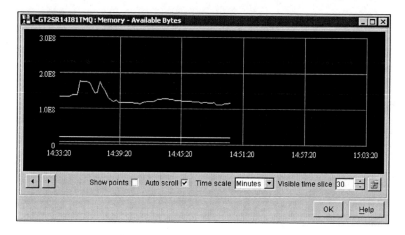

Figure 21.7   Graphing metrics.

In addition to server variables, you also can monitor the number of instances
of a particular application across the server farm. To set up this type of application monitoring, follow these steps:

1. Click the application name under the Applications folder.

2. Click the Resource Manager tab.

3. Right-click the Count variable and select Add/Remove Metrics.

4. From the Metrics screen, put a check next to Count.

You can now monitor and graph the count of the application instances just like you can for server metrics.

Setting Up Alerts

The last thing you will learn about Resource Manager is how to set up alerts. You can set up alphapage, email, and SNMP alerts very easily with Resource Manager. For each alert, you can set two different thresholds: a yellow threshold and a red threshold. When the monitored metric exceeds the threshold you set up for a specified time, the alert is sent.

For alerting to work for email alerts, you must first set up a dedicated email alerting server. This server must be running the Resource Manager Mailing service. This service is installed when you install Resource Manager, but it is set to be manually started rather than automatically. To set up an email alert server using Outlook and Exchange, follow these steps:

1. Install Resource Manager and the latest service pack on the server.

2. Create a user account on the domain called **Alerter**. Create an email account on the Exchange Server called **Alerter**, with an alias of **Alerter**. Give the Alerter user ID the rights to read the Alerter email

3. Install Microsoft Outlook on the server. This will install the necessary MAPI application components that are needed for the server to send email out.

4. Create an email profile named **Alerter** using the EMail Profile Creator tool in Control Panel.

5. Log on as Alerter and verify that you can bring up Outlook and send and receive email using the Alerter profile.

6. From Control Panel, Services set the startup for the Resource Manager Mailer service to Automatic. Change the user ID for the service to Alerter and enter the password for the Alerter account.

7. Select the Resource Manager from the CMC and click the EMail tab.

8. Click the Edit button and enter **Alerter** for the Profile Name and **Alerter** for the User ID. Enter the Alerter account's password for the password and click OK.

9. Click the Add button and add the email alerter server to the list and click the Test button to test. The test should come back green.

If you have problems setting up the email alerting, make sure of the following:

- You can open Outlook email from the console of the server and send and receive emails when logged on as Alerter.
- The Alerter is the default and only profile in Outlook.
- You set up the Resource Mail Manager service for Automatic start, and it is set up to log on with the Alerter account.

The next type of alert you can set up is SMS. SMS is a special standardized system used by many paging and cellular companies for the sending of alphanumeric pages to pagers and cellular devices. When sending an alpha-page, your server just dials the number for the SMS server for your particular pager or cellular and then sends special modem codes that are translated to an alphapage and sent to your pager. Most cellular and pager companies use what is referred to as the *TAP protocol* to do this. You can get the number for the SMS server and verify the protocol used and other settings by calling the technical support representatives for your cellular or pager company. The following instructions cover how to set up SMS alerting:

1. Install a modem on your server and make sure it works through HyperTerminal.

2. Highlight Resource Manager in the CMC and click the SMS tab.

3. Click the Add button under SMS Gateways.

4. Enter the phone number for the SMS system and select either TAPI or Orange as the protocol. Enter the gateway name and click OK.

5. Click Add under Users to add a new user. Enter the username, gateway to use and the cell phone/pager number.

6. Click Test to test an alphapage to the user.

You also can easily create paging groups by clicking the Groups button, entering the group name, and adding the users you want in the group.

To set up alerts on a particular server metric, follow these steps:

1. From the CMC, select the server you want to set the alert for and then click the Resource Manager tab.

2. Right-click the metric that you want to set the alert threshold for and select Properties.

3. Enter the threshold value you want for either the red or yellow alerts (the time the value must be past this threshold for an alert to be sent) and which alert you want to send (SMS, email, or SNMP). You also can set it to run a particular local script file if an alert threshold is exceeded.

22

Securing Your Server

I S YOUR SERVER SECURE? This is a tough question to answer. Security is more of a process than an attainable goal. Good security requires constant diligence on the part of the network administrator. As you make changes to your server, you need to keep in mind the effects that those changes have on security.

Having a secure system often means both controlling access to information and ensuring that information is accessible. First, if someone can obtain unauthorized access to information from your server, your server is not secure. Second, if someone can disable others from being able to access your server or its resources, your server is not secure. Reliability is directly related to security—if you want a reliable system, you first have to secure it.

This chapter discusses what it means to have a properly secured Terminal Server. While reading this chapter, keep in mind these two distinct goals: controlling access and ensuring accessibility. The tips throughout the chapter are geared toward both of these goals.

Planning Terminal Server Security

Terminal Server presents special security problems that you might not be used to if you're coming from a Novell or Windows server background. Users no longer are accessing your server's resources across a network through a file security barrier; instead, they are at your server working with its files as if they were sitting at the console. Imagine the security problems that could occur if a hundred different users were able to sit at the console of your Windows NT server in your computer room and access its resources, and the resources of the server were not locked down properly! If one user accidentally deletes a critical system file that's not locked down, all users are immediately affected. The use of file share security is no longer a shield, because users have direct access to the server's hard drive itself. For this, and many more reasons, security is a topic that you should take very seriously with Terminal Server.

In the military, information is protected by a "need to know" test. Likewise, with Terminal Server, you as the administrator need to determine a user's or group's "need to access." Ideal security happens when users are given the minimal level of access necessary to perform their jobs. Think of the simplicity of a mainframe terminal when setting up your user desktops. Give your users icons only for applications they need. If they need to use only one application, take them directly to it when they log on.

Documenting Your Security

Before going into the details of securing your Terminal Server, the importance of documenting your security must be emphasized. The following are some of the many reasons why documenting your security setup is important:

- **Application troubleshooting**   Setting up proper security for your system can quickly become very complex. As you implement more and more security measures, the likelihood increases that a security measure will cause an application problem. Security-related application problems can be very difficult to troubleshoot without meticulous documentation. Your documentation should include what security changes were made, why they were made, when they were made, and who made them.

- **Disaster recovery**   You should have enough information in your documentation to be able to re-create your security setup in case of disaster recovery or for setting up a new server. Automating your security setup with documented scripts also is recommended for quick recovery times.

- **Consistency**   Consistency is very important for effective security. Often, as an administrator, you'll encounter the same security issues. By documenting the correct security setup for a particular security issue, such as how to secure a particular application, you can re-create the security setup accurately in the future. By having those who work for you refer to the same documentation, you can keep your security approach consistent on all the servers both you and your team manage.

- **Justification**   Security often comes at the cost of convenience. After you've decided on the appropriate level of security for your Terminal Server, documented it, and obtained approval on the documentation, you can use that documentation as justification for the security measures you need to take.

Creating a System Security Manual

While going through the tips in this chapter, you should start a system security manual. Start the security manual with the assessment of threats. Which of your security threats are the most critical? How do you detect breaches in security? How do you recover from security problems?

Next, pick out the tips you think will work well in your environment and implement them. Then document them in the system security manual. This is the most important part. In this section, list every security measure that has been taken to secure your system.

The tips have been organized into the following categories to make it easier for you to document the ones you want to use in an organized fashion:

- **Physical security**   How is your system physically secured? Who is responsible for what aspects of the physical security?

- **Desktop security**   How are your desktops secured? What policies and profiles have you implemented, and why?

- **File security**   Include changes that were made to the default NTFS security and why. Also include information on the directories on your server. What is stored under them, and how they are secured (home directories, application directories, data directories, system directories, temporary directories)? Every directory on your server should have a specific purpose and should be locked appropriately. Remember that the users might have direct access to your server's drives.

- **Registry security**   Include what Registry keys were changed or added for security reasons. Also include changes to the default Registry permissions, and why.

- **System security**   What security changes apply to your entire system? What is your password policy? What are your backup and recovery procedures?

- **Monitoring**   What are your regularly scheduled security checks? How is auditing set up on your system?

Periodic Security Checks

No security can be ensured without setting up some type of system for periodically checking it. Over time, settings might change, applications might be added, and security might inadvertently be compromised. The best way to ensure your servers are always in the highest state of readiness is to start a periodic server security check program.

To start this program, just create a spreadsheet with a list of your servers in the left column. Across the top, put all the security checks that you need to do on each server. Because of the amount of time it can take to perform security checks, you should create three pages in this spreadsheet. The first page contains the weekly security checks, the second contains the monthly, and the third contains quarterly security checks. Whether a particular item is checked weekly, monthly, or quarterly depends on how much time you can dedicate to checking security. The following are some suggested checks that can be performed periodically:

- **Virus protection**   It is very important to check whether virus protection is working properly. You should have a check for whether the latest pattern is downloaded and whether virus scanning is active. You also might want to log any viruses detected.

- **File security**   You should maintain a list of all the shares necessary on your Terminal Server farm and the appropriate security for these shares. On a periodic basis, you should check that this security is set up properly. In addition, file-level security also should be documented and double-checked.

- **Domain Admin membership**   It is critical to maintain tight control of who is a member of the Domain Admin group. This definitely should be checked periodically.

- **Local security and admin password**   Local security should be checked regularly to ensure that only Domain Admins are part of the Local Administrators group and only Domain Users or TS Users are part of the local Users group. In addition, the Local Administrator account's password should be changed on a periodic basis.

- **Patch levels**   With the recent widespread exploits by viruses of common security holes, it is critical to ensure that your servers are patched properly. This need goes beyond just ensuring the patches are applied during setup. Once a month or quarter, you should run the Windows Update on all your Terminal Servers to ensure that all currently installed components on the server are patched properly. This is especially important if you are using IIS on any of your Terminal Servers.

Security Tips

This section covers some of the many things that you can do to help lock down your Terminal Servers. The tips are broken down by categories. Remember these tips are only a start. As an administrator, you need to decide which of the many tips make the most sense for your environment and apply them. Not all the tips will apply or even make sense for your situation. The final word on security lies with you. Through continual diligence and careful observation of the network administrator, a network and its servers are kept reliable and secure.

Physical Security

One often-overlooked area of security is the physical security of your server and network. If you want a reliable and secure Terminal Server solution, you need to control the physical security of your server. Good physical security helps prevent both accidental mishaps, such as the pulling of a plug, and malicious attacks, such as vandalism. The following are some commonsense tips on how to ensure good physical security:

- **Locked server room with access cards**   Having a locked server room is self-explanatory. Locking it by using access cards provides an audit trail of who came and left the server room and at what time. With readily available shareware utilities on the market, a potential hacker can retrieve the administrator password in seconds from your servers—all that's required is physical access to your console.

- **Floppy, case, and cabinet locks**   Nothing deters the curious or unwelcome as well as a good lock. Most cabinets are lockable, as well as most computer cases. Giving general floppy drive access to your servers is not recommended. Again with readily available utilities, administrator passwords can be obtained and NTFS partitions can even be read (from a bootable floppy disk). In addition, floppy disks are the most common and easiest way to infect a server with a virus. Some servers enable you to disable booting from floppy disks, which is a good idea.

- **Uninterruptible power supplies (UPS)**   Power problems are common in many areas of the country. Using a UPS you can protect yourself from many of the types of power problems that can occur. Most UPSs also come with notification software that can be set up to warn you via pager, email, broadcast message, or other means of an impending power failure.

- **High-temperature and fire alarms**   Security does not do too much good if your servers melt down. High-temperature alarms are an often-overlooked measure. You could toast a marshmallow with the heat that comes off most processors today. Don't make the mistake of thinking air conditioning just happens. Installing a fire-suppressant system or having electrically safe (Class C) fire extinguishers readily available in the server room is also a good idea.

- **Fireproof safe for backup tapes and offsite storage**   No matter what natural or unnatural disaster occurs, you should always be able to get back your backup tapes and original install media. By sending your tapes offsite using an offsite data storage service, you have recourse in case of a major disaster.

Desktop Security

Desktop security is perhaps the most important type of security. Remember, with Terminal Server, when you sit at a desktop, it's as though you're sitting at the console of the server itself. Desktops are windows onto your server that can be opened from any location for which you have given access.

The key to good desktop security is simplification. You need to decide exactly what your users need access to, provide them that access, and take away all else. If users need to run only two remote applications, for instance, do they need to have the Run program option in their Start menu or access to the command line or any other program icon in the Start menu or desktop except for the icons for those applications?

By default, desktops are riddled with potential security holes. The main tools you can use to control the desktop are policies and profiles. Policies are Registry settings that can restrict what users can do on their desktops. With policies, you can prevent a user from being able to use the run command or from getting access to the command line, and much more. Profiles contain all of a user's personal settings, such as the programs on the user's desktop and in the Start menu. With profiles, you can control which program icons users have and, therefore, which programs they can run. See Chapter 14, "Policies and Desktop Management," to learn more about both of these features. Here are some general guidelines on desktop security:

- **Simplicity**   The more options users are given, the greater the potential for security problems. User desktops should be devoid of any icons or options that they do not have an absolute need to use. Keeping desktops simple also makes them significantly easier to administer.

- **Application security**   The number of applications that your users need access to with Terminal Server is usually very short. With the Application Security tool, you can restrict the applications your users can run. The next section discusses this powerful tool.

- **Running applications directly after logon**   The most secure desktop is one that's bypassed completely. Desktops are merely launching pads for user programs. If users need remote access only to a few applications, it's best to run these applications directly after the user logs on to the system. You can set up a program to execute right after a user logs on by defining the program executable and working directory at the client (in User Manager or for the connection). When users exit an application, they are logged off the system.

- **Publishing applications**   If you're using MetaFrame, you have the option to publish your applications. This is the best way to provide application access for most systems. Not only can you control who has access to run an application, but you also can make a single application available from multiple servers using load balancing. This greatly increases reliability and performance and is a very secure alternative to providing the user with a desktop.

- **Disable access to the command prompt, run command, My Computer, Network Neighborhood, and Explorer**   These are all huge security holes that hackers with even a small amount of knowledge can exploit to gain further access to your system. Carefully weigh the potential security problems of giving access to these tools against the inconvenience of not having them available when setting up your user desktops. All of these can be restricted using the policies shown in Chapter 14. Also be careful of applications that have backdoors that can access the command prompt; these can be just as much of a security risk.

- **Add/Remove Programs dialog box**   Be careful of what's installed through the Add/Remove Programs dialog box during the initial install of Terminal Server. Never give your users' access to any program that could needlessly rob your other users of processing power. The main examples of this are games and screen savers. Games should not be installed, and no screen savers should be used except for those that require minimal processor power, such as the blank screen saver or logon screen saver. Animated cursors also should not be installed. It is also very important not to install unneeded services. If you install IIS and do not keep it patched properly, it can be subject to virus vulnerability attacks, such as the Red Worm attack.

- **User policies**   Access to the Control Panel, Registry (REGEDT32), Run option, Find option, Network Neighborhood, and much more can all be controlled through policies. Use policies to keep the desktop simple and to control what your users have access to. Chapter 14 discusses policies in detail.

- **Common folder**   Be careful of what's in the common folder, because this contains the icons that will appear in everyone's Start menu. To look at what's in the common folder, select Programs from the Start menu. All the icons and folders below the divider line in Windows NT 4.0 Terminal Server are in the common folder. Their folders will have a computer next to them to indicate that they are accessible by all users of this computer. They will appear in everyone's Start menu.

By default, most applications install their icons in the common folder. If the application is going to be used only by a select group of users, you might want to manually add the icon to their personal Start menu folder located in their profile directories. By doing this, the icon will be accessible only by those users. If the application is for general use and you want to put it in the common folder, make sure that only the proper icons are shown. For example, your application might create an Uninstall icon. It would be a good idea to remove this so that your users cannot uninstall the program by accident! Another problem with the common folders is the Administrative Tools folder. The Administrative Tools folder contains applications only an administrator should use. It should be moved to the administrator's personal folder.

To change what's in the common folder, right-click the Start button and select Open All Users. The icons in here are the ones that are in the common folder. You can delete them or move them to other locations, such as the personal folder (select Open from the Start menu), as necessary.

The simplest and perhaps best common folder is made up of the program icons your users need and nothing more. Specific examples of how best to set up your desktop are covered in Chapter 14.

File Security

Setting appropriate file security can be very challenging, especially with Terminal Server. To make sure the correct file security is implemented, you must make the appropriate choices; the first and most important of which is to choose NTFS during installation. The next choices you have to make occur when you install your users' applications. The following are some tips on securing your file system:

- **Choose NTFS during installation, not after.**   This is worth saying twice. If you use FAT for your system partition, you have little or no protection from a user wiping out a critical system file. You should choose NTFS for your system partition during installation. Don't plan to convert afterward from FAT to NTFS. During installation, if you choose NTFS, it will apply a default set of security rights. These rights are crucial for protecting your critical system files. If you convert to NTFS later using the `convert` command, these default rights are not applied.

- **Back up your data daily.** This is a self-explanatory item. Just remember, no matter how much security you have, you still have to trust someone with access to the data. If anyone breaks that trust and loses or destroys a file, the most recent backup might be your only recourse.

- **Choose a reliable storage solution.** One of the most common and reliable storage solutions is using RAID 5. With RAID 5, you can lose an entire drive, and the system will still function. Mirroring or duplexing are also good alternatives.

- **Set up Failure notification.** Make sure you are notified upon failure of any part of your Terminal Server, especially its storage devices. Many systems today offer various types of notification options, such as audible, pager, mail, and SMTP. If you lose one drive in a RAID or mirrored system, you're still okay. If you lose two, prepare for a restore. Performing a test failure of your RAID system during prototyping is also a good idea to ensure that the notification system you set up works properly and that the system can correctly handle a drive failure. Many administrators wisely dedicate a few minutes every morning checking the hardware status of all their servers.

- **Make a separate partition for user data or use a third-party disk quota program.** One problem with Terminal Server security is the lack of a space restriction per user. For this reason, you should make a separate partition for user data. If users are allowed to store data in the same partition as your system files and print queues, when the partition is filled up, users will lose their ability to print. What's more, the system and/or applications could crash. By keeping the data in a separate partition, your users will instead get an out-of-space error when trying to save, but they will otherwise not be affected.

- **Compartmentalize your data and applications.** This goes along with simplification. With a properly organized server, security problems become readily apparent and can be fixed quickly. Always compartmentalize your applications and data. Application directories should be kept together under a single directory. User data from the application also should be kept together in a separate directory or in individual user home directories, as appropriate. In general, users should be given read-only access to the application directories they need and read/write/change access to the user data directories. By treating applications and user data as separate security entities, administration is much easier.

- **Control access through groups.**   Using groups is the best way to control file access. Many administrators make local application groups, assign those groups the rights necessary to run a single application, and add global groups to them containing the users who need access to the application. For example, you could create an APP_OFFICE97 local group for users of Office 97. Remove the Everyone group from the access list to the Office 97 directories and give the APP_OFFICE97 group access to the application using the appropriate rights. When you want to give your domain users access to this application, add them to a global DOM1_APP_OFFICE97 group and add that group to the local APP_OFFICE97 group. This makes it easy to control who has access to applications on the Terminal Server.

- **Audit critical file access.**   The auditing tools included with Terminal Server are very powerful. You can use them to keep an eye on critical system files and data. You also can use them to record logon and logout times, which are also important. If you ever have a security problem, this will help provide proof of the culprit's actions.

- **Control what can be executed using the read permission.** Removing the read permission is one of the simplest ways to prevent users from executing programs they have no reason to execute. Take a look through your system directories for utilities and programs you do not want your users to execute. One particular program you should disable execute access to is REGEDT32.

Changing NT Security

When a user logs on to the system, the system generates an access token object that contains all the user's security-related information, including which groups he is a member of. This access token object is used to validate users whenever they try to access a secured resource.

What this means to an administrator is that if you make security changes, such as removing a user from a group such as Domain Admins, the user will still have Domain Admin rights until the user logs off. The reason is that although you have changed the user's security in the SAM, the user's access token list still has the user as a member of the Domain Admins group. Be careful which groups you make users a member of and always have a user log off after you make changes to his security.

Registry Security

This is probably one of the most often overlooked areas of security. Many administrators might not realize that the Registry has security at all. Fewer still might recognize how important this security can be. The Registry contains a wealth of information about your system that an intruder can take advantage of. Because many programs are loaded from the Registry with system-level access, the Registry is a common point of access for setting up Trojan horse attacks.

Microsoft has made great strides with Windows 2000 for locking down the Registry. However, these new security settings are only implemented if, during the installation of Terminal Services, you select Windows 2000 security rather than Windows NT 4.0-compatible security. This choice is a critical choice for security during the installation of Terminal Services. The majority of applications have no problem working with the heightened security in Windows 2000. You should always choose to use Windows 2000 security. If a particular application has a problem with the extra security, you can open up security to just that application's Registry keys.

The difference between Windows NT 4.0 or Windows 2000 Registry security in NT 4.0-compatible mode and that of Windows 2000's default heightened security is that in Windows NT 4.0, applications could write to most portions of the Registry. By default, in Windows NT 2000 only administrators are given full access to the Registry's folders.

In Windows NT 4.0, the Everyone group has read access to most of the machine Registry's keys (HKEY_LOCAL_MACHINE), and the Administrator group has full control. This means that only administrators will be able to change Registry entries that affect the hardware, such as which device drivers are loaded at startup. This is appropriate security.

In Windows NT 4.0 the Everyone group also has special access to the majority of the SOFTWARE key, underneath HKEY_LOCAL_MACHINE. The special access granted to Everyone includes the rights to view, create, and delete keys/values. This is a very important security vulnerability to realize. If users are given access to REGEDT32, if they can run any program that changes the Registry (REGINI for example), or if they start installing their own software, they have the ability to make changes to the Registry that will affect everyone on the system! In addition, many viruses are designed to write to the Registry keys under here, especially the Windows Registry keys where viruses can control what applications are run when users log on to the system.

If the solution to this problem were as simple as restricting users to read-only access to this key, life would be good. Unfortunately, some applications will not run or run properly unless users have read/write access to at least some of the applications' keys under SOFTWARE. Your job is to figure out which keys are used by an application and how best to secure them.

Understanding Registry Security

To best secure the Registry, you first need to understand it. As a Terminal Server administrator, you should have an excellent understanding of the Registry. This book goes into detail on components of the Registry that directly pertain to Terminal Server. However, full coverage of the Registry is beyond the scope of this book. It might be worthwhile to get a book dedicated specifically to the Windows NT Registry as a reference guide when you need it, such as *Windows NT Registry: A Settings Reference* by Sandra Osborne (New Riders, 1998) ISBN: 1562059416.

Although you need to understand the Registry to ensure that your server is secure, playing with the wrong parameters in the Registry can crash the system. If you need to test the effects of changes to the Registry or want to discover how your applications interact with it, perform the task on a test server. You could install Terminal Server on your own workstation using one of the many dual-boot techniques. Using third-party software, such as Partition Magic, you can set up a dual-boot Windows 95 (FAT)/Terminal Server (NTFS) workstation, or whatever operating system combination works best for you. It's better not to install Terminal Server on a FAT partition, just because Terminal Server on NTFS will give you the most accurate idea of how your applications will run.

Even if you test your changes carefully before you implement them, as well as document these changes thoroughly and take every precaution necessary, you should still perform a backup before making any changes. The REGBACK utility, included with the Windows NT Resource Kit, provides an easy way to do this. Just remember that the size of the Registry can be large with Windows Terminal Server. You also can back up the Registry by following these steps:

1. Run the Repair Disk utility by entering **rdisk.exe** in the Start menu's Run dialog box.

2. From the Repair Disk utility window, click Update Repair Info. This will make a copy of the current Registry files, AUTOEXEC.NT, CONFIG.NT, and set up information in the `%systemroot%\repair` directory on the server.

You also can make a copy of the repair information on floppy disk using this utility by clicking the Create Repair Disk button from the main window.

Some backup programs also will let you back up and restore down to a key level.

In general, the following tips will help keep you out of trouble:

- Always fully back up the Registry before any changes.
- Do any planned Registry work after-hours during system maintenance time when no one is logged on. Disable logon first, and then make sure all users are off.
- If you have to look at the HKEY_KEY_LOCAL_MACHINE key, stay out of the SYSTEM subkey. Manually changing parameters under this key is rarely necessary and can quickly crash the system if you change the wrong ones.
- Document any changes.

General Registry Tips

The following are some general tips on how to secure your Registry:

- **Replace the Everyone group with TS Users.**   Everyone means every user in the Windows NT domain that Terminal Server is a part of. The Everyone group is used in countless places to provide access to Terminal Server's Registry and file system. In reality, not everyone needs access to your file system and Registry. By replacing the Everyone group with the TS Users group in your system's *access control lists* (ACLs), you can increase security significantly.
- **Make sure your backup software is backing up the Registry.** The Registry is not always backed up by default. With many backup programs, you need to specify that the Registry is backed up. Make sure that Registry backup is part of your backup jobs.
- **Choose Windows 2000 not NT 4.0-compatible security.**   If you are using Windows 2000 Terminal Server, make sure to choose Windows 2000 security, not NT 4.0-compatible security, during the setup of Terminal Services. The most important effect of this change is that with Window 2000 security, only administrators have write access to HKLM\SOFTWARE. In NT 4.0-compatible security, the Everyone group is given read/write access to the HKLM\SOFTWARE key.
- **On Windows NT 4.0 Terminal Server, carefully restrict user access to application keys under HKLM\SOFTWARE.**   The emphasis here is on *carefully*. HKLM\SOFTWARE contains global settings for your applications. If users are allowed to change the application settings under this key, their changes will affect all users of the application. If, on the other hand, you arbitrarily restrict all users to read-only access to the entire SOFTWARE key, no user will be able to log on. Even if you restrict access to read-only on only a single subkey, you might disable an application that needs more

access. If you're serious about Registry security, refer to the developers of the applications you need to restrict. Whether your application will work with read-only access to these setting keys needs to be thoroughly tested.

- **Use auditing to tune security.** Auditing can be an excellent tool for helping secure the system. One approach is to lock down the Registry and file system tightly and then enable auditing upon access to the Registry keys and parts of the file system you locked. Then run your applications. If you encounter any errors during their execution because they cannot access certain parts of the Registry or file system, you should be able to see in the audit log which parts they were trying to access. Enable access to these parts and try the application again. Through this process, you can build a picture of your application's Registry and file system access needs.

- **Beware of the Trojan horse attack.** Many areas of the Registry are subject to Trojan horse attacks. If you allow users the right to create keys under the `HKEY_LOCAL_MACHINE\SOFTWARE\Classes` key, which contains file extension association, they could implant a Trojan horse that would be run the next time the administrator opens up a text file (*.TXT).

The TS Users Group

Creating a group that contains only Windows Terminal Server users is useful for many security and administrative reasons. One of the best ways to get around the "everyone has full access" problem is just to replace the Everyone group with the TS Users group and grant appropriate access in the system's various ACLs. This chapter refers to this group frequently. The TS Users name is arbitrary; you might want to choose a name that works better for your network.

System Security

The tips in this section cover general systemwide security settings and proper system setup for good security. These tips are very important for securing your environment properly.

Apply the Latest Service Packs and Hotfixes

It should almost go without saying; however, it is hard to overstress the importance of keeping your service packs and hotfixes current. Many fixes for known security vulnerabilities are included in patches from both Microsoft and from Citrix. This is especially important for systems exposed to the Internet.

The easiest way to check whether your patch level is current on Microsoft Terminal Server is to go to the `http://windowsupdate.microsoft.com` web site. This web site will automatically scan your system to determine whether all the latest service packs and hotfixes have been installed. It is a good idea to regularly check for new patches from these web sites. In addition, Microsoft has an excellent security web site and a mailing list that you can join to receive notice of the latest vulnerabilities. It is highly recommended to join this mailing list and search the site for information pertinent to your environment. You can access the security web site at `www.microsoft.com/security`. You also can find specific information on how to join the mailing list at `www.microsoft.com/technet/treeview/default.asp?url=/technet/security/bulletin/notify.asp`.

On the Citrix side, you can find the latest service packs and hotfixes at `www.citrix.com/download`. Because Citrix servers are designed to work together as a farm, and because service packs and hotfixes sometimes make changes to important aspects of farm behavior, it is critical to always apply service packs and hotfixes across all servers in a farm at the same time. Never apply a service pack or hotfix to just one server in the farm for testing, or do a slow rollout and apply the patch one server at a time over a period of several days. Instead, schedule a downtime where you can apply the patch to all servers in the same farm at the same time. If you are concerned that the service pack might cause problems, set up a small test farm to test the service pack on before rolling the service pack into production.

RDP and ICA Vulnerabilities

As of this writing, a known vulnerability in RDP can be used to cause a Denial of Service in both Windows 2000 and NT 4.0 Terminal Server. By applying the latest patches for your Terminal Server, you can eliminate this vulnerability. For more information, see `www.microsoft.com/technet/treeview/default.asp?url=/technet/security/bulletin/MS01-040.asp`.

In addition, Citrix has discovered a similar Denial of Service vulnerability in its ICA protocol. This vulnerability applies to both MetaFrame 1.8 and MetaFrame XP. It is currently available only as a hotfix and is not part of Service Pack 1 for XP. To download this hotfix, go to the Citrix download web site at `www.citrix.com/download`, select Hotfixes, and then select the version of Citrix MetaFrame you are running. As with all hotfixes, make sure to apply the hotfix to all the servers at the same time rather than just one server in the farm.

Set Up Virus Protection

You can protect your system from viruses in several ways. The first is to schedule periodic virus scans using third-party virus scanning software. The second is to prevent users from copying files to your server. The easiest way to do this is to disable the connection of client drives at logon. To do this, follow these steps:

1. Run the User Manager for Domains, located in the Administrative Tools folder in the Program menu.

2. Double-click the username of the user whose client drive mapping you want to disable.

3. In the User Properties window, click Config.

4. Uncheck Connect Client Drives at Logon and click OK.

Any way a file can get onto your server is a way a virus can enter. This means you also should consider things such as locking the floppy drive on the server, preventing users from connecting their own drives, and preventing users from downloading files to the server. The third way to protect your system is to enforce proper file security using NTFS.

In general, boot sector viruses cannot infect Terminal Server. The majority of virus problems you'll run into will be with infected files (macro viruses and Trojan horses). On the other hand, if you accidentally leave a floppy disk in the drive while the server is rebooting, it could easily be infected with a boot virus. This is why you should disable booting from the floppy drive (if your system has the capability).

Certified Virus Protection

At the time of this writing, only two virus protection solutions are specifically supported on Terminal Server. The first is the server virus protection from Trend Micro (www.trendmicro.com). The second is Syamantec's Norton Antivirus Corporate Edition version 7.6 (www.symantec.com). Version 7.6 is the first version from Symantec that is specifically designed, tested, and supported on Windows Terminal Server.

Whatever solution you choose, be certain that the publisher fully supports the virus protection running on Terminal Server. Terminal Server's multiuser and highly active environment places special demands on virus protection software. The software must be written and tested with Terminal Server in mind to function correctly on Terminal Server.

Create an Administrator Account and a Maintenance Account

Use an alphanumeric, 14-character password for the Administrator account and create a separate account for maintenance. The Administrator account is the only account that cannot be locked out by hacking attempts. It is therefore subject to brute-force password-guessing attempts. In general, you should choose as secure a password as possible for your Administrator account, lock the password up in a secure location, and then use a separate administrative account for system maintenance. Changing the administrative password periodically also is recommended.

Change the Administrator Name

It's common knowledge that the default administrator account name is Administrator on Terminal Server. With this knowledge, hackers are already halfway on their way to getting into your system. Just changing the administrator logon name to something less obvious can increase your server's and network's security. Do not use this as a substitute for proper password security, however. Your system's usernames are readily accessible for anyone on your network who has a little knowledge of NetBIOS.

Secure the Local Administrator Account

When you create a standalone server and then add it to a domain, you've allowed two administrative accounts access to your server: the local Administrator and the domain Administrator. The reason for this is that any Windows NT-based workstation or server has a user database. When you add your server to a domain, you are in essence telling it that you want to use the domain's user database for primary validation and not the local one. The local database remains and will still validate users. All users have to do is select the local computer name from the domain list when they log on and they will be validating against the local user account database.

What this means to an administrator is that the local Administrator account should be locked just as tightly as the domain Administrator account to protect the server. Always make sure while installing a new standalone server that you choose a secure password for the local Administrator account. Lock this password in a secure place and disable any other accounts besides Administrator. Do all of this before you add the server to the domain.

Disable Unnecessary Services

Services that run on Terminal Server are often run using the System account. With system-level access, a service can run anything. Terminal Server services, therefore, are another entry point for Trojan horse attacks. One particular service that's often the focus of such attacks is the Schedule service. The Schedule service handles running programs scheduled with the at command. A potential intruder who gains administrative access can use the at command to schedule the execution of a rogue program. If you're not using the at command, this service should be disabled by doing the following:

1. Select Services from the Control Panel.

2. Highlight the Schedule service and click Startup from Service window.

3. Select Disabled for Startup Type and click OK.

Restrict Connection Access to Terminal Server

By default, when you install Terminal Server into a domain, all users in the domain can log on to the server. To restrict access to Terminal Server to just your Terminal Server users, do the following:

1. Create a TS Users group in User Manager or in Active Directory Users and Computers and make your Terminal Server users members of the group.

2. Open the Terminal Services Connection Configuration tool, which is located in the Administrative Tools folder in the Start menu.

3. In the Terminal Services Connection Configuration main window, highlight one of the network connections in the list and select Permissions from the Security menu.

4. In the Connection Permissions window that appears, remove the Everyone, Guests, and Users groups from the access list by highlighting each one and clicking Remove.

5. Add the TS Users group and grant it user access by clicking Add.

6. In the Add Users and Groups window that appears, double-click the WTS_USER group to add it to the Add Names window. Make sure the type of access is User Access; then click OK.

7. Do this for each type of network connection you've defined.

Also it is a very good idea to delete any connection entries that you do not need. If you are using only ICA clients, for instance, delete any RDP connection entries and vice versa.

Restrict Network Access to TS Using User Rights

In general, user rights are adequate by default. To view the default user rights on a Windows NT 4.0 domain, go into User Manager and select User Rights from the Policies menu. This is where you define which groups and users are given which system rights. With Windows Terminal Server, you might want to change the following rights:

- **Access This Computer from the Network**   Take out the Everyone group and add the TS Users group. This ensures that only TS Users can access the shares of this computer from across the network.

- **Log On Locally** Take out the Everyone group and add the TS Users group. This, in effect, prevents anyone from using Windows Terminal Server who is not in the TS Users group. This is similar to restricting who can access the connections.

The same policies are available in Windows 2000; however, you need to modify them using the Group Policy Editor. For more information on how to do this, see Chapter 14.

Control Dial-In Access

Dial-in access is a big security risk. If you have dial-in access to your server, you might want to increase the level of password security. In addition, you might want to assign special dial-in user account names that are not as accessible as your regular account names. It's a good idea to create a WTS_DIALIN group for your dial-in users. Use file and Registry auditing to carefully monitor the WTS_DIALIN group's activity. Also be sure to audit logon/logoff times. If you have a MetaFrame server with dial-in async connections, use the Terminal Server Connection Configuration tool permissions, located in the Administrative Tools folder, to restrict anyone who is not a member of this group from being able to dial in. If you're using *Remote Access Services* (RAS), make sure that only members of the WTS_DIALIN group have dial-in permission.

Many security features, such as RAS dial-in permission, are controlled only on a user level rather than a group level in Windows NT 4.0. To ensure that only members of the WTS_DIALIN group can dial in using RAS in a Windows NT 4.0 domain, follow these steps. (Be aware that these instructions will disable RAS access for everyone on your domain except the members of the WTS_DIALIN group.)

1. Select all the users in the domain in User Manager by first highlighting the top user in the user list and then scrolling down and selecting the last user by pressing Shift while clicking. This will highlight all the users.

2. Press Enter to modify everyone's properties simultaneously.

3. In the User Properties window, click Dialin.

4. Remove the check next to Grant Dialin Permission to User under the Dialin section; click OK to save your changes. Click OK again to return to the User Manager main window.

5. Now select the members of the WTS_DIALIN group by selecting Select Users from the Users menu, highlighting the WTS_DIALIN group, and then clicking Select.

6. In the User Properties window, click Dialin.

7. Check the box next to Grant Dialin Permission to User so that WTS_DIALIN members are granted dial-in privilege.

This technique works well for any situation where you want to ensure that only members of a certain group have a particular setting in User Manager. Be aware that with Terminal Server, if you add another person to the WTS_DIALIN group at a later time that person will not automatically be given dial-in access. You will have to manually grant the permission.

With Windows 2000 and *Routing and Remote Access* (RRAS), you have significantly more control over logon security than in Windows NT 4.0. For more information on setting up RRAS for Windows 2000, see Chapter 16, "Dial-In and VPN Access."

Display a Legal Notice

The Terminal Server logon prompt can legally be construed as an invitation to enter the system without proper authorization! Therefore, to be able to prosecute potential system hackers, you should display a legal notice when users first log on. The legal notice normally warns the users that they will be held liable for unauthorized access to the system. You also might use the notice to tell your users about important system events, such as regularly scheduled downtimes.

To make it so that a legal notice window pops up before users log on, you need to change the following values of type REG_SZ under the following key:

Key name: HKEY_LOCAL_MACHINE\SOFTWARE\Microsoft\Windows NT\Current Version\Winlogon

Value name: (type REG_SZ) LegalNoticeCaption

Value name: (type REG_SZ) LegalNoticeText

As usual, take the appropriate precautions when working with the Registry. The LegalNoticeCaption value will become the window title, and the LegalNoticeText value will be the text inside of the window.

Don't Display Last User's Logon Name

Because Windows Terminal Server clears the last logon name by default when logging on remotely, this value is not as useful as with Windows NT Workstation. Even so, it will prevent the last logon name from appearing on the system console. This is most useful when you've changed the name of the administrator. To enable this security feature, add the value DontDisplayLastUserName of type REG_SZ (select Add Value from the Edit menu) under the previous key and set it to the number 1. Note that both this security feature and the legal notice also can be controlled with policies.

User Account Policies

With user account policies, you can set a password expiration age and a minimum password length, enforce password uniqueness, and even temporarily lock out accounts that fail logon attempts too many times.
User account policies are often confused with policies. These are two very different features of Terminal Server. User account policies are controlled from User Manager, whereas policies are controlled from the System Policy Editor.

To set user account policies for a Windows NT 4.0 domain, follow these steps:

1. Open User Manager, located in the Administrative Tools folder in Start menu, Programs.

2. Select Account from the Policies menu.

3. In the dialog box that appears, set the user account policies, as appropriate, for your system.

It's highly recommended that you set the Minimum Password Length field to at least six characters and enable account lockout after five attempts.

All these settings and more can be controlled using Windows 2000 group policies. For more information on setting security settings with group policy objects, see Chapter 14.

Use PASSFILT.DLL or Secure Password Policy

If you're installing Terminal Server in a situation where inconvenience at the cost of security is not an issue, you might want to consider enabling strong password filtering. Ever since Service Pack 2 with Windows NT 4.0, you can enable strong password filtering with the PASSFILT.DLL file. With Windows 2000, secure password filtering can now be enforced through the use of group policy objects.

With strong password filtering enabled, your users will have the following restrictions applied when choosing a password:

- Passwords must be at least six characters in length. (This can still be increased with the Password Length setting in User Account Policies.)

- Passwords must contain characters that are part of at least three of the following four classes:

  - English uppercase (A, B, C, and so on).

  - English lowercase (a, b, c, and so on).

  - Numbers: 0–9.

  - Nonalphanumeric characters (quotation marks, periods, commas, and so on).

- Passwords cannot contain the user's name or any part of the user's full name.

To enable password filtering on Windows NT 4.0, you must make a change under the HKLM\SYSTEM key. Make sure you create an emergency disk and back up the Registry before you do this. Full instructions on how to enable strong password filtering can be found in Microsoft Knowledge Base article Q151082, available in the online support section of the Microsoft web site.

Monitoring Your Server

No environment is secure without ongoing monitoring. The following sections provide some tips on how best to monitor the security of your server.

Use Third-Party Security Tools

As you've undoubtedly ascertained from this extensive list of Terminal Server security tips, security is very complex. Fully understanding the many security risks of Terminal Server and knowing what to do to prevent them can take an extraordinary amount of time. The reality is that most administrators do not have the luxury of time. Several third-party security analyst tools are available that might help you with securing your Terminal Server:

- **Internet Scanner for Windows NT by ISS (www.iss.net)**   If you're going to install Internet services on your server and publish applications on the web, this is a great tool to have.

- **Kane Security Analyst for NT by Intrusion Detection, Inc. (www.intrusion.com)**   A comprehensive security analysis tool for your Windows NT servers.

- **DumpACL and DumpEvt by Somarsoft (www.somarsoft.com)** DumpACL is similar to the ACLCHECK utility included with Windows Terminal Server. It scans the ACLs for your entire file system, Registry, printers, and shares and quickly highlights security holes. It's easier to use than ACLCHECK and its output is easier to read. DumpEvt helps you organize and sift through your event log. This is a very useful utility to have if you're heavy into auditing.

- **SuperCACLS by Trusted Systems (www.trustedsystems.com)**   A good collection of command-line utilities for automating the administration of ACLs lists.

Keep in mind that these applications were originally designed for Windows NT Server, not Terminal Server. Because they haven't been fully tested with Terminal Server, there's no guarantee they'll work properly in a multiuser environment. As always, test new applications in a test environment first, before implementing them into production. It's likely that security analyst programs specifically designed for Terminal Server will soon be available, so keep your eyes open for new products like these.

Set Up Logon/Logoff Audit Logs

Setting up auditing for logon and logoff attempts is strongly recommended. You'll be able to see both successful and failed logon attempts. Make sure you check this log on a regular basis for attempted intrusions. To set up auditing, follow these steps:

1. Open User Manager from the Administrative Tools folder in Start menu, Programs.

2. Select Audit from the Policies menu. The Audit Policy window will appear.

3. Select Audit These Events and check the Success and Failure boxes next to Logon and Logoff; this will audit both successful and failed user logon and logoff attempts. If you want to enable auditing for any other system events, check those boxes as well. Click OK when finished.

4. To check user logon and logoff attempts, open the Event Viewer, which also is located in the Administrative Tools folder, and select Security from the Log menu.

Log off and then log back on to the system. Go into the Event Viewer. You should see a record of your logoff and logon in the security log. Try logging off and then logging back on using an incorrect password at least once. When you log on with the correct password and look at the security log, you also should see your failed logon attempt.

By default, the security log will be overwritten after seven days. You can change this and other security log settings from the Log Settings dialog box, located by selecting Log Settings from the Log menu in Event Viewer.

Use a Directory Tree Sizing Utility

One of the more useful shareware utilities to purchase is a good directory tree sizing program. Quite a few are available, but their basic function is the same. They just graph out your hard drive, tallying the amount of space used under each directory. This way, you can get a better picture of where the majority of your data is and how fast it's growing.

> **Disk Frontier**
>
> One of the best tree-sizing or disk-sizing utilities is Disk Frontier by Choice Computing (www.choicecomp.com). It's simple, small, inexpensive, and elegant. It sums up the directory sizes under any drive or directory you specify using a simple bar graph. In addition to directory sizes, the bar graph also relays information on how much of the directory has been read from or written to within the last 30 days.

Monitor Security Sites on the Internet

This section closes with probably the most important security tip of all: Use the Internet as a resource! Literally hundreds of security-related web sites, mailing lists, and other sources of information are available on the Internet. The following are a few well-known resources to get you started. It's a good idea to join security mailing lists and periodically browse security-related sites for the most current Windows NT security news. Much of the security-related information for Windows NT available on these sites also applies to Terminal Server:

- **www.microsoft.com/security**   The authoritative source on security issues with Microsoft products. Scan this page frequently for the latest news. The page also has excellent links to other security resources on the Internet.

- **www.microsoft.com/technet/treeview/default.asp?url=/technet/ security/Default.asp**   The Microsoft Security Advisor site. One of the best ways to keep up with what is going on with Microsoft security is to become part of the Microsoft Security Advisory mailing list. At this web site you can join up with their mailing list. In addition you will find loads of useful tips and information on how to secure your servers properly. Microsoft publishes several security checklists that are available at this location.

- **www.incidents.org**   This is an excellent security site run by the highly respected SANS Institute. Every day they have a diary entry that covers current security concerns. They also work in conjunction with several businesses to be able to detect unusual hacker or scanning activity on the Internet and are often the first to know of unusual hacker activity.

- **www.ntsecurity.net**   A good compendium of Windows NT security problems and solutions, along with many links to other sites.

- **www.iss.net**   Makers of Internet Scanner 5.2 for Windows NT, a highly rated scanning tool. They also have lists of Windows NT security problems, with emphasis on problems that can occur when attaching a Windows NT server to the Internet (publishing applications on the web). In addition, they have a security-related mailing list that can provide a lot of good information.

- **www.cert.org/nav/index_red.html**   An excellent source of security advisories for multiple types of systems.

23

Advanced Application Installation and Installation Management

THE MAIN GOAL OF ANY TERMINAL SERVER solution is to deploy applications to users. However, those applications normally need to be manually installed on servers in the farm to deploy them. Because application installation is such a key piece of Terminal Server administration, it makes sense to automate this process as much as possible. Not only does automating application installation make it easier to install the application across multiple servers in a server farm, but it also ensures a high level of consistency in how an application is installed. This is especially important on Terminal Server, because often Registry changes or other changes to applications need to be made after they are installed for them to run well with Terminal Server.

This chapter discusses how to automate application installation by using application-imaging and deployment tools. Although the main focus of this chapter is on Citrix Installation Management tools for this purpose, many of the concepts are the same for other types of tools that you might use.

Automating Application Installations

You can automate the installation of applications in many ways. This section discusses some of the most common solutions.

Windows Installer Technology

In recent years, Microsoft has developed a new technology for helping auto-mate the process of application installation and upgrades. This technology is referred to as *Windows Installer Technology* and is included in Windows 2000 Server, Windows 2000 Workstation, and likely all future Windows operating system platforms. As part of this solution, Microsoft has standardized and clearly defined a new procedure for application installations that relies on a special installation definition file called a *Microsoft Installer* file or *.MSI* file. Every application that supports Windows Installer technology includes an .MSI file as part of its installation source. This file contains the following application information in a relational database format:

- **Application components** An application is broken down into a hier-archical structure of installable components in the .MSI file. In this way the option can be given to users and administrators as to which compo-nents will be installed.

- **Shortcuts** The shortcuts that will be created for running the applica-tion, along with their names are recorded in the .MSI file.

- **Files and locations** The relative location of the source files along with their intended destination during installation are included in the .MSI file. In some cases the actual content of the installation files can be included in compressed format inside of the .MSI file. In this way, you only need the .MSI file to install the application and no other installation files. GUID information for the registration of components and DLLs is also included in the installer package.

- **Services** Any services that need to be set up as part of the application installation are defined in the .MSI file.

- **Registry and .INI file changes** Any Registry and .INI file changes that are necessary as part of the installation are recorded in the .MSI file.

An application that supports Windows Installer technology can be installed using the MSIEXEC.EXE installer executable. This executable is included by default on all Windows 2000 platforms. This executable reads the applica-tion's .MSI file and walks the user through the installation choices using an installer wizard. Using special command-line options, you can use MSIEXEC.EXE to install an application with no user intervention or remove an application and all of its components.

In addition to the MSIEXEC.EXE executable, every Windows 2000 server or workstation includes the Windows Installer service. Like the MSIEXEC.EXE, the Windows Installer service is designed to handle application installation using .MSI installation files. Using group policy objects and the Windows Installer service, you can centrally deploy applications to workstations with no user intervention. The new group policy object technology in Windows 2000 enables you to specify .MSI packages that can be automatically installed on workstations or users that the group policy object applies to using that workstation's Windows Installer service. One very important advantage of this technology is that the Windows Installer service runs in the security context of the system itself. What this means is that you can remotely use the Windows Installer service to install applications, even though the user who is logged on may not have the rights to install the application.

Although Windows Installer Technology is not covered in detail in this chapter, it can definitely be used for automating the installation of applications on your Terminal Servers using group policies. In addition, software such as Veritas' WinINSTALL can be used to package or even repackage applications as .MSI files so that they can easily be deployed across your servers. If you are using Terminal Servers alone or you do not intend to purchase the XPe addition of Citrix MetaFrame XP, Windows Installer technology is definitely worth a close look. More specific instructions on how to use Windows Installer technology and group policies for automating application installation are provided in Chapter 14, "Policies and Desktop Management."

Ghost, WinINSTALL, and Other Third-Party Tools

Several excellent third-party tools that can be used for application imaging and deployment are available. Symantec Ghost (www.symantec.com) can be used to take an image of an entire server with all the applications installed. This image then can be used to build new identical servers to the original. Although more of a system-imaging solution than an application-imaging solution, Ghost can still significantly speed up both application and server deployment. Citrix MetaFrame now supports Ghost as an imaging solution.

Veritas' WinINSTALL (www.veritas.com) enables you to take a snapshot of a system before and after the installation of an application. It then uses the differences between the two snapshots to create an image of the changes that an application makes. This image can then be used to deploy the application to new platforms. One key advantage of WinINSTALL is that it can create and work with .MSI installer packages. This means you can use WinINSTALL to create an .MSI application image for any application that you install on your servers. You can then use Windows Installer technology and group policies to deploy the applications to your servers. You will find a limited edition version of WinINSTALL included on the Windows 2000 server CD under the `[cd]:\valueadd\3rdpart\mgmt\winstle` folder.

In addition to these tools, several others are available, including Microsoft SMS and Novell ZENworks, which can be used to automate application deployment for your environment.

Installation Manager in MetaFrame XPe

The final application–imaging solution, and the one covered in this chapter, is the Citrix Installation Manager. Installation Manager is an application-imaging and distribution package that comes only with Citrix MetaFrame XPe. It comes on a separate CD and is installed separately from the core Citrix MetaFrame XP package. The product works on both Windows NT 4.0 and 2000 Terminal Servers. In addition, the product installs as an add-on to the Citrix Management Console, making it easier for administration because only one tool is needed for controlling application distribution.

Using Installation Manager for Application Deployment

This section covers the basics of how the Installation Manager works, how it is installed, how to create an application image, and how to deploy it. To use the Installation Manager, you must have Citrix MetaFrame XPe.

How Installation Manager Works

The Citrix Installation Manager is a robust application-imaging and deployment solution with many features. The first step with any application-imaging solution is creating the image itself. For this task, the Citrix Installation Manager includes a special packager tool. You can use this tool to take a snapshot of a server before and then after an application installation. The changes that an application makes to server during installation can then be packaged into a .WMF file. Much like the .MSI files discussed earlier, the .WMF file contains all the Registry changes, file changes, and other system changes that an application makes. This file is referred to as the *application distribution file* or *.ADF* file by Citrix. The actual file that defines the shortcuts, Registry, and files used has a .WMF filename extension, however.

After you have created the application package, you use the application packager to add the application image to the Installation Manager database. The Installation Manager database supports both .WMF application packages and .MSI application packages. The ability to support .MSI packages is a very important feature in Installation Manager, because many applications are coming with their own .MSI file, especially those from Microsoft (such as Microsoft Office). Using an existing .MSI file for application installation can not only save you from having to create your own application images, but also ensures that you are installing the application in a manner that has been tested by the manufacturer.

After the .WMF or .MSI file has been added to the Installation Manager database, it can then be scheduled for deployment using the Citrix Management Console. After installing Installation Manager on your Citrix MetaFrame XPe server, you will see a new folder in the Citrix Management Console called Citrix Installation Manager (see Figure 23.1). Using the options within this folder, you can add the package you just created to the list of packages available to the Installation Manager. You can then schedule the application for deployment to a particular server, a specified group of servers, or all servers in the server farm.

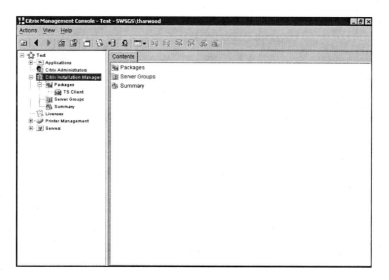

Figure 23.1 Citrix Installation Manager.

One important additional feature of Installation Manager is its capability to uninstall applications. If you need to remove a particular application from your server farm, just remove the package from the Installation Manager using the Citrix Management Console, and the application will automatically be removed from all the Citrix servers. This makes application uninstallation and upgrades as easy as application installations.

Planning for Citrix Installation Manager

Although Installation Manager is relatively simple to install and use, in larger farms it is very important to plan your installation carefully before actually installing and using Installation Manager.

Dedicating a Server for Application Imaging

If you have the resources, you should dedicate one server or even a workstation with Windows 2000 or NT 4.0 Server loaded on it as the imaging server. It is very important when you are taking the initial application image that the server is "clean." What this means is that the server you use to take the application image should have only the following:

- **Either Windows 2000 or Windows NT 4.0 operating system**   Your imaging server should be the same operating system as that of the rest of the servers in the farm. If you have multiple operating systems in the farm, ideally you should have one imaging server to take separate images for each operating system. This is not absolutely necessary; however, it is possible that an image taken on one operating system might cause problems when deployed to servers of another operating system.

- **MetaFrame XP and the Installation Manager Packager**   Make sure you install MetaFrame XP on this server and the Installation Manager Packager.

- **Latest Windows and MetaFrame service packs**   Install the same service packs that you have installed on the servers in the server farm. It is very important to standardize all your servers of the same operating system on the same Windows server pack for application deployment to go smoothly. In addition, all of your servers should be running the same MetaFrame service pack and hotfixes.

By not installing any other applications on top of the "clean" imaging server, you can ensure that the application images taken with that server will be as accurate as possible. The reason why having a clean server is important is that the packager creates an application image solely based on what changes it makes to the system. Suppose, for example, that you use a server that already has several applications installed to take the application images. When you install the application you want to package onto the system, it will not install files that already exist, such as .DLL files. These .DLL and other files are already installed as part of other applications on the system. This means that the application package itself will not include these files. Even though these files are needed by the application, they will not be part of the package.

When you now deploy this application package to other servers that do not have the files on them, the application will fail because those files will not be installed.

Ghosting the Application-Imaging Server

One problem you will run into with this technique is that even if you manually uninstall applications from the imaging server to clean it out, certain components will still be left on the server and might adversely affect future application images that you take. One technique to ensure that you always start with a clean application-imaging server is to use Symantec Ghost to take an image of the application-imaging server itself in a clean state. You could then quickly re-image the server after you have created an application package to bring the server back to the original state.

Dedicating a Package Server

After you have created your application packages, you need to store them in a network-accessible location. Ideally, you should choose a single server as the storage server for the application packages. This server could be one of the Citrix servers in the farm or it could be a central file server. Whichever server you choose, however, it should have plenty of storage space available. On this server, create a CTXPACKAGE share or similar and place all the packages underneath this share. When you are adding the packages to the Installation Manager, you can use the UNC path (\\[server name]\ctxpackage\[package name) to declare the packages on this server as the source for installations on the farm.

For small to medium-size deployments, this server could easily be used for other functions, such as serving applications through Citrix, or as a dedicated data collector server for the farm. For large deployments where application installation could be deployed across hundreds of servers at a time, however, it is important to dedicate the server for the sole purpose of holding the application packages.

Author's Note

Many administrators choose to use a powerful workstation as the dedicated package server instead of purchasing an entire server for this purpose alone.

Installing Installation Manager

The Installation Manager installation process is very easy. To install it, you will need the Application Packaging & Delivery CD, which is included with the set of CDs provided with MetaFrame XPe. The full Installation Manager application will take up about 12MB of drive space on your server. To install it, follow these steps:

1. Insert the Application Packaging & Delivery CD into the CD drive of the Citrix MetaFrame XP server on which you want to install the Installation Manager. A Citrix Installation Manager 2.0 window should display automatically. If it does not display, run the [cd]:\autoroot.exe file from the root of the CD.

2. Click the Citrix Installation Manager 2.0 Setup button to begin the installation.

3. Click Next at the main screen.

4. At the Select Components screen, make sure all the components are selected, and then click Next.

At this point the file installation process will begin. By default the following three components will be installed onto your system:

- **ADF Installer service**   This is a standard Windows NT or 2000 service that gets installed as part of the Installation Manager installation. This service runs in the background on your servers and is the one that is responsible for processing the application packages and handling the actual installation. When you schedule applications for deployment, the ADF Installer service on each server will actually handle the installation of the application on that server. Every Citrix server you want to deploy applications to must have this service installed and running.

- **Citrix Packager**   After the installation of Installation Manager you will find a shortcut for the Packager application in the Program menu, Citrix, Citrix Installation Manager folder. The Packager is the utility that you need to use to create the application images or packages that you will be deploying across the server farm. Using the Packager, you can take a before-and-after snapshot of an application installation to create the application package. This package can then be recorded into the Installation Manager database for deployment.

- **Citrix Installation Manager plug-in**   The final component installed is the plug-in to the Citrix Management Console. After installing the plug-in, you will be able to manage your application deployment from the Citrix Management Console using the settings available under the new Installation Management folder.

Packaging Applications

After Installation Manager has been installed on all the servers in your server farm that you want to install applications on, it is time to package your first application. As mentioned earlier, it is very important to do your application packaging on a "clean" server. Otherwise, your application packages might miss key application components, and the deployment will fail. This server needs to be a Windows 2000 or NT 4.0 Terminal Server with Citrix MetaFrame XPe and Installation Manager installed. In addition, you should have already installed the same service packs and hotfixes on this server that you use on the rest of the servers in the farm. After you have this server set up, follow these instructions to package an application:

1. Open up the Packager utility on the server from the Program menu, Citrix, Installation Manager folder.

2. Under the File menu, select Project Wizard.

3. Select the Package an Installation Recording and click Next.

4. Enter the name for the package and click Next. Notice that the package by default will be stored under the program folder for Installation Manager in a subfolder by the name of the package.

5. Browse to the location of your application's setup file and click Next.

6. Select the appropriate application compatibility script if there is one for your application and click Next.

7. Choose a build location and click Next. Normally the default of the root of the application package directory is acceptable.

8. At this point, the setup program for your application will be launched. In the background, the Recording window shown in Figure 23.2 will be launched. This window keeps track of your application installation.

9. When the application installation is complete, click the Stop Recording or Done button on the Recording window to build the application package.

At this point the Packager application will record any Registry and file changes that were made by the application to the application's project folder. It will build a .WMF file, which contains a list of all the application changes, and it will save a copy of any files that are installed by the application under the project folder.

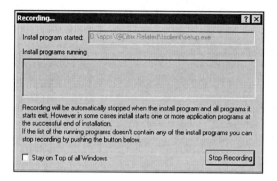

Figure 23.2   Recording window.

Note that the application is an exact copy of the shortcuts, files, and Registry changes that were made by the application installation program. If you want to modify or tweak the installation, you have two options. The first option is to just manually tweak the installation before ending the recording in step 9. After the application installation has completed and before you end the recording, do the following:

- **Remove, change, or add shortcuts.**   If you want to add any new shortcuts, change the name or location of existing shortcuts, or delete unneeded ones, take the time now to arrange the shortcuts as you want them to appear when the application is deployed.

- **Remove or add files.**   If there are any files you want to remove from the installation, or files that you want to add, add or remove them now.

- **Change application settings and modify the registry.**   If there are any settings that you want to record or any Registry changes you want deployed as part of the application installation, now is the time to make those changes.

- **Change application file locations.**   If there are any application settings for file locations, now is a good time to repoint those locations. This is especially important for applications that might try to save temporary files to a central location or have a default central data storage location. Because all users would use the same location, this can cause problems in a multiuser environment. Instead, change any location like this to point to a folder under the user's home drive. That way when a user runs an application, that instance of the application uses storage locations that do not conflict with other instances for other users.

After you have made the modification you want to record, click the End Recording button to build the package with the changes that you made.

The second way to make changes is to modify the actual package file itself. For more information on how to do this, see the following section on editing installation packages. Otherwise, if you are ready to deploy this package to your servers, go on to the section on deploying packages.

Adding to the Installation Package

After you have built your initial package, you will be brought back to the Packager window. In the window, you will now see your project (see Figure 23.3).

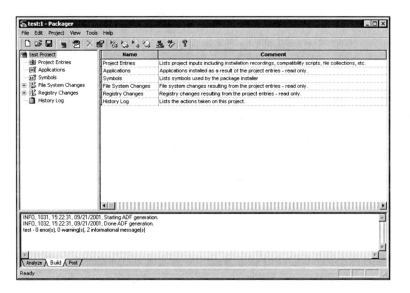

Figure 23.3 Application package.

Although you cannot edit the actual contents of your project from this window, you can view the following components that make up the package itself:

- **Project Entries** Project Entries is a list of all the different recording that you have added to this package. A package can consist of a recording for a single application, or it can consist of recordings for multiple applications. All of these recordings will be listed in this window.

- **Applications** This is a list of the applications and their shortcuts that are installed with this application.

- **Symbols** Symbols used throughout the .WMF file are listed here. For example, most application install recordings will create a `%targetdir%` symbol. This symbol contains the target directory for the application installation and is used as the reference point for where the application files are installed to.

- **File System Changes** Contains a list of all the files installed as part of the application, their size, destination location, and version number.

- **Registry Changes** A list of all the changes made to the Registry keys by the application are listed here.

- **History Log** The History Log records any changes that were made to the application package and the time the changes were made.

Unfortunately you cannot modify any of these settings through the GUI interface. At this point, however, you can do the following using the options under the Project menu:

- **Add a compatibility script** As you will see in the following section, you can create your own custom compatibility script to make changes to the original application installation.

- **Add unattended program** If you want to run a program as part of the application install, such as a script or batch file, you can use this option to specify the program. You also can use this option to reboot the server automatically upon the completion of an install, which is important for certain types of applications.

- **Add files** Finally, you can add files and folders of your choosing to the installation. These files and folders will be installed on the destination server in the same relative location as they were on the source.

Editing Installation Packages

One big disadvantage with the Packager utility is that it cannot be used to edit the contents of the package itself. For the more daring administrators, however, there is a way to modify the package after it has been built by editing the .WMF file that it creates. The .WMF file, much like an .MSI file, is the file that contains a list of all the changes that an application makes; this includes Registry changes, file changes, and shortcuts. Unlike an .MSI file that can be edited only with special utilities, however, a .WMF file is a text file and can be edited in Notepad.

To understand enough about the .WMF file format to make changes to it, create a simple application package of a small application, such as the Terminal Server client. You will find the .WMF file for the application under the ADF subfolder in the application package's project folder. Open up this file in Notepad.

The .WMF file uses standard .INI formatting. It is divided into several sections; each section has a section label enclosed in brackets. The first section you will see is the [Main] section. Under here are the general properties for the application package, including the application version and description.

The next section is the [GlobalSymbols] section. This is a very important section because it contains the `TARGETDIR` variable. If you want to change the destination folder for your application, you can change the `TARGETDIR` to point to the new destination.

After this section, the file format starts getting rather complicated. Basically you will see a Setup, User Setup, Repair, and Remove section. In each of these sections is a list of other sections that will be called to perform the setup or removal of the application. If you trace the steps as each section is called, you will get to the actual commands that are run for each step.

The following are the most commonly called commands that you will find in these sections:

- **`copyfile [source],[destination],...`** The `copyfile` command copies a particular file from the source location to the target location. If you want to remove a particular file from being installed, you can remove the associated `copyfile` command.

- **`addreg [hkcr or hklm],...`** Adds a Registry key to the system or user Registry.

- **`createshortcut [shortcut] ...`** Creates an application shortcut in the folder specified.

- **`deletefile [filename]`** Deletes the file listed. This command is normally used in the removal sections.

- **`deletereg [hklm or hkcr],[registry value]`** Deletes the particular Registry value from the Registry.

- **`deleteshortcut [shortcut] ...`** Deletes the particular shortcut from the machine.

Although specific documentation on these commands is not covered in this book, you can deduce the format of the commands fairly easily and modify the commands as needed to modify the installation. For more specific information on the layout of the installation files, see the "Installation Script Reference" whitepaper available on the Citrix web site at www.citrix.com/ support. This reference was written for v1.0 of the Installation Management Services; however, much of the material still applies to the .WMF file format in v2.0.

Importing Published Applications from MetaFrame 1.8

Many administrators might already have installation packages that have been deployed on their MetaFrame 1.8 servers that they need to be able to bring into MetaFrame XPe. During an upgrade install of MetaFrame XP, these packages are not brought in automatically. Instead, Citrix provides a special upgrade tool called IM_APP_UPGRD.EXE. You can find this tool in the [cd]:\support\debug\i386 folder of the Application Packaging & Delivery CD. To use this utility, just run it on your MetaFrame 1.8 server before you install MetaFrame XP.

This tool makes changes to the application installation path in the Registry so that these applications can be managed from MetaFrame XP. After you run this tool, these applications can no longer be managed from MetaFrame 1.8. In other words, if you try to uninstall them centrally, they will fail to be uninstalled from the server. If you now upgrade to MetaFrame XP and install Installation Manager, however, you will again be able to manage the applications centrally.

Author's Note

Realize that this issue relates only to applications that have been installed using Installation Management Services on MetaFrame 1.8. The actual installation packages for the applications in MetaFrame 1.8 can still be used in MetaFrame XP with no modification necessary.

Deploying Applications

The last step in the application installation process is the deployment of the packages. Although packaging application is handled by its own utility, the deployment of application packages is handled as part of the Citrix Management Console. To deploy the package you just created, follow these steps:

1. Open the Citrix Management Console and log on from the Program menu, Citrix folder.

2. Right-click the Citrix Installation Manager folder and select Properties. If you do not see this folder, the plug-in has not been installed correctly. You will need to reinstall the Installation Manager on this server.

3. Click the Edit button and enter the username and password of the user who will be used for the installation of applications. This user ID should be an administrative-level user, preferably a special service account dedicated for the purpose of installing applications on your server farm. In addition, this account must have read/write access to the packages on the network.

4. Right-click the Package folder underneath the Citrix Installation Manager folder and select Add Package.

5. Enter the UNC path for the .WMF or .MSI application package file and the package name, and then click OK. Note that UNCs are the only accepted type of path. Even if you click the Browse button, you will be able to browse only the Network Neighborhood and not local drives.

At this point the package should appear in the list of packages under the Package folder. One important thing to emphasize is the fact that you need to use a UNC path for the application package. This path must be accessible from all the servers that you intend to install the application on. As recommended earlier, it is normally best to dedicate a server as the application package server and share the application packages from that server. You can then specify the UNC (`\\[server name]\[share name]\[package name]`) for the package you want to add to the list very easily.

After all the packages you want to be able to deploy have been installed, it is time to schedule their deployment. If you intend to deploy an application to a particular group of servers, you should right-click the Server Groups folder, select Create, and then define the server groups you need before you schedule the application for deployment. After the groups you need have been defined, you can deploy the application as follows:

1. Right-click the package and select Install Package.

2. From the Servers window, add the servers or server groups that you want to deploy the package to and click Next.

3. At the Schedule window, click the Edit button to edit the time for the deployment. Otherwise, click Finish to accept the default of deploying the application immediately.

At the time scheduled, the application will be automatically installed on all the servers you selected.

Installing Applications on Farms Across a WAN

If your farm is split across a WAN, you need to be careful how you deploy your applications. If you set up only a single install source, servers across the WAN will attempt to download and install the application across the WAN. This would take up significant time and overtax the WAN circuit. A better way to handle this is to create a server group for the servers on each subnet by right-clicking the Server Groups and clicking Create. Add the servers that are at a particular location to a server group with the same name as that location.

Next, copy the packages that you need installed at the remote location to a file share that is at that location. If you are using Windows 2000 with Active Directory and there are domain controllers at both locations, you might want to consider putting your Citrix packages in the SYSVOL folder. Windows 2000 automatically replicates the contents of the SYSVOL folder to all locations. That way you can use the domain controllers as the source for your Citrix application package installations.

Define a separate package in the CMC for each location. If you have an Adobe Acrobat package on a file server in New York and one on a file server in Tokyo, for example, you would add the New York package as New York - Adobe Acrobat and the Tokyo package as Tokyo - Adobe Acrobat using the CMC. You would need to point the respective package to that location's package share.

Finally, when you deploy the application packages, deploy them to the local server group using the local package. For example, you would schedule only the deployment of the New York - Adobe Acrobat package to the New York server group.

In this way, the packages would be installed from a local file source rather than across the WAN.

Troubleshooting Application Deployment

You can check the status of a particular package's installation by highlighting the package and then clicking the Jobs tab. Under this tab you will see a list of the currently scheduled jobs and their status for all the servers. If you double-click one of these entries and then click the Job Details tab in the window that appears, you can view the exact status of the job installation and any error messages that occurred.

For an installation to occur successfully, the following must all be set up correctly:

- **The ADF Installer service must be running.**   The Installer service must be installed and running on all the servers on which you are installing the application. This service is installed as part of the Installation Manager program.

- **The Server must be licensed for MetaFrame XPe.** The server must be licensed for MetaFrame XPe; otherwise, you will not be able to install applications to it. You can verify which XP version your server is licensed for by highlighting the server under the Servers folder in the CMC and clicking the License tab. You will see a list of both the connection and product licenses assigned to this server. You need to see the product license for XPe for the installation to work correctly.

- **The installer user must have local administrator rights.** The user you defined as the installer user must have local administrative rights to the server. The installer user is the one you defined by right-clicking the Citrix Installation Manager folder in the CMC and selecting Properties. The user ID is the one defined in the Network Account section of the window.

- **The installer user must have read/write access to the package.** The best way to check this is to log on to the server you are having the problem with using the installer user account and verify that you have access to the installer package folder across the network.

24

Advanced Network Management and Monitoring

Any Terminal Server solution has a great reliance on the network. In a Terminal Server environment, the network can be looked upon as an extension to the workstation. The applications that a user runs off of Terminal Server appear as if they are running locally for the user. However, network failures and performance problems are much more critical in a Terminal Server environment than in an environment where users run applications locally. If the network fails, the connection for all Terminal Server users will fail. If the network is slow, all users' connections slow down.

This chapter covers some advanced techniques for ensuring the stability and performance of your network. You will first learn techniques for setting up performance simulation over a WAN to ensure that you have adequate bandwidth for the number of users you need to deploy. Next you will learn some of the many techniques you can use for monitoring the network and your servers to ensure that any problems are addressed quickly.

Finally, you will learn how to set up SNMP monitoring of your Terminal Servers and learn how to take advantage of the special SNMP monitoring capabilities available with Citrix MetaFrame XPe.

Prototyping the WAN

You need to make two main decisions when setting up Terminal Server on the WAN. First, you must determine what protocol to use. With Terminal Server, the choice is obvious: TCP/IP. With MetaFrame, you can use TCP/IP, IPX/SPX, or even NetBEUI with bridging. This choice is not always obvious and might depend on many factors. For one, you need to consider performance. TCP/IP, IPX/SPX, and NetBEUI vary in their performance and network bandwidth utilization.

Second, consider protocol standardization. There are many advantages to standardizing on a single protocol corporate-wide. The protocol of choice for this need is TCP/IP. It has become the de facto primary protocol for major network operating systems today. Even Novell NetWare, the most well-known operating system whose primary protocol has been IPX/SPX, has native TCP/IP support since version 4.x. Protocol standardization is very important for effective network monitoring. The focus of most major network monitoring packages is the monitoring of TCP/IP. You will find support for other protocols, such as IPX/SPX and NetBEUI, often lacking in comparison with the robust monitoring features available for TCP/IP.

Setting Up the WAN Lab

To effectively test the various WAN options available to you, you should set up a lab or test environment. The first part of every Terminal Server project plan should be dedicated to prototyping. Prototyping in a lab or test environment is critical for the success of any Terminal Server project, because in the prototyping stage you can best make the decisions about protocol type, necessary WAN bandwidth, and acceptable performance for your environment. Unfortunately, with WANs a true test environment is somewhat difficult to set up. Here are some options:

- **Establish a WAN link to the corporate site closest to you for testing.** If you have a hub-and-spoke type WAN configuration (in other words, a large corporate office with many branch offices), this option will probably work best for you. Setting up tests in this scenario gives you a very realistic picture of what to expect during the final rollout. Unfortunately, this works well only for new installations. Setting up testing across a WAN link that is already being relied on for daily use is not a good plan. Your testing could easily knock off current WAN users.

- **Perform after-hours testing on the WAN.** For many corporations, after-hours testing (when WAN utilization is low) is the only real testing option. The results of this testing provide real-world performance results that you can rely on for predicting the success of the actual rollout.

Whatever option you choose, the important thing is doing enough testing to ensure that when the project is finally rolled out, the level of performance across the WAN will be acceptable to users.

Using Existing WAN Links for Testing

Using existing WAN links can be the most accurate method for performance testing, but you must be careful about interfering with existing traffic. If the WAN links have not been set up yet and you plan to roll them out specifically for Terminal Server connections, you are fortunate. In this situation, make sure to roll out a site close to the main office first during the prototyping stage of the project. This site will become your test site, and you can run your performance tests to it. In this way, you can accurately estimate the amount of bandwidth that your Terminal Server application requires. This is important to know early in the project. Without accurate estimates of the amount of bandwidth Terminal Server will be using, you might quickly run into a situation in which there is not enough bandwidth for your Terminal Server needs at the sites. Depending on the type of line you ordered, you might end up being stuck ordering new routers and/or CSU/DSUs to increase the speed.

If you are like most administrators, however, you do not have the luxury of new installations. Instead you are probably trying to incorporate a Terminal Server solution into an existing WAN environment. In this situation, you will likely have to do two things. First, you must estimate the amount of current usage of the WAN. There are many ways to do this, depending on what equipment and network monitoring software you have at your disposal. Your local carrier often can be of great assistance by providing detailed wide area network utilization information—check with them first. Obtain the following information from them:

- The average bandwidth you are using
- The usage patterns during the week

This information will help greatly when planning for the additional traffic load caused by Terminal Server.

The second thing you must do is estimate this additional traffic load. Because this is a live WAN, you should probably do your testing after hours. Based on your traffic analysis, choose an off-peak time during which the testing results will not be skewed by background traffic.

To set up the actual test environment, you must deploy one or more test workstations to the remote site upon which you will be running performance tests. Try to use machines similar in capability to the ones you will be using in the rollout phase of the project. You should, of course, set up the Terminal Server client and protocol of choice on each workstation and establish connectivity to the Terminal Server.

A particular difficulty with this arrangement is ease of access. Every time you want to change a parameter on the workstation to test its effect on performance, you will probably need to dispatch someone to the site. If you are testing several different parameters, this can become tedious very quickly. One solution is to implement a remote control product such as pcAnywhere or Remotely Possible with dial-in access. In this way, you can dial in to the remote PC, set up the network and Terminal Server client the way you want, and commence the test, all without leaving the office! Be sure to close out of the remote control session after the tests have started. The screen updates for the remote control session also can affect the results because they take up processing time at the client.

Measuring WAN Bandwidth and Performance

After you have set up the testing environment, it is time to get some of the actual testing work done. It is recommended that you use these scripts to simulate user interaction across the WAN. Remember to keep the timing of these scripts realistic to mimic users' average use during the day. If the remote user will be using Terminal Server all day long, the amount of WAN bandwidth used is greater than if the user only occasionally needs access to the central office applications. Also be certain to set up simulation scripts that include all the applications that you will be rolling out to the remote sites in user simulation scripts.

You can use several methods, which are covered in the following sections, with Terminal Server to measure network bandwidth utilization.

Measuring Network Utilization Using the Terminal Server Administration Tool or Citrix Connection Manager

Using the Terminal Server Administration Tool or Citrix Connection Manager is a quick way to get a rough picture of your network utilization. With both of these tools, you can watch the number of packets input and output from your server. To gather this information, follow these steps:

1. Log on to Terminal Server from the test workstation across the WAN or simulated WAN connection.

2. For Terminal Server administrators, run the Terminal Server Administration Tool, highlight the test connection, and select the Status from the Actions menu. For Citrix administrators, double-click the ICA icon in the task tray, highlight the server under Active, and select Properties.

3. Start the user simulation script on the workstation that you created in Chapter 21, "Performance Tuning and Resource Management." If you did not have time to create the script, you can have a user work with you to simulate application activity.

4. Select Reset Counters from the Status window and start your stopwatch or an equivalent type of timer.

5. At the end of 10 minutes of user simulation, or however long you have decided to run the test, click the Print Screen button. This trick captures the screen to the Clipboard at the moment the clock stops. This makes it much easier to read the input and output byte totals.

6. Run the Clipboard view to see the results. To obtain an estimate of the network bandwidth utilization over the tested period of time, add the input and output bytes together and divide the total by the number of seconds you ran the test:

(input + output)/number of seconds $\star$ 8 / 1000

This gives you the amount of bandwidth utilization in kilobits per second, which is how most WAN connections are sized.

Measuring Network Utilization Using Performance Monitor

Performance Monitor is a great tool for getting a good picture of your network utilization pattern. You can use Performance Monitor for the following tasks:

- Testing to get a better idea of which application operations take the most network bandwidth
- Long-term network monitoring
- Base lining your network utilization over a long period of time
- Watching your traffic patterns throughout the day

Although there are many useful network-related parameters you can monitor, the one you should be most concerned with is Total Bytes. In Figure 24.1, you see that the Total Bytes counter, which is located under the Session object, is added to the chart view.

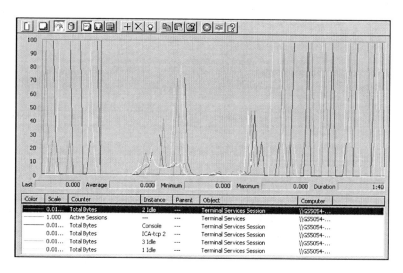

Figure 24.1   Monitor Terminal server network usage.

To add this counter to the chart, follow these steps:

1. Run Performance Monitor from the Administrative Tools folder located in Start menu, Programs.

2. Select Add to Chart from the Edit menu or click the plus sign (+) button on the screen.

3. Select Session on Windows NT 4.0 and Terminal Services Session on Windows 2000 from the Object drop-down list.

4. Select Total Bytes from the Counter list.

5. Select the instance for which you want to get a count for, from the Instance list. Each instance represents the Total Bytes from a different active session on Terminal Server.

6. Click OK to add the counter to the chart.

By default, the Total Bytes being transmitted are sampled every second, providing you with a good short-term picture of the network utilization patterns. For a longer sample rate, select Chart from the Options menu and raise the sample rate. On Windows 2000, the sample rate can be edited by clicking the Properties button at the top of the performance monitoring window (Notepad with a small hand).

Author's Note

For those who have purchased and installed Feature Release 1 on their MetaFrame XPe server farms, several new Performance Monitor counters have been added. Be sure to take a look at these, because several are related to network performance. You will find all of these counters under the ICA Session object in Performance Monitor. Even if you do not have MetaFrame XPe, you can monitor network latency under ICA Session.

For more useful long-term testing with Windows NT 4.0 Performance Monitor, go into the Performance Monitor logging section by selecting Log from the View menu. Here you can set up Performance Monitor to start logging the counters under the various objects. Again the main object of concern is the Session object for network utilization. It is recommended to log the Session counters while you are doing your performance testing. The best thing about the log is that you can view the results in the Chart view at any time after they are recorded. You also can view any session counter from any instance. This level of flexibility is great for obtaining an accurate picture of the application's network usage.

You can set up logging on Windows 2000 by setting up and starting a new performance log under the Performance Logs and Alerts, Counters Logs folder.

To get an idea of your network utilization patterns throughout the day or week, try changing the logging interval to something in the neighborhood of 15 minutes (900 seconds). Continue logging the session parameters for several days at this interval. By importing the results into a spreadsheet program such as Excel, you can generate traffic utilization charts. These charts can prove very beneficial for future planning. For example, you can use the first chart you create as a baseline. By sampling the network utilization every couple of months and overlaying the charts, you can watch how your utilization changes as the network grows. You also might want to include processor and memory object counters in your logging.

Author's Note

Chapter 21 provides more specific instructions on how to set up performance logging and export log files to other formats.

Other Ways to Measure Network Utilization

To measure network utilization, you must determine the number of bytes that have gone between the client and the server over a period of time. Most of the methods discussed so far use utilities that run from the server itself. Because the server has to waste extra processing time monitoring the network with these utilities, this can affect the results. Although the effect should be minimal, you can use some nonintrusive means to monitor network traffic:

- Run a packet sniffer and protocol analyzer on a separate box to capture the packets going between the test workstation and Terminal Server. There are many good network analysis packages on the market; however, one that is highly recommended and relatively inexpensive is Etherpeek by Wild Packets (www.etherpeek.com).

- If your test workstation is plugged into a switch, most switches keep statistics on the bytes sent and received for each port. You can use the network monitoring tools available with your switch to monitor this value.

- If your workstation is at a remote small office, and it is the only workstation at the office going across the WAN, you can use the statistics in the router. Most routers maintain traffic statistics.

- Using SNMP you can monitor many network statistics on your Terminal Servers and network devices. For more information, see the "SNMP Monitoring" section later in this chapter.

Monitoring the Network and Servers

Setting up a monitoring system for both the network and the Terminal Servers is an important part of any Terminal Server solution. Network monitoring will help you ensure that you are notified of any network outages and thus can respond to outages quickly. In addition, you can use many network monitoring packages to monitor the utilization of WAN circuits, so that you can better size those circuits in the long run. In addition, monitoring your Terminal Servers can give you advance notice of any problems with a particular server.

This section discusses the basics of how to set up your own network monitoring system.

Basic Network Monitoring and Notification Packages

Many different network monitoring packages are available on the market today. These packages range from simple network monitoring systems that can check whether a particular device is reachable to highly robust packages that can monitor the status of thousands of devices and use advanced network monitoring technologies such as SNMP to proactively prevent network problems. As the number of features increases, however, so do the costs. Enterprise-class network monitoring packages can easily run into the hundreds of thousands of dollars in large deployments.

For small to medium-size deployments, one highly recommended network monitoring package is WhatsUp Gold by IPSwitch software (www.ipswitch.com). Like many other monitoring packages in its class, it offers the ability to auto-discover your network devices, monitor their status, and notify administrators if a device fails; however, this package is relatively inexpensive compared to other packages available and is loaded with additional functionality.

Whether you choose to use WhatsUp Gold or some other basic network monitoring package to monitor your Terminal Server deployment, you should set up the following.

Server and Service Monitoring

It is important to add all the Terminal Servers in your server farm to the monitoring system and monitor them periodically. In addition to server monitoring, however, you also should monitor the services that your server runs. Many network monitoring packages, such as WhatsUp Gold, enable you to monitor whether a particular port or service on a server is responding. This is especially important for Citrix MetaFrame XP servers that have multiple ports for different services. The TCP/IP ports that you would need to monitor for different services are shown in Table 24.1.

Table 24.1 **TCP/IP Ports to Monitor**

Service	Port Number
Citrix XML Service for NFuse and TCP/IP+HTTP Access	80 or as set using CTXXMLS.EXE
Citrix ICA	1464
Citrix MetaFrame IMA Service	2512
Terminal Server	3389

What Causes Servers and Services to Fail?

It might seem unlikely that a server or service will just fail for no reason. As the number of servers in your server farm grows, however, you are likely to run into this type of issue often enough to justify monitoring it carefully. Services and servers can and do fail for a number of reasons ranging from software glitches to hardware failures.

By monitoring the issue carefully, you can ensure that you are the first to know of a serious server outage, instead of having to be informed by your user community or worse yet your supervisor. By knowing about the problem quickly, you can react to the issue much faster and fix the problem before the outage becomes extended.

In addition, most network monitoring packages will log the time of any outages. You can later use the logs to compare this time to what was happening on the server using the server's event logs or another system's logs to help discover the source of the problem.

Pager and Email Notification

In addition to monitoring, it is important to set up some type of notification if a device or server goes down. The following are the most common types of notification available and their advantages and disadvantages. (WhatsUp Gold supports all of these types of notification.)

- **Email**   Email is a great way to handle notification for all but the most serious of network outages. Most cell phones, pagers, and other portable personal devices have their own email address. Using packages such as WhatsUp Gold you can send notification directly to these devices when a service or server fails. Also it is a good idea to set up a special network monitoring account on your email server. If you send a copy of every outage to this account, this account can serve as a log of all outages on the network.

- **Pager**   If the network itself fails, email notification will not work. For the most reliable notification, alphanumeric paging is preferred. Systems that support the *Simple Messaging System* (SMS) can send alphapages to pagers via a modem. Two or three different protocols can be used; however, most pagers today support the TAPI protocol. You will need to attach a modem to your network monitoring server for it to be able to send the pages. Because it uses a modem to send the text page and not the network, it will be able to send a page even if the network fails.

- **Beeper**   Sending a numeric beep to your beeper if a system fails is possible on many systems. If you are monitoring numerous systems, however, it can be difficult to determine which system went down with only a numeric message.

- **Program**   Many monitoring systems enable you to run a particular program if a system goes down. This can be highly useful. For example, you can use this to remotely reset a service if a service continues to fail, log an outage to a file, or build more intelligence into the notification system.

Network Connection Monitoring

If you have users across the WAN who access your Terminal Servers, it is important to monitor whether their network connections are active. If the network connections fail, even for a moment, they will lose their connection to your Terminal Server and likely make a call into the help desk.

When setting up network connection monitoring, you should monitor both the primary WAN interface and the Ethernet interface of the remote device. This is important because it gives you good information as to the nature of the problem. Basically, two things can occur to make the connection go down. First, the WAN connection itself can fail. If this is the case, you will see indication that both the WAN interface and Ethernet interface are unreachable. If you have a backup WAN connection, however, it might be able to reestablish the connection automatically. In this case, you will see the WAN down, but the Ethernet up, meaning that the connection is still good and the backup link worked. The final possibility is that the WAN link is up, but the Ethernet is down. This could happen if they lose power to their Ethernet switch or the remote router becomes unplugged. As you can see, by just monitoring both the WAN and Ethernet you can gain important information as to the nature of the problem with the connection for the remote users.

Network Latency and Packet Loss

Network latency is very important in a WAN. Latency refers to the time it takes for a packet to travel to a remote location and back. Network latency is normally measured in milliseconds and can be monitored by most network monitoring packages.

The reason network latency is so important is that latency is closely related to a user's perception of the responsiveness of their Terminal Server connection. If the latency is too high, users will start perceiving that their connection or application is slow. Table 24.2 shows latency values and gives you a rough idea of what these values mean in terms of response time for a user.

Table 24.2   **Network Response Time**

Latency	Responsiveness	User Response Time Perception
0 to 25ms	Excellent	This is the typical response time on a local area network. Users will perceive no difference in response time between an application running locally and one running on Terminal Server.
25 to 250ms	Good	This is the typical response time you should get for most wide area network connections that are not being overused. Application response time might appear slightly slower to users, but response time will be good enough for typical remote application use through Terminal Server.

continues ▶

Table 24.2   **Continued**

Latency	Responsiveness	User Response Time Perception
250 to 750ms	Slow	This is the typical response time for slow dial-up connections, wireless connections, and heavily used WAN connections. Response time will be noticeably slower for users. This response time is adequate for short periods of remote access, but is not fast enough for working remotely for extended periods of time.
750ms and above	Unacceptable	In this range, a single packet is taking up to or more than one second to travel between the remote users and the Terminal Server. This is not fast enough for working remotely with Terminal Server. At this speed, connections will likely drop after timeout values are reached, causing users to have to reconnect. Response time will be so slow that typical tasks will take several times longer to complete.

To measure latency, network packages ping the remote device and measure how long it takes for the packet to return. Because response time will vary slightly with each packet, it is important to look at the average response time and not the minimum or maximum. Many network packages, such as WhatsUp Gold, automatically average the response time to a remote device for you. You also can manually get a rough idea of response time by just using the ping [device IP] -t command. This command will send a continual stream of pings out to a remote device. When you press Ctrl+C to end the ping, it will show you the minimum, maximum, and average response times in milliseconds, as follows in Listing 24.1.

Author's Note

Remember that after you have installed Service Pack 1 and Feature Release 1, new ICA Session performance counters available can be used to measure latency.

Listing 24.1   **Determining Latency Using Ping**

```
C:\>ping gsmeta1 -t

Pinging gsmeta1.southernwine.com [192.168.10.208] with 32 bytes of data:

Reply from 192.168.10.208: bytes=32 time=121ms TTL=125
Reply from 192.168.10.208: bytes=32 time=120ms TTL=125
```

```
Reply from 192.168.10.208: bytes=32 time=120ms TTL=125
Reply from 192.168.10.208: bytes=32 time=120ms TTL=125
Reply from 192.168.10.208: bytes=32 time=110ms TTL=125
Reply from 192.168.10.208: bytes=32 time=120ms TTL=125
Reply from 192.168.10.208: bytes=32 time=110ms TTL=125
Reply from 192.168.10.208: bytes=32 time=120ms TTL=125
Reply from 192.168.10.208: bytes=32 time=120ms TTL=125
Reply from 192.168.10.208: bytes=32 time=131ms TTL=125

Ping statistics for 192.168.10.208:
    Packets: Sent = 10, Received = 10, Lost = 0 (0% loss),
Approximate round trip times in milli-seconds:
    Minimum = 110ms, Maximum =  131ms, Average =  119ms
Control-C
```

The response time for each ping is shown next to the `time=` and is measured in milliseconds. Notice at the end of the example that the minimum, maximum, and average response times are shown. The average response time of 119ms means that it is taking approximately 1/10 of a second for a packet to travel to the Terminal Server and back to the workstation. This is well within the "good" range for response time. This means users could work for extended periods of time with applications on your Terminal Server without the response time becoming an issue.

Response time can vary significantly depending on many factors; however, the most common reason that response time will vary is that a WAN connection is being overused. Suppose, for example, that you test the response time for one of your remote sites early in the morning when no one is using the connection, and you get an average response time of 100ms. However, that day at around 10 a.m. several users at the remote location call the help desk complaining that the connection is slow. You then check the connection again and find that the response time has increased to 450ms. What has happened is that multiple people using the connection have slowed down the response time for everyone.

At this point you would need to use a network sniffer to view all the traffic on the connection. Look for any unusual traffic. Generally, extended data transfers, such as FTP transfers or large file copies, will take up enormous amounts of network bandwidth even on fast connections. If you see this type of transfer occurring, you can work with the users who started the transfer to have them schedule the file transfer for after-hours. If this is not possible, you might have to increase the line speed.

The advantage of monitoring network latency is that you can get advance warning of when large file transfers are affecting the performance of your network connections. In addition, you can use network latency to help determine whether a particular connection's speed needs to be increased.

SNMP Monitoring

Although network monitoring is focused on monitoring the connection between your users and your Terminal Servers, many other things on your servers and network devices can be important to monitor because they can affect their reliability and performance. For example, you might want to monitor server drive space or be alerted if a drive on a server fails. On the network side, you might want to determine the amount of packet loss or the percentage of utilization of a particular line.

To accomplish this type of monitoring, you need to use *Simple Network Management Protocol* (SNMP) monitoring. SNMP is a widely supported, standardized protocol that can be used for monitoring and even managing a large variety of devices. Both Windows NT 4.0 and 2000 Terminal Server fully support SNMP. In addition, nearly all network devices, such as routers, switches, and printers, have SNMP support.

For Citrix administrators, advanced SNMP support is available in with MetaFrame XPe. This enables you to remotely monitor specific Citrix parameters, such as license use and number of connections.

SNMP Monitoring Systems

To monitor your servers via SNMP, you first need to purchase and install an SNMP-capable network monitoring package. WhatsUp Gold includes simple SNMP monitoring capabilities, but is not designed to be an enterprise-class SNMP monitoring system. Most enterprise SNMP monitoring systems are expensive; however, they include several capabilities important for SNMP monitoring, such as the following:

- **Extended SNMP logging and graphs** The value of SNMP monitoring is normally realized over the long term. This means that the system you choose should have the capability to log SNMP parameters over an extended period of time and be able to graph those parameters. This will enable you to establish performance baselines so that you can better plan for future expansion. For example, a typical enterprise-class SNMP monitoring package will enable you to record the utilization of a network circuit over an extended period of time. You can then view this graph and determine whether a circuit is being overutilized and what time of day a circuit is the most heavily used.

- **Threshold alerts** Many systems enable you to set up alerts based on whether thresholds are exceeded. For example, using SNMP you can monitor the space available on your servers. You could then set up a threshold alert to send you an alert if the space available goes below a certain value.

- **SNMP traps** SNMP includes the capability to send out alert messages, called *traps*, when certain events happen or when settable thresholds are exceeded. The types of traps supported depend on the manufacturer of the device. For example, the SNMP implementation provided by Citrix with MetaFrame XPe can send out a trap when licenses are exceeded on a server. This trap is sent to the SNMP monitoring package, where it can be used to send out an alert or email message to an administrator notifying the person of the license outage.

- **Auto-discovery** Most SNMP monitoring packages can auto-discover the network. This means that they can discover all the devices on the network and set up monitoring of those devices without you having to enter them. This is a big time saver on large networks with thousands of devices that need to be monitored.

SNMP Monitoring Systems

Quite a few enterprise-class SNMP monitoring systems are available on the market with a large range of capabilities. You might want to review the following:

- HP OpenView (**www.hp.com**, search for OpenView) This is probably the best known and most widely used enterprise class SNMP monitoring system. Like most SNMP monitoring packages, it can be very expensive; however, this package can extend to the largest of networks. Citrix MetaFrame XPe includes plug-ins specifically for this package that provide enhanced management capabilities for your Citrix servers.

- IBM Tivoli NetView (**www.ibm.com**, search for Tivoli) This package is widely used in large IBM shops and includes a robust set of enterprise-class SNMP monitoring features. It can handle monitoring for networks of any size. Like OpenView, Citrix has a special plug-in available for NetView.

- SNMPc by CastleRock (**www.castlerock.com**) This is an inexpensive but full-featured SNMP monitoring package. No special Citrix plug-ins are included for this package; however, you can import the Citrix .MIB into the package manually and monitor specific parameters.

Setting Up the SNMP Service on Terminal Server

To set up SNMP monitoring on your Terminal Servers, you must first install the service. The SNMP service is available for installation on both Windows NT 4.0 and 2000 Server.

To install the SNMP service on Windows NT 4.0 Terminal Server, follow these steps:

1. Right-click the Network Neighborhood on the Windows NT 4.0 Terminal Server desktop and select Properties.

2. Click the Services tab, and then click Add.

3. From the Select Network Service window that appears, select SNMP Service, and then click OK.

4. Use the defaults for the SNMP setup.

5. Reapply the latest service pack to ensure that the SNMP service is patched properly.

To install the SNMP service on Windows 2000 Terminal Server, follow these steps:

1. Select Add/Remove Programs from the Control Panel.

2. Click the Add/Remove Windows Components button.

3. From the Components Wizards window, double-click Management and Monitoring Tools.

4. Check the box next to Simple Network Management Protocol, and then click OK.

5. Click Next to begin the installation and follow the wizard.

6. Re-apply the latest service pack.

Setting SNMP Security

It is very important to lock down the SNMP service properly after you install it. SNMP security is controlled using a simple security password referred to as a *community string*. A security string can be granted either read access, write access, or both to the SNMP parameters. Whereas read access is used only to gather information from a server, write access can be used to set important system parameters depending on the capabilities built into SNMP by the manufacturer.

When you set up the SNMP monitoring package, you need to enter the IP address of your Terminal Servers and the community string that they use. Using readily available tools, hackers can easily crack SNMP community strings on your servers if security is left open. In addition, the SNMP community string goes across the line in clear text. To prevent the threat of a hacker gaining access to the SNMP service, you should always restrict SNMP access to the IP address of your network monitoring station. In this way, only the network monitoring station can read from or write to the SNMP service.

To lock down the SNMP service on a Windows NT 4.0 Terminal Server, follow these steps:

1. Right-click the Network Neighborhood and select Properties.

2. Click the Services tab.

3. Highlight the SNMP service and click Properties.

4. Click the Security tab.

5. Under the Security tab, add the address(es) of your network monitoring stations and set the community string to a secure alphanumeric password. Grant the community string only read access if write access is not necessary. Remove the default community string of PUBLIC. Figure 24.2 shows a secure setup.

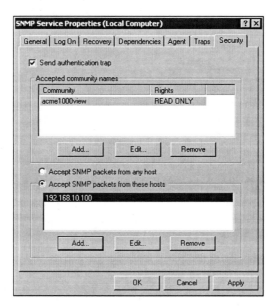

Figure 24.2 SNMP security.

6. If you want to set up traps to be sent to the network monitoring system, click the Traps tab and add the IP address of the monitoring system to the list of systems to which traps are sent. Figure 24.3 shows an example configuration.

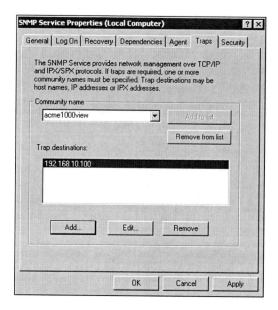

Figure 24.3   Setting up SNMP traps.

To lock down the SNMP service on a Windows 2000 Terminal Server, follow these steps:

1. Go to Control Panel, Administrative Tools, and select Services.
2. Double-click the SNMP Service in the Services window.
3. Click the Security tab.
4. Under the Security tab, add the address(es) of your network monitoring stations under the hosts area.
5. Set the community string to a secure alphanumeric password. Grant the community string only read access if write access is not necessary. Remove the default community string of PUBLIC.
6. If you want to set up traps to be sent to the network monitoring system, click the Traps tab and add the IP address of the monitoring system to the list of systems to which traps are sent.

Setting Up the Network Monitoring System

After your servers have been set up with SNMP, the next step is to set up the network monitoring system so that you can start gathering information on the servers. The basic process to do this for most network monitoring systems is as follows:

1. Add all the Terminal Servers to the network monitoring system's map.

2. Ensure that SNMP monitoring of these servers is enabled.

3. Enter the community string that you defined for each server when you set up the SNMP service. Normally the community string used for monitoring a particular network device can be found in that device's Properties screen on most network monitoring systems.

4. Set up the monitoring interval.

5. Configure whether traps will be captured and what the response to the SNMP traps will be. Remember that you also need to set up the SNMP service on the Terminal Server to send traps to the network monitoring system before these traps can be captured.

Understanding SNMP .MIBs

As mentioned earlier, a large variety of different parameters can normally be monitored using SNMP; however, the manufacturer determines the actual list of what can be monitored. Each manufacturer of a device that can be monitored by SNMP creates what is called a *Management Information Base* (.MIB) file. This file defines exactly what parameters or objects can be monitored on the system.

.MIB files can normally be found in the `%systemroot%\system32` directory on your Terminal Servers after you install the SNMP service. .MIB files are text files and can be easily read and edited in Notepad. The purpose of the .MIB file is basically to define the objects that can be monitored. Each object within an .MIB is identified by a unique number called an *object ID*. When the network monitoring system needs to retrieve the value of a particular object, it sends the object ID it needs and the community string to the Terminal Server. The Terminal Server then validates that the community string has access to read the .MIB and then sends back the value of the requested object.

Listing 24.2 is a sample excerpt from the LAN Manager .MIB (LMMIB2.MIB) file showing the definition of an object that holds the count of the number of sessions established with the server. Notice that each object has a full description. This makes it easier for you to find the object you need when you are browsing the .MIBs.

Listing 24.2   **Example .MIB**

```
svSessionNumber OBJECT-TYPE
    SYNTAX  INTEGER
    ACCESS  read-only
    STATUS  mandatory
    DESCRIPTION
        "The number of sessions have established to this server."
    ::= { server  19  }
```

Suppose, for example, that you want to find out the number of users logged on to the server. You would browse the appropriate .MIB from the network monitoring system and find the object that represents the number of currently logged on users. At this point, the network monitoring system sends out an SNMP message to the Terminal Server you were monitoring with the community string you defined and the object ID for the object that reports the number of logged-on users. The Terminal Server validates that the community string had read access and then returns the current value of the object ID, which contains the number of currently logged-on users. The network monitoring system would then display this value. With most network monitoring systems, you also could graph this value, meaning you could easily create a real-time graph showing the number of users currently logged on.

A large number of .MIBs are available with Windows 2000 and Windows NT 4.0 Terminal Server. Exactly what .MIBs are in use depends on what services you have installed. In addition, Citrix provides its own .MIB file with MetaFrame XPe that can be found on the Network Management CD. The following are some of the commonly installed .MIBs that you will find on your Terminal Server:

- **MIB_II.MIB**   This is one of the standard .MIBs defined by the SBMP RFC. This .MIB contains objects for information on the system itself, network interfaces, IP parameters, ICMP, TCP, UDP, and more. The main use of this .MIB is for monitoring information from the network interface of your Terminal Servers. Because this is one of the standard .MIBs, you will find it loaded by default on most network monitoring systems.

- **LMMIB2.MIB**   The LAN Manager .MIB is a very old .MIB from the days when Windows NT was first being developed. At the time, Windows NT design was heavily influenced by its predecessor OS/2 LAN Manager. With this .MIB, you can monitor many Windows NT-specific parameters, such as the domain that a server belongs to, the version of Windows, and more. You will often find this .MIB included with network monitoring packages by default.

- **DHCP.MIB, WINS.MIB, FTP.MIB, INETSRV.MIB, HTTP.MIB**
These .MIBs provides detailed information on the DHCP, WINS, FTP, and HTTP service respectively. You can monitor one or more of these .MIBs if your server is running the associated service.

- **CITRIX.MIB and MF.MIB**   These .MIBs are available only if you have purchased Citrix MetaFrame XPe. You will find these .MIBs under the [cd]:\mibs folder on the Network Management CD. They provide detailed Citrix-related information on your Citrix MetaFrame servers, including connection lists, user lists, connection status, license information, and performance information on sessions. These .MIBs must be manually added to the network monitoring system to use it.

Adding .MIBs to your Network Monitoring System

Many of the previously listed .MIBs are already included with most network monitoring systems. This means you should be able to browse the objects in these .MIBs on your Terminal Server using the network monitoring system. However, .MIBs such as the CITRIX.MIB and MF.MIB are not included with network monitoring systems. The only way to browse the objects included with these .MIBs is to add them to your network monitoring systems. The exact procedure for this varies from system to system; however, the basic procedure is as follows:

1. Open the network monitoring system.

2. Go to the area of the network monitoring system where you can see the list of .MIBs currently installed on the system.

3. Select Add a New MIB and browse for the .MIB you want to add. You can copy the .MIB you need from the %systemroot%\system32 directory of your Terminal Server or from the Network Management CD (as in the case of Citrix MetaFrame XPe).

The network monitoring system will now recompile its list of .MIBs by adding the new objects to its existing set of objects.

Now when you use the network monitoring package to browse the Terminal Servers, you will be able to view the values for the new objects you added.

Installing the Network Management Plug-Ins for Tivoli or OpenView

Citrix includes special network management plug-ins in MetaFrame XPe for both IBM Tivoli or HP OpenView. These plug-ins enable you to perform various Citrix management and monitoring tasks directly from the console of your IBM Tivoli or HP OpenView monitoring system. In addition, Citrix servers will display using a special icon to identify them on the console. To install these plug-ins, follow these steps:

1. Insert the Network Management CD into the CD drive of your IBM Tivoli or HP OpenView management console.

2. The Network Manager splash screen should appear; if it doesn't, run the `[cd]:\autorun.exe` executable on the CD.

3. Select to either Install Plug-in for NetView or Install Plug-in for OpenView as appropriate.

Top-Ten Networking Tips

The following are the top-ten tips for setting up your network for the highest level of performance and stability to support applications on Terminal Server

1. **Use a dial backup solution for critical WAN links.** A dial-up ISDN line works very well as a backup WAN link. Most major router manufacturers have equipment options that support ISDN as a backup WAN link. A major problem at your carrier can easily result in several hours of downtime for the sites on your WAN.

2. **Give higher priority to Citrix ICA (1494) and Microsoft RDP (3389) traffic.** Most routers can prioritize traffic. It is a very good idea normally to give higher priority to your Citrix ICA and/or RDP, especially if application performance is critical. By bumping up the priority, you can help ensure user response time will not be as badly affected as it would be normally when other traffic on the WAN starts to congest the circuit.

3. **Set up a network alerting system.** This is critical for ensuring the highest level of network reliability. On large networks, circuits go down relatively frequently. The important thing is to have backup circuit solutions available and to address problems quickly.

4. **Set up a secondary PVC.** If you are using Frame Relay, set up a secondary PVC that is routed through an alternate set of Frame Relay switches. This technique makes a huge difference in long-term reliability on Frame Relay networks. Most communication providers can handle this request. The cost for the additional backup PVC is generally very inexpensive.

5. **Set up an SNMP monitoring system.** Just as important as alerting on down circuits is the ability to monitor network utilization. Using most SNMP monitoring systems, you can monitor and record the utilization of any of your WAN circuits.

6. **Use high-performance network cards.** Always use the highest performance network cards you can afford. The network can be a bottleneck, especially for users accessing the server on the LAN. Using gigabit cards or bonding together two or more 100Mbps cards is a good idea to improve performance.

7. **Do not trust auto-negotiation.** Problems with the auto-negotiation process for network cards can quickly lead to very strange network-related problems on Citrix MetaFrame and poor performance. Check on the switch to make sure no malformed packets are coming from the server and that the auto-negotiate negotiated for the correct speed (100Mbps, full duplex).

8. **Size circuits correctly.** Make sure to always size your circuits correctly based on the maximum expected number of concurrent users. Remember to account for any other network traffic that normally occurs during peak usage times.

9. **Use switches not hubs.** This is a rather dated recommendation. In some environments, however, hubs might still be around. Using a hub with a Terminal Server rather than a switch is not a good idea. Terminal Servers use the network heavily.

10. **Monitor the network and postpone file transfers for after-hours.** A single extended file transfer can consume nearly the entire WAN circuit and cause session response time to slow down considerably. In addition, heavy printing can quickly bring a WAN connection to a crawl. Try to postpone large file transfers and printouts for after-hours, when they will not affect production use of the Terminal Server.

25

Terminal Server and NetWare

FOR ALL THE ADMINISTRATORS OUT THERE trying to integrate
Terminal Server into existing NetWare networks, this chapter is for you.
Terminal Server works very well with NetWare networks and has specific
features and tools designed to make the integration with NetWare as easy
and seamless as possible. In addition, Novell has made great strides in recent
years in ensuring that their software works well with both Terminal Server
and Citrix MetaFrame solutions.

This chapter begins with a discussion of the different options you have
available for connecting to Novell NetWare servers. Then the discussion
covers mapping drives to Novell NetWare file resources and connecting to
Novell printers. The chapter ends with detailed coverage of how to connect
to Citrix MetaFrame servers using the IPX/SPX protocol.

Connecting to Novell Networks

When setting up your Terminal Servers so that users can connect to Novell
networks, you basically have two choices, either use Gateway and Client
Services for Novell NetWare from Microsoft or use the Novell Client for
Windows NT/2000. Each option has its own advantages and disadvantages.
In this section, you will learn how to set up both.

Novell Client for Windows NT/2000

When you set up a Novell network, normally you deploy the Novell Client to all the network workstations and servers from which you need to log on. The Novell Client replaces the standard logon prompt with a specialized version that includes many options that are important in a Novell environment, such as the ability to set a user's context, full support for the NDS API, support for ZENworks, and the ability to run Novell administration tools. Although at one time this client was not supported on Terminal Server, it is now fully supported on both Terminal Server and Citrix MetaFrame by Novell as a means of connecting to Novell networks.

To install this client on your Terminal Server, follow these steps:

1. Download the latest version of the Novell Client for Windows NT/2000 as appropriate from the Novell web site (www.novell.com/downloads).

2. Install the latest service pack on your server.

3. Install the Novell Client for Windows NT/2000 by running the SETUPNW.EXE file from the download and then reboot the server.

Novell Support in MetaFrame XP's Feature Release 1

Those who are considering installing the Novell Client on their Citrix MetaFrame servers should definitely consider purchasing Feature Release 1 for Citrix MetaFrame XP. Not only is the Novell Client not supported by Citrix without Feature Release 1, but its installation will likely cause you problems on your server.

The main issue with the install of the Novell Client on Citrix MetaFrame XP is that MetaFrame XP relies on a new logon GINA called *CTXGINA*. The GINA is the graphical interface that displays your logon prompt for Citrix. When you install the Novell Client, however, it overwrites this GINA with its own. This is evident by the different logon prompt and logon options available when you log on to a server that has the Novell Client installed.

Feature Release 1 includes code to get around this problem. If you install the Novell Client before you install MetaFrame XP, you should have no problem with Feature Release 1. If you intend to install the Novell Client after the installation of MetaFrame XP, however, you might need to manually switch the logon GINA back to the default of MSGINA.DLL, before installing the Novell Client. To do so, follow these steps:

1. Run REGEDT32.EXE.

2. Browse to the following Registry key: HKLM\Microsoft\WindowsNT\Current Version\WinLogon.

3. Replace the CTXGINA.DLL string in the GinaDLL value with MSGINA.DLL.

Be very careful when performing this procedure because this value controls what is used for the logon prompt for your server. Make sure you test this procedure with your particular Novell Client version on a test MetaFrame server before trying it in production.

In addition to the ability to work with the Novell Client, Feature Release 1 also offers the following Novell-related enhancements:

- The ability to use pass-through authentication from the client using Novell credentials.

- Full support of application publishing to accounts in NDS (you can now publish to user and group objects in Novell trees in addition to Windows NT domains).

- Support of tree and context specification at the NFuse logon prompt.

The Novell Client and Authentication

One issue with using the Novell Client and Windows Terminal Server is with password and user ID synchronization. Because a user has to authenticate to Windows NT and to Novell, it is possible for users' passwords to become out of sync. For this process to work as seamlessly as possible, both the username and the password must match on both the Windows NT domain and in the Novell tree.

Suppose, for example, that you set up a username John Doe with a user ID of jdoe and password of temp123 on both Novell and Windows NT. During normal logon, John has to enter only his username and password once. Windows will finish the logon process automatically with Novell using the username and password pass through. Now suppose John's password expires on Novell and he changes it, but he does not change it on Windows NT. Now the passwords are out of sync. When John tries to log on, he will be able to log on to Windows using his old username and password. When the system attempts to log him on to Novell using the same user ID and password, however, the logon attempt fails. An error message will display and John will have to enter the correct username and password for Novell. In essence, he will have to log on twice.

To avoid this problem, it is very important to instruct your users on how to properly change their passwords. In addition, you should expire passwords only from either Novell or from Windows NT, but not from both.

The Novell Client and Published Applications

The second problem is related and happens with some versions of the Novell Client when using published applications through Citrix. Published applications use pass-through authentication for users to log on to the server farm. In some situations, however, this pass-through authentication does not work and a user will be prompted for his Novell logon name and password after he launches the published application. To fix this problem, you need to change the `TSClientAutoAdminLogon` value to 1 in the `HKLM\Software\Novell\Login` key. This value forces the pass-through authentication process, ensuring that the username and password used for logon to Windows also will be used for logon to Novell NetWare. As mentioned previously, however, it is still important that the user ID and password used for Windows be the same as that used for Novell.

The Novell Client and Context

The third and last issue relates to a user's context. In Novell each user has a context within the tree. When a user logs on, she must specify the context. The context defines where the user's user object is within the tree. Unfortunately, this is a per-machine and not a per-user setting. If you have users who are part of multiple contexts logging on to the same Terminal Server, it can quickly become confusing for your users. Every time they log on, their logon context will be set by default to the last user's context, meaning that they will have to manually change it to log on.

To avoid this hassle for users, it is highly recommended to set up Catalog Services for Novell. This feature is available in NetWare 5 and 6. Instead of requiring the context for a user to be specified, Novell automatically builds a catalog of all the user IDs in the tree. If the user enters her ID, Novell will automatically be able to log her in, because it can determine from the catalog what her context should be. For more information on how to set up this service, refer to the documentation that comes with your version of NetWare.

ZENworks and the Novell Client

One very powerful feature of Novell that is possible to take advantage of only if you use the Novell Client is ZENworks. In concept, ZENworks is much like the Citrix Program Neighborhood. Instead of publishing applications using Citrix administrative tools, however, you can publish them by assigning them to the user using the NetWare Administrator.

For administrators who are using Terminal Server only, and therefore cannot take advantage of published applications, ZENworks can provide a useful alternative. You can set up your Terminal Server clients so that they run the ZENworks client when they log on. The ZENworks client will query the NDS directory to determine what applications are assigned to the user and present the icons to those applications within the ZENworks window.

In addition to application publishing-like features, ZENworks has the capability to push down both user-specific and machine-specific policies and Registry changes. You can use this capability, instead of using Windows 2000 group policy objects, to help lock down users' desktops and handle other functionality normally available only through policies.

Using the Gateway and Client Services for NetWare

Although the Novell NetWare Client is the preferred way to connect to your NetWare servers, if you need the full set of functionality available from Novell, you can still attach to NetWare using the Gateway and Client

Services for NetWare from Microsoft instead. Although you cannot do the following things using this client, you can map drives to NetWare volumes and attach to NetWare printers:

- **No support for the NDS API** This means that various software such as Novell's GroupWise email package and the NetWare Administrator will not work from your Terminal Server.

- **Limited Explorer integration** With the full Novell Client, you can browse the objects in the NetWare trees on the network, perform searches for NetWare objects, and even perform advanced NetWare administration tasks from within Explorer. These capabilities are not available if you choose to use the Microsoft Gateway and Client Services for NetWare. However, you still will be able to attach to Novell volumes and printers from Explorer.

Installing the Gateway and Client Services for NetWare

To install the Gateway and Client Services for NetWare on a Windows NT 4.0 Terminal Server, follow these steps:

1. Open the Network Control Panel (Control Panel, Network) and select the Services tab.

2. Click the Add button on the Services tab to add a new service.

3. In the Select Network Service window, highlight Gateway (and Client) Services for NetWare, and click OK.

4. Enter the path to your Terminal Server CD-ROM's install directory in the Windows NT Setup window.

5. After the file install has finished, click Yes to shut down and restart.

6. The server will now reboot. When it comes back up, the Gateway and Client Services for NetWare will be started.

To set up Gateway and Client Services for NetWare on a Windows 2000 Terminal Server, follow these steps:

1. Open the Local Area Network connection from the Start menu, Settings, Network and Dial-Up Connections folder.

2. Click the Install button to add a new client.

3. Select Client and click Add.

4. Select the Gateway (and Client) Services for NetWare and then click OK.

5. Enter the preferred NetWare server and tree.

6. Reboot the server.

Setting Preferred Server or Default Tree

One important feature of the client is that it keeps track of NetWare settings separately for each user. In this way, two different users can log on to Terminal Server, each with a different preferred server or tree.

The disadvantage of this feature is that each user will be prompted for the preferred server or default tree that he wants to attach to the first time he logs on to Terminal Server. For users who are not NetWare-aware, this prompt will be confusing. If you have a small number of users, you might choose just to reset their passwords, log on to the server as each user, and set their NetWare parameters manually. After these parameters have been set, the users will not be prompted for them again. If you opt instead to have users enter the information based on written or verbal instructions, you can double-check that the parameters they enter are correct by running the Registry Editor (REGEDT32) and viewing the following Registry key:

```
HKLM\System\CurrentControlSet\Services\NWCWorkstation\Parameters\Option\
[User SID]
```

A SID entry under the Option key will be created as each user logs on and sets the NetWare parameters for the first time. Under the User SID key will be values for PreferredServer, LogonScript, and PrintOption. Out of these values, the PreferredServer value is of most interest. If the user chooses a preferred server, this value will be set to its name. If instead the user chooses a default tree and context, PreferredServer will be set to *[Tree Name]\ [Context]. Notice the preceding asterisk. This differentiates it from a preferred server.

This Registry key also can be handy to know if you need to change your server's name or a tree or container name in the future.

Mapping Drives to NetWare Servers

After you've authenticated with the NetWare server or tree, you can map drives in the same manner as you would with Windows NT servers and shares. Terminal Server looks at NetWare servers as servers with volumes, as opposed to Windows NT servers, which are viewed as servers with shares. There are three primary methods for mapping drive letters to NetWare: manual mappings using Explorer, mappings through the NetWare login script using the map command, and mappings using the built-in net use command.

Mapping NetWare Drives Using Explorer

Mapping NetWare drives using Explorer is similar to mapping drives to Windows NT shares, with one important difference—You can map-root a network drive to any directory in a NetWare volume, whereas with NT shares you can map-root a drive only to the root of the share itself. Map-rooting a drive makes it much easier to hide the complexities of the directory structure from the user. To map-root a drive letter to a directory on a NetWare volume, just follow these steps:

1. Run Explorer. (Go to the Start menu and choose Programs, Windows NT Explorer.)

2. Click the NetWare server you want to map to in Network Neighborhood; then go to the volume and directory you want.

3. Right-click and select Map Network Drive.

4. Select the drive letter you want to map-root to the selected directory and check whether you want to have the drive automatically reconnected at logon.

Mapping Drives Through the NetWare Logon Script

One advantage of mapping drives through the NetWare logon script is that you can create both search drives and standard mappings. To map a search drive to a server, add the following line to your NetWare login script:

```
MAP INSERT S1:=[Server]/[Volume]:\[Directory]
```

This drive will automatically be added to your search path and be available from the command prompt.

This might be self-explanatory for most NetWare administrators, but what you might not realize is that you also can easily incorporate mappings to Windows NT servers and shares in your NetWare logon script using the following syntax:

```
#NET USE [Drive letter]: \\[NT server name]\[Share name]
```

The leading pound sign (#) means to treat this as an external command.

By incorporating both the map root and net use statements into your NetWare logon script, you can fully control all your drive mappings from one central location.

Mapping Drives Through the *net use* Command

The syntax for the `net use` command for mapping drives to NetWare volumes is as follows:

```
NET USE [Drive letter]: \\[NetWare server name]\[Volume name]\[Directory]
```

Remember that the `net use` command will map-root the drive letter to that directory.

Printing to NetWare Printers

In many Novell NetWare environments, network administrators choose to set up their print queues on the Novell servers rather than on the Windows servers. This is fully supported by Terminal Server and Citrix MetaFrame, whether you choose to use the Novell Client, or if you use Gateway and Client Services for NetWare from Microsoft. In addition, printer auto-creation works in the same manner, even if clients are running the Novell Client and using printers on Novell servers.

Novell Directory Print Services and Terminal Server

Novell Directory Print Services (NDPS) is an advanced feature available in Novell NetWare 4.x and above. Using NDPS you can assign printers and print queues to users using the Novell NetWare Administrator tool. When those users log on to their workstations, those printers can be set up to be created automatically and the drivers installed automatically. This feature is only possible, however, if you are using the Novell Client.

In a Terminal Server environment, you need to be very careful with this feature because it can cause problems with printer auto-creation. In addition, the drivers that are pushed down to users on Terminal Server might not be compatible with Terminal Server. For this reason, it is highly recommended not to install NDPS support during the installation of the Novell Client. To control this, make sure you do a custom install of the client and remove the check mark next to NDPS in the list of components. If the client is already installed, you can remove the NDPPNT.DLL from the `%systemroot%\` `system32` folder on the server to disable NDPS functionality.

Printing from DOS to NetWare Print Queues

The easiest ways to print to a NetWare printer from a DOS-based program is to either capture a port to the printer in the logon script or use `net use` command. To capture a port in the logon script, add the following command to it:

```
#capture q=[queue name] l=[lpt port number]
```

This is the standard Novell NetWare `capture` command. This command will capture all output from the LPT port number you specified to the queue. For more information on the available settings, refer to your NetWare manual. Although the `capture` command will work from the logon script, you might have problems running it from the command prompt.

Here's the second way to capture your LPT ports to a NetWare print queue using the `net use` command:

```
NET USE LPT[n]: \\[NetWare Server Name]\[Queue name]
```

This command will map the queue to the port you specified. As with the `net use` command shown previously, if you want to add this command to your NetWare logon script, put a pound sign (#) in front of it.

NDS for NT

If you have a primarily NetWare NDS network with only a handful of Windows NT 4.0 servers, and if none of your Terminal Servers are PDCs or BDCs, NDS for NT might be a solution worth looking into. NDS for NT enables you to bring all the users from a Windows NT domain into the NDS tree. This centralizes your NT management by enabling you to control both NT and NetWare users with the NetWare Administrator tool. Although you won't learn how to install this product here, you will learn how it works.

NDS for NT works through authentication redirection. Normally when you log on to Terminal Server, Terminal Server authenticates with the domain by sending an encrypted logon request to either the domain's PDC or a BDC. This request will be handled at the PDC or BDC by SAMSRV.DLL. This .DLL takes the username and password hash and matches it against the username and password hash in the domain database. If they match, the user is then logged on to the server and receives the rights to the domain resources that have been assigned.

NDS for NT, on the other hand, replaces SAMSRV.DLL with its own version of the .DLL. This version authenticates with NDS rather than with the Windows NT user database. In this way, all NT authentications on that domain are redirected to the NDS tree.

For more information on the features of the NDS for NT product and how to integrate it with your network, go to `www.novell.com`.

Connecting to MetaFrame by Using IPX/SPX

The IPX protocol is commonly found on many Novell NetWare networks. Although TCP/IP is now fully supported by Novell, many shops still need to support IPX/SPX for backward compatibility. Citrix MetaFrame fully supports IPX/SPX connections to the server from IPX/SPX clients. This section discusses some of the details of how IPX/SPX works in a Citrix MetaFrame environment and how to set up a connection to a Citrix server using IPX/SPX.

Browsing for Citrix Services Using IPX/SPX

A MetaFrame server advertises itself on an IPX/SPX network by using the *Service Advertising Protocol* (SAP). With SAP, each type of service available on a network uses a unique SAP number to advertise itself. MetaFrame uses SAP number 0x83D.

When you set up an ICA client using the IPX/SPX protocol, and browse for the list of servers or applications available on the network, the client will query the network looking for this SAP number. Being able to select the server from this browse list is important. If you are not able to select it from the browse list, you will need to enter the exact IPX network address for the server, as shown in the following section.

As long as your network is set up so that the SAP list reaches the remote site's router, you should be able to see the MetaFrame server from the remote ICA client's browse list across a WAN connection. Many times network engineers block certain SAPs on the routers to reduce WAN traffic. If this is the case, you must ensure that SAP 0x83D is let through.

The Importance of IPX/SPX Frame Type

If you still cannot browse the MetaFrame servers when setting up a new entry at the client, you can try a few additional techniques. First, make sure you are using the same frame type. By default, MetaFrame attempts to auto-detect the frame type of the network to which it is attached. If it does not sense a frame type, MetaFrame uses frame type 802.2. It also can be manually set for other IPX/SPX frames, such as 802.3 and Ethernet II, in the Network Control Panel, on Windows NT 4.0, as follows:

1. Open the Network Control Panel from the Start menu, Settings, Control Panel.
2. Click the Protocol tab in the Network window.
3. Highlight NWLink IPX/SPX Compatible Transport under the Protocol tab and click the Properties button.
4. In the NWLink IPX/SPX Properties window that appears, select Manual Frame Type Detection and click Add. The Manual Frame Detection window appears.

5. Select the frame type that you want to bind to the server, enter the IPX network number for that frame type, and click OK to return to the NWLink IPX/SPX Properties window. The frame type you selected is shown in the Frame Type list in this window.

6. If you want to bind more frame types to the server, click the Add button and repeat step 5; otherwise, click OK.

7. Click Close from the Network window to finish binding the new IPX frame types to the server.

8. Shut down and restart the server.

On a Windows 2000 Server, do the following to change the frame type:

1. Open the Local Area Network connection from the Start menu, Settings, Network and Dial-Up Connections folder.

2. Select the NWLink IPX/SPX Protocol and click Properties.

3. From the Properties window, select Manual Frame Type and then add the frame type you need (see Figure 25.1).

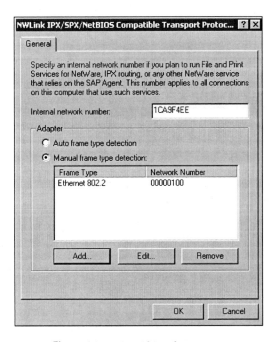

Figure 25.1   Specifying frame type.

To double-check the frame type being used at the MetaFrame server, run the `ipxroute config` command from the command prompt. Running this command displays the information in Listing 25.1.

Listing 25.1 **Running** *ipxroute*

```
c:> ipxroute config
NWLink IPX Routing and Source Routing Control Program v2.00
net 1: network number 00000000, frame type 802.2, device IEEPRO1 (00aa00a13711)
```

Note that this command shows not only all bound frame types, but also the IPX network number (0) and the MAC address of the card (00aa00a13711).

Windows clients generally use 802.2, by default, unless they detect another frame type on the network. The method of checking which frame type is selected varies with each type of client. If you are using Windows 95/98, you can check the frame type that is selected in the Network Control Panel under the Advanced Properties for the IPX/SPX protocol. A setting of Auto means that the client will auto-detect the protocol on the network. If you have a Novell server on the network using 802.3, Windows 95 chooses 802.3. If the MetaFrame server is running only 802.2, you will not be able to see the frame type. To get around these problems, change either the server or client to the same frame type.

Specifying Servers by the IPX/SPX Address

If you are still having a problem bringing up the list of MetaFrame servers, try entering the IPX/SPX address directly when setting up the connection at the ICA client.

The IPX/SPX address of the server is formatted as `[network number]:` `[MAC address]`. You can get this address by using the `ipxroute config` command. For the server in Listing 25.1, you would enter `0:00AA00A13711` in the Server field when setting up the ICA client connection. On a Windows 2000 server, you can use the same `ipxroute config` command to determine the address; however, look for the Network and Node Address next to Local Area Connection, as shown in Listing 25.2.

Listing 25.2 **Running** *ipxroute* **on 2000**

```
C:\Documents and Settings\tharwood>ipxroute config
NWLink IPX Routing and Source Routing Control Program v2.00
Num  Name                        Network    Node          Frame
==================================================================
0.   Internal                    1ca9f4ee   000000000001   [None ]
1.   IpxLoopbackAdapter          1ca9f4ee   000000000002   [802.2]
2.   Local Area Connection       00000000   0060083e2ebf   [802.2]
3.   {C2104951-62F5-4EB5-80F2-   00000000   444553544200   [802.2]
4.   NDISWANIPX                  00000000   96ef20524153   [EthII]
```

26

Disaster Recovery Techniques and Enhancing Reliability

As your Terminal Server farm grows, so does its importance to the business. In this chapter you will learn about the many ways to ensure the reliability and recoverability of your server farm.

The chapter starts with coverage of the options available for disaster recovery. You then learn how to set up your servers and clients to fail-over in a disaster scenario. Finally, you learn about the many specific techniques for enhancing the reliability of your server farm.

Disaster Recovery Planning

Disasters happen. A disaster can range from a temporary power failure or network failure to your building, to a full-blown natural disaster such as a hurricane, tornado, or earthquake that can shut down your main data center for an indefinite period of time. Although these disasters might adversely affect your business and the business of those around, business itself still goes on. For companies whose systems support customers around the country or around the world, it is very important that those systems' services remain available even in the event of disaster. The following sections discuss some of the many ways to build redundancy into your Terminal Server or Citrix MetaFrame solution, so that it is available in case of disaster.

Backing Up the Data Center

The first step in planning for disaster recovery is choosing where the backup data center will be. When choosing the location, realize that you need to consider several factors. The backup data center should meet all the following criteria:

- **Remotely accessible**   This is a very important criteria. In the event of disaster, your key personnel might be responding to personal issues or might not be able to travel to the backup data center. For this reason there must be easy remote access to the data center so that key personnel can access and manage the backup equipment remotely to handle any necessary reconfiguration.

- **Ease of voice communication**   Not only should you be able to easily make a data connection to the disaster recovery center, but there also should be sufficient phone lines and phones so that voice communication is easy.

- **Sufficient workspace**   Your disaster recovery center should have sufficient workspace so that the key staff who will be bringing up the backup systems have a place in which to work.

- **Reliable and appropriate facilities**   It is important to ensure that the backup data center has sufficient power and cooling capacity to handle the additional backup equipment that might be necessary. The backup data center should have an *uninterruptible power supply* (UPS) with generator backup for power. In addition, sufficient space and capacity must be available to handle any extra equipment that might need to be set up.

- **Close proximity to parts warehouses**   This is an important criterion, but an often-overlooked one. Check with your server vendor to find out what the closest parts depot is for that area. In many cases you should contract with that vendor to ensure that sufficient parts will be available in case of disaster. When choosing a location for your backup data center, make sure that you choose a location near a major city where it will be easier to obtain parts quickly.

Building a Corporate Disaster Recovery Center

For corporations with multiple locations that can support a data center, the best and least expensive disaster recovery solution is most often to set up a disaster recovery center at one of the remote locations. Suppose, for example, that your main data center is in Boston, Massachusetts. Suppose further that you have large offices in Denver, Colorado and in Austin, Texas. Instead of attempting to outsource the data center to a third party, make use of your existing offices as a backup data center to your main office's data center.

This approach is one of the best approaches for many reasons. First, you can make use of existing office space that you are already paying for. Second, the remote office already has employees who can assist or be trained to assist in any disaster recovery scenario. Third, you do not have to pay for special wide area network circuits that are used only in a disaster. Instead, the existing wide area network connection to the remote data center would be used in case of disaster.

Using NFuse as a Disaster Recovery Solution

Many people do not realize the importance of NFuse in disaster recovery. Using NFuse, you can create a "virtual workplace" anywhere you have an NFuse server and some Citrix MetaFrame servers. You can provide this virtual workplace to anyone who can connect to the NFuse server and has a web browser. In a disaster scenario, NFuse can be a critical part of your backup solution.

Suppose, for example, that a fire occurs at your main data center and takes out most of the equipment at the center. You have already set up a backup *disaster recovery center* (DRC) at an alternative location. At the DRC you have an NFuse web server, a couple of Citrix MetaFrame servers, a dial-in modem bank, and a backup set of your mission-critical data servers. Because you have set up access to your key corporate applications on the NFuse web server, the key people involved in the disaster recovery can easily connect. They just have to dial in to the modems at the DRC and establish a connection to these applications by just using their web browser and going to the NFuse web page. From this web page, they have access to all of their applications.

One big advantage of this solution is centralized control. Instead of having to reconfigure applications on users' workstations to point to the machines at the DRC, you have complete central control of the applications with NFuse because they are running on your Citrix MetaFrame. If you need to change the IP address that an application uses to point to the disaster recovery server for that application, for example, you can easily and quickly make the change on the disaster recovery Citrix MetaFrame servers.

In addition, by centrally changing the DNS entries that point to your NFuse web site, you can seamlessly switch users over from pointing to the address of the NFuse server at the destroyed data center to the backup NFuse server at the DRC. Suppose, for example, that your users access your primary NFuse web site at `http://nfuse.acme.com`. This hostname points to the address of the NFuse server at your corporate location. In the case of disaster, you switch the DNS entry for `http://nfuse.acme.com` to point to your backup NFuse server at the DRC. Users do not even notice the change because they are going to the same web address as they were before the disaster was declared.

One other important feature for disaster recovery available in NFuse 1.6 is the ability to bring together a user's applications from multiple farms into the same application list. This enables you to set up a backup server farm at a remote location. In the scenario where you have a backup NFuse server at a DRC location and backup Citrix MetaFrame servers, you could put those servers on a separate farm. You could then configure NFuse to pull the application list for users from both the primary server farm and the backup server farm. In case of disaster, users would use the icons for the applications on the backup server farm.

Outsourcing the Backup Data Center

If your business is highly centralized and the remote locations cannot serve as a data center, or if you have only one large location, you should consider outsourcing your backup data center needs. Many companies either specialize in offering backup data center solutions or have an offering available. Often you will find that larger hardware vendors, such as IBM and Compaq, have facilities that can handle this need. For companies that have a large number of the same vendor's hardware, check with that vendor to see whether it offers a backup data center solution.

In addition, many large communication and web-hosting companies also have a backup data center solution. The advantage of going with a disaster recovery solution from a company such as this is the abundance of data lines available. This can be a strong advantage for businesses that rely heavily on data connections, such as Internet businesses.

Backing Up the Hardware and the Data

As part of the decision about where your backup data center will be located, you need to determine how you will back up your hardware and your data. The goal is to be able to recover as quickly as possible from a disaster on a backup set of systems and data. However, the shorter the acceptable downtime window, the more expensive the backup solution will be. The following are some possible solutions, from the most expensive to the least expensive:

- **Full hardware backup and full data replication** If there is absolutely no window for downtime, this is the solution you need. For this solution to work, you must have a complete replica of your hardware at a remote location. In addition you must have a very high speed network connection between your main location and the remote location. Across this connection all transactions are replicated. In the event of a major failure at your main location, the systems should be designed to fail-over to the backup location. The biggest disadvantage with this solution is the enormous costs of having to purchase double the hardware and having to lease a highly expensive data line for the backup.

- **Partial hardware backup and full data replication** In this scenario, you have backup of only your most critical hardware at the remote location or have hardware with less capacity. Although full data replication still takes place, if a disaster were declared certain business functions would have to be scaled back or eliminated during the recovery period. This solution is much less expensive and a good alternative for many companies. You can still recover the most critical aspects of your business quickly; however, periphery functionality might not be available for a large period of time.

- **Partial or full hardware backup and offsite data storage** In this scenario you have a backup data center with hardware in place; however, data is not replicated. In a disaster, offsite data tapes would be sent to the backup center and restored. Downtime could be one or two days while this process was completed. This scenario is the least expensive and a good solution for many companies that can withstand this length of downtime.

Backing Up the Communications

The final step in planning the disaster recovery solution is planning how to restore communications. This is a critical component, especially with a Terminal Server solution because Terminal Servers are often used remotely. The following are some possible alternatives:

- **Partial mesh Frame Relay** In a partial mesh Frame Relay scenario, you build a connection from each remote site to the main data center and then a backup connection to the backup data center. If the main data center fails, the routers automatically switch communication to the backup data center. Many companies choose to have an additional backup Frame Relay connection to the main data center that travels through a different path or through a different carrier.

- **ISDN or analog dial backup**   With ISDN dial backup, each site has both a Frame Relay connection and an ISDN or analog connection. In this scenario, if the Frame Relay link to the main data center fails, the ISDN line is set to restore the connection by dialing an ISDN line at the main data center. If this fails, it can be set to dial the backup data center instead. The disadvantage of this solution is the high cost of long-distance ISDN. Dialing from a remote location using ISDN is normally charged at the same rate as making a long-distance call from the remote location. You need to compare this cost to the cost of a backup Frame Relay circuit.

ISDN as a Backup Solution

ISDN is one of the best backup solutions available today for many reasons. First, it is an alternative technology to Frame Relay. If you use Frame Relay to back up your Frame Relay, you are using a single technology, a single set of switches in many cases, and a single physical connection to your communication equipment. If this connection fails from a power surge or lightning strike, you have lost both your primary and secondary Frame Relay connections. By using an alternative communication technology, such as ISDN or analog dialup, you help ensure that you can recover from a failure of your main communication. Lightning strikes and power surges are relatively common sources of communication failure.

In addition, it is important to realize the flexibility you can achieve with ISDN. Not only can you set a remote ISDN router to dial any ISDN router nationwide, but you also can bond multiple ISDN connections together for higher speed. This means you can provide near instantaneous backup to any wide area network data connection regardless of the speed needed. This would enable you, for example, to establish a high-speed ISDN dialup to a backup data center in case of disaster. You would then have to pay only for your usage of the ISDN during the time of disaster, instead of having to pay the recurring costs for a leased line to the disaster recovery center. You also could easily dial in to another disaster recovery center if the need arose.

Measuring Reliability

One issue that you face with any steps you take to improve reliability is measuring the level of reliability on your network. Measuring reliability can be a tricky endeavor because reliability is hard to define. Because of the high costs of making systems more reliable, however, it is important to be able to justify to upper management that those funds are being effectively used.

Unfortunately, in the corporate world the perception of reliability is more important than the actual reliability of your systems. To measure this perception, you need to look at the services that your systems provide from a user's perspective. Users do not care about the technical details of how applications are run on your server farm; they just care about getting reliable access to the application, so that they can get their work done.

To measure reliability, you first need to make a list of the general services that your systems provide to users and for whom those services are provided. You can consider each application running on your Citrix MetaFrame server farm as a service provided to the user community. Put this list in a simple spreadsheet for easy reference. If you provide a large number of services, divide the list of services into different categories. Remember that this is a list of services and not servers. It is more important to upper-level management to speak in terms of services provided rather than to cover the details of what servers run what services. The following are some example services for Windows environments:

- Sales reporting on Citrix MetaFrame
- Accounting application on Citrix MetaFrame
- Email services from Exchange
- Office applications on Citrix MetaFrame

Now for each of these services, decide what the window of availability needs to be. For most services, you can either assign a window of availability of 24×7 or 12×5 (8 a.m. to 8 p.m., Monday through Friday).

These services are the ones that users care about and are the ones for which you need to ensure the reliability. Always remember to look at things from this service-oriented view. If a hardware failure causes you to lose a Citrix MetaFrame server, your users and upper-level management first concern is which services are lost. If your users automatically switched over to a backup server that was load managed with the lost server, the actual loss of service is very insignificant.

Now that you have a list of services, you need to prioritize those services and define different outage levels. The following is one suggested definition of outage levels that you can use:

- **Level 1**   A level 1 outage is one where all access is lost to multiple business-critical systems. This level of outage is characterized by widespread inability for users to work for extended periods of time. An example of this type of outage would be a major WAN or LAN failure, or complete failure of name resolution on the network.

- **Level 2**   A level 2 outage is an outage experienced in one or more business-critical systems for extended periods of time. This is a less serious outage than a level 1 outage. However, a level 2 outage means that one or more large groups of users are prevented from performing a business-critical function while the outage is in effect. Examples of this type of outage include failure of the primary Exchange server, failure of a WAN connection to a particular warehouse site, failure of the Internet connection, and failure of one or more Citrix MetaFrame servers.

- **Level 3** A level 3 outage is an outage characterized by either repeated loss of access to business-critical systems over a short period of time, degraded ability to access those systems, or a failure of one or more components within those systems. An example of a level 3 outage is the failure of the Print Spooler service on a Citrix MetaFrame server, degraded performance caused by an over-utilized WAN connection, failure of a WAN connection to a small site, or a major email virus outbreak in Exchange.

Now that you have clearly defined what an outage is and what services need to be tracked for outages, it is time to set up an outage tracking spreadsheet to start recording any outages when they occur. Remember that an outage is only an outage if it occurs during the window of availability for the system. If one of your Citrix MetaFrame servers fails in the middle of the night, but you are able to fix it by morning before users need to use it, the outage does not need to be recorded. Only those outages that affect users need to be recorded in the outage tracking spreadsheet. In this spreadsheet, you should record the outage level, the service name affected, the date and time of the start of the outage, the length of the outage in hours, and a description of the outage.

Using the information in this spreadsheet, you can easily and accurately calculate the reliability of the services that your systems provide. If there was no outage that affected any user of the Great Plains application running on your Citrix MetaFrame servers for the month of September, for instance, you could say that the reliability of this application was 100 percent. If the application was down for an entire hour because a drive failed on one of your servers, however, the reliability is less than 100 percent. In this case, the window of availability is supposed to be 12×5, which means there are roughly 240 (12 hours × 5 days per week × 4 weeks in a month) hours that the application needs to be in service a month. Because the application was available 239 of those 240 hours, just divide 239 by 240 to get an application uptime percentage of 99.58.

Using the information in the outage tracking spreadsheet, you can create periodic reports on the reliability of your systems. It is important to ensure that you always measure reliability from a user's perspective. If you fixed an outage within an hour, but you did not send the message out to users that they could reconnect until another hour later, the perceived outage is two hours, not one.

Reliability and Disaster Recovery Tips

The following are some of the many steps you can take to enhance the reliability and recoverability of your Terminal Server solution.

Terminal Server Disaster Recovery Tips

Even though Terminal Servers alone do not include many disaster recovery features, you can take several steps to help enhance their reliability and recoverability.

Use Network Load Balancing

Although you cannot perform automatic load balancing in Terminal Server, as you can with Citrix MetaFrame XPa and XPe, you can use Microsoft's Network Load Balancing to provide some level of redundancy. Network Load Balancing is a feature that is available only in Windows 2000 Advanced Server. Using Network Load Balancing, you can set up multiple Terminal Servers that share a single IP address. If one server fails, users will automatically be redirected to the remaining servers. This solution is covered in detail in Chapter 27, "Network Load Balancing for NFuse and Terminal Servers."

DNS Round-Robin

DNS round-robin is a load-sharing solution that uses a special mechanism in DNS to distribute incoming requests for Terminal Server. Basically the way it works is you create one DNS hostname for your Terminal Servers with multiple IP addresses. You then set up the Terminal Services clients to use this hostname to connect. When the client queries the DNS server for the IP address of the Terminal Server, the DNS server will respond with the next available address in sequence. The disadvantage with this technique is that if one server goes down, it will have to be manually removed from the DNS list. If not, incoming requests will still be directed to the down server.

On most DNS servers, setting up round-robin is just a matter of adding multiple host entries with the same name but different IP addresses. The following instructions cover how to setup DNS round-robin with Windows 2000 DNS:

1. Open the DNS management tool from the Administrative Tools folder in the Start menu.

2. Right-click the domain you want to add the host entry to and select Add Host.

3. Add the common hostname for your Terminal Server (for instance, **ACMETS1**) and then the IP address of the first server. Then click OK.

4. Right-click the domain again and select to add the host entry.

5. Enter the same hostname as in step 3 (that is, **ACMETS1**), but specify the IP address of another Terminal Server.

6. On client workstations, use the fully qualified hostname as the address for the Terminal Server (for instance, Acmets1.acmecorp.com).

Other Terminal Server Tips

The following are some of many things you can do to help improve the reliability of your Terminal Servers:

- **Separate data from applications.** This recommendation has been given often throughout this book and is very important. For the highest level of reliability and for quick recoverability, always store your data centrally and not on your Terminal Servers. Users' home directories, profiles, and application data should be centralized and not on your Terminal Servers.

- **Use server-imaging technologies.** Imaging your servers is a great way to ensure that they can be restored quickly. If you do not store data on your servers and use them only for applications, after they are set up little will change on them. After you have your servers installed with all the applications needed, take an image of them. If any server fails, you can get it back up quickly just by restoring the image.

- **Cluster data storage.** Although you cannot cluster Terminal Servers, you can cluster data storage. Both Microsoft SQL Server and file and print services can be clustered. This is another reason why it is important not to store data on Terminal Server. If you store it centrally, as the data becomes more critical you can cluster the data so that if one of the data servers fails, the other will pick up automatically.

- **Set up server and network monitoring.** Monitoring your servers and the network carefully is very important for ensuring the reliability of your Terminal Server solution. For more information on how to set this up, see Chapter 24, "Advanced Network Management and Monitoring."

- **Use more smaller servers rather than fewer larger servers.** This is a very important design philosophy. When you are determining how many Terminal Servers you need to meet a certain requirement, it is greatly preferred to use more servers with less capacity each. Although this is almost always more expensive, it buys a great amount of reliability and flexibility, which is important in many situations. For example, instead of purchasing a single 4-processor server to handle 100 users, purchase 2 dual-processor servers. Even if one of the dual-processor servers completely fails, you can handle at least part of the user load on the other server. If the 4-processor server bites the dust, none of your users can work.

- **Standardize on the latest service packs and hotfixes.** It is not only important to ensure your servers have the latest service packs, but it is also very important to ensure they are all at the same service pack level. If you run into any unusual issues on your servers and need technical support, the first question they will ask is what service pack level you are running. If the service pack level varies across your servers, they might want you to standardize the service pack level before they will help resolve the problem.

- **Schedule reboot.** Rebooting your servers on either a daily or weekly basis is highly recommended for many reasons, depending on the applications and services you have loaded. Rebooting a server will clear out server memory and system temp files, in addition to resetting system processes. Often you might want to run a special cleanup batch file as part of the reboot to help clean up application directories and system directories as part of the reboot process. The scheduling tools now available with Windows 2000 make it very easy to either run a batch file or just the `shutdown` command at a scheduled time. To schedule a shutdown, just add the following scheduled task from Control Panel, Scheduled Tasks: `tsshutdn /server:[server name] /reboot`. Notice that using this command you can schedule the shutdown of remote servers. This enables you to control all of your server shutdowns from a single server, which is easier to set up.

Citrix MetaFrame Disaster Recovery and Reliability Tips

Citrix MetaFrame offers a large number of features that are useful when planning for disaster recovery and enhancing the reliability of your solution. The following is a list of some of the most common tips:

- **Use Load management.** Load management is available in MetaFrame XPa and XPe and is by far the number one way to ensure the reliability of your Citrix MetaFrame server farm. If one server in a load-managed solution fails, the other servers will automatically pick up the users. Although users who were connected to the server that failed will have to reconnect, the farm will automatically direct them to the next most available server for the application. In addition, load balancing makes server maintenance significantly easier. If you run into a problem with one server or need to perform an update, you can just remove that server from the load-balancing group while you are doing the maintenance. For more information on how to set up load balancing, see Chapter 15, "Application Publishing and Load Management with Citrix MetaFrame."

- **Use SQL data store.** Using either a Microsoft SQL data store or an Oracle data store is greatly preferred over using Access for both reasons of performance and reliability. If you are currently using an Access data store, you can use the `dsmaint` command to move the data store to either Microsoft SQL or Oracle. For more information on how to do this, see Citrix technical article CTX773628.

- **Back up your data store daily.** It is very important to add the data store to your backup scheme. The data store is a critical piece of your server farm. If you are using a SQL or Oracle data store, you will need to either use special backup agents to back up the databases correctly or use their built-in backup software to back up the databases locally. If you are using an Access data store, you can use the `dsmaint backup [destination path]` command in a scheduled batch file to back up the data store periodically. This performs a clean backup of the data store. At this point, you can back up the data store backup to tape for restoration later.

- **Apply service packs evenly.** Always apply Citrix MetaFrame service packs to all servers in the farm, instead of just one server at a time. This is very important for reliability because service packs often make significant changes to farm functionality. If you apply a service pack to one server only, it might not communicate correctly with the other servers in the farm.

- **Manage change well.** It is critical to strictly manage changes to your server farm. If possible, set up a test Citrix MetaFrame server farm where you can test any changes or test applications before making those changes in a production environment.

- **Document well.** Good documentation is critical, not only for the ongoing upkeep of your server farm but also the recoverability. You should document all steps taken during the installation of applications on your server farm, especially special steps that need to be taken to secure an application or tweak application performance. This document should have enough information to rebuild your Citrix MetaFrame server farm and reinstall all the applications from scratch. To ensure consistent server setup, you also should create a checklist of the important security- and performance-related steps that you take on each server after it has been installed.

- **Use NFuse for disaster recovery.**   NFuse can make for a great disaster recovery solution. One of the biggest advantages of setting up a disaster recovery NFuse web site is that you can centrally control the configuration. This enables you to easily adjust for necessary changes, such as changes to IP addresses that often happen when users switch over to a disaster recovery center for access to their systems.

- **Set up backup server groups in Program Neighborhood.**   One alternative to using NFuse for disaster recovery is using the disaster recovery features built in to the Program Neighborhood. When setting up an application set in Program Neighborhood, you can specify a backup server group. You can point this backup server group to the addresses of your servers at the disaster recovery center. If the client cannot connect to the primary servers, it will attempt to connect to the backup servers instead to list the applications available.

- **Use DNS hostnames.**   Using DNS hostnames is a good idea, as long as you have taken steps to set up a redundant DNS system. The advantage of using DNS hostnames when configuring your Citrix ICA clients is that the hostnames can easily be switched to a disaster recovery Citrix MetaFrame server just by switching the hostname. By default, newer versions of the ICA client will automatically search for a server by the hostname of `ica.[domain name]`. You could build on this functionality also by creating hostnames in DNS for backup Citrix MetaFrame servers. If the domain name for your company is acme.com, for example, you could configure the server list with the following addresses: `ica.acme.com`, `ica2.acme.com`, `ica-drc.acme.com`, and `192.168.10.200` (IP address of `ica-drc.acme.com`). When the client attempts to connect to the application set, it would first try to resolve `ica.acme.com`. If that server was not available, it would try `ica2` and then `ica-drc`. If DNS was down, it would use the IP address instead.

Disaster Recovery Kit

Creating a disaster recovery kit is an important part of your administrative arsenal. If your Terminal Server ever goes down, you need to be prepared to quickly bring it back to life. The *disaster recovery kit* (DRK) will help you do this by providing you with the critical information you need to restore your server. The DRK can additionally serve as an administrative and troubleshooting tool for your server.

Creating the Disaster Recovery Kit

The best time to create your DRK is while you are installing Terminal Server. It is critical to record such information as license key codes, hardware configuration, and installation notes, so that you are prepared if you ever have to reinstall your server quickly in the future. The DRK is intended to serve this purpose and more.

The DRK can take many forms, depending on what you find the most useful for your environment. You could keep all the information in the DRK in electronic form on your local drive or on the drive of another server on the network. You also could print out all the information for the DRK and keep it in a binder in safe storage.

No matter which option you choose, it is important to gather sufficient information to quickly rebuild your server from scratch.

Gathering Server Information

Out of all the information you will be gathering, detailed server information is perhaps the most critical. Included with Terminal Server is an often-over-looked utility for gathering server information: the Windows NT Diagnostics program. With the Windows NT Diagnostics program, you can gather all the following information into either a printed report or text file:

- **Version**   Provides version information, including to whom Terminal Server is registered, the product number, and the service pack level.

- **System**   Includes the loaded HAL, system processors, processor speed, and BIOS version.

- **Display**   Provides information on the current resolution, VGA BIOS version, display adapter, and display drivers.

- **Drives**   Shows the total and free space of all system drives.

- **Memory**   Provides a large variety of information on memory, including total memory and memory available.

- **Services**   Lists the services and device drivers that are currently loaded.

- **Resources**   Shows the system resources currently being taken, including I/O ports, IRQs, DMAs, and memory ranges.

- **Environment**   Displays both the user and system environment variable settings.

- **Network**   Provides detailed network information, including logon domain, workstation name, protocols loaded, network adapter MAC addresses, network statistics, and network settings.

To create a report on your server with the Windows NT Diagnostics program, follow these steps:

1. Run the Windows NT Diagnostics program from Start menu by selecting Programs, Administrative Tools.

2. In the Windows NT Diagnostic program main window, click Print. The Create Report window appears.

3. In the Create Report window, select All Tabs under Scope. Selecting All Tabs creates a report with all the information listed previously.

4. Select Complete under Detail Level to create as detailed a report as possible on your server.

5. Select either File, Clipboard, or Default Printer under Destination, depending on the media format in which you want the report.

6. Click OK to create the report.

Besides the Windows NT Diagnostics program, server manufacturers often make utilities available for gathering server information. Compaq, for one, makes a survey utility for gathering detailed information on their servers. This utility is freely available on their web site (www.compaq.com). The survey utility can generate a report with Compaq-specific information, such as the model of all installed Compaq components, which is lacking in reports from the Windows NT Diagnostic program.

Application Installation

Because of the unique manner in which applications are installed on Terminal Server, it is important to maintain good records of their installation techniques. These records will help in both the administration and troubleshooting of your server. They also will make it easier for you to delegate server responsibilities, such as setting up new users with applications. The following is a list of some of the pertinent information you should keep on the applications installed on your server:

- Application basics, including a description of the application, its purpose, and who makes it

- Any notes taken from application testing, such as memory used by the application and any problems encountered

- Detailed installation steps of the initial application install, and instructions for setting up new users on the application

- Application troubleshooting tips

- Application technical support information, such as telephone numbers, contact names, and hours of operation for technical support

Other Information

The following are some of the many other pieces of information that should be kept on your server and network as part of the DRK:

- Take the time to record the licensing key codes for all the products that you will be installing on Terminal Server. It is especially important to record the MetaFrame license and product codes if you will be installing it.

- Any driver disks you needed during the installation should be kept with the DRK.

- Any unusual BIOS or jumper settings.

- Network diagrams.

- Maintenance logs for keeping track of server maintenance and for making notes on troubleshooting.

27

Network Load Balancing for NFuse and Terminal Servers

THE LAST FEATURE THAT WILL BE covered in this book is *Network Load Balancing* (NLB). NLB is a load-sharing feature from Microsoft that is available in Windows 2000 Advanced Server. Even though it is marketed as a load-balancing product, it is truly a rather simplistic load-sharing technology. Although it does not compare to the more advanced load-balancing capabilities with Citrix MetaFrame XPe and XPa, it is still very useful in many situations.

You can use NLB with both Terminal Server and with Citrix MetaFrame. With your Terminal Servers, you can use NLB to set up a Terminal Server server farm for serving your applications to multiple users across multiple load-shared servers. For Citrix MetaFrame administrators, you can use NLB to set up redundancy and load sharing for your NFuse web servers.

NLB Versus Citrix Load Management

It is important to note the difference in capabilities of NLB to Citrix Load Management. Citrix Load Management offers a more robust form of dynamic load balancing, whereas NLB is more of a load-sharing solution. What this means is that the Citrix load-balancing solution can dynamically assign users to the server with the least current load based on adjustable load factors. With Microsoft NLB, you need to manually control the load factors on the server to help move more users over to one server or the other.

How Network Load Balancing Works

It is important to understand how NLB works so that you can set up your network properly for load balancing. NLB is an optional service that you can install from the Local Area Connection Properties page for your server's network cards. This service is not available with Windows 2000 Server, only with Windows 2000 Advanced Server.

To set up NLB, you need to install this service on the network cards of every Terminal Server that you want to load balance. NLB is designed to handle up to 32 servers in a single load-balanced cluster.

On each server that you install the NLB service on, you will need to set the following parameters:

- **Cluster IP address and subnet mask** The cluster IP address and subnet mask parameter is the common IP address used by all servers in the cluster. This address should be set to the same IP address for every server.

- **Multicast support** As part of the decision of how you will be implementing the NLB cluster, you must decide whether you will be using unicast or multicast. This is a very important decision. See the section "Setting Up the Network for Network Load Balancing" later in this chapter.

- **Remote control** You have the option of setting each server up so that it can be remote controlled. This enables you to remote control the server from another server in the cluster using the wlbs.exe command.

- **Host priority** This is another very important parameter. Every server has to have a unique priority set or it will not be able to join the cluster. The priority determines which server is the master server in the cluster; there can be only one master server at a time. If the master server fails, the server with the next highest priority number will take over as the master.

- **Dedicated subnet mask and IP address** You need to set this to the IP address you will be using for direct communication to that server. You normally would set this to the actual IP address of the server.

- **Port rules** Enables you to define how network traffic on certain TCP or UDP ports will be handled. The default is that all network traffic will be handled by all servers using single affinity. This will work fine for Terminal Server. Single affinity is very important, because it controls how session state is handled. Because users need to establish and maintain sessions with Terminal Server, you must use single affinity. In addition, you can use port rules to adjust the load balance of the servers. By default, the load will be equally distributed across the servers.

After you have set up these parameters correctly for all of your servers, NLB can begin.

How Clients Are Load Balanced

To load balance incoming client connections, you need to first set up the Terminal Services clients to use the shared IP address of the cluster. If you are using NLB to load balance your NFuse web servers, you need to point the DNS hostname for your web server to the clustered IP address of your NFuse servers.

When a Terminal Services client or NFuse user attempts to establish a session to the cluster's IP address, that request gets sent to all the servers in the cluster. Each server in the cluster then does its own statistical calculation, based on the IP address of the client, the priority or host ID of the server, and the load-balance factor of the protocol, to determine whether it should be the server to handle the session. If you are using single affinity, the result of this calculation will always end up choosing the same server for a given client IP address; however, this calculation is set up to equally distribute the load across the servers based on the load-balance factors of each server.

Suppose, for example, that user John Doe attempts to establish a Terminal Server session to one of two load-balanced Terminal Servers. Although the dedicated IP address of server 1 and B are different, they both share a common cluster IP address of 192.168.10.100. When John sets up his Terminal Services client to make the connection, he needs to use the cluster address of 192.168.10.100.

When John attempts to make a connection to the load-balanced servers using the cluster address of 192.168.10.100, each server receives a copy of the initial connection request packet. Because this is a new connection request, each server performs the statistical calculation to determine whether it should handle the request or whether the other server should. The result of both calculations determines that John's request should be handled by server 1. Server 1 then begins the conversation with John to establish the Terminal Server session.

What is important to note is that the calculation is based in part on the client's source IP address, if you are using single affinity. That means that unless John's workstation address changes, he will always connect to server 1 in the cluster. If the number of servers in the cluster changes, the actual server John uses might change. As long as the number of servers stays the same, however, John will always use the same server for Terminal Server connections. Although this affinity characteristic is very important to turn on for Terminal Server's that are clustered, it is not necessary to turn on for clustered NFuse web servers.

The magic of how load balancing works is in the statistical calculation. Even though John will always use the same server, each server will go through the same calculation based on the source IP address of the next person trying to connect. Overall, traffic will be balanced equally between the servers. If 100 people try to connect, 50 will always use server 1 and 50 will always use server 2. Although equal load distribution is the default, you have the option of manually adjusting the percentage of the load distributed to each server. For specific instructions on how to do this, see the "Adjusting the Load Distribution" section later in this chapter.

Server Heartbeats and Convergence

One of the big advantages of NLB over load-sharing solutions such as DNS round-robin is that if one server in the cluster fails or is taken offline, the other servers will pick up its user load automatically as users attempt to reconnect. This process is referred to as *convergence*.

For convergence to begin, the servers need to know whether any of the servers go offline. To handle this need, every server in a load-balanced cluster automatically sends out a heartbeat packet every second to the other servers. This heartbeat packet basically lets the other servers know that it is alive. In addition, the heartbeat packet tells the other servers about the port rules that the server sending the heartbeat is using.

Each server in the load-balanced cluster uses these heartbeat packets to create its own list of the servers that are available and their port rules. If five heartbeat packets are missed in a row, the convergence process is initiated by the cluster. This process takes a few seconds to complete. During convergence, the servers all remove the missing server from their list and readjust the load values. The missing server's load weight is subtracted from the total load weight of all the servers and the load calculation is reinitiated with the new load value. The whole process takes about 10 seconds total from the time the missing server leaves the server farm to the point that all the servers have reconverged. During this time, the servers will still process incoming connection requests so there should be little or no noticeable effect for users, other than that users who were on the failed server will have to reconnect.

Setting Up the Network for Network Load Balancing

NLB can be run in two different modes, either unicast or multicast. Before you install NLB, you need to decide on what mode you want to run in and set up your network appropriately for it to work.

When a user makes a request to establish a Terminal Server connection to the clustered IP address, that request needs to be sent to all the servers in the cluster. By default, however, a switch will send a request only to one port on the switch and not all. To understand how NLB can get around this issue, you need to understand how switches themselves work.

When a workstation on a switch attempts to start a Terminal Server connection with a Terminal Server on the same switch, it will first broadcast an ARP request with the IP address of that server to the switch. The purpose of the ARP request is for the workstation to receive the server's hardware address or MAC address. The switch, seeing that this is a broadcast packet, will send a copy of the packet to every device that is plugged into the switch. Each device on the switch that receives the ARP request will check to see whether the IP address in the ARP request matches its own IP address. If it does, it sends a message back to the workstation with its hardware or MAC address, so that the conversation can begin.

In the case of the network load-balanced Terminal Servers, all the servers will receive the ARP request from the workstation for the IP address of the cluster. At this point the Terminal Servers know that the workstation is attempting to connect to the cluster, and they know the source IP address of the workstation. This is all the information they need to calculate which server should handle the connection request. Using the special statistical formula, each server determines whether it is the one that should handle the request from the workstation.

In unicast mode, which is the default mode, the server that is the one will then send back a "dummy" MAC address by default (02-xx-xx-xx-xx), not its own MAC address. This behavior is unique and very important to understand. Every server will send back the same "dummy" MAC address to the switch by default. Because the server sends back a "dummy" MAC address and not its true MAC address, the switch has no way of learning this address and associating it to a port. For this reason, when the workstation continues the conversation using the "dummy" MAC address, the switch will send the conversation to all ports on the switch. This means that all servers in the cluster will again receive the packet. This is important because if one of the servers fails, the client can switch over to another server easily. However, the problem with this is that if you have a large switch with many devices on it, this will flood the switch with traffic. In other words, all traffic going from the client to the Terminal Servers will be copied to each port of the switch. This can cause big problems on a large network.

The following sections cover the different options you can take to configure your network properly.

Set Up a Separate Subnet for Network Load Balancing

One simple alternative is to set up a separate switch on a separate subnet dedicated for use by the Terminal Servers that are using NLB. Because the servers are on a separate network, you do not need to worry about the switch flooding problem. The disadvantage of this approach is that you will need to put a router between your Terminal Servers and the clients. This router will have to process all traffic and can become overtaxed or slow down communications to your Terminal Servers. If you are providing access to your Terminal Servers across slower WAN connections, this should not be much of an issue. If you are providing access for large numbers of users in the same building or are greatly concerned about speed, however, you should consider the multicast option instead.

Use the Multicast Option

For large corporations, the multicast option is highly recommended. The difference between the behavior with multicast and with unicast is that when servers respond to client request, they will send back a unique multicast address to the clients rather than the "dummy" address. However, with nearly all switches, including the Cisco Catalyst switches, when the client attempts to reach the server using its multicast address, the switch will send that packet to every port on the switch.

To set it up properly, you need to configure the switch so that it knows that any packet destined to the multicast MAC address of one of the servers should be sent to every Terminal Server in the cluster. On most switches, you can manually assign a single MAC address to multiple ports on the switch. By assigning the MAC address to just those ports, you ensure that other devices connected into the switch do not have to process the Terminal Server traffic.

The following instructions cover how to do this on more recent versions of a Cisco Catalyst switch:

1. Put together a list of the ports on the switch to which the Terminal Servers are attached.

2. Go into the properties for NLB on each server and enable multicast support under the Cluster Parameters tab of the Properties for NLB.

3. Record the MAC or network address shown for each server in this Properties window.

4. For each server MAC address, run the following commands on the switch where the [term server *n* port] parameters represent the list of switch ports that the servers are connected to:

```
cam [server mac address] [term server 1 port],[term server 2 port], [term
server n port]
```

To verify that the setup is working properly, you will need to attach a network sniffer to one of the unused ports on the switch. If you attempt to start up a Terminal Server session to the network load-balanced Terminal Servers from a client on another port, you should not see any of the Terminal Server traffic (port 389) on the network sniffer. If you do, the traffic is being flooded on the switch. Verify that the CAM entries are correct. For further assistance, search for CAM entries on the Cisco web site or contact Cisco technical support.

Using a Hub

The last option is to just use a hub to help isolate network traffic. This option can be used to prevent the problem of switch flooding.

The basic steps to this technique are to attach all of your Terminal Servers in the cluster to the same network hub. Then attach this hub to one port on the switch. You will need to ensure that your switch is set up so that it can learn more than one MAC address per port. This is the default set up for nearly all switches; however, it is sometimes disabled by network administrators for security reasons.

For this technique to work, you also must disable the "dummy" MAC addresses so that the switch can learn the addresses for the Terminal Servers. If you do not do this, the switch will still flood the "dummy" MAC addresses to every port. To disable the "dummy" MAC addresses, change the MaskSourceMAC value to 0 in the `HKLM\SYSTEM\CurrentControlSet\Services\WLBS\Parameters` key.

Installing Network Load Balancing

NLB is very easy to install. It can be installed as a service for any network card in a server. In some situations, you might want to dedicate one of the network cards in the server for NLB and use the other card for normal network traffic. The following instructions cover how to set it up:

1. Open the Local Area Connection icon from the Start menu, Settings, Network and Dial-Up Connections folder.

2. Click the Install button, select Service, and then click OK.

3. Select the Network Load Balancing service, and then click OK.

4. Highlight the Network Load Balancing service and select Properties.

5. Under the Cluster Parameters tab, set the primary IP address and subnet mask for the cluster. This is the same IP address and subnet mask that you need to use for all of the servers in the cluster.

6. Enter the domain name for the cluster and enable remote control if needed. If you will be using multicast to access the cluster, check the Enabled box next to Multicast support.

7. Click the Host Parameters tab and set the Priority ID for the server. This priority ID must be unique among all the servers in the load-balanced cluster. The server with the lowest priority becomes the master server in the cluster.

8. Enter the dedicated IP address of the server. This is normally the IP address that you assigned to the server's network card.

9. Click the Port Rules tab and make any changes that you need to the port rules. Then click OK.

10. Reinstall the latest service pack on the server.

11. Repeat these steps for every server in the load-balanced cluster.

Remember that you need to ensure that the network is set up properly, depending on whether you choose unicast or multicast for load balancing. Whichever you choose, you need to choose the same for every server.

Verify that you can make an attachment to the servers using the cluster IP address. Remember that each workstation will always use the same Terminal Server. Make sure to try other workstations to ensure that incoming users are equally distributed across the servers.

If the load balancing is working properly, one thing you need to ensure before you put this into production is that the incoming network traffic is not being copied to all ports of the switch. As shown in the preceding section, you need to set up the network especially for load balancing to work as expected. If you do not set it up correctly, or if you just plug your servers into a switch without modifying anything at all, that network traffic going to your Terminal Servers will be broadcast to all ports of the switch. On large networks, this can have a huge detrimental effect if you put this into production.

To make sure that this is not the case, put a network sniffer or a workstation running network sniffer software on one of the ports on the same switch on which you have your Terminal Servers. Set up packet capturing to capture Terminal Server traffic (TCP port 389). While capturing packets, attempt to log on to the load-balanced Terminal Servers using the cluster IP from a different workstation. If you see that workstation's connection attempt, your switch is not set up properly. The only traffic you should see from that workstation is the original ARP request for the IP address of the servers. For more information on how to resolve this problem, see the earlier section "Setting Up the Network for Network Load Balancing" or refer to Microsoft technical article Q193602.

Adjusting the Load Distribution

By default, the incoming user load is equally distributed between all the Terminal Servers in the cluster. By modifying the port rules, however, you can adjust the balance of the servers. For each server you can define a particular load weight between 0 and 100. If you set a load weight of 0 for a server, it will not accept any connections. If you set any other weight, the server will receive a certain percentage of the incoming user load. The percentage is calculated using the following formula:

Server Load Weight $\star$ 100 = Total Load Weight of All Servers

Suppose, for instance, that you have a two-server load-balanced cluster and you set server 1's load weight to 25 and server 2's load weight to 75. The total load weight for the farm is 100. Twenty-five percent of the users will be sent to server 1 and 75 percent will be sent to server 2.

It is important to note that the load values of all the servers do not necessarily have to add up to 100. If you set server 1's load weight to 100 and server 2's load weight to 50, the total load weight for the server cluster would be 150. Sixty-six percent (100/150) of the users would be sent to server one and 33 percent (50/150) would be sent to server 2.

You can change the load-balancing value on your server as follows:

1. Open the Local Area Connection from the Start menu, Settings, Network and Dial-Up Connections folder.

2. Select Network Load Balancing from the list, and then click the Properties button.

3. Click the Port Rules tab.

4. Highlight the main port rule and remove the check mark next to the Equal box for Load Weight.

5. Change the Load Weight to the value desired.

6. Repeat this process for each server in the cluster.

Monitoring the Cluster Using *WLBS*

The best tool to use to monitor the status of the cluster is the `wlbs` command. This command is available on any server that has NLB installed. Using this command you can check the status of the convergence, check the settings of your server, stop or start clustering, and even perform these commands on other servers in the cluster. The `wlbs` command has many command-line options. You can view these options by just running the `wlbs` command with no parameters.

The two most useful commands available are the `wlbs display` and `wlbs query` commands. The `wlbs display` command will display all the current cluster settings for your server in one consolidated output, as shown in Listing 27.1. The `wlbs query` command will show you the status of server convergence and which servers are currently part of the cluster. You can use these commands to get a better idea of the status of your clustered solution.

Listing 27.1   Consolidated Output of the Current Cluster Settings

```
C:\Documents and Settings\tharwood>wlbs display
WLBS Cluster Control Utility V2.3. (c) 1997-99 Microsoft Corporation

=== Configuration: ===

Current time            = Wed Sep 26 13:36:36 2001
ParametersVersion       = 4
VirtualNICName          = \Device\{F116C85E-54BC-4A3A-ADB2-CB341079D9C
ClusterNICName          = PCI\VEN_10B7&DEV_9050&SUBSYS_00000000&REV_00
7F&0&48
AliveMsgPeriod          = 1000
AliveMsgTolerance       = 5
NumActions              = 50
NumPackets              = 100
NumAliveMsgs            = 66
ClusterNetworkAddress   = 02-bf-c0-a8-14-01
ClusterName             = cluster.domain.com
ClusterIPAddress        = 192.168.20.1
ClusterNetworkMask      = 255.255.255.0
DedicatedIPAddress      = 0.0.0.0
DedicatedNetworkMask    = 0.0.0.0
HostPriority            = 1
ClusterModeOnStart      = ENABLED
LicenseKey              =
DescriptorsPerAlloc     = 512
MaxDescriptorAllocs     = 512
ScaleSingleClient       = 0
NBTSupportEnable        = 1
MulticastSupportEnable  = 0
MulticastARPEnable      = 1
```

```
MaskSourceMAC             = 1
NetmonAliveMsgs           = 0
IPChangeDelay             = 60000
IPToMACEnable             = 1
ConnectionCleanupDelay    = 300000
RemoteControlEnabled      = 0
RemoteControlUDPPort      = 2504
RemoteControlCode         = 0x4ED64EB2
RemoteMaintenanceEnabled  = 0x0
CurrentVersion            = V2.3
InstallDate               = 0x39A857C9
VerifyDate                = 0x7B3B2DC4
NumberOfRules             = 1
PortRules
Start  End    Prot  Mode        Pri   Load   Affinity
    0  65535  Both  Multiple          Equal  S
```

V

Appendixes

A

Thin Client Hardware Solutions

For those interested in deploying thin client terminals in their environment, this appendix is for you. You will find a list of all the major thin client terminal vendors here, along with a basic technical description of their current offerings. You can use this information as a starting point for your research into the best thin client terminal solution for your environment.

In addition, solutions from some of the top handheld vendors that support Terminal Server technology also are covered.

Thin Client Terminal Solutions

In this section, you will learn about the leading thin client terminal solutions available on the market today. The term *thin client terminal* was chosen rather than *Windows-based terminal* because, as you will see in this section, not all manufacturers of thin client terminals use a platform based on Windows.

Because of the large variety of thin client solutions out there, the line between desktops and thin clients has begun to blur. In this appendix, the difference between a thin client terminal and a low-end desktop is the lack of moving parts. In other words, a thin client terminal is not considered a thin client terminal if it has a floppy drive or hard drive.

A lot has changed in the past few years in the thin client arena. You will now find that many big hardware companies, such as Compaq, HP, and IBM, now all have thin client offering. In addition, significant industry consolidation has occurred over the past few years. Wyse, a leading maker of all types of terminals, bought out Netier, and Neoware bought out Boundless's thin client terminal line.

As you research your thin client terminal solution, you will likely find that nearly all thin client offerings are less than $1000. The basic features of a thin client terminal normally include the following:

- RDP and/or ICA clients

- Simple terminal emulation

- Very low power consumption

- Usually based on Windows CE, Windows NT embedded (NTe), or Linux

- Centrally manageable

- Local Flash for system settings and applications and DRAM for running the thin client or terminal emulation software

- One or more communication ports, such as a serial, parallel, or USB port

As the price goes up, you tend to start finding one or more of the following features:

- **Additional DRAM** Additional DRAM allows a terminal to run more applications simultaneously. If your terminal has 16MB of DRAM, for example, you might be able to run one application through Citrix and a terminal emulation session at the same time. If you have 48MB of DRAM, however, you might be able to run Internet Explorer, an application through Citrix, and two terminal emulations sessions concurrently.

- **Additional Flash** Flash is used for a lot of things on terminals, and its exact use varies from one manufacturer to the next. If any local applications need to be installed, such as Internet Explorer, however, the application itself is normally burned to Flash. Flash upgrades are generally the method of adding additional features to your terminal in the future.

- **Advanced central management tools** Many manufacturers offer advanced central management tools for your terminal. These tools enable you to deploy settings, such as Terminal Emulation configuration changes or new connections for RDP, to all of your terminals from a central location. Some manufacturers offer these tools or a low-end version of these tools for free. Others charge you for them. These tools are very important for ease of management and should be thoroughly investigated while you are evaluating thin client terminal solutions.

- **Additional terminal emulation**   Some manufacturers offer limited terminal emulation, such as VT-100, in their base models and then give you additional terminal emulations in the higher end models. If you need your terminals to play both the role of a RDP or ICA client and a terminal emulator, be sure to check what emulations the terminals you are evaluating support.

- **Additional ports**   More serial, parallel, or USB ports are common in more expensive terminals. These ports enable you to handle such needs as local printing or in some cases dial-up access to Citrix.

- **Web browser**   Because of the prevalence of the Internet, many thin client terminal manufacturers have now begun to include web browsers with some of their offerings. Be sure to check the browser that is included and what features it has. One big limitation of using a browser on a terminal is the lack of ability to download plug-ins. They have no local hard drive, so there is no way to store plug-in software. Although many manufacturers will allow you to "burn-in" any plug-ins that you need, adding new plug-ins in the future can be difficult. Many administrators choose instead to run browsers through the Terminal Server.

- **Better video support**   More expensive thin client terminals generally support additional colors or video modes.

- **Audio**   With many thin client terminal offerings, you will now find the capability to play audio from applications. This opens the doors on using thin client terminals for training, multimedia communications, and other situations where audio is important.

- **NT Embedded**   Generally, many manufacturers choose NT Embedded for their high-end terminals. NT Embedded is basically Windows NT 4.0 on a chip. Using this operating system, a thin client terminal manufacturer can load most any application that can run on NT by burning it into the thin client's Flash.

Table A.1 shows a condensed sampling of the many thin client terminal offerings on the market today. Be aware that this table shows only one of the offerings in each manufacturer's product line, generally the lower end model. This is not intended to be a product comparison, but instead gives you an idea of the large variation in operating systems and configurations among vendors. For more detailed information, see the manufacturer's web page, as listed in this section.

Table A.1 **Sample of Thin Client Terminal Offerings**

Product	OS	Browser	RDP/ICA/ Term Emul	Ports (Ser/Par/ USB)
Compaq Evo	CE or NTe	IE 5.5	Y/Y/Y	0/0/4
IBM NetVista 2200	Turbo Linux	Net Nav 4.77	N/Y/Y	0/0/2
Keytronic ClienTerm	WinCE	None	N/Y/N	1/1/0
NCD ThinSTAR 232	WinCE	None	Y/Y/N	1/1/0
Neoware Eon 2000e	Linux	None	N/Y/Y	2/1/2
Wyse 3230 LE	WinCE	IE	Y/Y/Y	2/1/2

Compaq T1x10 and Evo

Compaq currently has two basic categories of thin client terminal product lines: the Compaq T1x10 and the newer Compaq Evo. Each offering has different models with slight variations in features.

The thin client terminals in the T1x10 product line, the T1010 and the T1510, are slightly larger than those in the Evo line. The T1010 is based on the Windows CE operating system. The base unit comes with 8MB of Flash and 32MB of DRAM, but is expandable to 16MB and 48MB of DRAM. They also support a PCMCIA slot for added expandability.

The Evo line of thin client terminals are a newer, sleeker offering by Compaq. They range from a low-end WinCE version with 16MB Flash/32MB DRAM and higher end NTe versions with up to 96MB Flash/128MB DRAM (upgradeable to 256/256).

Both platforms come with the WorkGroup version of Compaq's Rapport central thin client terminal management software. An Enterprise edition of this software is available for additional cost.

The contact information for Compaq is as follows:

Compaq Computer Corporation

20555 SH 249

Houston, TX 77070-2698

1-800-AT-COMPAQ (Pre-Sales)

www.compaq.com

IBM NetVista

IBM's longstanding presence in the computer hardware field, and its line of mid-range and mainframe systems, makes it an excellent choice for a thin client manufacturer, especially if you already have significant investment in IBM equipment.

IBM has a large variety of different offerings that make up its NetVista line. Starting with the low-end 2200l with a TurboLinux operating system and a based 32MB of RAM, to the high-end NetVista 2800 series that has more RAM and additional expandability. Nearly all the units in the NetVista series come with Netscape Navigator, Java Virtual Machine, ICA client, and terminal emulation. Other than that, the actual feature set and expandability options vary significantly.

IBM offers a separately purchased central management software package called the NetVista Thin Client Manager.

For more information on this line of thin client terminals, contact IBM at the following address:

IBM Corporation
New Orchard Road
Armonk, NY 10504
1-800-IBM 4 YOU
www.ibm.com

Neoware Eon and Capio Series

Neoware has been a mainstay in the world of thin client terminals since the inception of this new breed of devices more than five years ago. Purely focused on thin client terminals, this relatively small publicly held company has two main lines of thin client terminals to offer: the Eon and Capio.

The Eon is Neoware's flagship product. On the low-end, you will find the Eon 2000e, based on Linux, bare-bones thin client offering has an ICA client, RDP client, VTxxx emulation, and 32MB of DRAM (expandable to 128MB). On the high end you will find the Eon 5000s, which includes all that the 2000e offers plus a built-in IE 5.5 browser, Java Virtual Machine, 64MB of DRAM, and more terminal emulation offerings.

To centrally manage terminals in the Eon series, you need to purchase the ezRemoteManager software from Neoware.

The second line of products is the Capio line of thin client terminals. These terminals are actually the product line that was bought from Boundless Technologies. Neoware is marketing the Capio as a more affordable and simpler thin client terminal than the Eon series. They are based on the WinCE platform and include ICA clients.

For more information on either of these products, refer to the following contact information:

Neoware
400 Feheley Dr.
King of Prussia, PA 19406
1-800-NEOWARE
info@neoware.com
www.neoware.com

Key Tronic ClienTerm

Key Tronic has been well known for years for their keyboards. However, what is not as well known is that they also make thin client terminals. Their ClienTerm thin client terminal is one of the only thin client terminals that is built in to a keyboard! This wonder of miniaturized technology offers very basic thin client terminal features such as an ICA client, but not much else. Some models come with bar code wands, and touch screens are supported.

For a basic point-of-sale terminal, this space saver might be all you need. For more information, you can contact them as follows:

Key Tronic Corporation
P.O. Box 14687
Spokane, WA 99214-0687
1-800-262-6006
www.keytronic.com

Network Computing Devices (NCD) ThinSTAR

NCD has been around since 1988 and is one of the largest manufacturers of thin client solutions. NCD started with a UNIX focus and was one of the main manufacturers of X Windows terminals back in the early 1990s. With the advent of thin client terminal technology around the mid-1990s, NCD switched gears and now manufacturers one of the only lines of thin client terminals that can handle ICA, RDP, and X-11, the X Windows protocol.

NCD's line of terminals all support both the ICA and RDP protocols and are all based on the WinCE operating system. Instead of having to buy a different terminal to get more software features, however, NCD offers several separately purchased add-on software packages. For example, X Windows support is provided by the NCD ThinPATH X Windows software add-on. Add-ons are available for additional terminal emulations (ThinPATH Connect), centralized management (ThinPATH Manager), RDP protocol enhancements (ThinPATH Plus), and more.

For top-of-the-line capabilities, including a built-in Netscape Navigator browser, Java Virtual Machine, additional memory, and communication ports, take a look at NCD's network computer, the NCD 900. Although the term *network computer* has fallen somewhat out of favor in recent years, this thin client offering is worth a look. Especially for those who need as much functionality as possible without sacrificing ease of management.

For more information, you can contact them as follows:

Network Computing Devices, Inc.
350 North Bernardo Ave.
Mountain View, CA 94043-5207
1-800-800-9599
info@ncd.com
www.ncd.com

Wyse WinTerm

Last, but not least, is Wyse Technologies. Wyse is the leading manufacturer of thin client terminals. Starting back in 1981 with green screen text terminals, Wyse has long been known for their terminal technology. With the advent of thin client technology, in 1995 they introduced their first thin client terminal, the Wyse WinTerm. This product has been a leader now for several years in the thin client arena.

The Wyse WinTerm comes in a large variety of flavors. On the low end is the stateless Wyse WinTerm 1200LE. This thin client terminal supports the ICA protocol, but does not have any software loaded other than a simple bootstrap component. Instead it relies on DHCP to get it onto the network and FTP to download the software and configuration files it needs.

In the mid-range, you will find Wyse's 3xxx WinCE-based thin client terminals. These terminals all support both ICA and RDP and have a large number of additional features over the 1200LE.

On the high end are the Wyse 8xxx NT embedded-based thin client terminals. These are almost low-end desktops, and some models do have optional desktop functionality available, such as a local hard drive and floppy drive. These thin client offerings tend to be more modular in that many of the features are sold as add-on options.

Wyse sells a centralized management application called Wyse Rapport, which enables you to centrally control the settings and manage your Wyse thin client terminals.

For more information, you can contact them as follows:
Wyse Technology, Inc.
3471 N. First St.
San Jose, CA 95134
1-800-GET-WYSE
info@wyse.com
www.wyse.com

Low-End Desktop Versus Thin Client Terminal

As a final note, if you are considering a thin client solution, also be sure to consider some of the many low-end desktop solutions available. Many desktop manufacturers, such as Compaq, IBM, and Dell, now offer lower end desktop solutions with sufficient power to run most business applications at a price that is at or near what thin client terminal manufacturers charge for their products.

These desktop solutions have local storage, which allows for the installation of standard Windows applications locally; however, they are generally designed to be small and easy to manage, making them an excellent choice for corporations that want the most in terms of future flexibility and ease of management.

Many corporations find that thin client terminals significantly limit future flexibility. The biggest problem with using thin client terminals is that you are locked into that vendor's software solution; you do not have the option of just reloading the hard drive with a different OS or an application that you want to run locally instead of on Citrix or Terminal Server. Although you can often upgrade a thin client terminal Flash, you usually face significant limits as to what you can run on it.

Remember also that running applications on a Terminal Server does have its own set of costs. Some applications might be run more cost effectively on the local desktop (instead of taxing the expensive resources of a Terminal Server server farm).

Web browsers are a good example of this type of application. Unless web browsers are being used to provide access to business-critical applications, running web browsers on the local workstation is a better bet. Web browsers tend to be huge resource hogs on Terminal Servers unless locked down properly. Although you can run web browsers locally on many thin client terminal solutions, these browsers are significantly limited. With the upcoming Windows .NET Server technologies from Microsoft and the many other web technologies available today, one of the most powerful business capabilities of web browsers is their capability to download and run plug-ins. Most web-based business software requires some type of plug-in to run.

If you use a thin client terminal–based browser, plug-ins will have to be manually flashed onto the system, which is very tedious. If you choose a low-end desktop, however, you can run the browser locally, download and install plug-ins as needed, and still be able to run the majority of the workstation's applications off of your Terminal Servers.

On the other hand, thin client terminals can be an excellent device to choose as a replacement for green screen terminals. Most thin client terminals support terminal emulation locally. You can replace old green screens or other terminals with thin client terminals and give your users the ability to access their host systems just as before, plus be able to push out Windows applications to them through Citrix or Terminal Server. You will find that thin client terminals are often an excellent solution for 24×7 call centers, kiosks, points of sale, and educational labs. In these situations, they might be a better solution than a desktop because they are so easy to replace and get up and running quickly. As an administrator, the fact that there is no local storage can be a big benefit, especially if there is a lot of turnover of people who use the thin client terminals. If you deployed a desktop instead, and it was not locked down properly, users could store their documents or make changes to the desktop that would cause you extra work when you had to prepare the system for use by the next group of people.

Handheld Thin Client Solutions

Handhelds are some of the most sought after devices in the market. Most offer an incredible number of features in the smallest of packages. Their level of portability exceeds that of any other computing device. However, with all of these advantages they are often the bane of administrators. There is so much competition, so many offerings, and so much change in this industry that people tend to have their favorite one, and they change favorites often. Their tiny size also makes them more susceptible to damage and theft. As an administrator, if you have no control over the purchase of these devices, you can spend a good deal of your time supporting all the different varieties.

This section discusses the major handheld offerings available today that are capable of running either the RDP or ICA thin client. You will find that this list mainly includes those handhelds that use a Windows operating system, such as Windows CE. These type of handhelds can run either ICA or RDP client. For Citrix administrators, however, you have a greater amount of choice because of the recent availability of the ICA client for the handheld Symbian and EPOC operating systems. Although this list is far from exhaustive, it does include most of the larger players out there.

The difference between a handheld and a thin client terminal is fairly obvious: portability. With the incredible miniaturization now available for such devices as hard drives, however, the line between the capabilities of a handheld and a notebook is beginning to blur. In this review of these devices, size is the differentiating factor. For it to be considered a handheld or palmtop, you must just be able to put your hand around it and easily carry it with one hand.

Handhelds can range in price from around $100 to more than $1000 with all the accessories. The following is a list of the common features you will find in most of today's handhelds:

- Contact management software
- Calendar
- Calculator
- Some type of black-and-white or color graphical display
- Flash memory and DRAM
- Ability to load additional software
- Ability to synchronize with a desktop or transfer information to other devices
- Rechargeable battery pack

As you go higher in price you will start to find such features as the following:

- **Color display**   Many manufacturers are now making their handhelds available with color screens.

- **Additional DRAM**   Additional DRAM enables you to run more programs concurrently, run larger programs, and hold more information in memory.

- **Additional Flash**   Flash memory is the only means of storage for most handhelds. Additional Flash enables you to permanently store additional information, such as contacts, documents, programs, and even pictures.

- **Multimedia capabilities**   Some manufacturers have branched into the area of multimedia with such features as a built-in digital camera, audio, and video.

Windows CE Versus Pocket PC 2000 and 2002

One thing that is rather confusing about handheld operating systems is the difference between Windows CE and Pocket PC. Basically, Pocket PC is just the new name for the Windows CE operating system. Microsoft renamed the operating system for marketing reasons. On pocket-size devices, it is called *Pocket PC* and on handhelds it is called *Handheld PC*.

One important note is that several new features in Pocket PC 2002 were not available in Pocket PC 2000. One of the more important features is the availability of a VPN client. One problem with handhelds is that for them to connect into a device on your corporate network via wireless, you needed to open a port on your firewall. By using the PPTP VPN client that is now available in Pocket PC 2002, however, you can have them connect securely across the Internet into any device on your internal network using a secure VPN tunnel. For more information on setting up a VPN, see Chapter 16, "Dial-In and VPN Access."

Connecting Handhelds to the Terminal Servers

No matter how many features your handheld has, if your intention is to use it for running applications through Terminal Server you need some type of connection to the server. With thin client terminals, this connection was handled through a LAN connection. With handhelds, however, the following are the most common means of connecting them to Terminal Server.

Access Point Wireless

If your handheld users need access to Terminal Server applications only while in the building or in meetings, you can install one of the many access point wireless solutions in your office. These solutions use various technologies to provide you with normally around a 10Mbps connection to the network and thus to your Terminal Servers. For this solution to work, the handheld must support whatever wireless card you choose.

Open Air Wireless

This refers to the many wireless technologies currently available for wide-ranging access to the Internet, such as CDPD. Using this type of solution you would make your Terminal Servers accessible from the Internet. You would then put wireless cards on the handhelds and have them connect to the Internet, and then run the ICA or RDP client. Currently, the two biggest disadvantages to this approach are limited coverage and low speeds. Even the largest wireless service providers offer coverage in major cities only; the farther you get away from the cities, the worse the coverage becomes. Also, depending on the connection quality, the speeds can be downright dog slow. Most vendors today offer at least a 19.2Kbps connection rate if your connection is good. This is on the slow side, and although it is workable, people will tend to use it only out of necessity because of the slow response time. Depending on the application, however, this speed might be adequate for your needs.

Dial-In Access

This is one of the most popular and least expensive means of providing remote access. In this scenario, you would set up a modem bank and some remote access servers. Remote users would dial in to the modem bank to access the Terminal Servers. Alternatively, you might be able to use the ICA client for direct dial in to a Citrix server. Also some people might want their users to connect to the Internet locally using the dial-up connection and provide access to the Terminal Servers across the Internet. This approach saves costs because users do not have to make a long-distance call to dial in to a corporate modem bank.

Compaq iPAQ

Compaq's iPAQ line of handhelds is one of the most popular lines of handhelds on the market today. They are all based on the Windows CE operating system with the Intel StrongARM processor. They can easily be held in the palm of your hand and use a stylus for input rather than a keyboard.

Unlike many of the competitors, Compaq's iPAQ solution is highly modular. Using an add-on expansion pack, you can add up to two standard PCMCIA cards to the handheld. Using a PCMCIA card, you can give your iPAQ wireless capabilities, additional storage on PCMCIA-based hard drives, and even GPS navigational capabilities.

The iPAQ comes with pocket versions of Word, Excel, and Internet Explorer, and several built-in utilities. In addition, it comes with CDs loaded with more software you can add.

Either the RDP or ICA client can be loaded onto the iPAQ, enabling you to connect to your Terminal Servers. To make the connection, you can use the modem accessory to make a dial-in connection or the expansion pack to add a CDPD or access point wireless card.

For more information, contact them as follows:
Compaq Computer Corporation
20555 SH 249
Houston, TX 77070-2698
800-AT-COMPAQ (Pre-Sales)
www.compaq.com

HP Jornada

Much like the Compaq iPAQ, the HP Jornada series is a highly modular series of handhelds. They are all based on the Windows CE operating system and use either the Hitachi SH3 processor or Intel's StrongARM processor.

The Jornada comes with pocket version of Word, Excel, and Internet Explorer, along with several other built-in utilities. In addition, you can add on several other freely available software packages from the accompanying CD.

On the low end is the HP Jornada 5xx series. This handheld, or as HP refers to it *Pocket PC*, is very small in size and comes with a stylus for input. With the Jornada 5xx, you have numerous add-on connectivity options available, including using a Novatel wireless card, Socket Digital Phone Card, and Psion 56K modem.

On the high end are the HP Jornada 7xx series. These devices are larger than the 5xx series and have a foldout style case with a miniature keyboard. They both support standard PCMCIA style cards, and the 720 series comes with a built-in 56K modem.

For more information on the HP Jornada, you can contact them as follows:

Hewlett Packard
3000 Hanover Street
Palo Alto, CA 94304-1185
(650)857-1501
www.hp.com

Nokia 92xx

A cell phone company making a handheld personal digital assistant? Might seem strange, but that is the way many cell phone companies are heading today. With the growing business need for access to information from wherever you are, cell phone manufacturers are responding by making new devices that combine the wireless communication capabilities of a cell phone with other features traditionally supported only by handhelds, such as contact management, calendar, and now even access to applications through Citrix!

One phone is currently available in the 92xx series, with the next model projected to be released in the first half of 2002. The Nokia 9210 cell phone folds open to reveal a small color LCD screen and keyboard. This new cell phone will be based on the Symbian operating system. Although you will not be able to run an RDP client on it, Citrix has a version of the ICA client already available for the Symbian operating system. This client will enable you to run any application on your Citrix server from the palm of your hand on your cell phone! Currently, connection speeds range from 19.2 to 43Kbps, depending on your range to the cell phone tower.

For more information on this interesting new class of devices, you can contact them as follows:

Nokia Americas
6000 Connection Drive
Irving, Texas 75039
800-547-9810
www.nokia.com

Psion 5mx and Revo

For those who do not absolutely need color and can easily make do with grayscale display, Psion makes several interesting handheld solutions that will work with the Citrix ICA client. These handhelds are based on the EPOC operating system and support the Citrix EPOC ICA client. Using these handhelds, you can easily run full Windows applications from the palm of your hand.

For remote connectivity, Psion makes a small 56K wireless modem based on GSM technology. Using this modem, you can easily connect your Psion handheld to the Internet or a corporate RAS server and access your applications on Citrix remotely.

For more information on this solution, you can contact them as follows:

Psion Inc.
978-371-0310
www.psionusa.com

Sony Vaio Picturebook

Although an expensive solution because of its full laptop capabilities, this handheld is definitely worth mention because of its size. The Vaio picture book comes with either Windows ME or Windows 2000, 600+MHz processor, 1024×480 full-color LCD screen, and either a 12 or 15GB hard drive, all in a device that does not measure much larger than a piece of paper folded in half!

With this device, your mobile users can run most any application locally and be able to access corporate applications remotely using either RDP or ICA.

For remote connectivity, there is an integrated modem and an open slot for a PCMCIA card, such as a wireless card.

For more information on this device, you can contact them as follows:

Sony Corporation
888-595-VAIO
www.sonystyle.com/vaio/index.html

B

Third-Party Software and Utilities for Terminal Server and MetaFrame

IF YOU ARE LIKE MOST ADMINISTRATORS, you probably have your own treasure chest of favorite utilities. Generally very inexpensive, these after-market utilities have probably gotten you out of more than one sticky situation or have solved a difficult problem with surprising technical elegance. In this appendix you will learn about some of the many utilities and other types of available software that meet common needs for Terminal Server administrators.

Utilities from Microsoft and Citrix

You might be surprised to learn that some of the best utilities and resources are those available from Microsoft and Citrix. Here is a list of the most important ones:

- **Windows 2000 Server Resource Kit** The Resource Kit is an indispensable resource for Terminal Server administrators. You will find an almost unending multitude of useful utilities and other important information in the Resource Kit. You can find information on how to order the Resource Kit at www.microsoft.com/windows2000/techinfo/reskit/default.asp.

Thin Wizard Web Site
For an online version of all the links shown in this appendix, go to the book's companion web site at
`www.thinwizard.com`, which is also available from `www.awl.com/cseng/titles/0-735-71192-5`.

- **Terminal Server Scaling Tools**   This set of utilities available for free
from Microsoft includes useful information and utilities for appropriate
capacity planning. You can either download this utility at `www.microsoft.com/`
`windows2000/techinfo/reskit/tools/hotfixes/tscpt-o.asp` or do a search
on the Microsoft web site for TSSCALE.EXE.

- **Terminal Services Advanced Client**   The Terminal Services
Advanced Client is an essential download for any Terminal Server
administrator who does not intend to deploy Citrix technology. In addition to the much-heralded ActiveX web-based Terminal Services client,
you will find an MSI installer package for the Windows 32-bit client and
a plug-in for the Microsoft Management Console that enables you to
manage all of your Terminal Servers from one console. You can download
this client for free at `www.microsoft.com/windows2000/downloads/`
`recommended/TSAC/default.asp`.

- **Microsoft SysPrep**   If you intend to create images of your servers for
automated deployment, you need to take a look at this utility. SysPrep is a
powerful utility that can be used to prepare a system for imaging. It will
remove any SID-specific information from the machine and place a mini-
setup boot image on it so that the next time it is booted you can make
machine-specific changes, such as changing the computer name. It is
available for free download at `www.microsoft.com/windows2000/downloads/`
`tools/sysprep/default.asp`.

- **FAZAM 2000**   This is a freely available and very useful utility for assessing the effect of policies in Windows 2000. This utility also can be used
for advanced policy management. Although actually made by Full Armor
Corporation, you will find a reduced functionality version on the
Microsoft web site, `www.microsoft.com/windows2000/techinfo/reskit/`
`tools/existing/fazam2000-o.asp`.

- **Group Policy Verification Tool**   Another Group Policy–related tool
available from Microsoft. This tool is a must have if you are troubleshooting an issue with Group Policies in Windows 2000. It enables you to do
such things as check Group Policy replication, policy integrity, and more.
You can download it for free at `www.microsoft.com/windows2000/`
`techinfo/reskit/tools/existing/gpotool-o.asp`.

- **Group Policy Result**   Can't figure out which policies are being applied to a particular user or computer? If so, this freely available utility is for you. It provides a ton of useful information on how policies are being applied and why. See `www.microsoft.com/windows2000/techinfo/reskit/ tools/existing/gpresult-o.asp`.

- **RDP Clipboard File Copy**   Ever wanted to be able to cut and paste files from Terminal Server to the local client? If so, you can use this freely available utility to do so. Although this utility is part of the Resource Kit, the original version contains a bug. Be sure to download it instead from `www.microsoft.com/windows2000/techinfo/reskit/tools/hotfixes/ rdpclip-o.asp`.

- **User State Migration Tool**   Using this free tool, you can migrate a user's desktop and settings from one server to another. This can be very handy in a Terminal Server environment. You can download it at `www.microsoft.com/windows2000/techinfo/reskit/tools/new/usmt-o.asp`.

- **Drive Mapping in Terminal Server**   One of the most frustrating aspects of Terminal Server, for those who do not intend to purchase Citrix, is the lack of the ability to easily map to a user's local drives from a Terminal Server session. Using this freely available utility from Microsoft, you can do just that. Go to `www.microsoft.com/windows2000/techinfo/ reskit/tools/hotfixes/drmapsrv-o.asp`.

- **Citrix Client Server Test Kit**   If you want to test the capacity of your Citrix servers, you might try this freely available collection of scripts from the Citrix Developer Network web site at `http://apps.citrix.com/ CDN/SDK/cstk_sdk.asp`. You will need to sign on as a developer; however, you also will get access to useful SDKs and other detailed technical information on Citrix products.

- **Columbia NFuse web site**   Columbia is a very cool demo web site developed by Citrix that shows NFuse technology at its best. You can download a copy of the Columbia web code at either `www.citrix.com/cdn` (you will need to set up a free developer account) or in the file section of the Citrix South East Yahoo! Forum at `http://groups.yahoo.com/group/ citrixse/files` (you will need to sign onto Yahoo! Forum for access).

Third-Party Utilities and Software

You will find that many, many utilities are available out there. Some are specifically designed to work with Terminal Server and others offer enhanced Windows NT functionality that is important in a Terminal Server environment. The following sections list the major ones, broken down by category.

Outlook Profile Generation

The goal of any Terminal Server administrator should be quick and painless setup for users. One perpetual problem is that Outlook email profile generation always requires manual intervention. Suppose, for example, that you want to set up 20 users on your Terminal Server with access to Outlook or with an application out of which users needed to be able to email documents. You have to first grant the appropriate access to Terminal Server and possibly set up the profile directories. Then you have to log on as each user and manually set up each user's email profile correctly. This requires obtaining each user's password or walking each user through the steps. In other words, a big pain in the !@#!#. Fortunately, several companies have capitalized on this need by creating utilities that can automatically generate email profiles based on parameters you control from the logon script! Here are a few:

- **OProfile by Imanami**   Simple, powerful, easy to use. This utility runs in the logon script and will create profiles for your users automatically as they log on. It works great in a Terminal Server environment and is relatively inexpensive. There is a nice GUI interface for controlling profile settings or an extensive .INI file in which you can edit particular settings. You will find this utility at www.imanami.com.

- **Prfpatch by Microsoft**   This freely available collection of utilities from Microsoft enables you to centrally set profiles for Outlook from a script. Although not well documented or easy to use, this free utility might do the trick in a bind. You can find more information about Prfpatch, and the related Prfgen and Newprof, at www.microsoft.com/technet/treeview/default.asp?url=/TechNet/prodtechnol/office/deploy/confeat/prfpatch.asp.

Author's Note

For those who are more adventurous and do not want to have to purchase a third-party solution for this need, you might try experimenting with PROFGEN.EXE from Microsoft in the Outlook Developer Kit. You can download this kit for free at ftp://ftp.microsoft.com/softlib/mslfiles/odkidk98.exe.

Disk Usage and System Monitoring

Because Terminal Server is a multiuser environment, any user could potentially take up too much space and cause problems for the rest of the users. To proactively prevent problems due to insufficient space, Terminal Server administrators should periodically review space usage on their servers, especially space usage of profile folders. The following utilities offer an easy-to-read layout of space usage on whatever drive or directory you select:

- **Disk Frontier** Perhaps the simplest, easiest to use disk space management tool I have ever come across, and best of all it is free! Disk Frontier enables you to select any drive or folder and will scan that folder and all subfolder space usage. It will then present a bar chart showing the percentage usage and also indicate how often the data is used. You can download this free utility at www.choicecomp.com/diskfrontier.htm.

- **Free Meter** I recently came across this gem while looking for a better way to centrally monitor and manage our Windows servers. This very inexpensive utility helps you do just that. Not only will it enable you to continually monitor space usage, but you also can monitor other system resource parameters, such as processor and memory usage. You can click any drive or share for a detailed space breakdown or have it periodically logged to a comma-delimited file. You will find this utility atwww.tiler.com/freemeter.

- **LogCaster by RippleTech** This application is dedicated to Windows server monitoring. Much like more expensive server management products available from companies such as NetIQ, LogCaster enables you to monitor all aspects of your Windows servers and take action, such as pager notification, upon items such as certain event log messages or exceeding performance thresholds. In addition, LogCaster has special functionality for Citrix server monitoring, including the capability to set session limits and monitor per-session resource usage. For more information, go to www.rippletech.com.

Network Monitoring and Protocol Analysis

Server-based computing is all about the network. As a Terminal Server administrator, it is critical not only to ensure that your network is stable, but also to be able to respond quickly if a problem arises. In addition, for tougher issues you might need to dive deep into network protocol analysis to see exactly what is going on at a network layer. Although you can spend a small fortune on these types of tools, you really do not have to. The following tools are some of the least expensive, but still highly capable network monitoring and analysis applications available today:

- **WhatsUp Gold by IPSwitch**   This is probably the most robust network monitoring package you will find for less than $1000. WhatsUp gold is a versatile and feature-rich package that enables you to monitor the up or down status of any device on your network. If the device fails, you can have someone beeped, a message sent, an email sent, an alphanumeric page sent, or even a particular program run. WhatsUp Gold is robust enough to scale from a simple single-site network to networks that span the world with hundreds of sites and thousands of pieces of equipment that need to be monitored. In addition, WhatsUp comes with a very useful set of network tools that enables you to do things such as DNS name resolution, network throughput tests, port scanning, and more. You can find the latest version of this utility at www.ipswitch.com.

- **Etherpeek by WildPackets**   Have you ever wanted a robust, but easy-to-use protocol analyzer that did not cost an arm and a leg? Well, only a handful fit the bill, but Etherpeek is one of the best. With Etherpeek you can do detailed protocol analysis on more than 1000 different protocols. Like most protocol analysis packages available today, they do not yet have a decode for ICA or RDP; however, they can decode the TCP/IP on which these protocols rely. You will find this utility at www.wildpackets.com. Another application you might want to test out from WildPackets is NetDoplar. Using this software, you can better determine any sources of unusual latency on your network. If you are having problems with slow response time, NetDoplar can help you out.

Terminal Server Utilities

You would be surprised at the many after-market software packages available for Terminal Server and the functionality they can add. The following sections list of some of the major ones.

Tricerat Utilities

Tricerat, a small software company based out of Columbia, Maryland, has focused on solutions for both Citrix MetaFrame and Windows Terminal Server since 1997. They make the following useful utilities available for purchase from their web site at www.tricerat.com:

- **ScrewDrivers** ScrewDrivers offers something that Terminal Server and especially Citrix administrators have been longing for, for a long time: ease of printing. Printing issues are the bane of many Terminal Server administrators' existence. ScrewDrivers resolves these issues by using what is referred to as a *universal print driver*. In that way, printer auto-creation and driver matchup is unnecessary.

- **PMP** PMP is a very useful printer management application that can be used in conjunction with ScrewDrivers to ease many of the printer headaches that Terminal Server administrators face.

- **Thor** Thor is a robust desktop management application designed for either Terminal Server or Citrix MetaFrame deployments. If you provide desktops for your users, and you want more capabilities than are available with policies, this package is for you. Using Thor you can centrally control what is available on your users' desktops.

- **NTPass and NTAdmin** One difficulty many Citrix administrators face is providing users the ability to easily change passwords. This is especially the case for NFuse deployments entirely based on published applications. By publishing NTPass for your users, they can change their passwords easily through a GUI interface. The additional NT Admin utility is designed for help desk personnel and enables them to reset passwords easily without having to navigate through User Manager.

- **Reflect** Reflect enables Terminal Server administrators to replicate data across their server farm. Although there are other ways to do this, this utility is very easy to use and is especially useful in many situations when you need certain files to be available on all of your servers.

- **Tracker Express** This utility enables you to gather application and processor usage information on your users. This is a handy application, especially if you do not use Citrix MetaFrame or intend to purchase the Resource Management Services.

In addition to these utilities available for purchase, Tricerat offers a handful of free utilities. As of this writing, they include the following:

- **HFCheck** A utility for assisting with the installation of hotfixes on WinFrame.

- **ShowMSG** Displays a message from a text file to users as they log on.

- **WCopy** A very handy directory copy utility with file synchronization–like features.

- **NWLogout** Helps if you are having problems in a NetWare environment where NDS connections still remain open after a user logs off from Terminal Server.

AppSense Technologies

AppSense Technologies make the following two products that work well in a Terminal Server/Citrix MetaFrame environment:

- **AppSense** Similar in some ways to Thor from Tricerat, this security application enables administrators to lock down Terminal Server desktops so that only certain applications can be run. It has robust central management capabilities for application control and can audit application use.

- **TimePortal** Time portal solves a problem with older versions of Citrix MetaFrame—that users always had to work in the time zone of the server, even if they were logged on from a different time zone.

You can view more information regarding these products on the AppSense web site at www.appsense.com.

Emergent Online's Thin Essentials

Emergent Online is a Platinum Citrix reseller out of Virginia that also happens to have some of the most useful Terminal Server utilities around. Although not a dedicated software company, the utilities that they have available offer some very interesting and important features for both Terminal Server and Citrix MetaFrame:

- **EOL AppPortal** Have you ever wanted the ability to publish applications from Terminal Server without having to pay the premium for Citrix MetaFrame? Using AppPortal you can do just that. This application enables administrators to easily and centrally deploy applications across their Terminal Server farm. Although more advanced application publishing capabilities such as load balancing are not included, using AppPortal along with Network Load Balancing might be all you need.

- **EOL DesktopManager** Enables you to preconfigure and lock down a desktop configuration for your users.

- **EOL ProfileSweeper** A useful and inexpensive application that cleans up orphaned cached roaming profiles after they have not been used for a configurable number of days.

- **EOL TimeZone** Corrects the problem of the server time zone being different from the time zone of the user. This utility proves very useful for environments not using MetaFrame XP but that have users who access a central server farm from a multitude of different time zones.

- **EOL Universal Printer**   This utility gets around the problem of printer auto-creation by enabling users to print documents in PDF format and then streaming them to the user's local printer from the PDF.

- **Printer Driver Services**   Although not necessary if you are using MetaFrame XP, if you are using an earlier version of Citrix MetaFrame or Terminal Server alone, this application can help you out with your printer drivers. Using this application, you can push printer drivers out to every server in your server farm, instead of having to manually install drivers.

Although the applications just listed are all available for purchase, EOL has made the following applications available for free on their web site:

- **EOL ListDrivers**   Enables you to list all loaded print drivers on a Terminal Server.

- **EOL SetPassword**   A very handy and free password-changer utility. If you are using Citrix and only use published applications, you can publish this utility so that your users can change passwords. This also is a very handy utility to publish to your NFuse users, so that they can change their password.

- **EOL SetPrinter**   Enables a user to choose his own default printer.

You can find out more about these products and contact information for EOL on their web site at www.99point9.com.

WM Software's Terminal Server Tools

WM Software is a small, privately held software company based in Strongsville, Ohio. They have a large collection of useful software tools, many of which are designed specifically for the needs of Terminal Server administrators. The following is a brief description of their major offerings:

- **Shutdown Plus 5.0**   If you are on the lookout for a good utility to control the shutdown of your servers, this is it. Shutdown Plus goes beyond the normal ability of just scheduling shutdown times, by providing different versions with additional features customized for different needs.

- **Performance Sentinel**   Performance Sentinel is a simple performance monitoring utility that enables you to monitor various parameters on your server farm, such as CPU utilization, memory utilization, network utilization, and disk use.

- **Registry Sentinel**   This is a nice utility for those who want to easily be able to back up and restore their server's Registry. This utility runs as a service on your servers and can be scheduled to back up the Registry on a regular basis.

- **Server Sentinel TSE** This utility is similar to Performance Sentinel in that it can monitor system parameters; however, it has better notification capabilities and is custom designed for Terminal Server.
- **Service Restarter** This tool can be handy for troublesome services that get stuck frequently on your systems. Although not a substitute for proper troubleshooting and the pursuit of a long-term resolution, it will at least help stabilize the service by restarting it at defined intervals.
- **Profile Cleaner** Profile cleaner is a handy little utility that you can use to clean out unnecessary files from your system, such as *.TMP files, on a periodic basis.

You can download free trial versions of these products and find out more information on WM Software's web site at www.wmsoftware.com.

SysInternals Tools

If you have not been to the SysInternals web site, www.sysinternals.com, you need to go. Mark Russinovich, co-author of *Inside Microsoft Windows 2000* (ISBN: 0735610215, Microsoft Press, June 2000), and Bryce Cogswell, a frequent speaker on Windows system internals, have put together an incredible collection of utilities that provide deep insight into the inner workings of both Windows NT 4.0 and 2000 servers. Although not specifically designed for Terminal Servers, these tools will bring your understanding of how Terminal Server works to a new level and are important tools for troubleshooting tough application problems. The following are some of the most useful of these tools; and best of all, most of them are free:

- **Filemon** Monitors file system usage in real-time. You can use this handy, free utility to find out to where your applications are writing files.
- **Regmon** Similar to Filemon, except this tool monitors the Registry. This is a very important and free troubleshooting tool for Terminal Server administrators. You can use this tool to determine where in the Registry your application is writing to or reading from.
- **ListDLLs** You can use this utility to display a list of loaded DLLs and their version numbers. You can use this to help troubleshoot problems that might be related to incorrect DLL versions.
- **Process Explorer** Of all the tools on their web site, this tool is probably the best for seeing exactly what is going on in your system. Using this tool, you can "dissect" all of your running processes on your Terminal Server, by viewing what Registry keys, files, and other objects they have open.

- **PageDefrag**   One of the big limitations of the built-in defragmenter utility in Windows 2000 is the inability to defragment paging files. A heavily fragmented paging file on a heavily used Terminal Server can quickly lead to performance problems. It is highly recommended to periodically defragment your paging files using this tool on your most heavily used servers.

- **BgInfo**   Wouldn't it be nice if you could see the name of your server, processor speed, memory, and other system parameters on your desktop? With this utility, you can. When you run it, it will change your desktop background to display a number of useful system parameters.

In addition to the free utilities just listed, SysInternals sells a handful of more advanced, but very useful utilities for a Terminal Server administrator. One of the most useful is ERD Commander. This utility is a must have for Windows NT Server disaster recovery. Using this utility, you can boot from a floppy disk to a command-prompt-like interface on your server and access the system drive, even if it is formatted in NTFS!

HobLink Software

Hob Software, accessible online at www.hobsoftware.com, is a terminal emulation software developer based in Germany. They have been making useful terminal emulation software solutions for years. They have one very interesting piece of software that you need to know about as a Terminal Server administrator: HobLink JWT.

This software is currently the world's only Java version of the Terminal Services client. As a Terminal Server administrator, you might have been frustrated at the lack of support by Microsoft of other platforms besides Windows. If you do not intend to buy Citrix MetaFrame to meet this need, you might be interested in this software. Using this Java-based Terminal Server client, you can access your Terminal Server from any platform that supports Java, which is just about every major one.

Shareware Web Sites

Every day more useful utilities are coming out that can help you as a Terminal Server administrator. The following is a list of some of the best sites on the web to find utilities to meet your needs:

- **www.hotfiles.com**   This web site, run by Ziff-Davis publishing, is a personal favorite of mine. They have one of the largest collections of shareware on the Internet. Unlike other shareware sites that tend to show you more information than you need when you do a search, HotFiles shows you just the application title, size, rating, and number of times downloaded. Generally, you can focus in quickly on the best shareware titles by viewing those that have the highest ratings or are the most downloaded.

- **www.downloads.com**   This site is also very good, but is focused more on commercial software than shareware. You will find plenty of shareware here, however; and if you want to download a commercially available piece of software, you can do that too.

- **www.tucows.com**   A rather quirky, but very useful shareware site. They have a huge collection of shareware and an excellent rating system. Definitely worth a look.

- **www.windrivers.com**   Although not a shareware site, you need to know this site as a Terminal Server administrator. Have you ever spent days searching for the driver for some ancient printer or device that you have to get working? Well, if so, this site is for you. They have one of the largest collections of drivers available on the Internet in an easily searchable format. Definitely a keeper.

C

Web Sites, Newsgroups, and Other Resources

WITH SUCH A DIVERSE PRODUCT AS Terminal Server, it is impossible to do it full justice in print. Every day new products come out that add to or enhance its robust capabilities. In addition, the many knowledge bases, forums, and web sites that are available out there are continually being updated with new information. In this appendix, you will learn about some of the many resources available to you as a Terminal Server administrator to help you with the troubleshooting, support, and general administration of your Terminal Server environment.

> **Links on Thin Wizard**
> You will find links to all the sites mentioned here at this book's companion web site, www.thinwizard.com, which also is available from www.awl.com/cseng/titles/0-735-71192-5.

Web Sites

Following are some of the many web sites on the Internet that have information that will be of use to you as a Terminal Server administrator:

- **www.citrix.com**   The Citrix web site has loads of useful troubleshooting information, including a knowledge database and online forum. Even if you will not be installing the add-on product MetaFrame, this web site is worth a look.

- **www.microsoft.com**   The Microsoft Online Knowledge Base and their extensive documentation on their MSDN site make it a must use site for Terminal Server administrators. If you would rather have the Knowledge Base on CD, you can subscribe to the Microsoft monthly TechNet CD. This CD is loaded with important information and is a must have for any Terminal Server administrator.

- **www.thinplanet.com**   This site is a good place to go for information on all aspects of server-based computing. Although geared toward the ASP community, you will find a plethora of other useful information, such as an active online forum, interviews with industry leaders, and a calendar of server-based computing events.

- **www.jsiinc.com**   Home of the well-known and widely used NT Reg Hack list. If there is a Registry hack available that could help you with an issue that you are having with Terminal Server, you will likely find it here. In addition to Registry hacks, you will find several informative articles on various aspects of Windows NT administration and solutions to commonly encountered issues.

- **www.brainbuzz.com**   This all-around excellent tech community web site offers a plethora of forums on different topics, including Terminal Server and MetaFrame. In addition, they have job listings, online quizzes, and a must-see CramSession section, where you will find free and information-packed study guides for both the CCA and CCEA certifications.

- **www.systemtools.com**   You will find some of the best utilities for Terminal Servers available on the web here. The TSCmd utility enables you to change Terminal Server settings from the command line. Hyena supports user administration and enables you to modify Terminal Server properties. DumpReg, DumpACL, and DumpEvt are all very useful utilities for Terminal Server administration. Be sure to check this site out.

- **www.sysinternals.com**   Not only are there tons of great utilities on this web site, but most are free! This site, run by Mark Russinovich and Bryce Cogswell, is a Terminal Server administrator's dream site. Often when administering Terminal Server, you need to see "under the hood" to better troubleshoot or understand a problem you might be having. With the tools on this web site, you can do just that. For more information on the many utilities that are available, refer to Appendix B, "Third-Party Software and Utilities for Terminal Server and MetaFrame."

- **www.ccaheaven.com**   Not too extensive of a web site, but worth a look. This site is geared mainly toward those pursuing Citrix certifications, but has some tech tips, Citrix MetaFrame site links, and a Citrix MetaFrame support forum.

- `www.xs4all.nl/~soundtcr`   This is the home of the Citrix Hard Core User page. This site has one of the best collections of Citrix MetaFrame–related links of any site on the Internet. In addition you will find an interesting collection of utilities and some custom application compatibility scripts. Definitely worth a look.

- `http://thethin.net`   This site, run by Jim Kenzig, has links to one of the most extensive and widely used Citrix MetaFrame newsgroups on the web: The Thin List. This forum, now available through Yahoo! groups, is loaded with useful technical information and has a strong following of highly experienced Terminal Server and Citrix administrators who can help you with issues that you are having. In addition, on the `thethin.net` you will find an extensive FAQ, downloadable tools and utilities, an excellent collection of web links, and even some entertaining online games.

- `www.slider.demon.nl`   Run by "slider," a CCEA from the Netherlands— this site has links to useful sites for Citrix MetaFrame administrators and also some custom application compatibility scripts for free download.

- `http://beam.to/wtsmf`   You will find a collection of useful links to other sites and especially recent technical news on both Terminal Server and Citrix MetaFrame.

- `www.thinworld.co.uk`   This is an interesting site run out of the United Kingdom. You will find a decent collection of tips and tricks here.

- `www.winntmag.com/Techware/InteractiveProduct/TerminalServer`   Here on *Windows 2000 Magazine*'s site you will find a good list of links for third-party tools and add-ons for both Citrix MetaFrame and Terminal Server.

- `www.thinclientzone.com`   Here you will find a consistently updated list of the latest news and events in the world of thin clients and server-based computing.

- `www.99point9.com`   This site, run by Platinum Citrix Reseller Emergent Online, contains several very useful utilities and other information for Terminal Server and Citrix MetaFrame.

- `www.beachfrontdirect.com/citrix.html`   Beachfront is one of the few publishers of study exams for the CCA and CCEA certifications. If you are currently pursuing one of these certifications, be sure to check out their web site.

- **www.winntmag.com**   Although there are not any dedicated magazines yet for the thin client community, you will find some very useful information on Terminal Server and Citrix MetaFrame in *Windows 2000 Magazine*. Formerly referred to as *Windows NT Magazine*, this magazine is one of the top in the industry for good technical information on Windows administration. Periodically you will find articles with specific tips and tricks for Terminal Server and Citrix MetaFrame.

Forums and Newsgroups

Although web sites offer good general information on Citrix MetaFrame and Terminal Server administration, many administrators like the concept of an online community where they can learn from the experiences of other administrators. Luckily several very vibrant and feature-rich online communities are out there, dedicated to topics on server-based computing.

You will find many of these communities available through Yahoo! groups. Yahoo! groups is quickly becoming the most well known and widely used site for the establishment of online communities. Using Yahoo!'s freely available tools, you can build your own online forum, post a schedule, upload files, and more. In addition, if you subscribe to a forum on Yahoo!, you can have the forum messages automatically sent to you as they are posted or consolidated together into fewer mailings.

- **http://groups.yahoo.com/group/thin**   The Thin.Net newsgroup is undoubtedly the best out there. You will find a strong following of this newsgroup from Terminal Server administrators around the world. Jim Kenzig does an outstanding job of moderating this newsgroup and is constantly responding to user questions. In addition, you will find an extensive collection of files and utilities available for free download. Like all Yahoo! Groups, you can have the contents of this one emailed to you on a regular basis.

- **http://groups.yahoo.com/group/thinnews**   This group, also run by Jim Kenzig, is intended only for announcements and a periodic newsletter by Jim.

- **http://groups.yahoo.com/group/citrixstudy** or **http://groups.yahoo.com/group/ccalist**   Both of these newsgroups are excellent resources for those pursuing either the CCA or CCEA certifications.

- **http://groups.yahoo.com/group/citrixnw** This group, run by Rick Dehlinger from Citrix, is one of the better and more popular Citrix MetaFrame newsgroups. You will find lots of good tips here along with an excellent collection of files. Rick's widely used MetaFrame Install and Tuning Tips document is well worth the visit to this newsgroup.

- **http://groups.yahoo.com/group/citrixse** This is another excellent newsgroup run by Barry Flanagan and has become the standard for all other Yahoo! groups to follow. With more than 2500 members now, it is the largest of the Citrix Yahoo! groups out there servicing Citrix MetaFrame administrators around the world. Many utilities and white papers not found on the official Citrix web site can be found here, including Columbia for NFuse.

- **http://boards.brainbuzz.com** You will find lots of online bulletin boards at BrainBuzz.com's web site. They are generally very informative and well moderated.

Other Resources

Besides online forums and web sites, you can find a ton of other useful information and utilities out there, especially from Citrix and Microsoft, that are must-haves for a Terminal Server administrator. The following are the most recommended resources:

- **Citrix Solution Tools** An important resource is the Citrix Solution Tools program. You will find more information about this program at www.citrix.com/services/soltools. This is a yearly subscription-based program that gives you access to the latest Citrix support tools and information. This currently includes access to a special Solution Tools web site and a quarterly CD with technical information, presentations, and other information. The program currently includes quarterly CDs.

- **Microsoft TechNet** Microsoft offers a TechNet subscription-based program that is similar to the Citrix Solution Tools program. In this program you get monthly CDs sent to you that are loaded with important technical information, beta software, utilities, and operating system patches. This CD also has a complete copy of all the articles available in the Microsoft online Knowledge Base. For more information on this program, go to www.microsoft.com/technet.

- **Microsoft MSDN** For the more developer-oriented administrator, the Microsoft MSDN program is highly recommended. By joining this program, you get access to the latest Microsoft software, including beta software. In addition you get a monthly or quarterly MSDN CD, which contains detailed developer-level descriptions of various aspects of the Windows operating system, including specific information on Terminal Server. For more information on this program, go to `http://msdn.microsoft.com/subscriptions`.

D

History of Terminal Server and Citrix MetaFrame

ALTHOUGH HAVING A GOOD TECHNICAL GRASP of a topic is essential for technical administrators, it also can be beneficial to understand the technology from a historical perspective. This is especially true of Citrix MetaFrame and Terminal Server. These two products have a long and interesting history, which helps explain some of the complexities of how the products are deployed today.

The Story of Citrix

The story of Terminal Server begins with a South Florida software company called Citrix. Citrix was founded by Ed Iacobucci and 12 programmers in 1989. With the help of Iacobucci's strong OS/2 background at IBM, Citrix set to work on a DOS/Windows terminal server based on OS/2.

Multiuser OS/2 and WinView

Over the next year, the team worked diligently at creating a multiuser version of OS/2. The resulting Multiuser OS/2 product debuted in 1990 and was a significant technological accomplishment. It was the first product on the market that gave administrators the ability to distribute multiple OS/2 desktops to remote users from a single server.

Although Multiuser OS/2 had respectable sales, the market was hungry for a multiuser version of Windows 3.x. Using the Windows 3.x on OS/2 technology, Citrix was able to revamp their Multiuser OS/2 product to focus on distributing Windows 3.x and DOS desktops instead. This new product, called *WinView*, debuted in 1993 and was named "Networld + Interop: Best of Show" the following year.

WinView quickly became a significant player in the remote-access market. Businesses were hungry for the ability to give their employees access to applications from home and the Citrix WinView product was a good solution. From home, users could dial in to the WinView server and access a Windows 3.x desktop on the corporate network as though they were sitting on the network.

Meanwhile, in November 1992, Citrix licensed the source code for Windows NT 3.51 and began work on a multiuser version of this operating system. Like their multiuser versions of OS/2, this multiuser version of Windows NT 3.51 involved the rewrite of significant components of the operating system necessary for it to be able to support multiple users remotely running applications on the server simultaneously.

WinFrame

After three years of development, Citrix released its first version of this product, called *WinFrame*. WinFrame quickly gained industry-wide attention. The product split the user interface from the Windows applications running on the server, packaged it, and sent it across the network to a WinFrame client. It offered businesses the ability to simultaneously run multiple remote Windows NT desktops off a central Windows NT-based server, on nearly every type of workstation in their enterprise. Even legacy computers could run 32-bit Windows applications with the robust power of a Pentium-based server.

Enter Microsoft...

It did not take long for Microsoft to realize the potential of server-based computing technology.

With Citrix server-based computing technology, Windows applications could run on nearly every desktop in the enterprise, including UNIX, Macintosh, and OS/2. Citrix also was interested in working with Microsoft for several reasons, including access to large enterprise-class organizations and enhanced support.

Windows NT Server 4.0, Terminal Server Edition

In early 1997, a team of Citrix representatives, led by Mr. Iacobucci, went to Redmond to negotiate with Microsoft. In May 1997, the announcement was made: Microsoft had licensed significant portions of the WinFrame technology from Citrix and would be developing a multiuser version of Windows NT 4.0, called *Windows NT 4.0 Terminal Server Edition*. This product would incorporate all the current WinFrame MultiWin code, which enables a single Citrix server to support multiple Windows sessions. Microsoft, with the assistance of Citrix, began the integration this technology into Windows NT Server 4.0.

Citrix would now make and sell an add-on enhancement to Terminal Server called *MetaFrame*, which added such features as application publishing and device redirection. Although Microsoft would make clients only for Windows-based operating systems using TCP/IP, Citrix would continue to make clients for a larger range of operating systems and protocols.

Because Microsoft did not license the ICA protocol from Citrix, Microsoft developed a similar protocol on its own, called the *Remote Desktop Protocol* (RDP), which Microsoft based heavily on the communications protocol it was already using with its NetMeeting product.

MetaFrame

In 1998, Windows NT 4.0 Terminal Server Edition was released by Microsoft. For those who needed Terminal Server to work with more protocols and platforms, Citrix offered an add-on product to Terminal Server called *MetaFrame 1.0*.

This product was soon followed by MetaFrame 1.8 for Windows NT 4.0 Terminal Server, which included a more application-centric approach using the new Citrix Program Neighborhood, along with other significant feature enhancements.

With the release of Microsoft Windows 2000 Terminal Server, Citrix released a Windows 2000 version of its popular MetaFrame 1.8 product.

The widespread acceptance of Citrix and the rise of a new type of business called *application service providers*, led to the deployment of larger and larger server farms using both Microsoft Terminal Server and the Citrix add on product. Although MetaFrame 1.8 was an excellent product, its core design was not as scalable as some users demanded.

In the first part of 2001, Citrix launched MetaFrame XP. MetaFrame XP is a complete redesign of the core Citrix MetaFrame 1.8 architecture designed to easily scale from the smallest to the largest deployments. In addition, the numerous administrative tools in previous versions were consolidated into a single Java-based enterprise administrative console called the *Citrix Management Console.*

The Future of Terminal Server

Although Microsoft is continuing to add new functionality to its base Terminal Server product, such as drive mapping and additional color support, the focus is currently and mainly directed at the development of their .NET program and its related products.

Meanwhile, Citrix is diligently working on taking the best advantage of portal technologies to deploy applications across the web. Driven by the success of their NFuse application portal technology and the growing demand for corporate portals, Citrix purchased Sequoia Software in 2001. Sequoia, a leading maker of enterprise portals, is a good fit with existing Citrix technologies. The Sequoia XPs portal technology allows the integration of applications and a large variety of other content into a single consolidated web-enabled interface. This powerful combination of applications and information is attractive to many corporations that desire to centralize both.

Although both Microsoft and Citrix have come a long way with each of its respective server-based solutions, the story is far from over. Expect to see many new server-based innovations from both companies in the future.

E

Terminal Server and MetaFrame Command Reference

BOTH TERMINAL SERVER AND CITRIX METAFRAME have a rich set of commands that you can run from the command line. These commands can often provide more information than their graphical equivalents. In addition, many commands are useful for inclusion in either logon scripts or scripts that you can use to automate various Terminal Server administrative processes.

In this appendix you will learn about the many commands included with both Terminal Server and Citrix MetaFrame.

Command Index

The commands are first organized by their general purpose and then alphabetically as follows:

Windows 2000 Terminal Server Commands

The commands in this section are included with Windows 2000 Terminal Server and, in most cases, with Windows NT 4.0 Terminal Server. Be aware, however, that many commands available in Windows NT 4.0 Terminal Server have been renamed in Windows 2000 Terminal Server. You will see this noted in the command description if this is the case. Also unless otherwise noted, all Terminal Server commands will work with Citrix MetaFrame.

change client

Syntax   change client [/current | /flush | /view]

change client [/default | /default_drives | /default_printers]

change client [/persistent | /force_prt_todef]

change client [/delete *device name*]

change client [*host_device client_device*]

Source	Windows NT 4.0 or 2000 Terminal Server	
Description	This command allows you to view devices that are currently redirected to the host. This is a great command to use from a batch file to change or mappings to drives, LPT and COM ports on the client. With this command, you can display the currently mapped devices, delete device mappings, and map to new devices.	
Related Commands	N/A	N/A
Parameters	/current	Displays the current client device mappings.
	/flush	Flushes all the device mappings to the client.
	/view	Enables you to view all the devices on the client (\\client) that can currently be mapped to.
	/default_drives, /default_printers, /default	Resets either the client drive mappings, printer mappings, or both (default) to the defaults.
	/persistent	Makes the current mappings, persistent mappings.
	/delete device_name	Deletes the device name from the currently mapped devices (that is, /delete c:). Use /current to see the names of current mappings.
	[host_device client_device]	Maps the device on the host to the device on the client.
Example	``` M:\>change client c: c$ Mapping Host Device c: To Client Device c$ M:\>change client /delete c: M:\> ```	

change logon

Syntax	`change logon [/enable	/disable	/query]`
Source	Windows NT 4.0 or 2000 Terminal Server
Description	Enables you to change the logon status of your server. You can use this command to disable logons to a server, re-enable them, and query the current status.

continues ▶

Related Commands	N/A	N/A
Parameters	/enable	Enables logons to the server.
	/disable	Disables logons.
	/query	Returns the current logon status of the server.
| **Example** | ```
C:\>change logon /query
Session logins are currently ENABLED
C:\>
``` | |

change port

Syntax	change port [*port_a=port_b*]
	change port [/d *port* | /query]
Source	Windows NT 4.0 or 2000 Terminal Server
Description	Using this command you can map one port to another. This is some times useful with DOS applications that use ports on the Terminal Server.

Related Commands	N/A	N/A
Parameters	[*port_a=port_b*]	Maps input and output going to and from port a to port b.
	/d *port*	Deletes the port mapping.
	/query	Lists current port mappings.
| **Example** | ```
M:\>change port COM2=COM1
M:\>change port /query
AUX = \DosDevices\COM1
COM1 = \Device\Serial0
COM2 = \Device\Serial0
M:\>
``` | |

change user

Syntax	`change user [/install	/execute	/query]`
Source	Windows NT 4.0 or 2000 Terminal Server
Description	This is probably one of the most commonly run commands on Terminal Server, either directly or indirectly. You need to run the `change user /install` command before every installation. By default the server is in execute mode. Changing the server to install mode allows Terminal Server to capture important user-specific information about an application's installation. This information is then used to help the application run better in a multiuser environment.

Related Commands	N/A	N/A
Parameters	`/install`	Changes to install mode. Enter this mode before installing applications.
	`/execute`	Changes to execute mode. Execute mode is the default mode of operation and the mode in which you run applications.
	`/query`	Returns the current mode.

| **Example** | ```
M:\>change user /install
User session is ready to install applications.
M:\>change user /query
Application INSTALL mode is enabled.
M:\>
``` |
|---|---|

flattemp

Syntax	`flattemp [/query	/enable	/disable]`
Source	Windows NT 4.0 or 2000 Terminal Server
Description	Many applications store their temporary files in the folder designated as the temporary folder on the system. By default, with Terminal Server each user is given his own temporary folder so that other user's temporary files do not conflict with his own. Temporary folders are automatically created for each user either under the `%system drive%\temp\[session id]` folder on Windows NT 4.0 Terminal Server or under the `%userprofile%\localsettings\temp` folder on Windows 2000 Terminal Server. The `%temp%` and `%tmp%` environment variables are then set to this user-specific temporary file location.

continues ▶
```

Using the flattemp command, you can disable the creation of user-specific temporary file locations and instead have all users point to the same central temporary folder when they log on. This is necessary to set for a handful of legacy applications that do not recognize user-specific temporary locations. Unless you have one of these applications and are absolutely certain the application will not work with user-specific temporary locations, do not use this command.

Related Commands	N/A	N/A
Parameters	/query	Returns the status of temporary file locations.
	/enable	Enables flat or machine-specific temporary folder locations.
	/disable	The default option, which allows for user-specific temporary folder creation.
Example	N/A	

logoff

Syntax	logoff [*session_name* | *session_id*] [/server:*servername*] [/v]
Source	Windows NT 4.0 or 2000 Terminal Server
Description	This useful command-line utility enables you to log off a session by the session name or session ID. You can log off any session on any server using this command. To find the session ID or session name of a particular session, use the query session command. If you need to disconnect a session, rather than log off a session, use either the tsdiscon or discon command.
	To create a batch file that will log off all currently connected users, see the example shown in Microsoft Article Q259436.
Related Commands	tsdiscon — Disconnects user session (Windows 2000).
	discon — Disconnects user session (Windows NT 4.0).
	query session — Returns a list of currently logged-on session names and session IDs.

Parameters	[*session_name* | *session_id*]	Logs off the session with the entered session name or session ID.
	/server:*servername*	Logs off the session on the specified server. The default is the current server.
	/v	Verbose output.

Example

```
C:\>query session
  SESSIONNAME       USERNAME        ID      STATE   TYPE    DEVICE
 >console           tharwood        0       Active  wdcon
  ica-tcp                           65536   Listen  wdica
  rdp-tcp                           65537   Listen  rdpwd
  rdp-tcp#4         tharwood        1       Active  rdpwd
                                    2       Idle
                                    3       Idle

C:\>logoff 1 /v
Logging off session ID 1
C:\>
```

msg

Syntax

msg [*username* \| *session_name* \| *session id*]
[/server:*servername*] [/time:*seconds*] [/v] [/w] "*message*"

msg * [/server:*servername*] [/time:*seconds*] [/v] [/w] "*message*"

msg @*filename* [/server:*servername*] [/time:*seconds*] [/v] [/w]
"*message*"

Source Windows NT 4.0 or 2000 Terminal Server

Description This often-used command enables you to send a message to one or all (*) of the users on any Terminal Server. Use this command to send a message to users before resetting the system. You also can use this command in a batch file to warn users of something about to occur.

You have three options for specifying the intended audience of the message:

- Specify a particular username, session name, or session ID to which you want to send the message. You can retrieve a list of the currently logged on users, using the query user command.

continues ▶

- Specify the name of a text file that contains a list of the user names, session names, or session IDs. You must put the @ sign in front of the filename, so that it recognizes it as a file. In this text file, put each username, session name, or session ID on a separate line.

- To send the message to all users on the server, use the msg * *message* command.

One very useful feature of the message command is the wait and timeout parameters. You can use both of these parameters to pause a batch file for a given amount of time and wait for user input. The batch file will pause until either the time specified runs out or the user responds to the message; then the batch file continues. To send a message and wait for 10 seconds for users to respond, for example, use the command msg * /time:10 /w *message*.

Related Commands	query user	Displays the usernames, session IDs, and session names of currently connected users. You can use this information to send a message to a particular user.
Parameters	[*username* | *session_id* | *session_name*]	Sends a message to the specified username, session ID or session name.
	@*filename*	Sends the message to all of the usernames, session IDs, or session names that you specified in the file. You need to put the @ sign in front of the filename.
	*	Sends the message to all currently connected users.
	/server:*servername*	Sends a message to a particular server. The default is the current server.
	/time:*seconds*	Displays a message for a particular amount of time, after which the message box disappears. By default the message box will stay on the screen until the user clicks the OK button.

/v	Verbose output. Will display as each user acknowledges message if you use the /time:*seconds* /w parameters in addition.
/w	Pauses until the user responds to the message box by clicking the OK button. Use this in combination with the timeout value to pause a batch file for a given amount of time before continuing.
"*message*"	Specifies the message to be displayed. The message must be at the end of the command line. Quotes are optional.

Example

```
C:\>msg * /time:10 /w /v "test"
Sending message to session Console, display time 10
Message to session Console responded to by user
C:\>
```

query process

Syntax	query process [*	*username*	*session_name*	/ID:*session_id*	*program*] [/server:*servername*] [/system]
Source	Windows NT 4.0 or 2000 Terminal Server
Description	This command returns a list of currently running processes in the context specified. By default it returns a list of processes running in the current session. Using one of the *	*username*	*session_name*	/ID:*session_id* parameters, you can obtain a list of processes running on all sessions for a particular user, for a particular session name, or for a particular session ID, respectively.

Related Commands

tskill *process ID*	Kills a particular process (Windows 2000).
kill *process ID*	Kills a particular process (Windows NT 4.0).

Parameters

[*	*username*	*session_name*	/ID:*session_id*	*program*]	Displays processes running for all users, a username, session name, session ID, or for a particular program, respectively. By default, only processes running on the current session display.

continues ▶

	/server:*servername*	Displays process information for a particular server. The default is the current server.
	/system	Shows only the system processes.

Example

```
M:\>query process
    USERNAME          SESSIONNAME      ID    PID       IMAGE
   >tharwood          ica-tcp#7         7    4264      explorer.exe
   >tharwood          ica-tcp#7         7    4464      cmd.exe
   >tharwood          ica-tcp#7         7    2508      query.exe
   >tharwood          ica-tcp#7         7    4764      qprocess.exe

M:\>
```

query session

Syntax	query session [*username* | *session_name* | *session_id*] [/server:*servername*] [/mode] [/flow] [/connect] [/counter]
Source	Windows NT 4.0 or 2000 Terminal Server
Description	Use this command to list the users, session names, and session IDs on either the current server or a remote server.

Related Commands	query user	Returns the same information that query session does; in addition, it returns the logon time and idle time.
Parameters	[*username session_name* | *session_id*]	Returns the session information for the specified username, session name, or session ID. If not specified, all sessions are listed.
	/server:*servername*	Displays session information for the specified server. The default is the current server.
	/counter	Displays a count of total sessions, disconnected sessions, and reconnected sessions.
	/flow	Use to display flow-control settings for serially connected sessions.
	/connect	Shows the connection state of current connections to the server.

/mode   Displays serial communication information for serially attached sessions. This can be useful for MetaFrame administrators who use serial or modem connections to their server.

Example

```
M:\>query session
 SESSIONNAME        USERNAME          ID      STATE      TYPE      DEVICE
 console            0                 Conn    wdcon
 ica-tcp#1          cfoulger          1       Active     wdica
 ica-tcp                              65536   Listen     wdica
 ica-tcp#2          kwilliam          2       Active     wdica
 ica-tcp#3          CMCGINNI          3       Active     wdica
 ica-tcp#4          EWahl             4       Active     wdica
 ica-tcp#5          lcarreno          5       Active     wdica
 ica-tcp#6          tdweik            6       Active     wdica
>ica-tcp#7          tharwood          7       Active     wdica
                                      8       Idle
                                      9       Idle
                                      10      Idle
                                      11      Idle

M:\>
```

query termserver

Syntax   `query termserver [servername] [domain:domain] [/address]`

Source   Windows NT 4.0 or 2000 Terminal Server

Description   Returns a list of the current terminal servers on the local network. If you want to list just those servers that are a member of a particular domain, you can use the `[domain:domain]` parameter. You also can list the MAC address for all of your servers using the `query termserver /address` command.

The list of servers will be shown with an asterisk (*) next to the current server.

If you have a MetaFrame 1.8 environment or a MetaFrame XP environment running in mixed mode, use the `query server` command instead.

For MetaFrame XP administrators who are running in native mode, use the `query farm` command.

continues ▶

You will find descriptions of both of these commands in the "Citrix MetaFrame 1.8 and XP Commands" section.

Related Commands	query server	Displays a list of MetaFrame 1.8 servers or MetaFrame XP servers running in mixed mode.
	query farm	Displays a list of MetaFrame XP servers in the farm.
Parameters	[servername]	Optional parameter to list just a single server, use this command-line parameter in conjunction with the /address parameter to find the MAC address of a particular server.
	/domain:domain	Displays the servers on a particular domain.
	/address	Displays the MAC or node address of all network adapters on the Terminal Servers.

Example

```
M:\>query termserver /address
Known Terminal servers           Network    Node Address
---------------------            -------    ------------
GSMETA1                                     [   8C7917FCC]
GSMETA3                                     [  508B6470A3]

M:\>
```

query user

Syntax	query user [username	session_name	session_id] [/server:servername]
Source	Windows NT 4.0 or 2000 Terminal Server
Description	Use this command to list the users, session names, session IDs, logon times, and idles times on either the current server or a remote server.
Related Commands	query session	Returns similar information to the query user command, except for all sessions not just users. Does not include logon time or idle time.
Parameters	[username session_name	session_id]	Returns the session information for the specified username, session name, or session ID. If not specified, all sessions are listed.

	Example	M:\>query user

```
M:\>query user
 USERNAME      SESSIONNAME   ID   STATE    IDLE   TIME   LOGON TIME
 cfoulger      ica-tcp#1      1   Active          2:03   9/27/2001 7:05 AM
 kwilliam      ica-tcp#2      2   Active          40     9/27/2001 8:09 AM
 cmcginni      ica-tcp#3      3   Active          28     9/27/2001 8:12 AM
 ewahl         ica-tcp#4      4   Active          .      9/27/2001 8:14 AM
 lcarreno      ica-tcp#5      5   Active          5      9/27/2001 8:29 AM
 tdweik        ica-tcp#6      6   Active          .      9/27/2001 9:00 AM
>tharwood      ica-tcp#7      7   Active          .      9/27/2001 9:03 AM

M:\>
```

register

Syntax	register *filename* [/system | /user] [/v]
Source	Windows NT 4.0 or 2000 Terminal Server
Description	By default, most DLLs are registered for use by multiple users. In the background, Terminal Server can keep these DLL processes separated using the user's session ID. In some rare situations, the use of the session ID when referring to a DLL object may cause problems with DLLs in a multiuser environment.
	If you are running into DLL usage conflicts with one of your applications, you might try to register the DLLs for systemwide use by using the register *filename* /system command. With systemwide registration, there will be only a single instance of a DLL running in the global namespace.
	This command requires a reboot of the server for the registration change to take effect.
Related Commands	N/A	N/A
Parameters	*Filename*	Filename of the DLL. If you specify the filename without any parameters, the current registration status of a DLL will display.
	[/system | /user]	Registers the DLL for either systemwide or user-specific use.
	/v	Verbose output.

continues ▶

| Example | ```
C:\>register cards.dll /system
cards.dll registered SYSTEM GLOBAL

C:\>register cards.dll /user
cards.dll registered USER GLOBAL

C:\>
``` |

---

reset session

Syntax	reset session [*session_name* | *session_id*] [/server:*servername*] [/v]
Source	Windows NT 4.0 or 2000 Terminal Server
Description	You can use this command to reset a particular session on the server.
Related Commands	N/A N/A
Parameters	[*session_name* | *session_id*] Resets the session with the entered session name or session ID.
	/server:*servername* Resets the session on the specified server. The default is the current server.
	/v Verbose output.
| Example | ```
C:\WINNT\system32>reset session tharwood
Session tharwood not found

C:\WINNT\system32>
``` |

---

shadow

Syntax	shadow [*session_name* | *session_id*] [/server:*servername*] [/v]
Source	Windows 2000 Terminal Server Only
Description	This command enables you to remotely control another session running on the same server or a different server. This command does not work with Windows NT 4.0 Terminal Server unless you are running Citrix MetaFrame. However, you can use this command to remotely control both Terminal Server and Citrix MetaFrame sessions in Windows 2000.

	For you to shadow someone else's session, your video mode and colors must be at the same level or greater than the session you want to shadow.	
Related Commands	N/A	N/A
Parameters	`[session_name | session_id]`	Remotely controls the session with the entered session name or session ID.
	`/server:servername`	Remotely controls the session on the specified server. The default is the current server.
	`/v`	Verbose output
Example	N/A	

tscon

Syntax	`logoff [session_name | session_id] [/server:servername]` `[/dest:session_name] [/password:password] [/V]`
Source	Windows NT 4.0 (connect) or 2000 Terminal Server (tscon)
Description	tscon in Windows 2000 Terminal Server and connect in Windows NT 4.0 Terminal Server are identical commands that enable you to manually connect to a disconnected session.
	This command can be very useful in many situations. For example, you can leave several sessions running on a server in a disconnected state and then switch between them using this command. To look at what sessions are currently disconnected, use the `query session` command. Then log on to the server and use the `tscon session_id` to connect to that session.
	In addition, a help desk analyst could use this command to reconnect a user to one of his open sessions using the following syntax: `tscon current_session_id /dest:disconnected_session_id`.
	As with shadowing, you cannot reconnect to sessions from the server console.
Related Commands	`connect` This is the equivalent command to tscon with Windows NT 4.0 Terminal Server. The parameters you can use are identical.

continues ▶

	`query session`	Returns a list of currently logged-on session names and session IDs. You need to know either the session name or ID of the disconnected session to use this command.
Parameters	`[session_name	session_id]`	Connect to the disconnected session with the entered session name or session ID.
	`/server:servername`	Connects to the disconnected session on the specified server. The default is the current server.
	`/dest:session_name`	Use this parameter if you want to connect another user to one of her disconnected sessions.
	`/password:password`	If the session is not your own, you will need to enter the user's password.
	`/v`	Verbose output.
Example	N/A	

tsdiscon

Syntax	`tsdiscon [session_name	session_id] [/server:servername] [/v]`
Source	Windows NT 4.0 (`disconnect`) or 2000 Terminal Server (`tsdiscon`)
Description	Enables you to disconnect either the current session or another session. Remember that this command disconnects a session and does not log it off. This means that the session still remains running on the server. You can then use the `tscon` command at a later point to reconnect to this session.
	Using `tsdiscon` alone will disconnect the current session.
	On a Windows NT 4.0 Terminal Server, the equivalent command is `disconnect`, not `tsdiscon`.

Related Commands	`disconnect`	Disconnects user sessions. This is the equivalent command on Windows NT 4.0 Terminal Server to `tsdiscon`.

	tscon	Reconnects to a disconnected Terminal Server session.
	query session	Returns a list of currently logged-on session names and session IDs.
Parameters	[*session_name* | *session_id*]	Disconnects the session with the entered session name or session ID.
	/server:*servername*	Disconnects the session on the specified server. The default is the current server.
	/v	Verbose output.

Example

```
M:\>query session
 SESSIONNAME       USERNAME        ID      STATE     TYPE    DEVICE
 console                            0      Conn      wdcon
 ica-tcp                        65536      Listen    wdica
 ica-tcp#7         tharwood        7      Active    wdica
>ica-tcp#13        tharwood       13      Active    wdica
 ica-tcp#16        tharwood       15      Active    wdica
                                  17      Idle
                                  18      Idle

M:\>tsdiscon 7 /v
Disconnecting sessionID 7 from sessionname

M:\>
```

tskill

Syntax	tskill *process_ID* | *process_name* [/server:*servername*] [/ID:*session_ID* | /a] [/v]
Source	Windows NT 4.0 (kill) or 2000 Terminal Server (tskill)
Description	The tskill command enables you to kill particular processes running on a Terminal Server. One advantage of this command is that you also can stop processes running on remote servers.
Related Commands	kill — This is the equivalent command in Windows NT 4.0 Terminal Server. The syntax is the same.
	query process — Returns a list of all the processes running.

continues ▶

Parameters	*process_ID* | *process_name*	Kills the process with the specified process ID or name.
	/ID:*session_ID*	Kills a process on a particular session. The default is the current session.
	/a	Kills a process on all sessions.

Example

```
C:\>query process
 USERNAME              SESSIONNAME          ID    PID    IMAGE
>tharwood              console              0    1260    explorer.exe
>tharwood              console              0    2324    excel.exe
>tharwood              console              0    2700    iexplore.exe
                                                         wfcrun32.exe
>tharwood              console              0    2524    winhlp32.exe
>tharwood              console              0    1104    qprocess.exe

C:\>tskill 2324 /v
End Process(2324)
C:\>
```

---

tsshutdn

Syntax

```
tsshutdn [wait_time] [/server:servername] [/reboot]
[/powerdown] [/delay:logoff_delay] [/v]
```

Source

Windows NT 4.0 (shutdown) or Windows 2000 Terminal Server (tsshutdn)

Description

For administrators who want to periodically reboot their servers, this is the command to use. This powerful and simple-to-use command can be put in a batch file and scheduled to run at a particular time using the Windows 2000 Scheduler or the AT command in Windows NT 4.0. You also can use this command to remotely shut down and restart one of your servers.

The following is an example batch file that you can schedule to reboot your server:

```
Msg * /time:120 /w "Beginning the weekly server reboot,
please logoff within two minutes"
Tsshutdn 5 /reboot /delay:5
```

Related Commands	shutdown	The equivalent command (to shut down) in Windows NT 4.0 Terminal Server. The command-line parameters are the same.
	msg	Use this command to send a specific message to users before the shutdown. Otherwise they will get just a system shutdown warning prompt.
Parameters	[wait_time]	Specify the wait time in seconds.
	/server:servername	Logs off the session on the specified server. The default is the current server.
	/v	Verbose output.

Example

```
C:\>query session
 SESSIONNAME         USERNAME              ID  STATE  TYPE    DEVICE
>console             tharwood               0  Active wdcon
 ica-tcp                               65536  Listen wdica
 rdp-tcp                               65537  Listen rdpwd
 rdp-tcp#4           tharwood               1  Active rdpwd
                                           2  Idle
                                           3  Idle

C:\>logoff 1 /v
Logging off session ID 1
C:\>
```

Citrix MetaFrame 1.8 and XP Commands

The commands in this section are applicable only to Citrix MetaFrame 1.8 and XP servers.

altaddr

Syntax	altaddr [/server:servername] [/set alternate_address | /set adapter_address alternate_address |/delete | /delete adapter_address] [/v]
Source	Windows NT 4.0 or 2000 Terminal Server
Description	The alternate address (altaddr) command is useful if you want your servers to report an alternate address to your client. This is useful in situations where your servers are behind a firewall and there is address translation on the firewall.

continues ▶

Suppose, for example, that a server's address is 192.168.10.100; however, that Citrix server is behind a firewall. Outside the firewall the address for the server is translated to 145.100.100.100. You should use the following command so that your server can be connected:

```
altaddr /set 192.168.10.100 145.100.100.100
```

Make sure you run this command for all servers in a farm when that farm is behind a firewall. For more information on accessing Citrix servers through a firewall, see Chapter 17, "Firewalls and SSL Relay." Using altaddr by itself will display if there is any alternate address currently configured.

Related Commands	`ctxxmlss`	Changes the port number used by the XML service. You can use this service to provide access through a firewall to your Citrix servers.
Parameters	`/set adapter_address alternate_address`	Sets the alternate address for the specified adapter address.
	`/set alternate_address`	Sets the alternate address as the default alternate address for the server. Use this command form if your server only has one NIC card.
	`/delete`	Deletes all alternate address assignments on a server.
	`/delete adapter_address`	Deletes the alternate address assignment for a particular adapter.
	`/v`	Verbose output.

Example

```
C:\>altaddr /set 192.168.1.1

C:\>altaddr
Alternate TCP addresses for gs5054--home

Local Address            Alternate Address
--------------------     --------------------
Default                  192.168.1.1

C:\>
```

app

Syntax	`app script_name`
Source	Windows NT 4.0 or 2000 Terminal Server with Citrix MetaFrame 1.8 or XP.
Description	`app` is a unique utility that can be very useful in a lot of situations. The `app` utility is a script interpreter that you can use to run an application script from the `%systemroot%\scripts` folder. Using one of these scripts, you can copy files or delete files before and after running a particular application. This is good for application preparation and for cleanup.

Although you can do the same thing with a standard batch file, the advantage of using the `app` utility is that it runs in the background and does not keep a command prompt window open during application execution.

To make the script, just use Notepad. You need to save the script in the `%systemroot%\scripts` folder on the server from which you want to run it. You can use any of the following commands in the script:

- `copy source destination` Copies a file from the source location to the destination. Use it just like the equivalent DOS `copy` command.

- `delete path\filename` Deletes the specified file or files if you use standard DOS wildcard characters (`*.*`).

- `execute` Runs the application specified by the `path` command from the specified working directory.

- `path path\filename` Specifies the path for the application.

- `Workdir path` Sets the working directory for the application to `path`.

For example, the following script copies a text file over to the application directory and then runs the application:

```
Path c:\program files\app1\app.exe
Copy c:\appset.txt c:\program files\app1\
Execute
Delete c:\program files\app1\app.exe
```

After the application is completed the file is deleted.

Related Commands	N/A N/A

continues ▶

Parameters	`Script_name`	Runs the script name entered from the `%systemroot%\scripts` folder.
	`/server:servername`	Logs off the session on the specified server. The default is the current server.
	`/v`	Verbose output.
Example	N/A	

clicense

Syntax	`clicense [add license#	remove license#	force_remove license#	activate license_code]`
	`clicense [strings] [products] [connections]`
Source	Windows NT 4.0 or 2000 Terminal Server with Citrix MetaFrame XP
Description	This is the command you use to retrieve detailed licensing information in MetaFrame XP. This command has tons of different options and functionality. Only the most useful parameters are covered here. You can display your current licenses in several ways. To display a list of all the license strings you have entered and what they are for, use the `clicense strings` command.
	To display all the product licenses installed, use the `clicense product` command. This will show you the numbers that have actually been assigned.
	One of the most useful commands is `clicense connections`. Using this command, you can see the number of connection licenses available, the number assigned, and the number in use.
	You also can add, remove, and activate licenses from the command line. This can be useful for activating large numbers of licenses. This also enables you to put your license codes into a license batch file that you can run if you need to relicense your servers. However, realize that the activation code will need to be retrieved and entered manually for each license because it is different from the original if you have to reactivate a license.
Parameters	`/add license#` Adds the license number to the currently installed licenses.
	`/remove license#` Removes the license number from the license list.

/force_remove *license#*	Removes the specified license even if active users are using the connections.
/activate *license_code*	Activates a license using the activation.
strings	Displays the license strings currently installed.
connections	Displays currently installed connection licenses and the number used.
products	Displays the products licenses (either MetaFrame XP alone or MetaFrame XP Upgrade with MetaFrame 1.8).

Example

```
M:\>clicense products
Get Product License Capabilities:

License Set: MetaFrame XPe 1.0 English For Windows
    License Set ID: 0x04004000000186f7
    Status: Activated
    Count: (Unlimited)
    Pooled In Use: 50
    Pooled Available: (Unlimited)
    Number Assigned: 0
    Assigned In Use: 0
    Available For Assignment: 0

Completed successfully.

M:\>clicense connections
Get Connection License Capabilities:

License Set: MetaFrame Connection
    License Set ID: 0x0000000000000003
    Status: Activated
    Count: 1000
    Pooled In Use: 0
    Pooled Available: 1000
    Number Assigned: 0
    Assigned In Use: 0
    Available For Assignment: 1000


Completed successfully.

M:\>
```

cltprint

Syntax	`cltprint [/q	pipes:number]`
Source	Windows NT 4.0 or 2000 Terminal Server with Citrix MetaFrame XP
Description	Sets the number of virtual pipes or channels available for print jobs. This controls the number of simultaneous print jobs that you can send from a server to the client. The only time you might need to bump up this value from the default of 10 is in extremely heavy printing situations.
	After changing this setting, you will need to start and stop the spooler service for it to take effect.

Parameters		
	`/q`	Displays the current setting.
	`/pipes:number`	Sets the maximum number of concurrent printer pipes.

Example	`C:\>cltprint /pipes:10`
	`CLTPRINT Spooler must be stopped and restarted`
	`to enable new Pipe Instances setting`
	`C:\>`

ctxxmlss

Syntax	`ctxxmlss [/rnnn] [/u] [/knnn]`
Source	Windows NT 4.0 or 2000 Terminal Server with Citrix MetaFrame 1.8 FR1 or Citrix MetaFrame XP
Description	If you are using Citrix MetaFrame 1.8 Feature Release 1 or Citrix MetaFrame XP, you can use this command to change the port number for your XML service. By default, the XML service installs on port 80.
	The XML service is used for TCP/IP + HTTP connections from ICA clients. It also is used by NFuse for enumerating applications running on a server farm.

Parameters		
	`/rnnn`	Changes the port number to the number specified.
	`/u`	Uninstalls XML.
	`/knnn`	Changes the timeout file from the default of 9 seconds to whatever you specify.

Example

```
C:\>ctxxmlss /r400
Citrix XML Service: The service is now registered on port
number 400.

C:\>
```

dsmaint

Syntax

```
dsmaint config [/user:username] [/pwd:password] [/dsn:dsn]

dsmaint backup path

dsmaint failover servername

dsmaint compactdb [/ds] [/lhc]

dsmaint migrate [/srcdsn:dsn1 /srcuser:user1 /srcpwd:password]
[/dstdsn:dsn2 /dstuser:user2 /dstpwd:password]

dsmaint publishsqlds [/user:username /pwd:password]

dsmaint recover
```

Source   Windows NT 4.0 or 2000 Terminal Server and MetaFrame XP

Description   dsmaint is the Citrix MetaFrame XP command for data store maintenance and migration. Using dsmaint you can back up your data store, compact it, migrate it to another database, change its user configuration, and more.

The dsmaint backup *path* command is useful for backing up an Access data store to the path you specify. It is highly recommended to periodically back up your data store. For Access data store users, you can schedule this command to back up the data store periodically to a network location.

One of the most important parameters with this command is the migrate parameter. Using this parameter you can migrate a data store from one DSN source to another. You can use this command to migrate an Access data store to a SQL database. To do this, follow these steps:

1. Create the new SQL database.

2. Define a new file DSN for the SQL database and put it in the program directory for Citrix MetaFrame XP.

continues ▶

3. Run the `dsmaint migrate ...` command. Use the DSN used for the Access data store as the `/srcdsn`. Use the new DSN you created as the `/dstdsn`. Enter the appropriate username and password for the destination DSN.

4. After the migratation, you need to run the `dsmaint config ...` command on each server in the farm to point it to the new data store.

Parameters	config [`/user:username`] [`/pwd:password`] [`/dsn:dsn`]	Use this parameter to repoint your server to a different data store. The *dsn* is the path to a file DSN on your system that is configured for the new data store location.
	Backup *path*	Backs up an Access data store to the defined location. Does not work with SQL or Oracle.
	Failover *servername*	Used to switch the server used for indirect access to a data store.
	compactdb [`/ds`] [`/lhc`]	Compacts an Access data store (`/ds`) or the local host cache (`/lhc`).

	Migrate
	[`/srcdsn:dsn1`
	`/srcuser:user1`
	`/srcpwd:password`]
	[`/dstdsn:dsn2`
	`/dstuser:user2`
	`/dstpwd:password`]
		Migrates a data store from the source file DSN to the destination.

	publishsqlds [/user:*username* /pwd:*password*]	You can use this feature to publish your data store for a distributed data store setup on Microsoft SQL.
	Recover	Enables you to restore an Access data store. The source file is always the MF20.BAK file.
Example	N/A	

query farm

Syntax	query farm [*servername*] [`/addr` | `/app` | `/app` *appname* | `/load`] [`/tcp` | `/ipx`| `/netbios`] [`/continue`]
Source	Windows NT 4.0 or 2000 Terminal Server with MetaFrame XP

Description	This is the "Swiss Army knife" of Citrix MetaFrame commands and is useful for many purposes.	

The most basic use of this command is to list all of the servers in the farm. Running the `query farm` command alone will produce a list of all the servers, along with their network address. The data collector for the farm will be indicated with the letter *D* next to the server address.

One of the most important uses of this command is for getting detailed information on server and application load. You can use this information to help troubleshoot load-balancing problems and to check the current load of all your servers. If you run the `query farm /app` command, you will get a list of every application, what server the application runs on, and what the load is for that server and that application on that server.

This command is most useful for Citrix MetaFrame XP running in native mode. This command will not display any MetaFrame 1.8 servers. If you are running Citrix MetaFrame XP in mixed mode and you want to see all the MetaFrame 1.8 and XP servers in the mixed-mode farm, you need to use the `query server` command, not `query farm`. `query farm` is the replacement in XP for `query server`.

Related Commands	`query server`	Displays MetaFrame 1.8 servers in a farm and any MetaFrame XP servers in a farm that are running in mixed mode.
Parameters	`[servername]`	Shows information just for the specified server. The default is to show information for all servers in the farm.
	`/addr`	Displays the network address for a server. You must specify the server name.
	`/load`	Displays the server load for your servers. A server load of 20,000 indicates that the server is not licensed properly.
	`[/tcp | /ipx| /netbios]`	Displays just the servers for the specified protocol.
	`/continue`	Use this for a continuous display without the default pauses at the end of each page.

continues ▶

/app

Displays a list of all the published applications, what server they are on, and what their current server and application load are. An application load of 9999 means that the application is not load-balanced.

Example

```
R:\>query farm gsmeta1 /addr

Server                Transport Network Address
-------------------- --------- --------------------
GSMETA1               TCP/IP    192.168.10.208


R:\>query farm /app
App     Serv
Application Name                                 Server Name
Load    Load
--------------------------------------------- ---------------
------  ----
AD Users and Computers                          GSMETA4
99999   1200
Citrix Management Console                        GSMETAMB
99999   100
Crystal Reports                                 GSMETA4
99999   1200
SAP 46D4                                        GSMETA4
99999   1200
User Manager - terminal server edition  GSMETAMB
99999   100


R:\>query farm /load

Server Name           Server Load
-------------------- ------------
GSCTX-RPT1            0
GSMETA1              200
GSMETA3              1000
GSMETA4              1200
GSMETA5              200
GSMETA6              900
GSMETAMB             100


R:\>query farm
Server                Transport Network Address
-------------------- --------- --------------------
GSMETA1               TCP/IP    192.168.10.208
GSMETA6               TCP/IP    192.168.10.231
GSMETAMB              TCP/IP    192.168.10.251 D

R:\>
```

query server

Syntax	`query server [servername] [/stats	/app	/license]` `[/tcp	/ipx| /netbios] [/continue]`	
Source	Windows NT 4.0 or 2000 Terminal Server with MetaFrame 1.8 or MetaFrame XP in mixed mode	
Description	This used to be the main command for displaying server information in MetaFrame 1.8; however, it has now been replaced in MetaFrame XP with the `query farm` command.	
	Even so, the `query server` command can be very useful in MetaFrame XP if you are running your XP farm in compatibility mode. In this mode, your MetaFrame XP server acts like a MetaFrame 1.8 server so that it can communicate with other MetaFrame 1.8 servers in the same server farm. When running in this mode, the `query server` command is the only command that will list all the servers, both MetaFrame XP and 1.8, that are in the same farm.	
	In addition, this is the only command you can use to view how many licenses are truly available for MetaFrame 1.8 users. This can prove very useful for troubleshooting licensing problems when working in mixed mode. You will see how many licenses are available in the common pool.	
	One important use of this command is to show which server is the master browser in a MetaFrame 1.8 farm. When you run the `query server` command, the server that is the master browser will have an *M* next to its listing.	
Related Commands	`query farm`	The MetaFrame XP equivalent to MetaFrame 1.8. See this command's reference for more information.
Parameters	`[servername]`	Shows information just for the specified server. The default is to show information for all servers in the farm.
	`/app`	Displays the network address for a server. You must specify the server name.
	`/stats`	Displays browser statistics for a server
	`/license`	Displays number of licenses available and number taken across the farm.

continues ▶

[/tcp | /ipx| /netbios]	Displays just the servers for the specified protocol.
/continue	Use this for a continuous display without the default pauses at the end of each page.
/app	Displays a list of all the published applications, what server they are on, and what the current load is on that server.

Example

```
R:\>query farm gsmeta1

Server                Transport Network Address
-------------------- --------- --------------------
GSMETA1               TCP/IP    192.168.10.208

R:\>query farm
Server                Transport Network Address
-------------------- --------- --------------------
GSMETA1               TCP/IP    192.168.10.208
GSMETA6               TCP/IP    192.168.10.231
GSMETAMB              TCP/IP    192.168.10.251 M

R:\>
```

F

Citrix and Microsoft Technical Article Reference

MICROSOFT AND CITRIX BOTH HAVE AN extraordinary amount of detailed technical information available on their web sites. In many situations, this source is one of the best resources for resolving issues that you might have with either Terminal Server or Citrix MetaFrame. These technical articles also can supplement some of the material in this book, and might provide even deeper technical description in certain areas of a particular concept.

Thin Wizard Web Site

For an online version of all the links shown in this appendix, go to the book's companion web site at
www.thinwizard.com, which is also available from www.awl.com/cseng/titles/0-735-71192-5.

In this appendix you will find an organized list of the most important technical articles currently available on their web sites. This list is organized by the following subject areas:

- **Licensing**   Both Citrix and Terminal Server licensing are very complex. However, several technical articles on licensing are important to know about. Although licensing concepts were summarized well in Chapter 5, "Licensing Terminal Server and Citrix MetaFrame," you will find even more detailed information on different aspects of licensing in these articles.

- **Performance optimization, security, and reliability**   Both the Microsoft and Citrix web sites are a gold mine for finding performance-tuning tips, tips on securing the server, and ways to improve server reliability. Although the most important of these tips have already been covered, you will find additional tips and coverage in their technical articles.

- **Common errors and error codes**   One of the best uses for their web sites is for resolving common problems. The majority of problems can be fixed using the latest service pack or hotfix. The most commonly encountered of these types of errors are presented here.

Looking Up Knowledge Base Articles on the Citrix and Microsoft Web Sites

Much of the material in this appendix is a reference to technical articles contained on either the Microsoft or Citrix web sites. For those unfamiliar with how to navigate the Microsoft or Citrix web sites, you need to know some basic things.

Microsoft technical articles are referred to as "Q" articles because the article number always starts with the letter Q (for instance, Q112489). To look up any of the Q articles referenced in the tables in this chapter, just go to the Microsoft online knowledge base, http://support.microsoft.com, and search for the article number.

Citrix also assigns numbers to their technical articles; however, their technical numbers start with "CTX," not "Q" (for instance, CTX841082). To access any of the Citrix articles referenced in the tables in this chapter, go to http://knowledgebase.citrix.com and search for the CTX article number.

You also will find an easy-to-use online version of this reference chapter at the companion web site for this book, www.thinwizard.com (or www.awl.com/cseng/titles/0-735-71192-5).

Terminal Server and Citrix Licensing

Just covering licensing could almost be a book in itself. Well, it is not quite that bad, but understanding licensing and licensing your Terminal Server and Citrix MetaFrame solution correctly can definitely be a challenge. Besides the material provided in Chapter 5, you can find plenty of good technical articles on licensing on both the Microsoft and Citrix web sites. The tables in the following sections list them.

Planning and Setting Up Licensing

Table F.1 **Citrix Whitepapers**

URL	Whitepaper Title	Description
`ftp://ftp.citrix.com/doclib/licensing.pdf`	The Citrix License Activation Process activation process for licensing Citrix MetaFrame.	Description of the license
`ftp://ftp.citrix.com/doclib/licensepool.pdf`	Citrix License Pooling	An explanation of the ICA Browser Service as it relates to the storage and manipulation of pooled license data.
`ftp://ftp.citrix.com/doclib/citrix_licensing.pdf`	Citrix Licensing	Good general whitepaper on licensing.

Table F.2 **Citrix Licensing Articles**

Article Number	Article Title	Description
CTX222475	iLicense Frequently Asked Questions About MetaFrame XP License Meter and MetaFrame 1.8 License Audit Utility	Frequently asked questions about Citrix's special licensing program for ASPs.

continues ▶

Table F.2 **Continued**

Article Number	Article Title	Description
CTX244994	Understanding Windows 2000 Terminal Services Client Access Licenses for Non-Windows ICA Clients	How Windows 2000 Terminal Server licensing works with non-Windows clients.
CTX245514	Licenses Required for ICA Connectivity to a Windows 2000 Server with MetaFrame 1.8	Licensing required for Citrix MetaFrame 1.8 and Terminal Server 2000.
CTX300722	License Pool Recovery in a Server Farm	License pool recovery with MetaFrame 1.8.
CTX320069	Use Migration Licenses to Upgrade to a Newer Citrix Product	Using Migration licenses to upgrade Citrix.
CTX841082	Overview of the MetaFrame XP Evaluation and NFR Licenses	MetaFrame XP evaluation and Not-for-Resale licenses.
CTX998792	Licensing Scheme for Windows NT 4.0 Terminal Server and MetaFrame 1.8	Licensing explained for Windows NT 4.0 Terminal Server and MetaFrame 1.8. Also see CTX654838.

Table F.3 **Terminal Server Licensing Articles**

Article Number	Article Title	Description
Q187629	Terminal Server Licensing	Technical description of how licensing and the licensing service work in Windows NT 4.0 Terminal Server.
Q232520	Description of Terminal Services License Server Discovery	Description of how Windows 2000 Terminal Server licensing and license servers work.
Q237801	Windows 2000 Terminal Services Requires Licensing Service	Windows 2000 Terminal Services uses enforced licensing.
Q237811	How to Activate a Terminal Services License Server and Install CALs over the Internet	Description of the activation process for Terminal Services CALs.

Article Number	Article Title	Description
Q239107	Establishing Preferred Windows 2000 Terminal Services License Server	How to establish a preferred Windows 2000 Terminal Server license server.
Q244749	Licenses Required When Using Terminal Services Client Software	Required licenses for Windows 2000 Terminal Server.
Q248430	How to Transfer Terminal Services CAL from One Computer to Another	The rather complicated process for transferring a TS CAL from one workstation to another.
Q263315	How to Run the Terminal Services Licensing Tool from Another Computer	This is a rather useful article for setting up the Terminal Services Licensing tool for use on a machine besides the Terminal Server itself.
Q270898	Permissions Required to Install a Terminal Services Enterprise License Server	Active Directory permissions necessary to install a Terminal Services Enterprise license server.
Q272235	Internet Connector License Types for Windows 2000	Internet connector licenses explained.
Q275052	Terminal Services Licensing Technology for Application Service Providers	Windows 2000 Terminal Server licensing for ASPs.
Q287687	Terminal Services Licensing Enhancements	Terminal Server 2000 license recovery hotfix explained.
Q288379	Terminal Services Internet Connector License and ASPs	Describes various licensing options for ASPs, especially the Internet Connector License option.
Q291795	How to Locate a Phone Number for the Microsoft Clearinghouse	Has a short description of how to find the phone number for the Microsoft Clearinghouse. You need this number to register your TS CALs over the phone.
Q294655	Terminal Services Licensing Enhancements Frequently Asked Questions	This is a good article for gaining a basic understanding of how Terminal Services licensing works.

Resolving Licensing Problems

Table F.4   **Citrix Licensing Errors**

Article Number	Article Title
CTX585636	Error: "The License Could Not be Added Error 1073741823– (No Error Text Available)" When Attempting to Add a License
CTX395456	Seamless Windows Using More Than One License
CTX471666	Error: "The License Could Not Be Removed: Error Code 334/80060035"
CTX757104	Error: (The Citrix Server has no Licenses...) on a MetaFrame XP Server
CTX450326	Error: "The System Could not Log You On. You have Reached Your License Logon Limit" When Attempting to Connect to a MetaFrame 1.8 or MetaFrame XP Server

Table F.5   **Terminal Server Licensing Errors**

Article Number	Article Title
Q187629	Terminal Server Licensing Error Code 201 – Insufficient NT CAL Licenses
Q216159	Dr. Watson Starting TS License Service with Error 3221487623 in Event ID 7024
Q216843	Clients Receive "Error 1000 No Licenses Are Available" When Logging On to Terminal Server
Q232520	Description of Terminal Services License Server Discovery
Q234319	Client Registers a Second Terminal Services License After Clean Installation
Q238186	Simultaneous Multiple Terminal Server Client Logons Might Not Connect
Q239107	Establishing Preferred Windows 2000 Terminal Services License Server
Q248409	Terminal Services Licensing Problems After Upgrade to Release Version of Windows 2000
Q248430	How to Transfer Terminal Services CAL from One Computer to Another
Q251386	Several Terminal Services CALs Appear to Have the Same Computer Name

Article Number	Article Title
Q256854	Terminal Services OEM License Server Activation Does Not Validate PIN or Recognize License Server ID
Q257617	Terminal Server Service Might Stop Responding if the License Logging Service Hangs
Q258021	Event 52 When Starting Terminal Services
Q258045	Terminal Services Licensing Does Not Accept a Valid License Key Pack
Q261110	Windows 2000 Terminal Services in Windows NT 4.0 Domain Cannot Find Windows 2000 Terminal Services Licensing Server
Q262663	Error Message: The Licensing Wizard Cannot Connect to the Selected License Server
Q271245	Cannot Revoke Windows 2000 Terminal Services License from Client
Q274805	Error Message: Terminal Server Has Ended the Connection
Q281258	Event 1010 Is Reported After Specifying Default License Server
Q286272	Error Message: The System Cannot Log You On (573)
Q287687	Terminal Services Licensing Enhancements
Q294326	Event ID 1003: Terminal Service Client Has Provided an Invalid License
Q294655	Terminal Services Licensing Enhancements Frequently Asked Questions

Improving Server Performance, Security, and Reliability

A large number of technical articles have performance-tuning tips, but many of these require Registry hacks and should be used only in certain situations and with appropriate care. The most important ones are listed in this section. In addition, you will find listings of security- and reliability-related technical articles.

Rick's Tuning Tips

Although this appendix is dedicated just to listing technical articles and whitepapers, you can access many "unofficial" sources for tuning tips for your servers. One of the best is the Tuning Tips document from Rick Dehlinger. Rick is a field engineer for Citrix and has done an outstanding job of putting together a list of tuning tips for Citrix servers. These tuning tips include important tips on enhancing server reliability and security.

The guide can be a little difficult to get a hold of; however, it is currently available for download at the download area of Yahoo! Group forum that he runs at http://groups.yahoo.com/group/citrixnw/files. You must join the forum to access the files.

Performance

Table F.6   **Citrix Articles on Performance**

Article Number	Article Title	Description
CTX411514	Improving Display Performance on Windows 2000 with Terminal Services for All Users	How to improve display performance on Windows 2000 with Terminal Services for all users.
CTX757449	Improving Performance over the Internet or WAN Link	How to improve performance over a WAN or the Internet with Terminal Server or Citrix MetaFrame.
CTX846521	Comprehensive Application Tuning Document	Tuning DOS applications with doskbd in MetaFrame 1.8.

Table F.7   **Microsoft Articles on Performance**

Article Number	Article Title	Description
Q123747	Moving the Windows Default Paging and Spool File	Moving these files to a faster disk can greatly increase server performance. This article describes how to improve this performance.
Q130694	NTFS Performance with Numerous Long Filenames	Disabling the creation and use of 8.3 names can make a huge difference in the speed of file browsing, especially for directories with a large number of files. This article covers this tip in detail and the Registry change you need to make.
Q150355	Windows NT Nonresponsive During NTFS Directory Traversal	Every time you access a file or a folder, NTFS will update the access time in the background. This also can lead to very slow file browsing. This technical article shows how to disable it on your servers.
Q184419	How to Stop the NTExecutive from Paging to Disk	This is an often recommended tuning tip. This technical article provides good detail on the tip.

Article Number	Article Title	Description
Q226931	How to Minimize Graphics Use with Terminal Server	This simple Registry tweak is highly recommended to minimize desktop animations.
Q228766	How to Change the Server Service Properties	This is an often recommended performance tweak. However, according to Microsoft this recommendation is erroneous. For more information on exactly what this tweak is supposed to do and why it is not useful, see this article.
Q232476	Terminal Server Client Connections and Logon Limited by MaxWorkItem and MaxMpxCt Values	Error message: `System could not log you on because domain x is not available` or `You do not have access to logon to this session.` On the domain controllers, you might get `RPC server is unavailable or too busy`. Resolution involves changing the `MaxWorkItems`. Also see Q191370.
Q236573	How to Distribute Terminal Services Client Using Active Directory	This is a great article on how to use .MSI files to distribute the Terminal Services client to users.
Q243200	How to Modify Process Scheduling in Windows 2000 Terminal Services	It is important to ensure that priority is given to background services on Terminal Server for the best performance. This article describes how to change the setting for Windows 2000, and make sure it is set for Background Services. For Windows NT 4.0 Terminal Servers, set the bar to None under the Control Panel, System, Performance tab. For a detailed description of what this setting does, see article Q259025.

Reliability

Table F.8   **Citrix Articles on Reliability**

Article	NumberArticle Title	Description
CTX432257	How to Increase the Number of Idle ICA Listener Ports Available in Terminal Server	By default, there are only two idle sessions created to handle incoming sessions. On busy servers, these idle sessions might not be re-created fast enough, resulting in connection error messages. It is highly recommended to set idle Win Stations to at least four on busy servers. This article describes how to make the change.
CTX708444	How to Configure TCP and ICA KeepAlive Values So TCP/IP Users Go to Disconnected State	Problems with user sessions either going into a disconnected state unexpectedly or not going into a disconnected state soon enough when the connection drops. Also see Citrix article CTX895981.
		Changing the number of times TCP/IP attempts to retry a connection can also sometimes help when users are disconnecting frequently across an unreliable connection link. See article Q170359 on this.

Table F.9   **Microsoft Articles on Reliability**

Article Number	Article Title	Description
Q124594	Understanding and Configuring Registry Size Limit (RSL)	The Registry size on Terminal Server can grow very big, very quickly. It is highly recommended to increase the Registry size to at least 50MB if not more during server installation. This article describes the Registry size limitation in detail.

Article Number	Article Title	Description
Q188296	How to Disable Dr. Watson for Windows	Although Dr. Watson's can provide useful information for application troubleshooting, they can wreak havoc with Terminal Server and Citrix MetaFrame sessions. A Dr. Watson error can hang a session in a state where users cannot reconnect to the server, causing you to have to reset their session. It is highly recommended to disable them. This article covers how.
Q190162	Terminal Server and the 2048 Open File Limitation	This article describes the limit and how to fix the problem that it causes with applications that open large numbers of files. Also see Q233082.
Q279282	Slow File Write from Windows 2000 to Windows NT 4.0 Server	If you have an application that copies or moves large amounts of files from one server to another, you might want to adjust certain file and/or network buffers on your servers. This article shows you how. Also see Q223140.

Security

Table F.10 **Citrix Article on Security**

Article Number	Article Title	Description
CTX792384	Network Security Issues	Security issues in a network environment.

Table F.11 **Microsoft Articles on Security**

Article Number	Article Title	Description
Q101270	Disabling the POSIX Subsystem	Posix and OS/2 subsystems are rarely used, and they should be disabled, as shown in this article.

continues ▶

Table F.11   **Continued**

Article Number	Article Title	Description
Q182086	How to Clear the Windows Paging File at Shutdown	Clearing the paging file at shutdown is recommended to help achieve the highest level of server security.

Installing and Tuning Applications

Many applications need to be tweaked to work properly on Terminal Server. Citrix has an excellent collection of articles on how to properly install and configure various applications. Be sure to do a search for the name of the application you want to install in the Citrix online knowledge base. Besides those tips, Microsoft has quite a few useful documents on their own applications. The following articles in Table F.12 are important to read.

Table F.12   **Installing and Tuning Applications on Terminal Server**

Article Number	Article Title	Description
Q186499	Terminal Server Registry Settings for Applications	This article details some of the many special Registry changes you can make to tune or change the performance of particular applications.
Q212242	WD2000: Where Settings Are Stored in the Registry	Grammar checking is a performance hog. Make sure to turn AutoGrammar off by setting it to 0. This article shows the location of several keys that you can change with Office 2000, including this one. You might likely find more that you will want to tweak.
Q224299	How to Prevent the Internet Explorer "Welcome" Tour from Running	This article shows you how to disable the default welcome tour on IE4 only.

Error Messages

Table F.13 and Table F.14 list of some of the most commonly encountered errors and their resolution.

Table F.13 **Citrix Articles on Error Messages**

Article Number	Article Title
CTX450326	Error: "The System Could Not Log You On. You have Reached Your License Logon Limit" When Attempting to Connect to a MetaFrame 1.8 or MetaFrame XP Server
CTX471666	Error: "The License Could Not Be Removed: Error Code 334/80060035"
CTX585636	Error: "The License Could Not be Added Error 1073741823- (No Error Text Available)" When Attempting to Add a License
CTX757104	Error: (The Citrix Server has no Licenses…) on a MetaFrame XP Server

Table F.14 **Citrix and Terminal Server Articles on Error Messages**

Article Number	Article Title
Q126401 (Also see Q126402, Q259837, and Q142719.)	Err Msg: "Not Enough Server Storage Is Available to Process…"
Q187629	Terminal Server Licensing Error Code 201 - Insufficient NT CAL Licenses
Q216159	Dr. Watson Starting TS License Service with Error 3221487623
Q216843	Clients Receive "Error 1000 No Licenses Are Available" When Logging On to Terminal Server
Q232476	Terminal Server Client Connections and Logon Limited by MaxWorkItem and MaxMpxCt Values. Error Message "System could not log you on because domain x is not available" or "You do not have access to logon to this session."
Q256854	Terminal Services OEM License Server Activation Does Not Validate PIN or Recognize License Server ID
Q258021	Event 52 When Starting Terminal Services. Error Message "Cannot Connect, the server is busy" or "Terminal Server has ended the connection" or error message "Object Name not found" in event ID 52 on server.
Q258045	Terminal Services Licensing Does Not Accept a Valid License Key Pack
Q265382	Error Message: Your Interactive Logon Privilege Has Been Disabled. Please Contact Your System Administrator
Q274805	Error Message: Terminal Server Has Ended the Connection and Event ID 1004

continues ▶

Table F.14   **Continued**

Article Number	Article Title
Q281258	Event 1010 Is Reported After Specifying Default License Server
Q286272	Error Message: The System Cannot Log You On (573)
Q294326	Event ID 1003: Terminal Service Client Has Provided an Invalid License

General Interest

The articles in Table F.15 are larger articles of general interest or about miscellaneous topics.

Table F.15   **Terminal Server Articles about General Interest topics**

Article Number	Article Title	Description
Q120642	TCP/IP and NBT Configuration Parameters for Windows	This lengthy and detailed technical reference covers every single Registry tweak you can make that affects TCP/IP and NBT in detail.
Q161334	Guide To Windows NT 4.0 Profiles and Policies (Part 1 of 6)	This series of articles is one of the best references around on the inner workings of profiles and policies in Windows NT 4.0. Although profiles and policies have changed significantly with Windows 2000, you can still learn a lot about them in these references.
Q186498	Terminal Server Application Integration Information	Good, detailed technical article on implementing applications on Terminal Server.
Q186572	Terminal Server Walkthrough: Startup, Connection, and Application	Very detailed technical article that walks through the logon process all the way to the point of starting up an application. Discusses the components that are loaded each step of the way.

Article Number	Article Title	Description
Q244725	Using Drive Share with Terminal Services	There is actually a way to set up access to a client's local drives in Terminal Server using a special procedure and set of files in the Windows 2000 Resource Kit. This article shows you how.
Q245607	Windows NT Server 4.0, Terminal Server Edition Issues in a Domain Environment	This technical article has a huge list of different issues for Windows NT 4.0 Terminal Servers and is a great reference. It has many references to other technical articles.
Q250380	How to Remove Internet Connection Wizard and Outlook Express Icons from the Desktop in Windows 2000	One of the more annoying things with Internet Explorer is that every user is prompted to configure his Internet Explorer connection. If you are on a LAN, this is not necessary. To just prevent this prompt from popping up for your users and to remove the Outlook Express icon that appears for users, follow the instructions in this article. Also add a "Completed" value of 1 to the `HKEY_USERS\.Default\Software\ Microsoft\Internet Connection Wizard` key.
Q250776	Windows 2000 Terminal Services Issues in an Active Directory Domain Environment	This article, much like Q245607, is a great one-stop reference for many Terminal Server 2000 issues. It has loads of references to other technical articles.
Q260370	How to Apply Group Policy Objects to Terminal Services Servers	Sometimes you need to apply a computer policy to Terminal Server, but you do not want to affect other machines on the net work. This article provides a lot of information about how to do this. Also see Q192794 for Windows NT 4.0 Terminal Server users.
Q260711	How to Configure Automatic Logon to a Terminal Server	This is very useful for many situations.

Index

D

E

J-K

M

N

T

U

X-Z

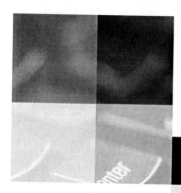

inform

YOUR GUIDE TO IT REFE

Articles

Keep your edge with thousands of free articles, in-depth features, interviews, and IT reference recommendations – all written by experts you know and trust.

Online Books

Answers in an instant from **InformIT Online Book's** 600+ fully searchable on line books. For a limited time, you can get your first 14 days **free**.

Catalog

Review online sample chapters, author biographies and customer rankings and choose exactly the right book from a selection of over 5,000 titles.

Colophon

The image on the cover depicts a road through Zion National Park in southwestern Utah captured by Macduff Everton. This rugged national park is filled with sandstone canyons, rocky deserts, and forested plateaus. Much of the park consists of old volcanoes and petrified wood from ancient forests. In the park, cliffs tower 2,000 feet above canyons narrowly carved by the Virgin River. Zion officially was made a National Park by an act of Congress in 1919.

This book was written and edited in Microsoft Word, and laid out in QuarkXPress. The fonts used for the body text are Bembo and MCPdigital. It was printed on 50# Husky Offset Smooth paper at R.R. Donnelley & Sons in Crawfordsville, Indiana. Prepress consisted of PostScript computer-to-plate technology (filmless process). The cover was printed at Moore Langen Printing in Terre Haute, Indiana, on 12pt, coated on one side.